# Fodor's 97

# Florida

" "When it comes to information on regional history, what to see and do, and shopping, these guides are exhaustive."

—*USAir Magazine*

"Usable, sophisticated restaurant coverage, with an emphasis on good value."

—Andy Birsh, *Gourmet Magazine* columnist

"Valuable because of their comprehensiveness."

—*Minneapolis Star-Tribune*

"Fodor's always delivers high quality...thoughtfully presented...thorough."

—*Houston Post*

"An excellent choice for those who want everything under one cover."

—*Washington Post* "

Fodor's Travel Publications, Inc.
New York • Toronto • London • Sydney • Auckland
http://www.fodors.com/

# Fodor's Florida

**Editors:** Glen Berger, Audra Epstein, Jennifer Paull

**Editorial Contributors:** Pamela Acheson, Rob Andrews, Robert Blake, Hannah Borgeson, David Brown, Marianne Camas, Karen Cure, Catherine Fredman, Herb Hiller, Ann Hughes, Andrea Lehman, Mary Meehan, Peter Oliver, Mike Radigan, Heidi Sarna, Helayne Schiff, Linda K. Schmidt, Mary Ellen Schultz, M. T. Schwartzman (Gold Guide editor), Dinah Spritzer, Rowland Stiteler

**Creative Director:** Fabrizio La Rocca

**Cartographer:** David Lindroth

**Cover Photograph:** Bob Krist

**Design:** Between the Covers

# Copyright

ISBN 0–679–03220–7

# Special Sales

Fodor's Travel Publications are available at special discounts for bulk purchases for sales promotions or premiums. Special editions, including personalized covers, excerpts of existing guides, and corporate imprints can be created in large quantities for special needs. For more information, contact your local bookseller or write to Special Markets, Fodor's Travel Publications, 201 East 50th Street, New York, NY 10022. Inquiries from Canada should be directed to your local Canadian bookseller or sent to Random House of Canada, Ltd., Marketing Department, 1265 Aerowood Drive, Mississauga, Ontario L4W 1B9. Inquiries from the United Kingdom should be sent to Fodor's Travel Publications, 20 Vauxhall Bridge Road, London SW1V 2SA, England.

PRINTED IN THE UNITED STATES OF AMERICA

10 9 8 7 6 5 4 3 2 1

# CONTENTS

## Maps

# ON THE ROAD WITH FODOR'S

**W**E'RE ALWAYS THRILLED to get letters from readers, especially one like this:

*It took us an hour to decide what book to buy and we now know we picked the best one. Your book was wonderful, easy to follow, very accurate, and good on pointing out eating places, informal as well as formal. When we saw other people using your book, we would look at each other and smile.*

Our editors and writers are deeply committed to making every Fodor's guide "the best one"—not only accurate but always charming, brimming with sound recommendations and solid ideas, right on the mark in describing restaurants and hotels, and full of fascinating facts that make you view what you've traveled to see in a rich new light.

## About Our Writers

Our success in achieving our goals—and in helping to make your trip the best of all possible vacations—is a credit to the hard work of our extraordinary writers.

Like a snowbird, **Pamela Acheson** flies south in the winter after a summer in the Northeast—only Pam's south is the Caribbean and her Northeast is northeast Florida. A former New York publishing exec, she stopped in the Sunshine State on her way to the islands and fell in love with it after discovering that there's much more to it than Walt Disney World. She likes nothing better than to drive around to neat little towns, undiscovered beaches, and other less-traveled places as she writes about her two homes.

With a sister and niece on the southwest coast and parents on the southeast coast, Orlando-based **Marianne Camas** is caught in a Florida family triangle. She's spent many an hour zipping across the Tamiami Trail and knows every inch by heart. Because of a similar longstanding relationship with I-95 and the Florida Turnpike, she has memorized the tile color in the rest rooms of each rest stop en route. When not on the road, Marianne works as a senior editor

of American Automobile Association's *Car & Travel* magazine.

**Ann Hughes,** former editor of *Indiana Business* magazine and a contributing editor to other travel and trade publications, is a passionate golfer. She lives in northwest Florida, which has more courses than you can swing a club at.

**Mike Radigan** evaluated thousands of lodgings, restaurants, and attractions during nearly a decade as field inspector and quality assurance mangager for the American Automobile Association inspections program. Now president of a consulting firm that gives hoteliers a guest's perspective on their property, he searches out serenity in Florida's endless miles of coastal surf, fishing pole in hand.

Confirmed aquaphile **Rowland Stiteler** owns no fewer than six boats and is a frequent traveler on the Intracoastal Waterway. Professionally, he has served as editor and dining critic of *Orlando* and *Central Florida* magazines.

We'd also like to thank the helpful staff at the Gulf Coast Ranger Station for providing us with insights into The Everglades' ecosystem.

## New This Year

This year we've reformatted our guides to make them easier to use. Each chapter of *Florida '97* begins with brand-new recommended itineraries to help you decide what to see in the time you have. You may also notice our fresh graphics, new in 1996. More readable and more helpful than ever? We think so—and we hope you do, too.

### On the Web

Be sure to check out Fodor's Web site (http://www.fodors.com/), where you'll find travel information on major destinations around the world and an ever-changing array of travel-savvy interactive features.

### Let Us Do Your Booking

Our writers have scoured Florida to come up with a well-balanced list of the best B&Bs, inns, resorts, rental condos, and hotels, both small and large, new and old. But you don't have to beat the bushes for a reservation. Now that we've teamed up with an established hotel-booking service, reserving a room at the property of your choice is easy. It's fast and free, and confirmation is guaranteed. If your first choice is booked, the operators can recommend others. Call 1–800/FODORS–1 or 1–800/363–6771 (0800–89–1030 in Great Britain; 0014–800–12–8271 in Australia; 1–800/55–9101 in Ireland).

## How to Use This Book

### Organization

Up front is the **Gold Guide.** Its first section, **Important Contacts A to Z,** gives addresses and telephone numbers of organizations and companies that offer destination-related services and detailed information and publications. **Smart Travel Tips A to Z,** the Gold Guide's second section, gives specific information on how to accomplish what you need to in Florida as well as tips on savvy traveling. Both sections are in alphabetical order by topic.

Chapters in *Florida '97* are arranged by region, from south to north. Each city chapter begins with an Exploring section, which is subdivided by neighborhood; each subsection recommends a walking or driving tour and lists sights in alphabetical order. Each regional chapter is divided by geographical area; within each area, towns are covered in logical geographical order and, within town sections, all restaurants and lodgings are grouped together.

To help you decide what to visit in the time you have, all chapters begin with recommended itineraries; you can mix and match those from several chapters to create a complete vacation. The A to Z section that ends all chapters covers getting there, getting around, and helpful contacts and resources.

### Icons and Symbols

★    Our special recommendations
✕    Restaurant
🏨    Lodging establishment
✕🏨   Lodging establishment whose restaurant warrants a detour
☺    Good for kids (rubber duckie)
☞    Sends you to another section of the guide for more information
✉    Address
☎    Telephone number

🕐    Opening and closing times (those we give don't apply on holidays; if you're visiting then, call ahead)
💳    Admission prices (those we give apply only to adults; substantially reduced fees are almost always available for children, students, and senior citizens)

Numbers in white and black circles—that appear on the maps, in the margins, and within the tours correspond to one another.

### Dining and Lodging

The restaurants and lodgings we list are the cream of the crop in each price range. Price categories are as follows:

For restaurants:

| CATEGORY | COST* |
| --- | --- |
| $$$$ | over $50 |
| $$$ | $35–$50 |
| $$ | $25–$35 |
| $ | under $20 |

*per person for a three-course meal, excluding drinks, service, and 6% sales tax (more in some counties)

For hotels:

| CATEGORY | COST* |
| --- | --- |
| $$$$ | over $150 |
| $$$ | $90–$150 |
| $$ | $60–$90 |
| $ | under $60 |

*All prices are for a standard double room, excluding 6% sales tax (more in some counties) and 1%–4% tourist tax.

### Hotel Facilities

We always list the facilities that are available—but we don't specify whether they cost extra: When pricing accommodations, always ask what's included.

### Restaurant Reservations and Dress Codes

Reservations are always a good idea; we note only when they're essential or when they are not accepted. Book as far ahead as you can, and reconfirm when you get to town. Unless otherwise noted, the restaurants listed are open daily for lunch and dinner. We mention dress only when men are required to wear a jacket or a jacket and tie. Look for an overview of local habits under Dining in Smart Travel Tips A to Z.

The following abbreviations are used: **AE**, American Express; **D**, Discover; **DC**, Diners Club; **MC**, MasterCard; and **V**, Visa.

## Don't Forget to Write

You can use this book in the confidence that all prices and opening times are based on information supplied to us at press time; Fodor's cannot accept responsibility for any errors. Time inevitably brings changes, so always confirm information when it matters—especially if you're making a detour to visit a specific place. In addition, when making reservations be sure to mention if you have a disability or are traveling with children, if you prefer a private bath or a certain type of bed, or if you have specific dietary needs or any other concerns.

Were the restaurants we recommended as described? Did our hotel picks exceed your expectations? Did you find a museum we recommended a waste of time? If you have complaints, we'll look into them and revise our entries when the facts warrant it. If you've discovered a special place that we haven't included, we'll pass the information along to our correspondents and have them check it out. So send your feedback, positive *and* negative, to the Florida editor at 201 East 50th Street, New York, New York 10022—and have a wonderful trip!

Karen Cure

*Editorial Director*

## Florida

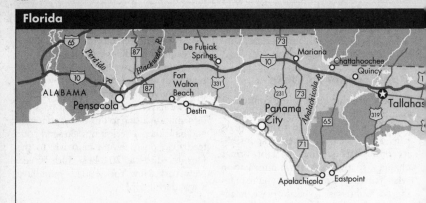

*Gulf of Mexico*

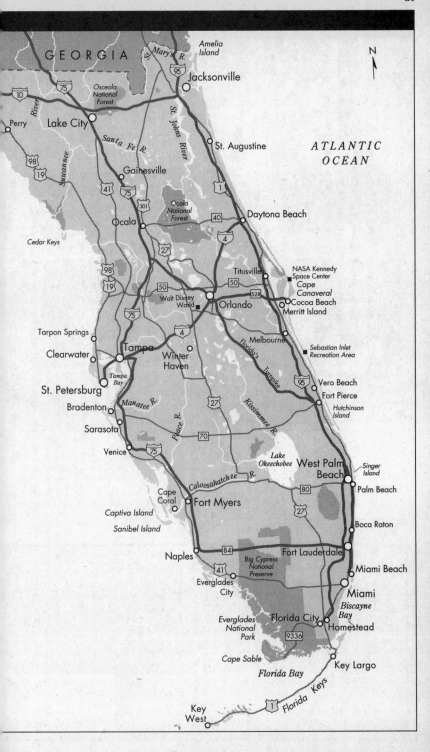

x

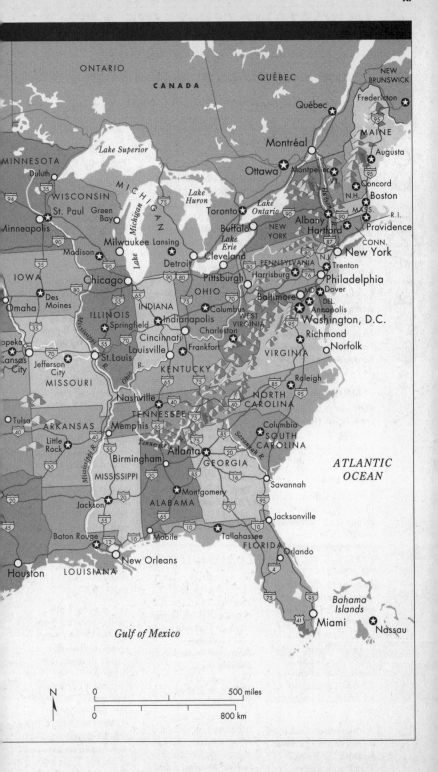

# IMPORTANT CONTACTS A TO Z

*An Alphabetical Listing of Publications, Organizations, and Companies that Will Help You Before, During, and After Your Trip*

## A

### AIR TRAVEL

The major gateways to Florida include **Miami International Airport** (☎ 305/876–7000), **Orlando International** (☎ 407/825–2001), **Tampa International** (☎ 941/870–8700), and **Palm Beach International** (☎ 561/471–7420). If you're destined for the north side of Dade (metro Miami), fly into more manageable **Fort Lauderdale–Hollywood International** (☎ 954/359–1200).

### FLYING TIME

Flying time to Miami is three hours from New York, six hours from Chicago, and seven hours from Los Angeles.

### CARRIERS

For regular flights into Florida's gateway airports, contact **American** (☎ 800/433–7300), **Continental** (☎ 800/525–0280), **Delta** (☎ 800/221–1212), **Midway** (☎ 800/446–4392), **Northwest** (☎ 800/225–2525), **Southwest** (☎ 800/435–9792), **TWA** (☎ 800/221–2000), and **United** (☎ 800/241–6522). Smaller, out-of-the-way airports are usually accessible via commuter carriers.

For inexpensive, no-frills flights, contact **Carnival Air Lines** (☎ 800/824–7386), which serves Ft. Lauderdale, Miami, and Tampa; **Kiwi International** (☎ 800/538–5494), serving Orlando, Tampa, and West Palm Beach; **Midwest Express** (☎ 800/452–2022), which serves Ft. Lauderdale, Ft. Myers, and Tampa; **Private Jet** (☎ 404/231–7571, 800/546–7571, or 800/949–9400), serving Miami and Orlando; and **ValuJet** (☎ 404/994–8258 or 800/825-8538), serving Ft. Myers, Jacksonville, Tampa, and West Palm Beach.

FROM THE U.K.➤ Contact **American** (☎ 0345/789–789), **British Airways** (☎ 0181/897–4000; outside London, 0345/222–111), **Continental** (☎ 0800/776–464), **Delta** (☎ 0800/414–767), **Northwest** (☎ 01293/561–000), **TWA** (☎ 0800/222–222), **United** (☎ 0800/888–555), and **Virgin Atlantic** (☎ 01293/747–747).

### COMPLAINTS

To register complaints about charter and scheduled airlines, contact the U.S. Department of Transportation's **Aviation Consumer Protection Division** (✉ C-75, Washington, DC 20590, ☎ 202/366–2220). Complaints about lost baggage or ticketing problems and safety concerns may also be logged with the **Federal Aviation Administration (FAA) Consumer Hotline** (☎ 800/322–7873).

### PUBLICATIONS

For general information about charter carriers, ask for the Department of Transportation's free brochure **"Plane Talk: Public Charter Flights"** (✉ Aviation Consumer Protection Division, C-75, Washington, DC 20590, ☎ 202/366–2220). The Department of Transportation also publishes a 58-page booklet, **"Fly Rights,"** available from the Consumer Information Center (✉ Supt. of Documents, Dept. 133B, Pueblo, CO 81009; $1.75).

For other tips and hints, consult the Consumers Union's monthly **"Consumer Reports Travel Letter"** (✉ Box 53629, Boulder, CO 80322, ☎ 800/234–1970; $39 1st year) and the newsletter **"Travel Smart"** (✉ 40 Beechdale Rd., Dobbs Ferry, NY 10522, ☎ 800/327–3633; $37 per year).

Other worthwhile publications on flying are *The Official Frequent Flyer Guidebook,* by Randy Petersen (✉ Airpress, 4715-C Town Center Dr., Colorado Springs, CO 80916, ☎ 719/597–8899 or 800/487–8893; $14.99 plus $3 shipping); *Airfare Secrets Exposed,* by Sharon Tyler and Matthew Wunder (✉ Studio 4 Productions,

Box 280400, Northridge, CA 91328, ☎ 818/700–2522 or 800/408–7369; $16.95 plus $2.50 shipping); *202 Tips Even the Best Business Travelers May Not Know,* by Christopher McGinnis (✉ Irwin Professional Publishing, 1333 Burr Ridge Pkwy., Burr Ridge, IL 60521, ☎ 800/634–3966; $11 plus $3.25 shipping); and *Travel Rights,* by Charles Leocha (✉ World Leisure Corporation, 177 Paris St., Boston, MA 02128, ☎ 800/444–2524; $7.95 plus $3.95 shipping).

If you experience motion sickness or ear problems in flight, get the brochures **"Ears, Altitude, and Airplane Travel"** and **"What You Can Do for Dizziness & Motion Sickness"** from the American Academy of Otolaryngology (✉ 1 Prince St., Alexandria, VA 22314, ☎ 703/836–4444, FAX 703/683–5100, TTY 703/519–1585).

## B

### BETTER BUSINESS BUREAU

In Miami, contact the **Better Business Bureau** (✉ 16291 N.W. 57th Ave., Miami 33014-6709, ☎ 900/225–5222, 90¢ per minute). For other local contacts, consult the **Council of Better Business Bureaus** (✉ 4200 Wilson Blvd., Suite 800, Arlington, VA 22203, ☎ 703/276–0100, FAX 703/525–8277).

### BUS TRAVEL

**Greyhound** (☎ 800/231–2222) passes through practically

every major city in Florida. For schedules and fares, contact your local Greyhound Information Center.

## C

### CAR RENTAL

Major car-rental companies represented in Florida are **Alamo** (☎ 800/327–9633; in the U.K., 0800/272–2000), **Avis** (☎ 800/331–1212; in Canada, 800/879–2847), **Budget** (☎ 800/527–0700; in the U.K., 0800/181181), **Dollar** (☎ 800/800–4000; in the U.K., 0990/565656, where it is known as Eurodollar), **Hertz** (☎ 800/654–3131; in Canada, 800/263–0600; in the U.K., 0345/555888), and **National InterRent** (☎ 800/227–7368; in the U.K., where National is known as Europcar InterRent, 01345/222525). **Value** (☎ 800/468–2583) offers some of the state's lowest rates. Rates in Miami start at $26 a day and $155 a week with unlimited mileage. This does not include tax, which is 6.5%.

Several local firms also offer good deals in major cities. In Fort Lauderdale: **Aapex Rent A Car** (☎ 917/782–3400) and **Florida Auto Rental** (☎ 305/764–1008 or 800/327–3791). In Orlando: **Ugly Duckling Rent-A-Car** (☎ 407/240–7368 or 800/843–3825) or **Snappy Car Rental** (☎ 407/859–8808). In Tampa–St. Petersburg: **Pinellas Rent-A-Car** (☎ 813/287–1872 or 800/526–5499). **Inter-**

**American Car Rental** (☎ 305/871–3030) is usually a good bet and has offices in Fort Lauderdale, Miami Beach, Orlando, and Tampa. In Key West try **Tropical Rent-a-Car** ☎ 305/294–8136).

### RENTAL WHOLESALERS

Contact **Auto Europe** (☎ 207/828–2525 or 800/223–5555).

### CHILDREN & TRAVEL

#### FLYING

Look into **"Flying with Baby"** (✉ Third Street Press, Box 261250, Littleton, CO 80163, ☎ 303/595–5959; $4.95 includes shipping), cowritten by a flight attendant. **"Kids and Teens in Flight,"** free from the U.S. Department of Transportation's Aviation Consumer Protection Division (✉ C-75, Washington, DC 20590, ☎ 202/366–2220), offers tips on children flying alone. Every two years the February issue of *Family Travel Times* (☞ Know-How, *below*) details children's services on three dozen airlines. **"Flying Alone, Handy Advice for Kids Traveling Solo"** is available free from the American Automobile Association (AAA) (✉ send stamped, self-addressed, legal-size envelope: Flying Alone, Mail Stop 800, 1000 AAA Dr., Heathrow, FL 32746).

#### GAMES

Milton Bradley can help keep children from fidgeting in planes, trains, and automobiles. Pack the Travel Battleship sea-battle game; Travel Connect Four, a vertical strategy game; Travel Yahtzee; the Travel Trouble dice and board game; and the Travel Guess Who mystery game. Parker Brothers has travel versions of Clue!, Sorry, and Monopoly. Games cost $6–$8.

### KNOW-HOW

*Family Travel Times,* published quarterly by Travel with Your Children (⊠ TWYCH, 40 5th Ave., New York, NY 10011, ☎ 212/477–5524; $40 per year), covers destinations, types of vacations, and modes of travel.

The *Family Travel Guides* catalog (⊠ Carousel Press, Box 6061, Albany, CA 94706, ☎ 510/527–5849; $1 postage) lists about 200 books and articles on traveling with children. Also check *Take Your Baby and Go! A Guide for Traveling with Babies, Toddlers and Young Children,* by Sheri Andrews, Judy Bordeaux, and Vivian Vasquez (⊠ Bear Creek Publications, 2507 Minor Ave. E, Seattle, WA 98102, ☎ 206/322–7604 or 800/326–6566; $5.95 plus $1.50 shipping). The Globe Pequot Press (⊠ Box 833, 6 Business Park Rd., Old Saybrook, CT 06475, ☎ 203/395–0440) publishes *100 Best Family Resorts in North America,* by Jane Wilson with Janet Tice ($14.95), and eastern and western editions of *50 Great Family Vacations in North America*

($18.95 plus $3 shipping).

### LODGING

Of the many hotels with organized children's programs, here are representative samples (not necessarily available at all times).

ORLANDO AREA➤ Look into the Kids Club program for ages 4–12 at **Westgate Lakes Resort** (⊠ 10000 Turkey Lake Rd., Orlando 32819, ☎ 800/424–0708), Camp Gator for children aged 5–12 at the **Hyatt Regency Grand Cypress** (⊠ 1 Grand Cypress Blvd., Orlando 32819, ☎ 407/239–1234 or 800/228–9000), Wally's Club Kids Creative Center for 6–12-year-olds at **Delta Orlando Resort** (⊠ 5715 Major Blvd., Orlando 32819, ☎ 800/877–1133), Shamu's Playhouse for ages 2–12 at the **Stouffer Renaissance Orlando Resort** (⊠ 6677 Sea Harbor Dr., Orlando 32821, ☎ 407/351–5555 or 800/468–3571), and the programs for ages 3–12 at **Holiday Inn Main Gate East** at Walt Disney World (⊠ 5678 Space Coast Hwy., Kissimmee 32741, ☎ 407/396–4488 or 800/465–4329) and for ages 2–12 at **Holiday Inn Lake Buena** (⊠ 13351 Rte. 535, Lake Buena Vista 32830, ☎ 800/366–6299).

MIAMI AREA➤ For Just Us Kids, ages 5–13, contact the **Sonesta Beach Hotel Key Biscayne** (⊠ 350 Ocean Dr., Key Biscayne 33149, ☎ 800/766–3782).

FORT LAUDERDALE➤ Look into the Beachside Buddies for ages 5–12 at **Marriott's Harbor Beach Resort** (⊠ 3030 Holiday Dr., Fort Lauderdale 33316, ☎ 305/525–4000 or 800/228–9290).

PALM BEACH AND THE TREASURE COAST➤ **Club Med** (⊠ 40 W. 57th St., New York, NY 10019, ☎ 800/258–2633) operates the Sandpiper resort village in Port St. Lucie; there's a Baby Club (4–24 months) and Mini Club (2–11 years). **Indian River Plantation** (⊠ 555 N.E. Ocean Blvd., Hutchinson Island, Stuart 34996, ☎ 407/225–3700 or 800/444–3389) has the Pineapple Bunch Children's Camp for children 4–12 plus a teen program.

THE KEYS➤ Florida's only environmentally oriented children's program, conducted by marine-science counselors, is Camp Cheeca for ages 6–12 at **Cheeca Lodge** (⊠ MM82, Upper Matecumbe Key, Box 527, Islamorada 33036, ☎ 800/327–2888). **Sheraton Key Largo** (⊠ MM 97, BS, Key Largo 33037, ☎ 305/852–5553 or 800/325–3535) has a Keys Kids Club for ages 5–12.

NORTHEAST FLORIDA➤ **Amelia Island Plantation Resort** (⊠ Rte. A1A, Amelia Island 32034, ☎ 904/261–6161 or 800/874–6878) for kids 3–12, has Sunday Night at the Movies and Kids Night Out.

MARCO ISLAND➤ Look for the year-round, seven-days-a-week Beach Bandits program for ages 5–13 at **Marriott's Marco Island Resort** (✉ 400 S. Collier Blvd., Marco Island 33937, ☎ 800/228–9290), which includes shell-hunting, and Radisson Rascals for ages 3–12 at **Radisson Suite Beach Resort** in Marco Island (✉ 600 S. Collier Blvd., Marco Island 33937, ☎ 800/333–3333).

## TOUR OPERATORS

Contact **Rascals in Paradise** (✉ 650 5th St., Suite 505, San Francisco, CA 94107, ☎ 415/978–9800 or 800/872–7225).

## CANADIANS

Contact **Revenue Canada** (✉ 2265 St. Laurent Blvd. S, Ottawa, Ontario K1G 4K3, ☎ 613/993–0534) for a copy of the free brochure **"I Declare/Je Déclare"** and for details on duty-free limits. For recorded information (within Canada only), call 800/461–9999.

## U.K. CITIZENS

**HM Customs and Excise** (✉ Dorset House, Stamford St., London SE1 9NG, ☎ 0171/202–4227) can answer questions about U.K. customs regulations and publishes a free pamphlet, **"A Guide for Travellers,"** detailing standard procedures and import rules.

## D
## DISABILITIES & ACCESSIBILITY

## COMPLAINTS

To register complaints under the provisions of the Americans with Disabilities Act, contact the U.S. Department of Justice's **Disability Rights Section** (✉ Box 66738, Washington, DC 20035, ☎ 202/514–0301 or 800/514–0301, FAX 202/307–1198, TTY 202/514–0383 or 800/514–0383). For airline-related problems, contact the U.S. Department of Transportation's **Aviation Consumer Protection Division** (☞ Air Travel, *above*). For complaints about surface transportation, contact the Department of Transportation's **Civil Rights Office** (☎ 202/366–4648).

## ORGANIZATIONS

TRAVELERS WITH HEARING IMPAIRMENTS➤ The **American Academy of Otolaryngology** (✉ 1 Prince St., Alexandria, VA 22314, ☎ 703/836–4444, FAX 703/683–5100, TTY 703/519–1585) publishes a brochure, **"Travel Tips for Hearing Impaired People."**

TRAVELERS WITH MOBILITY PROBLEMS➤ Contact the **Information Center for Individuals with Disabilities** (✉ Box 256, Boston, MA 02117, ☎ 617/450–9888; in MA, 800/462–5015; TTY 617/424–6855); **Mobility International USA** (✉ Box 10767, Eugene, OR 97440, ☎ and TTY 503/343–1284, FAX 503/343–6812); **Moss-**

**Rehab Hospital Travel Information Service** (☎ 215/456–9600, TTY 215/456–9602), a telephone information resource for travelers with physical disabilities; the **Society for the Advancement of Travel for the Handicapped** (✉ 347 5th Ave., Suite 610, New York, NY 10016, ☎ 212/447–7284, FAX 212/725–8253; membership $45); and **Travelin' Talk** (✉ Box 3534, Clarksville, TN 37043, ☎ 615/552–6670, FAX 615/552–1182) which provides local contacts worldwide for travelers with disabilities.

TRAVELERS WITH VISION IMPAIRMENTS➤ Contact the **American Council of the Blind** (✉ 1155 15th St. NW, Suite 720, Washington, DC 20005, ☎ 202/467–5081, FAX 202/467–5085) for a list of travelers' resources or the **American Foundation for the Blind** (✉ 11 Penn Plaza, Suite 300, New York, NY 10001, ☎ 212/502–7600 or 800/232–5463, TTY 212/502–7662), which provides general advice and publishes "Access to Art" ($19.95), a directory of museums that accommodate travelers with vision impairments.

## IN THE U.K.

Contact the **Royal Association for Disability and Rehabilitation** (✉ RADAR, 12 City Forum, 250 City Rd., London EC1V 8AF, ☎ 0171/250–3222) or **Mobility International** (✉ rue de Manchester 25, B-1080 Brussels, Belgium, ☎ 00–322–410–6297, FAX 00–

322–410–6874), an international travel-information clearinghouse.

## PUBLICATIONS

The free pamphlet **"Florida: Planning Companion for Travelers with Disabilities"** from the Florida Governor's Alliance (✉ 345 S. Magnolia Dr., Ste. D-11, Tallahassee,32301; ☎ 904/487–2222, FAX 904/922–9619, TTY 904/487–2223), lists resources by region.

Several publications for travelers with disabilities are available from the **Consumer Information Center** (✉ Box 100, Pueblo, CO 81009, ☎ 719/948–3334); call for a free catalog. The Society for the Advancement of Travel for the Handicapped (☞ Organizations, *above*) publishes the quarterly **Access to Travel** ($13 for 1-year subscription).

Fodor's **Great American Vacations for Travelers with Disabilities** (available in bookstores, or ☎ 800/533–6478; $18) details accessible attractions, restaurants, and hotels in U.S. destinations. The 500-page **Travelin' Talk Directory** (✉ Box 3534, Clarksville, TN 37043, ☎ 615/552–6670, FAX 615/552–1182; $35) lists people and organizations who help travelers with disabilities. For travel agents worldwide, consult the **Directory of Travel Agencies for the Disabled** (✉ Twin Peaks Press, Box 129, Vancouver, WA 98666, ☎ 360/694–2462 or 800/637–2256, FAX 360/696–3210; $19.95 plus $3 shipping). The Sierra

Club publishes **Easy Access to National Parks** (✉ Sierra Club Store, 730 Polk St., San Francisco, CA 94109, ☎ 415/776–2211 or 800/935–1056; $16 plus $3 shipping).

## TRAVEL AGENCIES & TOUR OPERATORS

The Americans with Disabilities Act requires that all travel firms serve the needs of all travelers. But some agencies and operators specialize in making travel arrangements for individuals and groups with disabilities, among them is **Access Adventures** (✉ 206 Chestnut Ridge Rd., Rochester, NY 14624, ☎ 716/889–9096), run by a former rehab counselor.

TRAVELERS WITH DEVELOPMENTAL DISABILITIES➤ Contact the nonprofit **New Directions** (✉ 5276 Hollister Ave., Suite 207, Santa Barbara, CA 93111, ☎ 805/967–2841) and **Sprout** (✉ 893 Amsterdam Ave., New York, NY 10025, ☎ 212/222–9575).

TRAVELERS WITH MOBILITY PROBLEMS➤ Contact **Hinsdale Travel Service** (✉ 201 E. Ogden Ave., Suite 100, Hinsdale, IL 60521, ☎ 708/325–1335 or 800/303–5521), a travel agency that benefits from the advice of wheelchair traveler Janice Perkins; and **Wheelchair Journeys** (✉ 16979 Redmond Way, Redmond, WA 98052, ☎ 206/885–2210 or 800/313–4751), which can handle arrangements worldwide.

## TRAVEL GEAR

The **Magellan's** catalog (☎ 800/962–4943, FAX 805/568–5406), sells products for travelers with disabilities.

## DISCOUNTS & DEALS

## AIRFARES

For the lowest airfares to Florida, call 800/FLY-4-LESS. Also try 800/FLY-ASAP.

## CLUBS

Contact **Entertainment Travel Editions** (✉ Box 1068, Trumbull, CT 06611, ☎ 800/445–4137; $28–$53, depending on destination), **Great American Traveler** (✉ Box 27965, Salt Lake City, UT 84127, ☎ 800/548–2812; $49.95 per year), **Moment's Notice Discount Travel Club** (✉ 163 Amsterdam Ave., Suite 137, New York, NY 10023, ☎ 212/486–0500; $25 per year, single or family), **Privilege Card** (✉ 3391 Peachtree Rd. NE, Suite 110, Atlanta, GA 30326, ☎ 404/262–0222 or 800/236–9732; $74.95 per year), **Travelers Advantage** (✉ CUC Travel Service, 49 Music Sq. W., Nashville, TN 37203, ☎ 800/548–1116 or 800/648–4037; $49 per year, single or family), or **Worldwide Discount Travel Club** (✉ 1674 Meridian Ave., Miami Beach, FL 33139, ☎ 305/534–2082; $50 per year for family, $40 single).

## HOTEL ROOMS

Contact the **Hotel Reservations Network** (☎ 800/964–6835).

## STUDENTS

Join Hostelling International–American Youth Hostels (☞ Students, *below*).

## PUBLICATIONS

Consult *The Frugal Globetrotter,* by Bruce Northam (⌧ Fulcrum Publishing, 350 Indiana St., Suite 350, Golden, CO 80401, ☎ 800/992–2908; $15.95). For publications that tell how to find the lowest prices on plane tickets, see Air Travel, above.

Also see Fodor's *Affordable Florida* (available in bookstores, or ☎ 800/533–6478; $16.00).

## G

### GAY & LESBIAN TRAVEL

## ORGANIZATIONS

The **International Gay Travel Association** (⌧ Box 4974, Key West, FL 33041, ☎ 800/448–8550, FAX 305/296–6633), a consortium of more than 1,000 travel companies, can supply names of gay-friendly travel agents, tour operators, and accommodations.

## PUBLICATIONS

*Fodor's Gay Guide to the USA* ($19.50; Fodor's Travel Publications, ☎ 800/533–6478 and in bookstores) is a comprehensive guide for gay and lesbian travelers. The premier international travel magazine for gays and lesbians is *Our World* (⌧ 1104 N. Nova Rd., Suite 251, Daytona Beach, FL 32117, ☎ 904/441–5367, FAX 904/441–5604; $35 for 10

issues). The 16-page monthly *"Out & About"* (☎ 212/645–6922 or 800/929–2268, FAX 800/929–2215; $49 for 10 issues and quarterly calendar) covers gay-friendly resorts, hotels, cruise lines, and airlines.

## TOUR OPERATORS

**Toto Tours** (⌧ 1326 W. Albion St., Suite 3W, Chicago, IL 60626, ☎ 312/274–8686 or 800/565–1241) takes worldwide groups.

## TRAVEL AGENCIES

The largest organizations serving gay travelers are **Advance Travel** (⌧ 10700 Northwest Fwy., Suite 160, Houston, TX 77092, ☎ 713/682–2002 or 800/695–0880), **Islanders/Kennedy Travel** (⌧ 183 W. 10th St., New York, NY 10014, ☎ 212/242–3222 or 800/988–1181), **Now Voyager** (⌧ 4406 18th St., San Francisco, CA 94114, ☎ 415/626–1169 or 800/255–6951), and **Yellowbrick Road** (⌧ 1500 W. Balmoral Ave., Chicago, IL 60640, ☎ 312/561–1800 or 800/642–2488). **Skylink Women's Travel** (⌧ 3577 Moorland Ave., Santa Rosa, CA 95407, ☎ 707/588–9961 or 800/225–5759) serves lesbian travelers.

## I

### INSURANCE

## IN CANADA

Contact **Mutual of Omaha** (⌧ Travel Division, 500 University Ave., Toronto, Ontario M5G 1V8, ☎ 800/268–8825 or 416/598-4321).

## IN THE U.S.

Travel insurance covering baggage, health, and trip cancellation or interruptions is available from **Access America** (⌧ Box 90315, Richmond, VA 23286, ☎ 804/285–3300 or 800/284–8300), **Carefree Travel Insurance** (⌧ Box 9366, 100 Garden City Plaza, Garden City, NY 11530, ☎ 516/294–0220 or 800/323–3149), **Near Travel Services** (⌧ Box 1339, Calumet City, IL 60409, ☎ 708/868–6700 or 800/654–6700), **Tele-Trip** (⌧ Mutual of Omaha Plaza, Box 31716, Omaha, NE 68131, ☎ 800/228–9792), **Travel Guard International** (⌧ 1145 Clark St., Stevens Point, WI 54481, ☎ 715/345–0505 or 800/826–1300), **Travel Insured International** (⌧ Box 280568, East Hartford, CT 06128, ☎ 203/528–7663 or 800/243–3174), and **Wallach & Company** (⌧ 107 W. Federal St., Box 480, Middleburg, VA 22117, ☎ 703/687–3166 or 800/237–6615).

## IN THE U.K.

The Association of British Insurers (⌧ 51 Gresham St., London EC2V 7HQ, ☎ 0171/600–3333) gives advice by phone and publishes the free pamphlet "Holiday Insurance," which sets out typical policy provisions and costs.

## L

### LODGING

## APARTMENT & VILLA RENTAL

Among the companies to contact are Interhome (⌧ 124 Little

**THE GOLD GUIDE / IMPORTANT CONTACTS**

Falls Rd., Fairfield, NJ 07004, ☎ 201/882–6864, FAX 201/808–1742), Property Rentals International (✉ 1008 Mansfield Crossing Rd., Richmond, VA 23236, ☎ 804/378–6054 or 800/220–3332, FAX 804/379–2073), Rent-a-Home International (✉ 7200 34th Ave. NW, Seattle, WA 98117, ☎ 206/789–9377 or 800/488–7368, FAX 206/789–9379), and Vacation Home Rentals Worldwide (✉ 235 Kensington Ave., Norwood, NJ 07648, ☎ 201/767–9393 or 800/633–3284, FAX 201/767–5510). Members of the travel club Hideaways International (✉ 767 Islington St., Portsmouth, NH 03801, ☎ 603/430–4433 or 800/843–4433, FAX 603/430–4444; $99 per year) receive two annual guides plus quarterly newsletters and arrange rentals.

## CAMPING & RV FACILITIES

Contact the national and state parks and forests you plan to visit directly, and the Florida Department of Environmental Protection (☞ National and State Parks in Parks and Preserves *below*) for information on camping facilities.

The free annual **"Florida Camping Directory"** lists 220 commercial campgrounds, with 66,000 sites. It's available at Florida welcome centers, from the Florida Division of Tourism, and from the **Florida Association of**

**RV Parks & Campgrounds** (✉ 1340 Vickers Dr., Tallahassee 32303-3041, ☎ 904/562–7151, FAX 904/562–7179).

## CONDOS

See *The Condo Lux Vacationer's Guide to Condominium Rentals in the Southeast*, by Jill Little ($9.95; Vintage Books/Random House, New York).

## HOME EXCHANGE

Some of the principal clearinghouses are HomeLink International/Vacation Exchange Club (✉ Box 650, Key West, FL 33041, ☎ 305/294–1448 or 800/638–3841, FAX 305/294–1148; $70 per year), which sends members three annual directories, with a listing in one, plus updates; and **Intervac International** (✉ Box 590504, San Francisco, CA 94159, ☎ 415/435–3497, FAX 415/435–7440; $65 per year), which publishes four annual directories.

## HOTELS

**The Florida Hotel & Motel Association** (✉ 200 W. College Ave., Box 1529, Tallahassee 32301-1529, ☎ 904/224–2888) publishes an "Annual Travel Directory," which you can obtain from the Florida Division of Tourism (✉ Dept. of Commerce, 126 Van Buren St., Tallahassee 32399, ☎ 904/487–1462).

## INNS & B&BS

**Inn Route, Inc.**(✉ Box 6187, Palm Harbor 34684, ☎ and FAX 813/786–9792 or 800/524–1880), a

statewide association of small, architecturally distinctive historic inns, will send you a free brochure. *Florida's Country Inns*, by Robert Tolf, published by Buchan Publications (✉ Box 7218, St. Petersburg 33734, ☎ 813/526–9121) describes 100 inns.

Bed-and-breakfast referral and reservation agencies in Florida include Bed & Breakfast Co., **Tropical Florida** (✉ Box 262, Miami 33243, ☎ and FAX 305/661–3270), **Bed & Breakfast Scenic Florida** (✉ Box 3385, Tallahassee 32315-3385, ☎ 904/386–8196), **RSVP Florida & St. Augustine** (✉ Box 3603, St. Augustine 32085, ☎ 904/471–0600), and **Suncoast Accommodations of Florida** (✉ 8690 Gulf Blvd., St. Pete Beach 33706, ☎ 813/360–1753).

## VACATION OWNERSHIP RESORTS

Most are affiliated with one of two major exchange organizations—**Interval International** (✉ 6262 Sunset Dr., Penthouse One, South Miami 33143, ☎ 305/666–1861 or 800/828–8200, FAX 305/665–2546) or **Resort Condominiums International** (✉ 3502 Woodview Trace, Indianapolis, IN 46268-3131, ☎ 317/876–8899 or 800/338–7777, FAX 317/871–9335).

To rent at vacation ownership resorts, contact the exchange organizations **Worldex** (☎ 800/235–4000, FAX 305/667–5372) or **Resort Condominiums International** (☎ 800/

338–7777), the individual resort, or a local real-estate broker in the area where you want to rent.

# M
## MARINE CHARTS

A packet of charts to the Keys (and elsewhere in Florida) helpful to boaters, divers, and fisherfolk is available for $7.95 ($3.60 each individual chart) from **Tealls, Inc.** (✉ 111 Saguaro La., Marathon 33050, ☎ 305/743–3942, FAX 305/743–3942), along with a free directory of what's available.

## MONEY

### ATMS

For specific Cirrus locations in the United States and Canada, call 800/424–7787. For U.S. **Plus** locations, call 800/843–7587 and enter the area code and first three digits of the number from which you're calling (or of the calling area in which you want to locate an ATM).

# P
## PACKING

For strategies on packing light, get a copy of **The Packing Book,** by Judith Gilford (✉ Ten Speed Press, Box 7123, Berkeley, CA 94707, ☎ 510/559–1600 or 800/841–2665, FAX 510/524–4588; $7.95).

## PARKS & PRESERVES

### NATIONAL PARKS

Consult the "Guide and Map of National Parks of the U.S." **(GPO No. 024005008527; $1.25 from the U.S. Govern-**ment Printing Office, Washington, DC 20402) and *The Complete Guide to America's National Parks* ($15.95; Fodor's Travel Publications, ☎ 800/533–6478 and in bookstores) for park addresses and facilities. For further details, contact individual sites.

Several passes are available for senior citizens, travelers with disabilities, and frequent visitors at any park that charges admission or by mail from the **National Park Service** (✉ Dept. of the Interior, Washington, DC 20240).

### STATE PARKS

**The Florida Department of Environmental Protection** (✉ Marjory Stoneman Douglas Bldg., MS 535, 3900 Commonwealth Blvd., Tallahassee 32399-3000, ☎ 904/488–2850, FAX 904/488–3947) is responsible for hundreds of historic buildings, landmarks, nature preserves, and parks. When requesting a free *Florida State Park Guide,* mention which parts of the state you plan to visit. For information on camping facilities at the state parks, ask for the free **"Florida State Parks, Fees and Facilities"** and **"Florida State Parks Camping Reservation Procedures"** brochures.

Responding to cutbacks in its budget, the DEP has established a citizen support organization, open to all, called **Friends of Florida State Parks** (✉ Dept. of Environmental Protection, 3900 Commonwealth Blvd.,

Tallahassee 32399, ☎ 904/488–8243).

## PRIVATE PRESERVES

**Contact the National Audubon Society** (✉ Sanctuary Director, Miles Wildlife Sanctuary, R.R. 1, Box 294, W. Cornwall Rd., Sharon, CT 06069, ☎ 203/364–0048), or, for information about **Nature Conservancy** preserves, contact its Florida chapter (✉ 2699 Lee Rd., Ste. 500, Winter Park 32789, ☎ 407/628–5887). Visitors are welcome at the Winter Park office and at offices in Tequesta (✉ 250 Tequesta Dr., Ste. 301, 33469, ☎ 407/575–2297), Key West (✉ 201 Front St., Ste. 222, 33040, ☎ 305/296–3880), Lake Wales (✉ 225 E. Stuart Ave., 33853, ☎ 813/678–1551), Tallahassee (✉ 625 N. Adams St., 32301, ☎ 904/222–0199), and West Palm Beach (✉ Comeau Bldg., 319 Clematis St., Ste. 611, 33401, ☎ 407/833–4226). All offices are open weekdays 9–5.

## PASSPORTS & VISAS

### U.K. CITIZENS

For fees, documentation requirements, and to request an emergency passport, call the **London Passport Office** (☎ 0990/210410). For U.S. visa information, call the **U.S. Embassy Visa Information Line** (☎ 01891/200–290; calls cost 49p per minute or 39p per minute cheap rate) or send a self-addressed stamped envelope to the **U.S. Embassy Visa Branch**

**THE GOLD GUIDE / IMPORTANT CONTACTS**

(✉ 5 Upper Grosvenor St., London W1A 2JB). If you live in Northern Ireland, write to the **U.S. Consulate General** (✉ Queen's House, Queen St., Belfast BTI 6EO).

The *Kodak Guide to Shooting Great Travel Pictures* (available in bookstores; or contact Fodor's Travel Publications, ☎ 800/533–6478; $16.50) explains how to take expert travel photographs. **The Kodak Information Center** (☎ 800/242–2424) answers consumer questions about film and photography.

## S

SAFETY

**"Trouble-Free Travel,"** from the AAA, is a booklet of tips for protecting yourself and your belongings when away from home. Send a stamped, self-addressed, legal-size envelope to **Flying Alone** (✉ Mail Stop 75, 1000 AAA Dr., Heathrow, FL 32746).

SENIOR CITIZENS

**EDUCATIONAL TRAVEL**

The nonprofit **Elderhostel** (✉ 75 Federal St., 3rd Floor, Boston, MA 02110, ☎ 617/426–7788), for people 60 and older, has offered inexpensive study programs since 1975. Courses cover everything from marine science to Greek mythology and cowboy poetry. Fees for programs in the United States and Canada, which usually last one week, run about $300,

not including transportation.

**ORGANIZATIONS**

Contact the **American Association of Retired Persons** (✉ AARP, 601 E St. NW, Washington, DC 20049, ☎ 202/434–2277; annual dues $8 per person or couple). Its Purchase Privilege Program secures discounts for members on lodging, car rentals, and sightseeing, and the AARP Motoring Plan (☎ 800/334–3300) furnishes domestic trip-routing information and emergency road-service aid for an annual fee of $39.95 ($59.95 for a premium version). Senior citizen travelers can also join the AAA for emergency road service and other travel benefits (☞ Discounts & Deals *in* Smart Travel Tips A to Z).

Additional sources for discounts on lodgings, car rentals, and other travel expenses, as well as helpful magazines and newsletters, are the **National Council of Senior Citizens** (✉ 1331 F St. NW, Washington, DC 20004, ☎ 202/347–8800; annual membership $12) and Sears's **Mature Outlook** (✉ Box 10448, Des Moines, IA 50306, ☎ 800/336–6330; annual membership $9.95).

**PUBLICATIONS**

*The 50+ Traveler's Guidebook: Where to Go, Where to Stay, What to Do,* by Anita Williams and Merrimac Dillon (✉ St. Martin's Press, 175 5th Ave., New York, NY 10010, ☎ 212/674–5151 or 800/288–2131;

$13.95), offers many useful tips. **"The Mature Traveler"** (✉ Box 50400, Reno, NV 89513, ☎ 702/786–7419; $29.95), a monthly newsletter, covers all sorts of travel deals.

**SPORTS**

The Governors Council on **Physical Fitness and Sports** (✉ 1330 N.W. 6th St., Ste. D, Gainesville 32601, ☎ 904/955–2120, FAX 904/373–8879) puts on the annual Senior Games Championships each December.

SPORTS

The Governor's Council on **Physical Fitness and Sports** puts on the Sunshine State Games each July in a different part of the state. The **Florida Sports Foundation** (✉ 107 W. Gaines St., Ste.466, Tallahassee 32399-2000, ☎ 904/488–8347) publishes guides on Florida boating, diving, fishing, golf, and baseball spring training.

New publications for guiding visitors to Florida's natural attractions include *Florida Wildlife Viewing Guide,* by Susan Cerulean and Ann Morrow ($7.95 plus $3 shipping; Falcon Press, Box 1718, Helena, MT 59624, ☎ 800/582–2665). The guide lists 96 marked wildlife-watching sites. The Florida Division of Tourism (☞ Visitor Information,) publishes **"Florida Trails: A Guide to Florida's Natural Habitats,"** a review of bicycling, canoeing, horseback riding, and walking trails, with additional information on camping, snorkeling, diving, and Florida ecosystems. The **"Official Florida Golf Guide"** is a free comprehensive listing of Florida courses published by the **Florida Sports Foundation** (✉ 107 W. Gaines St., Tallahassee 32399, ☎ 904/488–8347). You can request a free **"Recreation Guide to District Lands"**, with detailed descriptions of 32 marine, wetland, and upland recreational areas from the **St. Johns River Water Management District** (✉ Box 1429, Palatka 32178-1429).

Information on canoeing, kayaking, bicycling, and hiking trails statewide is available from the Florida Department of **Environmental Protection** (✉ Office of Greenways, Mail Station 585, 3900 Commonwealth Blvd., Tallahassee 32399-3000, ☎ 904/487–4784).

## BASEBALL
For information on all major-league baseball teams' exhibition games, call the **Florida Sports Foundation** (☎ 904/488–8347).

## BICYCLING
**Florida's Department of Transportation** (DOT) publishes free bicycle trail guides, which you can request from the state bicycle-pedestrian coordinator (E 605 Suwannee St., Mail Station 82, Tallahassee 32399-0450, P 904/487–1200); you can also request a free touring information packet. Also contact the DOT for names of bike

coordinators around the state.

## CANOEING
A free guide issued by the Florida Department of Environmental Protection (DEP); (☞ above), **Florida Recreational Trails System Canoe Trails**, describes nearly 950 miles of designated canoe trails among of a total canoe/kayak trail network now up to 1,550 miles. The DEP guide lists support services along 36 Florida creeks, rivers, and springs. Two additional guides are **Canoe Liveries and Outfitters Directory,** which lists rental services along the canoe trails in the system, and **Canoe Information Resources Guide,** which lists canoe clubs and organizations and printed records.

Two Florida canoe-outfitter organizations publish free lists of outfitters who organize trips and rent equipment: the Florida Association of **Canoe Liveries and Outfitters** (✉ Box 1764, Arcadia 33821) and the **Florida Canoeing and Kayaking Association** (✉ Box 20892, West Palm Beach 33416, ☎ 407/575–4530) which also publishes a quarterly newsletter, sponsors events, and can provide up-to-date information on trail conditions. "Canoe Outpost System" lists five outfitters on eight Florida rivers (✉ 2816 N.W. Rte. 661, Arcadia 33821, ☎ 813/494–1215).

## FISHING
For a free copy of the annual *Florida Fishing*

*Handbook,* which lists places to get a fishing license, write to the **Florida Game and Fresh Water Fish Commission** (✉ 620 S. Meridian St., Tallahassee 32399-1600, ☎ 904/488–1960). You can also request fishing guides for five Florida regions as well as educational bulletins on catch-and-release fishing and on largemouth and striped bass.

Write the **Florida Sea Grant Extension Program** (✉ Bldg. 803, University of Florida, Gainesville 32611, ☎ 904/392–5870) for a free list of publications on saltwater fishing, pier fishing, Florida varieties of fish, licenses and much more.

## HORSEBACK RIDING
Contact the **Sunshine State Horse Council** (✉ P.O. Box 4158, N. Fort Myers, 33918, ☎ 813/731–2999) or **Horse & Pony** (6229 Virginia La., Seffner 33584, ☎ 813/621–2510). You can also call the **Happy Wrangler Dude Ranch** (✉ 7586 S.W. 90th Ave., Bushnell, 33513, ☎ 352/793–DUDE), the only dude ranch in the state.

## JOGGING, RUNNING, AND WALKING
Local running clubs all over the state sponsor weekly public events for joggers, runners, and walkers. For a list of local clubs and events, call or send a SASE to **USA Track & Field–Florida** (✉ Attn. Event Marketing & Management Intl., 1322 N. Mills Ave., Orlando 32803, ☎ 407/895–

6323, FAX 407/897–3243), the Florida affiliate for the governing body of the sport. For information about South Florida events, contact the 1,600-member **Miami Runners Club** (✉ 7920 S.W. 40th St., Miami 33155, ☎ 305/227–1500, FAX 305/220–2450).

## PARI-MUTUEL SPORTS

You can request a schedule, updated every six months, from the Department of Business & Professional Regulations, **Division of Pari-Mutuel Wagering** (✉ 8405 N.W. 53rd St., Ste. C-250, Miami 33166, ☎ 305/470–5675, FAX 305/470–5686).

## TENNIS

For a schedule of tournaments and events, you can order the yearbook of the **United States Tennis Association Florida Section** (✉ 1280 S.W. 36th Ave., Ste. 305, Pompano Beach 33069, ☎ 305/968–3434, FAX 305/968–3986; $11).

## STUDENTS

### GROUPS

A major tour operator is **Contiki Holidays** (✉ 300 Plaza Alicante, Suite 900, Garden Grove, CA 92640, ☎ 714/740–0808 or 800/466–0610).

### HOSTELING

Contact **Hostelling International–American Youth Hostels** (✉ 733 15th St. NW, Suite 840, Washington, DC 20005, ☎ 202/783–6161 or 800/444–6111 for reservations at selected hostels, FAX 202/783–6171); in

Canada, **Hostelling International–Canada** (✉ 205 Catherine St., Suite 400, Ottawa, Ontario K2P 1C3, ☎ 613/237–7884); and in the United Kingdom, the **Youth Hostel Association of England and Wales** (✉ Trevelyan House, 8 St. Stephen's Hill, St. Albans, Hertfordshire AL1 2DY, ☎ 01727/855215 or 01727/845047). Membership (in the U.S., $25; in Canada, C$26.75; in the U.K., £9.30) gives you access to 5,000 hostels in 77 countries that charge $5–$30 per person per night.

### I.D. CARDS

To get discounts on transportation and admissions, get the **International Student Identity Card,** if you're a bona fide student, or the **GO 25: International Youth Travel Card,** if you're not a student but under age 26. Each includes basic travel-accident and illness coverage, plus a toll-free travel hot line. In the United States, either card costs $18; apply through the Council on **International Educational Exchange** (☞ Organizations, *below*). In Canada, cards are available for $15 each ($16 by mail) from Travel Cuts (☞ Organizations, *below*), and in the United Kingdom for £5 each at student unions and student travel companies.

### ORGANIZATIONS

A major contact is the Council on **International Educational Exchange** (✉ mail orders: CIEE, 205 E. 42nd St., 16th Floor,

New York, NY 10017, ☎ 212/661–1450); walk-in locations in Boston (✉ 729 Boylston St., 02116, ☎ 617/266–1926), Miami (✉ 9100 S. Dadeland Blvd., 33156, ☎ 305/670–9261), Los Angeles (✉ 10904 Lindbrook Dr., 90024, ☎ 310/208–3551), 43 other college towns in the U.S., and in the United Kingdom (✉ 28A Poland St., London W1V 3DB, ☎ 0171/437–7767). Twice per year, it publishes **"Student Travels"** magazine. The CIEE's Council Travel Service offers domestic air passes for bargain travel within the United States and is the exclusive U.S. agent for several student discount cards.

**The Educational Travel Centre** (✉ 438 N. Frances St., Madison, WI 53703, ☎ 608/256–5551 or 800/747–5551, FAX 608/256–2042) offers rail passes and low-cost airline tickets, mostly for flights that depart from Chicago.

In Canada, also contact **Travel Cuts** (✉ 187 College St., Toronto, Ontario M5T 1P7, ☎ 416/979–2406 or 800/667–2887).

## T

### TOUR OPERATORS

Among the companies that sell tours and packages to Florida, the following are nationally known, have a proven reputation, and offer plenty of options.

### GROUP TOURS

Deluxe➤ **Globus** (✉ 5301 S. Federal Circle, Littleton, CO 80123, ☎ 303/797–2800 or

800/221–0090, FAX 303/795–0962), **Maupintour** (✉ Box 807, Lawrence, KS 66047, ☎ 913/843–1211 or 800/255–4266, FAX 913/843–8351), and **Tauck Tours** (✉ Box 5027, 276 Post Rd. W, Westport, CT 06881, ☎ 203/226–6911 or 800/468–2825, FAX 203/221–6828).

FIRST CLASS➤ **Caravan Tours** (✉ 401 N. Michigan Ave., Chicago, IL 60611, ☎ 312/321–9800 or 800/227–2826), **Gadabout Tours** (✉ 700 E. Tahquitz Canyon Way, Palm Springs, CA 92262, ☎ 619/325–5556 or 800/952–5068), and **Mayflower Tours** (✉ Box 490, 1225 Warren Ave., Downers Grove, IL 60515, ☎ 708/960–3430 or 800/323–7064).

BUDGET➤ **Cosmos** (☞ Globus, *above*).

## PACKAGES

Independent vacation packages are available from major tour operators and airlines. Contact **Adventure Vacations** (✉ 10612 Beaver Dam Rd., Hunt Valley, MD 21030-2205, ☎ 410/785–3500 or 800/638–9040, FAX 410/584–2771), **American Airlines Fly AAway Vacations** (☎ 800/321–2121), **Continental Vacations** (☎ 800/634–5555), **Club Med** (✉ 40 W. 57th St., New York, NY 10019, ☎ 800/258–2633), **Delta Dream Vacations** (☎ 800/872–7786), **Globetrotters** (✉ 139 Main St., Cambridge, MA 02142, ☎ 800/333–1234 or 617/621–

9911), **SuperCities** (☎ 800/333–1234), **United Vacations** (☎ 800/328–6877), and **USAir Vacations** (☎ 800/455–0123). **Funjet Vacations,** based in Milwaukee, Wisconsin, **Gogo Tours,** based in Ramsey, New Jersey, and **Kingdom Tours,** based in Plains, Pennsylvania, sell Florida packages only through travel agents. For rail packages that combine air, hotel, and tour options, contact **Amtrak's Great American Vacations** (☎ 800/321–8684).

Regional operators specialize in putting together Florida packages for travelers in their local area. **Contact Apple Vacations** (✉ 25 N.W. Point Blvd., Elk Grove Village, IL 60007, ☎ 708/640–1150 or 800/365–2775), **Friendly Holidays** (✉ 1983 Marcus Ave., Lake Success, NY 11042, ☎ 800/344–5687), and **Travel Impressions** (✉ 465 Smith St., Farmingdale, NY 11735, ☎ 516/845–8000 or 800/284–0044, FAX 516/845–8095).

For independent self-drive itineraries, contact **Budget WorldClass Drive** (☎ 800/527–0700; in the U.K., 0800/181181).

FROM THE U.K.➤ Tour operators offering Florida packages include **Kuoni Travel** (✉ Kuoni House, Dorking, Surrey, RH5 4AZ, ☎ 01306/742–222), **British Airways Holidays** (✉ Astral Towers, Betts Way, London Rd., Crawley, West Sussex, RH10 2XA, ☎ 01293/723–111),

**Jetsave Travel Ltd.** (✉ Sussex House, London Rd., East Grinstead, West Sussex RH19 1LD, ☎ 01342/312–033), **Key to America** (✉ 1–3 Station Rd., Ashford, Middx. TW15 2UW, ☎ 01784/248–777), and **Virgin Holidays Ltd.** (✉ The Galleria, Station Rd., Crawley, West Sussex RH10 1WW, ☎ 01293/562–944).

Some travel agencies that offer cheap rates to Florida include **Trailfinders** (✉ 42–50 Earl's Court Rd., London W8 6FT, ☎ 0171/937–5400), **Travel Cuts** (✉ 295A Regent St., London W1R 7YA, ☎ 0171/637–3161), and **Flightfile** (✉ 49 Tottenham Court Rd., London W1P 9RE, ☎ 0171/700–2722).

## THEME TRIPS

ADVENTURE➤ **Outdoor Adventures** (✉ 6110-7 Powers Ave., Jacksonville, FL 32217, ☎ 904/739–1960, FAX 904/739–2216) runs kayaking, backpacking, bicycle, and tubing vacations in the wilderness of northeastern Florida.

FISHING➤ **Anglers Travel** (✉ 3100 Mill St., #206, Reno, NV 89502, ☎ 702/324–0580 or 800/624–8429, FAX 702/324–0583) offers fishing trips in central Florida. **Cutting Loose Expeditions** (✉ Box 447, Winter Park, FL 32790, ☎ 407/629–4700) can arrange a charter yacht or resort fishing vacation. Also try **Fishing International** (✉ Box 2132, Santa Rosa, CA 95405, ☎ 800/950–4242).

GOLF➤ **Golfpac** (✉ Box 162366, Altamonte Springs, FL 32716-2366, ☎ 800/327-0878, FAX 407/260-8989), **Great Florida Golf** (✉ Box 590, Palm Beach, FL 33480, ☎ 407/820-9336 or 800/544-8687), **Stine's Golftrips** (✉ Box 2314, Winter Haven, FL 33883-2314, ☎ 813/324-1300 or 800/428-1940, FAX 941/325-0384) and **World of Golf Tours** (✉ 255 Semoran Commerce Pl., Apopka 32703, ☎ 407/884-8300 or 800/729-1400) sell golf packages at resorts throughout the state.

HEALTH➤ Call **Spa-Finders** (✉ 91 5th Ave., #301, New York, NY 10003-3039, ☎ 212/924-6800 or 800/255-7727).

LEARNING➤ **Earthwatch** (✉ Box 403, 680 Mount Auburn St., Watertown, MA 02272, ☎ 617/926-8200 or 800/776-0188, FAX 617/926-8532) recruits volunteers as short-term assistants to scientists on research expeditions. Also contact **Oceanic Society Expeditions** (✉ Fort Mason Center, Bldg. E, San Francisco, CA 94123-1394, ☎ 415/441-1106 or 800/326-7491, FAX 415/474-3395).

MUSIC➤ **Dailey-Thorp Travel** (✉ 330 W. 58th St., #610, New York, NY 10019-1817, ☎ 212/307-1555 or 800/998-4677, FAX 212/974-1420) has March opera packages in Sarasota that include hotel stays, dining at fine restaurants, and sightseeing.

SAILING SCHOOL➤ **Annapolis Sailing School** (✉ Box 3334, 601 6th St., Annapolis, MD 21403, ☎ 410/267-7205 or 800/638-9192) has vacation packages to the Florida Keys that include sailing instruction. **Offshore Sailing School** (✉ 16731-110 McGregor Blvd., Fort Meyers, FL 33908, ☎ 813/454-1700 or 800/221-4326, FAX 813/454-1191) offers similar packages in St. Petersburg and Captiva Island.

SPORTS➤ **Championship Tennis Tours** (✉ 7350 E. Stetson Dr., #106, Scottsdale, AZ 85251, ☎ 602/990-8760 or 800/468-3664, FAX 602/990-8744) has packages to the Lipton Championships. For Daytona 500 packages, contact **Dan Chavez's Sports Empire** (✉ Box 6169, Lakewood, CA 90714-6169, ☎ 310/920-2350 or 800/255-5258). Orange Bowl packages including accommodations and transportation are available from **Spectacular Sport Specials** (✉ 5813 Citrus Blvd., New Orleans, LA 70123-5810, ☎ 504/734-9511 or 800/451-5772, FAX 504/734-7075).

YACHT CHARTERS➤ Contact **Huntley Yacht Vacations** (✉ 210 Preston Rd., Wernersville, PA 19565, ☎ 610/678-2628 or 800/322-9224, FAX 610/670-1767), **The Moorings** (✉ 19345 U.S. Hwy. 19 N, 4th floor, Clearwater, FL 34624-3193, ☎ 813/530-5424 or 800/535-7289, FAX 813/530-9474), **Ocean Voyages** (✉ 1709 Bridgeway, Sausalito, CA 94965, ☎ 415/332-4681, FAX 415/332-7460), **Russell Yacht Charters** (✉ 404 Hulls Hwy., Southport, CT 06490, ☎ 203/255-2783 or 800/635-8895), and **SailAway Yacht Charters** (✉ 15605 S.W. 92nd Ave., Miami, FL 33157-1972, ☎ 305/253-7245 or 800/724-5292, FAX 305/251-4408).

## ORGANIZATIONS

The **National Tour Association** (✉ NTA, 546 E. Main St., Lexington, KY 40508, ☎ 606/226-4444 or 800/755-8687) and the **United States Tour Operators Association** (✉ USTOA, 211 E. 51st St., Suite 12B, New York, NY 10022, ☎ 212/750-7371) can provide lists of members and information on booking tours.

## PUBLICATIONS

Contact the USTOA (☞ Organizations, *above*) for its **"Smart Traveler's Planning Kit."** Pamphlets in the kit include the "Worldwide Tour and Vacation Package Finder," "How to Select a Tour or Vacation Package," and information on the organization's consumer protection plan. Also get copy of the Better Business Bureau's **"Tips on Travel Packages"** (✉ Publication 24-195, 4200 Wilson Blvd., Arlington, VA 22203; $2). The National Tour Association will send you **"On Tour,"** a listing of its member operators, and a personalized package of information on group travel in North America.

**TRAIN TRAVEL**

**Amtrak** (☎ 800/872–7245) provides north–south service on two routes to the major cities of Jacksonville, Orlando, Tampa, West Palm Beach, Fort Lauderdale, and Miami and east–west service through Jacksonville, Tallahassee, and Pensacola, with many stops in between on all routes.

**TRAVEL GEAR**

For travel apparel, appliances, personal-care items, and other travel necessities, get a free catalog from **Magellan's** (☎ 800/962–4943, ℻ 805/568–5406), **Orvis Travel** (☎ 800/541–3541, ℻ 703/343–7053), or **TravelSmith** (☎ 800/950–1600, ℻ 415/455–0554).

**TRAVEL AGENCIES**

For names of reputable agencies in your area, contact the **American Society of Travel Agents**
(✉ ASTA, 1101 King St., Suite 200, Alexandria, VA 22314, ☎ 703/739–2782), the **Association of Canadian Travel Agents** (✉ Suite 201, 1729 Bank St., Ottawa, Ontario K1V 7Z5, ☎ 613/521–0474, ℻ 613/521–0805) or the **Association of British Travel Agents** (✉ 55-57 Newman St., London W1P 4AH, ☎ 0171/637–2444, ℻ 0171/637–0713).

**VISITOR INFORMATION**

Contact the **Florida Division of Tourism** (✉ 126 W. Van Buren St., Tallahassee 32399, ☎ 904/487–1462 or 904/487–1463, ℻ 904/487–0132). Canadian travelers can get assistance from **Travel, U.S.A.** (☎ 900/451–4050; US$2 per min).

The **Florida Division of Tourism** operates welcome centers on I–10, I–75, I–95, and U.S. 231 (near Graceville) and in the lobby of the New Capitol in Tallahassee (✉ Dept. of Commerce, 126 Van Buren St., Tallahassee 32399, ☎ 904/487–1462). Also contact regional tourist bureaus and chambers of commerce. (☞ individual chapters for listings).

**W**

**WEATHER**

For current conditions and forecasts, plus the local time and helpful travel tips, call the **Weather Channel Connection** (☎ 900/932–8437; 95¢ per minute) from a Touch-Tone phone.

The *International Traveler's Weather Guide* (✉ Weather Press, Box 660606, Sacramento, CA 95866, ☎ 916/974–0201 or 800/972–0201; $10.95 includes shipping), written by two meteorologists, provides month-by-month information on temperature, humidity, and precipitation in more than 175 cities worldwide.

# SMART TRAVEL TIPS A TO Z

*Basic Information on Traveling in Florida and Savvy Tips to Make Your Trip a Breeze*

## A
### AIR TRAVEL

If time is an issue, **always look for nonstop flights,** which require no change of plane. If possible, **avoid connecting flights,** which stop at least once and can involve a change of plane, even though the flight number remains the same; if the first leg is late, the second waits.

For better service, **fly smaller or regional carriers,** which often have higher passenger satisfaction ratings. Sometimes they have such in-flight amenities as leather seats or greater legroom and they often have better food.

### CUTTING COSTS

The Sunday travel section of most newspapers is a good place to look for deals.

MAJOR AIRLINES➤ The least-expensive airfares from the major airlines are priced for round-trip travel and are subject to restrictions. Usually, you must **book in advance and buy the ticket within 24 hours** to get cheaper fares, and you may have to **stay over a Saturday night.** The lowest fare is subject to availability, and only a small percentage of the plane's total seats is sold at that price. It's smart to **call a number of airlines, and when you are quoted a** good price, book it on the spot—the same fare may not be available on the same flight the next day. Airlines generally allow you to change your return date for a $25 to $50 fee. If you don't use your ticket, you can apply the cost toward the purchase of a new ticket, again for a small charge. However, most low-fare tickets are nonrefundable. To get the lowest airfare, **check different routings.** If your destination has more than one gateway, **compare prices to different airports.**

FROM THE U.K.➤ To save money on flights, **look into an APEX or Super-PEX ticket.** APEX tickets must be booked in advance and have certain restrictions. Super-PEX tickets can be purchased right at the airport.

### ALOFT

AIRLINE FOOD➤ If you hate airline food, **ask for special meals when booking.** These can be vegetarian, low-cholesterol, or kosher, for example; commonly prepared to order in smaller quantities than standard fare, they can be tastier.

SMOKING➤ Smoking is banned on all flights of less than six hours' duration within the United States and on all Canadian flights; the ban also applies to domestic segments of international flights aboard U.S. and foreign carriers. Delta has banned smoking system-wide.

## C
### CAMERAS, CAMCORDERS, & COMPUTERS

### LAPTOPS

Before you depart, **be prepared to turn of your computer;** at security you may be asked to prove that it is what it appears to be. At the airport, you may prefer to **request a manual inspection,** although security X-rays do not harm hard-disk or floppy-disk storage.

### PHOTOGRAPHY

If your camera is new or if you haven't used it for a while, **shoot and develop a few rolls of film** before you leave. Always **store film in a cool, dry place**—never in your car's glove compartment or on the shelf under the rear window.

The chances of your film growing cloudy increase with each pass through an X-ray machine. To protect against this, carry it in a clear plastic bag and **ask for hand inspection at security.** Such requests are virtually always honored at U.S. airports. Don't depend on a lead-lined bag to protect film in checked luggage—the airline may increase the radiation to see what's inside.

### VIDEO

Videotape is not damaged by X-rays, but it may be harmed by the magnetic field of a walk-through metal detector, so **ask that videotapes be hand-checked.**

### CUTTING COSTS

Florida is a bazaar of car rentals, with more discount companies offering more bargains—and more fine print—than any other state in the nation. For the best deal, **look for the best combination rate for car and airfare.**

To get the best deal, **book through a travel agent who is willing to shop around.** When pricing cars, **ask where the rental lot is located.** Some off-airport locations offer lower rates—even though their lots are only minutes away from the terminal via complimentary shuttle. You also may want to **price local car-rental companies,** whose rates may be lower still, although service and maintenance standards may not be as high as those of a national firm. Ask your agent to **look for fly-drive packages,** which also save you money, and **ask if local taxes are included** in the rental or fly-drive price. These can be as high as 20% in some destinations. Don't forget to find out about required deposits, cancellation penalties, drop-off charges, and

the cost of any required insurance coverage.

Also **ask your travel agent about a company's customer-service record.** How has it responded to late plane arrivals and vehicle mishaps? Are there often lines at the rental counter, and—if you're traveling during a holiday period—does a confirmed reservation guarantee you a car?

### INSURANCE

When driving a rented car, you are generally responsible for any damage to or loss of the rental vehicle, as well as any property damage or personal injury that you cause. Before you rent, **see what coverage you already have** under the terms of your personal auto insurance policy and credit cards.

For about $14 a day, rental companies sell protection, known as a collision- or loss- damage waiver (CDW or LDW), that eliminates your liability for damage to the car; it's always optional and should never be automatically added to your bill.

If you do not have auto insurance or an umbrella insurance policy that covers damage to third parties, purchasing CDW or LDW is highly recommended.

### FOR U.K. CITIZENS

In the United States you must be 21 to rent a car; rates may be higher if you're under 25. You'll pay extra for child seats (about $3 per day), compulsory for children under five, and for additional

drivers (about $2 per day). To pick up your reserved car you will need the reservation voucher, a passport, a U.K. driver's license, and a travel policy that covers each driver.

### SURCHARGES

Before you pick up a car in one city and leave it in another, **ask about drop-off charges or one-way service fees,** which can be substantial. Note, too, that some rental agencies charge extra if you return the car before the time specified on your contract. To avoid a hefty refueling fee, **fill the tank just before you turn in the car**—but be aware that gas stations near the rental outlet may overcharge.

When traveling with children, **plan ahead** and **involve your youngsters** as you outline your trip. When packing, **include things to keep them busy.** On sightseeing days, **schedule activities of special interest to your children,** like a trip to a zoo or a playground. If you **plan your itinerary around seasonal festivals,** you'll never lack for things to do. In addition, **check local newspapers for special events** mounted by public libraries, museums, and parks.

### BABY-SITTING

For recommended local sitters, **check with your hotel desk.**

### DRIVING

If you are renting a car, don't forget to **arrange for a car seat when you**

## THE GOLD GUIDE / SMART TRAVEL TIPS

**reserve.** Sometimes they're free.

### FLYING

On domestic flights, children under two not occupying a seat travel free, and older children are charged at the lowest applicable adult rate.

BAGGAGE➤ In general, the adult baggage allowance applies to children paying half or more of the adult fare.

SAFETY SEATS➤ According to the FAA, it's a good idea to **use safety seats aloft** for children weighing less than 40 pounds. Airline policies vary. U.S. carriers allow FAA-approved models but usually require that you buy a ticket, even if your child would otherwise ride free, since the seats must be strapped into regular seats.

FACILITIES➤ When making your reservation, **request for children's meals or freestanding bassinets** if you need them; the latter are available only to those seated at the bulkhead, where there's enough legroom. If you don't need a bassinet, **think twice before requesting bulkhead seats**—the only storage space for in-flight necessities is in the overhead bins.

### LODGING

Florida may have the highest concentration of hotels with organized children's programs in the United States; sometimes they are complimentary—sometimes there's a charge. Not all accept children still in diapers, and some offer programs when their central reservations services say they don't.

Most hotels allow children under a certain age to stay in their parents' room at no extra charge; others charge them as extra adults. Be sure to **ask about the cutoff age.** Often the best bet for traveling with children is to book space that comes with a kitchen and more than one bedroom. Such properties are especially plentiful around Orlando, where hoteliers expect steady family trade.

## CUSTOMS & DUTIES

### IN FLORIDA

Visitors from outside the United States age 21 or over may import the following: 200 cigarettes or 50 cigars or 2 kilograms of tobacco; one U.S. liter of alcohol; gifts to the value of $100. Restricted items include meat products, seeds, plants, and fruits. Never carry illegal drugs.

### IN CANADA

If you've been out of Canada for at least seven days, you may bring in C$500 worth of goods duty-free. If you've been away for fewer than seven days but for more than 48 hours, the duty-free allowance drops to C$200; if your trip lasts between 24 and 48 hours, the allowance is C$50. You cannot pool allowances with family members. Goods claimed under the C$500 exemption may follow you by mail; those claimed under the lesser exemptions must accompany you.

Alcohol and tobacco products may be included in the seven-day and 48-hour exemptions but not in the 24-hour exemption. If you meet the age requirements of the province or territory through which you reenter Canada, you may bring in, duty-free, 1.14 liters (40 imperial ounces) of wine or liquor *or* 24 12-ounce cans or bottles of beer or ale. If you are 16 or older, you may bring in, duty-free, 200 cigarettes, 50 cigars or cigarillos, and 400 tobacco sticks or 400 grams of manufactured tobacco. Alcohol and tobacco must accompany you on your return.

An unlimited number of gifts with a value of up to C$60 each may be mailed to Canada duty-free. These do not affect your duty-free allowance on your return. Label the package "Unsolicited Gift— Value Under $60." Alcohol and tobacco are excluded.

### IN THE U.K.

From countries outside the EU, including the United States, you may import, duty-free, 200 cigarettes, 100 cigarillos, 50 cigars, or 250 grams of tobacco; 1 liter of spirits or 2 liters of fortified or sparkling wine or liqueurs; 2 liters of still table wine; 60 milliliters of perfume; 250 milliliters of toilet water; plus £136 worth of other goods, including gifts and souvenirs.

## D
### DINING

One cautionary word: Raw oysters have been identified as a problem for people with chronic illness of the liver, stomach, or blood, or who have immune disorders. Since 1993, all Florida restaurants serving raw oysters are required to post a notice in plain view of all patrons warning of the risks associated with consuming them.

### DISABILITIES & ACCESSIBILITY

When discussing accessibility with an operator or reservationist, **ask hard questions.** Are there any stairs, inside *or* out? Are there grab bars next to the toilet *and* in the shower/tub? How wide is the doorway to the room? To the bathroom? For the most extensive facilities, meeting the latest legal specifications, **opt for newer accommodations,** which more often have been designed with access in mind. Older properties or ships must usually be retrofitted and may offer more limited facilities as a result. Be sure to **discuss your needs before booking.**

### DISCOUNTS & DEALS

You shouldn't have to pay for a discount. In fact, you may already be eligible for all kinds of savings. Here are some time-honored strategies for getting the best deal.

### LOOK IN YOUR WALLET

When you **use your credit card to make** travel purchases, you may get free travel-accident insurance, collision damage insurance, medical or legal assistance, depending on the card and bank that issued it. Visa and MasterCard provide one or more of these services, so **get a copy of your card's travel benefits.** If you are a member of the AAA or an oil-company-sponsored road-assistance plan, always **ask hotel or car-rental reservationists for auto-club discounts.** Some clubs offer additional discounts on tours, cruises, or admission to attractions. And don't forget that auto-club membership entitles you to free maps and trip-planning services.

### SENIORS CITIZENS & STUDENTS

As a senior-citizen traveler, you may be eligible for special rates, but you should mention your senior-citizen status up front. If you're a students or under 26 can also get discounts, especially if you have an official ID card (☞ Senior-Citizen Discounts *and* Students on the Road, *below*).

### DIAL FOR DOLLARS

To save money, **look into "1-800" discount reservations services,** which often have lower rates. These services use their buying power to get a better price on hotels, airline tickets, and sometimes even car rentals. When booking a room, always **call the hotel's local toll-free number** (if one is available) rather than the central reservations number—you'll often get a better price. Ask the reservationist about special packages or corporate rates, which are usually available even if you're not traveling on business.

### JOIN A CLUB?

Discount clubs can be a legitimate source of savings, but you must use the participating hotels and visit the participating attractions in order to realize any benefits. Remember, too, that you have to pay a fee to join, so **determine if you'll save enough to warrant your membership fee.** Before booking with a club, **make sure the hotel or other supplier isn't offering a better deal.**

### DRIVING

Three major interstates lead to Florida. I–95 begins in Maine, runs south through the Mid-Atlantic states, and enters Florida just north of Jacksonville. It continues south past Daytona Beach, the Space Coast, Vero Beach, Palm Beach, and Fort Lauderdale, eventually ending in Miami.

I–75 begins in Michigan at the Canadian border and runs south through Ohio, Kentucky, Tennessee, and Georgia then moves through the center of the state before veering west into Tampa. It follows the west coast south to Naples, then crosses the state, and ends in Fort Lauderdale.

California and all the most southern states are connected to Florida by I–10 which moves east from Los Angeles through Arizona, New Mexico, Texas,

Louisiana, Mississippi, and Alabama; it enters Florida at Pensacola and crosses the northern part of the state to Jacksonville.

## SAFETY

Before setting off on any drive, **make sure you know where you're going** and carry a map. When you rent your car or at your hotel **ask if there are any areas that you should avoid.** A new system indicates the main tourist routes in a series of red sunbursts on special directional signs. Always **keep your doors locked,** and ask questions only at toll booths, gas stations, or other obviously safe locations. Also, **don't stop if your car is bumped from behind** or if you're asked for directions. One hesitates to foster rude behavior, but at least for now the roads are too risky to stop any place you're not familiar with (other than as traffic laws require). If you'll be renting a car, **ask the car-rental agency for a cellular phone.** Alamo, Avis and Hertz are among the companies with in-car phones.

## SPEED LIMITS

Speed limits are 55 mph on state highways, 30 mph within city limits and residential areas, and 55–65 mph on interstates and Florida's Turnpike. Be alert for signs announcing exceptions.

## H
### HEALTH
### CONCERNS

If you are unaccustomed to strong subtropical sun, you run a risk of sunburn and heat prostration, even in winter. So hit the beach early in the day or in late afternoon. If you must be out at midday, limit strenuous exercise, drink plenty of liquids, and wear a hat. Before swimming, make sure there's no undertow.

## DIVERS' ALERT

Scuba divers take note: **Do not fly within 24 hours of scuba diving.**

## I
### INSURANCE

Travel insurance can protect your monetary investment, replace your luggage and its contents, or provide for medical coverage should you fall ill during your trip. Most tour operators, travel agents, and insurance agents sell specialized health-and-accident, flight, trip-cancellation, and luggage insurance as well as comprehensive policies with some or all of these coverages. Comprehensive policies may also reimburse you for delays due to weather—an important consideration if you're traveling during the winter months. Some health-insurance policies do not cover preexisting conditions, but waivers may be available in specific cases. Coverage is sold by the companies in Important Contacts A to Z, who act as the policy's administrators; the actual insurance is usually underwritten by a well-known company, such as The Travelers or Continental Insurance.

Before you make any purchase, **review your existing health and homeowner's policies** to find out whether they cover expenses incurred while traveling.

## BAGGAGE

Airline liability for baggage is limited to $1,250 per person on domestic flights. On international flights, it amounts to $9.07 per pound or $20 per kilogram for checked baggage (roughly $640 per 70-pound bag) and $400 per passenger for unchecked baggage. Insurance for losses exceeding the terms of your airline ticket can be bought directly from the airline at check-in for about $10 per $1,000 of coverage; note that it excludes a rather extensive list of items, shown on your airline ticket.

## COMPREHENSIVE

Comprehensive insurance policies include all the coverages described above plus some that may not be available in more specific policies. If you have purchased an expensive vacation, especially one that involves travel abroad, comprehensive insurance is a must; **look for policies that include trip delay insurance,** which will protect you in the event that weather problems cause you to miss your flight, tour, or cruise. A few insurers will also sell you a waiver for preexisting medical conditions. Some of the companies that offer both these features are Access America, Carefree Travel, Travel Insured International, and TravelGuard.

## FLIGHT

You should **think twice before buying flight insurance.** Often purchased as a last-minute impulse at the airport, it pays a lump sum when a plane crashes, either to a beneficiary if the insured dies or sometimes to a surviving passenger who loses his or her eyesight or a limb. Supplementing the airlines' coverage described in the limits-of-liability paragraphs on your ticket, it's expensive and basically unnecessary. Charging an airline ticket to a major credit card often automatically provides you with coverage that may also extend to travel by bus, train, and ship.

## U.K. TRAVELERS

According to the Association of British Insurers, a trade association representing 450 insurance companies, it's wise to **buy extra medical coverage when you visit the United States.** You can buy an annual travel insurance policy valid for most vacations during the year in which it's purchased. If you are pregnant or have a preexisting medical condition make sure you're covered before buying such a policy.

## TRIP

Without insurance, you will lose all or most of your money if you cancel your trip regardless of the reason. Especially if your airline ticket, cruise, or package tour is nonrefundable and cannot be changed, it's essential that you **buy trip-cancellation-and-inter-**ruption insurance. When considering how much coverage you need, look for a policy that will cover the cost of your trip plus the nondiscounted price of a one-way airline ticket should you need to return home early. Read the fine print carefully, especially sections that define "family member" and "preexisting medical conditions." Also **consider default or bankruptcy insurance,** which protects you against a supplier's failure to deliver. Be aware, however, that if you buy such a policy from a travel agency, tour operator, airline, or cruise line, it may not cover default by the firm in question.

## L

LODGING

## APARTMENT & VILLA RENTAL

If you want a home base that's roomy enough for a family and comes with cooking facilities, **consider taking a furnished rental.** This can also save you money, but not always—some rentals are luxury properties (economical only when your party is large). Home-exchange directories list rentals—often second homes owned by prospective house swappers—and some services search for a house or apartment for you (even a castle if that's your fancy) and handle the paperwork. Some send an illustrated catalog; others send photographs only of specific properties, sometimes at a charge; up-front registration fees may apply.

## HOME EXCHANGE

If you would like to find a house, an apartment, or some other type of vacation property to exchange for your own while on holiday, **join a home-exchange organization,** which will send you its updated listings of available exchanges for a year, and will include your own listing in at least one of them. Arrangements for the actual exchange are made by the two parties involved, not by the organization.

## HOTELS & MOTELS

Florida has every conceivable type of lodging, everything from treehouses to penthouses, from mansions for hire to hostels. Recession has discouraged wildfire expansion, but even with occupancy rates inching up above 70%, there are always rooms for the night, except maybe during Christmas and other holiday weekends. Affordable lodgings can be found in even the most glittery resort towns, typically motel rooms that may cost as little as $30–$40 a night; they may not be in the best part of town, mind you, but they won't be in the worst, either (perhaps along busy highways where you'll need the roar of the air-conditioning to drown out the traffic). Since beachfront properties tend to be more expensive, **look for properties a little off the beach for the best bargain;** still, many beachfront properties are surprisingly affordable, too, as in places like Olde Naples in the far southwest and

Amelia Island in the far northeast.

Vintage hotels are everywhere. The classics include the Breakers and the Boca Raton Resort & Club, both in Boca Raton; the Biltmore in Coral Gables; and the Casa Marina in Key West. Florida also has more than 200 historic inns, from the Miami River Inn in downtown Miami to the Governors Inn in Tallahassee and the New World Landing Inn in Pensacola.

Children are welcome generally everywhere in Florida. Pets are another matter, so **inquire ahead of time if you're bringing an animal with you.**

In the busy seasons— over Christmas, from late January through Easter, and during holiday weekends in summer—always reserve ahead for the top properties. St. Augustine stays busy all summer because of its historic flavor. Key West is jam-packed for Fantasy Fest at Halloween. If you're not booking through a travel agent, call the visitors bureau or the chamber of commerce in the area where you're going to check whether any special event is scheduled for when you plan to arrive. If demand isn't especially high for the time you have in mind, you can often **save by showing up at a lodging in mid- to late afternoon**—desk clerks are typically willing to negotiate with travelers in order to fill those rooms late in the day. In addition,

check with chambers of commerce for discount coupons for selected properties.

### INNS & B&BS

Small inns and guest houses are increasingly numerous in Florida. Many offer bed-and-breakfast in a homelike setting; many, in fact, are in private homes, and the owners treat you almost like family.

### VACATION OWNERSHIP RESORTS

Vacation ownership resorts sell hotel rooms, condominium apartments, and villas in weekly, monthly, or quarterly increments. The weekly arrangement is most popular; it's often referred to as "interval ownership" or "time sharing." Of more than 3,000 vacation ownership resorts around the world, some 500 are in Florida, with the heaviest concentration in the Walt Disney World/Orlando area. As an owner, you can join your resort's exchange organization and swap your interval for another someplace else in any year when you want a change of scene. Non-owners can also rent at many vacation ownership resorts.

## M
### MONEY

### ATMS

CASH ADVANCES➤ Chances are that you can **use your bank card, MasterCard, or Visa at ATMs** to withdraw money from an account or get a cash advance. Before leaving home, **check on frequency**

limits for withdrawals and cash advances.

TRANSACTION FEES➤ On credit-card cash advances you are charged interest from the day you receive the money, whether from a teller or an ATM. Transaction fees for ATM withdrawals outside your local area may be higher than those charged for withdrawals at home.

### TRAVELER'S CHECKS

Whether or not to buy traveler's checks depends on where you are headed; **take cash to rural areas and small towns, traveler's checks to cities.** The most widely recognized checks are issued by American Express, Citicorp, Thomas Cook, and Visa. These are sold by major commercial banks for 1%–3% of the checks' face value—it pays to **shop around.** Both American Express and Thomas Cook issue checks that can be countersigned and used by either you or your traveling companion. Before leaving home, **contact your issuer for information on where to cash your checks** without incurring a transaction fee. Record the numbers of all your checks, and keep this listing in a separate place, crossing off the numbers of checks you have cashed.

### WIRING MONEY

For a fee of 3%–10%, depending on the amount of the transaction, you can have money sent to you from home through Money-

GramSM or Western Union. The transferred funds and the service fee can be charged to a MasterCard or Visa account.

# N
## NATIONAL PARKS

If you are a frequent visitor, senior citizen, or traveler with a disability, you can **save money on park entrance fees** by getting a discount pass available at all national park entrances. The Golden Eagle Pass can be a good deal if you plan to visit several parks. Priced at $25, it entitles you and your companions to free admission to *all parks* for a year (but not fees for camping and parking). Both the Golden Age Passport, for U.S. citizens or permanent residents 62 or older, and the Golden Access Passport, for travelers with disabilities, entitle holders to free entry to all national parks plus 50% off fees for the use of all park facilities and services except those run by private concessionaires. Both passports are free; you must show proof of age and U.S. citizenship or permanent residency (such as a U.S. passport, driver's license, or birth certificate) or proof of disability.

# P
## PACKING
## FOR FLORIDA

The northern part of the state is much cooler in winter than the southern part. However, always **take a sweater or jacket,** just in case.

The Miami area and the Tampa–St. Petersburg area are warm year-round and often extremely humid in summer months. Be prepared for sudden summer storms, but keep in mind that plastic raincoats are uncomfortable in the high humidity.

Dress is casual throughout the state, with sundresses, jeans, or walking shorts appropriate during the day; **bring comfortable walking shoes or sneakers** for theme parks. A few restaurants request that men wear jackets and ties, but most do not. Be prepared for air-conditioning working in overdrive.

You can generally swim year-round in peninsular Florida from about New Smyrna Beach south on the Atlantic coast and from Tarpon Springs south on the Gulf Coast. Be sure to **take a sun hat and sunscreen** because the sun can be fierce, even in winter and even if it is chilly or overcast.

Bring an extra pair of eyeglasses or contact lenses in your carry-on luggage, and if you have a health problem, **pack enough medication** to last the trip. It's important that you **don't put prescription drugs or valuables in luggage to be checked,** for it could go astray.

## LUGGAGE

Airline baggage allowances depend on the airline, the route, and the class of your ticket; ask in advance. In general, on domestic flights you are entitled to

check two bags. A third piece may be brought on board, but it must fit easily under the seat in front of you or in the overhead compartment. In the United States, the FAA gives airlines broad latitude regarding carry-on allowances, and they tend to tailor them to different aircraft and operational conditions. Charges for excess, oversize, or overweight pieces vary.

SAFEGUARDING YOUR LUGGAGE➣ Before leaving home, **itemize your bags' contents** and their worth, and label them with your name, address, and phone number. (If you use your home address, cover it so that potential thieves can't see it readily.) Inside each bag, **pack a copy of your itinerary.** At check-in, **make sure that each bag is correctly tagged** with the destination airport's three-letter code. If your bags arrive damaged—or fail to arrive at all—file a written report with the airline before leaving the airport.

## PASSPORTS
## & VISAS

### CANADIANS

No passport is necessary to enter the United States.

### U.K. CITIZENS

British citizens need a valid passport to enter the United States. If you are staying for fewer than 90 days and traveling on a vacation, with a return or on-ward ticket, you probably will not need a visa. However, you will need to fill out the Visa Waiver Form, 1-94W, supplied by the airline.

THE GOLD GUIDE / SMART TRAVEL TIPS

Always **leave one photocopy of your passport's data page** with someone at home and keep another with you, separated from your passport, while traveling. If you lose your passport, promptly call the nearest embassy or consulate and the local police; having the data page information can speed replacement.

## S

### SENIOR-CITIZEN DISCOUNTS

To qualify for age-related discounts, **mention your senior-citizen status up front** when booking hotel reservations, not when checking out, and before you're seated in restaurants, not when paying the bill. Note that discounts may be limited to certain menus, days, or hours. When renting a car, **ask about promotional car-rental discounts**—they can net even lower costs than your senior-citizen discount.

### SPORTS

#### FISHING

In Atlantic and Gulf waters, fishing seasons and other regulations vary by location and by species. You will need to **buy a license for both freshwater and saltwater fishing.** Nonresident fees for a saltwater fishing license are $30. Nonresidents can purchase freshwater fishing licenses good for seven days ($15) or for one year ($30). Typically, you'll pay a $1.50 surcharge at most any marina, bait-and-tackle shop, Kmart, WalMart, or other license vendor.

### STUDENTS ON THE ROAD

To save money, **look into deals available through student-oriented travel agencies.** To qualify, you'll need to have a bona fide student ID card. Members of international student groups are also eligible (☞ Students *in* Important Contacts A to Z).

## T

### TELEPHONES

#### LONG-DISTANCE

The long-distance services of AT&T, MCI, and Sprint make calling home relatively convenient and let you avoid hotel surcharges; typically, you dial an 800 number in the United States.

### TOUR OPERATORS

A package or tour to Florida can make your vacation less expensive and more hassle-free. Firms that sell tours and packages reserve airline seats, hotel rooms, and rental cars in bulk and pass some of the savings on to you. In addition, the best operators have local representatives available to help you at your destination.

#### A GOOD DEAL?

The more your package or tour includes, the better you can predict the ultimate cost of your vacation. Make sure you know exactly what is covered, and **beware of hidden costs.** Are taxes, tips, and service charges included? Transfers and baggage handling? Entertainment and excursions? These can add up.

Most packages and tours are rated deluxe, first-class superior, first class, tourist, or budget. The key difference is usually accommodations. If the package or tour you are considering is priced lower than in your wildest dreams, **be skeptical.** Also, **make sure your travel agent knows the accommodations** and other services. Ask about the hotel's location, room size, beds, and whether it has a pool, room service, or programs for children, if you care about these. Has your agent been there in person or sent others you can contact?

#### BUYER BEWARE

Each year a number of consumers are stranded or lose their money when operators—even very large ones with excellent reputations—go out of business. To avoid becoming one of them, take the time to **check out the operator**—find out how long the company has been in business and ask several agents about its reputation. Next, **don't book unless the firm has a consumer-protection program.** Members of the USTOA and the NTA are required to set aside funds for the sole purpose of covering your payments and travel arrangements in case of default. Nonmember operators may instead carry insurance; look for the details in the operator's brochure—and for the name of an underwriter with a solid reputation. Note: When it comes to tour operators, **don't trust escrow accounts.** Although there are laws governing those of charter-flight operators, no governmental body prevents tour operators from raiding the till.

Next, **contact your local Better Business Bureau and the attorney general's offices** in both your own state and the operator's; have any complaints been filed? Finally, **pay with a major credit card.** Then you can cancel payment, provided that you can document your complaint. Always **consider trip-cancellation insurance** (☞ Insurance, *above*).

BIG VS. SMALL➢ Operators that handle several hundred thousand travelers per year can use their purchasing power to give you a good price. Their high volume may also indicate financial stability. But some small companies provide more personalized service; because they tend to specialize, they may also be more knowledgeable about a given area.

## USING AN AGENT

Travel agents are excellent resources. In fact, large operators accept bookings made only through travel agents. But it's good to **collect brochures from several agencies** because some agents' suggestions may be skewed by promotional relationships with tour and package firms that reward them for volume sales. If you have a special interest, **find an agent with expertise in that area**; ASTA can provide leads in the United States. (Don't rely solely on your agent, though;

agents may be unaware of small-niche operators, and some special-interest travel companies only sell direct.)

## SINGLE TRAVELERS

Prices are usually quoted per person, based on two sharing a room. If traveling solo, you may be required to pay the full double-occupancy rate. Some operators eliminate this surcharge if you agree to be matched up with a roommate of the same sex, even if one is not found by departure time.

### TRAVEL GEAR

For useful items that can save space when packing and make life on the road more convenient **check out travel gear catalogues.** Compact alarm clocks, travel irons, travel wallets, and personal-care kits are common.

## W
### WHEN TO GO

Florida is a state for all seasons, although most visitors prefer October–April, particularly in southern Florida.

Winter remains the height of the tourist season, when southern Florida is crowded with "snowbirds" fleeing cold weather in the North. Hotels, bars, discos, restaurants, shops, and attractions are all crowded. Hollywood and Broadway celebrities appear in sophisticated supper clubs, and other performing artists hold the stage at ballets, operas, concerts, and theaters. From mid-December through January 2, Walt Disney World's

Magic Kingdom is lavishly decorated, and there are daily parades and other extravaganzas, as well as overwhelming crowds. In the Jacksonville and Panhandle area, winter is off-season—an excellent bargain.

For the college crowd, spring vacation is still the time to congregate in Florida, especially in Panama City Beach and the Daytona Beach area; Fort Lauderdale, where city officials have refashioned the beachfront more as a family resort, no longer indulges young revelers, so it's much less popular with college students than it once was.

Summer in Florida, as smart budget-minded visitors have discovered, is often hot and very humid, but along the coast, ocean breezes make the season quite bearable and many hotels lower their prices considerably. In the Panhandle and central Florida, summer is peak season. Theme park lines shrink only after children return to school in September. Large numbers of international visitors keep year-round visitation high at theme parks.

For senior citizens, fall is the time for discounts for many attractions and hotels in Orlando and along the Pinellas Suncoast in the Tampa Bay area.

## CLIMATE

What follows are average daily maximum and minimum temperatures for major cities in Florida.

## Climate in Florida

### KEY WEST (THE KEYS)

| Jan. | 76F | 24C | May | 85F | 29C | Sept. | 90F | 32C |
|------|-----|-----|------|-----|-----|-------|-----|-----|
|      | 65  | 18  |      | 74  | 23  |       | 77  | 25  |
| Feb. | 76F | 24C | June | 88F | 31C | Oct.  | 83F | 28C |
|      | 67  | 19  |      | 77  | 25  |       | 76  | 24  |
| Mar. | 79F | 26C | July | 90F | 32C | Nov.  | 79F | 26C |
|      | 68  | 20  |      | 79  | 26  |       | 70  | 21  |
| Apr. | 81F | 27C | Aug. | 90F | 32C | Dec.  | 76F | 24C |
|      | 72  | 22  |      | 79  | 26  |       | 67  | 19  |

### MIAMI

| Jan. | 74F | 23C | May | 83F | 28C | Sept. | 86F | 30C |
|------|-----|-----|------|-----|-----|-------|-----|-----|
|      | 63  | 17  |      | 72  | 22  |       | 76  | 24  |
| Feb. | 76F | 24C | June | 85F | 29C | Oct.  | 83F | 28C |
|      | 63  | 17  |      | 76  | 24  |       | 72  | 22  |
| Mar. | 77F | 25C | July | 88F | 31C | Nov.  | 79F | 26C |
| 65   | 18  |     | 76   | 24  |     | 67    | 19  |     |
| Apr. | 79F | 26C | Aug. | 88F | 31C | Dec.  | 76F | 26C |
| 68   | 20  |     | 77   | 25  |     | 63    | 17  |     |

### ORLANDO

| Jan. | 70F | 21C | May | 88F | 31C | Sept. | 88F | 31C |
|------|-----|-----|------|-----|-----|-------|-----|-----|
|      | 49  | 9   |      | 67  | 19  |       | 74  | 23  |
| Feb. | 72F | 22C | June | 90F | 32C | Oct.  | 83F | 28C |
|      | 54  | 12  |      | 72  | 22  |       | 67  | 19  |
| Mar. | 76F | 24C | July | 90F | 32C | Nov.  | 76F | 24C |
|      | 56  | 13  |      | 74  | 23  |       | 58  | 14  |
| Apr. | 81F | 27C | Aug. | 90F | 32C | Dec.  | 70F | 21C |
|      | 63  | 17  |      | 74  | 23  |       | 52  | 11  |

THE GOLD GUIDE / SMART TRAVEL TIPS

# 1 Destination: Florida

# CATCH IT WHILE YOU CAN

ONLY YESTERDAY the world depicted in photos and displays at the Museum of the Florida Keys teems with bird and fish life, deer and gators, scrub flats laced by mangroves, and landscape randomly canopied by palm and hardwood hammocks. Over all hang the pewter skies of dawn, the blue skies of balmy afternoons, purple storms of summer, and red-orange sunsets. Rimming the shore for 220 miles is the reef, a magical other world beneath the sea.

But outside the museum, along the Overseas Highway, that splendor is eclipsed by motels, gas stations, RV parks, fast-food chains, convenience stores, shell shops, dive shops, and dives.

Florida these days is struggling to redress a century of environmental disaster. The state has lost more than half its wetlands and much of its upland forests, more than half its waters have been contaminated, and its coasts have been cankered with concrete. Lake bass carry dangerous levels of mercury, and the catch of bay shrimp continues to dwindle.

For more than 100 years, Florida's allure has engendered Florida's ruin. Drawn by the state's natural bounty and warm winters, early developers ravaged the state's bird populations, tore out its orchids, burned tree snail habitats, and massacred gators. The winter climate continues to draw hundreds of new year-round residents daily—swelling Florida's population to fourth place in the nation at a rate likely to surpass New York by the turn of the century.

It all began in 1513 when Juan Ponce de León stumbled on the peninsula that became Florida, in his now legendary search for a Fountain of Youth. But long before what amounted to Spanish invasion, Native Americans had discovered the area's restorative springs, rich fishing and hunting grounds along both coasts, and life-sustaining lakes and rivers. Spain named the region la Florida, land of flowers. But the Spanish never stopped to smell the fra-grance: Florida disappointed them. Gold was what they were after, and Florida produced none.

Even after acquisition by the United States in 1821 and following statehood in 1845, Florida attracted few permanent settlers. Except for cotton plantations that spread south from Georgia and railroads that linked Atlantic and Gulf ports to facilitate commerce in cotton and timber, settlement of the state had to wait for the end of the Civil War.

What would become the Sunshine State came into its own only in the last two decades of the 19th century. One early visionary was Ralph Middleton Munroe, a Staten Island yacht designer who shared Ralph Waldo Emerson's idea that humans had gotten the civilizing process wrong and needed to start over in wilderness. Finding his own piece of wilderness, Munroe settled at Jack's Bight, where he formed the community of Coconut Grove. He convinced early Grove settlers Charles and Isabella Peacock to open an inn, which in the winter of 1882–83 became the first lodging along Florida's lower east coast. When the inn was later closed, Munroe himself began putting up winter guests. His Camp Biscayne for years drew an intellectually prominent clientele, attracted by hospitality and the clean bay waters. Coconut Grove, when annexed into Miami in 1925, became the oldest district in that city. Although in the 1990s the Grove has become a playground for the rich and famous, it remains a sanctuary of vital Florida spirit.

Munroe's thoughtful style of development was the exception rather than the rule. State government, eager to overcome a legacy of debt, usually cast its lot with entrepreneurial monopolists eager to exploit Florida's resources. Chief among them were railroaders Henry Plant and Henry Flagler. Plant heaped sophistications on a barely civilized Gulf Coast; Flagler more grandly tamed the east.

The partner of John D. Rockefeller in Standard Oil, Flagler was one of the richest men in America, notorious for his ruthless and sometimes corrupt methods. When his sickly wife required a winter in the sun, he brought her to Florida. In 1884, widowed and remarried to his deceased wife's former nurse, he returned to St. Augustine and recruited a pair of New York architects to design the grandest hotel Florida had ever seen: the Ponce de León Hotel, opened in 1888. (Henry Plant did much the same thing for the west coast when he opened his $3 million Tampa Bay Hotel in 1891.)

Moving down the coast, Flagler bought an entire island, burned out the inhabitants, and created the opulent new American Riviera he called Palm Beach. His magnificent Royal Poinciana Hotel opened in 1894, and the Breakers—another of his great creations—remains, rebuilt, among Florida's finest accommodations.

**H**EALTHY, VIGOROUS people began coming to enjoy the climate, and sports and outdoor activities became a vital part of Florida vacations. Flagler indulged winter visitors with imaginative forms of recreation. Laborers pedaled wicker rickshaws. Sportier types raced their new motorcars on the hard-packed sand of Ormond and Daytona beaches.

Henry Plant, meanwhile, at another of his west-coast resorts, paved the first asphalt track for the newly popular sport of racing bicycles, and lavished an entire golf course—the first in Florida conceived as a resort amenity—on his immense Belleview Hotel, as popular today (now the Belleview Mido) as ever, on the bluffs of Clearwater Bay.

In 1896 Flagler brought his railroad to Miami (until then an Indian trading post). At the turn of the century, seized by his own manifest destiny, he began ruthlessly extending tracks to Key West. He proceeded unmindful of the havoc construction wreaked on the fisheries of Florida Bay and denying responsibility for the slavelike treatment of his workers. He even left crews unprepared for the 1906 hurricane that killed 200 railroad employees. But the railroad lived on, reaching Key West six years later. Flager, from then on hailed as one of history's great engineers, had little time to enjoy his accolades. He died within the year.

But his engineering achievement was just one example of Florida's quickly changing landscape. The draining of the Everglades was underway, and the sale of homesites floating in flooded swamplands to unsuspecting Northerners had begun. Citrus planters extended cultivation from along the lower St. Johns River south into the lakes district, fouling the water with pesticides. Phosphate mining lowered the water table and reduced to trickles the flows of springs that for years had supported the state's spa resorts. But even as the state's natural beauty was eroding, tourism grew.

Almost 100 years after Flagler's railroad extended tourism to the Keys, Walt Disney created another empire. Florida granted Disney extraordinary tax breaks and near-sovereign control over rule making throughout his fiefdom. (Many of those controls are still in place.) Typically, a compliant Orlando newspaper remained silent when it learned about Disney's plans in the early 1960s. The newspaper owner helped keep secret Disney's quiet acquisition of 28,000 acres for $5.5 million. The rest has been tourism magic. But Disney's environmental record has been mixed—on the one hand being fined for disrupting the natural environment and on the other, acquiring the vast Walker Ranch for public preservation. What may seem to outsiders as a disinterest in the state's invaluable natural assets, the grow-at-all-cost mentality that attracted Walt Disney World continues throughout Florida. In 1994 former owner of Blockbuster Video, Wayne Huizenga, faced only mild challenge in his attempts to create a Disneylike sports-and-entertainment empire in a well-field site west of Miami and Fort Lauderdale, an effort subsequently abandoned by a Blockbuster Video corporate successor.

The pluses have a way to go to catch up to the long accumulation of minuses, but simply because not everything has yet been trashed, what's left of Florida's natural beauty will continue to dazzle those who never knew the state's better days.

As Florida has grown disenthralled with its potentate developers, citizens have become more aware of the environmental problems facing the state. In reaction voters are demanding more green legislation, more parks and trails, and greater support of both culture and sports. Sports franchises ratify Florida's emergence from the ranks of the minor leagues. The state now supports nine major-league teams, including football's Miami Dolphins, basketball's Orlando Magic, and a new baseball franchise expected to begin play in St. Petersburg in 1997. Bahamians, who make up one of Florida's largest contingent of overseas visitors, fly over early each June to celebrate with mainland kin the annual Bahamian heritage festival called Goombay. In February, Latins come from around the Americas for Carnaval Miami and its hip-swiveling finale, the salsa-spiced Calle Ocho Festival. November's annual Miami Book Fair is now the largest book event in America.

Sports lovers come for the Breeders Cup at Fort Lauderdale's Gulfstream Track, the winter polo season at the Palm Beach Polo and Country Club, and for the London Philharmonic Orchestra's biannual summer seasons in Daytona Beach. As many as can find a room anywhere within 50 miles pack Key West for the annual Halloween Fantasy Fest.

In Fort Lauderdale, downtown's 1¼-mile Riverwalk is a magical setting for shaded promenades and alfresco entertainment, and there are new performing-arts and fine-arts venues. Along the beachfront—for years infamous for spring-break debauchery—2½ miles of shore road attest to the good life by the sea. Farther up the east coast, the rich and famous of Palm Beach County and the Treasure Coast willingly pay higher taxes to support and patronize their arts and recreational facilities, which are unequaled in the state.

In Miami—the big bad boy of Florida cities, its image tar-brushed by real-world Miami Vice—the South Beach Art Deco District has been expanded to include a revived Lincoln Road Mall. In Coconut Grove, CocoWalk and Mayfair malls, with their shops and smart bistros, have renewed that sense of life-as-art that dates from Ralph Munroe's days. To the far west is Everglades National Park.

Along the lower west coast in Naples, both the grandest hotels and baronial new residential estates lie to the back or to the side of coastal wetlands. Yet even here, mangroves are dying where marshes front the posh new communities, linked only by boardwalks to the beach. Lee County, farther north, stands out for its nature preserves, shelling beaches, and unbridged barrier islands. Since 1988 the county has collected ⅙ of its tourist-development tax solely to buy, protect, and improve beaches and parks.

**S**ARASOTA'S DOWNTOWN and Tampa's Ybor City stand out as the best revived urban neighborhoods of the west coast. Downtown Tampa shows off its new aquarium, a mix of museums, and big recreational facilities among its office high-rises, while downtown St. Petersburg has a beautiful park-lined waterfront.

Where beaches are few or where railroaders never laid track, along the mid-Gulf Coast north of Tampa Bay, nine counties have banded together as "The Nature Coast," to flaunt their lakes and bubbling springs, hilly inland stretches, and marshes. In upper midstate, 11 counties now constitute "The Original Florida," a region that includes America's landmark Suwannee River and Cross Creek, the setting for Marjorie Kinnan Rawlings's classic novel *The Yearling*. Nearby Paynes Prairie provides habitat for sandhill cranes and bison. At the Devil's Millhopper you can descend a 221-foot walkway to the bottom of a 120-foot deep sinkhole, and at O'Leno State Park watch the Santa Fe River swirl underground. At Ichetucknee State Park you can tube the mighty "Itch." Nearby you can dive into a dozen or more pellucid springs.

The Panhandle region has many of the state's most beautiful parks—Florida Caverns, Falling Waters, Natural Bridge, Eden State Gardens, Maclay State Gardens, and Torreya State Park—and Florida's finest beaches, including top-rated Grayton in south Walton County. And nearby, beside another white beach, is Seaside, perhaps America's most acclaimed new resort. With its shell- and picket-lined lanes too narrow for automobiles, Seaside harks back to early 20th-century town planning, trying to recapture that old-fashioned sense of community, leisure pace, and human scale. Seaside is just one of the answers that Florida is attempting for its problems.

East across the top of the state, St. Augustine and Fernandina Beach are two of the state's most historic towns. Metropolitan Jacksonville, Florida's largest city in land mass, is site of the most ambitious public-private effort to maintain natural preserves, centered on the 46,000-acre Timucuan Ecological and Historic Preserve, which, at Fort Caroline, includes Europe's earliest settlement site in North America. In downtown Orlando, Lake Eola Park has become the healthy heart of the city with a $900,000 amphitheater, swan boats, night-lit fountain, and landscaping. Church Street Station has helped bring downtown back to life, and the active theater, art, and music community north of downtown shows there is more to Orlando than theme parks.

The search continues for a solution to Florida's environmental distress. In one attempt at remedy, tourism promoters increasingly aim to attract visitors to natural resources—state parks, beaches, nature preserves, rivers—with the hope that politicians will accordingly pay more attention to preserving these resources. Although new, stronger coalitions have formed among hotel owners, the fishing industry, and environmentalists that may forestall worsening disaster, these same groups fight among themselves over a management plan for the new Florida Keys National Marine Sanctuary. The forecast for Florida's future is still unclear.

The ever-increasing threat to natural habitats by development shows that it is a small world after all. Still, much natural beauty remains. Enjoy it while you can.

*–Herb Hiller*

# WHAT'S WHERE

## The Everglades

Created in 1947, this national park in the southernmost extremity of the peninsula preserves a portion of the slow-moving "River of Grass"—a 50-mile-wide stream flowing through marshy grassland en route to Florida Bay. Biscayne National Park, nearby, is the largest national park in the continental United States with living coral reefs.

## The Florida Keys

This slender necklace of landfalls off the southern tip of Florida is strung together by a 110-mile-long highway. The Keys have two faces: one a wilderness of flowering jungles and shimmering seas amid mangrove-fringed islands dangling toward the tropics, the other a traffic jam with a view of billboards, shopping centers, and trailer courts. Embrace the first, avoid the latter. Come here for beaches, deep-sea fishing, snorkeling and diving and the balmy, semitropical weather.

## Fort Lauderdale

Once known for its wild spring breaks, this southern Florida city on the east coast is newly chic. Just as the beach has renewed itself, so has downtown—with residential construction and an emerging cultural arts district.

## Miami and Miami Beach

In the 1980s, a stylized television cop show called *Miami Vice* brought notoriety to this southernmost of big Florida cities; South Beach put it on the map again in the 1990s with its revamping of the Art Deco District. Stomping ground for celebrities such as Madonna and Sylvester Stallone, the city has gone from an enclave of retired northeasterners to an international crossroads with a Latin beat. Don't miss Coconut Grove, South Florida mainland's oldest settlement. It's chic and casual, full of bistros, cafés, and galleries.

## Northeast Florida

The northeast corner of the state is an area of remarkable diversity. Only a short drive separates the 400-year-old town of St. Augustine from the spring-break and auto-racing mecca of Daytona Beach. In between are slender barrier islands—some relatively pristine, all with fabulous beaches. Inland is the university town of Gainesville, Ocala horse country, and the backwoods scrub made famous by Marjorie Kinnan Rawlings.

## Palm Beach and the Treasure Coast

For 100 years, high society has made headlines along South Florida's Atlantic shore from Palm Beach to Boca Raton—part of the Gold Coast. The coast north of Palm Beach County, called the Treasure Coast, is also worth exploring. Comprising Martin, St. Lucie, and Indian River counties, it's dotted with nature preserves, fishing villages, and towns with active cultural scenes.

## The Panhandle

With its magnolias, live oaks, and loblolly pines, northwest Florida has more in common with the Deep South than with the Florida of the Everglades. Even the high season is different: By May, when activities are winding down south of Tampa, the Panhandle is just gearing up. The fabulous beaches, however, are a constant. A recent coastal research study named Grayton Beach, St. Andrews State Recreation Area, St. Joseph Peninsula State Park, and St. George Island among the top 10 beaches in the country.

## Southwest Florida

This region is subtropical to the core. It's most noted for Sanibel Island, a low-key spot that's home to world-class shelling, and Naples, a once-sleepy fishing village that's developed fast. Unlike the East Coast, much of the building here has been inland of the mangrove swamps, and the area prides itself on the number of access points along its 41 miles of strand.

## The Tampa Bay Area

The west coast cities of Tampa and St. Petersburg are diverse and busy. Inland is typical suburban sprawl, tempered by a bit of Africa (the Busch Gardens theme park). To the north, along what's billed as the Manatee Coast, are extensive nature preserves and parks. Tarpon Springs has been known for its Greek population for decades, Ybor City for its Cuban community. South of the bay, the cities of Sarasota and Bradenton—and the offshore keys that line the Gulf Coast—feel like the restful resort towns they are, plus Sarasota has a thriving arts community.

## Walt Disney World and the Orlando Area

When Walt Disney chose 28,000 acres in central Florida as the site of his eastern Disneyland, he forever changed the face of a cattle-and-citrus town called Orlando. Today, Disney isn't the only show in town: Universal Studios, Sea World, and Church Street Station give Mickey a run for his money. It's easy to spend weeks here lost in these artificial worlds.

# PLEASURES AND PASTIMES

## Beaches

Florida rates 12 of the top 20 U.S. beaches, and no point in the state is more than 60 miles from salt water. The long, lean peninsula is bordered by a 526-mile Atlantic coast from Fernandina Beach to Key West and a 792-mile coast along the Gulf of Mexico and Florida Bay from Pensacola to Key West. If you were to stretch Florida's convoluted coast in a straight line, it would extend for about 1,800 miles. What's more, if you add in the perimeter of every island surrounded by salt water, Florida has about 8,500 miles of tidal shoreline—more than any other state except Alaska. Florida's coastline comprises about 1,016 miles of sand beaches.

Along the Atlantic Coast from the Georgia border south through the Daytona Beach area the beaches are broad and firm. In Daytona Beach you can drive on them (though the number of cars is restricted). Some beachfront communities in this area charge for the privilege; others provide free beach access for vehicles.

From Daytona south, Hurricane Gordon caused considerable beach erosion late in 1994, and the usual cycle of seasonal tides and winds has so far been slow to repair the damage; the Panhandle was hard hit by hurricane season again in 1995. Major beach-rehabilitation projects have been completed or are near completion in Fort Lauderdale, the Sunny Isles area of north Dade County, Miami Beach, Key Biscayne. The experimental renourishing of beaches in metro Miami's Surfside and at John U. Lloyd Beach State Recreation Area is also nearly complete.

In the Florida Keys, coral reefs and prevailing currents prevent sand from building up to form beaches. The few Keys beaches are small, narrow, and generally have little or no sandy bottom. A happy exception is the beach at Bahia Honda State Park.

The waters of the Gulf of Mexico are somewhat murky, and Tampa Bay is polluted, though improving. But the Gulf Coast beaches are beautiful. The Panhandle is known for its sugary white sand;

around Sarasota the sand is particularly soft and white. The barrier islands–especially Sanibel—off Fort Myers are known for excellent shelling.

Although the state owns all beaches below the high-tide line, even in front of hotels and private resorts, gaining access to them can be a problem along much of Florida's coastline. You must pay to enter and/or park at most state, county, and local beachfront parks. Where hotels dominate the beach frontage, public parking may be limited or nonexistent.

## Biking

Florida has many cyclists on the road traveling many miles. The key to cycling's popularity is the terrain—flat in the south and gently rolling along the central ridge and in much of the Panhandle. Most cities of any size have bike-rental shops, which are good sources of information on local bike paths.

Florida's Department of Environmental Protection has developed three overnight bicycle tours of different areas of the state. The tours vary in length between 100 and 450 miles (for two to six days of cycling) and use state parks for rest stops and overnight camping. The office can also provide information on recreational cycling trails, rail-trails, and the rim trail atop the levee around Lake Okeechobee.They can also provide you with a list of the more than 30 Bicycle Coordinators in the state who have current information on local biking maps and activities.

## Canoeing

The Everglades has areas suitable for flat-water wilderness canoeing that are comparable to spots in the Boundary Waters region of Minnesota. Other popular canoeing rivers include the Blackwater, Econlokahatchee, Juniper, Loxahatchee, Peace, Oklawaha, Suwannee, St. Marys, and Santa Fe. The Florida Department of Natural Resources provides maps and brochures of the 36 canoe trails it maintains in various parts of the state; the trails run for 950 miles. Also contact individual national forests, parks, monuments, reserves, and seashores for information on their canoe trails. Local chambers of commerce have information on canoe trails in county parks. The best time to canoe in Florida is winter, the dry season, when you're less likely to get caught in a torrential downpour or become a snack for mosquitoes.

## Dining

Florida's cuisine changes as you move across the state, based on who settled the area and who now operates the restaurants. You can expect seafood to be a staple on nearly every menu, however, with greater variety on the coasts, and catfish, frogs' legs, and gator tail popular around inland lakes and at Miccosukee restaurants along the Tamiami Trail. Florida has launched some big-league culinary stars. Restaurateurs like Fort Lauderdale's Mark Militello are nationally acclaimed, while others who got their start here, such as Douglas Rodriguez, formerly of Yuca in Coral Gables, have gone on to glory in Manhattan.

South Florida's diverse assortment of Latin American restaurants offers the distinctive national fare of Argentina, Brazil, Colombia, Cuba, El Salvador, Mexico, Nicaragua, and Puerto Rico, and it's also easy to find island specialties born of the Bahamas, Haiti, and Jamaica. A new fusion of tropical, Continental, and nouvelle cuisine—some call it Floribbean—has gained widespread popularity. It draws on exotic fruits, spices, and fresh seafoods. The influence of earlier Hispanic settlements remains in Key West and Tampa's Ybor City.

All over Florida, Asian cuisine no longer means just Chinese. Indian, Japanese, Pakistani, Thai, and Vietnamese specialties are now available. Continental cuisine (French, German, Italian, Spanish, and Swiss) is also well represented all over Florida.

Every Florida restaurant claims to make the best Key lime pie. Pastry chefs and restaurant managers take the matter very seriously—they discuss the problems of getting good lime juice and maintaining top quality every day. Traditional Key lime pie is yellow, not green, with an old-fashioned graham cracker crust and meringue top. The filling should be tart and chilled but not frozen. Some restaurants serve their Key lime pie with a pastry crust; most substitute whipped cream for the more temperamental meringue. Each pie will be a little different. Try several. It is, after all, a vacation.

## Fishing

Opportunities for saltwater fishing abound from the Keys all the way up the Atlantic Coast to Georgia and up the Gulf Coast to Alabama. Many seaside communities have fishing piers that charge admission to anglers (and usually a lower rate to spectators). These piers generally have a bait-and-tackle shop. It's easy to find a boat-charter service that will take you out into deep water. Some of the best are in the Panhandle, where Destin and Fort Walton Beach have huge fleets. The Keys, too, are dotted with charter services, and Key West has a big sportfishing fleet. Depending on your taste, budget, and needs, you can charter anything from an old wooden craft to a luxurious, waterborne palace with state-of-the-art amenities.

Inland, there are more than 7,000 freshwater lakes. The largest—448,000-acre Lake Okeechobee, the third largest natural lake in the United States—is home to bass, bluegill, speckled perch, and succulent catfish (which the locals call "sharpies"). In addition to the state's many natural freshwater rivers, South Florida also has an extensive system of flood-control canals. In 1989 scientists found high mercury levels in largemouth bass and warmouth caught in parts of the Everglades in Palm Beach, Broward, and Dade counties, and warned against eating fish from those areas. Those warnings remain in effect, and warnings have been extended to parts of northern Florida.

## Golf

Except in the heart of the Everglades, you'll never be far from one of Florida's nearly 1,100 golf courses. Palm Beach County, the state's leading golf locale, has 150 courses, and the PGA, LPGA, and National Golf Foundation all have headquarters in the state. Many of the best golf courses in Florida (☞ Chapter 2) allow visitors to play without being members or hotel guests.

Especially in winter, you should reserve tee times in advance. Ask about golf reservations when you make your lodging reservations.

## Horseback Riding

Trail and endurance riding are popular throughout the state. Sixteen Florida parks and recreation areas include horse trails, while five parks have overnight facilities for campers and their horses. Amelia Island offers horseback riding on the beach. Florida's only dude ranch is located in Bushnell. Equestrians meet twice a year, during the fall in Altoona in the Ocala National Forest, and during the spring at a location that changes annually.

## Jogging, Running, Walking

All over Florida, you'll find joggers, runners, and walkers on bike paths and city streets—primarily in the early morning and after working hours in the evening. Some Florida hotels have their own running trails; others provide guests with information on measured trails in the vicinity. The first time you run in Florida, be prepared to go a shorter distance than normal because of higher heat and humidity.

Two major Florida festivals include important running races. Each year in December the Orange Bowl 10K, one of the state's best-known running events, brings world-class runners to Miami. In April, as part of the Florida Keys annual Conch Republic Days, runners congregate near Marathon on one of the world's most spectacular courses for the Seven Mile Bridge Run. Other major events include the Office Depot Corporate Challenge, which attracts 15,000 runners to Miami the first week of May, and the Heart Run, which takes place February 4 each year in Fort Lauderdale.

## National and State Parks

Although Florida is the fourth-most-populous state in the nation, more than 10 million acres of public and private recreation facilities are set aside in national forests, parks, monuments, reserves, and seashores; state forests and parks; county parks; and nature preserves owned and managed by private conservation groups. All told, Florida now has some 3,500 miles of trails, encompassing 1,550 miles of canoe and kayak trails, about 670 miles for bicycling and other uses, 900 miles exclusively for hiking, about 350 exclusively for equestrian use, plus some 30 miles of purely interpretive trails, chiefly in state parks. An active greenways development plan, which seeks to protect wildlife habitat as much as foster recreation, identified 150 greenways in use or under development by 1995.

On holidays and weekends, crowds flock to Florida's most popular parks—some on islands that are accessible only by boat. Come early or risk being turned away. In winter, the flocking crowds are replaced by northern migratory birds descending on the state. Many resident species breed in the warm summer months, but others (such as the wood stork) time their breeding cycle to the winter dry season. In summer, mosquitoes are voracious and daily afternoon thundershowers add to the state's humidity, but it's during the early part of this season that sea turtles come ashore to lay their eggs and you're most likely to see frigate birds and other tropical species.

NATIONAL PARKS> In 1993 **Fort Jefferson National Monument** in the Dry Tortugas was declared a national park. **Everglades National Park** was established in 1947, and **Biscayne National Park** in 1980. Other natural and historic sites in Florida under federal management include **Big Cypress National Preserve** in the Everglades, **Canaveral National Seashore** in central Florida, **Castillo de San Marcos National Monument** in north Florida, **De Soto National Memorial** in Bradenton, the 46,000-acre **Timucuan Ecological & Historic Preserve** on the St. Johns River in Jacksonville, **Fort Matanzas National Monument** south of St. Augustine, and **Gulf Islands National Seashore** in northwest Florida. The federal government maintains no centralized information service for its natural and historic sites in Florida.

NATIONAL FORESTS> The federal government operates three national forests in Florida. The **Apalachicola National Forest** encompasses 557,000 acres of pine and hardwoods across the northern coastal plain. The 336,000-acre **Ocala National Forest** includes the sandhills of the Big Scrub. Cypress swamps and numerous sinkhole lakes dot the 157,000-acre **Osceola National Forest.**

NATIONAL WILDLIFE REFUGES> National wildlife refuges in Florida include the **Great White Heron National Wildlife Refuge, Crocodile Lakes National Wildlife Refuge,** and **National Key Deer Refuge** in the Keys; Pelican Island National Wildlife Refuge (America's first) in Indian River County; Loxahatchee National Wildlife Refuge near Palm Beach; J. N. "Ding" Darling National Wildlife Refuge in southwest Florida; and Merritt Island National Wildlife Refuge. The federal government also operates the Key Largo National Marine Sanctuary, Looe Key National Marine Sanctuary, and the Florida Keys National Marine Sanctuary, largest in the national system.

STATE PARKS> The Florida Department of Environmental Protection manages hundreds of historic buildings, landmarks, and nature preserves as well as beaches, recreation areas, and parks as part of an expanding state park system.

PRIVATE NATURE PRESERVES> Wood storks nest at the National Audubon Society's **Corkscrew Swamp Sanctuary** near Naples. At the **National Audubon Society Wildlife Sanctuary** on Lake Okeechobee, a concessionaire operates boat tours. Audubon also controls more than 65 other Florida properties, including islands, prairies, forests, and swamps. Visitation at these sites is limited.

The Nature Conservancy admits the public to five of its preserves: the 6,267-acre **Apalachicola Bluffs & Ravines Preserve** in Liberty County; **Blowing Rocks Preserve,** with its unique anastasia limestone rock formations; the 970-acre **Cummer Sanctuary** in Levy County; the 4,500-acre **Tiger Creek Preserve,** near Lake Wales in Polk County; and the 150-acre **Spruce Creek Preserve,** which has restored historic buildings, in Volusia County.

## Pari-Mutuel Sports

Florida has a big variety of venues for sports you can lawfully bet on. These include 18 greyhound race tracks, six tracks for harness and Thoroughbred racing, and seven jai-alai frontons.

## Scuba Diving and Snorkeling

South Florida and the Keys attract most of the divers and snorkelers, but the more than 300 statewide dive shops schedule drift-, reef-, and wreck-diving trips for scuba divers all along Florida's Atlantic and Gulf coasts. The low-tech pleasures of snorkeling can be enjoyed throughout the Keys and elsewhere where shallow reefs hug the shore.

Inland in north and central Florida divers explore more than 100 grottoes, rivers, sinkholes, and springs. In some locations, you can swim near endangered manatees ("sea cows"), which migrate in from the sea to congregate around warm springs during the cool winter months.

## Shopping

ANTIQUES➤ Antiques lovers should explore beautifully restored Havana, just north of Tallahassee; Micanopy, south of Gainesville off I–75; the Antiques Mall in St. Augustine's Lightner Museum; Beach Street in Daytona Beach; downtown and along the outskirts of Mt. Dora, near Orlando; U.S. 17/92 between Orlando and Winter Park; U.S. 1 north of Dania Beach Boulevard in Dania; and S.W. 28th Lane and Unity Boulevard in Miami (near the Coconut Grove Metrorail station).

CITRUS FRUIT➤ Fresh citrus is available most of the year, except in summer. Two kinds of citrus grow in Florida: the sweeter and more expensive Indian River fruit from a thin ribbon of groves along the east coast, and the less-costly fruit from the interior, south and west of Lake Okeechobee.

Citrus is sold in ¼, ½, ¾, and full bushels. Many shippers offer special gift packages with several varieties of fruit, jellies, and other food items. Some prices include U.S. postage; others may not. Shipping may exceed the cost of the fruit. If you have a choice of citrus packaged in boxes or bags, take the boxes. They are easier to label and harder to squash.

NATIVE AMERICAN CRAFTS➤ Native American crafts are abundant, particularly in the southern part of the state, where you'll find billowing dresses and shirts, hand-sewn in striking colors and designs. At the Miccosukee Indian Village, 25 miles west of Miami on the Tamiami Trail (U.S. 41), as well as at the Seminole and Miccosukee reservations in the Everglades, you can also find handcrafted dolls and beaded belts.

SEASHELLS➤ The best shelling in Florida is on the beaches of Sanibel Island off Fort Myers. Shell shops, selling mostly kitschy items, abound throughout Florida. The largest such establishment is the Shell Factory, near Fort Myers. The coral and other shells sold in shops in the Florida Keys have been imported for sale because of restrictions on harvesting these materials.

## Tennis

Many Florida hotels have a resident tennis pro and offer special tennis packages with lessons. Many local park and recreation departments throughout Florida operate modern tennis centers like those at country clubs, and most such centers welcome nonresidents, for a fee.

# FODOR'S CHOICE

## Beaches

★ **Canaveral National Seashore, New Smyrna Beach to Titusville.** With its 24 miles of undeveloped coastline and miles of wind-swept dunes, this 57,000-acre park is remarkable—all the more so because its beach is virtually empty. Check on the lively ranger programs, with everything from canoe trips to turtle talks.

★ **Grayton Beach, near Destin.** Blue-green waters, white sand beaches, and salt marshes make it one of the most scenic spots along the Gulf Coast. There's also camping and snorkeling.

★ **St. Andrews State Recreation Area, eastern tip of Panama City Beach.** This highly visited park has an artificial reef that creates a calm, shallow area perfect for young children.

★ **South Lido Park, Sarasota.** These 130 acres of sugary sand draw everyone from bird-watchers to anglers to picnickers.

## Theme Parks and Attractions

★ **Busch Gardens, Tampa.** Two of the world's largest roller coasters, good shows, and live animals are loosely brought together under a turn-of-the-century Africa theme at these 335 acres.

★ **Florida Aquarium, Tampa.** Follow the path of a drop of water, and along the way see exhibits on springs and wetlands, bay and barrier beach, a spectacular coral reef, and the Gulf Stream and open ocean.

★ **Spaceport USA, Cocoa Beach.** Here is the home of the real Apollo 13. A garden of old rockets, current launch facilities and Space Shuttle sites, great films, and exhibits illuminating the romance of the early space program make this one of Florida's best entertainment bargains.

★ **Universal Studios Florida, Orlando.** It's saucy, sassy, and hip, with great special effects—a grown-up theme park packed with thrill rides.

⭐ **Walt Disney World, Orlando.** It's everything it's cracked up to be—and there's more of it every year.

⭐ **Everglades National Park from the tower on Shark Valley Loop.** This 50-foot observation tower yields a splendid panorama of the wide "River of Grass" as it sweeps southward toward the Gulf of Mexico.

⭐ **Inland waterway, Sanibel.** Scattered here are dozens and dozens of tiny mangrove islets, a lovely sight.

⭐ **Ocean Drive in the Art Deco District, Miami Beach.** Feast your eyes on brilliantly restored vintage Art Deco hotels at every turn. Since their restoration, this palm-lined beachfront has been hopping 24 hours a day.

⭐ **Sunset scene at Mallory Square, Key West.** Here, sunset draws street performers, vendors, and thousands of onlookers to Mallory Dock and the eponymous square nearby.

⭐ **Sunshine Skyway across Tampa Bay.** One of the world's great monumental sculptures carries six lanes of traffic soaring across the mouth of Florida's largest estuary.

⭐ **Castillo de San Marcos National Monument, St. Augustine.** The 300-year-old fort comes complete with moat, turrets, and 16-foot-thick walls. For a big boom, watch one of the artillery demonstrations, held periodically on the gun deck.

⭐ **Edison's winter home and museum, Fort Myers.** With everything just as the inventor left it, you can imagine him tinkering around to build the first phonograph.

⭐ **Morikami Museum and Japanese Gardens, Delray Beach.** The leading U.S. center for Japanese and American cultural exchange is housed in a model of a Japanese imperial villa. On display is a permanent exhibition on the area's Yamato Colony, a turn-of-the-century settlement of immigrant Japanese farmers.

⭐ **Vizcaya Museum and Gardens, Coconut Grove.** The estate of industrialist James Deering, overlooking Biscayne Bay, has an Italian Renaissance–style villa containing Renaissance, Baroque, Rococo, and Neoclassical art and furniture.

⭐ **Casa Grande, Miami Beach.** It's the first hotel on Ocean Drive and still the best for both style and trend—and with spacious baths. $$$$

⭐ **Registry Resort, Naples.** Sure there are sumptuously decorated rooms, exceptional service, and 3 miles of glistening white beach awaiting you after a walk through a mangrove forest, but there's also a Sunday brunch that makes others pale in comparison. $$$$

⭐ **Ritz-Carlton Amelia Island.** Ritz-Carltons may be known for stylish elegance, superb comfort, and excellent service, but this one also comes with a pristine beach, its own golf course, and the outstanding and unusual Grill restaurant. $$$$

⭐ **Sandestin Beach Resort, Destin.** This 2,600-acre resort is a town unto itself. Accommodations range from simple to extravagant, and all rooms have a view, either of water, golf course, or bird sanctuary. $$–$$$$

⭐ **Orlando Heritage Inn, Orlando.** Reproduction turn-of-the-century furnishings, French windows, brass lamps, and a scattering of 19th-century antiques make this property far more charming than you might expect from the rates. $$

⭐ **Cafe des Artistes, Key West.** Chef Andrew Berman's brilliant tropical version of French cuisine is served in a series of intimate dining rooms filled with tropical art and an upstairs, outdoor patio. $$$

⭐ **Mark's Place, North Miami Beach.** The deco-style dining room is as much a feast for the eyes as owner-chef Mark Militello's absolutely fresh, contemporary Florida fare is a feast for the palate. $$$

⭐ **Columbia, Tampa.** Flamenco dancing and paella set the scene at this Ybor City institution. $$

⭐ **Le Coq au Vin, Orlando.** The traditional French cuisine is as expertly prepared as any you'll find in the area, but the setting, in a small but charming house, is delightfully unstuffy. $$

# FESTIVALS AND SEASONAL EVENTS

WINTER

DEC.➤ **Month-long Victorian Seaside Christmas** takes place oceanside on Amelia Island (☎ 904/277–0717).

MID-DEC.➤ **Walt Disney World's Very Merry Christmas Parade in the Magic Kingdom** celebrates the season at the Magic Kingdom (Lake Buena Vista, ☎ 407/931–7369).

MID-DEC.➤ **Christmas in St. Augustine** is a three-week festival with caroling, tours of turn-of-the-century churches and cottages, and musical performances (☎ 904/829–5681).

MID-DEC.➤ **Winterfest Boat Parade** is on the Intracoastal Waterway, Fort Lauderdale (☎ 305/767–0686).

LATE DEC.➤ **Coconut Grove King Mango Strut** is a parody of the Orange Bowl Parade (☎ 305/858–6253).

EARLY JAN.➤ **Polo Season** opens at the Palm Beach Polo and Country Club (☎ 407/793–1440).

JAN. 6➤ **Greek Epiphany Day** includes religious celebrations, parades, music, dancing, and feasting at the St. Nicholas Greek Orthodox Cathedral in Tarpon Springs (☎ 813/937–6109).

MID-JAN.➤ **Art Deco Weekend** spotlights Miami Beach's historic district with an Art Deco street fair, a 1930s-style Moon Over Miami Ball, and live entertainment (☎ 305/672–2014).

MID-JAN.➤ **Taste of the Grove Food and Music Festival** is a popular fundraiser put on in Coconut Grove's Peacock Park by area restaurants (☎ 305/444–7270).

MID-JAN.➤ **Martin Luther King, Jr., Festivals** are celebrated throughout the state—including, for example, Tampa (☎ 813/223–8518) and Orlando (☎ 407/246–2221).

LATE JAN.➤ **Miami Rivers Blues Festival** takes place on the south bank of the river next to Tobacco Road (☎ 305/374–1198).

FEB.➤ **Gasparilla Festival** celebrates the legendary pirate's invasion of Tampa with street parades, an art festival, and music (☎ 800/448–2672).

FEB.➤ **Edison Festival of Lights,** in various locations around Fort Myers, celebrates Thomas A. Edison's long winter residence in the city (☎ 813/334–2550).

FEB.➤ **International Carillon Festival** takes place at the Bok Tower Gardens, Lake Wales (☎ 813/676–1408).

FEB.➤ **Florida Strawberry Festival** in Plant City has for more than six decades celebrated the town's winter harvest with two weeks of country-music stars, rides, exhibits, and strawberry delicacies (☎ 813/752–9194).

FEB.➤ **Olustee Battle Festival** in Lake City is the second-largest Civil War reenactment in the nation after the one in Gettysburg (☎ 904/752–3610 or 904/758–1312).

FEB.➤ **Speed Weeks** is a three-week celebration of auto racing that culminates in the famous Daytona 500, at the Daytona International Speedway in Daytona Beach (☎ 904/254–2700 or 800/854–1234).

FEB.–MAR.➤ **Winter Equestrian Festival** at the Palm Beach Polo and Country Club in West Palm Beach includes more than 1,000 horses and three grand-prix equestrian events (☎ 407/798–7000).

MID-FEB.➤ **Florida State Fair** in Tampa includes carnival rides and 4-H competitions (☎ 813/621–7821).

MID-FEB.➤ **Miami Film Festival** sponsored by the Film Society of America is 10 days of international, domestic, and local films (☎ 305/377–3456).

MID-FEB.➤ **Florida Manatee Festival** in Crystal River focuses on both the river and the endangered manatee (☎ 904/795–3149).

MID-FEB.➤ **Florida Citrus Festival and Polk County Fair,** in Winter Haven, showcases the citrus harvest with displays and entertainment (☎ 813/967–3175).

MID-FEB.➤ **Coconut Grove Art Festival** is the state's largest (☎ 305/447–0401).

LAST FULL WEEKEND IN FEB.➤ **Labelle Swamp Cabbage Festival** is a salute to the state tree, the cabbage palm (☎ 813/675–0125).

## SPRING

EARLY MAR.➤ The **Annual Sanibel Shell Fair,** which runs for four days starting the first Thursday of the month, is the largest event of the year on Sanibel Island (☎ 813/472–2155).

EARLY MAR.➤ **Azalea Festival** is a beauty pageant, arts and crafts show, and parade held in downtown Palatka and Riverfront Park (☎ 904/328–1503).

EARLY MAR.➤ **Carnaval Miami** is a carnival celebration staged by the Little Havana Tourist Authority (☎ 305/644–8888).

EARLY MAR.➤ **Bike Week,** one of Daytona's biggest annual events, draws 400,000 riders from across the U.S. for 10 days of races, plus parades and even cole slaw wrestling (☎ 904/255–0981).

MID-MAR. AND EARLY JULY➤ **Arcadia All-Florida Championship Rodeo** is professional rodeo at its best (☎ 813/494–2014 or 800/749–7633).

MID-MAR.–EARLY MAY➤ **Springtime Tallahassee** is a major cultural, sporting, and culinary event in the capital (☎ 904/224–5012).

LATE MAR.➤ On Palm Sunday the **Blessing of the Fleet** is held on the bayfront in St. Augustine (☎ 904/829–5681).

LATE MAR.–EARLY APR.➤ The gala **Concourse d'Elegance,** held at the Amelia Island Ritz-Carlton on Easter weekend, shows off over 150 exquisitely preserved collector cars (☎ 904/277–1100).

APR.➤ **Arts in April** is a series of visual- and performing-arts events produced by independent Orlando arts organizations (☎ 407/425–0277).

EARLY APR.➤ **Delray Affair** is the biggest event in the area and features arts, crafts, and food (☎ 407/278–0424).

EARLY APR.–LATE MAY➤ The **Addison Mizner Festival** in Boca Raton celebrates the arts in Palm Beach County (☎ 407/241–7432 or 407/930–6400).

MID-APR.➤ **Cedar Key Sidewalk Arts Festival** is celebrated in one of the state's most historic towns (☎ 904/543–5600).

LATE APR.➤ **River Cities Festival,** a three-day event in Miami Springs and Hialeah, focuses attention on the Miami River and the need to keep it clean (☎ 305/887–1515).

LATE APR.–EARLY MAY➤ **Sun 'n' Fun Festival** in Clearwater includes a bathtub regatta, golf tournament, and nighttime parade (☎ 813/462–6531).

LATE APR.–EARLY MAY➤ **Conch Republic Celebration** in Key West honors the founding fathers of the Conch Republic, "the small island nation of Key West" (☎ 305/296–0123).

LATE APR.–EARLY MAY➤ The **Daytona Beach Music Festival,** held over four consecutive weekends, features concerts by marching bands; jazz and stage bands; an orchestra; and men's, womens', and mixed choirs (☎ 800/881–2473).

FIRST WEEKEND IN MAY➤ **Sunfest** in West Palm Beach includes a wide variety of cultural and sporting events (☎ 407/659–5980 or 800/833–5733).

MID-MAY➤ **Arabian Nights Festival** in Opa-locka is a mix of contemporary and fantasy-inspired entertainment (☎ 305/758–4166).

MID-MAY➤ **Tropicool Fest** draws thousands to more than 30 concerts as well as arts and sports events for two weeks all around Naples (☎ 813/262–6141).

MEMORIAL DAY WEEKEND➤ **Florida Folk Festival** takes place in White Springs at the Stephen Foster State Folk Culture Center (☎ 904/397–2192).

## SUMMER

FIRST WEEKEND IN JUNE➤ **Miami-Bahamas Goombay Festival,** in Miami's Coconut Grove, celebrates the city's Bahamian heritage (☎ 305/443–7928 or 305/372–9966).

EARLY–MID-JUNE➤ **Billy Bowlegs Festival,** in Fort Walton Beach, is a week of entertaining activities in memory of a pirate who ruled the area in the late 1700s (☎ 800/322–3319).

EARLY–MID-JUNE➤ **International Mangrove Fest** in Naples is an eco-tourism event that combines musical concerts, kid's activities, and sand sculpting contests, canoe tours through the mangroves, and a program of activities by the Nature Conservancy (☎ 941/594–6038).

JULY 4➤ **Firecracker Festival,** in Palm Bay, is one of the state's most colorful Independence Day celebrations (☎ 407/727–0457).

MID-JULY➤ **Hemingway Days Festival,** in Key West, includes plays, short-story competitions, and a Hemingway look-alike contest (☎ 305/294–4440).

EARLY AUG.➤ **Annual Wausau Possum Funday & Parade** is held in Possum Palace, Wausau (☎ 904/638–1460).

**AUTUMN**

LABOR DAY➤ **Worm Fiddler's Day** is the biggest day of the year in Caryville (☎ 904/548–5571).

EARLY SEPT.➤ **Anniversary of the Founding of St. Augustine** is held on the grounds of the Mission of Nombre de Dios (☎ 904/829–8379).

EARLY SEPT.➤ Annual Outdoor Art Show is a weekend sidewalk show dislaying the works of artists from around the state (☎ 352–376–6062).

OCT.➤ **Jacksonville Jazz Festival** is three days of jazz performances, arts and crafts, and food, plus the Great American Jazz Piano Competition (☎ 904/353–7770).

OCT.➤ **Destin Seafood Festival** gives you two days to sample smoked amberjack, fried mullet, and shark kabobs (☎ 800/322–3319).

MID-OCT.➤ **Fall RiverFest Arts Festival** takes place downtown along the St. Johns River in Palatka (☎ 904/328–8998).

MID-OCT.➤ **Biketoberfest** is highlighted by championship racing at the Daytona International Speedway, the Main Street Rally, concerts, and swap meets that last four days (☎ 904/255–0415).

MID-OCT.➤ **Boggy Bayou Mullet Festival** is a three-day hoedown in celebration of the "Twin Cities," Valparaiso and Niceville, and the famed scavenger fish, the mullet (☎ 904/678–1615).

MID-OCT.➤ **Cedar Key Seafood Festival** is held on Main Street in Cedar Key (☎ 904/543–5600).

LATE OCT.➤ **Fantasy Fest** in Key West is a no-holds-barred Halloween costume party, parade, and town fair (☎ 305/296–1817).

EARLY NOV.➤ **Florida Seafood Festival** is Apalachicola's celebration of its famous oyster harvest, with oyster-shucking-and-consumption contests and parades (☎ 904/653–9419.)

EARLY NOV.–LATE FEB.➤ The **Orange Bowl** and **Junior Orange Bowl Festival,** in the Miami area, are best known for the King Orange Jamboree Parade and the Orange Bowl Football Classic, but also include more than 20 youth-oriented events (☎ 305/371–3351).

MID-NOV.➤ **Jensen Beach Pineapple Festival** is at the Martin County Fairgrounds (☎ 407/334–3444).

MID-NOV.➤ **12th Annual Miami Book Fair International,** the largest book fair in the United States, is held on the Miami-Dade Community College Wolfson Campus (☎ 305/237–3258).

# 2 The Florida Fifty

*Golfing Throughout the State*

Updated by
Ann Hughes

**H**OW COULD GOLFERS FEEL UNDER PAR in the sunshine state? One out of every 10 rounds of golf
played in the United States is played here, and
golfers visit Florida more than any other state. Florida is twice as popular as its nearest rivals, Arizona and South Carolina, and three times
as popular as runners-up California and North Carolina.

But there is plenty of green to go around. Florida has more golf courses
than any other state. The present count tallies 1,098, with another 63
courses either planned or under construction. According to National
Golf Foundation figures, Palm Beach County, with 147, has more
courses than any other county in the country.

Many of Florida's courses are private. Still, at last count roughly two-
thirds were either public, "semiprivate," or private but offering limited access for nonmembers (for example, courses extending privileges
to guests of nearby hotels). So if you're on your way to Florida with
a mind to play golf, you'll have more than 600 places to get teed off.

A big part of the appeal of Florida golf is its year-round availability.
Although a few courses might close for a day or two in fall to reseed
greens and a few in northern Florida might delay morning tee times in
winter when there's frost, it's still fair to say that you can find a fair-
way here 365 days a year. That's why a large number of touring professionals—including Jack Nicklaus, Gary Player, and Payne
Stewart—have settled here.

What sort of play can golfers expect? It's no state secret that Florida
is flat. With its highest elevation at 345 feet, it can't claim many naturally rolling courses. The world's leading golf-course designers, including Tom Fazio, Jack Nicklaus, and Ed Seay, have added the rolls
and undulations that nature omitted. No designer, however, has been
more notable in this regard than Pete Dye, pioneer of stadium-style
courses, those designed for large tournament audiences.

Deep rough is uncommon as a penalizing element in Florida play,
short rough is especially prevalent during winter, and water and sand
are common. Often, lakes and canals have to be carved out to make
fairways. Although Florida fairways are characteristically wide, greens
tend to be heavily bunkered or protected by water. A diabolically popular invention of Florida course builders is the island green, completely surrounded by water. Sand is also a natural part of the Florida
environment, although a special fine-grain sand is sometimes imported;
it isn't unusual to come across a hole in Florida with 10 or more traps,
and several courses have more than 100 traps each. On the other
hand, because the sandy soil drains well, the playing surface is more
forgiving of iron shots than denser, clay-rich soil.

What this adds up to is a premium on accuracy when it comes to approach shots.

Wind also comes into play in Florida, particularly at courses near the
state's 3,000 miles of coastline. Inland, it swirls and becomes unpre-
dictable as it moves through tall pine and palm trees.

Finally, keep in mind that for most of the year, Florida greens are seeded
with Bermuda grass. If you're familiar with putting on the bent-grass
greens found in other parts of the country, you may find that the speed
(on the slow side) and grain of Bermuda greens takes getting used to.

# The Florida Fifty

In a state with nearly 1,100 courses, coming up with a mere 50 recommendations isn't easy. Even after discounting nine-hole courses, par-3 (sometimes called "executive") courses, courses that are private, and those with policies for public play that are unusually restrictive, hundreds of top-notch courses remain.

A sampling of what is available, from inexpensive municipal courses to luxurious resort courses, this index includes those repeatedly cited among Florida's best.

This does not mean these are the only ones worth playing. Also, although just one course has been highlighted at each of the multicourse resorts cited (for example, Doral, Grand Cypress, PGA National), other courses at these resorts may also be among Florida's best. For that reason, the *total* number of holes at any resort is listed, not just the holes of the featured course.

Yardages included are of the featured course and are intended as an indication of one course's length relative to others; yardages are calculated from the championship, or blue, tees. The championship length represents a course at its most difficult near the listed length. Courses are typically 400 to 800 yards shorter from the regular men's tees and between 1,000 and 1,500 yards shorter from the regular women's tees. With its large retirement population, Florida also has many facilities with "seniors" tees, usually in front of the women's tees and often designated as gold. A few designers—notably Jack Nicklaus—include five or more sets of tee boxes to make courses playable for everyone.

The United States Golfing Association (USGA) ratings are also from the championship tees and indicate a course's relative difficulty; the rating is the average a scratch (0-handicap) golfer should expect to score. Any course with a rating of two or more strokes higher than par is considered especially demanding and generally suitable only for experienced golfers. If you're less experienced, look for courses with ratings below par.

Keep in mind that a golf course tends to be a work-in-progress; holes are often lengthened or shortened, greens are rebuilt, traps added, and so forth. The statistics and descriptions here were accurate at the time of publication, but courses may have undergone changes—even major overhauls—by the time you play them.

Because Florida courses tend to be flat, most are easy to walk, but unfortunately for people who enjoy walking, this is rarely an option anymore. Carts are usually required, although a few courses allow late-afternoon players to walk and some public courses allow you to stroll between holes. The official reason is that carts help speed up play, which is generally true. Operators, however, concede that cart rental means extra revenue. A note for anyone interested in walking, when and where it is permitted: In Florida, where the "golf community" is a pervasive concept, walking distances *between* holes can be substantial, a real-estate ploy to allow more space for course-side homes and condos.

Greens fees are per person, regular-season rates, with mandatory cart fees (per person) included, where applicable. Greens fees, especially at resort courses, can be as much as 50% more during the high season—which runs generally from February to May—and substantially lower in slow summer months.

# Florida Golf Courses

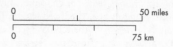

*Gulf of Mexico*

0              50 miles

0              75 km

### Panhandle
Bluewater Bay Resort, **3**
Hombre Golf Club, **6**
Killearn Country Club & Inn, **7**
Marriott's Bay Point Resort, **5**
Perdido Bay Resort, **1**
Sandestin Beach Resort, **4**
Tiger Point Golf & Country Club, **2**

### Northeast Florida
Amelia Island Plantation, **8**
Golden Ocala Golf Club, **15**
Indigo Lakes Golf Club, **14**
Marriott at Sawgrass, **9**
Ponce de Leon Golf and Conference Resort, **12**
Ponte Vedra Inn & Club, **10**
Ravines Golf & Country Club, **11**
Sheraton Palm Coast, **13**

### Orlando Area
Falcon's Fire Golf Club, **20**
Grand Cypress Golf Resort, **19**
Grenelefe Golf & Tennis Resort, **22**
Mission Inn Golf & Tennis Resort, **17**

Palisades Country Club, **18**
Timacuan Golf & Country Club, **16**
Walt Disney World Resort, **21**

### Tampa Bay Area
Bloomingdale Golfers Club, **27**
Buffalo Creek, **28**
Innisbrook Hilton Resort , **25**
Plantation Golf & Country Club, **31**
Plantation Inn & Golf Resort, **23**
The Resort at Longboat Key, **29**
Saddlebrook Golf and Tennis Resort, **26**
Sun 'n Lake Golf Club, **30**
World Woods Golf Club, **24**

### Southwest Florida
Cape Coral Golf & Tennis Resort, **33**
Eastwood Golf Club, **32**
Lely Flamingo Island Club, **35**
Naples Beach Hotel & Golf Club, **36**
Pelican's Nest Golf Course, **34**

### Palm Beach
Boca Raton Resort & Club, **43**
Boynton Beach Municipal Golf Course, **42**
Breakers Hotel Golf Club, **39**
Emerald Dunes Golf Club, **40**
Indian River Plantation Beach Resort, **37**
Palm Beach Polo and Country Club, **41**
PGA National Resort & Spa, **38**

### Fort Lauderdale
Bonaventure Resort & Spa, **45**
Colony West Country Club, **46**
The Oaks Golf & Racquet Club, **44**

### Miami
Don Shula's Hotel & Golf Club, **49**
Doral Golf Resort and Spa, **48**
Links at Key Biscayne, **50**
Turnberry Isle Resort & Club, **47**

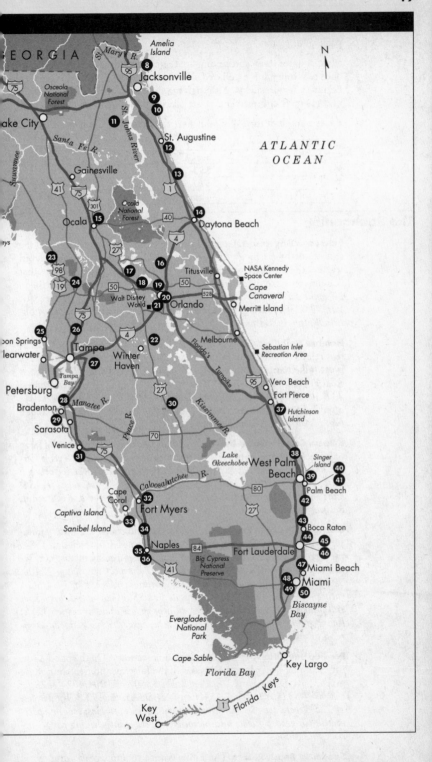

Many resorts also offer golf packages, with greens fees included at a considerable discount. There are also companies specializing in golf packages.

Most courses (even some municipal ones) have dress codes. The standard requirement is a collared shirt and long pants (often no jeans) or Bermuda-length shorts. Although many courses are less than militant in dress-code enforcement, come prepared to play by the rules.

Prices quoted in the following chart refer to greens fees:

| CATEGORY | COST |
| --- | --- |
| **$$$$** | over $75 |
| **$$$** | $50–$75 |
| **$$** | $20–$50 |
| **$** | under $20 |

# The Panhandle

**Bluewater Bay Resort.** Generally ranked among the top courses in the state's northwest by golf magazines, the Tom Fazio–designed layout features thick woods, water, and marshes on four nine-hole courses that combine to make six different 18–hole routes. ⊠ *1950 Bluewater Blvd., Niceville 32578,* ☎ *904/897–3241 or 800/874–2128. Yardage: 6,803. Par: 72. USGA rating: 73. Total holes: 36.* ⌸ *Greens fees $$. Cart optional after 1. Restaurant, driving range, accommodations.*

**Hombre Golf Club.** Site of the Nike Panama City Beach Golf Classic, this relatively flat, bunker-laden layout is one of the Sunshine State's most talked about courses. ⊠ *120 Coyote Pass, Panama City Beach 32407,* ☎ *904/234–3673. Yardage: 6,820. Par: 72. USGA rating: 73.4. Total holes: 18.* ⌸ *Greens fees $$–$$$. Cart optional weekdays after 2. Special policies: tee times available a week in advance. Snack bar, restaurant, driving range.*

**Killearn Country Club & Inn.** Gently rolling fairways and clusters of large oak trees give this course its distinctive character. ⊠ *100 Tyron Circle, Tallahassee 32308,* ☎ *904/893–2186 or 800/476–4101. Yardage: 7,025. Par: 72. USGA rating: 73.9. Total holes: 27.* ⌸ *Greens fees $$. Cart optional. Special policies: inn guests and members. Restaurant, accommodations.*

**Marriott's Bay Point Resort.** The Lagoon Legend course is a watery monster, with the beast coming into play on 16 holes. Completed in 1986, the Lagoon Legend has been rated by magazines among the top courses in the U.S. ⊠ *100 Delwood Beach Rd., Panama City Beach 32408,* ☎ *904/235–6909 or 800/874–7105. Yardage: 6,942. Par: 72. USGA rating: 73. Total holes: 36.* ⌸ *Greens fees $$$. Cart mandatory. Special policies: tee times available 2 months in advance for resort guests; lower greens fees for resort guests. Restaurant, driving range, accommodations.*

**Perdido Bay Resort.** This course demands accuracy: On the par-5 11th, for example, water lines both sides of the fairway and the front of the green. ⊠ *1 Doug Ford Dr., Pensacola 32507,* ☎ *904/492–1223 or 800/874–5355. Yardage: 7,154. Par: 72. USGA rating: 73.8. Total holes: 18.* ⌸ *Greens fees $$. Cart mandatory. Special policies: tee time preference for resort guests and members. Restaurant, driving range, accommodations.*

**Sandestin Beach Resort.** The Links course requires play around and across canals on most of its holes. After little water on the first three holes, the fourth—a par-5 of 501 yards and ranked as one of Florida's toughest—is flanked by a lagoon and marsh. ⊠ *9300 U.S. 98W, Destin 32541,* ☎ *904/267–8211 or 800/277–0800. Yardage: 6,710. Par: 72. USGA rating: 72.8. Total holes: 63.* ⊡ *Greens fees $$$. Cart optional. Special policies: tee time preference and reduced greens fees for resort guests. Restaurants, driving range, accommodations.*

**Tiger Point Golf & Country Club.** In the design of the East Course, Jerry Pate and Ron Garl built many "spectator mounds," a relatively modern design feature that frames greens. ⊠ *1255 Country Club Rd., Gulf Breeze 32561,* ☎ *904/932–1333. Yardage: 7,033. Par: 72. USGA rating: 73.8. Total holes: 36.* ⊡ *Greens fees $$. Cart mandatory. Special policies: tee times available a week in advance. Restaurant, driving range.*

# Northeast Florida

**Amelia Island Plantation.** The Tom Fazio–designed Long Point Course is unusual for Florida: It features water on only three holes. Cedars, oaks, marshes, and ocean views make for unusually scenic play. ⊠ *3000 First Coast Hwy., Amelia Island 32034,* ☎ *904/261–6161 or 800/874–6878. Yardage: 6,775. Par: 72. USGA rating: 72.9. Total holes: 45.* ⊡ *Greens fees $$$$. Cart mandatory. Special policies: must be a resort guest. Restaurant, driving range, accommodations.*

**Golden Ocala Golf Club.** Ron Garl designed this course with several "replica" holes, including one of the famed, par-3 Postage Stamp hole at Royal Troon, Scotland, and also of the 12th and 13th holes at Augusta National, home of the Masters. ⊠ *7300 U.S. 27 NW, Ocala 34482,* ☎ *904/622–0172. Yardage: 6,755. Par: 72. USGA rating: 72.2. Total holes: 18.* ⊡ *Greens fees $$. Cart mandatory. Special policies: tee times available 2 weeks in advance. Driving range.*

**Indigo Lakes Golf Club.** Indigo Lakes is distinguished by its oversize greens, each averaging more than 9,000 square feet. ⊠ *312 Indigo Dr., Daytona Beach 32114,* ☎ *904/254–3607. Yardage: 7,123. Par: 72. USGA rating: 73.5. Total holes: 18.* ⊡ *Greens fees $$. Cart mandatory. Special policies: public tee times available a day in advance. Restaurant, driving range, accommodations.*

**Marriott at Sawgrass.** With 99 holes, this is one of Florida's largest golfing compounds. The Pete Dye–designed TPC Stadium Course—famed for its island 17th hole—vexes even top pros who compete in the Tournament Players Championship. ⊠ *110 TPC Blvd., Ponte Vedra Beach 32082,* ☎ *904/273–3235 or 800/457–4653. Yardage: 6,857. Par: 72. USGA rating: 74. Total holes: 99.* ⊡ *Greens fees $$$$. Cart mandatory. Special policies: hotel guests, members, and guests of members. Restaurant, driving range, accommodations.*

**Ponce de Leon Golf and Conference Resort.** This is an older-style Florida course, originally designed by Donald Ross. Here, marshland tends to be more of a backdrop to play than a hazard, as opposed to newer courses, where marshy areas are often converted into ponds or lakes that are very much in play. ⊠ *4000 U.S. 1N, St. Augustine 32095,* ☎ *904/824–2821. Yardage: 6,878. Par: 72. USGA rating: 72.9. Total holes: 18.* ⊡ *Greens fees $$. Cart mandatory. Special policies: tee times available a week in advance. Restaurant, driving range, accommodations.*

**Ponte Vedra Inn & Club.** Designed by Robert Trent Jones, Sr., the Ocean Course features an island hole—the 147-yard 9th said to have inspired Pete Dye's design of the 17th at the nearby TPC Stadium Course—and plays tough when the wind is up. ⊠ *200 Ponte Vedra*

*Blvd., Ponte Vedra Beach 32082,* ☎ *904/273–7710 or 800/234–7842. Yardage: 6,593. Par: 72. USGA rating: 71.5. Total holes: 36.* ✉ *Greens fees $$$. Cart mandatory. Special policies: inn guests and guests of members only. Restaurant, driving range, accommodations.*

**Ravines Golf & Country Club.** Trees, rolling terrain, and deep ravines are atypical in Florida, where longer, flat courses with many water hazards are the norm. ✉ *2932 Ravines Rd., Middleburg 32068,* ☎ *904/282–7888. Yardage: 6,733. Par: 72. USGA rating: 72.4. Total holes: 18.* ✉ *Greens fees $$. Cart mandatory. Special policies: tee times available a week in advance. Restaurant, driving range, 18-hole putting course, accommodations.*

**Sheraton Palm Coast.** The Matanzas Woods course, one of several open to resort guests, is an Arnold Palmer/Ed Seay design, featuring rolling fairways and large greens. ✉ *398 Lakeview Blvd., Palm Coast 32137,* ☎ *904/446–6330 or 800/874–2101. Yardage: 6,985. Par: 72. USGA rating: 73.3. Total holes: 90.* ✉ *Greens fees $$. Cart mandatory. Restaurant, driving range, accommodations.*

## Orlando Area

**Falcon's Fire Golf Club.** One of Orlando's newest courses, this layout designed by respected golf architect Rees Jones features strategically placed fairway bunkers that demand accuracy off the tee. ✉ *3200 Seralago Blvd., Kissimmee 34746,* ☎ *407/397–2777. Yardage: 6,901. Par: 72. USGA rating: 72.5. Total holes: 18.* ✉ *Greens fees $$$. Cart mandatory. Special policies: tee times available a week in advance. Restaurant, driving range.*

**Grand Cypress Golf Resort.** The New Course is a Jack Nicklaus re-creation of the famed Old Course in St. Andrews, Scotland—hidden in the fairways are "pot" bunkers deep enough to have stairs for entry and exit. ✉ *1 N. Jacaranda, Orlando 32836,* ☎ *407/239–4700. Yardage: 6,773. Par: 72. USGA rating: 72.1. Total holes: 45.* ✉ *Greens fees $$$$; $10 reduction for walkers. Cart optional. Special policies: guests only; tee times available 2 months in advance. Restaurant, driving range, accommodations.*

**Grenelefe Golf & Tennis Resort.** Length is the key here: The West Course, designed by Robert Trent Jones, Sr., plays to 7,325 yards from the championship tees. An absence of water hazards (there are just two ponds) ease the challenge—a little. ✉ *3200 Rte. 546, Haines City 33844,* ☎ *813/422–7511 or 800/237–9549. Yardage: 7,325. Par: 72. USGA rating: 75.4. Total holes: 54.* ✉ *Greens fees $$$$. Cart mandatory. Special policies: tee times available 90 days in advance. Restaurant, driving range, accommodations.*

**Mission Inn Golf & Tennis Resort.** Originally built 60 years ago, this course is a mixed bag, featuring island greens typical of Florida as well as elevated tees and tree-lined fairways more characteristic of courses in the Carolinas and the Northeast. ✉ *10400 Rte. 48, Howey-in-the-Hills 34737,* ☎ *904/324–3885 or 800/874–9053. Yardage: 6,852. Par: 72. USGA rating: 73.5. Total holes: 36.* ✉ *Greens fees $$$. Cart mandatory. Special policies: tee times available a week in advance. Restaurant, accommodations.*

**Palisades Country Club.** Overlooking Lake Minneola, this Joe Lee–signed course is known for its roller-coaster-like fairways and generous landing areas. ✉ *16510 Palisades Blvd., Clermont 34711,* ☎ *904/394–0085. Yardage: 7,004. Par: 72. USGA rating 73.8. Total holes:*

*18.* ☒ *Greens fees $$. Cart mandatory. Special policies: tee times available a week in advance. Restaurant, driving range.*

**Timacuan Golf & Country Club.** This is a two-part course designed by Ron Garl: Part I, the front nine, is open, with lots of sand; Part II, the back nine, is heavily wooded. ☒ *550 Timacuan Blvd., Lake Mary 32746,* ☎ *407/321–0010. Yardage: 7,019. Par: 72. USGA rating: 73.5. Total holes: 18.* ☒ *Greens fees $$$. Cart mandatory. Special policies: tee times available 3 days in advance. Restaurant, driving range.*

**Walt Disney World Resort.** Where else would you find a sand trap shaped like the head of a well-known mouse? There are five championship courses here—all on the PGA Tour. Eagle Pines, a Pete Dye design, has small, undulating greens and bunker-punctuated fairways. Ospley Ridge, by Tom Fazio, incorporates a relaxing tour into forested, undeveloped Walt Disney World acreage. The Magnolia is long but forgiving, with extra-wide fairways. The Palm is shorter, narrower, and more tree-covered. For novice and preteen golfers there's the nine-hole Oak Trail. ☒ *1950 W. Magnolia Palm Dr., Lake Buena Vista 32830,* ☎ *407/824–2270. Yardage: 7,190. Par: 72. USGA rating: 73.9. Total holes: 99.* ☒ *Greens fees $$$$. Cart mandatory. Special policies: tee times available 30 days in advance for resort guests, a week in advance for the public. Restaurant, driving range, accommodations.*

## Tampa Bay Area

**Bloomingdale Golfers Club.** Playing on this water- and tree-lined course can be like playing in an open-air aviary, because there are, reportedly, more than 60 bird species (including a bald eagle) in residence on the course. For golfers, however, birdies and eagles are hard to come by. ☒ *1802 Natures Way Blvd., Valrico 33594,* ☎ *813/685–4105. Yardage: 7,165. Par: 72. USGA rating: 74.4. Total holes: 18.* ☒ *Greens fees $$. Cart mandatory. Special policies: reserved for members Fri.–Sun. after 11:30 AM. Restaurant, driving range.*

**Buffalo Creek.** This Manatee County–owned course resembling a Scottish links and designed by Lakeland, Florida–based golf architect Ron Garl is in as good condition as most private clubs. It's challenging but playable, with few water-lined fairways or traps in front of the greens. ☒ *8100 Erie Rd., Palmetto 34221,* ☎ *813/776–2611. Yardage: 7,005. Par: 72. USGA rating: 73.1. Total holes: 18.* ☒ *Greens fees $–$$. Cart optional. Special policies: tee times available 2 days in advance. Restaurant, driving range.*

**Innisbrook Hilton Resort.** Innisbrook's Copperhead course, generally ranked among Florida's toughest, has several long, dog-leg par-4s. ☒ *U.S. 19, Tarpon Springs 34684,* ☎ *813/942–2000. Yardage: 7,087. Par: 71. USGA rating: 74.4. Total holes: 63.* ☒ *Greens fees $$$$. Cart mandatory. Special policies: must be a resort guest or a member of a U.S. or Canadian golf club. Restaurant, driving range, accommodations.*

**Plantation Golf & Country Club.** Local knowledge can be helpful on the Bobcat course: With water on 16 holes and greens not visible from the tee on 12 holes, shot placement and club selection are critical. ☒ *500 Rockley Blvd., Venice 34293,* ☎ *813/493–2000. Yardage: 6,840. Par: 72. USGA rating: 73. Total holes: 36.* ☒ *Greens fees $$. Cart mandatory. Special policies: Bobcat course reserved for resort guests and members Oct.–Apr.; tee times available 2 days in advance. Restaurant, driving range, accommodations.*

**Plantation Inn & Golf Resort.** The Championship Course winds through pines and natural lakes. An assortment of tees makes the course playable for golfers of varying ability levels. ⊠ *9301 W. Fort Island Trail, Crystal River 34423,* ☎ *904/795–7211 or 800/632–6262. Yardage: 6,502. Par: 72. USGA rating: 71.6. Total holes: 27.* ▧ *Greens fees $$. Cart optional off-season. Special policies: tee times available a week in advance, 2 days in advance in Feb. and Mar. Restaurant, driving range, accommodations.*

**The Resort at Longboat Key.** Water, water everywhere: Amid canals and lagoons, the Islandside Course brings water into play on all but one hole, and play can be especially tough when the wind comes off Sarasota Bay or the Gulf of Mexico. ⊠ *301 Gulf of Mexico Dr., Longboat Key 34228,* ☎ *813/383–8821. Yardage: 6,792. Par: 72. USGA rating: 73.8. Total holes: 45.* ▧ *Greens fees $$$. Cart mandatory. Special policies: must be a resort guest or a member; tee times required 3 days in advance. Restaurant, driving range, accommodations.*

**Saddlebrook Golf and Tennis Resort.** The Saddlebrook course, designed by Arnold Palmer, is relatively short, but the premium is on accuracy, with lots of water to avoid. Large undulating greens make four-putting a constant concern. ⊠ *5700 Saddlebrook Way, Wesley Chapel 33543,* ☎ *813/973–1111 or 800/729–8383. Yardage: 6,564. Par: 70. USGA rating: 72. Total holes: 36.* ▧ *Greens fees $$$$. Cart mandatory. Special policies: tee times available 2 months in advance for resort guests. Restaurant, driving range, accommodations.*

**Sun 'n Lake Golf Club.** The original 18-hole course has a "wilderness" reputation: Deer are often spotted on the fairways, and playing from the rough can feel like playing from a jungle. ⊠ *5223 Sun 'n Lake Blvd., Sebring 33872,* ☎ *813/385–4830. Yardage: 6,731. Par: 72. USGA rating: 72. Total holes: 27.* ▧ *Greens fees $$. Cart mandatory. Special policies: tee times available 6 days in advance; Wed. morning, women members only; Thurs. morning, men members only. Restaurant, driving range, accommodations.*

**World Woods Golf Club.** The Rolling Oaks course, designed by Tom Fazio, is aptly named. Numerous large trees frame undulating fairways, providing both beauty and challenge. ⊠ *17590 Ponce de Leon Blvd., Brooksville 34614,* ☎ *904/796–5500. Yardage: 6,985. Par: 72. USGA rating: 73.5. Total holes: 48.* ▧ *Greens fees $$$. Cart mandatory. Special policies: tee times available a month in advance. 22-acre practice area with 4-sided driving range, 2-acre putting course.*

## Southwest Florida

**Cape Coral Golf & Tennis Resort.** This course tests those who think themselves expert in sand play. Although not long and not difficult, the course is guarded by more than 100 bunkers. ⊠ *4003 Palm Tree Blvd., Cape Coral 33915,* ☎ *813/542–7879. Yardage: 6,649. Par: 72. USGA rating: 71.6. Total holes: 18.* ▧ *Greens fees $–$$. Cart mandatory. Special policies: tee times available 3 days in advance. Restaurant, driving range, accommodations.*

**Eastwood Golf Club.** Included on many lists of America's best public courses, Eastwood demands accuracy, with tight fairways, water, and well-bunkered greens. ⊠ *4600 Bruce Herd La., Fort Myers 33905,* ☎ *813/275–4848. Yardage: 6,772. Par: 72. USGA rating: 73.3. Total holes: 18.* ▧ *Greens fees $$. Cart mandatory before 3 in season. Driving range.*

**Lely Flamingo Island Club.** This Robert Trent Jones course was completed in 1991 and was the first of three planned at this resort-in-the-making. Multilevel greens are guarded by a fleet of greedy bunkers, but the wide, rolling fairways generally keep errant drives in play. ⊠ *8004 Lely Resort Blvd., Naples 33962,* ☎ *813/793–2223. Yardage: 7,171. Par: 72. USGA rating: 73.9. Total holes: 36.* ☒ *Greens fees $$$–$$$$. Cart mandatory. Special policies: tee times available 3 days in advance. Restaurant, driving range.*

**Naples Beach Hotel & Golf Club.** Originally built in 1930, this is one of Florida's oldest courses. Although it is short and flat, the strategic bunkering can make for challenging play. ⊠ *851 Gulf Shore Blvd. N, Naples 33940,* ☎ *813/261–2222 or 800/237–7600. Yardage: 6,497. Par: 72. USGA rating: 71.2. Total holes: 18.* ☒ *Greens fees $$$–$$$$. Cart mandatory. Special policies: tee times available 3 days in advance. Restaurant, driving range, accommodations.*

**Pelican's Nest Golf Course.** Tom Fazio–designed, the Seminole and Hurricane courses are bordered with swamp and thick vegetation—cypress, pine, oak, and palm trees. The elegant and enormous clubhouse and meticulous groundskeeping make the Pelican's Nest a haven for guests of Naples's luxury resorts. ⊠ *4450 Pelican's Nest Dr. SW, Bonita Springs 33923,* ☎ *813/947–4600. Yardage: 6,972. Par: 72. USGA rating: 74.3. Total holes: 36.* ☒ *Greens fees $$$–$$$$. Cart mandatory. Restaurant, driving range.*

# Palm Beach

**Boca Raton Resort & Club.** It's not so much the resort course as the celebrity aura that serves as an attraction here. When you play this one, you follow in the footsteps (or cart tracks) of Frank Sinatra and Gerald Ford, among others. ⊠ *501 E. Camino Real, Boca Raton 33432,* ☎ *407/395–3000 or 800/327–0101. Yardage: 6,523. Par: 71. USGA rating: 71.5. Total holes: 72.* ☒ *Greens fees $$$. Cart mandatory. Special policies: must be a resort guest or a member; tee times available 5 days in advance. Restaurant, driving range, accommodations.*

**Boynton Beach Municipal Golf Course.** The rolling terrain of this relatively short public course is unusual around generally flat Palm Beach. ⊠ *8020 Jog Rd., Boynton Beach 33437,* ☎ *407/969–2200. Yardage: 6,340. Par: 71. USGA rating: 70.1. Total holes: 27.* ☒ *Greens fees $. Cart mandatory until 3. Snack bar, driving range.*

**Breakers Hotel Golf Club.** The Ocean Course, designed by Donald Ross and among Florida's oldest, compensates for its shortness with tight fairways and small greens. ⊠ *1 S. County Rd., Palm Beach 33480,* ☎ *407/655–6611 or 800/833–3141. Yardage: 6,017. Par: 70. USGA rating: 69.3. Total holes: 36.* ☒ *Greens fees $$$$. Cart mandatory. Special policies: must be a hotel guest or a member; free shuttle bus to West Course, 11 mi off-site. Restaurant, driving range, accommodations.*

**Emerald Dunes Golf Club.** This Tom Fazio–designed course gets official credit as the 1,000th course to open in Florida and was considered one of the best new courses in the United States in 1990. ⊠ *2100 Emerald Dunes Dr., West Palm Beach 33411,* ☎ *407/684–4653. Yardage: 7,006. Par: 72. USGA rating: 73.8. Total holes: 18.* ☒ *Greens fees $$$–$$$$. Cart mandatory. Special policies: tee times available 30 days in advance. Restaurant, driving range.*

**Indian River Plantation Beach Resort.** This par-61 course is classic Florida—flat, with lots of palms and bunkers, and made tricky by ocean breezes. ⊠ *555 N.E. Ocean Blvd., Hutchinson Island, Stuart 34996,* ☎ *407/225–3700 or 800/444–3389. Yardage: 4,048. Par: 61. USGA* *rating: 57. Total holes: 18.* ⌨ *Greens fees $$. Cart mandatory. Special policies: must be a resort guest or a member; tee times available a month in advance for resort guests. Restaurant, driving range, accommodations.*

**Palm Beach Polo and Country Club.** The Dunes course—the resort's newest—is a Ron Garl/Jerry Pate design with Scottish touches, such as pot bunkers and grass traps. ✉ *11830 Polo Club Road, West Palm Beach 33414,* ☎ *407/798–7000. Yardage: 7,050. Par: 72. USGA rating: 73.6. Total holes: 45.* ⌨ *Greens fees $$$$. Cart mandatory. Special policies: must be a resort guest or a member; tee times available 2 days in advance. Restaurant, driving range, accommodations.*

**PGA National Resort & Spa.** The Champion Course, redesigned by Jack Nicklaus, demands length and accuracy, with water on 17 holes and more than 100 traps. It is the site of the PGA Seniors Championship. ✉ *1000 Ave. of the Champions, Palm Beach Gardens 33418,* ☎ *407/627–1800. Yardage: 7,022. Par: 72. USGA rating: 74.7. Total holes: 90.* ⌨ *Greens fees $$$–$$$$. Cart mandatory. Special policies: must be a resort guest, a member, or a golf pro; higher greens fees for Champion Course. Restaurant, driving range, accommodations.*

## Fort Lauderdale

**Bonaventure Resort & Spa.** Plenty of trees, water, and bunkers line the East Course. The highlight hole is the par-3 third, where the green fronts a waterfall. ✉ *200 Bonaventure Blvd., Fort Lauderdale 33326,* ☎ *954/389–2100 or 800/327–8090. Yardage: 7,011. Par: 72. USGA rating: 74.2. Total holes: 36.* ⌨ *Greens fees $$$. Cart mandatory. Special policies: tee times available 3 days in advance. Restaurant, driving range, accommodations.*

**Colony West Country Club.** There is water on 14 of the Championship Course's holes. The most interesting hole is the 12th, a par-4 through a cypress forest. ✉ *6800 N.W. 88th Ave., Tamarac 33321,* ☎ *954/726–8430. Yardage: 6,864. Par: 71. USGA rating: 73.9. Total holes: 36.* ⌨ *Greens fees $$. Cart mandatory. Special policies: tee times available 3 days in advance. Restaurant.*

**The Oaks Golf & Racquet Club.** The Cypress, the more challenging of two courses, has familiar Florida features: lots of palms and greens well protected by sand and water. ✉ *3701 Oaks Clubhouse Dr., Pompano Beach 33069,* ☎ *305/978–1737. Yardage: 6,910. Par: 72. USGA rating: 73.3. Total holes: 54.* ⌨ *Greens fees $$–$$$. Cart mandatory. Special policies: tee times available a day in advance. Restaurant, driving range, accommodations.*

## Miami

**Don Shula's Hotel & Golf Club.** Large greens and elevated tees—unusual in south Florida—are features of the championship course. For golfers who can't get enough, there's also a par-3 course that's lighted at night. ✉ *7601 Miami Lakes Dr., Miami Lakes 33014,* ☎ *305/821–1150. Yardage: 7,055. Par: 72. USGA rating: 73. Total holes: 36.* ⌨ *Greens fees $$–$$$. Cart optional, $20. Special policies: tee times available a week in advance for members, a day in advance for nonmembers. Restaurant, driving range, accommodations.*

**Doral Golf Resort and Spa.** The 18th hole on the Blue Course, nicknamed "the Blue Monster" and venue for the Doral-Ryder Open, rates among the hardest finishing holes on the PGA Tour. Veteran pro Ray Floyd reportedly called it the toughest par-4 in the world. ✉ *4400 N.W.*

*87th Ave., Doral 33178, ☎ 305/592–2000 or 800/713–6725. Yardage: 6,939. Par: 72. USGA rating: 72. Total holes: 81. ✉ Greens fees $$$–$$$$. Cart optional. Special policies: tee time preference for hotel guests; higher greens fees for Blue Course. Restaurant, driving range, accommodations.*

**Links at Key Biscayne.** Regularly rated highly among U.S. public courses, this one—the site of the Royal Caribbean Classic on the PGA Seniors Tour—is surrounded by mangrove swamps and inhabited by many bird species and alligators. ✉ *6700 Crandon Blvd., Key Biscayne 33149, ☎ 305/361–9129 or 305/669–9500. Yardage: 7,099. Par: 72. USGA rating: 75.2. Total holes: 18. ✉ Greens fees $$–$$$. Cart optional after 1. Special policies: tee times available a week in advance. Restaurant, driving range.*

**Turnberry Isle Resort & Club.** The Robert Trent Jones South Course, which has hosted the PGA Seniors Championship, mixes old and new: a double green, similar to those at the Old Course at St. Andrews, Scotland, and a modern island green (on the 18th hole). ✉ *19999 W. Country Club Dr., Aventura 33180, ☎ 305/932–6200 or 800/327–7028. Yardage: 7,003. Par: 72. USGA rating: 73.7. Total holes: 36. ✉ Greens fees $$$. Cart mandatory. Special policies: must be a hotel guest or a member; tee times available 2 days in advance. Restaurant, driving range, accommodations.*

# 3 Miami and Miami Beach

*In the 1980s, a stylized television cop show called* Miami Vice *brought notoriety to this southernmost of big Florida cities; in the 1990s the revamped Art Deco District of South Beach put it on the map again. Through all this, the city went from an enclave of retired northeasterners to the ultimate international joyride with a Latin beat—more than half the city's population is Latin. Don't miss Coconut Grove, South Florida's oldest settlement. It's chic and casual, full of bistros, cafés, and galleries.*

By Herb Hiller

Updated by
Marianne
Camas

**W**HAT MAKES MIAMI DIFFERENT from the rest
of the United States is quickly apparent from
the air. With the vast Everglades at the west-
ern edge and the Atlantic to the east, Miami clings to a ribbon of drained
land near the southeastern tip of the country. Still vulnerable to
mosquitoes, periodic flooding, and potential devastation by hurricanes, Miami a hundred years after its founding is still the wrong
place for a city, but it's the right place for an international crossroads.
And that's exactly what this hot, humid melting pot has become.

Long before Spain's gold-laden treasure ships passed through the Gulf
Stream offshore, the Calusa Indians who lived here had begun to trade
with mainland neighbors to the north and island brethren to the south.
Repeating this pattern, more than 150 U.S. and multinational companies
now locate their Latin American headquarters in Greater Miami. The
city has unparalleled airline connections to the Western Hemisphere,
its cruise port ranks No. 1 in the world, and it leads the nation in the
number of Edge Act banks. Miami hosts 20 foreign trade offices, 29
binational chambers of commerce, and 49 foreign consulates. No city
of the Western Hemisphere is so universally simpatico.

First-time visitors are always struck by the billboards in Spanish. Ini-
tially these seem an affectation, an attempt to promote Miami's exotic
international image. But the language and the Latin influence is everywhere. Only after you hear Spanish spoken all around you or after a
computerized elevator announces the floor stops as *primer piso* and
*segundo piso* do you realize that the city *Newsweek* called "America's
Casablanca" is really the capital of Latin America. Metro Miami is more
than half Latin. Cubans make up most of this Spanish-speaking population, but there are also significant communities from Colombia, El
Salvador, Nicaragua, Panama, Puerto Rico, and Venezuela. The Spanish place-names George Merrick affixed to the streets in Coral Gables
75 years ago—Alhambra, Alcazar, Salzedo—may have been romantic
pretense, but today's renamed Avenida Gen. Maximo Gomez and Carlos Arboleya Way are earnest celebrations of a contemporary city's
heroes. Frank Sinatra and Barbra Streisand have given way in the
hearts of Miamians to Julio Iglesias and Gloria Estefan.

In addition to the dominant Spanish-speaking population, Miami is
home to some 200,000 Haitians, along with Brazilians, Chinese, Ger-
mans, Greeks, Iranians, Israelis, Italians, Jamaicans, Lebanese,
Malaysians, Russians, and Swedes—all speaking a veritable Babel of
tongues. Most either know or are trying to learn English. Communi-
cation is eased by speaking slowly and distinctly.

Established Miami has warmed up to its newcomers. That's a big step
forward. Only a few years ago metropolitan government enacted an
ordinance forbidding essential public information from appearing in
Spanish. In 1993 that restrictive affront was rescinded, and resisters
have adjusted or moved north. Yesterday's immigrants have become
today's citizens, and the nation's most international city now offers a
style expressed in its many languages, its world-beat music, and its wealth
of exotic restaurants.

Miami has changed fast. Not too long ago, old Miami Beach was a
rundown geriatric center. Today it's South Beach, the deco darling of
the world. Summer especially brings young people; two of every three
are male, and three of every four are single. Lincoln Road, once the
5th Avenue of the South and only recently an embarrassing derelict row,

has been stunningly brought back to life. On weekends it rivals the pedestrian malls of Cambridge, Lyons, or Munich for crowds and sheer hoi polloi festivity. Next slated for revival is North Beach, as all of Miami Beach becomes a real-world Magic Kingdom, proving it's possible and relatively inexpensive to build community by preserving distinctive architecture rather than by "imagineering" pseudo worlds. (Miamians—especially Miami's immigrant newcomers—still adore Disney, however.)

More changes are in store in this city that seems fueled by caffeine. (Stop by the window serving station of any Cuban café for a *tinto*, the city's high-test coffee.) Not surprisingly, much of the change is taking place in areas to the south, those hardest hit by Hurricane Andrew in 1992. In the Redlands district, the Redlands Conservancy is introducing bicycle trails and B&Bs as a way of preserving South Dade County's agricultural heritage. Coral-rock walls and avocado groves may prove as distinctive in their own way as Art Deco hotels. A network of 200 miles of trails should link Biscayne and Everglades national parks by the end of the decade. For those interested in a quicker pace, Homestead has become a state-of-the-art hub for America's love affair with car racing (☞ Chapter 4).

As a big city, Miami also earns its bad rap. A high percentage of its citizens live in poverty. It is ranked fourth in the United States for traffic congestion. It ranks first in violent and property crimes and does the worst job of any city in putting and keeping criminals behind bars. Yet some widely publicized crimes against tourists in 1993 led to stepped-up visitor-safety programs that increased the margin of visitor safety. Police patrols have increased in areas frequented by tourists. Highway direction signs with red sunburst logos are now installed at ¼-mile intervals on major roads. Identification making rental cars conspicuous to would-be criminals has been removed, and multilingual pamphlets on avoiding crime are widely distributed. Despite all the problems and hyped headlines, Miami still has heated allure with a climate, beaches, and international sophistication that few places can match.

A slew of international celebrities have moved here: Madonna, Sylvester Stallone, Cher, Gianni Versace. Four major-league sports franchises call Miami home along with the Doral-Ryder Open Tournament, the Lipton Championships, the Miami City Ballet, and Florida Grand Opera. On the verge of its centennial year and barely two years after Hurricane Andrew roared through, Miami played host to both the Summit of the Americas and the Super Bowl. Visitors find in Miami a multicultural metropolis that works and plays with vigor and that welcomes the world to celebrate its diversity.

## Pleasures and Pastimes

### Beaches

Greater Miami has beaches to fit every style. A sandy, 300-foot-wide beach extends for 10 miles from the foot of Miami Beach to Haulover Beach Park, with several distinct sections. Amazingly, it's all man-made. Seriously eroded during the mid-1970s, the beach was restored by the U.S. Army Corps of Engineers in a $51.5 million project between 1977 and 1981. Between 23rd and 44th streets, Miami Beach built boardwalks and protective walkways atop a sand dune landscaped with sea oats, sea grape, and other native plants whose roots keep the sand from blowing away.

### Biking

Dade County has about 100 miles of off-road bicycle trails, and there are many places to rent cycles.

### Boating

It's not uncommon for traffic to jam at boat ramps, especially on weekend mornings. But the waters are worth the wait. The calm waves of Key Biscayne are made for sailing and powerboats are always popular. There are numerous marinas in Greater Miami. Dock masters can provide information on other marine services you may need. Ask them for *Teall's Tides and Guides, Miami-Dade County,* and other local nautical publications.

### Dining

You can eat your way around the world in Greater Miami, enjoying just about any kind of cuisine imaginable, in every price category. The rich mix of nationalities encourages individual restaurateurs and chefs to celebrate their culinary roots. Miami offers dishes native to Spain, Cuba, and Nicaragua as well as specialties of China, India, Thailand, Vietnam, and other Asian cultures. However, innovative American cooking ranks among the best to be found. In recent years the city has gained eminence for the distinctive cuisine introduced by chefs who have migrated north from the tropics and combined fresh, natural foods—especially seafoods—with classic dishes in a style that is sometimes called Floribbean because of a tangy island influence.

### Diving

Summer diving conditions in Greater Miami have been compared to those in the Caribbean. Winter diving can be adversely affected when cold fronts come through. Dive-boat schedules vary with the season and with local weather conditions.

Fowey, Triumph, Long, and Emerald reefs are all shallow 10- to 15-foot dives good for snorkelers and beginning divers. These reefs are on the edge of the continental shelf, ¼ mile from depths greater than 100 feet. You can also paddle around the tangled prop roots of the mangrove trees that line Florida's coastline, peering at the fish, crabs, and other onshore creatures hiding there.

In 1994 a greatly expanded artificial-reef program was begun off the shores of Miami. The first units of 100,000 tons of lime-rock boulders were placed on the mostly sand and silt sea bottom where sea life had been destroyed by Hurricane Andrew. Early reports confirm fish life has quickly been attracted to the new sites.

### Golf

From the famed "Blue Monster" at the Doral Golf Resort and Spa to the scenic Links at Key Biscayne, overlooking Biscayne Bay, Greater Miami has more than 30 private and public courses.

### Lodging

Few urban areas can match Greater Miami's diversity of accommodations. The area has hundreds of hotels, motels, and B&Bs with lodgings in all price categories, from $8 for a night in a dormitory-style hostel to $2,000 for a night in a luxurious presidential suite.

### Nightlife

Greater Miami has a new concentration of nightspots in South Beach along Ocean Drive, Washington Avenue, and most recently along Lincoln Road Mall. Other nightlife centers on Little Havana, Coconut Grove, and on the fringes of downtown Miami.

Individual clubs offer jazz, reggae, salsa, various forms of rock, and Top 40 sounds on different nights of the week. Some clubs refuse entrance to anyone under 21; others 25. (If that is a concern, call ahead.) On South Beach, where the sounds of jazz and reggae spill into the streets, fashion models and photographers frequent the lobby bars of small Art Deco hotels. Throughout Greater Miami, bars and cocktail lounges in larger hotels operate nightly discos, with live weekend entertainment. Many hotels extend their bars into open-air courtyards, where patrons dine and dance under the stars throughout the year. It's a good idea to ask in advance about cover charges; policies change frequently.

## Sailing
Dinner Key and the Coconut Grove waterfront remain the center of sailing in Greater Miami, although sailboat moorings and rentals are located along other parts of the bay and up the Miami River.

## Shopping
Except in the heart of the Everglades, visitors to Greater Miami are never more than 15 minutes from a major shopping area and the soothing shoosh, shoosh sound of a credit card machine. Downtown Miami ceased to be the community's central shopping hub long ago when most residents moved to the suburbs. Today Dade County has more than a dozen major malls, an international free-trade zone, and hundreds of miles of commercial streets lined with stores and small neighborhood shopping centers. Many of these local shopping areas have an ethnic flavor, catering to Greater Miami's immigrant cultures.

In the Latin neighborhoods, for example, children's stores sell *vestidos de fiesta* (party dresses) made of organza and lace. Men's stores sell the *guayabera,* a pleated, embroidered shirt that replaces the tie and jacket in much of the tropics. Traditional bridal shops display formal dresses that Latin families buy or rent for a daughter's *quince,* a lavish 15th-birthday celebration.

No standard store hours exist in Greater Miami, though most malls observe the typical seven-day hours of malls everywhere. Call ahead. When you shop, expect to pay Florida's 6% sales tax (6.5% in Dade County), unless you have the store ship your goods out of the state.

## Spectator Sports
Greater Miami has franchises in all major-league sports—baseball, basketball, football, and ice hockey—plus top-rated events in boat racing, jai alai, and tennis. In addition to contacting the addresses below directly, you can get tickets to major events from **Ticketmaster** (Dade County, ☎ 305/358–5885; Broward County, ☎ 305/523–3309; Palm Beach, ☎ 407/839–3900), and charge them to your credit card. (There is a service charge.) Generally you can find daily listings of local sports events in the sports section of the *Miami Herald*. Friday's Weekend section carries detailed schedules and coverage of spectator sports.

Activities of the annual **Orange Bowl** and **Junior Orange Bowl Festival** take place from early November to late February. Best known for its King Orange Jamboree Parade and the Federal Express/Orange Bowl Football Classic, the festival also includes two tennis tournaments: the Rolex–Orange Bowl International Tennis Tournament, for top amateur tennis players 18 and under, and an international tournament for players 14 and under. The Junior Orange Bowl Festival is the world's largest youth festival, with more than 20 events between November and January, including sports, cultural, and performing arts activities. The showcase event is the HealthSouth/Junior Orange Bowl Parade, held in downtown Coral Gables.

# EXPLORING MIAMI AND MIAMI BEACH

Disney captured Miami's family trade; a television cop show called *Miami Vice* smacked the city upside the head with notoriety; the winds of Hurricane Andrew literally shook its foundation; and South Beach made it a global resort for the turn of the 21st century. Through this, the city went from an enclave of retired northeasterners to the ultimate joyride with a Latin beat. Hardly any part of the city isn't caught up in change. Meanwhile sightseeing—which used to be pretty much limited to picking fruit off citrus trees and watching alligator wrestling—has become a fun way to glimpse the city at work and at play.

Finding your way around Greater Miami is easy if you know how the numbering system works. Miami is laid out on a grid with four quadrants—northeast, northwest, southeast, and southwest—which meet at Miami Avenue and Flagler Street. Miami Avenue separates east from west, and Flagler Street separates north from south. Avenues and courts run north–south; streets, terraces, and ways run east–west. Roads run diagonally, northwest–southeast.

Many named streets also bear numbers. For example, Unity Boulevard is N.W. and S.W. 27th Avenue, and LeJeune Road is N.W. and S.W. 42nd Avenue. However, named streets that depart markedly from the grid, such as Biscayne Boulevard and Brickell Avenue, have no corresponding numerical designations. Dade County and most other municipalities follow the Miami numbering system.

In Miami Beach, avenues run north–south; streets, east–west. Numbers rise along the beach from south to north and from the Atlantic Ocean in the east to Biscayne Bay in the west.

In Coral Gables, all streets bear names. Coral Gables uses the Miami numbering system for north–south addresses, but begins counting east–west addresses westward from Douglas Road (S.W. 37th Ave.).

Hialeah has its own grid. Palm Avenue separates east from west; Hialeah Drive separates north from south. Avenues run north–south and streets east–west. Numbered streets and avenues are designated west, east, southeast, southwest, northeast, or northwest.

## Great Itineraries

Most visitors to the Greater Miami area don't realize that Miami and Miami Beach are separate cities. Miami, on the mainland, is south Florida's commercial hub. Miami Beach, on 17 islands offshore in Biscayne Bay, is sometimes considered America's Riviera, luring refugees from winter with its warm sunshine, sandy beaches, graceful, shady palms, and ever-rocking nightlife.

Downtown has become the lively hub of the mainland city, now more accessible thanks to the Metromover extension (☞ Getting Around by Train *in* Miami A to Z, *below*). Other major attractions include Coconut Grove, Little Havana, and the South Beach/ Art Deco District, but since these districts are spread out beyond the reach of public transportation, you'll have to drive. Rent a convertible if you can—there's nothing quite like the sensation of having the wind in your hair as you drive across one of the causeways en route to Miami Beach. (Dark glasses are a must with the car.)

*Numbers in the text correspond to numbers in the margin and on the maps.*

IF YOU HAVE 3 DAYS

Take a few hours to explore downtown Miami via the Metromover. Then check out the shops at Bayside Marketplace. Drive across the MacArthur Causeway (U.S. 41) and hang out with the beautiful people in trendy South Beach. Do some more people-watching and shopping at the **Lincoln Road Mall** ④ then head north on Collins Avenue to the **Fontainebleau Hilton** ⑨. On the second day visit **Vizcaya** ㊲, Virginia Key, and Key Biscayne. For your third day explore Coconut Grove or South Dade, home of the first-class **Metrozoo** ㊺.

IF YOU HAVE 5 DAYS

Spend your first day exploring shops and museums in downtown Miami. On Day Two, drive across the MacArthur Causeway, take a leisurely walking tour of South Beach and **Lincoln Road Mall** ④, then drive north on Collins Avenue to the landmark **Fontainebleau Hilton** ⑨. Use Day Three to see **Vizcaya** ㊲, Virginia Key, and Key Biscayne. Spend Day Four exploring Coral Gables, South Miami, and Coconut Grove. On the fifth day visit South Dade, site of the **Miami Metrozoo** ㊺ and **Monkey Jungle** ㊼.

IF YOU HAVE 7 DAYS

A week gives you time to fully experience the multicultural, cosmopolitan, tropical mélange that is Greater Miami and its beaches. The theme for your first day is urban; use the Miami Metromover to zip around downtown Miami. Day Two is for the beach: drive across the MacArthur Causeway, take a leisurely walking tour of South Beach and drive north on Collins Avenue to the landmark **Fontainebleau Hilton** ⑨. Use Day Three to see historic **Vizcaya** ㊲ and Miami's tropical enclaves, Virginia Key and Key Biscayne. On Day Four explore Little Havana and Little Haiti. Spend the fifth day seeing the sights in Coral Gables and South Miami and the next day relaxing and exploring the cafés and boutiques that line the streets of Coconut Grove. On Day Seven visit South Dade, site of the **Miami Metrozoo** ㊺ and **Monkey Jungle** ㊼.

# South Beach/Miami Beach

The hub of South Beach (SoBe, to the truly hip) is the mile-square Art Deco District, fronted on the east by Ocean Drive. SoBe is trendy, it's tropical, and it's a tricky place to find a parking space. From mid-morning on, parking is scarce along Ocean Drive. You'll do better on Collins or Washington avenues, the next two streets parallel to Ocean Drive to the west. Be warned: Tickets are handed out freely when meters expire, and towing charges are high. Additional parking garages are supposed to be on the horizon, but don't count on it.

Less than 15 years ago, South Beach's vintage hotels were badly run down, catering mostly to infirm retirees. But a group of visionaries saw this collection of buildings as an architectural treasure to be salvaged from a sea of mindless urban renewal. It was, and is, peerless grouping of Art Deco modern architecture from the 1920s and 1930s. In the early 1980s, investors started fixing up the interiors of these hotels and repainting their exteriors with vibrant colors. International bistro operators then moved in, sensing the potential for a new café society. The media took note, and celebrities like singer Gloria Estefan, designer Gianni Versace, and record executive Chris Blackwell bought a piece of the action. (The list continues to expand and now includes the artist formerly known as Prince.) Now SoBe buzzes 24 hours a day, as fashion photographers pose beautiful models for shoots that make backdrops of the throngs of visitors.

## A Good Tour

*Numbers in the text below correspond to numbers in the margin and on the Miami Beach map.*

The Art Deco District is a 10-block stretch of Ocean Drive that has become the most talked-about beachfront in America. Palm-fringed **Lummus Park** ①, at Ocean Drive and 5th Street, is a good starting point. Facing north the first—and most obvious—things to notice about the Art Deco district are its buildings, painted with a pastel palette. About 650 significant buildings in the district are listed on the National Register of Historic Places. As you progress up Ocean Drive, notice that the forms and decorative detail of buildings are drawn both from nature and the streamlined shapes of modern transportation and industrial machinery.

At 5th Street cross to the west side of Ocean Drive, where there are many sidewalk cafés. As you walk north on Ocean Drive take note of the Park Central Hotel, built in 1937 by Deco architect Henry Hohauser. Next up is the Beacon, built in 1936. Its vertical fluting and racing stripes recall the principles of aerodynamics, a science in its infancy when the Beacon was constructed.

At 10th Street recross Ocean Drive to the beach side and visit the **Art Deco District Welcome Center** ② in the Oceanfront Auditorium, a 1950s building, not Deco.

Walk back across 10th Street, where you'll find the Clevelander, with its wonderful flying-saucer architecture. On the next block, at Number 1114, is the Amsterdam Palace, purchased by designer Gianni Versace and now restored. At Number 1144 is the eight-story Victor Hotel, which has an ocean-liner motif. Its lobby was frequently used as a setting for episodes of *Miami Vice*.

At Number 1244 the Leslie stands guard with its graceful fluted columns. At 1250 the Carlyle, built in 1941, is one of the few buildings on Hotel Row that no longer functions as a hotel.

The Cardozo is a classic example of streamlined architecture. Its unique facade was first noticed by filmmakers in 1959, when it was used as a setting for the Frank Sinatra film *A Hole in the Head*. Now owned by pop star Gloria Estefan, it's one of SoBe's hottest spots.

Make a right at 13th Street and walk one block to Washington Avenue, a mix of chic restaurants, avant-garde shops, delicatessens, and produce markets. Turn left on Washington and walk 2½ blocks south to the **Wolfsonian Foundation Gallery** ③, home of a 50,000-plus-item collection of modern design and so-called propaganda arts and political design amassed by Miami native Mitchell Wolfson, Jr.

Back on Washington Avenue turn right and walk four blocks north to 14th Street and Espanola Way, a narrow street of Mediterranean-revival buildings constructed in 1925 and frequented through the years by artists and writers. In the 1930s Cuban bandleader Desi Arnaz performed in the Village Tavern, which is now part of the Clay Hotel & AYH International Youth Hostel. One block of Espanola Way, west of Washington Avenue to Drexel Avenue, has been narrowed to a single lane, and Miami Beach's trademark pink sidewalks have been widened to accommodate new sidewalk cafés and shops selling imaginative clothing, jewelry, and art.

Continue two blocks beyond Drexel to Meridian Avenue and turn right. Three blocks north of Espanola Way is **Lincoln Road Mall** ④. At 541–545 Lincoln Road you'll see a classical four-story Deco gem with

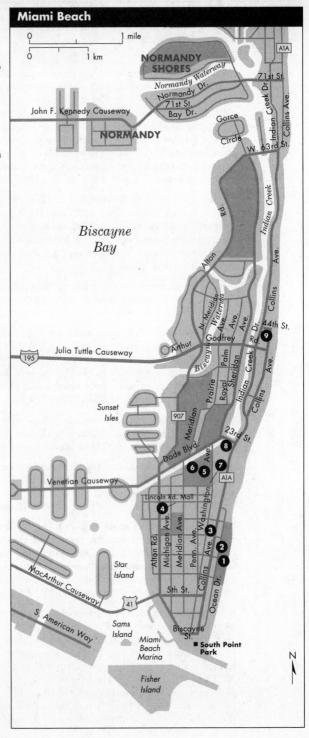

friezes—this is where the New World Symphony, a national advanced-training orchestra led by Michael Tilson Thomas, rehearses and performs. As you walk west toward Biscayne Bay the street is lined with chic food markets, cafés, and boutiques. Go farther west and you'll find the South Florida Art Center, home to one of the first arts groups to help resurrect the area. Farther on, a black-and-white Deco movie house with a Mediterranean barrel-tile roof has become the Colony Theater.

The first main street north of Lincoln Road Mall is 17th Street, named Hank Meyer Boulevard for the publicist who persuaded the late comedian Jackie Gleason to broadcast his TV show from Miami Beach in the 1950s. East on 17th Street, beside the entrance to Miami Beach City Hall, stands *Red Sea Road,* a huge red sculpture by Barbara Neijna. Also to your left across Convention Center Drive is the **Miami Beach Convention Center** ⑤, Miami's largest convention space.

Behind the Convention Center north along Convention Center Drive, at the northwest end of the parking lot near Meridian Avenue, is the **Holocaust Memorial** ⑥, a monumental sculpture and graphic record in memory of the 6 million Jewish victims of the Holocaust.

Just south of the convention center, at 17th Street and Washington Avenue, you'll see another large sculpture, *Mermaid,* by Roy Lichtenstein, in front of the **Jackie Gleason Theater of the Performing Arts** ⑦, where one of Gleason's TV shows originated. Go one block east to Collins Avenue and head north. At 21st Street turn left beside the Miami Beach Public Library in Collins Park, walk two blocks to Park Avenue, and turn right. You're approaching the **Bass Museum of Art** ⑧, which houses a diverse collection of European art.

If you've got the energy, return on 21st or 22nd Street to Collins Avenue and turn left. Head north toward the impressive **Fountainbleau Hilton Resort and Towers** ⑨. Locals call the 1,206-room hotel Big Blue. It's the giant—both physically and historically—of Miami Beach. Turn left on 65th Street, left again at the next corner onto Indian Creek Drive, and right at 63rd Street, which leads to Alton Road, a winding, landscaped boulevard of gracious homes styled along Art Deco lines.

TIMING

To see only the Art Deco buildings on Ocean Drive, allow one hour minimum. Depending upon your interests (and the heat, which in summer can wilt even the hardiest soul), schedule at least five hours and include a drink or meal at a café and browsing time in the shops on Ocean Drive and at Lincoln Road Mall.

Start your walking tour as early in the day as possible; in winter the street becomes crowded as the day wears on, and in summer, afternoon heat and humidity can be unbearable.

## Sights to See

**Amsterdam Palace.** In the early 1980s, before South Beach became the hotbed of chicness, Italian designer Gianni Versace purchased this rundown residence. After spending $8 million on the restoration, Versace's home-sweet-elaborate home is a modern-day Xanadu, an ornate three-story palazzo with a guest house and a copper-dome rooftop observatory. The structure is not open for tours, but gawkers line up along the street anyway. ⊠ *1114 Ocean Dr.*

**Ancient Spanish Monastery.** The oldest building in the Western Hemisphere was built in 1141 in Segovia, Spain. Newspaper magnate William Randolph Hearst had it removed in pieces and stored in California for 25 years. In 1954 Miami developers rebuilt it at its present site. ✉ *16711 W. Dixie Hwy., North Miami Beach,* ☎ *305/945–1461.* ⌨ *$4.* ◷ *Mon.–Sat. 10–4, Sun. noon–4.*

**②  Art Deco District Welcome Center.** Run by the Miami Design Preservation League, this clearinghouse in the Oceanfront Auditorium provides information about the buildings in the Art Deco district. A well-stocked gift shop sells 1950s and Art Deco memorabilia and books on Miami's history. Saturday-morning walking tours start here. ✉ *1001 Ocean Dr. (Barbara Capitan Way),* ☎ *305/531–3484.* ⌨ *Free.* ◷ *Daily 11–6, open later Thurs.–Mon. in season.*

**❽  Bass Museum of Art.** Works on display include *The Holy Family,* a painting by Peter Paul Rubens; *The Tournament,* one of several 16th-century Flemish tapestries; and works by Albrecht Dürer and Henri de Toulouse-Lautrec. A current expansion project will double the museum's size to 40,000 square feet in time for the 1997–98 winter season. ✉ *2121 Park Ave.,* ☎ *305/673–7530.* ⌨ *$7, donation Tues., more for some exhibitions.* ◷ *Tues.–Sat. 10–5, except 2nd and 4th Wed. of each month 1–9; Sun. 1–5.*

★ **❾  Fountainebleau Hilton Resort and Towers.** A triumphal archway looms over Collins Avenue, framing a majestic white building set in lush vegetation beside a waterfall and tropical lagoon. This vista is an illusion—a 13,000-square-foot outdoor mural on an exterior wall of the hotel. Artist Richard Haas designed the mural to illustrate how the hotel and its rock-grotto swimming pool would look behind the wall. ✉ *4441 Collins Ave.* ☎ *305/538–2000.*

**❻  Holocaust Memorial.** The focus of the memorial is a 42-foot-high bronze arm rising from the ground, with sculptured people climbing the arm seeking escape. A memorial wall with victims' names and a meditation garden complement the sculpture. ✉ *1933–1945 Meridian Ave.,* ☎ *305/538–1663.* ⌨ *Free.* ◷ *Daily 9–9.*

**❼  Jackie Gleason Theater of the Performing Arts.** The 3,000-seat theater, renamed for Gleason after his death (☞ Nightlife and the Arts, *below*) hosts touring Broadway shows and classical-music concerts. In front of the building the **Walk of the Stars** contains the footprints and signatures in concrete of the performers who have appeared in the theater since 1984, including Julie Andrews, Leslie Caron, Carol Channing, Edward Villella, and the late George Abbott. ✉ *1700 Washington Ave.,* ☎ *305/673–7300.*

★ **❹  Lincoln Road Mall.** A new, playful redesign of this grande dame of Miami Beach includes a grove of 20 towering date palms, five linear pools divided by strips of jungle, and a simulated aquarium behind a curtain-like waterfall. The mall is paired with Ocean Drive as part of must-see South Beach, especially on Saturday night, when art galleries schedule openings. ✉ *Lincoln Rd. between Collins Ave. and Alton Rd.*

🄲 **❶  Lummus Park.** This palm-shaded oasis on the beach side of Ocean Drive attracts beach-going families with its children's play area. It is a stark contrast to the ultrachic atmosphere just across the street. ✉ *East of Ocean Dr. between 5th and 15th Sts.*

**❺  Miami Beach Convention Center.** One of Jackie Gleason's TV shows originated in this building, a stucco 1960s structure that gained its peach-tone, Art Deco look in a 1990 renovation and expansion. ✉ *1901 Convention Center Dr.,* ☎ *305/673–7311.*

**South Pointe Park.** From the 50-yard Sunshine Pier, which adjoins the mile-long jetty at the mouth of Government Cut, you can fish while watching huge ships pass. No bait or tackle is available in the park.

Other facilities include two observation towers and volleyball courts.
⊠ *1 Washington Ave.*

**❸ Wolfsonian Foundation Gallery.** An elegantly renovated 1927 warehouse
is now home to the 50,000-plus item collection of modern design and
so-called "propaganda arts" amassed by Miami native Mitchell Wolfson, Jr., a world traveler and connoisseur. Included in the museum's
eclectic holdings are 8,000 matchbooks collected by King Farouk.
(The name "Wolfsonian," by the way, is intended to echo "Smithso-
nian.") Visitors are advised to call ahead for reservations, due to the
building's small capacity. ⊠ *1001 Washington Ave.,* ☎ *305/531–
1001.* 🖅 *$1.* ⊙ *Weekdays 1–5.*

# Downtown Miami

From a distance you see downtown Miami's future—a 21st-century
skyline already stroking the clouds with sleek fingers of steel and glass.
By day this icon of commerce and technology sparkles in the strong
subtropical sun; at night it basks in the man-made glow of neon and
floodlights.

Here staid, suited lawyers and bankers share the sidewalks with Latino
merchants wearing open-neck, intricately embroidered shirts called
guayaberas. Fruit merchants sell their wares from pushcarts. Young European travelers with backpacks stroll the streets. Foreign businesspeople
haggle over prices in import-export shops. You hear Arabic, Chinese,
Creole, French, German, Hebrew, Hindi, Japanese, Portuguese, Spanish, Swedish, Yiddish, and even a little English now and then.

This metropolis has become one of the great international cities of the
Americas, yet Miami's downtown is sorely neglected. Although office
workers crowd the area by day, the city, except for Bayside and the
Miami Arena, is deserted at night, and patrons of the Arena rarely linger
downtown. Those who live close to downtown stay at its fringes, as
on Claughton Island at the mouth of the Miami River, where a half
dozen residential towers have risen to house thousands in the last
decade. Visitors, too, spend as little time here as possible, since most
tourist attractions are in other neighborhoods. Miami's oldest downtown buildings date from the 1920s and 1930s—not very old compared
to the historic districts of St. Augustine and Pensacola. What's best in
the heart of downtown Miami today is its Latinization and the sheer
energy of Latin shoppers.

Thanks to the **Metromover** (☞ Getting Around by Train *in* Miami Es-
sentials, *below*), which has inner and outer loops through downtown
plus north and south extensions, this is an excellent tour to take by
rail. Attractions are conveniently located within about two blocks of
the nearest station, so the tour approximately follows the outer loop.
Parking downtown is no less convenient or more expensive than in any
city, but the best idea is to leave your car at an outlying Metrorail station and take the train downtown.

## A Good Tour
*Numbers in the text below correspond to numbers in the margin and
on the Downtown map.*

Get off the Metrorail train at Government Center Station, where the
21-mile elevated Metrorail commuter system connects with **Metromover.** As you leave the station, notice the Dade County Courthouse.
It's the building to the east with a pyramid at its peak, where turkey
vultures roost in winter. Built in 1928, it was once the tallest building
south of Washington, D.C.

On N.W. 1st Street stands Metro-Dade Center, the county government's sleek 30-story office building. Designed by architect Hugh Stubbins, it opened in 1985.

Across N.W. 1st Street stands the **Metro-Dade Cultural Center** ⑩, one of the focal points of Miami's downtown. The city's main art museum, historical museum, and library are here.

Take the Metromover to the next stop, **Ft. Dallas Park Station,** and walk one block south to the **Miami Avenue Bridge,** one of 11 bridges on the Miami River that open to let ships pass. From the bridge approach, watch freighters, tugboats, research vessels, and luxury yachts ply this busy 5-mile waterway.

At the next Metromover stop, **Knight Center Station,** you can transfer to the inner loop and ride one stop to the Miami Avenue Station, a block south of Flagler Street, downtown Miami's commercial spine. Or you can ride the Metromover spur that links downtown with the Brickell District, across the Miami River along Brickell Avenue, a southward extension of S.E. 2nd Avenue. Heading south on Brickell Avenue through a canyon of tall buildings, you'll pass the largest concentration of international banking offices in the United States. From the end of the Metromover line you can look south to where several architecturally interesting condominiums rise between Brickell Avenue and Biscayne Bay. Israeli artist Yacov Agam painted the rainbow exterior of Villa Regina. Arquitectonica, a nationally prominent architectural firm based in Miami, designed three of these buildings: the Palace, the Imperial, and the Atlantis.

The next stop on the outer loop is **Bayfront Park Station,** opposite **Claude and Mildred Pepper Bayfront Park** ⑪. South of the park the lobby of the Hotel Inter-Continental Miami contains *The Spindle,* a huge sculpture by Henry Moore. West of Bayfront Park Station stands the tallest building in Florida, the 55-story Southeast Financial Center; towering royal palms grace the 1-acre Palm Court plaza beneath its steel-and-glass frame.

As you continue north on the Metromover take in the fine view of Bayfront Park's greenery, the bay beyond, the Port of Miami in the bay, and Miami Beach across the water. The next Metromover stop, **First Street Station,** places you a block north of Flagler Street and the landmark **Gusman Center for the Performing Arts** ⑫, an ornate former movie palace restored as a concert hall.

The **College/Bayside Station** Metromover stop serves the downtown campus of **Miami-Dade Community College** ⑬, which has two fine galleries.

As Metromover rounds the curve after College/Bayside Station, look northeast to see **Freedom Tower** ⑭, where the Cuban Refugee Center processed more than 500,000 Cubans who entered the United States to flee Fidel Castro's regime in the 1960s. To see the tower up close, walk north from **Edcom Station** to N.E. 6th Street then two blocks east to Biscayne Boulevard. At this point in the loop the spur curves north to the Omni District.

A two-block walk south from Edcom Station will bring you to the **U.S. Courthouse** ⑮, a handsome building of coquina coral stone, erected in 1931 as Miami's main post office. As you round the northwest corner of the loop, at **State Plaza/Arena Station,** look two blocks north to see the round, squat, windowless, pink **Miami Arena** ⑯.

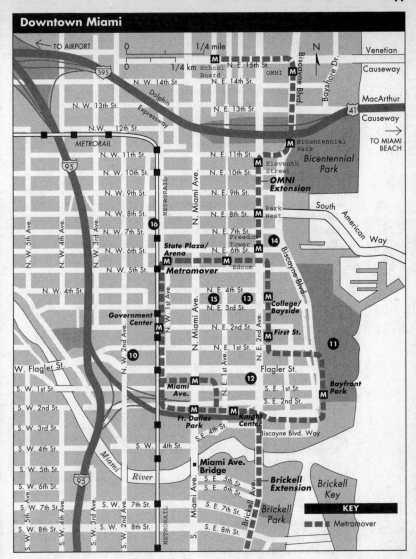

# Downtown Miami

TO AIRPORT

0      1/4 mile

0      1/4 km

N

Venetian

Causeway

MacArthur

Causeway

TO MIAMI BEACH

School Board

N. E. 15th St.

N. W. 14th St.

N. E. 14th St.

OMNI

Dolphin Expressway

N. W. 13th St.

N. E. 13th St.

Bayshore Dr.

Biscayne Blvd.

N. W. 12th St.

METRORAIL

Bicentennial Park

Bicentennial Park

N. W. 11th St.

N. E. 11th St.

Eleventh Street

N. W. 10th St.

N. E. 10th St.

OMNI Extension

N. W. 9th St.

N. E. 9th St.

N. W. 8th St.

N. E. 8th St.

Park West

South American Way

N. W. 7th St.

N. E. 7th St.

Freedom Tower

State Plaza/ Arena

N. E. 6th St.

Metromover

Edcom

N. W. 5th St.

N. W. 4th St.

N. E. 4th St.

N. E. 3rd St.

College/ Bayside

Government Center

N. E. 2nd St.

First St.

N. E. 1st St.

W. Flagler St.

Flagler St.

S. W. 1st St.

S. E. 1st St.

Bayfront Park

S. W. 2nd St.

S. E. 2nd St.

Miami Ave.

S. W. 3rd St.

Ft. Dallas Park

Knight Center

S. W. 4th St.

Biscayne Blvd. Way

Miami River

S. W. 5th St.

Miami Ave. Bridge

S. E. 5th St.

Brickell Extension

Brickell Key

S. W. 6th St.

S. E. 6th St.

Brickell Park

S. W. 7th St.

S. E. 7th St.

S. W. 8th St.

S. E. 8th St.

**KEY**

Metromover

Claude and Mildred Pepper Bayfront Park, **11**

Freedom Tower, **14**

Gusman Center for the Performing Arts, **12**

Metro-Dade Cultural Center, **10**

Miami Arena, **16**

Miami-Dade Community College, **13**

U.S. Courthouse, **15**

TIMING

To walk and ride to the various points of interest, allow two hours. If you want to spend additional time eating and shopping at Bayside, allow at least four hours. To include museum visits, allow six hours.

## Sights to See

**American Police Hall of Fame and Museum.** This museum exhibits more than 10,000 law enforcement–related items, including weapons, a jail cell, and an electric chair, as well as a 400-ton marble memorial listing the names of more than 3,000 police officers killed in the line of duty since 1960. ⊠ *3801 Biscayne Blvd.,* ☎ *305/573–0070.* ▧ *$6.* ⊙ *Daily 10–5:30.*

**⑪ Claude and Mildred Pepper Bayfront Park.** An oasis among downtown Miami's skyscrapers, this park extends east from busy, palm-lined Biscayne Boulevard to the edge of the bay. Japanese sculptor Isamu Noguchi redesigned the park just before his death in 1989; it now includes a memorial to the *Challenger* astronauts, an amphitheater, and a fountain (usually turned off as a budget-tightening measure) honoring the late Florida congressman Claude Pepper and his wife. ⊠ *Biscayne Blvd. between 2nd and 3rd Sts.*

**⑭ Freedom Tower.** Built in 1925 for the *Miami Daily News,* this imposing Spanish-baroque structure was inspired by the Giralda, an 800-year-old bell tower in Seville, Spain. ⊠ *600 Biscayne Blvd.*

**⑫ Gusman Center for the Performing Arts.** This ornate former movie palace has been restored as a concert hall. Resembling a Moorish courtyard with twinkling stars in the sky, it hosts performances by the Miami City Ballet and the New World Symphony. ⊠ *174 Flagler St.*

★ ⓒ **⑩ Metro Dade Cultural Center.** Here the city's main art museum **Center for the Fine Arts,** gives major touring exhibitions of work by international artists. The focus is on work completed since 1850. Also part of the 3.3 acre complex is the **Historical Museum of Florida,** which interprets human experience in southern Florida from prehistory to the present. The **Main Public Library** contains nearly 4 million holdings and offers art exhibits in the auditorium and second-floor lobby. ⊠ *101 W. Flagler St.,* ☎ *305/375–1700.* ▧ *Center for Fine Arts and Museum of Southern Florida $8.* ⊙ *Tues.–Sat. 10–5, Thurs. 10-9.*

**⑯ Miami Arena.** This is the home of the National Basketball Association's Miami Heat, and the National Hockey League's Florida Panthers. The arena also hosts a variety of sports and entertainment events. ⊠ *701 Arena Blvd.,* ☎ *305/530–4444.*

**⑬ Miami-Dade Community College.** The campus houses two fine galleries: the third-floor **Centre Gallery,** which hosts various exhibitions, and the fifth-floor **Frances Wolfson Art Gallery,** which houses traveling exhibits of contemporary art. ⊠ *300 N.E. 2nd Ave.,* ☎ *305/237–3278.* ⊙ *Weekdays 10–6.*

**⑮ U.S. Courthouse.** In what was once the second-floor central courtroom is *Law Guides Florida Progress,* a huge Depression-era mural by Denman Fink. Surrounding the central figure of a robed judge are several images that define the Florida of the 1930s: fish vendors, palm trees, beaches, and a Pan Am airplane winging off to Latin America. No cameras or tape recorders are allowed in the building. ⊠ *300 N.E. 1st Ave.* ⊙ *Building weekdays 8:30–5, security guards open courtroom on request.*

# Little Havana★

Nearly 40 years ago the tidal wave of Cubans fleeing the Castro regime flooded into an older neighborhood west of downtown Miami. This area became known as **Little Havana**. Today, with a million Cubans and other Latins—more than half the metropolitan population—dispersed throughout Greater Miami, Little Havana and neighboring East Little Havana remain magnets for Hispanics and Anglos alike, who come to experience the flavor of traditional Cuban culture. That culture, of course, functions in Spanish. Many Little Havana residents and shopkeepers speak little or no English.

## A Good Tour

*Numbers in the text below correspond to numbers in the margin and on the Miami, Coral Gables, and Key Biscayne map.*

From downtown go west on Flagler Street across the Miami River. Drive west on West Flagler Street to Teddy Roosevelt Avenue (S.W. 17th Ave.), and pause at **Plaza de la Cubanidad** ⑰ on the southwest corner. Red-brick sidewalks surround a fountain and monument with a quotation from José Martí, a hero to Cuban refugees and immigrants who resettled in Miami.

Turn left at Douglas Road (S.W. 37th Ave.), drive south to **Calle Ocho** ⑱ (S.W. 8th St.), and turn left again. You are now on the main commercial thoroughfare of Little Havana. Drive east on Calle Ocho. After you cross Unity Boulevard (S.W. 27th Ave.), Calle Ocho becomes a one-way street eastbound through the heart of Little Havana, where every block deserves exploration. If your time is limited, try the three-block stretch from S.W. 14th Avenue to S.W. 11th Avenue. Parking is more plentiful west of Ronald Reagan Avenue (S.W. 12th Ave.).

At Avenida Luis Muñoz Marín (S.W. 15th Ave.) stop at **Dominoes Park** ⑲, where elderly Cuban men dressed in guayaberas pass the day with their black-and-white play tiles. At Calle Ocho and Memorial Boulevard (S.W. 13th Ave.) stands the **Brigade 2506 Memorial** ⑳, which commemorates the victims of the unsuccessful 1961 Bay of Pigs invasion. A block south on Memorial Boulevard are several other monuments relevant to Cuban history, including a statue of José Martí. Drive five blocks south on Ronald Reagan Avenue to the **Cuban Museum of Arts and Culture** ㉑.

TIMING

If the history hidden in the monuments is your only interest, set aside two hours. Allow more time for a strong cup of Cuban coffee on Calle Ocho and a glimpse of Latin culture in the Cuban Museum.

## Sights to See

⑳ **Brigade 2506 Memorial.** An eternal flame burns atop a simple stone monument with the inscription: CUBA—A LOS MARTIRES DE LA BRIGADA DE ASALTO ABRIL 17 DE 1961. The monument also bears a shield with the Brigade 2506 emblem, a Cuban flag superimposed on a cross. ⊠ *Calle Ocho and Memorial Blvd. (S.W. 13th Ave.).*

⑱ **Calle Ocho.** Here, in the commercial heart of Little Havana, experience Cuban customs in hand-rolled cigars or in a good Cuban sandwich piled high with meats and cheeses and topped with hot and mild sauces. ⊠ *S.W. 8th St. near Unity Blvd.*

㉑ **Cuban Museum of Arts and Culture.** Created by Cuban exiles to preserve and interpret the cultural heritage of their homeland, the museum has expanded its focus to embrace the entire Hispanic arts community and work produced by young local artists. The collection includes the art of exiles and of artists who continue to live on the island. Other exhibits are drawn from the museum's small permanent collection. ⊠ *1300 S.W. 12th Ave.,* ☎ *305/858–8006.* ▱ *Donations welcome.* ☉ *Tues.–Fri. 11–3, Sat. noon–5.*

⑲ **Dominoes Park.** Officially known as Maximo Gomez Park, this is a major gathering place for elderly Cuban males, who pass the day playing dominoes while arguing anti-Castro politics. A recent addition is a mural of the hemispheric Summit of the Americas, held in Miami in late 1994; included are portraits of every leader who took part in the event. ⊠ *S.W. 8th St. and S.W. 15th Ave.* ☉ *Daily 9–6.*

⑰ **Plaza de Cubindad.** Here, an important momument preserves the words of José Martí, a leader in Cuba's struggle for independence from Spain—LAS PALMAS SON NOVIAS QUE ESPERAN (The palm trees are girlfriends who will wait)—counseling hope and fortitude to the Cubans.

# Coral Gables and South Miami

Coral Gables, a planned community of broad boulevards and Spanish Mediterranean architecture, justifiably calls itself "the City Beautiful," a nickname it shares with Orlando. George E. Merrick began selling Coral Gables lots in 1921 and incorporated the city in 1925. He named most of the streets for Spanish explorers, cities, and provinces. Street names are at ground level beside each intersection on whitewashed concrete cornerstones.

The 1926 hurricane and the Great Depression prevented Merrick from fulfilling many of his plans. The city languished until after World War II but then grew rapidly. Today Coral Gables has a population of about 41,000. In its bustling downtown more than 140 multinational companies maintain headquarters or regional offices. The University of Miami campus in the southern part of Coral Gables brings a youthful vibrance to the area.

## A Good Tour

From downtown Miami drive south on S.E. 2nd Avenue across the Miami River, where the street becomes Brickell Avenue. One-half mile south of the river turn right on Coral Way, which at this point is S.W. 13th Street. Within ½ mile Coral Way turns left under I–95 and becomes S.W. 3rd Avenue. It continues another mile to a complex five-point intersection and doglegs right to become S.W. 22nd Street.

Along the S.W. 3rd Avenue and S.W. 22nd Street segments of Coral Way, banyan trees planted in the median strip in 1929 arch over the roadway. The banyans end at the Miami–Coral Gables boundary, where Miracle Mile begins. Actually only ½ mile long, this five-block retailing stretch of Coral Way, from Douglas Road (37th Ave.) to Le Jeune Road (42nd Ave.), is the heart of downtown Coral Gables.

The Colonnade Building on Miracle Mile once housed the sales office for Coral Gables's original developer, George Merrick. Its rotunda bears an ornamental frieze and a Spanish-tile roof 75 feet above street level. The Colonnade Building has been restored and connected to the 13-story Colonnade Hotel and an office building that echoes the rotunda's roofline.

Immediately west of LeJeune Road bear left onto Biltmore Way. The ornate Spanish Renaissance structure facing Miracle Mile is **Coral Gables City Hall** ㉒, opened in 1928.

Continue west on Biltmore Way to the corner, turn right on Segovia, left on Coral Way, and right again on Toledo Street to park behind **Coral Gables Merrick House and Gardens** ㉓, George Merrick's boyhood home. As you leave the parking lot turn left on Toledo Street and continue to South Greenway Drive. You'll see the Granada Golf Course, a gorgeously green nine-hole course in the midst of the largest historic district of Coral Gables.

Turn left on South Greenway Drive, follow it to Alhambra Circle, and turn right. One block ahead on your left, at the intersection of Alhambra Circle, Greenway Court, and Ferdinand Street, is the restored **Alhambra Water Tower** ㉔, a city landmark dating from 1924.

Now drive south on Alhambra Circle four short blocks to Coral Way. Turn left and after six blocks turn right on Granada Boulevard. You are now approaching De Soto Plaza and Fountain, a classical column on a pedestal with water flowing from the mouths of four sculpted faces. The closed eyes of the face looking west symbolize the day's end. Denman Fink designed the fountain in the early 1920s.

Follow the traffic circle almost completely around the fountain to northeast-bound De Soto Boulevard. On your right in the next block is **Venetian Pool** ㉕. A neighborhood fixture, it's one of the few municipal swimming complexes in this tony part of Miami and was built in the days before the majority of private homes had their own pools.

Return to the De Soto Fountain and follow De Soto Boulevard southwest to the recently restored **Biltmore Hotel** ㉖. To the west, in a separate building, is the Biltmore Country Club. This richly ornamented Beaux Arts–style structure with a superb colonnade and courtyard was reincorporated into the hotel in 1989. From the hotel, turn right on Anastasia Avenue, go east to Granada Boulevard, and turn right. Continue south on Granada Boulevard over a bridge across the Coral Gables Waterway, which empties into Biscayne Bay. In the hotel's heyday, Venetian gondolas plied the waterway, bringing guests to a bayside beach.

At Ponce de León Boulevard turn right. On your left is Metrorail's Stonehenge-like concrete structure, and on your right is the main campus of the **University of Miami** ㉗. Turn right at the first stoplight (Stanford Dr.) to enter the campus, and park in the lot on your right designated for visitors to U.M.'s Lowe Art Museum. Exit the U.M. campus on Stanford Drive, pass under the Metrorail, and cross Dixie Highway. Beyond the Burger King on your right, bear right on Maynada Street. Turn right at the next stoplight, onto Sunset Drive. Fine old homes and stately trees line this city-designated Historic and Scenic Road. Sunset Drive leads to and through South Miami, a pioneer farm community that grew into a suburb but retains its small-town charm.

Drive south on Red Road and turn right just before Killian Drive (S.W. 112th St.), into the 13-acre grounds of **Parrot Jungle** ㉘, one of Greater Miami's oldest and most popular commercial tourist attractions.

From Parrot Jungle follow Red Road ½ mile south and turn left on scenic Old Cutler Road, which curves north along the uplands of southern Florida's coastal ridge. Visit the 83-acre **Fairchild Tropical Garden** ㉙, the largest tropical botanical garden in the continental United States. Just north of the gardens, Old Cutler Road traverses Dade County's oldest and most scenic park, **Matheson Hammock** ㉚. Allow yourself time to relax at the park's unique swimming area.

# Miami, Coral Gables and Key Biscayne

OCEAN

Fisher Island

Virginia Key

Marine Stadium

Rickenbacker Ca

MIAMI BEACH

Bay

JFK Causeway

Biscayne Blvd.

N.E. 2nd Ave.

Julia Turtle Causeway

Venetian Causeway

Alton Rd.

MacArthur Causeway

A1A

195

41

43

1

N. Miami Ave.

Miami International Arts and Design District

395

95

441

27

S.W. 13th St.

S.W. 3rd Ave.

Brickell Ave.

38

39

37

35

36

41

21

N.W. 17th Ave.

S.W. 12th Ave.

19

20

17

COCONUT GROVE

1

N.W. 54th St.

N.W. 62nd St.

N.W. 79th St.

N.W. 36th St.

N.W. 20th St.

Robert Frost Expwy.

9

944

18

S.W. 8th St.

S.W. 22nd St.

Coral

7th Ave.

E. 25th St.

Hialeah Dr.

Miami River

N.W. 27th Ave.

N.W. 7th St.

Flagler St.

Ponce de Leon Blvd

Douglas Rd.

le Jeune Rd.

Miracle Mile

Granada Blvd

Sevilla Ave.

Tamiami Trail

953

22

25

23

26

24

972

h Ave.

HIALEAH

East-West Expressway

Miami International Airport

959

836

968

Coral Way

Dairy Rd.

N.W. 39th

St.

N.W. 72nd Ave.

Palmetto Expwy

S.W. 8th St.

Coral Way

826

27

MIAMI

N

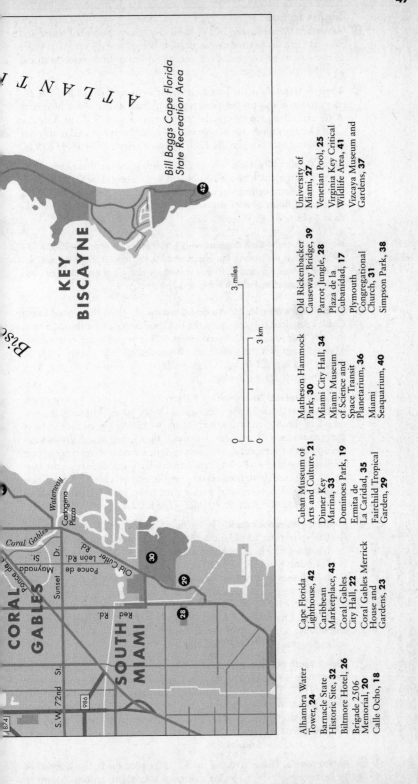

## Sights to See

**㉔ Alhambra Water Tower.** In 1924 this city landmark stored water and was clad in a decorative moresque, lighthouselike exterior. After more than 50 years of disuse and neglect the tower was completely restored in 1993 with a copper-rib dome and multicolor frescoes.

**㉖ Biltmore Hotel.** Like the Freedom Tower in downtown Miami the 26-story tower of this property is a replica of the Giralda Tower in Seville. After extensive renovations the hotel reopened in 1992. The Biltmore Golf Course, known for its scenic layout, has been restored to its original Donald Ross design. ⊠ *1200 Anastasia Ave.,* ☎ *305/445–1926.*

**㉒ Coral Gables City Hall.** This 1928 building has a three-tier tower topped with a clock and a 500-pound bell. A mural by Denman Fink inside the dome ceiling depicts the four seasons and can be seen from the second floor. ⊠ *405 Biltmore Way,* ☎ *305/446–6800.* ☉ *Weekdays 8–5.*

---

NEED A BREAK?

Have lunch at the **Café Cappuccino** (⊠ 550 Biltmore Way, ☎ 305/441-2959), which sits among the Shops at 550, the toniest shopping mall in the city. Between 8 and 2:30 you can enjoy muffins or an entrée or two among the marble, Persian rugs, and haute couture.

---

**㉓ Coral Gables Merrick House and Gardens.** In 1976 the city of Coral Gables acquired this dwelling, the boyhood home of George Merrick, the city's developer. Restored to its 1920s appearance, it contains Merrick family furnishings and artifacts. ⊠ *907 Coral Way,* ☎ *305/460–5361.* ☞ *House $2, grounds free.* ☉ *House Sun. and Wed. 1–4, grounds daily 8–sunset.*

**㉙ Fairchild Tropical Garden.** This 83-acre attraction is the largest tropical botanical garden in the continental United States. Although the gardens lost most of their tropical foliage to 1992's Hurricane Andrew, the cycads survived, and the gardens are flourishing again. Visitors can get an idea of how tropical plants regenerate themselves after severe storms by visiting a portion of the gardens left untouched since the hurricane. The rare-plant house is open again, concerts are a frequent new feature, and the entry and parking lot have been relandscaped. ⊠ *10901 Old Cutler Rd.,* ☎ *305/667–1651.* ☞ *$7.*

**㉚ Matheson Hammock Park.** The Civilian Conservation Corps developed the 100-acre tract of upland and mangrove swamp in the 1930s on land donated by a local pioneer, Commodore J. W. Matheson. The park, Dade County's oldest and most scenic, features a bathing beach where the tide flushes a saltwater "atoll" pool through four gates. A 90-slip marina is open, with an additional 162 slips to follow by 1997. Pool lifeguards are on duty winter, daily 8:30–5, and summer, daily 7:30–7. ⊠ *9610 Old Cutler Rd.,* ☎ *305/667–3035.* ☞ *Parking for beach and marina $3 per car, $5 per car with trailer, $6 per RV; limited free upland parking.* ☉ *Daily 6–sunset.*

**Miami Youth Museum.** Housed in temporary facilities on Coral Way, the museum is scheduled to move into larger space in neighboring Kendall by late 1997. This lively museum features arts exhibits, hands-on displays, and activities to enhance children's creativity and inspire interest in artistic careers. ⊠ *3301 Coral Way (Miracle Center),* ☎ *305/446–4368.* ☞ *$3.* ☉ *Mon. and Fri. 10–5, Tues.–Thurs. 1–5, weekends 11–5; closed holidays.*

**㉘ Parrot Jungle.** Home to more than 1,100 exotic birds, this opened in 1936 as one of South Florida's original tourist attractions. Many of the parrots, macaws, and cockatoos fly free, and they'll come to you for seeds, which you can purchase from old-fashioned gum-ball machines. Attend a trained-bird show, watch baby birds in training, and pose for the ultimate tourist photo, with colorful macaws perched on your arms. The "jungle" is a natural hammock surrounding a sinkhole. Stroll among orchids and other flowering plants nestled among ferns, bald cypress, and massive live oaks. Other highlights include a primate show, small-wildlife shows, a children's playground, and a petting zoo. Also see the cactus garden and Flamingo Lake, whose breeding population of 75 Caribbean flamingos was featured on the opening credits of *Miami Vice*. ⊠ *11000 S.W. 57th Ave.,* ☎ *305/666–7834.* ☞ *$10.95.* ⊙ *Daily 9:30–6, last admission at 5; café daily 8–6.*

㉗ **University of Miami.** With almost 14,000 full-time, part-time, and noncredit students, U.M. is the largest private research university in the southeast. On the campus of the University of Miami is the **Lowe Art Museum,** with a permanent collection of 8,000 works that includes Renaissance and Baroque art, American paintings, Latin American art, and Navajo and Pueblo Indian textiles and baskets. The museum also hosts traveling exhibitions. ⊠ *1301 Stanford Dr.,* ☎ *305/284–3535 or 305/284–3536.* ☞ *$4.* ⊙ *Tues.–Sat. 10–5, Sun. noon–5.*

☙ ㉕ **Venetian Pool.** This unique municipal swimming pool was sculpted from a rock quarry. Despite the proliferation of private swimming pools in the area, it remains quite popular. ⊠ *2701 De Soto Blvd.,* ☎ *305/460–5356.* ☞ *Nonresidents $4, free parking across De Soto Blvd.* ⊙ *Weekends 10–4:30; plus June–Aug., weekdays 11–7:30; Sept., Oct., Apr., and May, Tues.–Fri. 11:30–5:30; and Nov.–Mar., Tues.–Fri. 10–4:30.*

# Coconut Grove★

Coconut Grove is southern Florida's oldest settlement, inhabited as early as 1834 and established by 1873, two decades before Miami. Its early settlers included Bahamian blacks, "Conchs" from Key West, and New England intellectuals. They built a community that attracted artists, writers, and scientists to establish winter homes. By the end of World War I more people listed in *Who's Who* gave addresses in Coconut Grove than any other place in the country.

To this day Coconut Grove reflects its pioneers' eclectic origins. Posh estates mingle with rustic cottages, modest frame homes, and stark modern dwellings, often on the same block. To keep Coconut Grove a village in a jungle, residents lavish affection on exotic plantings while battling to protect remaining native vegetation.

The historic center of the Village of Coconut Grove went through a hippie period in the 1960s, laid-back funkiness in the 1970s, and a teeny-bopper invasion in the early 1980s. Today the tone is upscale and urban, with a mix of galleries, boutiques, restaurants, bars, and sidewalk cafés. On weekends the Grove is jam-packed.

## A Good Tour

From downtown Miami follow U.S. 1 south to S.W. 27th Avenue (Grapeland Blvd.), turn left, and drive south to South Bayshore Drive. Turn right and follow this road until it jogs right and becomes McFarlane Road. At the next intersection turn left on Main Highway, which passes through the heart of the Village of Coconut Grove. Before you explore this trendy area, go on to Devon Road and turn right in front of **Plymouth Congregational Church** ㉛. Opened in 1917, this handsome coral-rock structure resembles a Mexican mission church.

Return to Main Highway and head northeast toward the historic Village of Coconut Grove. Parking can be a problem, especially on weekend evenings, when police direct traffic and prohibit turns at some intersections to prevent gridlock. Be prepared to walk several blocks from the periphery into the heart of the Grove.

As you enter the village center, note the apricot-hue Spanish-rococo Coconut Grove Playhouse to your left. Built in 1926 as a movie theater, it became a legitimate theater in 1956 and is now owned by the state of Florida.

Benches and shelter opposite the playhouse mark the entrance to the **Barnacle State Historic Site** ㉜, a pioneer residence built by Commodore Ralph Munroe in 1891.

Leaving the village center, follow McFarlane Road east from its intersection with Grand Avenue and Main Highway. Peacock Park, site of the first hotel in southeast Florida, is on your right. In an iron enclosure to the side of the Coconut Grove Library (a branch of the main library system) is the Eva Hewitt Munroe grave. Ralph Munroe's first wife was reburied here at the site Munroe donated for the library.

If you turn north at the end of McFarlane Road onto South Bayshore Drive you'll pass the 150,000-square-foot Coconut Grove Convention Center, where antiques, boat, and home shows are held, and **Dinner Key Marina** ㉝, where seabirds soar and sailboats ride at anchor.

At the northeast corner of the same lot is the Art Deco **Miami City Hall** ㉞. Continue north on South Bayshore Drive past Kirk Street to Kennedy Park, where you can park your car and walk toward the water. From a footbridge over the mouth of a small tidal creek you'll enjoy an unobstructed view across Biscayne Bay to Key Biscayne. Film crews often use the park to make commercials and Italian westerns.

Drive north on South Bayshore Drive. At the entrance to Mercy Hospital, South Bayshore Drive becomes South Miami Avenue. At the next stoplight turn right on a private road that passes St. Kieran's Church or **Ermita de La Caridad** ㉟. A mural above the shrine's altar depicts Cuba's history.

Another ³⁄₁₀ mile up South Miami Avenue turn left to the **Miami Museum of Science and Space Transit Planetarium** ㊱, a participatory museum with animated displays for all ages.

Across South Miami Avenue is the entrance to **Vizcaya Museum and Gardens** ㊲, an estate with an Italian Renaissance–style villa built between 1912 and 1916 as the winter residence of Chicago industrialist James Deering.

Continue north on South Miami Avenue to 17 Road and turn left to **Simpson Park** ㊳, where you saunter through a jungle of tropical flora and fauna. You may follow South Miami Avenue the rest of the way downtown or go back two stoplights and turn left to the entrance to the Rickenbacker Causeway and Key Biscayne.

TIMING

The best time to take this tour is during the day, when the Dinner Key Marina and Simpson Park are at their best. Set aside a minimum of two hours to simply cover Cocunut Grove and at least three more for the museums.

## Sights to See

㉜ **Barnacle State Historic Site.** A broad sloping roof and deeply recessed verandas channel sea breezes into the house. A central stairwell and rooftop vent allow hot air to escape. Many furnishings are original. Reservations are essential for groups of eight or more; other visitors should meet the ranger on the porch. ⊠ *3485 Main Hwy.,* ☎ *305/448–9445.* ⌹ *$2.* ⊙ *Thurs.–Mon. 9–4; tours 10, 11:30, 1, and 2:30, but call ahead.*

| NEED A BREAK? | Cafés at both corners overflow the brick sidewalks around Commodore Plaza. Try the **Green Streets Cafe** (⊠ 3110 Commodore Plaza, ☎ 305/567-0662) on the south side. It features a bar, breakfast until 3, and pastas, pizzas, salads, and sandwiches. |
|---|---|

**㉝ Dinner Key Marina.** Named for a small island on which early settlers held picnics, this is Greater Miami's largest marina, with 581 moorings at nine piers. ⊠ *3400 Pan American Dr.,* ☎ *305/579–6980.*

**㉟ Ermita de La Caridad (Our Lady of Charity Shrine).** This conical building 90 feet high and 80 feet wide overlooks Biscayne Bay, so worshipers face Cuba. ⊠ *3609 S. Miami Ave.,* ☎ *305/854–2404.* ⊙ *Daily 9–9.*

**㉞ Miami City Hall.** Built in 1934 as the terminal for the Pan American Airways seaplane base at Dinner Key, the building retains its nautical-style Art Deco trim. ⊠ *3500 Pan American Dr.,* ☎ *305/250–5357.* ⊙ *Weekdays 8–5.*

**㊱ Miami Museum of Science and Space Transit Planetarium.** This museum is chock-full of hands-on sound, gravity, and electricity displays for children and adults alike. A wildlife center houses native Florida snakes, turtles, tortoises, birds of prey, and large wading birds—175 live animals in all. Outstanding traveling exhibits appear throughout the year. ⊠ *3280 S. Miami Ave.,* ☎ *305/854–4247; planetarium information, 305/854–2222.* ⌹ *$6; planetarium $5, laser-light rock-and-roll concert $6.* ⊙ *Daily 10–6.*

**㉛ Plymouth Congregational Church.** The front door, made of hand-carved walnut and oak with original wrought-iron fittings, came from an early 17th-century monastery in the Pyrenees. Also on the 11-acre grounds are natural sunken gardens; the first schoolhouse in Dade County (one room), which was moved to this property; and the site of the original Coconut Grove waterworks and electric works. Call the office one day in advance if you'd like to see the inside of the church. ⊠ *3400 Devon Rd.,* ☎ *305/444–6521.* ⊙ *Weekdays 9–4:30, Sun. service 10 AM.*

**㊳ Simpson Park.** Enjoy a fragment of the dense tropical jungle—large gumbo-limbo trees, marlberry, banyans, and black calabash—that once covered the 5 miles from downtown Miami to Coconut Grove. You'll get a rare glimpse of how things were before the high-rises towered. Avoid the park during summer, when mosquitoes are unrelenting. ⊠ *55 S.W. 17th Rd.,* ☎ *305/856–6801.* ⊙ *Daily sunrise–sunset.*

**★ ㊲ Vizcaya Museum and Gardens.** The house and gardens overlook Biscayne Bay on a 30-acre tract that includes a native hammock and more than 10 acres of formal gardens and fountains. The house contains 70 rooms, with 34 rooms of paintings, sculpture, antique furniture, and other decorative arts, open to the public. These objects date from the 15th through the 19th centuries and represent the Renaissance, Baroque, Rococo, and Neoclassical styles. Guided 45-minute tours are available, and group tours are given by appointment. ⊠ *3251 S. Miami Ave.,* ☎ *305/250–9133.* ⌹ *$8.* ⊙ *House and ticket booth daily 9:30–4:30, garden daily 9:30–5:30.*

# Virginia Key and Key Biscayne

Government Cut and the Port of Miami separate the dense urban fabric of Miami from two of the city's playground islands, Virginia Key and Key Biscayne—the latter no longer the laid-back village where Richard Nixon set up his presidential vacation compound. Parks occupy much of both keys, providing facilities for golf, tennis, softball, picnicking, and basking on the beach, plus uninviting but ecologically valuable stretches of dense mangrove swamp. These islands were hit hard in 1992 by Hurricane Andrew, and, although all of the hotels have reopened, the tourist attractions—many of which are outdoors and near the water—are still recovering their foliage.

## A Good Tour

To reach Virginia Key and Key Biscayne take the Rickenbacker Causeway ($1 per car) across Biscayne Bay from the mainland at Brickell Avenue and S.W. 26th Road, about 2 miles south of downtown Miami. The causeway links several islands in the bay.

The William M. Powell Bridge rises 75 feet above the water to eliminate the need for a draw span. The panoramic view from the top encompasses the bay, keys, port, and downtown skyscrapers, with Miami Beach and the Atlantic Ocean in the distance.

Just south of the Powell Bridge, a stub of the **Old Rickenbacker Causeway Bridge** ㊴, built in 1947, is now a fishing pier. Park at its entrance, about a mile from the tollgate, and walk past anglers tending their lines, to the gap where the center draw span across the Intracoastal Waterway was removed.

Next along the causeway, on Virginia Key, stands the 6,536-seat Miami Marine Stadium, formerly the site of summer pop concerts, occasional shows by name entertainers, and a spectacular Fourth of July fireworks display. The stadium has been closed due to underuse and the need for repairs, and there's no date scheduled for reopening.

Down the causeway from Marine Stadium, look for the gold dome of the **Miami Seaquarium** ㊵, one of the country's first marine attractions. Opposite the causeway from the Seaquarium a road leads north to Virginia Key Beach, a City of Miami park with a 2-mile stretch of oceanfront. Plans are in the works to safeguard the 400-acre portion of this mangrove-edged island that has been christened the **Virginia Key Critical Wildlife Area** ㊶.

From Virginia Key the causeway crosses Bear Cut to the north end of Key Biscayne, where it becomes Crandon Boulevard. The boulevard bisects 1,211-acre Crandon Park, which has a popular 3½-mile Atlantic Ocean beach with a nature center. On your right are entrances to the Links at Key Biscayne and the Tennis Center at Crandon Park.

From the traffic circle at the south end of Crandon Park, Crandon Boulevard continues for 2 miles through the developed portion of Key Biscayne. You'll come back that way, but first detour to the site of President Nixon's home. Turn right on Harbor Drive at the first stoplight, go about a mile, and turn right at Matheson Drive. A recent owner enlarged and completely changed the house.

Continue south on Harbor Drive to Mashta Drive; turn left and return to Crandon Boulevard. Turn right to reach the entrance to Bill Baggs Cape Florida State Recreation Area, a 406-acre park. Although devastated by Hurricane Andrew, the park has reopened, having been greatly transformed. Also in the park is the oldest structure in South Florida, the brick **Cape Florida Lighthouse** ㊷.

As you leave Cape Florida, follow Crandon Boulevard back to Crandon Park through Key Biscayne's commercial center, a mixture of posh shops and more-prosaic stores catering to the everyday needs of the neighborhood. On your way back to the mainland, pause as you approach the Powell Bridge to admire the downtown Miami skyline. At night the brightly lighted NationsBank Tower looks from this angle like a clipper ship running under full sail before the breeze.

TIMING

Set aside the better part of a day. Start out for the Keys in the morning, allowing time to stop at the bridge. Save the afternoon for the Miami Seaquarium and for bird-watching at the Virginia Key Critical Wildlife Area. You might want to spend a few hours at Crandon Park before an evening jaunt to the Cape Florida Lighthouse.

## Sights to See

42 **Cape Florida Lighthouse.** South Florida's oldest structure was erected in 1845 to replace an earlier lighthouse destroyed in an 1836 Seminole attack, in which the keeper's helper was killed. Climb 95 feet to the top, where you can visit a replica of the keeper's house. ⊠ *1200 S. Crandon Blvd.*, ☎ *305/361–5811.* ▣ *Park $3.25 per vehicle with up to 8 people.* ☉ *Park daily 8–sunset.*

NEED A BREAK?
Enjoy that rarity among Miami-area restaurants, a freestanding waterfront dining room, at **Sundays on the Bay** (⊠ 5420 Crandon Blvd., ☎ 305/361-6777). A 60-item brunch is served Sunday 10:30–3:30, and lunch and dinner are served daily.

★ 40 **Miami Seaquarium.** This is a popular attraction, with six daily shows featuring sea lions, dolphins, and Lolita, a killer whale who cavorts in a huge tank. Exhibits include a shark pool, a 235,000-gallon tropical-reef aquarium, and manatees. ⊠ *4400 Rickenbacker Causeway*, ☎ *305/361–5705.* ▣ *$18.95.* ☉ *Daily 9:30–6, last admission at 4:30.*

39 **Old Rickenbacker Causeway Bridge.** Here you can watch boat traffic pass through the channel, pelicans and other seabirds soar and dive, and dolphins cavort in the bay. ⊠ *South of Powell Bridge.*

41 **Virginia Key Critical Wildlife Area.** Residents include reddish egrets, black-bellied plovers, black skimmers, and roseate spoonbills—but they're here only in May, June, and July. The area is left undisturbed during the other nine months, to make it attractive to migratory shorebirds. Enter at Virginia Key Beach.

# Little Haiti

Of some 200,000 Haitians who have settled in south Florida, almost half live in Little Haiti, an area on Miami's northeast side covering about 200 city blocks. More than 400 small Haitian businesses operate in Little Haiti. Yet the future of the district is uncertain: Immigration from Haiti has virtually ceased, and many Haitians already in Miami question their economic future in the ghetto. As their fortunes improve, many move out. Still the neighborhood is one of the city's most distinctive. If you walk or drive along its side streets, you might see Haitian women carrying their burdens atop their heads, as they do on their home island.

For many Haitians, English is a third language. French is Haiti's official language, but much day-to-day conversation takes place in Creole, a French-based patois.

## A Good Tour

From downtown Miami, follow Biscayne Boulevard north to N.E. 38th Street; turn left about ⅒ mile west, as the street curves and becomes 39th Street. At North Miami Avenue turn right and at 40th Street turn right again onto the main street of the Miami International Arts and Design District. Here, near Little Haiti, some 225 wholesale stores, showrooms, and galleries feature interior furnishings and decorative arts. Since 1993 the district has undergone a revival, and there are several new art studios and showrooms.

Immediately north is the gentrified neighborhood of Buena Vista, which merges with Little Haiti. The area contains some of Miami's oldest dwellings, dating from the dawn of the 20th century through the 1920s land-boom era. Drive the side streets to see elegant Mediterranean-style homes and bungalows with distinctive coral-rock trim.

Return to North Miami Avenue and head north. A half block east on 54th Street is the tiny storefront office of the Haitian Refugee Center, a focal point of activity in the Haitian community. The building's facade is decorated by the painting of an uncomprehending Haitian standing in front of the Statue of Liberty, which denies him entry to America. Continue north on North Miami Avenue past the former Cuban consulate, an ostentatious Caribbean-Colonial mansion that is now the clinic of Haitian physician Lucien Albert.

North of 85th Street cross the Little River Canal into El Portal, a tiny suburban village of modest homes, where more than a quarter of the property is now Haitian-owned. Turn right on N.E. 87th Street and right again on N.E. 2nd Avenue. You are now southbound on Little Haiti's tree-lined main commercial street. Along N.E. 2nd Avenue between 79th and 45th streets, rows of storefronts in faded pastels reflect a first effort by area merchants to dress up their neighborhood and attract outsiders. The lovely **Caribbean Marketplace** ㊸ shows the strains of uncertainty in this immigrant community.

TIMING

This tour provides a look at an immigrant community currently in flux. An incredibly depressed section of Miami, it is not very safe at night. Tour during daylight hours.

## Sights to See

㊸ **Caribbean Marketplace.** This building, opened in 1990 by the Haitian Task Force (an economic-development organization) beautifully evokes the Iron Market in Port-au-Prince. Its handful of merchants surrounding a medical clinic sell handmade baskets, Caribbean art and craft items, books, records, videos, and ice cream. ✉ *5927 N.E. 2nd Ave.*

# South Dade

This tour directs you to major attractions in the suburbs southwest of Dade County's urban core. Although the population was largely dislocated by Hurricane Andrew in August 1992, little damage is evident today. All attractions have reopened.

## A Good Tour

*Numbers in the text below correspond to numbers in the margin and on the South Dade map.*

From downtown Miami follow the Dolphin Expressway (Rte. 836) west to the Palmetto Expressway (Rte. 826) southbound. Exit westbound onto Kendall Drive (S.W. 88th St.) and continue westbound on Kendall

**South Dade**

Drive to Lindgren Road (S.W. 137th Ave.). Turn left and drive south to S.W. 128th Street, the entrance to the Tamiami Airport and **Weeks Air Museum** ㊹. Although virtually destroyed by Hurricane Andrew, the museum has been rebuilt and currently has about 35 planes on display, most of World War II vintage.

Continue south on Lindgren Road to Coral Reef Drive (S.W. 152nd St.). Turn left and drive east to **Metrozoo** ㊺, a first-class zoo where animals roam on islands surrounded by moats. Devastated by the hurricane, the zoo has reopened but is without its signature exhibit, "Wings of Asia," a tropical-bird showcase. Next to the zoo the **Gold Coast Railroad Museum** ㊻ displays historic railroad cars.

Drive south on the Homestead Extension of Florida's Turnpike, exit at Hainlin Mill Drive (S.W. 216th St.), and turn right. Cross South Dixie Highway (U.S. 1), drive 3 miles west, and turn right into **Monkey Jungle** ㊼.

Continue west on Hainlin Mill Drive, past Krome Avenue (S.W. 177th Ave.) to Redland Road (S.W. 187th Ave.), and turn left to Coconut Palm Drive (S.W. 248th St.). Here you'll find the **Redland Fruit & Spice Park** ㊽, a Dade County treasure since 1944.

Drive east on Coconut Palm Drive (S.W. 248th St.) to Newton Road (S.W. 157th Ave.). Continue south on Newton Road to South Dixie Highway (U.S. 1) and turn left. Almost immediately you'll find **Coral Castle of Florida** ㊾, one of South Florida's original tourist attractions.

To return to downtown Miami after leaving Coral Castle, take South Dixie Highway to Biscayne Drive (S.W. 288th St.) and go east to the turnpike. Follow the turnpike back to the Don Shula Expressway (Rte. 874), which leads to the Palmetto Expressway (Rte. 826), which leads to the Dolphin Expressway (Rte. 836).

TIMING

To enjoy the parks and museums to the fullest, split the tour into two days. None of these sights has evening hours, so the trip must be made during the day.

## Sights to See

**⑭ Coral Castle of Florida.** Built by Edward Leedskalnin, a Latvian immigrant, between 1920 and 1940, the 3-acre castle has a 9-ton gate a child can open (expected to function again in 1997), an accurate working sundial, and a telescope of coral rock aimed at the North Star. ✉ *28655 S. Dixie Hwy.,* ☎ *305/248–6344.* ☞ *$7.75.* ⊙ *Daily 9–6.*

**㊻ Gold Coast Railroad Museum.** Displays include a 1949 *Silver Crescent* dome car and the *Ferdinand Magellan,* the only Pullman car constructed specifically for U.S. presidents, which was used by Franklin Delano Roosevelt, Harry Truman, Dwight Eisenhower, and Ronald Reagan. ✉ *12450 Coral Reef Dr. (S.W. 152nd St.),* ☎ *305/253–0063.* ☞ *$4 including train ride.* ⊙ *Weekdays 11–3, weekends 11–4.*

**㊺ Metrozoo.** One of the only zoos in America in a subtropical environment, this cageless 290-acre park is state-of-the-art. Major attractions include the Tiger Temple, where white tigers roam, and the African Plains exhibit, where giraffes, ostriches, and zebras graze in a simulated habitat. "Paws," a petting zoo for children, features three shows daily; during the Wildlife Show, trained animals demonstrate natural behavior on cue. Kids can touch Florida animals such as alligators and possums at the Ecology Theater. ✉ *12400 Coral Reef Dr. (S.W. 152nd St.),* ☎ *305/251–0401 or 305/251–0400.* ☞ *$8, 45-min. tram tour $2.* ⊙ *Daily 9:30–5:30, last admission at 4.*

**㊼ Monkey Jungle.** Home to more than 300 monkeys representing 25 species—including orangutans from Borneo and Sumatra and golden lion tamarins from Brazil—this popular attraction is high on kids' lists of things to do. The park's rainforest trail, damaged in the hurricane, reopened in 1996. Four different performing-monkey shows begin at 10 and run continuously at 30-minute intervals. The walkways of this 30-acre attraction are caged; the monkeys roam free. ✉ *14805 Hainlin Mill Dr. (S.W. 216th St.),* ☎ *305/235–1611.* ☞ *$10.50.* ⊙ *Daily 9:30–5, last admission at 4.*

**㊽ Redland Fruit & Spice Park.** This attraction has been a Dade County treasure since 1944, when it was opened as a 20-acre showcase of tropical fruits and vegetables. It has since expanded to 30 acres, and a 3-acre lake was added in 1996. Two of the park's three historic buildings were ruined by the hurricane, as well as about half of its trees and plants, but relandscaping has begun and the park has reopened. Plants are now grouped by country of origin and include more than 500 varieties of exotic fruits, herbs, spices, nuts, and poisonous plants from around the world. A sampling reveals 65 varieties of bananas, 40 varieties of grapes, and 150 varieties of citrus. A gourmet-and-fruit shop offers many varieties of tropical-fruit products, jellies, seeds, aromatic teas, and reference books. ✉ *24801 Redland Rd. (S.W. 187th Ave.),* ☎ *305/247–5727.* ☞ *$1, guided tour $1.50.* ⊙ *Daily 10–5, tours weekends at 1 and 3.*

**㊹ Weeks Air Museum.** Rebuilt since its destruction by the hurricane, the museum now displays 30–35 planes, including a B-17 Flying Fortress bomber and a P-51 Mustang from World War II. Most of the fragile

World War I planes were destroyed by the storm. ⊠ *14710 S.W. 128th St.,* ☎ *305/233–5197.* ⊠ *$5.* ☉ *Daily 10–5.*

# BEACHES

## Key Biscayne

**Crandon Park.** This 3½-mile county beach is popular with families and rated among the top 10 beaches in North America by many. The sand is soft, and parking is both inexpensive and plentiful. At the north end of the beach, the **Marjory Stoneman Douglas Biscayne Nature Center** explores a variety of natural habitats through exhibits and year-round tours. ⊠ *4000 Crandon Blvd.,* ☎ *305/361–5421 or 305/642–9600.* ⊠ *Park $3.50 per vehicle, nature center free.* ☉ *Park daily 8–sunset, nature center hours vary.*

**Bill Baggs Cape Florida State Recreation Area.** This beach is as far as you can go on Key Biscayne, lying at the island's southern tip. Badly damaged by Hurricane Andrew, the park is no longer as lush as it once was. But there are new boardwalks, 18 picnic shelters, and a café that serves light lunches. A stroll along the pathway and boardwalk provides a wonderful view of Miami's dramatic skyline. ☎ *305/361–5811.* ⊠ *Park $3.25 per private vehicle (maximum 8); $1 per person on bicycle, bus, motorcycle, or foot; parking free.* ⊠ *Daily 8 AM–dusk.*

**Virginia Key Beach.** A City of Miami park with a 2-mile stretch of oceanfront, it offers shelters, barbecue grills, ball fields, nature trails, and a fishing area. Ask for directions at the entrance gate. Likely to be added later this decade are an RV park with various ball fields and an improved beach with windsurfing facilities. Plans are in progress to safeguard the 400-acre portion of Virginia Key that has become the Virginia Key Critical Wildlife Area. ⊠ *Parking $2.*

## Miami Beach Area

**1st–15th streets.** Seniors predominate early in the day. The section from 5th to 15th, known as Lummus Park lies in the heart of the Deco District. Volleyball, in-line skating along the paved upland path, and a lot of posing go on here, while children's playgrounds make this a popular area for families. Along these beaches, city officials don't enforce the law against female bathers going topless, so long as everyone on the beach behaves with decorum. Gays like the beach between 11th and 13th streets. Sidewalk cafés parallel the entire beach area, which makes it easy to come ashore for everything from burgers to quiche. At 23rd Street, the boardwalk begins, and no skates or bicycles are allowed.

**72nd Street Beach.** Parlez-vous Français? If you do, you'll feel quite comfortable here, or on the beach from **Surfside to 96th Street.** This stretch of beach is the French Canadian enclave. Many folks here have spent their winters in Miami Beach for years.

**North Beach.** Families and those who like things quiet prefer this stretch of sand along Ocean Terrace between 73rd and 75th streets. Metered parking is ample right behind the dune and on Collins Avenue, a block behind, along a pleasant, old shopping street. The area, however, is slated for redevelopment with the intensity, if not the size, of South Beach.

**North Shore State Recreation Area.** This 40-acre park is backed by lush tropical growth rather than hotels. ⊠ *Collins Ave. between 79th and*

87th Sts., Miami Beach; office, Oleta/North Shore GEOpark, 3400
N.E. 163rd St., North Miami Beach, ☎ 305/940–7439. 🎫 $2 plus
parking. ⊘ Daily 9–6.

**96th to 103rd streets.** During the winter, wealthy condominium owners cluster on this stretch of prime real estate in tony Bal Harbour.

**Haulover Beach Park–Sunny Isles.** Older visitors especially complain
about just how wide the beaches have become—feet burn easily on long
marches across hot sand. If you want the water closer to the upland,
try these beaches. Eroded sand was never replaced here, and the strand
is mercifully narrow. ⊠ 10800 Collins Ave., Miami, ☎ 305/947–
3525. 🎫 $3 per vehicle. ⊘ Daily 8–sunset.

# DINING

## American

### Coral Gables

$$
★
✕ **Restaurant St. Michel.** The setting is utterly French, the little hotel
it's in (☞ Lodging, below) is Mediterranean, the town is very Span-
ish, but the cuisine is American. Stuart Bornstein's window on Coral
Gables is a lace-curtained café with sidewalk tables that could be
across the street from a railroad station in Avignon or Bordeaux. A
sculpted bust here, a circus poster there, newly repainted deco chan-
deliers, a mirrored mosaic in the shape of palm fronds all create a whim-
sical, foreign feel. Lighter dishes include moist couscous chicken and
pasta primavera. Among the heartier entrées are a plum, soy, and
lemon-glazed fillet of salmon; sesame-coated loin of tuna; and local
yellowtail snapper. ⊠ 162 Alcazar Ave., ☎ 305/444–1666. AE, DC,
MC, V.

### Downtown Miami

$$$$
★
✕ **Le Pavillon.** The mahogany, jade marble, and leather appointments
of the dining room evoke the conservative air of an English private club.
Beautiful floral displays enhance the mood as the attentive staff serves
regional American fare from a limited but frequently changing menu,
including items low in calories, cholesterol, and sodium. Specialties are
char-grilled bluefin tuna fillet, poached yellowtail snapper, panfried corn-
fed squab, roasted free-range chicken, spring lamb, and roasted fillet
of milk-fed veal. For a light dessert try red berry soup with vanilla ice
cream. The wine list is extensive. ⊠ 100 Chopin Plaza, ☎ 305/577–
1000, Ext. 4494 or 4462. Jacket required. AE, DC, MC, V. No lunch
(except Sun. brunch, noon–3) or Sun. dinner.

### Kendall

$
✕ **Shorty's Bar-B-Q.** Shorty Allen opened his barbecue retaurant here
in 1951 in a log cabin, and the place has since become a tradition in
this suburb southwest of the city. Parents bring their children here to
show them where Mom and Dad ate on their honeymoon. Meals are
served family-style at long picnic tables. Cowboy hats hang on the walls,
along with horns, saddles, and the mounted heads of boar and cari-
bou. Longtime fans are drawn to the barbecued pork ribs, chicken, and
pork steak slow-cooked over hickory logs and drenched in Shorty's own
warm, spicy sauce, with side orders of tangy baked beans and big chunks
of pork, corn on the cob, and coleslaw. ⊠ 9200 S. Dixie Hwy., ☎
305/670–7732; 5989 S. University Dr., Davie, ☎ 305/680–9900 or
305/944–0348 from Miami. MC, V.

## Miami Beach

**$$-$$$** ✕ **Embers.** The Embers was a steak-and-potatoes house on 21st Street when cholesterol was still unpronounceable and gay just meant happy. A bunch of Beach High kids grew up eating dinner there with their families. Thirty years later "kids" Sid Lewis, Steven Polisar, and Larry Schwartz, wealthy from Ocean Drive investments, put their money where their memories are. The new Embers is five blocks south of the old, around the corner from Lincoln Road. The decor is derived from the past; saucer lights emitting an amber glow dangle from the ceiling, and collections of early Beach photos hang on the walls. Although Embers' classic recipes are still used for the steaks, apple fritters, and mashed potatoes, pastas and à la carte vegetables have been added to the menu. ⊠ *1661 Meridian Ave.,* ☎ *305/538–0997. AE, MC, V. No lunch.*

**$$** ✕ **Max's South Beach.** Famed South Florida restaurateur Dennis Max has extended his bijou collection of eateries to South Beach with celebrity chef Kerry Simon in charge of the kitchen. The result is an immensely popular seen-and-be-seen addition to Deco District dining. The dining area, with a mix of high-top tables, booths, starched white linen, and black leather seats, is surrounded by photo displays from *Rolling Stone* magazine, which helped make a star of Simon by naming him one of 1991's 100 hottest personalities. He dares to turn out an authentic meat loaf and mashed potatoes or grilled and roasted vegetables with organic grains. But there's also a salmon tandoori with black beans and cayenne onion rings, a big choice of grills, and baked sea bass with basil, carrots, and a carrot-orange vinaigrette. Desserts include a Butterfinger chocolate cake with banana ice cream and Jack Daniel caramel and old-fashioned strawberry shortcake. ⊠ *764 Washington Ave.,* ☎ *305/532–0070. AE, D, DC, MC, V. No lunch.*

**$** ✕ **News Café.** This is the hippest joint on Ocean Drive. Owners Mark Soyka, who trained on the cosmopolitan beach scene in Tel Aviv, and Jeffrey Dispenzieri, from New York, are right on the money. Although there's a raw bar with 15 stools in back, most visitors prefer sitting outside, where they can feel the salt breeze and gawk at the beautiful people inside. Offering a little of this and a little of that—bagels, pâtés, chocolate fondue—the café attracts a big crowd all the time, with people coming in around the clock for a snack, a light meal, or an aperitif and, invariably, to indulge in the people parade. ⊠ *800 Ocean Dr.,* ☎ *305/538–6397. AE, DC, MC, V.*

**$** ✕ **Van Dyke Café.** Mark Soyka's second restaurant quickly attracted the artsy crowd, just as his News Café (☞ *above*) draws the fashion crowd. Of course, tourists like it too. It has the same style menu, but instead of facing south, this place, in the restored 1924 Van Dyke Hotel, faces north and is shadier. Save the News Café for winter, the Van Dyke for summer. Three meals are served, and a 15% gratuity is included. ⊠ *846 Lincoln Rd.,* ☎ *305/534–3600. AE, DC, MC, V.*

## North Miami

**$$$** ✕ **Mark's Place.** Behind the adobe facade lies a stylish, Deco-detailed
★ dining room, a work of art itself, while in the kitchen, owner-chef Mark Militello cooks contemporary Florida fare in a special oak-burning oven imported from Genoa. The menu changes nightly, based on the availability of fresh ingredients (many of the vegetables are organically grown by staffers), but typical appetizers are Australian stir-fry with red-tip crawfish, ginger, lemongrass, chili, and garlic, and pan-seared foie gras with fresh huckleberry. Among the entrées are several pizzas and pastas (saffron fettuccine with Maine lobster, black beans, roast corn, chilies, tomato, and cilantro, for instance) and, among the specialties, grilled marinated breast of duck with acorn-squash flan, wilted

61

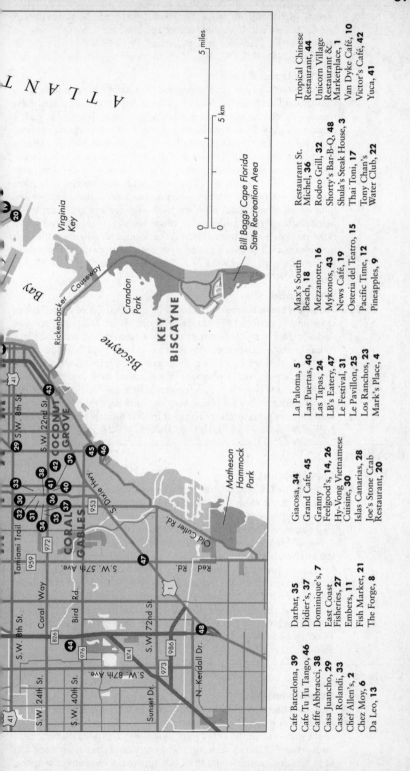

ATLANTIC

Rickenbacker Causeway

Virginia
Key

Biscayne
Bay

Crandon
Park

KEY
BISCAYNE

Biscayne

Bill Baggs Cape Florida
State Recreation Area

0        5 km

0        5 miles

Mathesen
Hammock
Park

COCONUT
GROVE

S.W. 8th St.
S.W. 22nd St.

CORAL
GABLES

Old Cutler Rd.

S. Dixie Hwy.

Red Rd.
S.W. 57th Ave.

953
972

959
Tamiami Trail

Coral Way
Bird Rd.

S.W. 72nd St.

S.W. 87th Ave.
N. Kendall Dr.

Sunset Dr.

S.W. 8th St.
S.W. 24th St.
S.W. 40th St.

826
976
874

41
41

1

973
986

48
44

29
33
32 30
31 34
36 37
41 40
38 42 39
45 46
43
47
20

Cafe Barcelona, **39**
Cafe Tu Tu Tango, **46**
Caffe Abbracci, **38**
Casa Juancho, **29**
Casa Rolandi, **33**
Chef Allen's, **2**
Chez Moy, **6**
Da Leo, **13**

Darbar, **35**
Didier's, **37**
Dominique's, **7**
East Coast
Fisheries, **27**
Embers, **11**
Fish Market, **21**
The Forge, **8**

Giacosa, **34**
Grand Cafe, **45**
Granny
Feelgood's, **14, 26**
Hy-Vong Vietnamese
Cuisine, **30**
Islas Canarias, **28**
Joe's Stone Crab
Restaurant, **20**

La Paloma, **5**
Las Puertas, **40**
Las Tapas, **24**
LB's Eatery, **47**
Le Festival, **31**
Le Pavillon, **25**
Los Ranchos, **23**
Mark's Place, **4**

Max's South
Beach, **18**
Mezzanotte, **16**
Mykonos, **43**
News Café, **19**
Osteria del Teatro, **15**
Pacific Time, **12**
Pineapples, **9**

Restaurant St.
Michel, **36**
Rodeo Grill, **32**
Shorty's Bar-B-Q, **48**
Shula's Steak House, **3**
Thai Toni, **17**
Tony Chan's
Water Club, **22**

Tropical Chinese
Restaurant, **44**
Unicorn Village
Restaurant &
Marketplace, **1**
Van Dyke Café, **10**
Victor's Café, **42**
Yuca, **41**

greens, and dried-fruit sauce. For dessert there may be warm chocolate decadence with chocolate sorbet and blackberry *coulis*. There's a second Mark's Place in Fort Lauderdale. ✉ *2286 N.E. 123rd St.,* ☎ *305/893–6888. AE, DC, MC, V. C. No lunch weekends.*

### North Miami Beach

**$$$**   ✕ **Chef Allen's.** In this Art Deco world of glass block, neon trim, fresh
★     flowers, and art from the Gallery at Turnberry, your gaze nonetheless remains riveted on the kitchen. Chef Allen Susser designed it with a picture window 25 feet wide, so you can watch him create contemporary American masterpieces. The menu changes nightly. After a salad of baby greens and warm wild mushrooms or the Caribbean antipasto or rock-shrimp hash with roast corn, consider *orecchiette* pasta with sun-dried tomato, goat cheese, spinach, and toasted pine nuts; swordfish with conch-citrus couscous, macadamia nuts, and lemon; honey-chili roasted duck with stir-fried wild rice and green-apple Armagnac chutney; or grilled lamb chops with eggplant timbale and a three-nut salsa. A favorite dessert is the double-chocolate soufflé with lots of nuts. A four-course, fixed-price menu with two wine selections is offered nightly. ✉ *19088 N.E. 29th Ave.,* ☎ *305/935–2900. AE, DC, MC, V. No lunch.*

### West Dade

**$$–$$$**   ✕ **Shula's Steak House.** Surrounded by memorabilia of retired coach Don Shula's perfect 1972 season with the Miami Dolphins, you can drink or dine in this shrine for the NFL-obsessed. The certified Black Angus beef is almost an afterthought to the icons, which include quarterback Earl Morall's rocking chair, assistant coach Howard Schnellenberger's pipe, and a playbook autographed by President Richard Nixon. Steaks, prime rib, and fish (including dolphin) are served in a woody setting with a fireplace. Also for Shula fans, there's Shula's All-Star Cafe, a sports celebrity hangout in Don Shula's Hotel. ✉ *15400 N.W. 77th Ave., Miami Lakes,* ☎ *305/822–2324. AE, DC, MC, V.*

## Brazilian

### Coral Gables

**$$**   ✕ **Rodeo Grill.** Skewers aloft, the wait staff at the imaginative Rodeo
★     Grill race about, ready to carve off hunks and slices of 10 kinds of meats. The restaurant's name and "Eat 'til you drop" philosophy are inspired by *rodizio,* a Portuguese word referring to a continuous feed—or "rodeo." Here that means every conceivable type of meat, served with sides of rice, potatoes, fried yucca, and a big salad bar. If you have room for dessert you might want to split an order of *quindim,* a cake-and-custard combination of coconuts and eggs. Restaurateur Tito Valiente, a native of São Paulo, and his wife, Teresa, have made the Rodeo Grill a great favorite among the 40,000 Brazilians living in Dade County. The dining room is filled with Brazilian art, much of it for sale. ✉ *2121 Ponce de León Blvd.,* ☎ *305/447–6336. AE, D, DC, MC, V. No lunch Sun.*

## Chinese

### Downtown Miami

**$$**   ✕ **Tony Chan's Water Club.** One of a pair of outstanding Chinese
★     restaurants on the mainland, this beautiful dining room just off the lobby of the high-rise Grand Prix Hotel looks onto a bayside marina. Filled with art and chrome, the long room is modern rather than stock Chinese. On the menu of more than 100 appetizers and entrées is minced quail tossed with bamboo shoots and mushrooms wrapped in lettuce leaves. Indulge in a seafood spectacular with shrimp, conch, scallops,

fish cake, and crabmeat tossed with broccoli in a bird's nest or pork chops sprinkled with green pepper in a black bean–garlic sauce. ✉ *1717 N. Bayshore Dr.,* ☎ *305/374–8888. AE, MC, V.*

## South Dade

$–$$ ✕ **Tropical Chinese Restaurant.** The big, laqueur-free room feels as open
★ and busy as a railway station. You'll find unfamiliar items on the menu—for example, the early spring leaves of snow pea pods sublimely tender and flavorful. The extensive menu is filled with tofu combinations, poultry, beef, and pork, as well as tender seafood. A dim sum lunch is served on great carts. In the big open kitchen 13 chefs prepare everything as if for dignitaries. ✉ *7991 S.W. 40th St., Miami,* ☎ *305/262–7576 or 305/272–1552. AE, MC, V.*

# Continental

## Coconut Grove

$$$ ✕ **Grand Cafe.** Understated elegance is the hallmark of this bi-level room
★ with fanlight windows, brass details, pink tablecloths, and floral bouquets. French chef Pascal Oudin's starter specialties include pan-seared Florida crab cake and chilled home-smoked salmon Bavarian (with Reggiano cheese ruffle, crème fraîche, Ikura caviar, and roasted tomato dressing). Among the main courses, favorites are the baked macadamia-and-ginger-crusted salmon and crusted black-bean seared rare yellowfin tuna. For dessert try the white-chocolate-and-pistachio mousse with blackberry sauce and Beaujolais essence. ✉ *2669 S. Bayshore Dr.,* ☎ *305/858–9600. AE, DC, MC, V.*

$$ ✕ **Cafe Tu Tu Tango.** Local artists set up their easels in the rococo-modern arcades of this eclectic café-lounge on the second story of Coconut Grove's highly popular CocoWalk. You'll be blown away, whether you sit indoors or out. Outside offers some of the best people-watching in the South. Inside, guests graze on chips, dips, breads, and spreads. House specials include frittatas, crab cakes, *picadillo empanadas* (spicy ground beef served with cilantro sour cream), and chicken and shrimp orzo paella, all to be enjoyed with some of the best sangria in the city. ✉ *3015 Grand Ave. (CocoWalk),* ☎ *305/529–2222. AE, MC, V.*

## Miami Beach

$$$ ✕ **The Forge.** A courtyard has been added in an effort to rehabilitate this landmark, which suffered a disastrous fire in 1991. Often compared to a museum, the Forge stands behind a facade of 19th-century Parisian mansions, where an authentic forge once stood. Each intimate dining salon has its own historical artifacts, including a 250-year-old chandelier that hung in James Madison's White House. The wine cellar contains an inventory of 380,000 bottles—including more than 500 dating from 1822 (and costing as much as $35,000) and recorked in 1989 by experts from Domaines Barons de Rothschild. Specialties include Norwegian salmon served over fresh garden vegetables with spinach vinaigrette, veal tenderloin roasted Tuscan-style over oak wood and marinated with fresh blackberries, and free-range Wisconsin duck roasted with black currants. For dessert try the famous blacksmith pie. ✉ *432 Arthur Godfrey Rd.,* ☎ *305/538–8533. AE, DC, MC, V. No lunch.*

## North Miami

$$$ ✕ **La Paloma.** This Swiss Continental restaurant offers a total sensory experience: fine food, impeccable service, and the ambience of an art museum. Since 1977, owners Werner and Maria Staub have displayed the ornate European antiques they've been collecting for decades: Baccarat crystal, Limoges china, Meissen porcelain, and Sèvres clocks. The

staff speaks Spanish, French, German, Portuguese, and Arabic. Specialties include fresh local fish and shellfish; wiener schnitzel; lamb chops coated with bread crumbs, mustard, garlic, and herbs; veal chop with morel sauce; and, for dessert, lemon sherbet with fresh kiwi fruit and vodka. ⊠ *10999 Biscayne Blvd.,* ☎ *305/891–0505. AE, MC, V. Closed 2 weeks in late summer. No lunch weekends.*

# Cuban

### Coral Gables

$$$  ✕ **Yuca.** Top-flight Cuban dining can be had at this bistro-chic restau-
★     rant in a storefront on restaurant row. The name stands for the pota-
tolike staple of Cuban kitchens and is also used to refer to upscale young
Cuban-Americans. High standards are first evident in the setting—a
trendy blend of blond wood, tile, black-iron rails, track lighting, and
modern art. Still more impressive is the follow-through on food: tra-
ditional corn tamale filled with conch and a spicy jalapeño and Cre-
ole cheese pesto, the namesake yuca stuffed with *mamacita's picadillo*
and dressed in wild mushrooms on a bed of sautéed spinach, and
plantain-coated dolphin with a tamarind tartar sauce. Featured desserts
include classic Cuban rice pudding in an almond basket, and coconut
pudding in its coconut. ⊠ *177 Giralda Ave.,* ☎ *305/444–4448. Reser-
vations essential. AE, DC, MC, V. No lunch Sun.*

### Little Havana

$$–$$$  ✕ **Victor's Cafe.** This popular restarant draws its inspiration from the
traditional Cuban *casona,* the great house of colonial Cuba. The mood
is old Havana, with Cuban art and antiques, high ceilings, and a glass-
covered fountain courtyard. Owner Victor del Corral, who emigrated
from Cuba in 1957, first made his mark in Manhattan before branch-
ing out to Miami. Now he works with his daughter Sonia Zaldivar and
her son Luis. Come on Friday afternoon, when the *tapas* (hors d'oeu-
vres) bar is packed and lunch often lasts through dusk, in true Cuban
fashion. All entrées are accompanied by rice and black beans. The hot
appetizers, such as a puff pastry filled with aromatically herbed lump
crabmeat or a savory cassava turnover filled with Florida lobster are
enough for a meal. Try the exceptional red-snapper fillet Miralda
(marinated in bitter orange juice and garlic, sautéed in olive oil, and
served over strips of fire-roasted pimentos, green peppers, and scallions);
truly jumbo shrimp are served with yam quenelles in a creamy cham-
pagne sauce sprinkled with salmon roe. Romantic music is played
nightly. ⊠ *2430 S.W. 32nd Ave.,* ☎ *305/445–1313. AE, DC, MC, V.*

$  ✕ **Islas Canarias.** Since 1976 this has been a gathering place for Cuban
poets, pop-music stars, and media personalities. Wall murals depict a
Canary Islands street scene (owner Santiago Garcia's grandfather came
from Tenerife). The menu includes such Canary Islands dishes as baked
lamb, ham hocks with boiled potatoes, and tortilla *Española* (Span-
ish omelet with onions and chorizo), as well as Cuban standards like
palomilla steak and fried kingfish. Don't miss the three superb vari-
eties of homemade chips—potato, malanga, and plantain. ⊠ *285 N.W.
Unity Blvd. (N.W. 27th Ave.),* ☎ *305/649–0440. Westchester; Coral
Way and S.W. 137th Ave.,* ☎ *305/559–6666. No credit cards.*

# Family Style

### Coral Gables

$  ✕ **LB's Eatery.** Town and gown meet at this sprout-laden haven a half
block from the University of Miami's baseball stadium. Kitschy food-
related posters cover the walls, and there is no wait staff: You order
at the counter and pick up your food when called. Vegetarians thrive

on LB's salads and daily meatless entrées, such as lasagna and moussaka. The place is famous for Saturday-night lobster—if you plan to come after 8, call ahead to reserve one. Other specialties include barbecued baby-back ribs, lime chicken, croissant sandwiches, and carrot cake. ⊠ *5813 Ponce de León Blvd.,* ☎ *305/661–7091. D, MC, V. Closed Sun. and holidays.*

## French

### Coral Gables

$$$ ✕ **Le Festival.** The canopied entrance to this classical French restaurant belies the elegance within, where decor celebrates Parisian *moderne* with etched-glass filigree, posh burgundy, mahogany, and rose-tinted details. A second room for smokers, is more gilded. Main courses include fillet of grouper in bouillabaisse sauce; stuffed quail with grape and red-wine sauce; milk-fed veal sautéed with mushrooms, grapes, and brandy cream sauce; and chateaubriand for two. Desserts comprise various pastries, mousses, and soufflées. The wine list includes 100 selections, many priced less than $30. ⊠ *2120 Salzedo St.,* ☎ *305/442–8545. Reservations essential for dinner and for lunch parties of 5 or more. AE, D, DC, MC, V. Closed Sun. No lunch Sat.*

$$ ✕ **Didier's.** Flower boxes with seasonal blooms show through the eye-
★ let-curtained windows, tulips brighten tables in spring, and floral embellishment continues on menus. For starters, choose fresh basil soup or snails cooked in clay pots with garlic butter. Follow that up with a seafood entrée, such as bouillabaisse; a free-range chicken marinated in rosemary and served with wild mushrooms and glazed shallots; or roasted rack of lamb with herbs and fava beans in a fresh mint sauce. Desserts include crème brûlée, apple tart, and a strawberry with passion-fruit sabayon. ⊠ *2530 Ponce de León Blvd.,* ☎ *305/567–2444. AE, DC, MC, V. Closed Sun.*

### Miami Beach

$$$$ ✕ **Dominique's.** Woodwork and mirrors create an intimate setting for a unique experience in contemporary cuisine. Dine in either of two enclosed patios, both walled in glass to provide ocean views. Among the eclectic appetizers are buffalo sausage, sautéed alligator tail, and rattlesnake-meat salad. Entrées include rack of lamb and fresh seafood. The wine list is extensive. Sunday brunch is also served. ⊠ *Alexander Hotel, 5225 Collins Ave.,* ☎ *305/865–6500 or 800/327–6121. AE, DC, MC, V.*

## Greek

### Five Points, Miami

$ ✕ **Mykonos.** This Miami fixture since 1973 brightens the intersection at Five Points in the Roads section of town with a beautiful mural of the Aegean. Inside a sparkling blue-and-white setting is dressed up with Greek travel posters. Specialties include gyro, moussaka, marinated lamb and chicken, calamari and octopus sautéed in wine and onions, and sumptuous Greek salads thick with feta cheese and briny olives. Vegetarian moussaka, eggplant roll, lasagna, and a Greek-style omelet are also on the menu. ⊠ *1201 Coral Way,* ☎ *305/856–3140. AE, DC, MC, V. Closed July 4, Thanksgiving, Dec. 24–25, Dec. 31, and Jan. 1. No lunch Sun.*

# Haitian

### Little Haiti

$  ✕ **Chez Moy.** At this neighborhood fixture, the music is Haitian, the TV in the corner plays Haitian programs, everyone speaks Creole, and the food is as authentic as on the rue Delmas in Port-au-Prince. You can sit outside on a shaded patio or in a pleasant room with oak tables and high-back chairs. Specialties include *grillot* (pork boiled then fried with spices), fried or boiled fish, stewed goat, and conch with garlic and hot pepper. Try a tropical fruit drink such as sweet sop (also called *anon* or *cachiman*) or sour sop (also called *guanabana* or *corrosol*), blended with milk and sugar, and sweet-potato pie for dessert. ⊠ *1 N.W. 54th St.,* ☎ *305/757–5056. No credit cards.*

# Indian

### Coral Gables

$$  ✕ **Darbar.** Owner Bobby Puri's impeccably arranged Darbar (Punjabi
★  for "Royal Court") is the glory of Miami's Indian restaurants. It's authentic, right down to the portraits of turbaned Puri ancestors, kings, and princes. Flavors rise as if in a dance from the *bangan bharta,* a dish of eggplant skinned and mashed with onions, tomatoes, herbs, and spices and baked in a tandoor. The limited menu's focus is on northern Indian or frontier cuisine—various kebabs, tandoori platters, and *tikkas* (chicken or lamb marinated in yogurt and spices and cooked tandoori style)—although there are also curries from different regions and *biryani* specialties prepared with basmati rice and garnished with boiled egg, tomato, nuts, and raisins. Everything, including the unusual Indian breads, is cooked to order. ⊠ *276 Alhambra Circle,* ☎ *305/448–9691. AE, DC, MC, V. No lunch Sun.*

# Italian

### Coral Gables

$$$  ✕ **Casa Rolandi.** Brick ovens, open beams and weathered village walls provide the setting for Northern Italian Cuisine. The menu features the expected antipasti and *caldi,* but on the way to the *gelati* and *dolci* you'll want to tour through risottos and pastas—smoked salmon and shrimp bathed in a creamy tomato rice; bow ties with ground veal, chicken, onions, and carrots; and a succulent Maine lobster bedded on spaghetti, fresh tomatos, and basil—or through such local choices as grouper baked with mushrooms, leeks, and saffron on a bed of arugula. ⊠ *1930 Ponce de León Blvd.,* ☎ *305/444–2187. AE, DC, MC, V. Closed Sun. and Mon. No lunch Sat.*

$$–$$$  ✕ **Caffe Abbracci.** Although the kitchen closes at 11, the last wave of
★  customers—usually Brazilians—is still partying to flamenco or salsa music on weekends at 2. The setting is graciously deco, with huge bursts of flowers, frosted glass, gallery lighting, and fresh roses on white linens; lights above each table are on individual dimmers. After the cold and hot antipasti—various carpaccios, porcini mushrooms, calamari, grilled goat cheese, shrimps, mussels—come festive entrées. Most of the pasta is made fresh, so consider sampling two or three, maybe with pesto sauce, Gorgonzola, and fresh tomatoes. The *agnolotti al pesto* are pasta pockets filled with ricotta cheese and spinach; the *dentice alla maggiorana* is red snapper sautéed in white wine, fresh marjoram, and lemon and topped with sliced grilled tomatoes. Room for dessert? Napoleons and tiramisù are made here daily, and there's always a choice of fresh fruit tarts. ⊠ *318 Aragon Ave.,* ☎ *305/441–0700. Reservations essential. AE, DC, MC, V. No lunch weekends.*

**$$-$$$** ✕ **Giacosa.** Named for one of Puccini's librettists, this is another of
★ the superbly evocative—and just plain superb—restaurants in Coral
Gables. The ambience is wonderfully informed—a thickly carpeted room
like a smart Venetian salon, fresh flowers, chair cushions inspired by
tapestry. From putting your napkin in your lap to whisking a tower of
airy pita bread with olive oil in a carafe to the table, the smooth staff
is the standard of competence. Parmesan is freshly grated to the plate.
A salad *tricolore* imparts the bitter kiss of arugula; pastas, veals, and
fresh seafood are all prepared for peak taste. ⊠ *394 Giralda Ave.,* ☎
*407/445–5858. AE, DC, MC, V. No lunch weekends.*

## Miami Beach

**$$$** ✕ **Osteria del Teatro.** Thanks to word of mouth, this Northern Ital-
★ ian restaurant is constantly full. Orchids grace the tables in the inti-
mate, gray, gray, and gray room with a low, laced canvas ceiling, deco
lamps, and the most refined clink and clatter along Washington Av-
enue's remarkable restaurant row. You'll start with large, unevenly sliced
hunks of homemade bread lightly toasted. Then try an appetizer of grilled
portobello mushrooms topped with fontina cheese and served over a
bed of arugula with a green peppercorn-brandy sauce, and for the main
course, linguine sautéed with chunks of jumbo shrimp, roasted pep-
pers, capers, black olives, fresh diced tomato, and herbs in a tangy gar-
lic-olive oil sauce. ⊠ *1443 Washington Ave.,* ☎ *305/538–7850.
Reservations essential. AE, DC, MC, V. Closed Tues. No lunch.*

**$$** ✕ **Mezzanotte.** Sometime between 6 and 10 each night, the big square
room with the square bar in the middle transforms from an empty cater-
ing hall to a New Year's Eve party. Trendoids call for their capellini
with fresh tomato and basil; calamari in clam juice, garlic, and red wine;
or scaloppine with mushroom, pepper, and white wine and then top
it off with their dolci: fresh napoleon, chocolate mousse, or tiramisù.
Chic but not intimate, Mezzanotte has been known since 1988 for fine
food at moderate prices, but watch out for the coffee at $2.25 a pop!
⊠ *1200 Washington Ave.,* ☎ *305/673–4343. AE, DC, MC, V. No lunch.*

**$-$$** ✕ **Da Leo.** Tables from this little restaurant spill all over the Lincoln
Road Mall, staying full thanks to consistently good food at prices only
half of what trendier places charge. The volume keeps the mood festive and the standards high. You'll be amazed by the art, which covers the walls so completely you might think the canvasses provide
structural support. The look is ancient Roman town house (though owner
Leonardo Marchini hails from Lucca), with banquettes along one wall
and wainscoting along the other. Pastas, fish, veal, and fowl make up
most of the entrées. ⊠ *819 Lincoln Rd. Mall,* ☎ *305/674–0350. AE,
DC, MC, V. No lunch weekends.*

# Mexican

## Coral Gables

**$$** ✕ **Las Puertas.** The restaurant row along Coral Gables' Giralda Av-
enue seems touched by magic, and this storefront dining room filled
with native arts and crafts is no exception. Handsome arches and
white tablecloths redeem south-of-the-border cuisine from the limits
of quick lunch food. The tastes of several Mexican states are repre-
sented. The chicken in green *pipian* sauce (breast grilled and poached
in a sauce of ground sesame, pumpkin seeds, tomatillos, cilantro, and
dark green poblanos chiles) hails from Puebla. Yucatán suckling pig
comes baked inside banana leaves, and the red snapper from Veracruz
is sautéed with capers, tomatoes, and green olives. Of several desserts
you've never seen on franchised Mexican menu boards, the best, when

available, is the cheesecake of fresh peaches and cream. ⊠ *148 Giralda Ave.,* ☎ *305/442–0708. AE, D, MC, V. No lunch weekends.*

## Natural

### Downtown Miami

$$    ✕ **Granny Feelgood's.** "Granny" is a shrewd gentleman named Irving Field, who caters to the health-conscious. Specialties include chicken salad with raisins, apples, and cinnamon; spinach fettuccine with pine nuts; grilled tofu; apple crumb cake; and carrot cake. ⊠ *190 S.E. 1st Ave.,* ☎ *305/358–6233;* ⊠ *111 N.W. 1st St.,* ☎ *305/579–2104;* ⊠ *647 Lincoln Rd. Mall, Miami Beach,* ☎ *305/673–0408. AE, MC, V. Closed Sun. No lunch.*

### Miami Beach

$$    ✕ **Pineapples.** Art-filled, tropical pink-and-green café seating occupies half of this popular mid-Beach neighborhood emporium; the other side is a health-food store. Daily seafood, chicken, and vegetarian specials add variety to longtime favorites lasagna filled with tofu and mushrooms, spinach fettuccine with feta cheese, and salads. Organic wine and beer are recent additions. ⊠ *530 Arthur Godfrey Rd.,* ☎ *305/532–9731. AE, MC, V.*

### North Miami Beach

$$    ✕ **Unicorn Village Restaurant & Marketplace.** In an outdoor setting of
★    free-form ponds and fountains by a bayfront dock, or in the plant-filled interior under three-story-high wood-beam ceilings, guests enjoy seitan medallions (wheat meat in a mushroom gravy sauce) and a line of homemade organic pizzas. Other favorites include a Tuscan vegetable sauté with Italian seasonings; grilled honey-mustard chicken; spicy seafood cakes; and the Unicorn's spring roll of uncooked veggies wrapped in thin rice paper with cellophane noodles. Very popular are the early dinner specials—typically eight entrées with soup or salad, basket of rolls, vegetables, and coffee—offered 4:30–5:30 for up to $10.95. The nondairy, fat-free chocolate-mocha cake is tasty, and there are organic cappuccinos. The adjacent market is the largest natural-foods source in Florida and desserts are baked on site. ⊠ *3565 N.E. 207th St.,* ☎ *305/933–8829. AE, MC, V.*

## Nicaraguan

### Downtown Miami

$$    ✕ **Los Ranchos.** Carlos Somoza, owner of this beautiful bayside es-
★    tablishment, is a nephew of Nicaragua's late president Anastasio Somoza. Carlos sustains a tradition begun more than 30 years ago in Managua, when the original Los Ranchos instilled in Nicaraguan palates a love of Argentine-style beef—lean, grass-fed tenderloin with *chimichurri,* a green sauce of chopped parsley, garlic, oil, vinegar, and other spices. Nicaragua's own sauces are a tomato-based marinara and the fiery *cebollitas encurtidas,* with slices of jalapeño pepper and onion pickled in vinegar. Specialties include chorizo, *cuajada con maduro* (skim cheese with fried bananas), and shrimp sautéed in butter and topped with creamy jalapeño sauce. Don't look for veggies or brewed decaf, but you do get live entertainment at lunch and dinner. ⊠ *Bayside Marketplace, 401 Biscayne Blvd.,* ☎ *305/375–8188 or 305/375–0666;* ⊠ *125 S.W. 107th Ave., Little Managua,* ☎ *305/221–9367;* ⊠ *Kendall Town & Country, 8505 Mills Dr., Kendall,* ☎ *305/596–5353;* ⊠ *The Falls, 8888 S.W. 136th St., Suite 303, South Miami,* ☎ *305/238–6867;* ⊠ *2728 Ponce de León Blvd., Coral Gables,* ☎ *305/446–0050. AE, DC, MC, V.*

## Seafood

### Downtown Miami

$$-$$$   ✕ **Fish Market.** If fish are truly running scarce in Florida waters, as
★   some claim, the last of what's available should be reserved for this superior dining room tucked in a corner of the Crowne Plaza Miami lobby.
The room is as beautiful as the kitchen staff is fluent in seafood's com-
plexities. Modern chrome and comfortable cushions combine in urban
sophistication. Though the menu is limited, whatever's fresh is highlighted. Look for seared swordfish with Oriental vinaigrette, broiled
Florida lobster with Creole sauce and onion risotto, or sautéed Florida
dolphin with roasted peppers in a beurre blanc. The chocolate-pecan
tart and pistachio-chocolate terrine with orange-cream sauce are two
of the featured desserts. There's free valet parking. ✉ *Biscayne Blvd.
at 16th St.,* ☎ *305/374–4399. AE, D, DC, MC, V. Closed Sun. No
lunch Sat.*

$$   ✕ **East Coast Fisheries.** This family-owned restaurant and retail fish
★   market on the Miami River offers fresh Florida seafood from its own
38-boat fleet in the Keys. From tables along the second-floor balcony,
watch the cooks prepare your dinner in the open kitchen below. Spe-
cialties include a complimentary fish-pâté appetizer, blackened pom-
pano with owner David Swartz's personal herb-and-spice recipe, lightly
breaded fried grouper, and a homemade Key lime pie. ✉ *360 W. Flag-
ler St.,* ☎ *305/373–5515. AE, MC, V. Beer and wine only.*

### Miami Beach

$$$   ✕ **Pacific Time.** This cool California-style restaurant is packed nearly
★   every night. It's rare that you can get in without a reservation or a 45-
minute wait. The superb eatery, co-owned by chef Jonathan Eismann,
has a high blue ceiling and banquettes, accents of mahogany and brass,
recessed lights, paddle fans, plank floors, and an open-windowed
kitchen. Entrées include a cedar-roasted salmon, rosemary-roasted
chicken, and shiitake mushroom-grilled, dry-aged Colorado beef.
Rices, potatoes, and vegetables are à la carte; however, a pre-theater
prix fixe dinner, served from 6 to 7 PM, is more affordable at $20 and
includes a noodle dish, Szechuan mixed grill and grilled ginger chicken.
Desserts (mostly around $7) include baked apricots and fresh black-
berries in phyllo pastry and a warm bittersweet-chocolate bombe.
There's an extensive California wine list. ✉ *915 Lincoln Rd.,* ☎
*305/534–5979. AE, DC, MC, V.*

$$   ✕ **Joe's Stone Crab Restaurant.** "Before SoBe, Joe Be," touts this
★   fourth-generation family restaurant, which reopened for the 1996 sea-
son with a chest-puffing facade on Washington Avenue. You go to wait,
people-watch, and finally settle down to an ample à la carte menu. About
a ton of stone-crab claws is served daily, with drawn butter, lemon
wedges, and piquant mustard sauce (recipe available). Popular side or-
ders include salad with a brisk vinaigrette house dressing, creamed gar-
lic spinach, french-fried onions, fried green tomatoes, and hash browns.
Save room for dessert—Key lime pie with a graham-cracker crust and
whipped cream or apple pie with a crumb-pecan topping. To minimize
the wait, come for lunch at 11:30 or 2:00, for dinner at 5 or after 9.
✉ *227 Biscayne St.,* ☎ *305/673–0365; takeout, 305/673–4611;
overnight shipping, 800/780–2722. AE, D, DC, MC, V. Closed May
15–Oct. 15.*

# Spanish

### Coral Gables

$$ ✕ **Cafe Barcelona.** This room with high-ceilings and coral walls is highlighted by gilt-framed art and beautiful, slender ceiling lamps with tiny fluted green shades. The dim glow illuminates the food but little else, yielding an ambience that's part art gallery and part private home. Exceptional food matches the exceptional mood, and in a city where fresh fish has gotten priced off the deep end, entrées here range a good $5 below comparable dishes at first-class restaurants. They do a sea bass in sea salt for two, a traditional codfish with garlic confit, and a grouper in a clay pot with seafood sauce as well as lamb, duck, and several affordable rice dishes, including three versions of a paella. The *crema Catalana,* a version of flan, is not to be missed. ✉ *160 Giralda Ave.,* ☎ *305/448–0912. AE, D, DC, MC, V. No lunch weekends.*

### Downtown Miami

$$ ✕ **Las Tapas.** Overhung with dried meats and enormous show breads, this popular spot with terra-cotta floors and an open kitchen offers a lot of imaginative creations. Tapas ("little dishes") give you a variety of tastes during a single meal. Specialties include *la tostada* (smoked salmon on melba toast, topped with a dollop of sour cream, baby eels, black caviar, capers, and chopped onion) and *pincho de pollo a la plancha* (grilled chicken brochette marinated in brandy and onions). Also available are soups, salads, sandwiches, and standard-size dinners. ✉ *Bayside Marketplace, 401 Biscayne Blvd.,* ☎ *305/372–2737. Reservations essential for large parties. AE, D, DC, MC, V.*

### Little Havana

$$–$$$ ✕ **Casa Juancho.** A meeting place for the movers and shakers of
★ Miami's Cuban community and a haven for lovers of fine Spanish food, Casa Juancho serves a cross section of Spanish regional cuisines. The exterior is marked by *tinajones,* the huge earthen urns of eastern Cuba, but the interior recalls old Castile. Strolling balladeers (university students from Spain) will serenade you among brown brick, rough-hewn dark timbers, walls hung with hooks of smoked meats and adorned with colorful Talavera platters. Ask about the hake prepared in a fish stock with garlic, onions, and white wine that's flown in from Spain or the *carabineros a la plancha* (jumbo red shrimp with head and shell on, split and grilled). Other specialties include roast suckling pig and *parrillada de mariscos* (fish, shrimps, squid, and scallops grilled in a light garlic sauce) from the Pontevedra region of northwest Spain. For dessert, the *crema Catalana* has a delectable crust of burnt caramel atop a rich pastry custard. The house features the largest list of reserved Spanish wines in the U.S. ✉ *2436 S.W. 8th St.,* ☎ *305/642–2452. AE, D, DC, MC, V.*

# Thai

### Miami Beach

$$ ✕ **Thai Toni.** Thai silks, bronze Buddhas, dramatic ceiling drapes, private dining alcoves, and two raised platforms for those who want to dine seated on cushions set this exceptional restaurant apart from other trendy eateries in South Beach. The mellow Thai Singha beer complements the spicy jumping squid appetizer with chili paste and hot pepper or the hot, hot pork. Choose from a large variety of inexpensive noodle, fried-rice, and vegetarian dishes or such traditional entrées as beef and broccoli, basil duck, or hot-and-spicy deep-fried whole snapper with basil leaves and mixed vegetables. The homemade lemonade

is distinctly tart. ⊠ *890 Washington Ave.,* ☎ *305/538–8424. AE, MC, V. No lunch.*

## Vietnamese

### Little Havana

$ ✕ **Hy-Vong Vietnamese Cuisine.** Beer-savvy Kathy Manning has in-
★ troduced a half dozen top brews since taking over in 1989 (Double
Grimbergen, Moretti, and Spaten, among them), and magic continues
to pour forth from the tiny kitchen of this plain little restaurant. Come
before 7 to avoid a wait. Favorites include spring rolls (a Vietnamese
version of an egg roll, with ground pork, cellophane noodles, and black
mushrooms wrapped in homemade rice paper), whole fish panfried with
*nuoc man* (a garlic-lime fish sauce), and thinly sliced pork, barbecued
with sesame seeds and fish sauce, served with bean sprouts, rice noodles, and slivers of carrots, almonds, and peanuts. ⊠ *3458 S.W. 8th
St.,* ☎ *305/446–3674. No credit cards. No smoking. Closed Mon.,
and 2 weeks in Aug. No lunch.*

# LODGING

As recently as the 1960s, many hotels in Greater Miami opened only
in winter, to accommodate Yankee snowbirds. Now all hotels stay open
all year. In summer they cater to European and Latin American vacationers, who find Miami congenial despite the heat, humidity, and intense afternoon thunderstorms.

Although some hotels (especially on the mainland) have adopted steady
year-round rates, many still adjust their rates to reflect seasonal demand.
The peak occurs in winter, with a dip in summer (prices are often more
negotiable than rate cards let on), when families with school-age children take vacation. You'll find the best values between Easter and Memorial Day (a delightful time in Miami but a difficult time for many people
to travel) and in September and October (the height of hurricane season).

## Coconut Grove

$$$$ ▦ **Grand Bay Hotel.** Combining the classical and flawless elegance of
★ Greece, a stepped facade that feels vaguely Aztec, a hint of the South,
and a brush of the tropical, this hotel is like no other in South Florida—
distinctive in look and supremely restful. Detailed moldings highlight
the inside, while artwork and fresh flowers enhance the beautiful
lobby. Guest rooms are filled with superb touches: a canister of sharpened pencils giving off the fresh aroma of shaved wood, an antique
sideboard that holds house phones, and matched woods, variously in-
laid and fluted. The piano in 814 is tuned when Pavarotti is in residence, but your needs will be met equally well. Rooms at the northeast
corner have the best views, looking out on downtown Miami. An afternoon tea is served. ⊠ *2669 S. Bayshore Dr., 33133,* ☎ *305/858–
9600 or 800/327–2788,* ℻ *305/858–1532. 132 rooms, 49 suites.
Restaurant, bar, lounge, pool, beauty salon, hot tub, massage, saunas,
health club. AE, DC, MC, V.*

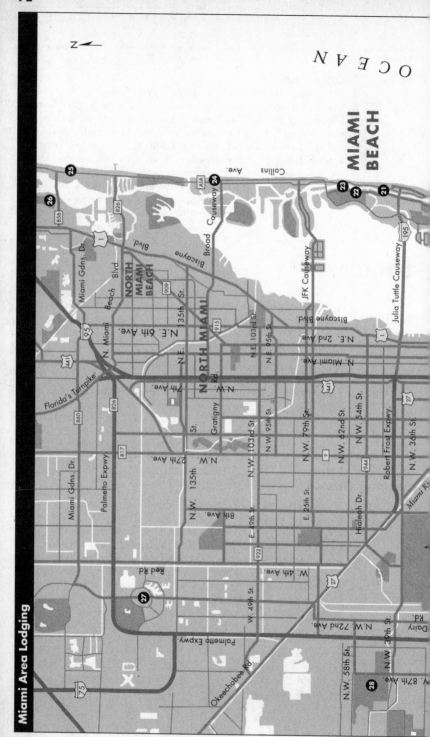

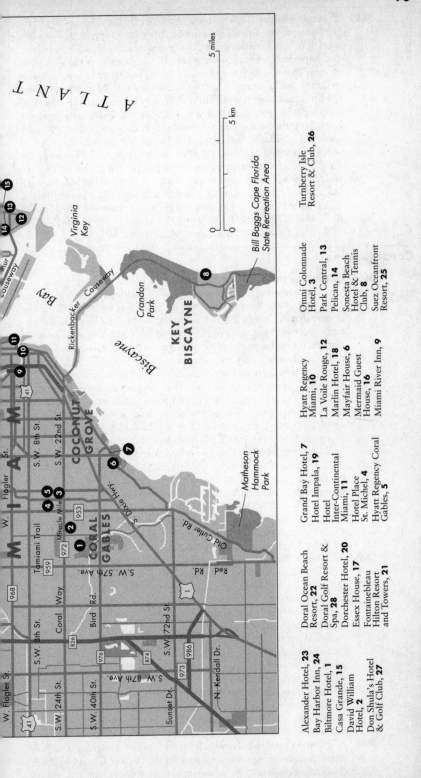

ATLANT

Virginia
Key

Rickenbacker Causeway

Bay

Crandon
Park

Biscayne

KEY
BISCAYNE

Biscayne

Bill Baggs Cape Florida
State Recreation Area

Matheson
Hammock
Park

COCONUT
GROVE

CORAL
GABLES

S.W. 8th St.

S.W. 22nd St.

Tamiami Trail

Miracle Mile

Coral Way

Bird Rd.

S.W. 57th Ave.

Old Cutler Rd.

S. Dixie Hwy.

Red Rd.

W. Flagler St.

W. Flagler St.

S.W. 3th St.

S.W. 24th St.

S.W. 40th St.

S.W. 87th Ave.

S.W. 72nd St.

Sunset Dr.

N. Kendall Dr.

MIAM

0   5 km
0   5 miles

Alexander Hotel, **23**
Bay Harbor Inn, **24**
Biltmore Hotel, **1**
Casa Grande, **15**
David William
Hotel, **2**
Don Shula's Hotel
& Golf Club, **27**

Doral Ocean Beach
Resort, **22**
Doral Golf Resort &
Spa, **28**
Dorchester Hotel, **20**
Essex House, **17**
Fontainebleau
Hilton Resort
and Towers, **21**

Grand Bay Hotel, **7**
Hotel Impala, **19**
Hotel
Inter-Continental
Miami, **11**
Hotel Place
St. Michel, **4**
Hyatt Regency Coral
Gables, **5**

Hyatt Regency
Miami, **10**
La Voile Rouge, **12**
Marlin Hotel, **18**
Mayfair House, **6**
Mermaid Guest
House, **16**
Miami River Inn, **9**

Omni Colonnade
Hotel, **3**
Park Central, **13**
Pelican, **14**
Sonesta Beach
Hotel & Tennis
Club, **8**
Suez Oceanfront
Resort, **25**

Turnberry Isle
Resort & Club, **26**

$$$$ 🏨 **Mayfair House.** This European-style luxury hotel sits within Mayfair Shops at the Grove, an exclusive open-air shopping mall. Public areas have Tiffany windows, polished mahogany, marble walls and floors, and imported ceramics and crystal. Also impressive is the glassed-in elevator that whisks you to the corridor on your floor; a balcony overlooks the mall's central fountains and walkways. All rooms are suites (22 for nonsmokers), with outdoor terraces facing the street, screened from view by vegetation and wood latticework. Each has a Japanese hot tub on the balcony or a Roman tub in the suite; otherwise, each room is individually furnished. The Sunset (Room 505) is one of 50 suites with antique pianos. Other luxury touches: All bathrooms have double sinks, makeup lights, and scales, and all closets are lighted. An added bonus is a roof-top recreation area. Revival of the Mayfair mall has also led to the reopening of the hotel's nightclub, Ensign Bitters. You'll want to ask to make sure you get a quiet suite. ⊠ *3000 Florida Ave., 33133,* ☎ *305/441–0000 or 800/433–4555,* ℻ *305/447–9173. 182 suites. Snack bar, pool, sauna. AE, D, DC, MC, V.*

## Coral Gables

$$$$ 🏨 **Biltmore Hotel.** This is Miami's grand boom-time hotel, one of a
★    handful remaining recapturing an era of uncompromised elegance. Now part of the Westin chain, the Biltmore was built in 1926 as the centerpiece of George Merrick's "city beautiful," and it rises like a sienna-color wedding cake in the heart of the Coral Gables residential district. A championship golf course, tennis courts, and waterway surround the hotel. The lobby is spectacularly vaulted with hand-painted rafters on a background sky of twinkling blue; travertine marble, Oriental rugs, and palms in blue porcelain pots set the tone that continues through the fountain patio and opulent ballrooms. Guest rooms are twice as large as they were when the hotel was built but may still appear small by today's grand hotel standards. They were completely modernized in a restrained Moorish style during a $55 million overhaul in 1986, when the hotel reopened after decades of neglect. A second, $5 million renovation, after its acquisition by Westin in 1992, brought a fitness center and spa with three workout areas in a 15,000-square-foot facility. Historical tours of the property take place Sun. at 1:30, 2:30, and 3:30. ⊠ *1200 Anastasia Ave., 33134,* ☎ *305/445–1926 or 800/445–2586,* ℻ *305/442–9496. 237 rooms, 38 suites. Restaurant, coffee shop, lounge, pool, sauna, spa, 18-hole golf course, 10 lighted tennis courts. AE, DC, MC, V.*

$$$$ ✕🏨 **Hyatt Regency Coral Gables.** In keeping with historic Gables
★    style, the exterior of this Hyatt makes an overt Spanish statement, courtesy of tile roofs, white-frame casement windows, and pink stucco. Spanish influences in the interiors, newly redone, are more subliminal: traces in the headboard design, a stair-stepped outline at guest information, the styling of antique furniture, and the fall browns and blonds that evoke peninsular Spain. The staff is savvy and helpful, as befits a business-oriented hotel. Yet the mood remains comfortable and residential. The large meeting facilities are all to the side, so vacationers don't feel they've stumbled into the corporate world they're trying to get away from. There are no bad views, but the best look onto the pool. ⊠ *50 Alhambra Plaza, 33134,* ☎ *305/441–1234,* ℻ *305/443–7702. 192 rooms, 50 suites. Restaurant, lounge, pool, sauna, steam rooms, health club. AE, D, DC, MC, V.*

$$$$ ✕🏨 **Omni Colonnade Hotel.** The twin 13-story towers of this hotel,
★    office, and shopping complex dominate the heart of Coral Gables. Architectural details echo the adjoining two-story Corinthian-style rotunda on Miracle Mile, from which 1920s developer George Merrick sold

lots in his fledgling city. Merrick's family provided old photos, paintings, and other heirlooms that are on display throughout the hotel. The oversize rooms come in 26 floor plans, each with a sitting area, built-in armoires, and traditional furnishings of mahogany. The hospitality bars feature marble counters and gold-plated faucets with 1920s-style ceramic handles. The pool on a 10th-floor terrace looks south toward Biscayne Bay. Ask for a room with a private balcony. ⊠ *180 Aragon Ave., 33134,* ☎ *305/441–2600 or 800/533–1337,* FAX *305/445–3929. 157 rooms, 17 bilevel suites. 2 restaurants, pool, 2 saunas, exercise room. AE, DC, MC, V.*

$$$ 🏨 **David William Hotel.** Easily the most affordable of the top Gables hotels, the DW (as aficionados call it) was the first high rise of Miami's modern era, standing 13 stories tall with a distinctive waffled facade. The hotel is solidly built, like a fort, so the rooms are very private and very quiet. Guest rooms are large, with marble baths; all those facing south (the sunnier exposure) have balconies. Many rooms have kitchens. The decor features new furniture trimmed with braids of varicolored wood, upholstered in tan and blue. The lobby is a bit tacky, with tables outside the elegant Chez Vendôme, a popular traditional French restaurant. Rooftop cabana guest rooms are the best bargains. ⊠ *700 Biltmore Way, 33134,* ☎ *305/445–7821; outside FL, 800/327–8770;* FAX *305/445–5585.*

$$$ ✕🏨 **Hotel Place St. Michel.** Art-nouveau chandeliers suspended from ★ vaulted ceilings grace the public areas of this intimate jewel in the heart of downtown. The historic low-rise hotel, built in 1926 and restored from 1981 to 1986, is filled with the scent of fresh flowers, circulated by the paddle fans hanging from the ceilings. Each room has its own dimensions, personality, and imported antiques from England, Scotland, and France. A complimentary Continental breakfast is served. ⊠ *162 Alcazar Ave., 33134,* ☎ *305/444–1666 or 800/247–8526,* FAX *305/529-0074. 24 rooms, 3 suites. Restaurant, lounge. AE, DC, MC, V.*

# Downtown Miami

$$$$ ✕🏨 **Hotel Inter-Continental Miami.** Stand outside on the fifth-floor pool ★ deck for the best view of downtown. You see only the clean upper stories of the city, nothing of the ragtag street—the view Miami likes best of itself, with its Disneyesque Metromover, the booming port, the beautiful bay. The marble grain in the lobby of this 34-story landmark matches that in *The Spindle,* a massive centerpiece sculpture by Henry Moore. With all that marble, the lobby could easily look like a mausoleum—and did before the addition of palm trees and oversize wicker chairs and tables. Sunlight streams through the atrium from a skylight high overhead. Guest rooms are traditional with a Latin flavor—in grays and beige and the darkest imaginable chintz. The Inter-Con, as guests call it, is altogether the most manorial property in the city—as well, as it happens, the most committed to waste reduction and recycling. ⊠ *100 Chopin Plaza, 33131,* ☎ *305/577–1000 or 800/327–0200,* FAX *305/577–0384. 644 rooms, 34 suites. 3 restaurants, lounge, pool, spa, jogging. AE, DC, MC, V.*

$$$$ 🏨 **Hyatt Regency Miami.** The blend of leisure and business should position the Hyatt well for the downtown renaissance that began with the opening of the new Miami Avenue Bridge in late 1996. Public spaces more colorful than the more businesslike, but no less distinctive, guest rooms, done in unusual avocado, beige, and blond and yielding views of the river or port. The best are on upper floors. The James L. Knight International Center is accessible without stepping outside, as is the

downtown Metromover, with its Metrorail connection, and there's a free shuttle to Coconut Grove. ⊠ *400 S.E. 2nd Ave., 33131,* ☎ *305/358–1234 or 800/233–1234,* FAX *305/358–0529. 615 rooms, 25 suites. 2 restaurants, lounge, pool. AE, D, DC, MC, V.*

**$$**   🏨 **Miami River Inn.** Preservationist Sallye Jude has restored these five 1904 clapboard buildings, the oldest continuously operating inn south of St. Augustine and the only concentration of houses in Miami remaining from that period. The inn is an oasis of country hospitality in a working-class neighborhood—one of Miami's safest even if it doesn't look that way. The heart of the city is only a 10-minute walk across the 1st Street Bridge, and José Martí Park, one of the city's prettiest but lately a haven for the homeless, is only a few hundred feet from the inn gates. There are 40 antique-filled rooms (some with tub only), a breakfast area, small meeting space, outdoor pool and patio, and an oval lawn. Guests receive a complimentary Continental breakfast and have use of a refrigerator. The best rooms look over and down the river from the second and third stories. Avoid the tiny rooms in Building D with a view of the stark condo to the west. As part of the same property— officially designated the Riverside Historic District—four modified-deco mid-century masonry buildings house long-term renters. ⊠ *118 S.W. South River Dr., 33130,* ☎ *305/325–0045 or 800/468–3589,* FAX *305/325–9227. 40 rooms (2 with shared bath). Pool. AE, D, DC, MC, V.*

## Key Biscayne

**$$$$**   🏨 **Sonesta Beach Hotel & Tennis Club.** The Sonesta was always one of
★      Miami's best and now is more tropical than ever, with reef pastels and stunning views of the sea, at least from those rooms facing east. Two villas are actually three-bedroom homes with full kitchen and screened pool. Don't miss the displays of museum-quality modern art by prominent painters and sculptors, especially Andy Warhol's drawings of rock star Mick Jagger in the hotel's disco bar, Desires. The 750-foot beach, one of Florida's best, has a big variety of recreational facilities. ⊠ *350 Ocean Dr., 33149,* ☎ *305/361–2021 or 800/766–3782,* FAX *305/365–2096. 284 rooms, 14 suites, 2 villas. 3 restaurants, bar, snack bar, pool, massage, steam rooms, 9 tennis courts (3 lighted), aerobics, health club, beach, windsurfing, children's program. AE, DC, MC, V.*

## Miami Beach

**$$$$**   🏨 **Alexander Hotel.** Located amid the high-rises of the mid-Beach dis-
★      trict, this 16-story hotel represents the elegance for which the Beach was once famous. It has immense suites furnished with antiques and reproductions, each with a terrace affording ocean or bay views, each with a living and dining room. Everything is understated, from the marquetry-paneled and landscaped lobby to the oceanfront dining rooms. Service is of the highest standard and includes twice-daily maid service. ⊠ *5225 Collins Ave., 33140,* ☎ *305/865–6500 or 800/327–6121,* FAX *305/864–8525. 158 1- and 2-bedroom suites with 2 baths and kitchen. Restaurant, coffee shop, 2 pools, spa, beach, boating. AE, D, DC, MC, V.*

**$$$$**   🏨 **Doral Ocean Beach Resort.** Of the great Miami Beach hotels, this
★      18-story glass tower that opened in 1962 still remains a standout. It has the only roof-top restaurant in town (Alfredo, the Original of Rome), the only roof-top ballroom (with 8,000 twinkling lights), two presidential suites designed in consultation with the Secret Service, an FAA-licensed helipad, and the kind of service that's kept the Beach going through the years. Some of the staff have worked here for 20 or 30

years, and the hotel remembers hospitality as it was before voice mail. Guest rooms are done in warm colors and are filled with details that make a difference : small fridges; three sets of drapes including black-out curtains; and big closets. Bathrooms have high-quality toiletries, two lavatories, a magnifying mirror, and a sliding door between toilet and shower-bath. Free transportation to Doral Golf Resort and Spa is provided. ⊠ *4833 Collins Ave., 33140,* ☎ *305/532–3600 or 800/223–6725,* ⅀ *305/534–7409. 293 rooms, 127 suites. 3 restaurants, 4 lounges, pool, 2 lighted tennis courts, exercise room, beach, helipad. AE, DC, MC, V.*

$$$$  🏨 **Fontainebleau Hilton Resort and Towers.** This is the Grand Central of Miami area hotels—the busiest, the biggest, and the most ornate. Its convention facilities rank second only to Miami's city-owned convention center. Tower rooms are now country in spirit, light and flowery, yet they come with traditional amenities and the added security of special elevator keys. Other themes vary from a 1950s look to one that's more contemporary. Even the smallest rooms are large by most standards. The Continental breakfast is more like a banquet, and the view extends halfway to the Azores. ⊠ *4441 Collins Ave., 33140,* ☎ *305/538–2000 or 800/548–8886,* ⅀ *305/531–9274. 1,146 rooms, 60 suites. 12 restaurants, 4 lounges, 2 pools, saunas, 7 lighted tennis courts, health club, volleyball, beach, windsurfing, boating, parasailing, children's programs. AE, DC, MC, V.*

$$$$  🏨 **Hotel Impala.** It seems there's nothing more routine on South Beach
★ than a crack house transformed into a sybarite's playpen. The difference here, at the former La Flora, built in the 1930s, is that the style is tropical Georgian, rather than deco. Iron, mahogany, and stone on the inside are in synch with the sporty white-trimmed ocher exterior. Rooms, though small, come across as complete and elegantly comfortable. It's all very European—from mineral water and orchids to Mediterranean-style armoires, wrought-iron furniture, Italian fixtures, draperies hung from heavy ornamental rods, and Spanish surrealist art above the white-on-white, triple-sheeted, modified Eastlake sleigh beds. (Not surprisingly, Continental breakfast is included.) Wastebaskets in the unusually large baths are galvanized fire buckets, and everything from towels to toilet paper is of exceptional quality. ⊠ *1228 Collins Ave., 33139,* ☎ *305/673–2021 or 800/646–7252,* ⅀ *305/673–5984. 17 rooms, 3 suites. Restaurant, lounge. AE, DC, MC, V.*

$$$$  🏨 **La Voile Rouge.** So thoroughly does the Red Sail (as the name trans-
★ lates) immerse you in Continental style and service, that you might imagine yourself transported to your favorite French watering place (complete with the highest prices on the Beach). The boutique-size hotel is blessed with the only beachfront setting among the luxury properties of South Beach, and with astonishing facilities considering its few rooms. Tropical gardens and decks are secluded behind high, iron gates. Inside, the Mimosa Dining Room glows with crystal-reflected mahogany beneath coffered ceilings and walls hung with exquisite reproductions of the past century's masterpieces. The oversize suites, some with private terrace and Jacuzzi, all have king-size beds and immense baths. Each comes with Evian water, hand-painted vases, floral arrangements and robes and slippers for padding about hardwood floors. A separate bath compartment contains toilet and bidet. Continental breakfast is included in the rate. ⊠ *455 Ocean Dr., 33139,* ☎ *305/535–0099 or 800/528–6453,* ⅀ *305/532–4442. 8 suites. Restaurant, indoor and outdoor bars, 2 pools, beach. AE, DC, MC, V.*

$$$$  🏨 **Marlin Hotel.** The Marlin is so Jamaican that it could be the island's
★ cultural showcase. Shabeen, the brilliant bar/café version of a north coast beach shack explodes in color. Jamaican art complements strik-

ing hand-painted furniture, woven grass rugs, batiklike shades, and rattan and mahogany furniture. Every room is different, some with sharp accents of ocher and plum, some with pale sky blue, but all completely detailed. Even the studio suites, with rattan sitting areas, are sizeable; larger suites are like villas. ⊠ *1200 Collins Ave., 33139,* ☎ *305/673–8770,* FAX *305/673–9609. 11 suites. Bar-café. AE, D, DC, MC, V.*

**$$$$** ⊞ **Pelican.** Dazzling, brilliant spaces with Deco-inspired frivolity have turned another tired Ocean Drive home for the elderly into pop-eyed digs for the hip. Rooms, with names like Leafforest, Best Whorehouse, People from the 1950s, and Cubarrean, all have their own special touch. What they have in common are small deco dimensions in the sleeping chambers with bathrooms tripled in size and outfitted with outrageously industrial piping. Best Whorehouse envelops you in thoroughly red flocked wallcoverings flecked with gold, and gilt, black silk, and silver. Ornaments are bordello extravagant: a heart-shape red velvet chair, hideously aqua night tables, whorish art, and griffins with voluptuous mammaries. Each room comes with its own cylindrical entertainment center. The ground floor of this four-story hotel has its own restaurant and sidewalk café. ⊠ *826 Ocean Dr., 33139,* ☎ *305/673–3373 or 800/773–5422,* FAX *305/673–3255. 25 units, penthouse. Restaurant, bar, concierge. AE, MC, V.*

**$$$–$$$$** ✕⊞ **Park Central.** Across the street from the glorious beach, this seven-story Deco hotel—painted blue, with wraparound corner windows—makes all the right moves to stay in the forefront of the Art Deco revival. Most of the fashion models visiting town come to this property, which dates from 1937. Black-and-white photos of old beach scenes, hurricanes, and familiar faces attest to its longevity. Rooms are decorated with Philippine mahogany furnishings—originals that have been restored. Newly incorporated in the property, the Imperial Hotel next door has an additional 36 rooms. The Barocco Beach restaurant of three years ago, which became Le Zebre, has now become Burt Reynolds's Backstage, assuming that if you can't count on trendy Italian or French-Continental, you ought to be able to count on American. ⊠ *640 Ocean Dr., 33139,* ☎ *305/538–1611 or 800/727–5236,* FAX *305/534–7520. 121 rooms. Restaurant, bar, espresso bar, pool, exercise room. AE, DC, MC, V.*

**$$$** ⊞ **Essex House.** This was one of the premier lodgings of the Art Deco era, now painted in cool pastel gray with sulphur-yellow trim. They got it right from the start: designed by architect Henry Hohause and Everglades mural by Earl LaPan. Here are the ziggurat arches, the hieroglyph-style ironwork, etched-glass panels of flamingos under the palms and 5-foot rose-medallion Chinese urns. Hallways have recessed showcases with original Deco sculptures. The 66 rooms from 1938 are now 60, including petite and grand suites. Amenities include designer linens and towels, feather-and-down pillows and sofa rolls, and individually controlled air-conditioning and central heat plus ceiling fans. The rooms are soundproofed from within (otherwise unheard of in beach properties of the 1930s), and rooms to the east have extra-thick windows to reduce the band noise from a nearby hotel. The smallest rooms are yellow and face north. Continental breakfast is included. ⊠ *1001 Collins Ave., 33139,* ☎ *305/534–2700 or 800/553–7739,* FAX *305/532–3827. 51 rooms, 9 suites. Breakfast room. AE, DC, MC, V.*

**$$–$$$** ⊞ **Bay Harbor Inn.** Here you'll find down-home hospitality in the most affluent zip code in the county. Retired Washington lawyer Sandy Lankler operates this 38-unit lodging in two sections and two moods. Townside is the oldest building in Bay Harbor Islands, vaguely Georgian in style but dating from 1940. Behind triple sets of French doors under fan windows, the lobby is full of oak desks, hand mills, grandfather clocks, historical maps, and potted plants. Rooms are antique-filled, and no two are alike. Along Indian Creek the inn incorporates the former Albert Pick Hotella, a shipshape tropical-style set of rooms on two floors, off loggias surrounded by palms, with all rooms facing the water. Rooms are mid-century modern, with chintz. A complimentary Continental breakfast and the *Miami Herald* are provided. The popular Miami Palm restaurant is located townside and B.C. Chong's Seafood Garden creekside, with the London Bar serving the best ½-pound hamburger in the city. ⊠ *9660 E. Bay Harbor Dr., Bay Harbor Islands 33154,* ☎ FAX *305/868–4141. 25 rooms, 12 suites, penthouse. 2 restaurants, lounge, pool. AE, DC, MC, V.*

$$–$$$ ⊞ **Casa Grande.** This was the first of the new top-flight hotels in South
★ Beach, and it's still the best. Luxurious suites capture the fashionable air of the street out front, yet in fine taste. In the lobby, teak, tile, and recessed lighting create a warm look that's welcoming and relaxing. There's nothing showy here, just luxurious space. Corridors are handsome and wide; suites are done in teak and mahogany, with dhurrie rugs and beautiful Indonesian fabrics and artifacts, two-poster beds with ziggurat turns, full electric kitchens equipped with fine European utensils, and large baths—absolutely unheard of in the Deco District—adorned with green decorator tiles. Goodies range from a daily newspaper and in-room coffee service to fresh flowers, complete TV/VCR/CD/radio entertainment stations, and evening turndown with Italian chocolates. Book well in advance for peak periods. ⊠ *834 Ocean Dr., 33139,* ☎ *305/672–7003 or 800/688–7678,* FAX *305/673–3669. 32 suites. Café, laundry service and dry cleaning, concierge. AE, DC, MC, V.*

$$–$$$ ⊞ **Dorchester Hotel.** It's wonderful that such value-oriented, untrendy
★ places remain in the Art Deco District. Here you'll find echoes of an older Miami Beach, the pre-Disney era when all you had to do was offer good lodging and service, and the family trade was yours. This hotel maintains those standards at year-round, affordable rates. Plus, it's set back from the avenue for peace and quiet. A big pool in a tropical garden, a large lobby, and a dining room for inexpensive breakfasts top off the list of reasons to stay here. Guest rooms are spacious and carpeted. The $5 extra for a kitchenette is worth it. ⊠ *1850 Collins Ave., 33139,* ☎ *305/534–6971, 305/531–5745, or 800/327–4739,* FAX *305/673–1006. 94 rooms, 6 suites. Grills, pool, table tennis, billiards, free parking. AE, DC, MC, V.*

$$ ⊞ **Mermaid Guest House.** Part Caribbean hideaway, part Bohemian youth hostel, the place oozes the same kind of exuberance that early on sparked the birth of the Deco District. Everything is framed in color: a back-of-the-house patio set in a jungle waiting to burst loose and retake Miami Beach; dresser drawers, each painted a different, vivid color; and louvered shutters outlined in bold graphics that bring the outdoor garden in. Beds are shrouded in mosquito netting, though rooms have air-conditioning (but not phones or TV), and small deco baths have tub-showers. There's a shared kitchen outside and a pay phone in the garden. A Continental breakfast is included, and frequent BYOB guest cookouts add to the family atmosphere. A youthful and young-at-heart clientele adores this place. ⊠ *909 Collins Ave., 33139,* ☎ *305/538–5324. 10 units. MC, V.*

$$ ✕▦ **Suez Oceanfront Resort.** They call this Miami Beach, and though it is on the beach, it's several miles north of the municipality of Miami Beach, in the section called Sunny Isles—more popularly referred to as Motel Row. This is affordable Miami Beach, chockablock with fancy motels but few of distinction. The carousel-stripe Suez, however, stands out; generous with space, it has been family run since the 1960s. Get past the tacky sphinx icons, walk upstairs in the main building, and you're in a quiet, gardenlike rattan-and-palm lounge. A landscaped palm courtyard leads to the beach, where you find a popular bar and beachside restaurant, two pools, a tennis court, and playground. Rooms are done with matched chinois furniture and dazzling color that counteracts the generally small spaces. The 46 rooms in the north wing are the smallest and the least expensive; they have views of the parking lot. Modified American Plan dining, fridges in all the rooms, and kitchens in some, along with special kids' rates make this an especially good value. Free laundry service is a bonus. ⊠ *18215 Collins Ave., 33160,* ☎ *305/932–0661 or 800/327–5278; in FL, 800/432–3661;* FAX *305/937–0058. 196 rooms. Restaurant, bar, freshwater and saltwater pools, wading pool, lighted tennis court, shuffleboard, volleyball, beach, playground, laundry service. AE, D, DC, MC, V.*

# North Dade

$$$$ ▦ **Turnberry Isle Resort & Club.** Finest of the Miami-area grand resorts,
★ Turnberry sits on 300 superbly landscaped acres by the bay, and it's recently been done over with an $80 million three-wing Mediterranean-style annex. Guests can also choose from the intimate Marina Hotel, the Yacht Club on the Intracoastal Waterway, or the Mizner-style Country Club Hotel, beside one of the two Robert Trent Jones–designed golf courses. Interiors of the oversize rooms have light woods and earth tones, large curving terraces, Jacuzzis, honor bar, and in-room safes. The marina has moorings for 117 boats up to 150 feet, and there's free shuttle service from the hotel to the beach club and the Aventura Mall. ⊠ *19999 W. Country Club Dr., Aventura 33180,* ☎ *305/932–6200 or 800/327–7028,* FAX *305/933–6560. 300 rooms, 40 suites. 6 restaurants, 5 lounges, 4 pools, saunas, spa, steam rooms, 2 18-hole golf courses, 24 tennis courts (18 lighted), health club, jogging, racquetball, beach, dive shop, windsurfing, boating, helipad. AE, DC, MC, V.*

# West Dade

$$$$ ▦ **Don Shula's Hotel & Golf Club.** This low-rise suburban resort is part of Miami Lakes, a planned town developed by Florida senator Bob Graham's family about 14 miles northwest of downtown Miami. The golf resort opened in 1962 and added two wings in 1978; facilities include a championship course, a lighted executive course, and a golf school. Its decor is English-traditional throughout, rich in leather and wood. All rooms have balconies. The hotel opened in 1983 with a typically Florida-tropics look—light pastels and furniture of wicker and light wood. In both locations the best rooms are near the lobby for convenient access; the worst are near the elevators. ⊠ *6840 Main St., Miami Lakes 33014,* ☎ *305/821–1150 or 800/247–4852,* FAX *305/879–8298. 269 rooms, 32 suites. 3 restaurants, 2 lounges, 2 pools, saunas, steam rooms, 2 18-hole golf courses, 9 lighted tennis courts, aerobics, basketball, health club, racquetball, volleyball. AE, D, DC, MC, V.*

**$$$$** ✕🍴 **Doral Golf Resort and Spa.** Millions of airline passengers annually peer down upon this 2,400-acre jewel of an inland golf-and-tennis resort while fastening their seat belts. It's 4 miles west of Miami International Airport and consists of eight separate three- and four-story lodges nestled beside the golf links (four championship and three executive courses). The entire resort has been undergoing a $17 million renovation since 1994, with about half the rooms so far done. Given the resort's division into separate lodges, guests are in no way inconvenienced by the rebuilding, which takes on a lodge at a time. Restaurants have been redesigned, adding Champions Bar & Grill, across from the pro shop, and Terraza, an informal Italian trattoria, as well as a lobby bar. The Provare Restaurant has become the more elegant Windows, specializing in seafood, with views of four golf courses. Outdoors, the famed Blue Monster course has been redesigned, as the remaining courses will be by 1997. The resort is site of the annual Doral-Ryder Open Tournament, one of the most popular on the PGA tour. Transportation to the beach is provided. ⊠ *4400 N.W. 87th Ave., Doral 33178-2192,* ☎ *305/592–2000 or 800/223–6725,* ℻ *305/594–4682. 592 rooms, 102 suites. 4 restaurants, 3 lounges, pool, spa, 7 golf courses, 15 tennis courts (4 lighted), health club, jogging, fishing, bicycles, pro shop. AE, DC, MC, V.*

# NIGHTLIFE AND THE ARTS

For information on what's happening around town, Greater Miami's English-language daily newspaper, the *Miami Herald,* publishes reliable reviews and comprehensive listings in its Weekend section on Friday and in the Lively Arts section on Sunday. Call ahead to confirm details.

If you read Spanish, check *El Nuevo Herald* (a Spanish version of the *Miami Herald*) or *Diario Las Américas* (the area's largest independent Spanish-language paper) for information on the Spanish theater and a smattering of general performing-arts news.

Another good source of information on the performing arts and nightspots is the calendar in *Miami Today,* a free weekly newspaper available each Thursday in downtown Miami, Coconut Grove, and Coral Gables. The best, most complete source is the *New Times,* a free weekly distributed throughout Dade County each Wednesday. Various tabloids reporting on Deco District entertainment and society come and go on Miami Beach. *Wire* reports on the gay community; *Ocean Drive* out-glosses everything else.

The free *Greater Miami Calendar of Events* is published twice a year by the Dade County Cultural Affairs Council (⊠ 111 N.W. 1st St., Suite 625, 33128, ☎ 305/375–4634).

*Guide to the Arts/South Florida* is a pocket-size publication produced 10 times a year ($2 per issue, $15 per year) that covers all the cultural arts in Dade, Broward, and Palm Beach counties and is available from Kage Publications ⊠ *3800 S. Ocean Dr., Hollywood 33019,* ☎ *305/456–9599.*

Real Talk/WTMI (93.1 FM) provides classical concert information on its **Cultural Arts Line** (☎ 305/358–8000, Ext. 9398), as well as on-air reports three times daily at 7:30 AM and 12:50 and 6:30 PM. WLVE (93.9 FM) sponsors an **Entertainment Line** (☎ 305/654–9436) with information on touring groups of all kinds except classical. **Blues Hot Line** (☎ 305/666–6656) lists local blues clubs and bars. **Jazz Hot Line** (☎ 305/382–3938) lists local jazz programs.

# The Arts

Performing-arts aficionados in Greater Miami will tell you they survive quite nicely, despite the area's historic inability to support a county-based professional symphony orchestra. In recent years this community has begun to write a new chapter in its performing-arts history.

The **New World Symphony,** a unique advanced-training orchestra, begins its 10th season in 1997. The Miami City Ballet has risen rapidly to international prominence in its 11-year existence. The Florida Grand Opera ranks among America's largest and best, and a venerable chamber-music series brings renowned ensembles here to perform. Several churches and synagogues run classical-music series with international performers. In theater, Miami offers English-speaking audiences an assortment of professional, collegiate, and amateur productions of musicals, comedy, and drama. Spanish theater also is active. In the cinema world, the Miami Film Festival attracts more than 45,000 people annually to screenings of new films from all over the world—including some made here.

To order tickets for performing-arts events by telephone, call **Ticketmaster** (Dade County, ☎ 305/358–5885; Broward County, 305/523–3309; Palm Beach, 407/839–3900) and charge tickets to a major credit card.

## Dance

**Miami City Ballet.** Under the direction of Edward Villella (who was a principal dancer with the New York City Ballet under George Balanchine), Florida's first major, fully professional, resident ballet company has become a world-class ensemble. Miami City Ballet re-creates the Balanchine repertoire and introduces new works of its own during its September–March season. Performances are held at TOPA in Miami Beach; at the Broward Center for the Performing Arts; Bailey Concert Hall, also in Broward County; the Raymond F. Kravis Center for the Performing Arts; and at the Naples Philharmonic Center for the Arts. Demonstrations of works in progress take place at the 800-seat Lincoln Theater in Miami Beach. Villella narrates the children's and works-in-progress programs. ⊠ *905 Lincoln Rd., Miami Beach 33139,* ☎ *305/532–7713 or 305/532–4880.*

## Film

**Alliance Film/Video Project.** The company presents cutting-edge cinema from around the world, with special midnight shows. ⊠ *Sterling Building, Suite 119, 927 Lincoln Rd. Mall, Miami Beach 33139,* ☎ *305/531–8504.*

**Miami Film Festival.** Screenings of new films from all over the world are held 10 days every February in the Gusman Center for the Performing Arts. ⊠ *444 Brickell Ave., Ste. 229, Miami 33131,* ☎ *305/377–3456.*

## Music

**Concert Association of Florida.** This not-for-profit organization directed by Judith Drucker, is the South's largest presenter of classical artists. ⊠ *555 Hank Meyer Blvd., Miami Beach 33139,* ☎ *305/532–3491.*

**Friends of Chamber Music.** This group presents an annual series of chamber concerts by internationally known guest ensembles, such as the Beaux Arts Trio, the Tokyo Quartet, and the Juilliard String Quartet. ⊠ *44 W. Flagler St., Miami 33130,* ☎ *305/372–2975.*

**Gusman Concert Hall.** This 600-seat concert hall on the University of Miami's campus has good acoustics and plenty of room. Parking is a problem when school is in session. ⊠ *1314 Miller Dr., Coral Gables 33146,* ☎ *305/284–2438.*

**New World Symphony.** Greater Miami has no resident symphony orchestra, and this group, conducted by Michael Tilson Thomas, helps fill the void. Performances are held Oct. –May. Musicians ages 22–30 who have finished their academic studies perform here before moving on to other orchestras. ⊠ *541 Lincoln Rd., Miami Beach 33139,* ☎ *305/673–3331 or 305/673–3330.*

## Opera

**Florida Grand Opera.** South Florida's leading opera company presents five operas each year in the Dade County Auditorium, featuring the Florida Philharmonic Orchestra (James Judd, artistic director). The annual series brings such luminaries as Placido Domingo and Luciano Pavarotti. (Pavarotti made his American debut with the company in 1965 in *Lucia di Lammermoor.*) All operas are sung in the original language, with subtitles in English projected onto a screen above the stage. The box office is open weekdays 10–4. ⊠ *1200 Coral Way, Miami 33145,* ☎ *305/854–7890.*

## Performing-Arts Centers

**Colony Theater.** What was once a movie theater has become a 465-seat, city-owned performing-arts center featuring dance, drama, music, and experimental cinema. ⊠ *1040 Lincoln Rd., Miami Beach 33139,* ☎ *305/674–1026.*

**Dade County Auditorium.** This venue satisfies patrons with 2,498 comfortable seats, good sight lines, and acceptable acoustics. Opera, concerts, and touring musicals are usually on the schedule. ⊠ *2901 W. Flagler St., Miami 33135,* ☎ *305/545–3395.*

**Gusman Center for the Performing Arts.** This downtown Miami landmark has 1,739 seats seemingly made for sardines—and the best acoustics in town. Concerts, ballet, and touring stage productions are seen here. An ornate former movie palace, the hall resembles a Moorish courtyard. Lights twinkle, starlike, from the ceiling. ⊠ *174 E. Flagler St., Miami 33131,* ☎ *305/372–0925.*

**Jackie Gleason Theater of the Performing Arts (TOPA).** After years of botched repair jobs, the theater has finally brought its acoustics and visibility up to par for all 2,750 seats. The Broadway Series each year presents five or six major productions (or other performances). ⊠ *1700 Washington Ave., Miami Beach 33139,* ☎ *305/673–7300; box office,* ⊠ *505 17th St., Miami Beach 33139,* ☎ *305/673–8300.*

## Theater

**Acapai.** The name stands for African Caribbean American Performing Artists, Inc. The company mounts productions year-round at various area stages. ⊠ *6161 N.W. 22nd Ave., Miami 33142,* ☎ *305/758–3534.*

**Acme Acting Company.** This innovative company presents thought-provoking, on-the-edge theater by new playwrights in its winter and summer seasons. ⊠ *955 Alton Rd., Miami Beach 33139,* ☎ *305/372–9077.*

**Actor's Playhouse.** This ten-year-old professional Equity company moved into the renovated Miracle Theater but still presents adults' and children's productions year-round. ⊠ *280 Miracle Mile, Coral Gables 33134,* ☎ *305/444–9293.*

**Area Stage.** This company performs provocative off-Broadway-style productions throughout the year. ⊠ *645 Lincoln Rd., Miami Beach 33139,* ☎ *305/673–8002.*

**Coconut Grove Playhouse.** This Grove fixture stages tried-and-true Broadway plays and musicals as well as experimental productions in its main theater and cabaret-style Encore Room. ⊠ *3500 Main Hwy., Coconut Grove 33133,* ☎ *305/442–4000 or 305/442–2662.* ⌘ *Parking $2 day, $4 evening.*

**Florida Shakespeare Festival.** Classic and contemporary theater is on the bill, with one Shakespeare production a year at the 200-seat **Carrusel Theater.** ⊠ *2304 Salzedo Ave., Coral Gables 33134,* ☎ *305/446–1116.*

**Gold Coast Mime Company.** The company performs October through June in the studios of the Miami City Ballet ⊠ *905 Lincoln Rd., Miami Beach 33139,* ☎ *305/538–5500.*

**New Theatre.** This is a showcase for contemporary and classical plays. ⊠ *65 Almeria St., Coral Gables 33134,* ☎ *305/443–5909.*

**Ring Theater.** Located on the campus of the University of Miami is this 311-seat hall of UM's Department of Theatre Arts, where eight plays a year are performed. ⊠ *1380 Miller Dr., Coral Gables 33146,* ☎ *305/284–3355.*

SPANISH THEATER

Spanish theater prospers, although many companies have short lives. About 20 Spanish companies perform light comedy, puppetry, vaudeville, and political satire. To locate them, read the Spanish newspapers. When you call, be prepared for a conversation in Spanish—few box-office personnel speak English.

**Prometeo.** Now in its 24th year, this company produces major plays and holds many workshop productions. Admission is free. ⊠ *Miami-Dade Community College, New World Center Campus, 300 N.E. 2nd Ave., Miami 33132,* ☎ *305/237–3263.*

**Teatro de Bellas Artes.** This 255-seat theater on Calle Ocho, Little Havana's main commercial street, presents eight Spanish plays and musicals year-round. ⊠ *2173 S.W. 8th St., Miami 33135,* ☎ *305/325–0515.*

# Nightlife

## Bars and Lounges

COCONUT GROVE

**Hungry Sailor** (⊠ 3064½ Grand Ave., ☎ 305/444–9359), with two bars, serves Jamaican-English food, British beer, and music Wednesday to Saturday. **Taurus Steak House** (⊠ 3540 Main Hwy., ☎ 305/448–0633) is an unchanging oasis in the trendy Grove. The bar, built in 1922 of native cypress, draws an over-30 singles crowd nightly that drifts outside to a patio. A band plays Wednesday through Saturday.

CORAL GABLES

In a building that dates from 1926, **Stuart's Bar-Lounge** (162 Alcazar Ave., ☎ 305/444–1666) was named one of the best new bars of 1987 by *Esquire*; 10 years later, locals still favor it. The style is fostered by beveled mirrors, mahogany paneling, French posters, pictures of old Coral Gables, and art-nouveau lighting. Stuart's is closed Sunday.

MIAMI

**Tobacco Road** (⊠ 626 S. Miami Ave., ☎ 305/374–1198), opened in 1912, holds Miami's oldest liquor license. Upstairs, in space occupied by a speakeasy during Prohibition, local and national blues bands perform nightly. There's excellent bar food and a dinner menu.

MIAMI BEACH

**Bash** (⊠ 655 Washington Ave., ☎ 305/538–2274) has bars inside and out and dance floors with music—sometimes reggae, sometimes Latin, plenty of loud disco, and world-beat sounds in the garden, where there are artsy benches. Inside it's grotto like. **Blue Steel** (⊠ 2895 Collins Ave., ☎ 305/672–1227) is a cool but unpretentious hangout with pool tables, darts, live music, comfy old sofas, and beer paraphernalia. Open-mike night is Friday, and there's a jam on Monday. **Mac's Club Deuce** (⊠ 222 14th St., ☎ 305/673–9537) is a South Beach gem where top international models pop in to have a drink and shoot some pool. All you get late at night are mini-pizzas, but the pizazz lasts long. In a nondescript motel row with nudie bars, baby stores, and bait-and-tackle shops **Molly Malone's** (⊠ 166 Sunny Isles Blvd., ☎ 305/948–9143) is the only cool, down-to-earth spot that thrives in this neighborhood. The Irish pub, a big local fave, has live Irish music Friday, acoustic sounds Saturday, and poetry readings Thursday. **Rose's Bar & Lounge** (⊠ 754 Washington Ave., ☎ 305/532–0228) has the best in local bands from Hendrix-style rock and rap/funk to jazz jams and Afro-Cuban/world beat, with the occasional national act. Though it doesn't take credit cards, there is an ATM. It's open seven nights, but it's packed Wednesday through Saturday. **Shabeen Cookshack and Bar** (⊠ 1200 Collins Ave., ☎ 305/673–8770) in SoBe's Marlin Hotel is Jamaican all the way with brilliant island decor and upbeat Caribbean music. **Union Bar** (⊠ 653 Washington Ave., ☎ 305/672–9958) has progressive/alternative music complete with pool table, informal dining area, strobe lighting, an unusual bubble fish tank in back-to-back rooms, and an immense dog sculpture all on a bare concrete floor.

## Discos and Rock Clubs

COCONUT GROVE

**Baja Beach Club** (⊠ 3015 Grand Ave., ☎ 305/445–0278), the number-one party place in CocoWalk and the number-one shopping place in the Grove, has waiters and waitresses dressed in beach attire.

KEY BISCAYNE

**Stefano's of Key Biscayne** (⊠ 24 Crandon Blvd., ☎ 305/361–7007) is a northern Italian restaurant with disco; the music's live Tuesday through Sunday.

MIAMI BEACH

**Amnesia** (⊠ 136 Collins Ave., ☎ 305/531–5535) feels like a luxurious amphitheater in the tropics, complete with rain forest, what used to be called go-go dancers, and frenzied dancing in the rain when showers pass over the open-air ground-level club. The full-service Portobello restaurant, on an upper level, has picture windows for taking in the scene without the decibels. Amnesia is closed Monday–Wednesday. **Bermuda Bar & Grille** (⊠ 3509 N.E. 163rd St., ☎ 305/945–0196) plays LOUD MUSIC for disco dancing. Male bartenders wear knee-length kilts with female bartenders in matching minis. The atmosphere and crowd though, are stylish island casual, and there's a big tropical forest scene, booths you can hide in, and six bars and pool tables. One drawback is there's no draft brew. Bermuda Bar & Grille is closed Monday. **Glam Slam** (⊠ 1235 Washington Ave., ☎ 305/672–4858), open Wednesday–Sunday, is where Club Z, 1235, and Paragon all hit the heights of fashion before falling out of favor. The artist formerly known as Prince has dressed the place up by parking his motorcycle from *Purple Rain* in the foyer, and creating a secret passage for his celeb pals.

Theme nights include Southern Fried Soul, Glamour Girls, Gay Night, and Saturday's wild, packed Disco Party Time. **Ruby's** (⊠ 300 Alton Rd., Miami Beach Marina, ☎ 305/673–3444), not quite hip but still yearning to be seen, is for that denim-shirt-and-tie-wearing yuppy crowd. The ritzy disco is filled with overstuffed seating, wall-to-wall tropical-print carpeting, and a fortune in audiovisual gear. The club is open Thursday–Sunday.

### Jazz Club

MIAMI BEACH

**MoJazz Cafe** (⊠ 928 71st St., ☎ 305/865–2636) arrived on the scene in 1993 with its easy neighborhood style, combining a local café with real (nonfusion) jazz. It's in the Normandy Isle section—a long over-looked neighborhood just right for hosting the occasional national name, like Mose Allison, and local talents like Ira Sullivan, Little Nicky, Joe Donato worthy of national attention. Highlights include a nightly happy hour, food from the country kitchen, and late-night breakfast.

### Nightclubs

MIAMI

**Les Violins Supper Club** (⊠ 1751 Biscayne Blvd., ☎ 305/371–8668) is a reliable standby owned for 35 years by the Cachaidora-Currais family, who ran a club and restaurant in Havana. There's a live dance band and a wooden dance floor. The cover charge is $15, and reservations are essential.

MIAMI BEACH

**Club Tropigala at La Ronde** (⊠ 4441 Collins Ave., ☎ 305/672–7469)—lately discovered by such stars as Sylvester Stallone, Madonna, and Elton John, this nightclub in the Fountainebleau Hilton is a four-tier round room decorated to create the effect of a tropical jungle with orchids, banana leaves, philodendrons, and cascading waterfalls. The band plays standards as well as Latin music for dancing on the wooden floor. Reservations are essential.

# OUTDOOR ACTIVITIES AND SPORTS

### Auto Racing

**Hialeah Speedway.** The Greater Miami area's only independent race-way holds stock-car races on a ⅓-mile asphalt oval in a 5,000-seat stadium. Five divisions of stock cars run weekly. The Marion Edwards, Jr., Memorial Race for late-model stock cars is held in November. The speedway is on U.S. 27, ¼ mile east of the Palmetto Expressway (Rte. 826). ⊠ *3300 W. Okeechobee Rd., Hialeah, ☎ 305/821–6644. ☞ $10, special events $12. ☉ Late Jan.–early Dec., Sat.; gates open at 5, racing 7–11.*

**The Toyota Grand Prix of Miami.** This race is typically held in February or March on a 1.9-mile, E-shaped track in downtown Miami, south of MacArthur Causeway and east of Biscayne Boulevard. Drivers race for three hours; the driver completing the most laps wins. Contact Miami Motor Sports, Inc. ⊠ *1110 Brickell Ave., Suite 206, Miami 33131, ☎ 305/379–5660 or 305/379–7223.*

### Baseball

The **Florida Marlins** (⊠ 100 N.E. 3rd Ave., Fort Lauderdale 33301, ☎ 305/626–7400) begin their fifth season in 1997 in the Eastern Division of the National League. Home games are played at Joe Robbie Stadium—also home to the Miami Dolphins (☞ Football, *below*)—which is 16 miles northwest of downtown Miami. On game days the Metro-Dade Transit Agency runs buses to the stadium.

## Basketball

The **Miami Heat** (⊠ Miami Arena, 701 Arena Blvd., 33136-4102, ☎ 305/577–4328), Miami's National Basketball Association franchise, plays home games November–April at the Miami Arena, a block east of Overtown Metrorail Station.

## Biking

A color-coded map outlining Dade's 4,000 miles of roads suitable for bike travel is available for $3.50 from area bike shops and from the **Dade County Bicycle Coordinator** (⊠ Metropolitan Planning Organization, 111 N.W. 1st St., Suite 910, 33128, ☎ 305/375–4507). For information on dozens of monthly group rides contact the **Everglades Bicycle Club** (⊠ Box 430282, South Miami 33243-0282, ☎ 305/598–3998). Among the best shops for renting bicycles are **Dade Cycle** (⊠ 3216 Grand Ave., Coconut Grove, ☎ 305/444–5997 or 305/443–6075) and **Gary's Megacycle On the Beach** (⊠ 1260 Washington Ave., Miami Beach, ☎ 305/534–3306).

## Boating

**Crandon Park Marina.** This popular marina sells bait and tackle. ⊠ *4000 Crandon Blvd., Key Biscayne,* ☎ *305/361–1281.* ⊙ *Office 7–6.*

**Dinner Key Marina.** This marina has dockage with space for transients and a boat ramp. ⊠ *3400 Pan American Dr., Coconut Grove,* ☎ *305/579–6980.* ⊙ *Daily 7 AM–midnight.*

**Haulover Marine Center.** This marina is low on glamour but high on service. It offers a bait-and-tackle shop, marine gas station, and boat launch. ⊠ *10800 Collins Ave., Miami Beach,* ☎ *305/945–3934.* ⊙ *Weekdays 9–5, bait shop and gas station.*

**Miami Beach Marina.** This waterfront mecca is now the "happening" marina with restaurants, charters, boat and vehicle rentals, a complete marine hardware store, dive shop, large grocery store, fuel dock, concierge services, and 400 boat slips accommodating vessels up to 190 feet. New, too, is the Thursday evening Art al Fresco, a sunset celebration with original art, crafts, and music, plus free admission and parking. Facilities include air-conditioned restrooms, washers and dryers, U.S. Customs clearing, and a heated swimming pool. This is the nearest marina to the Deco District, about a 15-minute walk away. ⊠ *300 Alton Rd., Miami Beach,* ☎ *305/673–6000.* ⊙ *Daily 8–6.*

**Watson Island Marina.** This operation will probably become a mega-yacht marina with a boutique hotel before the end of the decade, while maybe keeping a few charter and dive boats operating out of a facility dilapidated from official neglect. Chalk's International Airlines will likely remain, and a new heliport could be added. A potential botanical garden may include a refurbished Japanese Garden. Currently 10 slips are available. ⊠ *1050 MacArthur Causeway, Miami,* ☎ *305/579–6955.* ⊙ *Call for hours.*

## Diving

**Bubbles Dive Center.** This is an all-purpose dive shop with PADI affiliation. Its boat, *Divers Dream,* is kept on Watson Island on MacArthur Causeway. ⊠ *2671 S.W. 27th Ave., Miami,* ☎ *305/856–0565.* ⊙ *Weekdays 10–7, Sat. 9–6.*

**Divers Paradise of Key Biscayne.** This site has a complete dive shop and diving-charter service, including equipment rental and scuba instruction, with PADI affiliation. ⊠ *4000 Crandon Blvd., Key Biscayne,* ☎ *305/361–3483.* ⊙ *Weekdays 10–6, weekends 7:30–6.*

**The Diving Locker.** This 25-year-old, PADI-affiliated dive shop offers three-day and three-week Professional Diving Instructors Corporation certification courses, wreck and reef dives aboard *The Native Diver*, and full sales, service, and repairs. ⊠ *223 Sunny Isles Blvd., North Miami Beach,* ☎ *305/947–6025.* ⊙ *Weekdays 9–9:30, Sat. 8–9:30, Sun. 8–6.*

**Team Divers.** This PADI five-star facility is located in the Miami Beach marina (☞ Boating, *above*). It's the only dive shop in the South Beach area. Daily dives are arranged. ⊠ *300 Alton Rd.,* ☎ *305/673–0101 or 800/543–7887.* ⊙ *Oct.–Mar., weekdays 10–7, weekends 9–6; Apr.–Sept., weekdays 10–7, weekends 7:30–6.*

## Dog Racing

The Biscayne and Flagler greyhound tracks divide the annual racing calendar. Check with the individual tracks for dates.

**Biscayne Greyhound Track.** Here greyhounds chase a mechanical rabbit around illuminated fountains in the track's infield. ⊠ *320 N.W. 115th St., near I–95, Miami Shores,* ☎ *305/754–3484.* ☜ *table seats and grandstand $1, sports room $2, clubhouse $3, parking 50¢–$2.*

**Flagler Greyhound Track.** Located in the middle of Little Havana, this track is five minutes east of Miami International Airport off the Dolphin Expressway (Rte. 836) and Douglas Road (N.W. 37th Ave. and 7th St). ⊠ *401 N.W. 38th Ct., Miami,* ☎ *305/649–3000.* ☜ *$1, clubhouse $3, parking 50¢–$2.*

## Fishing

A few ocean fishing-charter operators sailing out of various parts of town are: **Abracadabra** (⊠ 4000 Crandon Blvd., Key Biscayne, ☎ 305/361–5625), **Blue Waters Sportfishing Charters** (⊠ 16375 Collins Ave., Sunny Isles, ☎ 305/944–4531), **Therapy IV** (⊠ Haulover Marine Center, 10800 Collins Ave., Miami Beach, ☎ 305/945–1578), and **Reward II** (⊠ Miami Beach Marina, 300 Alton Rd., MacArthur Causeway, Miami Beach, ☎ 305/372–9470).

## Football

The **Miami Dolphins** of the National Football League play at state-of-the-art Joe Robbie Stadium—JRS, as the fans call it—which has 73,000 seats and a grass playing-field surface with built-in drainage under the sod to carry off rainwater. It's on a 160-acre site 16 miles northwest of downtown Miami, 1 mile south of the Dade–Broward county line, accessible from I–95 and Florida's Turnpike. On game days the Metro-Dade Transit Agency (☎ 305/638–6700) runs buses to the stadium. ⊠ *Joe Robbie Stadium, 2269 N.W. 199th St., Miami 33056,* ☎ *305/620–2578.* ⊙ *Box office weekdays 10–6, also Sat. during season.*

The **University of Miami Hurricanes** (⊠ 1 Hurricane Dr., Coral Gables 33146, ☎ 305/284–2655), perennial contenders for top collegiate ranking, will be playing their 1997 home games at Joe Robbie Stadium (☞ *above*), after calling the venerable Orange Bowl their home for many years, from September through November.

## Golf

For information on Miami's private and public golf courses contact the appropriate parks-and-recreation department: City of Miami (☎ 305/575–5256), City of Miami Beach (☎ 305/673–7730), or Metro-Dade County (☎ 305/857–6868). Some 18-hole courses open to the public include: Biltmore Golf Course (⊠ 1210 Anastasia Ave., Coral Gables, ☎ 305/460–5364), Don Shula's Hotel & Golf Club (⊠ 7601 Miami Lakes Dr., Miami Lakes, ☎ 305/821–1150), Doral Golf Resort and Spa (⊠ 4400 N.W. 87th Ave., Doral, ☎ 305/592–2000 or 800/713–6725), Links at Key Biscayne (⊠ 6700 Crandon Blvd., Key Biscayne, ☎ 305/361–9129), Normandy Shores Golf Course (⊠ 2401 Biarritz Dr., Miami Beach, ☎ 305/868–6502), Presidential Country Club (⊠ 19650 N.E. 18th Ave., North Miami Beach, ☎ 305/933–5266), Williams Island California Club (⊠ 20898 San Simeon Way, North Miami Beach, ☎ 305/651–3590).

## Horse Racing

**Calder Race Course,** opened in 1971, is Florida's largest glass-enclosed, air-conditioned sports facility. Calder often has an unusually extended season, from late May to early Jan., though it's a good idea to call the track for specific starting and wrap-up dates. **Calder and Hialeah Park** (☞ *below*) rotate their race dates, so be sure to check with each park to see where the horses are running. Each year between November and early January, Calder holds the **Tropical Park Derby** for three-year-olds. The track is on the Dade–Broward county line near I–95 and the Hallandale Beach Boulevard exit, ¾ mile from Joe Robbie Stadium. ⊠ *21001 N.W. 27th Ave., Miami,* ☎ *305/625–1311.* ☞ *$2, clubhouse $4, parking $1–$3; gates open at 11, racing 1–5:30.*

A superb setting for thoroughbred racing, **Hialeah Park** has 228 acres of meticulously landscaped grounds surrounding paddocks, and a clubhouse built in a classic French-Mediterranean style. Since it opened in 1925, Hialeah Park has survived hurricanes and now seems likely to survive even changing demographics, as the racetrack crowd has steadily moved north and east. Although Hialeah tends to get the less prestigious racing dates from Mar.–May, it still draws crowds. The park is open year-round for free sightseeing, during which you can explore the gardens and admire the park's breeding flock of 800 Cuban flamingos. Metrorail's Hialeah Station is on the grounds. ⊠ *2200 E. 4th Ave., Hialeah,* ☎ *305/885–8000.* ☞ *Weekdays grandstand $1, clubhouse $2; weekends grandstand $4 clubhouse $4; parking $1–$4.* ⊘ *Gates open at 10:30, racing 1–5:30.*

## Ice Hockey

The **Florida Panthers** made the playoffs in their inaugural season in the National Hockey League. They play their fifth season in 1997–98 at the Miami Arena, one block east of Overtown Metrorail Station. ⊠ *Miami Arena, 701 Arena Blvd., Miami 33136-4102,* ☎ *305/577–4328.*

## Jai Alai

Built in 1926, the **Miami Jai-Alai Fronton,** a mile east of the airport, is the oldest fronton in America. Each evening it presents 13 games—14 on Friday and Saturday—some singles, some doubles. This game, invented in the Basque region of northern Spain, is the world's fastest. Jai-alai balls, called *pelotas,* have been clocked at speeds exceeding 170 mph. The game is played in a 176-foot-long court called a fronton. Players climb the walls to catch the ball in a *cesta*—a woven basket—with an attached glove. You can bet on a team to win or on the order in which teams will finish. Dinner is available. ⊠ *3500 N.W. 37th Ave., Miami,* ☎ *305/633–6400.* ☞ *$1, reserved seats $3, Courtview Club $5.* ⊘ *Mon., Wed., Fri., and Sat. noon–5 and 7–midnight; Tues., Thurs., and Sun. 7–midnight.*

## Jogging

Try these recommended jogging routes: in Coconut Grove, along the pedestrian/bicycle path on South Bayshore Drive, cutting over the causeway to Key Biscayne for a longer run; from the south shore of the Miami River, downtown, south along the sidewalks of Brickell Avenue to Bayshore Drive, where you can run alongside the bay; in Miami Beach, along Bay Road (parallel to Alton Road); and in Coral Gables, around the Riviera Country Club golf course, just south of the Biltmore Country Club. Two good sources of running information are the **Miami Runners Club** (⌧ 7900 S.W. 40th St., Miami, ☎ 305/227–1500) and **Foot Works** (⌧ 5724 Sunset Dr., South Miami, ☎ 305/667–9322), a running-shoe store.

## Sailing

**Easy Sailing.** This sailing center offers a fleet ranging from 19 to 127 feet for rent by the hour or the day. Services include sailboat lessons, scuba-diving lessons and certification, and on-board catering. Reservations and an advance deposit are essential. ⌧ *Dinner Key Marina, 3360 Pan American Dr., Coconut Grove,* ☎ *305/858–4001.* ☉ *Daily 9–sunset.*

## Tennis

Greater Miami has more than 60 tennis centers, of which more than a dozen are open to the public. All public tennis courts charge nonresidents an hourly fee. A sampling around the county includes:

**Biltmore Tennis Center.** This facility has 10 hard courts. ⌧ *1150 Anastasia Ave., Coral Gables,* ☎ *305/460–5360.* ▤ *Nonresident day rate $4.30, night rate $5 per person per hour* ☉ *Weekdays 8 AM–9 PM, weekends 8–8.*

**Flamingo Tennis Center.** Very popular with the locals, this facility has 19 clay courts. ⌧ *1000 12th St., Miami Beach,* ☎ *305/673–7761.* ▤ *Day rate $2.67, night rate $3.20 per person per hour.* ☉ *Weekdays 8 AM–9 PM, weekends 8–7.*

**Lipton Championships.** A 10-day spring tournament at the 64-acre Tennis Center at Crandon Park, this tournament is one of the largest in the world in terms of attendance, and, with $4.1 million in prize money in 1996, was fifth largest in purse. It's played in a new permanent stadium that seats 7,500 for big events. ⌧ *7300 Crandon Blvd., Key Biscayne,* ☎ *305/442–3367.*

**North Shore Tennis Center**. This park has 6 clay and 5 hard courts. ⌧ *350 73rd St., Miami Beach,* ☎ *305/993–2022.* ▤ *Day rate $2.66, night rate $3.20 per person per hour.* ☉ *Weekdays 8 AM–9 PM, weekends 8–7.*

**Tennis Center at Crandon Park.** This new $18 million facility is one of America's best. It's best known as the site of the annual Lipton Championships held each March (the only time when the courts are off-limits to the public). Included are two grass, eight clay, and 17 hard courts. Reservations required for night play. ⌧ *7300 Crandon Blvd., Key Biscayne,* ☎ *305/365–2300.* ▤ *Laykold courts day rate $2, night rate $3 per person per hour; clay courts $4 per person per hour.* ☉ *Daily 8 AM–10 PM.*

## Windsurfing

The safest and most popular windsurfing area in city waters is south of town at Hobie Island and Virginia Key on Key Biscayne. The best windsurfing on Miami Beach is at 1st Street, just north of the Government Cut jetty, and at 21st Street. You can also windsurf at Lummus Park at 10th Street and in the vicinity of 3rd, 14th, and 21st streets. Lifeguards discourage windsurfing from 79th to 87th streets.

**Sailboards Miami.** This sailboard shop on Hobie Island, just past the tollbooth for the Rickenbacker Causeway to Key Biscayne, rents windsurfing equipment. ⊠ *Key Biscayne,* ☎ *305/361–7245.* 🎫 *1 hour $17, 10 hours $95, 2-hour lesson $39.* ☉ *Daily 10–5:30.*

# SHOPPING

## Malls

**Aventura Mall** (⊠ 19501 Biscayne Blvd., Aventura ☎ 305/935–1110), in a northern suburb that became Dade's 28th municipality in 1995, has more than 200 shops anchored by Macy's, Lord & Taylor, JCPenney, and Sears. **Bal Harbour Shops** (⊠ 9700 Collins Ave., Bal Harbour ☉ Weekdays10–6; stores open until 9 on Mon., Thurs., and Fri.; Sun. 11–6) in a tropical garden setting, is a swank collection of 100 shops and boutiques such as Chanel, Gucci, Cartier, Nina Ricci, Fendi, Bruno Magli, Neiman Marcus, and Florida's largest Saks Fifth Avenue. Free buses run twice a day Monday–Saturday from several hotels in Coconut Grove, downtown Miami, and Miami Beach. The shops are open Monday, Thursday, Friday, and Saturday 10–9; Tuesday and Wednesday 10–6; and Sunday 11–6. **Bayside Marketplace** (⊠ 401 Biscayne Blvd., ☎ 305/577–3344), the 16-acre shopping complex on Biscayne Bay, has 150 specialty shops, entertainment, tour-boat docks, and a food court. It's open late (10 during the week, 11 on Friday and Saturday), but its restaurants stay open even later. A complex of clapboard, coral-rock, and stucco buildings, **Cauley Square** (⊠ 22400 Old Dixie Hwy., Goulds) was erected in 1907–20 for railroad workers who built and maintained the line to Key West. Saunter in and out of crafts, antiques, and clothing shops. **CocoWalk** (⊠ 3015 Grand Ave., Coconut Grove ☎ 305/441–0777, FAX 305/441–8936) has three floors of nearly 40 specialty shops (Victoria's Secret, the Gap, Banana Republic, among others), that stay open almost as late as the popular restaurants and clubs. A 16-screen AMC Theatre is also here. The oldest retail mall in the county but always upgrading, **Dadeland** (⊠ 7535 N. Kendall Dr., ☎ 305/665–6226) sits at the south side of town close to the Dadeland North and Dadeland South Metrorail stations. Retailers include Florida's largest Burdines, Saks Fifth Avenue, JCPenney, Lord & Taylor, and more than 175 specialty stores plus 17 restaurants. **The Falls** (⊠ 8888 S.W. 136th St., ☎ 305/255–4570), which derives its name from the several waterfalls inside, is the most upscale mall on the south side of the city. It contains Miami's only Bloomingdale's and Macy's, as well as another 50 specialty stores, restaurants, and a 12-theater multiplex. **Omni International Mall** (⊠ 1601 Biscayne Blvd.), rises vertically alongside the atrium of the Crowne Plaza Miami, where the eye-popping feature is an old-fashioned carousel. Among the 85 shops are a JCPenney, many restaurants, and 10 movie screens. The shortest and most elegant shopping arcade in the metropolis, the **Shops at 550** (⊠ 550 Biltmore Way, Coral Gables) is in the marble halls of the Aztec-like 550 Building. Shops include Stones of Venice (☞ *below*) and Allure couture.

## Outdoor Markets

**Coconut Grove Farmers Market** (⊠ Grand Ave., 1 block west of MacDonald Ave. [S.W. 32nd Ave.], Coconut Grove), open Saturday 8–2, originated in 1977 and was the first in the Miami area. At the **Farmers Market at Merrick Park** (⊠ LeJeune Rd. [S.W. 42nd Ave] and Biltmore Way, Coral Gables) some 25 produce and plant vendors sell their wares during high season. Gardening workshops, cooking demonstrations, and children's activities are standard features. **Lincoln Road Farmers Market** (⊠ Lincoln Rd. between Meridian and Euclid Aves., Miami Beach, open Sundays November–March), brings some 15 local produce vendors coupled with plant workshops and children's activities. Every weekend since 1984, more than 500 vendors sell a variety of goods at the **Flagler Dog Track** (⊠ 401 N.W. 38th Ct., Miami) from 9 to 4.

## Shopping Districts

There are 500 garment manufacturers in Miami and Hialeah, and many sell their clothing locally in the **Miami Fashion District** (⊠ 5th Ave. east of I–95, between 25th and 29th Sts.), making Greater Miami the fashion marketplace for the southeastern United States, the Caribbean, and Latin America. Most of the more than 30 factory outlets and discount fashion stores are open Monday–Saturday 9–5. The **Miami International Arts & Design District** (☞ Little Haiti, *above*), also known as 40th Street, is full of showrooms and galleries specializing in interior furnishings and decorative arts. **Miracle Mile** (⊠ Coral Way between 37th and 42nd Aves., Coral Gables) consists of some 160 shops along a wide, tree-lined boulevard. Shops range from posh boutiques to bargain basements, from beauty salons to chain restaurants. As you go west, the quality increases.

## Specialty Shops

### ANTIQUES

**Alhambra Antiques Center** (⊠ 3640 Coral Way, Coral Gables ☎ 305/446–1688) is a collection of four antiques dealers that sell high-quality decorative pieces from Europe. The center is open weekdays noon–6.

### BOOKS

Greater Miami's best English-language bookstore, **Books & Books, Inc** (⊠ 296 Aragon Ave., Coral Gables, ☎ 305/442–4408; ⊠ Sterling Bldg., 933 Lincoln Rd., Miami Beach, ☎ 305/532–3222) specializes in books on the arts, architecture, Florida, and contemporary and classical literature. Collectors enjoy browsing through the rare-book room upstairs, which doubles as a photography gallery. There are frequent poetry readings and book signings.

### CHILDREN'S BOOKS AND TOYS

**A Kid's Book Shoppe** (⊠ 1895 N.E. Miami Gardens Dr., Skylake Center, North Miami Beach, ☎ 305/937–2665), an excellent children's book resource, has been at this location since 1984. **A Likely Story** (⊠ 5740 Sunset Dr., South Miami, ☎ 305/667–3730) has been helping Miamians choose books and educational toys appropriate to children's interests and stages of development since 1978.

### CLOTHING

**Allure** (⊠ 550 Biltmore Way, Coral Gables, ☎ 305/448–6163) sells colorful, trendy crafts items. **Ninth Street Bizaare** (⊠ 900 Ocean Dr., Miami Beach, ☎ 305/534–2254) is a trendy South Beach minimart with vendors selling clothing and accessories from around the world.

### DECORATIVE AND GIFT ITEMS

**American Details** (⊠ 3107 Grand Ave., Coconut Grove, ☎ 305/448–6163) sells colorful, trendy arts and crafts handmade by American artists. Jewelry and handblown glass are popular sellers. The **Indies Company** (⊠ 101 W. Flagler St., Miami, ☎ 305/375–1492), the Historical Museum of Southern Florida's gift shop offers interesting artifacts reflecting Miami's history, including some inexpensive reproductions.

### JEWELRY

**Stones of Venice** (⊠ 550 Biltmore Way, Coral Gables, ☎ 305/444–4474), operated by a three-time winner of the DeBeers Diamond Award for jewelry, sells affordable creations. Customers have included

Orange juice concession, Florida
Photo © 1990 Peter Guttman,
author of *Fodor's Nights to Imagine*

Elliott Gould, Pope John Paul II, and film director Barbet Schroeder, among others.

# MIAMI A TO Z

## Arriving and Departing

### By Boat

If you're entering the United States along Florida's Atlantic Coast south of Sebastian Inlet, you must call the **U.S. Customs Service** (☎ 800/432–1216). Customs clears by phone most boats of less than 5 tons, but you may be directed for further inspection to one or another marina.

### By Bus

**Greyhound** (☎ 800/231–2222) buses stop at five bus terminals in Greater Miami (✉ 700 Biscayne Blvd., Miami; 4111 N.W. 27th St., Miami; 16250 Biscayne Blvd., North Miami; 7101 Harding Ave., Miami Beach; 5 N.E. 3rd Rd., Homestead). There are no reservations.

### By Car

The main highways into Greater Miami from the north are Florida's Turnpike (a toll road) and I–95. From the northwest take I–75 or U.S. 27 into town. From the Everglades to the west, use I–75 or the Tamiami Trail (U.S. 41), and from the south use U.S. 1 and the Homestead Extension of Florida's Turnpike. Continuous reconstruction of I–95 forever slows traffic at one place or another in South Florida. A $400 million, 46-mile widening project between Miami and West Palm Beach was completed in 1995, and the huge plate of spaghetti known as the Golden Glades interchange, north of downtown, which carries between 300,000 and 400,000 vehicles a day, has a new nine-story-high, $32 million car-pool overpass. On the flip side, a three- to four-year repaving project will keep I–95 from operating at peak capacity through most of the decade. The new Brickell Avenue Bridge, from the south into downtown, opened in 1996; meanwhile, drivers must cross the Miami River on the Miami Avenue twin bridges, across I–95, or on the S.W. 3rd Avenue Bridge. On the other hand, driving across the newly widened MacArthur Causeway, which connects downtown with Miami Beach, has become easier, thanks to a new high-rise span that eliminates frequent openings for boat traffic.

### By Plane

**Miami International Airport (MIA),** 6 miles west of downtown Miami, is Greater Miami's only commercial airport. With a daily average of 1,450 flights, it handled 30.2 million passengers in 1994, 43% of them international travelers. (It's also the nation's busiest airport for air cargo.) Altogether 149 airlines serve 188 cities around the world with nonstop or one-stop service. MIA has 118 aircraft gates and eight concourses; the newest, Concourse A, opened in late spring of 1995.

Anticipating continued growth, the airport has begun a more than $3 billion expansion program that will require much of the decade to complete. Passengers will mainly notice rebuilt and expanded gate and public areas, which should reduce congestion.

A greatly underused convenience for passengers who have to get from one concourse to another in this long, horseshoe-shape terminal is the Moving Walkway, on the skywalk level, with access points at every concourse. Also available on site is the 263-room **Miami International Airport Hotel** (Concourse E, upper level, ☎ 305/871–4100), which has the Top of the Port restaurant on the seventh floor and Port Lounge on the eighth. MIA, the first to offer duty-free shops, now boasts 14, carrying liquors, perfumes, electronics, and various designer goods.

When you fly out of MIA, plan to check in 55 minutes before departure for a domestic flight and 90 minutes before departure for an international flight. Services for international travelers include 24-hour multilingual information and paging phones and foreign-currency conversion booths throughout the terminal. There is an information booth with a multilingual staff and 24-hour currency exchange at the entrance of Concourse E on the upper level. Other tourist information centers are available at the customs exit, Concourse E, lower level (open daily 5 AM–11 PM); customs exit, Concourse B, lower level, (open daily 11–7); Concourse G, lower level (open daily 11–7); Concourse D, lower level, (open daily 11–11); and Satellite Terminal, (open daily 11–7).

Airlines that fly into MIA include **ACES** (☎ 305/265–1272), **Aero Costa Rica** (☎ 800/237–6274), **Aeroflot** (☎ 800/995–5555), **Aerolineas Argentinas** (☎ 800/333–0276), **Aeromexico** (☎ 800/237–6639), **AeroPeru** (☎ 800/777–7717), **Air Aruba** (☎ 800/882–7822), **Air Canada** (☎ 800/776–3000), **Air France** (☎ 800/237–2747), **Air Guadeloupe** (☎ 800/522–3394), **Air Jamaica** (☎ 800/523–5585), **Air South** (☎ 800/247–7688), **Airways International** (☎ 305/887–2794), **Alitalia** (☎ 800/223–5730), **ALM** (☎ 800/327–7230), **American** and **American Eagle** (☎ 800/433–7300), **American TransAir** (☎ 800/225–2995), **APA** (☎ 305/599–1299), **Avensa** (☎ 800/428–3672), **Avianca** (☎ 800/284–2622), **Aviateca** (☎ 800/327–9832), **Bahamasair** (☎ 800/222–4262), **British Airways** (☎ 800/247–9297), **BWIA** (☎ 305/371–2942), **Caribbean Airlines** (☎ 305/594–3232), **Carnival** (☎ 800/437–2110), **Cayman Airways** (☎ 800/422–9626), **Comair** (☎ 800/354–9822), **Continental** (☎ 800/525–0280), **Copa** (☎ 800/359–2672), **Delta** (☎ 800/221–1212), **Dominicana** (☎ 800/327–7240), **El Al** (☎ 800/223–6700), **Faucett** (☎ 800/334–3356), **Finnair** (☎ 800/950–5000), **Gulfstream International** (☎ 800/871–1200), **Guyana Airways** (☎ 800/242–4210), **Haiti Trans Air** (☎ 800/394–5313), **HANAIR** (☎ 305/757–7247), **Iberia** (☎ 800/772–4642), **LAB** (☎ 800/327–7407), **Lacsa** (☎ 800/225–2272), **Ladeco** (☎ 305/670–3066), **Lan Chile** (☎ 800/735–5526), **LAP** (☎ 800/677–7677), **Lauda Air** (☎ 800/645–3880), **LTU** (☎ 800/888–0200), **Lufthansa** (☎ 800/645–3880), **Martinair Holland** (☎ 800/366–4655), **Mexicana** (☎ 800/531–7921), **Nica** (☎ 800/831–4396), **Northwest** (☎ 800/225–2525), **Paradise Island** (☎ 800/432–8807), **Saeta** (☎ 800/827–2382), **Sahsa** (☎ 800/327–1225 or 800/432–9818 in FL), **Servivensa** (☎ 800/428–3672), **South African Airways** (☎ 800/722–9675), **Surinam Airways** (☎ 800/432–1230), **Taca** (☎ 800/535–8780), **Tower Air** (☎ 800/348–6937), **Transbrasil** (☎ 800/872–3153), **TWA** (☎ 800/221–2000), **United** (☎ 800/241–6522), **USAir** and **USAir Express** (☎ 800/842–5374), **ValuJet** (☎ 800/825–8538), **Varig** (☎ 800/468–2744), **VASP** (☎ 800/732–8277), **Viasa** (☎ 800/468–4272), **Virgin Atlantic** (☎ 800/862–8621), and **Zuliana** (☎ 800/223–8780).

## BETWEEN THE AIRPORT AND CENTER CITY

**By Bus:** The county's **Metrobus** (☎ 305/638–6700) still costs $1.25, though equipment has improved. From the airport you can take Bus 7 to downtown (weekdays 5:30 AM–9 PM every 40 minutes; weekends 6:30 AM–7:30 PM every 40 minutes), Bus 37 south to Coral Gables and South Miami (6 AM–11:30 PM every 30 minutes) or north to Hialeah (5:30 AM–11:30 PM every 30 minutes), Bus J south to Coral Gables (6 AM–12:30 AM every 30 minutes) or east to Miami Beach (4:30 AM–11:30

PM every 30 minutes), and Bus 42 to Coconut Grove (5:40 AM–7 PM hourly).

**By Limousine:** Miami, where it seems everyone is on stage, has more than 100 limousine services, though they're frequently in and out of business. If you rely on the Yellow Pages, look for a company with a street address, not just a phone. One of the oldest companies in town is **Vintage Rolls Royce Limousines of Coral Gables** (⊠ 4501 Monserrate St., Coral Gables 33146, ☎ 305/662–5763), which operates a 24-hour reservation service and provides chauffeurs for privately owned cars.

**By Rental Car:** Six rental-car firms—**Avis** (☎ 800/831–2847), **Budget** (☎ 800/527–0700), **Dollar** (☎ 800/800–4000), **Hertz** (☎ 800/654–3131), **National** (☎ 800/227–7368), and **Value** (☎ 800/468–2583)—have booths near the baggage-claim area on MIA's lower level.

**By Taxi:** Except for the flat-fare trips described below, cabs cost $1.70 per mile plus a $1 toll for trips originating at MIA or the Port of Miami. Approximate fares from MIA include $10 to Coral Gables, $15–$20 to downtown Miami, and $25–$30 to Key Biscayne. Newly established flat fares to the beaches are $38 to Golden Beach and Sunny Isles, north of Haulover Beach Park; $32 from Surfside through Haulover Beach Park; $27 between 63rd and 87th streets; and $22 from 63rd Street south to the foot of Miami Beach. These fares are per trip, not per passenger, and include tolls and $1 airport surcharge but not tip. The flat fare between MIA and the Port of Miami, in either direction, is $15.75.

For taxi service to destinations in the immediate vicinity, ask a uniformed county taxi dispatcher to call an **ARTS (Airport Region Taxi Service)** cab for you. These special blue cabs offer a short-haul flat fare in two zones. An inner-zone ride is $5.60; the outer-zone fare is $9. The area of service is north to 36th Street, west to the Palmetto Expressway (77th Avenue), south to N.W. 7th Street, and east to Douglas Road (37th Avenue). Maps are posted in cab windows on both sides.

**By Van: SuperShuttle** (from MIA, ☎ 305/871–2000; from Broward [Fort Lauderdale], 305/764–1700; from elsewhere, 800/874–8885) vans transport passengers between MIA and local hotels, the Port of Miami, and even individual residences on a 24-hour basis. The company's service area extends from Palm Beach to Monroe County (including the Lower Keys). Drivers provide narration en route. Service from MIA is available around the clock, on demand, but for the return it's best to make reservations 24 hours in advance, although the firm will try to arrange pickups within Dade County on as little as four hours' notice. The cost from MIA to downtown hotels is about $8. Additional members of a party pay a lower rate for many destinations, and children under four ride free with their parents. There's a pet transport fee of $5 for animals in kennels.

## By Train
**Amtrak** (☎ 800/872–7245) runs two trains daily between New York City and Miami (⊠ 8303 N.W. 37th Ave.; for recorded arrival and departure information; ☎ 305/835–1221; for shipping, 305/835–1222); the *Silver Meteor* and *Silver Star* make different stops along the way. The thrice-weekly *Sunset Limited* operates between Miami and Los Angeles, stopping in Jacksonville and Pensacola and other Florida towns en route.

The eight-year-old **Tri-Rail** (⊠ 1 River Plaza, 305 S. Andrews Ave., Suite 200, Fort Lauderdale, ☎ 305/728–8445 or 800/874–7245) commuter train system connects Miami with Broward and Palm Beach daily.

## Getting Around

Greater Miami resembles Los Angeles in its urban sprawl and traffic congestion. You'll need a car to visit many of the attractions and points of interest listed in this book. Some are accessible via the public transportation system, run by a department of the county government—the **Metro-Dade Transit Agency,** which consists of almost 600 **Metrobuses** on 71 routes, the 21-mile **Metrorail** elevated rapid-transit system, and the **Metromover,** an elevated light-rail system. Free maps, schedules, and a "First-Time Rider's Kit" are available. ⊠ *Government Center Station, 111 N.W. 1st St., Miami 33128; Maps by Mail,* ☎ *305/654–6586; route information,* ☎ *305/638–6700 weekdays 6 AM–10 PM, weekends 9–5.*

### By Bus

**Metrobus.** Stops are marked by blue-and-green signs with a bus logo and route information. The frequency of service varies widely, so call in advance to obtain specific schedule information. The fare is $1.25 (exact change), transfers 25¢; 60¢ with 10¢ transfers for people with disabilities, seniors (65 and older), and students. Some express routes carry surcharges of $1.50. Reduced-fare tokens sold 10 for $10 are now available from Metropass outlets. Lift-equipped buses for people with disabilities are available on 16 routes, including one from the airport that links up with many routes in Miami Beach as well as Coconut Grove, Coral Gables, Hialeah, and Kendall. All but four of these routes connect with Metrorail (☎ 305/638–6700). Those unable to use regular transit service should call **Special Transportation Services** (☎ 305/263–5400) for information on such services as curb-to-curb van pickup.

### By Car

In general, Miami traffic is the same as in any big city, with the same rush hours and the same likelihood that parking garages will be full at peak times. Many drivers who aren't locals and don't know their way around might turn and stop suddenly, or drop off passengers where they shouldn't. Some drivers are short-tempered and will assault those who cut them off or honk their horn.

Motorists need to be careful even when their driving behavior is beyond censure, however, especially in rental cars. Despite the removal of identifying marks, cars piled with luggage or otherwise showing signs that a tourist is at the wheel remain prime targets for thieves. Long-time residents know that reports of crime against tourists are blown way out of proportion by the media and that Miami is more or less as safe for a visitor as any American city its size. For more safety advice on driving in Miami, *See* Smart Travel Tips A to Z.

### By Taxi

One cab "company" stands out immeasurably above the rest. It's actually a consortium of drivers who have banded together to provide good service, in marked contrast to some Miami cabbies, who are rude, unhelpful, unfamiliar with the city, or dishonest, taking advantage of visitors who don't know the area. To plug into this consortium—they don't have a name, simply a number—call the dispatch service (☎ 305/888–4444). If you have to use another company, try to be familiar with your route and destination.

Since 1974 fares have been $1.75 per mile, 25¢ a minute waiting time, with no additional charge for extra passengers, luggage, or tolls. Taxis can be hailed on the street, although you may not always find one when you need one—it's better to call for a dispatch taxi or have a hotel doorman hail one for you. Some companies with dispatch service are **Central Taxicab Service** (☎ 305/532–5555), **Diamond Cab Company** (☎ 305/545–5555), **Metro Taxicab Company** (☎ 305/888–8888), **Miami-Dade Yellow Cab** (☎ 305/633–0503), **Miami Springs Taxi** (☎ 305/888–1000), **Society Cab Company** (☎ 305/757–5523), **Speedy Cab** (☎ 305/861–9999), **Super Yellow Cab Company** (☎ 305/888–7777), **Tropical Taxicab Company** (☎ 305/945–1025), and **Yellow Cab Company** (☎ 305/444–4444). Many now accept credit cards; inquire when you call.

### By Train

Elevated **Metrorail** trains run from downtown Miami north to Hialeah and south along U.S. 1 to Dadeland, daily 5:30 AM–midnight. Trains run every five minutes in peak hours, every 15 minutes at other times. The fare is $1.25. Transfers, which cost 25¢, must be bought at the first station entered. Parking at train stations costs $1.

**Metromover** has two loops that circle downtown Miami, linking major hotels, office buildings, and shopping areas. The system has been expanded from 1.9 miles to 4.4 miles, including the 1.4-mile Omni extension, with six stations to the north, and the 1.1-mile Brickell extension, with six stations to the south. Service runs daily every 90 seconds, 6 AM–midnight. The fare is 25¢. Transfers to Metrorail are $1.

### By Water Taxi

The service inaugurated in 1987 in Fort Lauderdale began Miami area operations in 1994 and expanded service between Miami Beach Marina and the Eden Rock Hotel in 1995. Canopied boats, 28 feet and longer, connect Miami Beach, Coconut Grove, and Key Biscayne from Bayside Marketplace. Routes cover downtown and Miami Beach hotels and restaurants and the Watson Island airboat station. Taxis operate daily 10 AM–2:30 AM. One-way fares around downtown Miami are $3, longer runs $7. For information, call 305/858–6292.

## Contacts and Resources

### Doctors and Dentists

**Dade County Medical Association** (✉ 1501 N.W. North River Dr., Miami, ☎ 305/324–8717) is open weekdays 9–5 for medical referral.

**East Coast District Dental Society** (✉ 420 S. Dixie Hwy., Suite 2E, Coral Gables, ☎ 305/667–3647) is open weekdays 9–4:30 for dental referral. Services include general dentistry, endodontics, periodontics, and oral surgery.

### Emergencies

Dial 911 for **police** or **ambulance.** You can dial free from pay phones.

AMBULANCE

**Randle Eastern Ambulance Service Inc.** (✉ 35 S.W. 27th Ave., Miami 33135, ☎ 305/642–6400) operates at all hours.

HOSPITALS

The following hospitals have 24-hour emergency rooms:

In Miami Beach: **Miami Heart Institute** (✉ 4701 N. Meridian Ave., Miami Beach, ☎ 305/672–1111; physician referral, 305/674–3004), **Mt. Sinai Medical Center** (✉ off Julia Tuttle Causeway, I–195 at 4300 Alton Rd., Miami Beach, ☎ 305/674–2121; emergency, 305/674–2200; physician referral, 305/674–2273), and **South Shore Hospital & Medical Center** (✉ 630 Alton Rd., Miami Beach, ☎ 305/672–2100).

In the north: **Golden Glades Regional Medical Center** (✉ 17300 N.W. 7th Ave., North Miami, ☎ 305/652–4200). Golden Glades offers physician referral.

In central Miami: **Coral Gables Hospital** (✉ 3100 Douglas Rd., Coral Gables, ☎ 305/445–8461), **Jackson Memorial Medical Center** (✉ 1611 N.W. 12th Ave., near Dolphin Expressway, Miami, ☎ 305/585–1111; emergency, 305/585–6901; physician referral, 305/547–5757), **Mercy Hospital** (✉ 3663 S. Miami Ave., Coconut Grove, ☎ 305/854–4400; emergency, 305/285–2171; physician referral, 305/285–2929), and **Pan American Hospital** (✉ 5959 N.W. 7th St., Miami, ☎ 305/264–1000; emergency, 305/264–6125; physician referral, 305/264–5118).

In the south: **Baptist Hospital of Miami** (✉ 8900 N. Kendall Dr., Miami, ☎ 305/596–1960; emergency, 305/596–6556; physician referral, 305/596–6557) and **South Miami Hospital** (6200 S.W. 73rd St., South Miami, ☎ 305/661–4611; emergency, 305/662–8181; physician referral, 305/633–2255).

## Guided Tours

### AIR TOURS

**Air Tours of Miami** (✉ 1470 N.E. 123rd St., Suite 602, Miami, ☎ 305/893–5874) flies over Miami, the Everglades, and nearby waters in a one-hour sightseeing tour on a Piper Seneca II six-seater. Tours depart from Opa-Locka Airport (ask for directions), and the cost is $75, with a minimum of three adults. Reservations are required.

**Chalk's International Airlines** (✉ 1000 MacArthur Causeway, Miami, ☎ 305/371–8628 or 800/424–2557, FAX 305/359–5240) has seaplane tours that depart from Watson Island every Saturday at 1:45. They last 25 minutes and include the Vizcaya Museum and Gardens, Miami Seaquarium, Fisher Island/Star Island, the Art Deco District, and Orange Bowl Stadium. The fee is $39.50.

### BOAT TOURS

**Heritage of Miami II** offers sightseeing cruises on board a two-masted, 85-foot topsail schooner. Tours start and end at Bayside Marketplace (✉ 401 Biscayne Blvd., ☎ 305/442–9697). One-hour sails cost $5 per person, and two-hour sails are $10. Tours loop through lower Biscayne Bay with views of the Vizcaya Museum and Gardens, movie-star homes, Cape Florida Lighthouse, the Port of Miami, and several residential islands.

**Island Queen, Island Lady,** and **Pink Lady** are 150-passenger double-decker tour boats docked at Bayside Marketplace (✉ 401 Biscayne Blvd., ☎ 305/379–5119). They go on daily 90-minute narrated tours of the Port of Miami and Millionaires' Row, costing $10.

### ECOTOURS

**EcoTours Miami** (✉ Box 22, Miami 33256-0022, ☎ 305/232–5398), consisting of longtime environmentalist Ginni Hokanson and friends, conduct customized interpretive tours of the Everglades, Big Cypress Swamp, Fackahatchee Strand, Florida Bay, and wherever else in South Florida's native environment visitors want to explore. Tour guides—environmental educators and natural history specialists—are available who speak German, Italian, Portuguese, and Spanish. Price quotes are given on request.

### HISTORIC TOURS

**Art Deco District Tour** (✉ 1001 Ocean Dr., Miami Beach, ☎ 305/672–2014), operated by the Miami Design Preservation League, is a 90-minute guided walking tour departing from the league's welcome center at the

Ocean Front Auditorium at 10:30 AM Saturday. Private group tours can be arranged with advance notice. A two-hour bike tour at 10:30 Sunday leaves from Cycles on the Beach (⊠ 713 5th St., Miami Beach, ☎ 305/673–2055). The walking tour costs $6; the bike tour is $10 with a rental bike, $5 with your own bike.

**Deco Tours Miami Beach** (⊠ 420 Lincoln Rd., Suite 412, Miami Beach, ☎ 305/531–4465) also offers walking tours of the Art Deco District. These 90-minute tours, which cost $10, depart from various locations and take in Lincoln Road, Washington Avenue, Espanola Way, Ocean Drive, Lummus Park, and the Art Deco Welcome Center.

**Professor Paul George** (⊠ 1345 S.W. 14th St., Miami, ☎ 305/858–6021), a history professor at Miami-Dade Community College and past president of the Florida Historical Society, leads a variety of walking tours as well as boat tours and tours that make use of Metrorail and Metromover. Tours generally last about two hours and 20 minutes. Covering downtown and other historic neighborhoods, they start Saturday at 10 and Sunday at 11 at various locations, depending on the tour. Call for each weekend's schedule and for additional tours by appointment. The fee is $10.

RICKSHAW TOURS

**Majestic Rickshaw** (⊠ 75 N.E. 156 St., Biscayne Gardens, ☎ 305/256–8833) has two-person rickshaws along Main Highway in Coconut Grove's Village Center, nightly 8 PM–2 AM. It's $3 per person for a 10-minute ride through Coconut Grove or $6 per person for a 20-minute lovers' moonlight ride to Biscayne Bay.

SELF-GUIDED TOURS

The **Junior League of Miami** (⊠ 2325 Salzedo, Coral Gables 33134, ☎ 305/443–0160) publishes excellent self-guiding tours to architectural and historical landmarks in downtown Miami, the northeast, and South Dade. Coconut Grove and Coral Gables tours are out of print but can sometimes still be found at bookstores. Each costs $3.

The **Miami Design Preservation League** (⊠ Bin L, Miami Beach 33139, ☎ 305/672–2014) sells the *Art Deco District Guide,* a book of six detailed walking or driving tours of the Art Deco District, for $10.

## Late-Night Pharmacies

**Eckerd Drug** (⊠ 1825 Miami Gardens Dr. NE, at 185th St., North Miami Beach, ☎ 305/932–5740; ⊠ 9031 S.W. 107th Ave., Miami, ☎ 305/274–6776). **Terminal Rexall Pharmacy** (⊠ Concourse F, Miami International Airport, Miami, ☎ 305/876–0556). **Walgreen** (⊠ 500–B W. 49th St., Palm Springs Mall, Hialeah, ☎ 305/557–5468; ⊠ 12295 Biscayne Blvd., North Miami, ☎ 305/893–6860; ⊠ 5731 Bird Rd., Miami, ☎ 305/666–0757; ⊠ 1845 Alton Rd., Miami Beach, ☎ 305/531–8868; ⊠ 791 N.E. 167th St., North Miami Beach, ☎ 305/652–7332).

## Services for People with Hearing Impairments

**Fire, police, medical, rescue** (TDD ☎ 305/595–4749).
**Operator and directory assistance** (TDD ☎ 800/855–1155).
**Deaf Services of Miami** (⊠ 9100 S. Dadeland Blvd., Suite 104, Miami 33156; voice, ☎ 305/670–9099) operates 24 hours year-round.
**Florida Relay Service** (voice ☎ 800/955–8770, TDD 800/955–8771).

## Visitor Information

**Greater Miami Convention & Visitors Bureau** (⊠ 701 Brickell Ave., Suite 2700, Miami 33131, ☎ 305/539–3063 or 800/283–2707). Satellite tourist information centers are located at Bayside Marketplace (⊠ 401

Biscayne Blvd., Miami 33132, ☎ 305/539–2980), Miami Beach Chamber of Commerce, and South Dade Visitor Information Center (✉ 160 U.S. 1, Florida City 33034, ☎ 305/245–9180 or 800/388–9669, FAX 305/247–4335).

**Coconut Grove Chamber of Commerce** (✉ 2820 McFarlane Rd., Coconut Grove 33133, ☎ 305/444–7270, FAX 305/444–2498). **Coral Gables Chamber of Commerce** (✉ 50 Aragon Ave., Coral Gables 33134, ☎ 305/446–1657, FAX 305/446–9900). **Florida Gold Coast Chamber of Commerce** (✉ 1100 Kane Concourse, Suite 210, Bay Harbor Islands 33154, ☎ 305/866–6020) serves the beach communities of Bal Harbour, Bay Harbor Islands, Golden Beach, North Bay Village, Sunny Isles, and Surfside. **Greater Miami Chamber of Commerce** (✉ 1601 Biscayne Blvd., Miami 33132, ☎ 305/350–7700, FAX 305/374–6902). **Greater South Dade/South Miami Chamber of Commerce** (✉ 6410 S.W. 80th St., South Miami 33143-4602, ☎ 305/661–1621, FAX 305/666–0508). **Key Biscayne Chamber of Commerce** (✉ Key Biscayne Bank Bldg., 95 W. McIntyre St., Key Biscayne 33149, ☎ 305/361–5207). **Miami Beach Chamber of Commerce** (✉ 1920 Meridian Ave., Miami Beach 33139, ☎ 305/672–1270, FAX 305/538–4336). **North Miami Chamber of Commerce** (✉ 13100 W. Dixie Hwy., North Miami 33181, ☎ 305/891–7811, FAX 305/893–8522). **Surfside Tourist Board** (✉ 9301 Collins Ave., Surfside 33154, ☎ 305/864–0722 or 800/327–4557, FAX 305/861–1302).

# 4 The Everglades

*Created in 1947, this national park in the southernmost extremity of the peninsula preserves a portion of the slow-moving "River of Grass"—a 50-mile-wide stream flowing through marshy grassland en route to Florida Bay. Biscayne National Park, nearby, is the largest national park with living coral reefs within the continental United States.*

Updated by
Marianne
Camas

**T**HE ONLY METROPOLITAN AREA in the United States
with two national parks in its backyard is Miami. Everglades National Park, created in 1947, was meant
to preserve the slow-moving "River of Grass"—a freshwater river 50
miles wide but only 6 inches deep, flowing from Lake Okeechobee
through marshy grassland into Florida Bay. Along the Tamiami Trail
(U.S. 41), marshes of cattails extend as far as the eye can see, inter-
spersed only by hammocks or tree islands of bald cypress and mahogany,
while overhead southern bald eagles make circles in the sky. A wide
variety of trees and flowers, including ferns, orchids, and bromeliads,
share the brackish waters with otters, turtles, marsh rabbits, and, occasionally, that gentle giant the West Indian manatee. Not so gentle
though, is the sawgrass. Deceptively graceful, these tall, willowy sedges
have small sharp teeth on the edges of their leaves.

Biscayne National Park, established as a national monument in 1968
and 12 years later expanded and designated a national park, is the nation's largest marine park and the largest national park with living coral
reefs within the continental United States. A small portion of the park's
almost 274 square miles consists of mainland coast and outlying islands, but 96% is under water, much of it in Biscayne Bay. The islands
contain lush, heavily wooded forests with an abundance of ferns and
native palm trees. Of particular interest to visitors are the mangroves—
tangled masses of stiltlike roots and stems that thicken the shorelines.
The "walking trees," as locals sometimes call them, have many supports reaching out to the ground; striking curved properates arch
down from the trunk of the tree and aerial roots drop from the
branches. Mangroves reproduce by dropping little trees, or propagules,
that look like 6- or 12-inch-long green cigars. They float in the dense
water for six months to a year, until they become waterlogged, then
slowly begin to float vertically instead of horizontally. Eventually,
roots pop out and grab onto oyster beds or mud flats. These maritime
trees draw fresh water from saltwater and create a coastal nursery ca-
pable of sustaining all types of marine life.

Unfortunately, Miami's backyard is being threatened by suburban
sprawl and by the proximity of an agricultural district that is one of
the most productive in the United States, albeit shrinking. What results
is competition between environmental, agricultural, and development
interests—for government money, and for control of the rules governing
this unique region's future.

The biggest issue is water. Originally, alternating floods and dry periods maintained wildlife habitat and regulated the water flowing into
Florida Bay. The brackish seasonal flux sustained a remarkably vigorous bay, including the most productive shrimp beds in American waters with thriving mangrove thickets and coral reefs at its Atlantic edge.
The system nurtured sea life and attracted anglers and divers. Starting
in the 1930s, however, a giant flood-control system began diverting
water to canals running to the Gulf and the Atlantic. As you travel
Florida's north–south routes, you cross this network of canals sym-
bolized by a smiling alligator representing the South Florida Water Management District, ironicallly known as"Protector of the Everglades."

The unfortunate side effect of flood control has been devastation of
the South Florida wilderness. Park visitors decry diminished bird
counts (citing a 90% reduction over 50 years); the black bear has been
eliminated, and the Florida panther nears extinction. Exotic plants once
imported to drain the Everglades and feral pigs released for hunting

are crowding out indigenous species. In 1995, the nonprofit group American Rivers again ranked the Everglades among the most threatened rivers of North America. Meanwhile the loss of all that fresh water has made Florida Bay more salty, devastating sea-life breeding grounds and creating dead zones where pea-green algae has replaced sea grasses and sponges.

Even while the ecosystem continues to fade, new policies, still largely on paper, hold promise. Some 40% of of what is commonly called Big Cypress Swamp was established as Big Cypress National Preserve in 1974, to protect the watershed of Everglades National Park. More recently, tourism and fishing industries, preservationists, and aggressive park management have pushed for improvement. Federal and state governments are now working together to push environmental protection toward the top of water-management priorities. Congressional appropriations to study restoration of the Everglades have increased. The state has acquired the Frog Pond, some 1,800 acres of critical farmland east of the Everglades, in order to allow more natural flooding. Passage in 1994 of Florida's Everglades Forever Act mandates creation of 40,000 acres of filtration marshes to remove harmful nutrients before they enter the protected wetlands. Within the next decade, farming must sharply reduce its phosphorus runoff, and the U.S. Army Corps of Engineers, which maintains Florida's flood-control system, proposes restoring a more natural flow of water into the Everglades and its related systems. Although the future of the natural system hangs uncertainly in this time of transition, these are certainly promising signs.

## Pleasures and Pastimes

### Biking and Hiking
In the Everglades, there are several nice places to ride and hike. The Shark Valley Loop Road (15 miles round-trip) makes a good bike trip, "Foot and Canoe Trails of the Flamingo Area," a leaflet, lists others. A vast network of almost 200 miles of bicycle and hiking trails is under development along the banks of flood-control canals. Inquire about water levels and insect conditions before you go. And plan accordingly, stocking up if necessary on repellent—both water and insect. Bike rentals are available in several areas.

### Boating and Canoeing
One of the best ways to experience the River of Grass is by boat, and almost all of Biscayne National Park is accessible only by water. Boat rentals are available in both parks.

In the Everglades, the 99-mile inland Wilderness Waterway between Flamingo and Everglades City is open to motorboats as well as canoes, although powerboats may have trouble navigating the route above Whitewater Bay.

The area also offers plentiful flat-water canoeing. It's best in winter, when temperatures are moderate, rainfall is minimal, and the mosquitoes are tolerable. You don't need a permit for day trips, as you do for camping, but tell someone where you're going and when you expect to return. Getting lost out here is easy, and spending the night without proper gear can be unpleasant, if not dangerous.

In the Gulf Coast area, you can explore the nooks and crannies and mangrove islands of Chokoloskee Bay, as well as the many rivers near Everglades City. The Turner River Trail through Everglades and Big Cypress mangrove, dwarf cypress, coastal prairie, and freshwater slough ecosystems makes a good day trip.

## Dining

Although both the Everglades and Biscayne National parks are wilderness areas, there are restaurants within a short drive. Most are between Miami and Shark Valley along the Tamiami Trail (U.S. 41), in the Homestead–Florida City area, in Everglades City, and in the keys along the Overseas Highway (U.S. 1). The only food service in either park is at Flamingo in the Everglades, but many of the independent restaurants will pack picnics. (You can also find fast-food establishments with carryout service on the Tamiami Trail and in Homestead–Florida City.)

## Fishing

Largemouth bass are plentiful in freshwater ponds, while snapper, redfish, and sea trout can be caught in Florida Bay. The mangrove shallows of the Ten Thousand Islands along the Gulf of Mexico yield tarpon and snook. Whitewater Bay is also a favorite spot. Note: The state has issued health advisories for large mouth bass and sea trout due to high mercury content. Signs are posted throughout the park.

## Lodging

Homestead, southwest of Miami, has become a bedroom community for both parks. You'll find well-kept, older properties, as well as chain motels and independents. Prices tend to be somewhat lower than in Greater Miami. There are also a few lodgings closer to the Everglades themselves, off U.S. 41.

## Shopping

For the sheer fun as well as the bargain, stop in at any of the local farms where you can pick your own produce. The harvest season runs from November through April and you can expect to find strawberries for maybe $2 a pound, corn at $1.25 a dozen ears, and tomatoes for 50¢ a pound. Look for signs—in season they're everywhere among the fields. You can also buy fresh-picked produce at stands that border fields.

# Exploring the Everglades

The best way to experience the real Everglades is to get your feet wet—but most visitors won't do that. Boat tours at Everglades City and Flamingo, a tram ride at Shark Valley, and boardwalks along the main park road allow you to see the park with dry feet.

In Biscayne National Park you can see the coral reefs through the floor of a glass-bottom boat, or take a closer look by snorkeling or scuba diving. Elliott Key, accessible by private boat only, has a nature trail with a variety of tropical plant life, including native gumbo limbo, mahogany, and satin leaf trees.

Most of the sports and recreational opportunities in Everglades and Biscayne national parks are based on water, the study of nature, or both. Even on land, be prepared to get a bit damp on the region's marshy hiking trails. In summer, save your outdoor activities for early or late in the day to avoid the sun's strongest rays, and use a sunscreen. Carry mosquito repellent at any time of year.

A watery wilderness, Big Cypress is devoted to balanced land use, which includes preservation, research, and also visitor use. Some activities allowed here but not in most national parks include hunting, off-road vehicle use (airboats, swamp buggies), and cattle grazing. The preserve's politically dictated policy is "use without abuse."

## Great Itineraries

The Everglades and Biscayne National Park are relatively compact, compared with the national parks of the West. Traveling time through the

Everglades tends to be long, however, since the park highways are narrow, two-lane roads. That most of Biscayne National Park is accessible only by boat, also requires plenty of sightseeing time.

*Numbers in the text below correspond to numbers in the margin and on the map.*

IF YOU HAVE 1 DAY

You'll have to make a choice—the Everglades or Biscayne? If you want a quiet, rural experience with nature, go with the Everglades. If you're interested in boating as well as seeing underwater flora and fauna, Biscayne is your best bet. Either way, you'll experience a little of what's left of the "real" Florida.

If you opt to spend the day in the Everglades, begin in **Homestead** near the entrance to the park for a visit to historic **City Hall** ①. Continue to **Florida City,** gateway to the park and site of a museum on Florida pioneer life. Head to the **Main Visitor Center** ② for an overview of the park and its ecosystems. Continue to the **Royal Palm Visitor Center** ③ for a look at several unique plant systems. Then go to **Flamingo Visitor Center** ④, in Flamingo, where you can rent a boat or take a tour of Florida Bay.

If Biscayne is your preference, begin at the **Convoy Point Visitor Center** ⑪ for an orientation. You'll then have to forsake dry land; the rest of the park is accessible only by water. Explore the offshore islands: **Elliott Key** ⑫, **Boca Chita Key** ⑬, or **Adams Key** ⑭.

IF YOU HAVE 3 DAYS

You'll have the opportunity to explore both the northern and southern ends of the Everglades as well as Biscayne National Park. On day one, explore the south. Begin in 🎦 **Homestead,** near the entrance to the park. Then continue to Florida City, and the **Main Visitor Center** ② for an overview of the park and its ecosystems. Next head to the **Royal Palm Visitor Center** ③. Then go to Flamingo and the **Flamingo Visitor Center** ④, where you can rent a boat or take a tour of Florida Bay. Day two is for exploring the northern Everglades. You'll be driving along the Tamiami Trail (U.S. 41) from Miami to Everglades City. Begin your tour at **Everglades Safari Park** ⑤. Then continue on to 🎦 **Shark Valley** ⑥ and take a tram tour. Visit the **Miccosukee Indian Village** ⑦, then head to little **Ochopee** ⑧. Next stop is 🎦 **Everglades City,** home of the **Gulf Coast Ranger Station** ⑨. Finally, visit historic **Smallwood's Store** ⑩. Day three will be your day at sea. Begin your tour of Biscayne National Park at the **Convoy Point Visitor Center** ⑪. Then head for the ocean in a tour boat or rent one on your own. Explore the offshore islands: **Elliott Key** ⑫, **Boca Chita Key** ⑬, and **Adams Key** ⑭.

## When to Tour

Winter is the best time to visit Everglades National Park. Temperatures and mosquito activity are moderate. Low water levels concentrate the resident wildlife around sloughs that retain water all year. Migratory birds swell the avian population. Winter is also the busiest time in the park. Make reservations and expect crowds at the most popular visitor service areas—Flamingo, the Main Visitor Center, and Royal Palm.

In spring the weather turns increasingly hot and rainy, and tours and facilities are less crowded. Migratory birds depart, and you must look harder to see wildlife. Be especially careful with campfires and matches; this is when the wildfire-prone sawgrass prairies and pinelands are most vulnerable.

Summer brings intense sun and billowing clouds unleashing torrents of rain almost every afternoon; water levels rise and wildlife disperses.

Mosquitoes hatch, swarm, and descend on you in voracious clouds. Although the power of a summer storm over the marshlands is something to behold, basically it's a good time to stay away. Europeans constitute 80% of the summer visitors.

In mid-October, the first cold front usually sweeps through. The rains diminish, water levels start to fall, and the ground begins to dry out. Wildlife moves toward the sloughs. Flocks of migratory birds and tourists swoop in, and the cycle of seasons begins once more.

# THE SOUTHERN EVERGLADES
## From Homestead and Florida City to Flamingo

The farm towns of Homestead and Florida City, flanked by Everglades National Park on the left and Biscayne National Park to the right, provide the closest visitor facilities to the two parks. Homestead is in the southeastern portion of the state, with Florida City just south of it. They date from early in the century, when Henry Flagler extended his railroad to Key West but soon decided that farming would do more for rail revenues than ferrying passengers. Devastated in 1992 by Hurricane Andrew, both towns have fully recovered. Homestead Air Force Base is becoming a civil air facility with commercial development. Downtown Homestead has become a preservation-driven Main Street city and has attracted several antiques stores. The area's better restaurants are here, but the best choices for overnighting are in Florida City. Flamingo, at the end of the road on Florida Bay, is an outpost resort providing more dining and lodging.

## Sights to See

*Numbers in the margin correspond to points of interest on the Everglades and Biscayne National Parks map.*

**❶ City Hall.** Before going to the Everglades National Park, you might want to stop off and view a portion of an historic photo collection at this restored 1917 Homestead landmark, which also houses the chamber of commerce. More of the collection is displayed in a storefront across the street. ✉ *43 N. Krome Ave., Homestead,* ☎ *305/247–1801.*

**Everglades Park Road.** The main park road (Rte. 9336), travels 38 miles from the Main Visitor Center to Flamingo, across a section of the park's eight distinct ecosystems: hardwood hammock, freshwater prairie, pineland, freshwater slough, cypress, coastal prairie, mangrove, and marine/estuarine. Highlights of the trip include a dwarf cypress forest, the ecotone (transition zone) between saw grass and mangrove forest, and a wealth of wading birds at Mrazek and Coot Bay ponds. Boardwalks and trails along the main road and several short spurs allow you to see the Everglades on dry land.

**❹ Flamingo Visitor Center.** Tour boats and fishing expeditions of Florida Bay leave from here. The center provides an interactive display, and you can also make use of a lodge, restaurant, lounge, gift shop, marina, and campground. *Park Service,* ☎ *305/242–7700; Flamingo Lodge, 305/253–2241.* ☉ *Visitor center daily 8–5.*

**❷ Main Visitor Center.** This gateway to the park has a full range of interactive materials. ✉ *11 mi west of Homestead on Rte. 9336,* ☎ *305/242–7700.* 🎟 *Park $5 per car, $3 per person on foot, bicycle, or motorcycle.* ☉ *Daily 8–5.*

**❸ Royal Palm Visitor Center.** A visit here is a must for anyone who wants to experience the real Everglades. You can stroll along the Anhinga Trail

# The Everglades and Biscayne National Parks

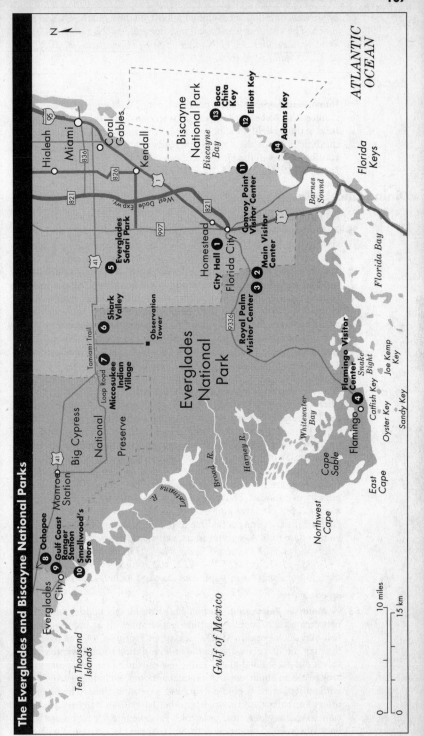

ATLANTIC OCEAN

Biscayne National Park

Biscayne Bay

13 Boca Chita Key
12 Elliott Key
14 Adams Key
11 Convoy Point Visitor Center

Hialeah
Miami
Coral Gables
Kendall

Barnes Sound

Florida Keys

Everglades Safari Park
5
Homestead
Florida City
City Hall 1
2 Main Visitor Center
3 Royal Palm Visitor Center

Florida Bay

6 Shark Valley
Observation Tower

Tamiami Trail

7 Miccosukee Indian Village
Loop Road

Big Cypress National Preserve

Everglades National Park

Whitewater Bay

Flamingo Visitor Center
4 Flamingo
Snake Bight
Catfish Key
Oyster Key
Joe Kemp Key
Sandy Key

Cape Sable

East Cape

Northwest Cape

8 Ochopee
9 Gulf Coast Ranger Station
10 Smallwood's Store
Everglades City
Monroe Station

Lostmans R.
Broad R.
Harney R.

Gulf of Mexico

Ten Thousand Islands

0    10 miles
0    15 km

boardwalk or follow the Gumbo Limbo Trail through a hardwood hammock. The visitor center has an interpretive display, a bookstore, and vending machines. ⊠ *41 N. Krome Ave., Homestead,* ☎ *305/247–2332,* ☉ *Call for hours.*

## Beaches

**Homestead Bayfront Park** is popular among local families and teenagers. Adjacent to Biscayne Bay is a saltwater atoll pool that is flushed by tidal action. Highlights include a playground, ramps for people with disabilities (including a ramp that leads into the swimming area), and four barbecues in the picnic pavilion. ⊠ *9698 S.W. 328th St., Homestead,* ☎ *305/230–3034.* ⌑ *$3 per car.* ☉ *Daily 7–sunset.*

## Dining and Lodging

### FLAMINGO

**$$**  ✕ **Flamingo Restaurant.** The grand view, convivial lounge, and casual style are great. Big picture windows on the visitor center's second floor overlook Florida Bay, revealing soaring eagles, gulls, pelicans, terns, and vultures. Dine at low tide, and you get to see the birds flock to the sandbar just offshore. Less satisfying is the food itself. All the seafood comes frozen—unless it's your own catch, which the kitchen will prepare after you've cleaned it at the marina. Otherwise look for pastas and a few grills. Service is limited to buffets in summer, though the snack bar at the marina store stays open all year to serve pizza, sandwiches, and salads, and you can always order a picnic basket. ⊠ *Flamingo Lodge, 1 Flamingo Lodge Hwy.,* ☎ *305/253–2241 or 941/695–3101. AE, D, DC, MC, V.*

**$$**  ▣ **Flamingo Lodge Marina & Outpost Resort.** This plain low-rise motel offers the only lodging inside Everglades National Park. Accommodations are basic but well kept, and an amiable staff with a sense of humor helps you adjust to the bellowing alligators from down the road, raccoons roaming the pool enclosure at night, and the flock of ibis grazing on the lawn. Rooms have carpeting, wood-paneled and plaster walls, contemporary furniture, floral bedspreads, and art prints of bird life. Bathrooms are tiny. All motel rooms face Florida Bay but don't necessarily overlook it. The cottages, in a wooded area on the margin of a coastal prairie, have kitchenettes and accommodate six people, except for the two units accessible to people with disabilities, which accommodate four. Ask about tours, skiffs, and canoes when you make reservations. ⊠ *1 Flamingo Lodge Hwy., 33034,* ☎ *305/253–2241, 941/695–3101, or 800/600–3813. 101 rooms, 24 cottages. Restaurant, lounge, snack bar, pool, coin laundry. AE, D, DC, MC, V.*

### FLORIDA CITY

**$$**  ✕ **Mutineer Restaurant.** Former Sheraton Hotels builder Allan Bennett created this upscale roadside restaurant with its indoor-outdoor fish and duck pond in 1980, back when Florida City was barely on the map. Etched glass divides the bi-level dining rooms, where striped velvet chairs, stained glass, and a few portholes set the scene; in the lounge are an aquarium and nautical antiques, including a crow's nest with stuffed crow, a gold parrot, and a treasure chest. The big menu offers 18 seafood entrées plus another half dozen daily seafood specials, as well as game, ribs, and steaks. Favorites include barbecued baby-back ribs, whole Dungeness crab, and snapper Oscar (topped with crab and asparagus). There's live music Thursday through Saturday evenings. ⊠ *11 S.E. 1st Ave.,* ☎ *305/245–3377. AE, D, DC, MC, V.*

$–$$ ✕ **Richard Accursio's Capri Restaurant** and **King Richard's Room.** One
★ of the oldest family-run restaurants in Dade County—since 1958—this
is where locals dine out. (The Rotary Club meets each Wednesday at
noon.) Specialties include pizza with light, crunchy crusts and ample
toppings; mild, meaty conch chowder; mussels in garlic-cream or marinara sauce; Caesar salad with lots of cheese and anchovies; antipasto
with a homemade, vinegary Italian dressing; pasta shells stuffed with
rigatoni cheese in tomato sauce; yellowtail snapper française; and Key
lime pie with plenty of real Key lime juice. A choice of six early-bird
entrées is offered 4:30–6:30 for $7.95, including soup or salad and
potato or spaghetti. ✉ *935 N. Krome Ave.,* ☎ *305/247–1544. AE,
D, MC, V.*

$$ 🏨 **Best Western Gateway to the Keys.** This two-story motel sits well
back from the highway and contains such amenities as full closets, a
heat lamp in the bathroom, and complimentary Continental breakfast.
More expensive rooms come with wet bar, fridge, microwave, and cof-
fee maker. Otherwise it's a standard modern motel with floral prints
and twin reading lamps. ✉ *1 Strano Blvd., 33034,* ☎ *305/246–5100,*
FAX *305/242–0056. 114 units. Pool, spa, laundry. AE, D, DC, MC, V.*

$$ 🏨 **Hampton Inn.** This two-story motel just off the highway has good
clean rooms (including a post–Hurricane Andrew wing) and public-
friendly policies, including free Continental breakfast, local calls, and
movie channels. All rooms have at least two upholstered chairs, twin
reading lamps, and a desk and chair. Units are color-coordinated and
carpeted. Baths have tub-showers. ✉ *124 E. Palm Dr., 33034,* ☎
*305/247–8833 or 800/426–7866,* FAX *305/247–8833. 122 units. Pool.
AE, D, DC, MC, V.*

HOMESTEAD

$ ✕ **El Toro Taco.** The Hernandez family came to the United States from
★ San Luis Potosí, Mexico, to pick crops. In 1976 they opened what has
become an area institution, where they make their own salt-free tortillas and nacho chips with Texas corn ground on site. The cilantro-
dominated salsa is mild for American tastes; if you like more fire on
your tongue, ask for a side dish of minced jalapeño peppers to mix in.
Specialties include *chile rellenos* (green peppers stuffed with ground
beef and topped with cheese) and chicken fajitas. ✉ *1 S. Krome Ave.,*
☎ *305/245–8182. MC, V. BYOB.*

$ ✕ **Potlikker's.** This Southern country-style restaurant takes its name
from the broth—pot liquor—left over from the boiling of greens.
Plants dangle from the sides of open rafters in the lofty pine-lined dining room. Specialties include a lemon-pepper chicken breast with
lemon sauce, roast turkey with homemade dressing, and at least 11 different vegetables served with lunch and dinner entrées. For dessert, try
a 4-inch-tall Key lime pie. ✉ *591 Washington Ave.,* ☎ *305/248–
0835. AE, MC, V.*

$ ✕ **Tiffany's.** This country-French cottage with shops and a restaurant
under a big banyan tree looks like a converted pioneer house with its
high-pitched roof and lattice. Teaberry-colored tables, satinlike floral
place mats, marble-effect floor tiles, fresh flowers on each table, and
lots of country items make for a very quaint atmosphere. Featured entrées include hot crab meat au gratin and asparagus supreme (rolled
in ham with hollandaise sauce). Homemade desserts are to die for: a
very tall carrot cake, strawberry whipped-cream cake, and a harvest
pie with double crust that has layers of apples, cranberries, walnuts,
raisins, and a caramel topping. There's also a Sunday brunch ✉ *22
N.E. 15th St.,* ☎ *305/246–0022. MC, V. Closed Mon. No dinner.*

## Outdoor Activities and Sports

### Auto Racing

The **Homestead Motorsports Complex** (✉ 1707 S.E. 43rd Ave., Homestead, ☎ 305/247–1801) is a state-of-the-art facility with an 8-degree banked-turn track resembling the Indianapolis Motor Speedway. The oval is the key element of the 2.21-mile road course. A schedule of year-round manufacturer and race-team testing, club racing, and other events climaxes with Indy Car Grand Prix racing and the season-ending NASCAR Busch Series Grand National Division event.

### Biking

Bike rentals are available from **Flamingo Lodge Marina & Outpost Resort** for $12 a day, $7 per half day, or $2.50 an hour.

### Boating

NEAR HOMESTEAD

Listed below are the major marinas serving the two parks. Dock masters can provide information on other marine services.

**Black Point Park** is a 155-acre Metro-Dade County Park with a hurricane-safe harbor basin. **Black Point Marina's** facilities include a bait-and-tackle shop, canoe-launching ramp, powerboat rentals, and a restaurant. From Florida's Turnpike, exit at S.W.112th Avenue, go two blocks north, turn east on Coconut Palm Drive (S.W. 248th St.), and drive to the end. ✉ 24777 S.W. 87th Ave., Miami, ☎ 305/258–3500. ☉ Office daily 8:30–5 (later in summer), park daily 6–sunset.

**Homestead Bayfront Park,** just 5 miles south of Black Point Park, has a marina with a dock, bait and tackle, ice, boat hoist, and ramp; the park also has a tidal swimming area and concessions. ✉ 9698 S.W. 328th St., Homestead, ☎ 305/230–3033. ☞ $3 per car, boat ramp $5, hoist $10. ☉ Daily 7–sunset.

FLAMINGO

**Flamingo Lodge Marina & Outpost Resort** has a marina and canoes, 10 power skiffs, and houseboats; several private boats are also available for charter. There are two ramps, one for Florida Bay, the other for Whitewater Bay and the backcountry. The hoist across the plug dam separating Florida Bay from the Buttonwood Canal can take boats up to 26 feet long. A small store sells food, camping supplies, bait and tackle, and fuel. ✉ 1 Flamingo Lodge Hwy., Flamingo, ☎ 305/253–2241 or 941/695–3101.

### Camping

Everglades National Park includes three developed campgrounds with drinking water, sewage dump station, and rest rooms. **Long Pine Key** has 108 campsites with a 24-hour attendant and rest rooms. **Flamingo** has 235 drive-in sites, 60 walk-in sites, and cold showers. **Chekika** has 20 sites, cold showers, and swimming facilities. Come early to get a good site, especially in winter. ☎ 305/242–7700. ☞ $8–$10 per site in winter; free in summer except walk-in sites at Flamingo, which are $4.

Deep in Everglades National Park are 48 designated back country sites, many inland and some on the beach. Two are accessible by land, the others only by canoe; 15 have chickees (raised wood platforms with thatch roofs). All have chemical toilets. Several are within an easy day's canoeing of Flamingo; five are closer to Everglades City. Carry all your food, water, and supplies in; carry out all trash. You'll need a free permit, issued for a specific site. Free permits are required, available on a first-come, first-served basis. For details contact the **Flamingo** or **Gulf**

**Coast Ranger Station** (*See* Contacts and Resources *in* Everglades A to Z, *below,* for both).

### Skydiving

**Skydive Miami** offers jumps above Homestead General Aviation Airport. All first jumps start with an hour of classroom instruction, leading to an aerial flight to altitude and a tandem dive with an instructor. ⊠ *Homestead General Aviation Airport, 28700 S.W. 217th Ave., Homestead,* ☎ *305/759–3483.* ☞ *$129.* ☉ *Jumps weekends 7–sunset with 1-hour notice for more than 2 people, weekdays by appointment with 24 hours notice.*

## Shopping

In addition to Homestead Boulevard (U.S. 1) and Campbell Drive (S.W. 312th St. and N.E. 8th St.), **Krome Avenue** (Rte. 997) is popular for shopping. In the heart of old Homestead, it has a brick sidewalk and many antique stores.

**Florida Keys Factory Shops** (⊠ 250 E. Palm Dr., Florida City) has 50 discount stores plus a small food court. **Robert Is Here** (⊠ 19200 Palm Dr. [S.W. 344th St.], Florida City, ☎ 305/246–1592), a remarkable fruit stand, sells vegetables, milk shakes, and, seasonally, some 40 kinds of tropical fruits, including carambola, egg fruit, monstera, sapodilla, soursop, sugar apple, and tamarind, as well as fresh juices.

# THE NORTHERN EVERGLADES
## Along the Tamiami Trail

Another way to see the Everglades is via a 15-mile probe extending south from the Tamiami Trail (U.S. 41) between Miami and Naples. Local Miccosukee Indians operate a range of cultural attractions and restaurants. The remaining entrance to the park is Everglades City, 35 miles southeast of Naples just off the Tamiami Trail. This community, around since the late 19th century, offers lodgings, restaurants, and guided tours.

## Sights to See

**Big Cypress National Preserve.** Part of the Big Cypress Swamp, which encompasses more than 2,400 miles of south Florida, this preserve, with its variegated pattern of wet prairies, ponds, marshes, sloughs, and strands provides a sanctuary for a variety of wildlife. ⊠ *Visitor Center, 20 mi east of Ochopee on U.S. 41,* ☎ *941/695–4111.* ☉ *Daily 8:30–4:30.*

**⑤ Everglades Safari Park.** This commercial attraction includes an airboat ride, jungle trail, observation platform, alligator wrestling, wildlife museum, and restaurant. ⊠ *Tamiami Trail,* ☎ *305/226–6923 or 305/223–3804,* ℻ *305/554–5666.* ☞ *$14 adults.* ☉ *Daily 8:30–5.*

**⑨ Gulf Coast Ranger Station.** This visitor center at the Everglades' western entrance offers interpretive exhibits about local flora and fauna. Backcountry campers can pick up the required free permits and for those in need of a little more guidance, there are ranger-led boat trips. The station offers access to the Ten Thousand Islands region along the Gulf of Mexico, but there are no roads from here to other sections of the park. ⊠ *Rte. 29,* ☎ *941/695–3311.* ☞ *Free.* ☉ *Nov.–Apr., daily 7–4:30; reduced hours May–Oct.*

**❼ Miccosukee Indian Village.** You can watch Miccosukee families cooking and making clothes, dolls, beadwork, and baskets and then buy their very unusual crafts. ✉ *Near Shark Valley entrance,* ☎ *305/223–8380.* ⊙ *Daily, 9–5.*

**❽ Ochopee.** This tiny town, site of the smallest post office in North America, is just east of Route 29. Buy a picture postcard of the little one-room shack and mail it to a friend, thereby helping to keep this picturesque post office in business.

**Rod and Gun Club.** This inn (☞ Dining and Lodging, *below*) is like a time-warp trip back to the '20s, when wealthy hunters, anglers, and yachting parties from all over the world came to Florida for the winter season. This landmark inn on the banks of the Barron River with a veranda and pool, dark cypress fixtures and a nautical theme, is a vestige of Florida's cracker glory days when imperial developer Barron Collier greeted U.S. presidents, Barrymores, and Gypsy Rose Lee for days of leisurely fishing. Most of them flew to the private landing strip; in the evenings they dined on one of Collier's big catches, prepared by a chef who once worked for Kaiser Wilhelm. Sit on the screened porch, have a beer, and watch the yachts and the fishing boats go by. ✉ *200 Riverside Dr., Everglades City,* ☎ *941/695–2101.*

**❻ Shark Valley.** This small town is the site of a park entrance and a visitor center with rotating exhibits and a bookstore. From here you can walk along a ¼-mile boardwalk, follow hiking trails, or take one of the **Shark Valley Tram Tours** (☞ Guided Tours *in* Everglades A to Z, *below*), which visits a 50-foot observation tower built on the site of an oil well drilled in the 1940s. From atop the tower you can view the vast river of grass sweeping south toward the Gulf of Mexico. ✉ *Visitor center, Tamiami Trail,* ☎ *305/221–8776.* 🎫 *Park $4 per car, $2 per person on foot, bicycle, or motorcycle.* ⊙ *Visitor center; daily 8:30–5.*

**❿ Smallwood's Store.** This perfectly restored old trading post dates back to 1906. Ted Smallwood pioneered this last American frontier deep in the Everglades and built a 3,000-square-foot pine store raised on pilings in Chokoloskee Bay. Smallwood's granddaughter Lynn McMillin reopened it in 1989 after it had been closed several years, and installed a small museum and gift shop. ✉ *360 Mamie St., Chokoloskee Island,* ☎ *941/695–2989.* 🎫 *$2.50.* ⊙ *Dec.–May, daily 10–5; May–Nov., Fri.–Tues. 10–4.*

# Dining and Lodging

EVERGLADES CITY

**$–$$** ✕ **Oyster House.** An established local favorite, this rustic seafood
★     house is accented by mounted swampcats, gator heads, deer, crabs, nets, shells, and anchor chains. Lanterns hang from the A-frame ceiling over burnished plank walls. You sit at booths and tables set without cloths. They'd serve on the porch, too, but the insects can get too pesty—though in winter, when the bugs relent, guests sit outside with a drink from the bar to wait for a table. Fresh oysters are shucked daily. Main-course favorites include pompano, black-tip shark, frogs' legs, gator tail, and steaks. Desserts include a homemade Key lime pie, carrot cake, and Black Forest cake. ✉ *Rte. 29 (Chokoloskee Causeway),* ☎ *941/695–2073. MC, V.*

**$** ✕ **Susie's Station.** You'd swear the place dates from Everglades City's heyday, with its white-balustered screened porch, the gas station memorabilia, and the 1898 horse-drawn oil tanker. Replica '20s lamps are strung over booths set with beige cloths. There are three dining areas, one with original area art by Camille Baumgartner, another fixed up like an old general store, and the third on the screened porch. Biss serves stone crabs in season, a cold seafood plate with lobster salad, seafood, steaks, and pizzas. The best buy is the nightly dinner special—maybe lasagna, baked chicken, or Salisbury steak. The homemade Key lime pie sells out daily. ⊠ *103 S.W. Copeland Ave.,* ☎ *941/695–2002. No credit cards.*

**$$** 🍴 **Rod and Gun Club.** The old guest rooms upstairs from the restaurant and bar aren't open anymore, but you can stay in comfortable cottages (no phone, however). The food is more than passable. Breakfast, lunch, and dinner are still served in the original dining room or on the wide veranda, and, as in Collier's day, if you catch a "keeper," the chef will prepare it for your dinner. ⊠ *200 Riverside Dr., 33929,* ☎ *941/695–2101. 25 rooms. Restaurant, lounge, pool, tennis courts. No credit cards.*

**$** 🍴 **Ivey House.** It's clean, homey, friendly, and a bargain, run by the folks who operate North American Canoe Tours. New manager Catlin Maser is a B&B-style innkeeper, and there are always adventure travelers around in the big living room—and lots of chatter over breakfast. The house is trailerlike, set upon blocks, and was a popular boardinghouse when workers were building the Tamiami Trail. Earl and Agnes Ivey ran it from 1928 to 1974. There was nothing at all fancy about it then, or now. Baths are down the hall, but the rooms are private. ⊠ *107 Camellia St., 33929,* ☎ *941/695–3299. 10 rooms with shared baths. Bicycles, recreation room, library. MC, V. Closed May–Oct.*

### NEARBY MIAMI

**$** ✕ **Coopertown Restaurant.** This rustic restaurant just into the Everglades, west of Miami, has been around for over 51 years. It's full of old Florida style—alligator skulls, stuffed alligator heads, and gator accessories (belts, key chains, and so on). Try the alligator and frogs' legs, breaded and deep-fried in vegetable oil, available for breakfast, lunch, or dinner. ⊠ *22700 S.W. 8th St.,* ☎ *305/226–6048. MC, V. Beer and wine only.*

**$** ✕ **Pit Bar-B-Q.** The intense aroma of barbecue and blackjack-oak smoke will overwork your salivary glands. Order at the counter; then pick up your food when called. Specialties include barbecued chicken and ribs with a tangy sauce, french fries, coleslaw, and a fried biscuit as well as catfish, frogs' legs, and breaded shrimp deep-fried in vegetable oil. ⊠ *16400 S.W. 8th St.,* ☎ *305/226–2272. MC, V.*

### SHARK VALLEY

**$** ✕ **Miccosukee Restaurant.** Murals here depict Native American women cooking and men engaged in a powwow. Favorites are catfish and frogs' legs breaded and deep-fried, Indian fry bread (a flour-and-water dough), pumpkin bread, Indian burger (ground beef browned, rolled in fry bread dough, and deep-fried), and Indian tacos (fry bread with chili, lettuce, tomato, and shredded Cheddar cheese on top). ⊠ *Tamiami Trail, near Shark Valley park entrance,* ☎ *305/223–8380, Ext. 332. No credit cards.*

**$** 🍴 **Everglades Tower Inn.** If you're overnighting in Shark Valley, odds are you just need a plain, serviceable, and affordable room, and that's just what you get here. This Miccosukee family-run lodging is 1 mile west of the Shark Valley entrance to Everglades National Park. Rooms have double beds and baths but no phones. Next door are the affordable **Gator Hut Cafe,** and the **Everglades Shark Valley Crafts Center.** ⊠ *Tamiami Trail, Mile Marker 70, SR Box E–4910, Ochopee 33943,* ☎ *305/559–7779; in FL, 800/423–6218. 20 rooms. MC, V.*

## Outdoor Activities and Sports

### Biking

**North American Canoe Tours,** in Everglades City, rents bikes for $3 per hour and **Shark Valley Tram Tours** for $3.25 per hour (☞ Guided Tours *in* Everglades A to Z, *below,* for all).

### Camping

**Everglades Gator Park,** on the Tamiami Trail, has an RV park with full hookups for up to 80 RVs. It also offers Everglades airboat tours for sightseeing, hunting, and fishing. ⊠ *24050 S.W. 8th St., Miami (mailing address, 13800 S.W. 8th St., Box 107, Miami 33184),* ☎ *305/559–2255 or 800/559–2205.* ☑ *$25 per night, $100 per week. MC, V.*

### Canoeing

The Everglades has six well-marked canoe trails in the Flamingo area, including the southern end of the 99-mile Wilderness Trail from Everglades City to Flamingo.

**Everglades National Park Boat Tours** (⊠ Gulf Coast Ranger Station, Everglades City, ☎ 941/695–2591; in FL, 800/445–7724) rents canoes for $15 per half day, $20 per full day.

**North American Canoe Tours** (⊠ Ivey House, 107 Camellia St., Box 5038, Everglades City 33929, ☎ 941/695–4666), is an established source for canoes, sea kayaks, and guided Everglades trips (November–April). Canoes cost $20 the first day, $18 for every day after. Kayaks are $35–$45 per day. Car shuttles for canoeists paddling the 99-mile Wilderness Trail from Chokoloskee (Everglades City) to Flamingo are $135 with NACT canoe ($150 with your own) plus $5 park entrance fee.

## Shopping

The larger of two Miccosukee-run crafts depots, **Everglades Shark Valley Crafts Center** (⊠ Tamiami Trail, Mile Marker 76, Shark Valley, ☎ 305/223–5055), carries a broad selection of interesting Native American crafts and, in addition, offers airboat rides. Some of the most unusual crafts in south Florida are the beadwork, dolls, baskets, and patchwork dresses and jackets sold at the **Miccosukee Indian Village** ½ mile east of the Everglades Shark Valley Crafts Center.

# BISCAYNE NATIONAL PARK

The park occupies the southern portion of Biscayne Bay, below Miami and north of the Florida Keys. Its area combines four distinct zones of water and land formed during the Ice Age, some 10,000 years ago. From shore to sea, the zones are: mangrove forest along the coast; Biscayne Bay, a shallow nursery for marine life; the undeveloped upper Florida keys; and coral reefs. The park is 96% below water and ranges from 4 feet above sea level to 10 fathoms, or 60 feet, below. From December through April when the mosquito population is relatively quiescent, you can comfortably explore several of the keys by boat.

Much like Florida Bay, Biscayne Bay functions as a lobster sanctuary and a nursery for fish, sponges, and crabs. Manatees and sea turtles frequent its warm, shallow waters, and the ocean east of the islands harbors the northernmost sections of Florida's tropical reef. At the park's boundary, the continental shelf runs 60 feet deep; farther east, the shelf falls rapidly away to a depth of 400 feet at the edge of the Gulf Stream. Lamentably, this bay, too, is under assault from forces similar to those in Florida Bay, and coral is additionally damaged by boat anchors and commercial ships that run off course onto the reefs.

Another 3 miles east of the keys lies the park's main attraction: living coral reefs, some the size of a student's desk, others as large as a football field. Once again, you can take a boat ride to see this underwater wonderland, but you really have to snorkel or scuba dive to appreciate it fully. A diverse population of colorful fish—angelfish, gobies, grunts, parrotfish, pork fish, wrasses, and many more—flits through the reefs. Fortunately, Hurricane Andrew did the reefs only minor damage and, scientists now believe, may actually have helped regenerate them. However, many of the park's facilities were destroyed by Hurricane Andrew and more than four years later are still in varying stages of construction.

## Sights to See

**⑭ Adams Key.** Rest rooms and a picnic shelter were destroyed by Hurricane Andrew. At press time, reconstruction was scheduled for mid-1996, when the island will be reopened for day use. A public dock and nature trail will be available. Access will be by private boat.

**⑬ Boca Chita Key.** This island was once owned by Mark C. Honeywell, former president of Minneapolis's Honeywell Company. Most of the historical structures damaged by Hurricane Andrew have been repaired and stabilized. Revegetation, harbor repair, and rest room construction were scheduled to be completed in May of 1996. Overnight docking and camping is allowed. Access is by private boat only.

**⑪ Convoy Point Visitor Center.** Because it was badly damaged by Hurricane Andrew, the center may not reopen until 1997. A temporary visitor center offers books for sale, limited exhibits, an eleven-minute slide orientation, and an 18-minute video on Hurricane Andrew's effects on the park. A short trail and boardwalk lead to a jetty and launch ramp. ☎ 305/230–7275. ⊠ Free. ☉ Park: daily 8–sunset; visitor center: weekdays 8:30–4:30 (until 5:30 June–Aug.), weekends 8:30–5.

**⑫ Elliott Key.** The harbor and campground, for which there are neither fees nor reservations, are open (☞ Outdoor Activities and Sports, *below*). The only access is by boat (on your own or by special arrangement with the concessionaire). Outdoor exhibits at ground level under the ranger station are being constructed.

## Beaches

**Elliott Key**'s 30-foot-wide sandy beach is the only one in Biscayne National Park; boaters like to anchor off it for a swim. It's about a mile north of the harbor on the west bay side of the key.

## Outdoor Activities and Sports

### Camping

In **Biscayne National Park,** you can camp for free on Boca Chita and Elliott keys. Bring plenty of insect repellent. Inquire at the park concessionaire office about boats to the keys, as there are no regular ferries or boats for rent.

### Canoeing

A firm called **Biscayne National Underwater Park, Inc,** (⊠ Convoy Point, Biscayne National Park, ☎ 305/230–1100, FAX 305/230–1120), the official concessionaire for Biscayne National Park, rents canoes for $7 an hour, $20 for four hours, $25 per day. It's open daily 9–5:30.

### Diving

**Biscayne National Underwater Park, Inc.,** rents and sells equipment and conducts trips aboard *Boca Chita,* a 43-foot boat dedicated to snorkeling and scuba diving. Trips include 1¼ hours on the reefs. Scuba instruction is available. ⊠ *Convoy Point, Box 1270, Homestead 33090,* ☎ *305/230–1100,* FAX *305/230–1120.* ⊠ *snorkeling $27.95, scuba $34.50.* ☉ *Office daily 9–5:30, trips daily 1:30–5.*

## Hiking

In Biscayne National Park, rangers lead informal nature walks on **Elliott Key.** The morning "walk" is actually a glass-bottom boat trip to Elliott Key. Departure times depend upon the seas. You can walk the 7-mile length of the key on your own along a rough path locally referred to as the "spite highway," which developers bulldozed before the park was created.

# EVERGLADES A TO Z

## Arriving and Departing

### By Boat

If you're entering the United States by boat, you must phone **U.S. Customs** (☎ 800/432–1216) either from a marine phone or on first arriving ashore. At its option, customs will direct you to Dodge Island Seaport (Miami), will otherwise rendezvous with you, or will clear you by phone.

### By Car

From Miami, the main highways to Homestead–Florida City are U.S. 1, the Homestead Extension of Florida's Turnpike, and Krome Avenue (Rte. 997 [old U.S. 27]).

To reach the western gateway to Everglades National Park, take the Tamiami Trail (U.S. 41). From Naples, it's 35 miles east to Everglades City's Gulf Coast Ranger Station and 70 miles east to the Shark Valley Information Center. From Miami, it's 40 miles west to Shark Valley and 83 miles west to Everglades City.

To reach Biscayne National Park, take the Florida Turnpike extension from Miami to the Tallahassee Road (S.W. 137th Ave.) exit, turn left, and go south. Turn left at North Canal Drive (S.W. 328th St.), go east, and follow signs to park headquarters at Convoy Point. The park is about 30 miles from downtown Miami.

### By Plane

**Miami International Airport** (MIA) is 34 miles from Homestead and 83 miles from the Flamingo resort in Everglades National Park.

BETWEEN THE AIRPORT AND TOWNS
**Airporter** (☎ 800/830–3413) runs shuttle buses three times daily offseason, four times daily in winter, that stop at the Hampton Inn in Florida City on their way between MIA and the Florida Keys. Shuttle service, which takes approximately an hour, runs 6:10 AM–5:20 PM from Florida City, 7:30 AM–6 PM from the airport. Reserve in advance. Pickups can be arranged for all baggage-claim areas. The cost is $20 oneway.

**Greyhound Lines** operates three buses daily in each direction between the Homestead bus stop (⊠ 5 N.E. 3rd Rd., ☎ 305/247–2040) and Miami's Greyhound depot (⊠ 4111 N.W. 27th St., ☎ 305/871–1810), from which it's about a $5 cab ride to MIA. You can take a blue ARTS (Airport Region Taxi Service) car from MIA to the Greyhound depot for about $5.

**Metrobus** Route 1A runs from Homestead to MIA only during peak weekday hours (6:30–9 AM and 4–6:30 PM). Fare is $1.25.

**SuperShuttle** (☎ 305/871–2000) operates 11-passenger air-conditioned vans to Homestead. Service from MIA is available around the clock, on demand; booths are located outside most luggage areas on the lower level. For the return to MIA, reserve 24 hours. The cost is $40 for the first person, $12 for each additional person at the same address.

## Getting Around

### By Boat

Bring aboard the proper *NOAA Nautical Charts* before you cast off to explore park waters. The charts run $15–$15.95 at many marine stores in South Florida, at the Convoy Point Visitor Center in Biscayne National Park, and at Flamingo Marina in the Everglades.

The annual *Waterway Guide* (southern regional edition) is widely used by boaters. Bookstores all over South Florida sell it, or you can order it directly from the publisher (✉ Argus Business, Book Department, 6151 Powers Ferry Rd., Atlanta, GA 30339, ☎ 800/233–3359) for $33.95 plus $3 shipping and handling.

### By Car

If you don't have your own car, you'll want to rent one to get from Homestead–Florida City to the parks. Agencies in the area include **A&A Auto Rental** (✉ 30005 S. Dixie Hwy., Homestead 33030, ☎ 305/246–0974), **Enterprise Rent-a-Car** (✉ 30428 S. Federal Hwy., Homestead 33030, ☎ 305/246–2056), and **Thrifty Car Rental** (✉ 406 N. Krome Ave., Homestead 33030, ☎ 305/245–8992).

To reach Everglades National Park's Main Visitor Center and Flamingo, turn right (west) onto Route 9336 in Florida City, and follow signs to the park. From Homestead, the Main Visitor Center is 11 miles, and Flamingo is 49 miles.

To get to the south end of Everglades National Park in the Florida Keys, take U.S. 1 south from Homestead. It's 27 miles to the Key Largo Ranger Station (between Mile Markers 98 and 99, BS, Overseas Hwy.), which is not always staffed but has maps and information.

To reach Biscayne National Park from Homestead, take U.S. 1 or Krome Avenue to Lucy Street (S.E. 8th St.), and turn east. Lucy Street becomes North Canal Drive (S.W. 328th St.). Follow signs for about 8 miles to the park headquarters.

### By Taxi

The local cab company is **New Taxi** (☎ 305/247–7466). Others servicing the area include **Action Express Taxi** (☎ 305/743–6800) and **South Dade Taxi** (☎ 305/256–4444).

## Guided Tours

Tours of Everglades and Biscayne national parks typically focus on native wildlife, plants, and park history. Concessionaires operate tram tours in the Everglades and boat cruises in both parks. In addition, the National Park Service organizes a variety of free programs at Everglades National Park. ✉ *Biscayne National Park Convoy Visitors Center, 9700 S.W. 328th St., Homestead,* ☎ *305/230–7275; Everglades Main Visitor Center, 305/242–7700.*

### Boat Tours

**Back Country Tour** gives two-hour cruises aboard a 40-passenger catamaran. The cost (including tax) is $12. **Everglades National Park Boat Tours** in Everglades City (✉ Gulf Coast Ranger Station, Rte. 29, ☎

941/695–2591; in FL, 800/445–7724) carry 40 to 140 passengers (the two largest boats have food and drink concessions) on three separate 14-mile tours through the Ten Thousand Islands region along the Gulf of Mexico on the western margin of the park. The cost is $11. **Flamingo Lodge Marina & Outpost Resort** (⊠ TW Recreational Services Inc., Everglades National Park, 1 Flamingo Lodge Hwy., Flamingo 33034, ☎ 305/253–2241 or 941/695–3101, FAX 941/695–3921), offers a number of services, including help in arranging for individualized tours given by charter fishing-boat captains. The cost is $265 a day for up to two people, $25 each additional person. **Florida Bay Cruise** runs 90-minute tours of Florida Bay aboard *Bald Eagle,* a 90-passenger catamaran. It costs $8.50. **Majestic Tours** (⊠ Box 241, 33929, ☎ 941/695–2777) are led by exceptionally well-informed guides Frank and Georgia Garrett. The 3½- to 4-hour trips, on a 24-foot pontoon boat, depart from Glades Haven, just shy of a mile south of the circle in Everglades City; take in the Ten Thousand Islands and visit the Watson Place, site of a turn-of-the-century wilderness plantation run by a fearsome outlaw. Tours are limited to six passengers and include brunch or afternoon snacks. The cost is $60 per person.

**North American Canoe Tours** (⊠ Ivey House, 107 Camellia St., Box 5038, Everglades City 33929, ☎ 941/695–4666 or 941/695–3299; May–Sept., 203/739–0791; FAX 941/695–4155) leads one-day to six-night Everglades tours November through April. Highlights include bird and gator sightings, mangrove forests, no-man's-land beaches, relics of the hideouts of infamous and just plain reclusive characters, and spectacular sunsets. Included in the cost of extended tours ($450–$750) are canoes, all necessary equipment, a guide, meals, and lodging for the first and last nights at the Ivey House B&B in Everglades City. Day trips cost $40, and one-day bicycling and hiking tours are also offered.

## Orientation Tours

Tours at Biscayne National Park are now run by people-friendly **Biscayne National Underwater Park,** the park concessionaire (⊠ Convoy Point, east end of North Canal Dr. [S.W. 328th St.], Box 1270, Homestead 33090, ☎ 305/230–1100, FAX 305/230–1120). Daily trips (10–1) explore the park's living coral reefs 10 miles offshore on *Reef Rover IV,* a 53-foot glass-bottom boat that carries up to 49 passengers. On days when the weather is unsuitable for reef viewing, an alternative two-hour, ranger-led, interpretive tour visits Elliott Key. Reservations are recommended, especially in summer. The cost is $16.50 adults, $15.50 seniors, and $8.50 children under 13.

## Special-Interest Tours

**Everglades Air Tours** (⊠ Homestead General Aviation Airport, 28790 S.W. 217th Ave., Homestead, ☎ 305/248–7754) gives bird's-eye tours of the Everglades and Florida Bay that last 50 minutes and cost $55 per person.

In Everglades City, **Florida Boat Tours** (⊠ 200 Rte. 29, ☎ 941/695–4400; in FL, 800/282–9194) runs 30- to 40-minute backcountry tours aboard custom-designed jet airboats. The cost is $11.95. **Swampland Airboat Tours** (⊠ Box 619, 33929, ☎ 941/695–2740 or 800/344–2740) offers custom tours of the Everglades or the Big Cypress National Preserve. The cost is $60 per hour for up to six persons. Reservations are required. **Wooten's Everglades** (⊠ Wooten's Alligator Farm, Tamiami Trail, ☎ 941/695–2781 or 800/282–2781) runs a variety of airboat and swamp-buggy tours through the Everglades. (Swamp buggies are giant tractorlike vehicles with oversize rubber wheels.) Tours of approximately 30 mins cost $12.

Southwest of Florida City near the entrance to Everglades National Park, **Everglades Alligator Farm** (⊠ 40351 S.W. 192nd Ave., ☎ 305/247–2628) runs a 4-mile, 30-minute tour of the River of Grass with departures 20 minutes after the hour. The tour includes free hourly alligator shows and feedings. Costs are $11 for the tour and show, or $5 for the show only. No reservations are necessary.

From Shark Valley, **Buffalo Tiger's Florida Everglades Airboat Ride** (⊠ 12 mi west of Krome Ave., 20 mi west of Miami city limits on Tamiami Trail, ☎ 305/559–5250) is led by a former chairman of the Miccosukee tribe. The 35- to 40-minute trip through the Everglades includes a stop at an old Native American camp. Tours cost $10 and operate Monday through Thursday and Saturday 10–sunset and Sunday 11–sunset. Reservations are not required. **Coopertown Airboat Ride** (⊠ 5 mi west of Krome Ave. on Tamiami Trail, ☎ 305/226–6048) operates the oldest airboat rides in the Everglades (since 1945). The 30- to 35-minute tour through the Everglades saw grass visits two hammocks (subtropical hardwood forests) and alligator holes. The charge is $9, with a $22 minimum for the boat. **Everglades Gator Park** (⊠ 12 mi west of Florida's Turnpike on Tamiami Trail, ☎ 305/559–2255) offers free tours of a Native American village and 45-minute airboat tours. Rates (including tax) are $12 adults and $6.50 children 6–12. A gift shop and restaurant are also on the premises.

## Tram Tours

In Flamingo, **Wilderness Tram Tour** (⊠ Flamingo Lodge, ☎ 305/253–2241 or 941/695–3101) visits Snake Bight, an indentation in the Florida Bay shoreline, aboard a 42-passenger screened tram. This two-hour tour passes through a mangrove forest and a coastal prairie to a 100-yard boardwalk over the mud flats at the edge of the bight. The cost (including tax) is $7.95.

Starting at the Shark Valley visitor center off the Tamiami Trail, **Shark Valley Tram Tours** (⊠ Box 1729, Tamiami Station, Miami 33144, ☎ 305/221–8455) follow a 15-mile loop road into the interior, stopping at a 50-foot observation tower especially good for viewing gators in winter. Tours cost $8. Reservations are recommended December through March.

# Contacts and Resources

## Emergencies

Dial 911 for **police** or **ambulance.** In the national parks, rangers answer police, fire, and medical emergencies. Phone the park switchboards: **Biscayne** (☎ 305/230–1144) or **Everglades** (☎ 305/242–7700). **Florida Marine Patrol** (☎ 305/325–3346), a division of the Florida Department of Natural Resources, maintains a 24-hour telephone service for reporting boating emergencies and natural resource violations. **Miami Beach Coast Guard Base** (⊠ 100 MacArthur Causeway, Miami Beach, ☎ 305/535–4300 or 305/535–4314) responds to local marine emergencies and reports of navigation hazards. The base broadcasts on VHF-FM Channel 16. The National Weather Service supplies local forecasts through its **National Hurricane Center** (⊠ Tamiami Trail Campus of Florida International University, ☎ 305/665–0429).

## Hospitals

**SMH Homestead Hospital** (⊠ 160 N.W. 13th St., Homestead, ☎ 305/248–3232; physician referral, ☎ 305/633–2255).

## Visitor Information

**Biscayne National Park:** Convoy Point Visitor Center (✉ 9700 S.W. 328th St., Box 1369, Homestead 33090-1369, ☎ 305/230–7275). **Everglades City Chamber of Commerce** (✉ Rte. 29 and Tamiami Trail, Everglades City 33929, ☎ 941/695–3941). **Everglades National Park:** Main Visitor Center (✉ 40001 Rte. 9336, Florida City 33034-6733, ☎ 305/242–7700), Gulf Coast Ranger Station (✉ Rte. 29, Everglades City 33929, ☎ 941/695–3311), Flamingo Ranger Station (✉ 1 Flamingo Lodge Hwy., Flamingo 33034-6798, ☎ 941/695–2945). **Homestead–Florida City Chamber of Commerce** (✉ 43 N. Krome Ave., Homestead 33030, ☎ 305/247–2332). **South Dade Visitor Information Center** (✉ 160 U.S. 1, Florida City 33034, ☎ 305/245–9180 or 800/388–9669, FAX 305/247–4335).

# 5 Fort Lauderdale

*Once known for its wild spring breaks, this southern Florida city on the east coast is newly chic. Just as the beach has renewed itself, so has downtown— with residential construction and an emerging cultural arts district.*

By Herb Hiller

Updated by
Rowland Stitler

**W**ITH ITS REJUVENATED BEACHFRONT and downtown acting like balanced weights on the ends
of a barbell, Fort Lauderdale has bench-
pressed its way out of a reputation for rowdy spring breaks, and the
renewed urban center has replaced scantily clad collegians as the most-
talked-about attraction of vacationing here. You can drive between beach
and town along beautiful Las Olas Boulevard, ride the free midweek
trolley, or—the best bet for experiencing this canal-laced city—cruise
aboard the city's water taxi. All this, plus the new expressway system
that connects city and airport (including Florida's only vehicular tunnel), makes getting around Fort Lauderdale remarkably hassle-free—
unusual in congested Florida.

Unusual in a state where gaudy tourist zones stand aloof from worka-
day downtowns, Fort Lauderdale exhibits uncommon consistency at
both ends of the 2-mile Las Olas corridor. The sparkling new look results from a decision to thoroughly improve both beachfront and downtown as opposed to focusing design attention in town and letting the
beachfront fall prey to development solely by T-shirt retailers. For 2
miles beginning just north of the new welcome center and the big
Radisson Bahia Mar Beach Resort, strollers and café goers along Atlantic Boulevard enjoy clear views, typically across rows of colorful
beach umbrellas, to the sea and ships passing in and out of nearby Port
Everglades. Those on the beach can look back to an exceptionally graceful promenade.

Pedestrians rank ahead of cars in Fort Lauderdale. Broad walkways
line both sides of Ocean Boulevard, the shore road, and traffic has been
trimmed to two gently curving northbound lanes, where in-line skaters
dance alongside the slow-moving cars. On the beach side, a low ma-
sonry wall, which serves as an extended bench for pedestrians, edges
the promenade. Where side streets reach the shore road, the wave crests
and then breaks for pedestrian access to the beach. At night, the wall
is wrapped in ribbons of fiber-optic color. On the west side of Atlantic
Boulevard, the inland side, the 17-story Beach Place residential, retail,
and entertainment complex two blocks north of Las Olas, opened in
late 1996. Otherwise there are mostly low-rise hotels plus a defining
row of smart cafés, restaurants, bars, and shops that seem to have sprung
up overnight.

North of the redesigned beachfront are another 2 miles of open and
natural coastal landscape. Much of the way parallels the Hugh Taylor Birch State Recreation Area, which preserves a patch of primeval
Florida.

The downtown area along the New River, site of a new arts and entertainment district, is as lovely as the renewed beach. Where drug deals
went down less than five years ago, pricey tickets now sell for Broadway shows at the riverfront Broward Center for the Performing Arts.
Clustered within a five-minute walk are the Museum of Discovery and
Science with its Blockbuster IMAX Theater, the expanding Fort Lauderdale Historical Society Museum, and the Museum of Art with its leading collection of works from the 20th-century CoBrA (Copenhagen,
Brussels, and Amsterdam) movement. Restaurants, sidewalk cafés,
delis, and blues, folk, jazz, reggae, and rock clubs flourish. Brickell Station, along several blocks once owned by pioneers William and Mary
Brickell, opened its multistory entertainment stages, restaurants, and
shops in 1996. The $40 million New World Aquarium is opening in
1997, and, in 1998, a living-history complex called Old Fort Lauderdale,

with reenactments and docents in pioneer dress centered on the Museum of History is scheduled to debut.

Tying this district together is the Riverwalk, which extends a mile along the New River's north bank and a half mile along the south. Tropical gardens with benches and interpretive displays fringe the walk on one side, boat landings on the other. East along Riverwalk is the 19th-century Stranahan House. A block away, Las Olas attractions begin. Tropical landscaping and trees separate the traffic lanes in some blocks, setting off fine shops, restaurants, and popular nightspots. From here it's five minutes by car or 30 minutes by water taxi back to the beach.

Broward County is named for Napoleon Bonaparte Broward, Florida's governor from 1905 to 1909, whose drainage schemes around the turn of the century opened much of the marshy Everglades region for farming, ranching, and settlement (in retrospect an environmental disaster). Fort Lauderdale's first known white settler, Charles Lewis, established a plantation along the New River in 1793. Major William Lauderdale built a fort at the river's mouth in 1838 during the Seminole Indian wars—hence the city's name.

Incorporated in 1911, with just 175 residents, Fort Lauderdale grew rapidly during the Florida boom of the 1920s. Today the city has a population of 150,000, and its suburban areas keep growing and growing—1.3 million live in the county. New homes, offices, and shopping centers have filled in the gaps between older communities along the coastal ridge. Now they're marching west along I–75, I–595, and the Sawgrass Expressway. Broward County is blessed with near-ideal weather, with some 3,000 hours of sunshine a year. The average temperature is about 66°F–77°F in winter, 84°F in summer. Once a home for retirees, the county today attracts younger, working-age families. It's always been known as a sane and pleasant place to live (spring break aside). Now it's also becoming one of Florida's most diverse and dynamic places to vacation.

# Pleasures and Pastimes

## The Arts
In forging a new image over the past 20 years, Fort Lauderdale has made a massive commitment to the arts. The centerpiece of the city's arts district is the **Broward Center for the Performing Arts,** with more than 500 events a year, including Broadway shows, ballet, opera, symphony and children's theater. This, complemented by the many galleries and museums in the city, makes taking in the arts a part of any trip to Fort Lauderdale.

## Beaches
Fort Lauderdale's beachfront extends for miles without interruption, although the character of the communities behind the beach changes. For example, in Hallandale at far south Broward County, the beach is backed by towering condominiums; in Hollywood, by motels and the hoi-polloi Broadwalk; and just north of there—blessedly—there's nothing at all.

## Biking
Fort Lauderdale is a great place for cycling. Although the traffic along many of the main thoroughfares can be heavy, there are several bike paths, including the 2.2-mile boardwalk on Hollywood Beach. A 7-mile bike path running along Rte. 84 and the New River leads to Markham Park, which has mountain bike trails. Most area bike shops have county cycling maps.

## Diving

Good diving can be enjoyed within 20 minutes of the shore along Broward County's coast. Among the most popular of the county's 80 dive sites is the 2-mile-wide, 23-mile-long **Fort Lauderdale Reef,** the product of Florida's most successful artificial reef–building program. The project began in 1984 with the sinking of a 435-foot freighter donated by an Oklahoma marine electronics manufacturer. Since then more than a dozen houseboats, ships, and oil platforms have been sunk in depths of 10 to 150 feet to provide a habitat for fish and other marine life, as well as to help stabilize beaches. The most famous sunken ship is the 200-foot German freighter *Mercedes,* which was blown onto Palm Beach socialite Mollie Wilmot's pool terrace in a violent Thanksgiving storm in 1984; the ship is now underwater a mile off Fort Lauderdale beach.

## Fishing

Four main types of fishing are available in Broward County: bottom or drift-boat fishing from party boats, deep-sea fishing for large sport fish on charters, angling for freshwater game fish, and dropping a line off a pier.

## Golf

In addition to having a tropical climate that's perfect for playing almost every day of the year, Broward County features great golf bargains. More than 50 courses, public and private, green the landscape in metro Fort Lauderdale, including famous championship links, and many hotels offer golf packages.

## Horse Racing

From mid-January to mid-March, you can place your bets at Gulfstream Park Race Track, home of the popular Florida Derby. Just north of Fort Lauderdale there's 11 months of harness racing at Pompano Harness Track.

## Lodging

In Fort Lauderdale, Pompano Beach, and the Hollywood-Hallandale area, dozens of hotels open onto the Atlantic Ocean beaches. In much of Fort Lauderdale, however, lodgings are limited to the upland side of the beach roads and in much of Hollywood to the upland side of the Broadwalk, leaving the beaches open to pedestrians and motorists. Lodgings range from economy motels—most notably those along much of the Hollywood beachfront and in the non-oceanfront areas of Fort Lauderdale—to a few opulent beachfronts and canalfront resorts in Fort Lauderdale. Good choices are found, too, in Lauderdale-by-the-Sea, a small suburb just north of Fort Lauderdale, graced with an accessible cultural life and high standards. Major chain hotels inland along I-95 north and south of the airport cater primarily to business travelers and overnight visitors en route to somewhere else.

An innovative Superior Small Lodging program, set up by the Greater Fort Lauderdale Convention & Visitors Bureau and administered by the hospitality department of Broward County's Nova University, has led to substantial upgrading of many smaller properties, without appreciable elevation of their usually modest rates.

## Nightlife

A dazzling and varied nightlife makes this oceanside city an excellent place to party. The same canals that are lined with waterfront restaurants also have bars and clubs, and the city's Water Taxi service even has a "pub crawl" service two nights a week so you don't have to drive after you drink. Many clubs around the city have live music or stand-up comedians.

## Shopping

Fort Lauderdale offers two kinds of shopping—the individual shops and boutiques found along Las Olas Boulevard and along Ocean Boulevard on the beach, and the groups of shops found at that ubiquitous American institution—the mall. The metro area has four major malls, including the Sawgrass Mill in Sunrise, with more than 250 stores. The new Beach Place shopping, lodging, and dining complex opened near Port Everglades in 1996.

## Spas

Two world-famous spas, the **Bonaventure Resort & Spa** in Fort Lauderdale and the **Palm-Aire Spa Resort** in Pompano Beach, have put Fort Lauderdale firmly on the spa-goers map. Both offer massages, facials, body wraps, and the kind of pampering and health rituals that people travel miles to experience. Several major hotels, also eager to join the fitness revolution, have their own spas that are somewhat less elaborate.

# EXPLORING FORT LAUDERDALE

The metro area is laid out in a basic grid system and only the hundreds of canals and waterways interrupt the straight-line path of the streets and roads. Nomenclature is important here. Streets, roads, courts, and drives run east–west. Avenues, terraces, and ways run north–south. Boulevards can run any which way. Las Olas Boulevard is one of the most important east-west thoroughfares while Atlantic runs along the north-south oceanfront.

The boulevards, those that are paved and those made of water, give Fort Lauderdale its distinct character—it's been called the Venice of America and the yachting capital of the world. Honeycombed with more than 260 miles of navigable waterways, the city is home port for about 40,000 privately owned boats. You won't see the gondolas you'd find in Venice, but you will see just about every other craft imaginable docked beside the thousands of homes and businesses that each have a little piece of waterfront. Visitors can tour the canals via the city's water-taxi system, made up of small motor launches that provide transportation and quick, narrated tours. Larger, multideck touring vessels and motorboat rentals for self-guided tours are other options. The Intracoastal Waterway, a massive canal that parallels Atlantic Boulevard, is the nautical equivalent of an interstate highway. It runs north–south through the metro area and provides easy access to neighboring beach communities; Deerfield Beach and Pompano Beach lie to the north and Dania and Hollywood lie to the south. All are within a 15-mile radius of the city center.

## Great Itineraries

The most enjoyable sights of Fort Lauderdale are relatively close to each other. You can catch a lot of the history, the museums, and the shops and bistros in the downtown area and along Las Olas Boulevard. From there, the beach is only a 10-minute drive to the east. Once you've reached the intersection of Las Olas and Atlantic Boulevard, you're there. Enjoy the sand and surf or work your way either north or south. Many of the neighboring suburbs, with attractions of their own, are just north or south of Fort Lauderdale. You can have a great visit to the city and hit most of the high points in three days. But if you have as many as seven to ten days, you can see virtually all of Fort Lauderdale's mainstream charms, and still have time for a quick ocean cruise.

*Numbers in the text below correspond to numbers in the margin and on the map.*

IF YOU HAVE 3 DAYS

On the first day, see the downtown area including **Stranahan House** ①, the oldest standing structure in Fort Lauderdale. Take time to shop and dine along Las Olas Boulevard between E. 6th and SE 11th avenues, sampling international bistros like Café Europa. The second day is for the beach. The Fort Lauderdale municipal beach runs north, adjacent to the intersection of Atlantic Boulevard and Las Olas. Don't miss the downtown **Riverwalk** ④, which you can see at a leisurely pace in half a day. Tour the canals on the third day, either on a rented boat from one of the various marinas along Atlantic Boulevard, or via the Water Taxi or a sighseeing boat, both of which can be boarded all along the Intracoastal Waterway.

IF YOU HAVE 5 DAYS

You can see more of the beach and more of the arts district and work in some outdoor sports like fishing if you have five days. On the first day, try Eco-Float, the tour sponsored by the Museum of Discovery & Science and the Water Taxi, a local commercial transportation company. The 30-minute tour explores the flora, fauna, history, and legends of the New River. You can get lost in the museum itself, which has seven permanent exhibits and a Blockbuster IMAX Theater showing stunning films on a five-story screen. Set aside the next day for an offshore adventure. Sign up for a deep-sea charter boat fishing trip at the Radisson Bahia Mar Resort in Fort Lauderdale or book a dive trip to the 23-mile long Fort Lauderdale Reef at several dive shops, like Pro Dive at the Bahia Mar Resort, or Lauderdale Diver. On the third day, shop and dine along the **Fort Lauderdale beachfront** ⑧ and at the end of the day, sneak a peak at the **Hillsboro Light** ⑫. Another good day can be spent at the **Hugh Taylor Birch State Recreation Area** ⑨ just off Rte. A1A at Sunrise Boulevard. The 180-acre park has a nature trail through tropical greenery as well as a museum, picnic area, and a place to rent canoes. Spend the fifth day at **Deerfield Island Park** ⑬, near the northern Broward County town of Deerfield Beach. The park, which can only be reached by a free ferry ride, is an 8-acre man-made island that features a mangrove swamp that sustains gopher tortoises, gray foxes, raccoons, and armadillos.

IF YOU HAVE 7 DAYS

With a full week in the Fort Lauderdale area, there's plenty of time to relax and pamper yourself, and there are few places better than **Bonaventure Resort & Spa** or the **Palm-Aire Spa Resort.** Spend a day at each, enjoying massages, body wraps, and facials. On the third day, tour the canals on a sightseeing boat or water taxi, and explore one of the area's greatest natural assets. Then shop and dine along Las Olas. The fourth day might be devoted to the many museums in downtown Fort Lauderdale; spend time studying art from all genres at the **Museum of Art** ②, move to the **Arts and Science District** ⑤, then partake of a little local history at the Fort Lauderdale Historical Society museum. On the fifth day, take an airboat ride at Sawgrass Recreation Park, at the edge of the Everglades. Fort Lauderdale offers plenty of facilities for outdoor recreation—spend Day Six fishing and picnicking on one of the area's many piers or playing a few rounds at top golf courses. Set aside the seventh day for Hollywood, where you can stroll along the scenic **Broadwalk** ⑮ or through a walk-through aviary at Flamingo Gardens before relaxing in peaceful **Hollywood North Beach Park** ⑯.

# Downtown Fort Lauderdale

Downtown Fort Lauderdale has at least three things going for it as a place to visit. First, there's Las Olas Boulevard, which combines quaint shops, sidewalk cafés, and historic buildings. Second, the city center hosts a crowd of museums representing art, history, and science. The third draw is the New River, which winds through downtown. From the Riverwalk, a sidewalk that runs alongside the New River, you can spend hours gazing at a rainbow of colorful yachts—many from foreign ports—that are docked curbside along the walkway.

With a bigger concentration of hotels, restaurants, and sights to see than its suburban neighbors, Fort Lauderdale makes a logical base of operations for any visit. There's nothing like settling into a beachfront hotel, turning up the air conditioner a few notches if you have arrived during the eight months of heat that qualify as summer, and getting ready to hit the beaches. After you've gotten your feet wet, literally, you'll find that there are almost a limitless number of other funs things to do.

## A Good Tour

*Numbers in the text below correspond to numbers in the margin and on the Fort Lauderdale Area map.*

Start on S.E. 6th Avenue at Las Olas Boulevard, where you'll find **Strana-han House** ①, home of pioneer businessman Frank Stranahan and the oldest standing structure in Fort Lauderdale. Then go north on S.E. 6th Avenue to Las Olas Boulevard proper. Between S.E. 6th and S.E. 11th avenues, Las Olas is an upscale shopping street with Spanish-Colonial buildings housing high-fashion boutiques, jewelry shops, and art galleries. If you drive east on Las Olas, you'll cross into The Isles, Fort Lauderdale's most expensive and prestigious neighborhood, where the homes line a series of canals with large yachts beside the seawalls.

Return West on Las Olas to Andrews Avenue, turn right, and park in one of the municipal garages so you can walk around downtown Fort Lauderdale. First stop is the **Museum of Art** ②, which has a major collection of works from the CoBrA movement. Walk one block north to the **Broward County Main Library** ③. On display here are many works from Broward's Art in Public Places program.

Go west on S.E. 2nd Street to S.W. 2nd Avenue, turn left, and head toward palm-lined **Riverwalk** ④, for a leisurely stroll. Head north toward a cluster of new facilities collectively known as the **Arts and Science District** ⑤. The district includes the outdoor Esplanade, which has several exhibits, including a hands-on display of the science and history of navigation. The adjacent Broward Center for the Performing Arts, a massive glass and concrete structure by the river, opened in 1991.

East of the Esplanade along the Riverwalk is the Fort Lauderdale Historical Society Musem, which surveys the city's history from the Seminole era to World War II.

Finally, go five blocks west along Las Olas Boulevard to S.W. 7th Avenue and the entrance to **Sailboat Bend** ⑥. You can return to the start of the tour by traveling east along Las Olas Boulevard.

### TIMING

Depending on how long you like to linger in museums and how many hours you want to spend in the quaint shops on Las Olas Boulevard, you can spend anything from half a day to an entire day on this tour. Budget at least a day to cover the museum district or set aside an af-

## Fort Lauderdale Area

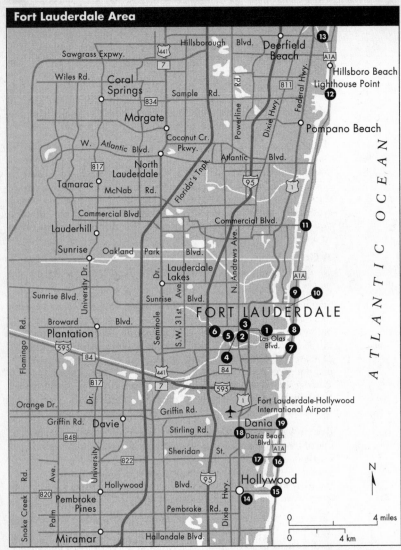

Art and Culture Center of Hollywood, **14**

Arts and Science District, **5**

Bonnet House, **10**

Broadwalk, **15**

Broward County Main Library, **3**

Deerfield Island Park, **13**

Fort Lauderdale beachfront, **8**

Graves Museum of Archeology & Natural History, **18**

Hillsboro Light, **12**

Hollywood North Beach Park, **16**

Hugh Taylor Birch State Recreation Area, **9**

International Swimming Hall of Fame Museum and Aquatic Complex, **7**

John U. Lloyd Beach State Recreation Area, **19**

Lauderdale-by-the-Sea, **11**

Museum of Art, **2**

Riverwalk, **4**

Sailboat Bend, **6**

Stranahan House, **1**

West Lake Park, **17**

ternoon to see just a few museums. Leave the rest of the day for a canal cruise along Fort Lauderdale's water highways.

## Sights to See

★ ☺ ❺ **Arts and Science District.** The major science attraction here is the $30 million **Museum of Discovery and Science.** It contains a 55-foot-by-71-foot screen in the Blockbuster IMAX Theater, which has six-channel sound and interactive exhibits on ecology, health, and outer space. Many displays focus on the local environment, including a replica of an oak forest complete with mosses, lichens, and air plants, which grow without soil. Another unusual exhibit offers a cutaway of an Indian shell mound. For a sunny respite from the dim labyrinth of indoor diplays, check out the exhibits on the Esplanade outside. ⊠ *401 S.W. 2nd St.; museums,* ☎ *954/467–6637; IMAX, 954/463–4629.* ▨ *Museum $6, IMAX $5, both $8.* ☺ *Weekdays 10–5, Sat. 10–8:30, Sun. noon–5.*

❸ **Broward County Main Library.** This distinctive building was designed by Marcel Breuer. Works on display from Broward's Art in Public Places program include a painting by Yaacov Agam; a wood construction by Marc Beauregard; an outdoor, aluminum-and-steel sculpture by Dale Eldred; and ceramic tile by Ivan Chermayeff. (Art in Public Places displays more than 200 works—painting, sculpture, photographs, weaving—by nationally renowned and Florida artists. Pieces can be found at 13 major sites, including the main bus terminal and the airport.) Productions from theater to poetry readings are presented in a 300-seat auditorium. ⊠ *100 S. Andrews Ave.,* ☎ *954/357–7444; self-guided Art in Public Places walking tour brochure, 954/357–7457.* ▨ *Free.* ☺ *Mon.–Thurs. 9–9, Fri. and Sat. 9–5, Sun. noon–5:30.*

**Fort Lauderdale Historical Society Museum.** In 1996, this museum expanded into several historic buildings, including the King-Cromartie House and the old New River Inn. The complex surveys the city's history from the Seminole era to World War II. A model in the lobby depicts old Fort Lauderdale. The building also houses a research library and a bookstore. ⊠ *219 S.W. 2nd Ave.,* ☎ *954/463–4431.* ▨ *$2.* ☺ *Tues.–Sat. 10–4, Sun. 1–4.*

★ ❷ **Museum of Art.** Works from the CoBrA movement, plus Native American, pre-Columbian, West African, and Oceanic ethnographic art are on display here. Edward Larrabee Barnes designed the museum building, which opened in 1986. The museum has a notable collection of works by celebrated Ashcan School artist William Glackens and other early 20th-century American painters. ⊠ *1 E. Las Olas Blvd.,* ☎ *954/525–5500.* ▨ *$5.* ☺ *Tues. 11–9, Wed.–Sat. 10–5, Sun. noon–5.*

★ ❹ **Riverwalk.** This lovely, paved promenade on the north bank of the New River is great for entertainment as well as views. On the first Sunday of every month SunTrust Bank sponsors a jazz brunch here. And by the late 1990s, the walk will extend 2 miles on both sides of the beautiful urban stream, connecting the facilities of the **Arts and Sciences District.**

❻ **Sailboat Bend.** Between Las Olas and the river, as well as just across the river, lies a neighborhood with much of the character of Old Town in Key West and historic Coconut Grove in Miami. No shops or services are located here.

❶ **Stranahan House.** The oldest standing structure in the city was once the home of pioneer businessman Frank Stranahan. Stranahan arrived in 1892 and, with his wife Ivy, befriended the Seminole Indians, traded with them, and taught them "new ways." In 1901 he built a store and later made it his home. Now it's a museum with many of his original furnishings on display. ⊠ *1 Stranahan Pl. (S.E. 6th Ave. at Las Olas Blvd.),* ☎ *954/524–4736.* 🖭 *$5.* ⊘ *Wed.–Sat. 10–4, Sun. 1–4.*

# North on Scenic 1A1

No trip to the Fort Lauderdale area would be complete without breathing in the salt air and feeling the sand against your skin. The beachfront area of Fort Lauderdale offers the best of all possible worlds, with easy access to restaurants and shops. Several oceanside communities are lined up along A1A; Pompano beach is the place for those who like to fish for sport, and Deerfield Beach, farther north, is home to a paradise of coastal hammock, or tree islands, where armadillos make an occasional appearance.

## A Good Tour

Go east on S.E. 17th Street across the Brooks Memorial Causeway over the Intracoastal Waterway and bear left onto Seabreeze Boulevard (Rte. 1A1). You will pass through a neighborhood of older homes set in lush vegetation before emerging at the south end of Fort Lauderdale's beachfront strip. On your left is the newly renovated Radisson Bahia Mar Beach Resort, where novelist John McDonald's fictional hero, Travis McGee, is honored with a plaque at marina slip F-18, where he docked his houseboat. Three blocks north, visit the **International Swimming Hall of Fame Museum and Aquatic Complex** ⑦, which celebrated its 31st anniversary in 1996. As you approach Las Olas Boulevard, you will see the lyrical new styling that has given a distinctly European flavor to the **Fort Lauderdale beachfront** ⑧.

Turn left off Route A1A at Sunrise Boulevard, then right into **Hugh Taylor Birch State Recreation Area** ⑨ where there are many outdoor activities to be enjoyed amidst picturesque flora and fauna. Cross Sunrise Boulevard and visit the **Bonnet House** ⑩ where you'll marvel at both the mansion and subtropical 35-acre estate. North of Birch Park, Route A1A edges back from the beach through the section known as the Galt Ocean Mile, marked by beach-blocking high-rises. The pattern changes again in **Lauderdale-by-the-Sea** ⑪. One block east of Route A1A, you can drive along lawn-divided El Mar Drive, lined by garden-style motels. North of Lauderdale-by-the-Sea, Route A1A enters Pompano Beach where the high-rise procession begins again. Take Atlantic Boulevard east to the beach road, which is first called Pompano Beach Boulevard and then again A1A. Behind a low coral rock wall, a park extends north and south of Fisherman's Wharf along the road and beach. The road swings back from the beach, and returns to it crossing Hillsboro Inlet. To your right across the inlet you can see **Hillsboro Light** ⑫.

Route A1A now enters on to the so-called Hillsboro Mile (actually more than 2 miles), which only a few years ago was one of Florida's outstanding residential corridors—a millionaire's row. Changes in zoning laws, however, have altered it; except for sections in the south and north, the island seems destined to sink under the weight of its massive condominiums. The road runs along a narrow strip of land between the Intracoastal Waterway and the ocean, with bougainvillea and oleanders edging the way and yachts docked along both banks. In winter, the traffic often creeps at a snail's pace along here, as vacationers and retirees gawk at the views.

Turn left on Hillsboro Boulevard (Rte. 810). Make a sharp right just over the bridge onto Riverview Road, and park at the Riverview Restaurant to take a free boat ride to **Deerfield Island Park** ⑬, where the armadillos dwell.

This branch of Fort Lauderdale is all about recreation and leisure. To enjoy it as it's meant to be, allow at least a day to loll on the beach or rent a fishing boat. Depending on the season, traffic along the Hillsboro Mile can be quite congested. Consider this as you head for Deerfield Island Park via the Hillsboro Mile.

## Sights to See

★ ❿ **Bonnet House.** Closed in winter, when Evelyn Fortune Bartlett (now 108) is in residence, this charming mansion, built by Mrs. Bartlett's late husband, artist Frederic Clay Bartlett, stands on land he was given by his first father-in-law, Hugh Taylor Birch. Both the mansion and estate contain original works of art, whimsically carved animals, a swan pond, and, most of all, tranquillity. ⊠ *900 N. Birch Rd.,* ☎ *954/563–5393.* ☞ *$8, by reserved tour only.*

☜ **Butterfly World.** This screened butterfly-breeding farm sits in a tropical rain forest on 3 acres of land. Thousands of caterpillars representing as many as 150 species pupate and emerge as butterflies in a laboratory. A screened aviary called North American Butterflies is reserved for native species. Tropical Rain Forest is a 30-foot-high construction with observation decks, waterfalls, ponds, and tunnels, where colorful butterflies sail and shift about. ⊠ *3600 W. Sample Rd.,* Coconut Creek, ☎ *954/977–4400.* ☞ *$8.95.* ☉ *Mon.–Sat. 9–5, Sun. 1–5.*

⓭ **Deerfield Island Park.** This 8½-acre island, officially designated an urban wilderness area, resulted from the dredging of the Intracoastal Waterway and from construction of the Royal Palm Canal. Its mangrove swamp provides a critical habitat for gopher tortoises, gray foxes, raccoons, and armadillos. ⊠ *1 Deerfield Island, Deerfield Beach,* ☎ *954/360–1320.* ☞ *Free.* ☉ *Wed. and Sat. 8:15–sunset.*

★ ❽ **Fort Lauderdale beachfront.** A wave theme unifies the setting—from the low, white wave wall between the beach and widened beachfront promenade to the widened and bricked inner promenade in front of shops, restaurants, and hotels. Alone among Florida's major beachfront resorts, Fort Lauderdale Beach remains open and unbuilt-upon, and throughout the beach area, you'll see distinctive signs and street furniture. More than ever, the boulevard is worth promenading. ☉ *May–Nov., Tues.–Thurs. 10 and 1:30, Sun. 1:30.*

⓬ **Hillsboro Light.** To your right across Hillsboro Inlet, capture the brightest light in the Southeast. Mariners have used this landmark for decades: from the ocean, you can see the light almost halfway to the Bahamas. Although the lighthouse is on private property and is inaccessible to the public, it's well worth a peek.

❾ **Hugh Taylor Birch State Recreation Area.** Amid the tropical greenery of this 180-acre park you can stroll along a nature trail, visit the Birch House Museum, picnic, play volleyball, pitch horseshoes, and paddle a canoe. ⊠ *3109 E. Sunrise Blvd.,* ☎ *954/564–4521.* ☞ *$3.25 per vehicle with up to 8 people.* ☉ *8–sunset; ranger-guided nature walks Fri. at 10:30.*

★ ❼ **International Swimming Hall of Fame Museum and Aquatic Complex.** This monument to underwater accomplishments has two 10-lane, 50-meter pools and an exhibition building featuring photos, medals, and other souvenirs from major swimming events around the world, as well as a theater that shows films of onetime swimming stars Johnny Weissmuller and Esther Williams. ⊠ *1 Hall of Fame Dr.; museum,* ☎ *954/462–6536 for museum or 954/468–1580 for pool.* ☞ *Museum*

*$3, pool $3.* ☉ *Museum and pro shop daily 9–7; pool weekdays 8–
4 and 6–8, weekends 8–4; closed mid-Dec.–mid-Jan.*

⑪ **Lauderdale-by-the-Sea.** Construction over three stories is banned from
this low-rise family resort town. Dozens of good restaurants and shops
are nearby, so you don't need a car.

NEED A
BREAK?

Where Commercial Boulevard meets the ocean, you can walk out onto
**Anglin's Fishing Pier,** stretching 875 feet into the Atlantic. Stop in at the
coffee shop or at any of the popular restaurants clustered around the
seafront plaza. **Aruba Beach Cafe** (☎ 954/776–0001) is your best bet.
A big beachside barn of a place, always crowded, always fun, it serves
large portions of Caribbean conch chowder, Cuban black-bean soup,
fresh tropical salads, burgers, sandwiches, and seafood.

🐊 **Sawgrass Recreation Park.** This 16½-acre former fish camp is at the
edge of the Everglades. Here you can rent fishing boats, get bait and
tackle, and enjoy a 90-minute series of three tours, one of which includes an airboat ride, a tour of a Native American village replica, and
a live reptile exhibit with alligators and caimans. ⊠ *2 mi north of I–75
on U.S. 27,* ☎ *954/389–0202 or 800/457–0788.* 🎫 *Tour package
$13.40.* ☉ *Tours daily 9–5, shop daily 6–6.*

# Hollywood

This 70-year-old oceanfront community has virtually nothing in common with its California namesake, but it does have the same feeling
as a Los Angeles County beach town. With trendy shops, an occasional
surfer or two, and young people on Rollerblades, this place could easily be in California, if it weren't 15 minutes south of downtown Fort
Lauderdale. And this small town is diverse. It has everything from a
classic beachfront area to a full-fledged Indian reservation.

## A Good Tour

Begin exploring at the junction of U.S. 1 and Hollywood Boulevard,
called Young Circle after Joseph W. Young, a California real estate developer who in 1921 began developing the community of Hollywood
from the woody flatlands. Just east of here, you can visit the **Art and
Culture Center of Hollywood** ⑭, a visual and performing arts center.
Drive east along wide Hollywood Boulevard, a reminder of the glory
of the Young era. Cross the Intracoastal Waterway in front of the Hollywood Beach Resort Hotel, opened by Young in 1922 and now a time-
share with some units available by the night. To the rear of the hotel
is the retail and entertainment center known as Oceanwalk—a good
idea that only inconsistently achieves the right execution.

Take the ramp north onto Route A1A. The Intracoastal Waterway parallels it to the west, and the beach and ocean lie just on the other side
of the 2.2-mile paved promenade, **Broadwalk** ⑮. The Broadwalk ends
at **Hollywood North Beach Park** ⑯.

Turn west onto Sheridan Street and proceed ½ mile. On your left, enter
1,400-acre **West Lake Park** ⑰, a new resource-preserving nature facility with a wide range of recreational activities. Drive West to Federal Highway (U.S. 1), turn right (you have now entered Dania), and
continue past one of Florida's largest antiques districts (☞ Specialty
Stores *in* Shopping, *below*) to the **Graves Museum of Archaeology &
Natural History** ⑱. On display here are Greco-Roman materials, a
3-ton quartz crystal, and dioramas of Tequesta Indian life and jaguar
habitat.

Continue north to Dania Beach Boulevard (Rte. A1A), turn right, and drive to the beach. Just before turning left to enter the **John U. Lloyd Beach State Recreation Area** ⑲, you'll find the Dania Pier (☞ Fishing *in* Outdoor Activities and Sports, *below*) and the colorful SeaFair, a small collection of shops and diversions yet to hit their stride.

From here return via A1A and Hollywood Boulevard to where you began, or take Dania Beach Boulevard north into Fort Lauderdale.

TIMING

You could easily see the high points of Hollywood in half a day, but if you want to gamble at the bingo and poker parlor at the Seminole Indian Village, you may want to stay overnight.

## Sights to See

🖐 **Anhinga Indian Museum and Art Gallery.** Here Joe Dan and Virginia Osceola display a collection of artifacts from the Seminoles and other tribes and sell contemporary Native American arts and crafts. ⊠ *5791 S. Rte. 7, Fort Lauderdale,* ☎ *954/581–0416.* ☉ *Daily 9–5.*

⑭ **Art and Culture Center of Hollywood.** This visual and performing arts center has an art reference library, outdoor sculpture garden, arts school, and museum store. ⊠ *1650 Harrison St.,* ☎ *954/921–3274.* 🖾 *Wed.–Sat. $3, Sun. $5 (including classical or jazz concert); donations welcome Tues.* ☉ *Tues.–Sat. 10–4, Sun. 1–4.*

⑮ **Broadwalk.** Since 1924 this scenic stretch has been popular with pedestrians and cyclists. Expect to hear French spoken, especially during the winter; Hollywood Beach has been a favorite winter getaway for Québecois ever since Joseph Young hired French-Canadians to work here in the 1920s.

NEED A BREAK?

One-half mile north of the Broadwalk on the left is **Le Tub** (⊠ 1100 N. Ocean Dr., ☎ 954/921-9425), formerly a Sunoco gas station and now a quirky waterside saloon with a seeming affection for clawfoot bathtubs. Hand-painted tubs are everywhere, under ficus, sea grape, and palm trees. Le Tub is highly favored by locals for affordable food, mostly shrimp and barbecue.

🖐 **Flamingo Gardens.** Gators, crocodiles, river otters, and birds of prey can be seen here, as well as a 23,000-square foot walk-through aviary, a plant house, and an Everglades Museum in the pioneer Wray Home. Admission includes a half-hour guided tram ride through a citrus grove and wetlands area. ⊠ *3750 Flamingo Rd., Davie,* ☎ *954/473–0010.* 🖾 *$8.* ☉ *Daily 9–5.*

⑱ **Graves Museum of Archaeology & Natural History.** Exhibits include collections of pre-Columbian art and underwater artifacts from St. Thomas harbor as well as a 9,000-square-foot dinosaur hall and additional wildlife dioramas. Monthly lectures, conferences, field trips, and a summer archaeological camp are offered. The museum bookstore is one of the best in Florida. ⊠ *481 S. Federal Hwy.,* ☎ *954/925–7770,* 🖾 *954/925–7064.* 🖾 *$5.* ☉ *Tues.–Wed., Fri., and Sat. 10–4; Thurs. 10–8; Sun. 1–4.*

⑯ **Hollywood North Beach Park.** No high rises overpower the scene, nothing hip or chic, just a laid-back old-fashioned place for enjoying the sun, sand, and sea. ⊠ *Rte. A1A and Sheridan St.,* ☎ *954/926–2444.* 🖾 *Free; parking $5 until 2, $3 after.* ☉ *Daily 8–6.*

★ ⑲ **John U. Lloyd Beach State Recreation Area.** This pleasant plot of land has a pine-shaded beach and a jetty pier where you can fish, and it has good views to the north of Palm Beach County and south Miami

Beach. From the road, look west across the waterway to the deep-water freighters and cruise ships in Port Everglades. ⊠ *6503 N. Ocean Dr.,* ☎ *954/923–2833.* ☐ *$3.25 per vehicle.* ☉ *8–sunset.*

**Seminole Native Village.** This is a reservation where Seminole Indians sell their arts and crafts. (The village also has a high-stakes bingo parlor and low-stakes poker tables, but these are not open to kids.) ⊠ *4150 N. Rte. 7, Hollywood,* ☎ *954/961–5140 or 954/961–3220.*

**⑰ West Lake Park.** Canoes, kayaks, and boats with electric motors (no fossil fuels allowed in the park) are available, and more than $1 million in nature exhibits are on display at the Anne Kolb Nature Center, with a shop carrying a large stock of books on the region's environment. Extensive boardwalks traverse a mangrove community, and a 65-foot observation tower allows views of the entire park. ⊠ *1200 Sheridan St.,* ☎ *954/926–2410.*

**☙ Young at Art Children's Museum.** Kids can work in paint, graphics, sculpture, and crafts according to themes that change three times a year, and take their masterpieces home with them. ⊠ *801 S. University Dr. in Fountains Shoppes, Plantation,* ☎ *954/424–0085.* ☐ *$3.* ☉ *Tues.–Sat. 11–5, Sun. noon–5.*

# BEACHES

The most crowded portion of beach is along **Ocean Boulevard,** between Las Olas Boulevard and Sunrise Boulevard in Fort Lauderdale. This is the onetime "strip" famed from *Where the Boys Are* and the era of spring-break madness, now but a memory. Parking is readily available, often at parking meters.

**Dania, Lauderdale-by-the-Sea, Pompano Beach,** and **Deerfield Beach** each have fishing piers in addition to beaches.

# DINING

### American

**$$$ ✕ Burt & Jack's.** Situated at the far end and most scenic lookout of Port Everglades, this local favorite has been operated by veteran restaurateur Jack Jackson and fronted by actor Burt Reynolds since 1984. Behind the heavy mission doors and bougainvillea, guests are presented with Maine lobster, steaks, and chops. The main ingredients are displayed in the raw by the waitstaff before orders are taken. The two-story gallery of haciendalike dining rooms surrounded by glass has views of both the Intracoastal Waterway and John U. Lloyd Beach State Recreation Area. Come Saturday or Sunday in early evening for cocktails and watch the cruise ships steam out. The dining area is non-smoking. ⊠ *Berth 23, Port Everglades, Fort Lauderdale,* ☎ *954/522–2878 or 954/525–5225. Jacket required. AE, D, DC, MC, V. No lunch.*

**$$$ ✕ Cafe Maxx.** New-wave epicurean dining had its South Florida start
**★** here in the early 1980s, and Cafe Maxx remains very popular among regional food lovers. The setting is ordinary, in a little strip of stores, but inside there's a holiday glow year-round. Chef Oliver Saucy demonstrates ritual devotion to the preparation of fine cuisine. A menu changing nightly showcases foods from the tropics: jumbo stone crab claws with honey-lime mustard sauce, Florida lobster with *salsa verde,* and black-bean and banana pepper chili with Florida avocado. Desserts, too, reflect a tropical theme, from praline macadamia mousse over chocolate cake with butterscotch sauce to candied ginger with pears poached in muscatel and sun-dried cherry ice cream. More than 200 wines are

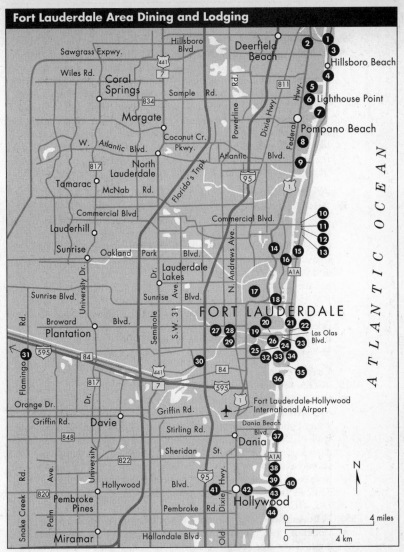

## Fort Lauderdale Area Dining and Lodging

**Lodging**

Bahia Cabana Beach Resort, **24**

Banyan Marina Apartments, **20**

Blue Seas, **12**

Bonaventure Resort & Spa, **31**

Carriage House Resort Motel, **4**

Driftwood on the Ocean, **44**

Hyatt Regency Pier Sixty-Six, **33**

Lago Mar Resort Hotel & Club, **35**

Lauderdale Colonial, **25**

A Little Inn by-the-Sea, **11**

Maison Harrison, **42**

Manta Ray Inn, **43**

Marriott's Harbor Beach Resort, **34**

Nina Lee Motel, **23**

Ocean Terrace Suites, **3**

Palm-Aire Spa Resort, **8**

Pier Pointe Resort, **13**

Riverside Hotel, **26**

Royal Flamingo Villas, **1**

Sea Downs, **38**

Spa LXVI of the Hyatt Regency Pier Sixty-Six, **32**

Tropic Seas Resort Inn, **10**

**Dining**

Brooks, **2**

Burt & Jack's, **36**

Cafe Arugula, **6**

Cafe Grazia, **5**

Cafe Maxx, **9**

Cap's Place, **7**

Down Under, **16**

Evangeline, **22**

Good Planet Cafe, **28**

Istanbul, **39**

Juice Extractor, **27**

La Coquille, **17**

Las Brisas, **40**

Mark's Las Olas, **19**

Martha's, **37**

Mistral, **21**

Rustic Inn Crabhouse, **30**

Sage, **14**

Sea Watch, **15**

Sheffield's, **34**

Shirttail Charlie's, **29**

Studio One French Bistro, **18**

Sushi Blues Cafe, **41**

offered by the bottle, another 20 by the glass. ⊠ *2601 E. Atlantic Blvd., Pompano Beach,* ☎ *954/782–0606. AE, D, DC, MC, V. No lunch.*

$$$ ✕ **Mark's Las Olas.** Mark's is an expansion of the acclaimed Mark's
★ Cafe in North Dade with chef Mark Militello in command. Entrées change daily, but typical choices include Gulf shrimp, dolphin, yellowtail snapper, grouper, swordfish, Florida lobster, and vegetables like callaloo (a West Indian spinach variety), chayote (cho-cho on Mark's menu), ginger, jicama, and plantain, all brilliantly presented and combined in sauces that tend to the low fat. Pastas and full-size dinner pizzas are thoughtful offerings. Tables are close together in a long, almost office-like row. Metallic finishes bounce the hubbub around the room, making conversation difficult. ⊠ *1032 E. Las Olas Blvd., Fort Lauderdale,* ☎ *954/463–1000. AE, DC, MC, V.*

## Argentinian

$$ ✕ **Las Brisas.** There's a wonderful bistro atmosphere at this small and cozy restaurant with Mexican tiles and blue-and-white checked tablecloths beneath paddle fans. Right next to the beach, Las Brisas offers eating inside or out, and food is Argentinian with an Italian flair. Antipasto salads are prepared for two; the roasted vegetables are crunchy and flavorful. A small pot sits on each table filled with *chimichurri* (a paste made of oregano, parsley, olive oil, salt, garlic, and crushed pepper) for spreading on steaks. Grilled or deep-fried fish are favorites, as are pork chops, chicken, and pasta entrées. Desserts include a rum cake, a flan like *mamacita* and a *dulce con leche* (a sweet milk pudding). The wine list is predominantly Argentine. ⊠ *600 N. Surf Rd., Hollywood,* ☎ *954/923–1500. AE, MC, V. Closed Mon. No lunch.*

## Continental

$$$ ✕ **Cafe Arugula.** Chef Dick Cingolani draws upon the culinary tradi-
★ tions of warm climates from Italy to the American Southwest. The decor, too, blends southwestern with Mediterranean looks—a row of mauve velvet booths beneath steamboat-wheel windows surrounds an entire wall of chili peppers, corn, cactus, and garlic cloves. A frequently changing menu may include succulent fresh hogfish with capers and shaved almonds over fettuccine or a free-range loin of venison with juniper–wild mushroom sauce, quesadilla, and stir-fried vegetables. ⊠ *3110 N. Federal Hwy., Lighthouse Point,* ☎ *954/785–7732. AE, D, DC, MC, V. No lunch.*

$$$ ✕ **Down Under.** When Leonce Picot and the late Al Kocab opened Down
★ Under in 1968, the Australian government sent them a boomerang as a gift. The name actually describes the restaurant's location, below a bridge approach at the edge of the Intracoastal Waterway. This was the first in a chain of the Gold Coast cluster of Kocab and Picot dining rooms combining gourmet cuisine with gracious old-house settings. Over the years the number has dwindled to a precious two: this and La Vieille Maison in Boca Raton, still draw devotees. Specials include Florida farm–raised striped bass with fennel and broth, spinach flan, tomato strips, and potatoes; a classic duck confit with crunchy red cabbage, roasted new potatoes, and truffle sauce; and many grills, from a hot spicy Jamaican jerked roast pork tenderloin with Calvados apples to a trio of lamb chops, thick-cut prime rib, and a prime 12-ounce sirloin or steak au poivre. Desserts include a classic Key lime pie, raspberry tiramisù, fresh-fruit cobbler, and a Grand Marnier sabayon with fresh berries. ⊠ *3000 E. Oakland Park Blvd., Fort Lauderdale,* ☎ *954/563–4123. AE, D, DC, MC, V.*

$$$ ✕ **Martha's.** This restaurant is dressy downstairs—tables adorned with orchid buds, fanned napery, etched-glass dividers, brass, rosewood, and an outdoor patio surrounded by a wild floral mural. Piano music

accompanies dinner, and later a band plays for dancing, setting a supper-club mood. The menu features chiefly Florida seafoods: flakey dolphin in a court bouillon; shrimp dipped in a piña colada batter, rolled in coconut, and panfried with orange mustard sauce; and snapper prepared 17 ways. For dessert, try fresh sorbet and vanilla and chocolate ice cream topped with meringue and hot fudge brandy sauce. ⊠ *6024 N. Ocean Dr., Hollywood,* ☎ *954/923–5444. Reservations essential. AE, D, DC, MC, V.*

$$$ ✕ **Sheffield's.** You'd expect dishes like this in a formal restaurant at Fort Lauderdale's most upscale luxury hotel: Beef Wellington, chateaubriand, rack of lamb. But the skillful preparation keeps these entrées from becoming Continental clichés. The symphony of shellfish, made with lobster, shrimp, and scallops is excellent eating. This oceanfront restaurant has an extensive seafood selection including salmon, grouper, swordfish, tuna, tilapia, red snapper, dolphin, and lobster; all can be ordered sautéed, grilled, blackened, poached, or broiled. The curried mango glaze and fresh raisin butter are two excellent toppings to choose from. ⊠ *Marriott's Harbour Beach Resort, 3030 Holiday Dr., Fort Lauderdale,* ☎ *954/525–4000. AE, D, DC, MC, V.*

$$ ✕ **Brooks.** This is one of the city's best and most affordable restau-
★ rants thanks to a French perfectionist, Bernard Perron. Meals are served in a series of rooms filled with replicas of Old Masters, cut glass, antiques, and tapestrylike floral wallpapers, though the shedlike dining room still feels very Florida. Fresh ingredients go into distinctly Floridian cuisine. Main courses include red snapper in papillotte, broiled fillet of pompano with seasoned root vegetables, and a sweet lemongrass linguine with bok choy and julienne of crisp vegetables. Desserts include pecan pie with banana ice cream, a filo purse filled with chocolate *ganache* and strawberries, and rum-basted bananas with coconut ice cream and toasted macadamia nuts. ⊠ *500 S. Federal Hwy., Deerfield Beach,* ☎ *954/427–9302. AE, D, MC, V.*

$$ ✕ **Mistral.** As part of a novelty dinner you can board a choo-choo replica
★ for a progressive dinner that includes Mistral's two sister restaurants: Evangeline, just down the oceanfront walk, and Sage, in town. The dining room, surrounded by tropical art and pottery, rates high in both taste and looks. The kitchen staff turns out hearty pastas such as a *primavera* redolent with garlic and herbs and *tagliolini* (an angel-hair pasta) with prosciutto, pine nuts, and tomato. Other favorites from the sun-drenched cuisine are grilled shrimp and black-bean cakes as well as panseared dolphin. Pizzas, big salads, and a strong selection of affordable wines, including by the glass, are also served. ⊠ *201 Rte. A1A, Fort Lauderdale,* ☎ *954/463–4900. AE, D, DC, MC, V.*

## Creole

$$$ ✕ **Evangeline.** Set inside and out on the ocean drive just south of its sister restaurant Mistral, Evangeline celebrates Acadian Louisiana in decor and food. The mood is set with paneled wainscoting and plank floors—a tankard and tavern look—highlighted by verse from Longfellow's legendary poem inscribed along the turn of the ceiling. Traditional favorites include oyster and artichoke pie, smoked rabbit gumbo with andouille sausage, a crawfish Caesar salad, jambalaya (clams, mussels, shrimp, and chicken andouille with a Creole sauce), sautéed alligator in a meunière sauce topped with flash-fried oysters, and crisp roasted duckling with poached plums and prunelle brandy. There's music nightly, and a Dixieland band plays weekends, including Sunday afternoon. ⊠ *211 Rte. A1A, Fort Lauderdale,* ☎ *954/522–7001. AE, D, DC, MC, V.*

## French

$$ ✕ **La Coquille.** Excellent French fare in a country-French setting. Although the restaurant sits at the edge of busy Sunrise Boulevard, it seems worlds apart thanks to French doors, pastel coral and green, faux open beams, and 18 tables set with double white covers and topped by carnations and baby's breath and a new tropical garden. Service is friendly and helpful accompanied by a delightful French accent, and the cuisine is equally authentic: Dubonnet and vermouth cassis aperitifs lead to escargots Provençal and various pâtés, followed by seared sea scallops with spring vegetables, honey-glazed duckling with lingonberry sauce and wild rice, sweetbreads in a morel and truffle sauce, and veal with shallots and sweet bell peppers. There's always a soufflé among the desserts and a dinner-savings special, such as a four-course dinner for two with bottle of wine for $47.50 (excluding tax and tip; not valid Saturday or holidays). ⊠ *1619 E. Sunrise Blvd., Fort Lauderdale,* ☎ *954/467–3030. AE, MC, V. Closed Sun. and Mon. June–Sept., Aug. No lunch Sat.–Thurs.*

$ ✕ **Sage.** This joyous, country-French café has a country-American setting: exposed brick walls, captain's chairs, lace curtains, herbal art, and baskets of dried grains and flowers. The menu is a happy mix of very affordable quiches and pâtés, salads, main-course specialties and dessert crepes. Entrées include coq au vin, beef bourguignon, *cassoulet à l'Armagnac* (layers of duck and garlic sausage with white beans), and a platter of fresh vegetables that's a veritable garden of legumes. Early-bird dinners (weekdays 4:30–6) feature four courses for $12.50. There are good selections of beers and wines by the glass. ⊠ *2378 N. Federal Hwy., Fort Lauderdale,* ☎ *954/565–2299. AE, D, MC, V.*

$ ✕ **Studio One French Bistro.** More like an art gallery—intimate, black-and-white, mirrored—this restaurant serves up bountiful portions at ★ ridiculously low prices. Food is thoughtfully presented, from high-gluten breads through a dozen or so appetizers, dinner-size salads, and entrées that include a grilled salmon in puff pastry with lobster sauce, Camembert-stuffed chicken breast with French cranberry sauce, and crispy roasted duckling with vanilla sauce. For dessert try the mildly sweet custard apple tart. Chef Bernard Asendorf now has charge of the kitchen, and his wife, Roberta, carries on the tradition of greeting by name the locals who return time and again, often bringing out-of-town guests. ⊠ *2447 E. Sunrise Blvd., Fort Lauderdale,* ☎ *954/565–2052. AE, DC, MC, V. Closed Mon. mid-May–mid-Dec. No lunch.*

## Italian

$–$$ ✕ **Cafe Grazia.** This happy green-red-and-white recreation of an Italian garden is so close to the highway that its bar glasses jiggle to the ★ passing of 18-wheelers. Not to worry—exuberance is what really shakes the scene. Chef Ace Gonzalez and his wife Estelita have created the best for less: dinners on the low side of moderate and downright inexpensive if you come between 4:30 and 5:30 for the early-bird specials, a choice of three-course dinners priced at $6.95–$9.95 year-round. Wallet-pleasing, too, are the regular menu's 15 pasta selections, including penne pasta with hot chilies, vodka, tomatos, and cream, and fresh pasta rosettes with fontina cheese, smoked ham, and spinach in a blush cream sauce. Other entrées include fowl, veal, and grills. ⊠ *3850 N. Federal Hwy., Lighthouse Point,* ☎ *954/942–7206. AE, MC, V. No lunch weekends.*

## Japanese

$–$$ ✕ **Sushi Blues Cafe.** First-class Japanese food, accompanied by live music Thursday through Saturday evenings, is served up in a cubicle setting that's so jammed you wonder where this hip group goes by day. Chef

Yozo Masuda prepares conventional and macrobiotic-influenced dishes that range from a variety of sushi and rolls (California, tuna, and the "Yozo roll" with snapper, flying-fish eggs, asparagus, and Japanese mayonnaise) to steamed veggies with tofu and steamed snapper with miso sauce. Also available are a few wines by the glass or bottle, a selection of Japanese beers, and some very un-Japanese desserts—fried banana and Swiss chocolate mousse cake. ⊠ *1836 S. Young Circle, Hollywood,* ☎ *954/929–9560. No credit cards. Closed Sun. No lunch.*

## Natural

$ ✕ **Juice Extractor.** Three guys from Pittsburgh, Philadelphia, and New York have made a splash in the arts district's Himmarshee Village with their inexpensive, deli-style organic foods and Champion-blended juices. Frothy and light, juices are made from fresh apples, pears, strawberries, citrus, and veggies and can be enjoyed with bagels, whitefish salads, and homemade breads for breakfast. Lunch features veggie burgers, pita sandwiches, and organic salads (at least three pasta versions). Entrées: free-range chicken prepared with mushrooms and vegetables; steamed salmon; bison steaks, whole or ground; a vegetarian choice with brown rice and beans. There is seating both inside (nosmoking) and outside. ⊠ *320 S.W. 2nd St., Fort Lauderdale,* ☎ *954/524–6935. D, MC, V.*

## Seafood

$$–$$$ ✕ **Cap's Place.** On an island that was once a bootlegger's haunt, this
★ restaurant is reached by launch and has served such luminaries as Winston Churchill, Franklin D. Roosevelt, and John F. Kennedy. "Cap" was Captain Theodore Knight, born in 1871, who, with partner-in-crime Al Hasis, floated a derelict barge to the area in the 1920s. Today the rustic restaurant, built on the barge, is run by descendants of Hasis'. Baked wahoo steaks are lightly glazed and meaty, the long-cut french fries arouse gluttony, hot and flaky rolls are baked fresh several times a night, and tangy lime pie a great finishing touch. Turn east off Federal Highway onto N.E. 24th Street (two blocks north of Pompano Fashion Square); follow the double yellow line to the launch. ⊠ *Cap's Dock, 2765 N.E. 28th Ct., Lighthouse Point,* ☎ *954/941–0418. AE, MC, V. No lunch.*

$$ ✕ **Rustic Inn Crabhouse.** Wayne McDonald started with a cozy one-room roadhouse in 1955, when this was a remote service road just west of the little airport. Now, the plain, rustic place is huge. Steamed crabs seasoned with garlic and herbs, spices, and oil are served with mallets on tables covered with newspapers; peel-and-eat shrimp are served either with garlic and butter or spiced and steamed with Old Bay seasoning. The big menu includes other seafood items as well. Pies and cheesecakes are offered for dessert. ⊠ *4331 Ravenswood Rd., Fort Lauderdale,* ☎ *954/584–1637. AE, D, DC, MC, V.*

$$ ✕ **Sea Watch.** It's back from the road and easy to miss—but not missed by many. Waiting for a table, you're likely to hear announced, "Party of 47, your tables are ready!" After more than 20 years, this nautical-theme restaurant by the sea stays packed during lunch and dinner. Waits can be as long as 30 minutes, but time passes quickly in the sumptuous upstairs lounge with comfy sofas and high-back rattan chairs. The menu has all the right appetizers: oysters Rockefeller, Gulf shrimp, clams casino, and Bahamian conch fritters. Typical daily specials might be sautéed yellowtail snapper, oat-crusted with roasted red bell pepper sauce and basil, or a charbroiled dolphin fillet marinated with soy sauce, garlic, black pepper, and lemon juice. Desserts include a Granny Smith apple crisp cheesecake, cappuccino brownie, and strawberries Romanoff. Good early-bird specials are offered in the off

season. ⊠ *6002 N. Ocean Blvd., Fort Lauderdale,* ☎ *954/781–2200. AE, MC, V.*

**$$**    ✕ **Shirttail Charlie's.** Overlooking the New River, diners watch the world go by from the outdoor deck or upstairs dining room of this restaurant, named for a yesteryear Seminole Indian who wore his shirttails out. Diners may take a free 30- to 40-minute after-dinner cruise on Shirttail Charlie's Express, which chugs upriver past an alleged Al Capone speakeasy, or across the river to and from the Broward Center. Charlie's is built to look old, with a 1920s tile floor that leans toward the water. Florida-style seafood offerings include an alligator-tail appetizer served with tortuga sauce (a béarnaise with turtle broth and sherry), conch served four ways, crab balls, blackened tuna with Dijon mustard sauce, crunchy coconut shrimp with a not-too-sweet piña colada sauce, three fresh catches nightly, and a superbly tart Key lime pie with graham-cracker crust. ⊠ *400 S.W. 3rd Ave., Fort Lauderdale,* ☎ *954/463–3474. AE, D, MC, V.*

### Southwestern

**$–$$**    ✕ **Good Planet Cafe.** A half block from the Florida East Coast Railroad track in a neighborhood that's turned from rundown to trendy (thanks to the Broward Center for the Performing Arts and all the nearby museums), this 50-seat eatery has primed the scene for food. Modeled after the Last Ditch Cafe in Silver City, New Mexico, run by sister Julie, the Good Planet is run by the Good family, especially brother Jonathan. Mom and Pop handle the contracting and pick out the thrift shop furniture that, with local art on the walls, creates a feel of hand-me-down chic. Most of the long list of entrées are served with *posole* (a corn chowder) or rice and beans. Try the bite-size chunks of lean pork marinated in red chili and fruit juices with a fresh mango-pineapple salsa, and the Szechuan scallop and shrimp angel hair. Portions are big. ⊠ *214 S.W. 2nd St., Fort Lauderdale,* ☎ *954/527–4663. AE, MC, V. Closed Sun.*

### Turkish

**$**    ✕ **Istanbul.** Turkish fast-food? Who knew? Actually fast food is a misnomer, since everything is prepared from scratch: hummus, tabouli, *adana* kebab (partially grilled, chopped lamb on skewers on a bed of yogurt-soaked pita squares, oven finished with hot butter sauce), pizza, salads, soups, and filo pie fingers filled with spinach, chicken, or meat. The creamy rice pudding, baklava, and pastries are equally transportable. You can dine in, but how often can you lounge on the beach with a reasonably priced Turkish picnic? ⊠ *707 N. Broadwalk, Hollywood,* ☎ *954/921–1263. No credit cards.*

# LODGING

Wherever you stay, reservations are a good idea. Tourists from the northern United States and Canada fill the hotels from Thanksgiving through Easter. In summer, southerners and Europeans create a second season that's almost as busy.

### Deerfield Beach

**$$$–$$$$**    ▥ **Ocean Terrace Suites.** This four-story motel is in one of the quieter sections of north Broward, just south of Boca Raton, across the narrow shore road from the beach. Large units—efficiencies and one- and three-bedroom apartments—all have big balconies overlooking the sea. Colors are from shore washed to bright; pink and green pastels tint the bedrooms. The furniture is rattan, and units are clean and neat. Art is throwaway, flowers are artificial, and materials are bargain quality. Still, for size, location, and price this is a good buy. ⊠ *2080*

*E. Hillsboro Blvd., 33441,* ☎ *954/427–8400,* [FAX] *954/427–0555. 30 units. Grill, pool. AE, D, DC, MC, V.*

$$–$$$  ⊞ **Carriage House Resort Motel.** Very clean and tidy, this good beach-front motel sits one block from the ocean. Run by a French-American couple, the two-story, black-shuttered white Colonial-style motel is actually two buildings connected by a second-story sundeck. Steady improvements have been made to the facility, including the addition of Bahama beds that feel and look like sofas. Kitchenettes are equipped with good-quality utensils. Rooms are self-contained and quiet and have walk-in closets and room safes. ⊠ *250 S. Ocean Blvd., 33441,* ☎ *954/427–7670,* [FAX] *954/428–4790. 6 rooms, 14 efficiencies, 10 apartments. Pool, shuffleboard, coin laundry. AE, MC, V.*

## Fort Lauderdale
### ON THE BEACH

$$$$  ⊞ **Lago Mar Resort Hotel & Club.** No sooner had Walter Banks opened
★   a new signature wing in 1993 as part of an ambitious $5 million project than he turned to renovating older hotel rooms, adding suitelike areas, balconies, and new furniture. The sprawling Lago Mar has been owned by the Banks family since the early 1950s. The lobby is luxurious, with fanlight surrounds, a coquina-rock fireplace, and an eye-popping saltwater aquarium behind the registration desk. Allamanda trellises and bougainvillea plantings edge the swimming lagoon, and guests have the use of the broadest beach in the city. Lago Mar is less a big resort than a small town—still a family-run operation after all these years and, in its way, a slice of Old Florida. ⊠ *1700 S. Ocean La., 33316,* ☎ *954/523–6511 or 800/524–6627,* [FAX] *954/524–6627. 32 rooms, 123 1-bedroom suites, 15 2-bedroom suites. 4 restaurants, 2 pools, miniature golf, 4 tennis courts, shuffleboard, volleyball. AE, DC, MC, V.*

$$$$  ⊞ **Marriott's Harbor Beach Resort.** No other hotel gives you so many options. Located south of the big public beach, it's a property of imperial dimensions—16 acres on the sea. Seen at night from upper stories (14 in all), the grounds, with their waterfall-pool beset by tall palms, shimmer like a jewel. The spacious guest rooms were refurbished in 1994 and 1995 with more tropical colors, lively floral prints, rattan, wicker, and wood. Each has a balcony facing either the ocean or the Intracoastal Waterway. There are in-room minibars. Sheffield's, one of five restaurants, is one of the city's culinary top spots. ⊠ *3030 Holiday Dr., 33316,* ☎ *954/525–4000 or 800/228–6543,* [FAX] *954/766–6152. 588 rooms, 36 suites. 5 restaurants, 3 lounges, pool, massage, saunas, 5 tennis courts, fitness center, beach, windsurfing, boating, parasailing, children's program (ages 5–12). AE, DC, MC, V.*

$$$  ⊞ **Bahia Cabana Beach Resort.** *Boating Magazine* ranks the waterfront bar and restaurant here among the 10 best in the world. It's far enough from guest rooms so that the nightly entertainment is not disturbing. Rooms are spread among five buildings furnished in tropical-casual style, last redone with new carpets, paint, tiles, landscaping, and patio furniture in 1992–93. Added at the same time was a video bar with a sweeping view of the marina. Rooms in the 500 Building are more motel-like and overlook the parking lot, but rates here are lowest. ⊠ *3001 Harbor Dr., 33316,* ☎ *954/524–1555 or 800/922–3008; in FL, 800/232–2437;* [FAX] *954/764–5951. 52 rooms, 37 efficiencies, 10 suites. Restaurant, 2 bars, café, 3 pools, hot tub, saunas, shuffleboard. AE, D, DC, MC, V.*

$$$  ⊞ **Lauderdale Colonial.** This 1950 resort motel, consisting of two
★   two-story buildings with good overhangs, occupies a prime location, right where the New River empties into the Intracoastal Waterway, 600 yards from the beach. The setting keeps it from feeling commercial,

and the views are spectacular. Every unit—motel rooms, efficiencies, and one- and two-bedroom apartments—has a view of the water, and the best ones have full views. Most are large, done in tropical rattan and mock French provincial: whites, pastels, chintz, and stripes. Even the small motel rooms are desirable, since the space is used well; each has an alcove with an eight-drawer double dresser, so the double bed isn't squeezed in. Motel rooms have a coffeepot and small fridge, while other units have full kitchens. ⊠ *3049 Harbor Dr., 33316–2491,* ☎ *954/525–3676,* FAX *954/463–3787. 14 units. Pool, dock, fishing, laundry. MC, V.*

$$      🏨 **Nina Lee Motel.** This is typical of the modest, affordable 1950s-style lodgings that can be found within a block or two of the ocean along the Fort Lauderdale shore. Be prepared for plain rooms—homey and clean, but not tiny, with at least a toaster, coffeepot, and fridge; efficiencies have gas kitchens, large closets, and tub-showers. The pool is set in a garden, and the entire property is just removed enough from the beach causeway to be quiet. ⊠ *3048 Harbor Dr., 33316,* ☎ *954/524–1568. 14 units. Pool. MC, V.*

### DOWNTOWN AND BEACH CAUSEWAYS

$$$$      🏨 **Bonaventure Resort & Spa.** Complimentary caffeine-free herbal teas are offered in the morning and fresh fruit in the afternoon. The staff nutritionist follows American Heart Association and American Cancer Society guidelines and can accommodate macrobiotic and vegetarian diets. The full-service beauty salon is open to the public. In addition there are luxury guest rooms and suites. Spacious rooms done in tropical colors with rattan seating overlook a lake or golf course. The oversize baths have dressing areas. The resort offers combination spa-tennis and spa-golf packages. ⊠ *250 Racquet Club Rd., Fort Lauderdale,* ☎ *954/389–3300 or 800/327–8090,* FAX *954/384–0563. 493 units. 4 restaurants, 2 lounges, 5 pools, 2 golf courses, 24 tennis courts, horseback riding, bowling, roller-skating rink, boutique, gift shop. AE, D, MC, V.*

$$$$      🏨 **Hyatt Regency Pier Sixty-Six.** The trademark of this high-rise re-
★      sort is its rooftop Pier Top Lounge, which revolves every 66 minutes and is reached by an exterior elevator. The 17-story tower dominates a 22-acre spread that includes the complete spa. Tower and lanai lodgings are tops from the ground up. In the early evening, guests try to perch at the Pelican Bar; at 6:06 a cannon is fired, and anybody around the bar gets a drink on the house. ⊠ *2301 S. 17th St., 33316,* ☎ *954/525–6666 or 800/327–3796,* FAX *954/728–3541. 380 rooms, 8 suites. 3 restaurants, 3 lounges, pool, hot tub, spa, 2 tennis courts, snorkeling, boating, parasailing, waterskiing, fishing. AE, D, MC, V.*

$$$      🏨 **Banyan Marina Apartments.** French doors have been added to
★      guest quarters, further fine-tuning these already outstanding waterfront apartments on a residential island just off Las Olas Boulevard. Imaginative landscaping includes a walkway through the upper branches of a banyan tree. Luxurious units with leather sofas, springy carpets, real potted plants, sheer curtains, custom drapes, high-quality art, and jalousies for sweeping the breeze in make these apartments as comfortable as any first-class hotel—but for half the price. Also included are a full kitchen, dining area, water view, beautiful gardens, dock space for eight yachts, and exemplary housekeeping. ⊠ *111 Isle of Venice, 33301,* ☎ *954/524–4430,* FAX *954/764–4870. 10 rooms, 1 efficiency, 4 1-bedroom apartments, 2 2-bedroom apartments. Pool. MC, V.*

$$$      🏨 **Riverside Hotel.** This six-story hotel, on Fort Lauderdale's most fashionable shopping thoroughfare, was built in 1936 and has been steadily upgraded. A sidewalk café fronts Bob Jenny's tropical murals, one of which is a New Orleans–style work that stretches across 725 square

feet of the hotel's facade. The poolside bar in back of the building offers a great view of the New River. An attentive staff includes many who have been with the hotel for two decades or more. The hotel hallways are like a pictorial museum, with old Fort Lauderdale photos gracing the walls. Each room is distinctive, with antique oak furnishings, framed French prints on the walls, in-room refrigerators, and European-style baths. The best rooms face south, overlooking the New River; the least desirable are the 36 series, where you can hear the elevator. Nonsmoker rooms available. ⊠ *620 E. Las Olas Blvd., 33301,* ☎ *954/467–0671 or 800/325–3280,* FAX *954/462–2148. 103 rooms, 7 suites. 2 restaurants, bar, pool, volleyball, dock. AE, DC, MC, V.*

## Hillsboro Beach

**$$$$** ⊞ **Spa LXVI of the Hyatt Regency Pier Sixty-Six.** Located on the Intracoastal Waterway, this resort's 22-acre tropical gardens and 142-slip marina contrast with the busy beach scene down the road. When you want to swim in the ocean, hail the water taxi at the resort's dock for a three-minute trip to the beach. Rooms have ocean, Intracoastal, or pool views, as well as private baths, air-conditioning, television, and telephone. Aerobics classes are offered poolside, and all guests can join an exercise session in the swimming pool. ⊠ *2301 S.E. 17th Street, Fort Lauderdale,* ☎ *954/525–6666,* FAX *954/728–3541. 380 units. 2 pools, beauty salon, 2 tennis courts, golf privileges, snorkeling, parasailing. AE, D, MC, V.*

**$$$–$$$$** ⊞ **Royal Flamingo Villas.** This small community of houselike villas, built in the 1970s, reaches from the Intracoastal Waterway to the sea. The roomy and comfortable 1- and 2-bedroom villas are all condominium owned, so they're fully furnished the way owners want them. All are so quiet that you hear only the soft click of ceiling fans and kitchen clocks. The development is wisely set back a bit from the beach, which is eroding but enjoyable at low tide. Lawns are so lushly landscaped you might trip. If you don't need lavish public facilities, this is your upscale choice at a reasonable price. ⊠ *1225 Hillsboro Mile (Rte. A1A), 33062,* ☎ *954/427–0669, 954/427–0660, or 800/241–2477,* FAX *954/427–6110. 40 villas. Pool, putting green, shuffleboard, beach, dock, boating, coin laundry. D, MC, V.*

## Hollywood

**$$–$$$** ⊞ **Sea Downs.** This three-story lodging directly on the Broadwalk is a good choice for efficiency or apartment living (one-bedroom apartments can be joined to make two-bedroom units). Views vary from full on the beach to rear-of-the-house prospects of neighborhood motels. Luck of the draw determines what you get. All units are comfortably done in chintz, however, with blinds, not drapes. Kitchens are fully equipped and most units have tub-showers and closets. Every room has a ceiling fan, air-conditioning, a TV, and phone. Housekeeping is provided once a week. In between, guests receive fresh towels daily and sheets on request, but they make their own beds. ⊠ *2900 N. Surf Rd., 33019-3704,* ☎ *954/923–4968,* FAX *954/923–8747. 5 efficiencies, 8 1-bedroom apartments. Pool. No credit cards.*

**$$** ⊞ **Driftwood on the Ocean.** This attractive 36-year-old resort motel faces the beach at the secluded south end of Surf Road. The setting is what draws guests, but attention to maintenance and frequent refurbishing are what make it a value. Most units have a kitchen, 1-bedroom apartments have a daybed, and standard rooms have a queen-size Murphy bed. All have balconies. ⊠ *2101 S. Surf Rd., 33019,* ☎ *954/923–9528,* FAX *954/922–1062. 10 rooms, 39 efficiencies. Pool, shuffleboard, beach, bicycles, laundry. AE, MC, V.*

$$    🏨 **Maison Harrison.** This house is reflective of the 1920s and 1930s, when developer Joseph Young planned and built Hollywood. The building originally housed Young's salesmen, so bedrooms have private baths. Rooms are complete, if a little overdone. Here and there a closet or bathroom-cabinet door doesn't quite close, or unplugged screw holes remain where a towel rack once hung. Beds are firm and there's plenty of hot water. Furnishings are mostly traditional, with much upholstery and Oriental-style rugs. An expanded Continental breakfast is included. This is a good option for those who want neither a sterile motel nor that sense of obligation that sometimes comes with doting hosts. ✉ *1504 Harrison St., 33020,* ☎ *954/922–7319. 4 rooms. V.*

$$    🏨 **Manta Ray Inn.** Canadians Donna and Dwayne Boucher run this
★ exemplary two-story lodging on the beach and haven't failed to keep the place immaculate and the rates affordable. Dating from the 1940s, the inn offers casual, comfortable beachfront vacationing Hollywood is famous for. Nothing's fussy—white spaces with burgundy trim and rattan furniture—and everything's included. Kitchens are equipped with pots, pans, and mini-appliances that make housekeeping convenient. All apartments have full closets. All, except for 2-bedroom units with stalls, baths have tub-showers. ✉ *1715 S. Surf Rd., 33019,* ☎ *954/921–9666,* 𝗙𝗔𝗫 *954/929–8220. 12 units. Grills, beach. No credit cards.*

## Lauderdale-by-the-Sea

$$$–$$$$    🏨 **Tropic Seas Resort Inn.** It's only a block off A1A, but it might as well be a mile. It's a million-dollar location—directly on the beach, two blocks from municipal tennis courts. Built in the 1950s, units are plain but clean and comfortable, with tropical rattan furniture and ceiling fans. Managers Sandy and Larry Lynch tend to the largely repeat, family-oriented clientele. The complimentary Sunday brunch and weekly wiener roast and rum swizzle party are good opportunities to mingle with other guests. ✉ *4616 El Mar Dr., 33308,* ☎ *954/772–2555 or 800/952–9581,* 𝗙𝗔𝗫 *954/771–5711. 16 rooms, 6 efficiencies, 7 apartments. Pool, beach. AE, D, DC, MC, V.*

$$$    🏨 **A Little Inn by-the-Sea.** In 1992, the former owners renovated a pair of old motels to create one of the better lodging establishments in this low-rise town. With the addition of balconies to all units, the inn is even better today. Room themes reflect much of what Florida is about: shells and boats and birds and fish. All floors are newly tiled, and all rooms have at least a refrigerator, if not a complete kitchen. Plantings surround the pool, and the furniture can be taken onto the beach. The fountain lobby, where complimentary Continental breakfast is served, is given over to guest use. A daily newspaper is provided. ✉ *4546 El Mar Dr., 33308,* ☎ *954/772–2450 or 800/492–0311,* 𝗙𝗔𝗫 *954/938–9354. 10 rooms, 13 efficiencies, 6 apartments. Pool, hot tub, beach, bicycles. AE, D, DC, MC, V.*

$$$    🏨 **Pier Pointe Resort.** Built in the 1950s, this oceanfront resort one block off the main street (Rte. A1A) and one block from the fishing pier is reminiscent of the Gold Coast 40 years ago. The aqua canopied entry opens onto two- and three-story buildings set among brick pathways on cabbage-palm lawns. The wood pool deck is set off by sea grapes and rope-strung bollards. Rooms are plain and comfortable and have balconies; most have a kitchen. There's a complimentary barbecue on Wednesday. ✉ *4320 El Mar Dr., 33308,* ☎ *954/776–5121 or 800/331–6384,* 𝗙𝗔𝗫 *954/491–9084. 40 suites, 31 efficiencies, 27 apartments. 3 pools, volleyball, beach, coin laundry. AE, D, DC, MC, V.*

$–$$    🏨 **Blue Seas.** Bubbly innkeeper Cristie Furth runs this one- and two-story motel with her husband, Marc, and small as it is, they keep investing their future in it. Newly added are lattice fencing and gardens of cactus and impatiens in front, so there's more privacy around the brick patio and garden-set pool. Guest quarters feature kitchenettes, terra-cotta tiles, bright Haitian and Peruvian art, and generally Tex-Mex and Danish furnishings, whose woody textures work well together. Handmade painted shutters and indoor plants add to the look. This remains an excellent buy in a quiet resort area just a block from the beach. ⊠ *4525 El Mar Dr., 33308,* ☎ *954/772–3336. 13 units. Pool, coin laundry. MC, V.*

### Pompano Beach

**$$$$** 🏨 **Palm-Aire Spa Resort.** This 750-acre health, fitness, and stress-reduction spa offers exercise activities, personal treatments, and calorie-controlled meals. Separate men's and women's pavilions have private sunken Roman baths, Swiss showers, and some of the most experienced hands in the massage business. There are 166 spacious rooms and 18 golf villas with private terraces. All have separate dressing rooms and some have two baths. The resort is 15 minutes from downtown Fort Lauderdale. ⊠ *2601 Palm-Aire Dr. N, Pompano Beach,* ☎ *954/972–3300 or 800/272–5624. 184 units. Restaurant, pools, 37 tennis courts, 3 golf courses, 2 raquetball courts, indoor squash court. AE, D, MC, V.*

# NIGHTLIFE AND THE ARTS

For the most complete weekly listing of events, read the "Showtime!" entertainment insert and events calendar in the Friday *Fort Lauderdale News/Sun Sentinel.* "Weekend" in the Friday edition of the *Herald,* the Broward edition of the *Miami Herald,* carries similar listings. The weekly *XS* is principally an entertainment and dining paper with a relic "underground" look. A 24-hour **Arts & Entertainment Hotline** (☎ 954/357–5700) provides updates on art, attractions, children's events, dance, festivals, films, literature, museums, music, opera, and theater.

Tickets are sold at individual box offices and through **Ticketmaster** (☎ 954/523–3309). (There is a service charge.)

## The Arts

**Bailey Concert Hall** (⊠ Central Campus of Broward Community College, 3501 S.W. Davie Rd., Davie, ☎ 954/475–6884) is a popular place for classical music concerts, dance, drama, and other performing arts activities, especially Oct.–Apr.

**Broward Center for the Performing Arts** (⊠ 201 S.W. 5th Ave., Fort Lauderdale, ☎ 954/462–0222) is the waterfront centerpiece of Fort Lauderdale's new cultural arts district. More than 500 events a year are scheduled at the performing arts center, including Broadway musicals, plays, dance, symphony and opera, rock, film, lectures, comedy, and children's theater.

## Nightlife

So that you don't have to designate a driver, Fort Lauderdale's famous water taxi offers a Tues.–Thurs. evening "pub crawl" from 7 to midnight except holidays. The price is about $30 per person, including visits to three clubs with a drink at each. For pickup and drop-off points, call 954/565–5507.

### Bars and Lounges

**Baja Beach Club** (⊠ Coral Ridge Mall, 3200 N. Federal Hwy., Fort Lauderdale, ☎ 954/561–2432) offers trendy entertainment: karaoke, lip sync, virtual reality, performing bartenders, temporary tatoos—plus a 40-foot free buffet. There are free drinks for women Wednesday night. **Cheers** (✉ 941 E. Cypress Creek Rd., Fort Lauderdale, ☎ 954/771–6337) is a woody nightspot with two bars and a dance floor. Every night has something special. **Confetti** (✉ 2660 E. Commercial Blvd., Fort Lauderdale, ☎ 954/776–4080) is a high-energy "in" spot for adults up to 50. A long-running venue for the best of blues, jazz, rock-and-roll, and reggae performers, **Musicians Exchange** (✉ 729 W. Sunrise Blvd., Fort Lauderdale, ☎ 954/764–1912) has a new Italian-American café. Events include national acts on weekends and a Monday blues jam. **O'Hara's Pub & Sidewalk Cafe** (✉ 722 E. Las Olas Blvd., Fort Lauderdale, ☎ 954/524–2801) features live jazz and blues nightly. It's packed for TGIF, though usually by the end of each day the trendy crowd spills onto this prettiest of downtown streets. The **Parrot Lounge** (✉ 911 Sunrise La., Fort Lauderdale., ☎ 954/563–1493) is a loony feast for the eyes, with a very casual, friendly, local crowd. Fifteen TVs and frequent sing-alongs add to the fun. A jukebox jams all night. **Squeeze** (✉ 401 S. Andrews Ave., Fort Lauderdale, ☎ 954/522–2068) welcomes a wide-ranging clientele—hard-core new-wavers to yuppie types.

### Comedy Clubs

The **Comic Strip** (✉ 1432 N. Federal Hwy., Fort Lauderdale, ☎ 954/565–8887) headlines stand-up comedians from New York and nationally touring comics who perform among framed old newspaper funnies. **Uncle Funny's Comedy Club** (✉ 9160 Rte. 84, Davie, ☎ 954/474–5653) has national and local comics in two shows Friday and Saturday.

### Country-and-Western Clubs

**Desperado** (✉ 2520 S. Miami Rd., Fort Lauderdale, ☎ 954/463–2855) features a mechanical bull and free line-dance lessons.

# OUTDOOR ACTIVITIES AND SPORTS

### Biking

For a schedule of public hours and spectator events, as well as a copy of the new "Bicycling in Fort Lauderdale" brochure, contact the **County Bicycle Coordinator** (✉ 115 S. Andrews Ave., Fort Lauderdale 33301, ☎ 954/357–6661). The most popular routes include Route A1A and Bayview Drive, especially early in the morning before traffic builds and a 7-mile bike path that parallels Route 84 and the New River and leads to Markham Park, which has mountain-bike trails.

### Diving

**Lauderdale Diver** (✉ 1334 S.E. 17th St. Causeway, Fort Lauderdale, ☎ 954/467–2822 or 800/654–2073), which is PADI affiliated, arranges dive charters throughout the county. Dive trips typically last four hours. Nonpackage reef trips are also open to divers for $35, to snorkelers for $25; scuba and snorkel gear are extra.

**Pro Dive** (✉ Radisson Bahia Mar Beach Resort, 801 Seabreeze Blvd., Fort Lauderdale, ☎ 954/761–3413 or 800/772–3483), a PADI five-star facility, is the area's oldest diving operation and offers packages with Radisson Bahia Mar Beach Resort, from where its 60-foot boat departs. Snorkelers can go out for $25 on the four-hour dive trip or $20 on the two-hour snorkeling trip, which includes snorkel equipment but not scuba gear. Scuba divers pay $35 using their own gear or $85 with all rentals included.

## Dog Racing

**Hollywood Greyhound Track** has plenty of dog-racing action during its December–April season. There is a clubhouse dining room. ⊠ *831 N. Federal Hwy., Hallandale,* ☎ *954/454–9400.* ☒ *Box seats 50¢–$1, grandstand $1, clubhouse $2.* ⊙ *Racing; Tues., Thurs., Sat. 12:30 and 7:30; Sun., Mon., Wed., and Fri. 7:30.*

## Fishing

For bottom fishing, party boats typically charge between $20 and $22 per person for up to four hours, including rod, reel, and bait. Three operators are **Captain Bill's** (⊠ South dock, Radisson Bahia Mar Beach Resort, 801 Seabreeze Blvd., Fort Lauderdale, ☎ 954/467–3855), *Fish City Pride* (⊠ Fish City Marina, 2621 N. Riverside Dr., Pompano Beach, ☎ 954/781–1211), and *Sea Leg's III* (⊠ 5400 N. Ocean Dr., Hollywood, ☎ 954/923–2109).

Two primary centers for saltwater charter boats are **Radisson Bahia Mar Beach Resort** (⊠ 801 Seabreeze Blvd., Fort Lauderdale, ☎ 954/764–2233) and the **Hillsboro Inlet Marina** (⊠ 2629 N. Riverside Dr., Pompano Beach, ☎ 954/943–8222). Half-day charters for up to six people now run up to $325, six-hour charters up to $495, and full-day charters (eight hours) up to $595. Skipper and crew, plus bait and tackle, are included. Split parties can be arranged at a cost of about $85 per person for a full day.

Among marinas catering to freshwater fishing are **Sawgrass Recreation** (⊠ U.S. 27 north of I–595, ☎ 954/426–2474) and **Everglades Holiday Park** (⊠ 21940 Griffin Rd., ☎ 954/434–8111). For $47.50 for five hours, you can rent a 14-foot, flat-bottom John boat (with a 9.9-horsepower Yamaha outboard) that carries up to four people. A rod and reel rent for $9 a day, and bait is extra. For two people, a fishing guide for a half day (four hours) is $110, for a full day (eight hours) $170; a third person adds $25 for a half day, $50 for a full day. You can also buy a freshwater fishing license (mandatory) here.

Fishing piers draw anglers for pompano, amberjack, bluefish, snapper, blue runners, snook, mackerel, and Florida lobsters. Pompano Beach's **Fisherman's Wharf** (☎ 954/943–1488) extends 1,080 feet into the Atlantic. The cost is $2.65 for adults, $1.06 for children under 10; rod-and-reel rental is $10.07 (including admission and initial bait). **Anglin's Fishing Pier** (☎ 954/491–9403), in Lauderdale-by-the-Sea, reaches 876 feet and is open for fishing 24 hours a day. Fishing is $3 for adults and $2 for children up to 12, tackle rental is an additional $10 (plus $10 deposit), and bait averages $2. The 920-foot **Dania Pier** (☎ 954/927–0640), in Dania, is open around the clock. Fishing is $3 for adults (including parking), tackle rental is $6, bait's about $2, and spectators pay $1.

## Golf

Off-season (May–Oct.) greens fees range $15–$45, peak-season (Nov.–Apr.) charges run $25–$65. Fees can be trimmed by working through **Next Day Golf** (☎ 954/772–2582), which customizes hotel-golf packages as well as providing 10%–25% discounts to golfers willing to wait until after 5 pm to book tee times for next-day play. Some private clubs even provide access to non-members through the service.

The public usually can arrange to play at: **Bonaventure Country Club** (⊠ 200 Bonaventure Blvd., Fort Lauderdale, ☎ 954/389–2100 or 800/327–8090), 36 holes; **Broken Woods Country Club** (⊠ 9000 Sample Rd., Coral Springs, ☎ 954/752–2270), 18 holes; **Colony West Coun-**

try Club (⊠ 6800 N.W. 88th Ave., Tamarac, ☎ 954/726–8430), 36
holes; **Diplomat Resort & Country Club** (⊠ 501 Diplomat Pkwy., Hallandale, ☎ 954/457–2082), 18 holes; **Emerald Hills** (⊠ 4100 Hills Dr.,
Hollywood, ☎ 954/961–4000), 18 holes; **Jacaranda Golf Club** (⊠ 9200
W. Broward Blvd., Plantation, ☎ 954/472–5855), 18 holes; **Oaks
Golf & Racquet Club** (⊠ 3701 Oaks Clubhouse Dr., Pompano Beach,
☎ 954/978–1737), 36 holes; **Rolling Hills** (⊠ 3501 Rolling Hills Circle, Davie, ☎ 954/475–3010), 27 holes; **Sabal Palms Golf Course** (⊠
5101 W. Commercial Blvd., Fort Lauderdale, ☎ 954/731–2600), 18
holes; and **Sunrise Country Club** (⊠ 7400 N.W. 24th Pl., Sunrise, ☎
954/742–4333), 18 holes.

### Horse Racing

**Gulfstream Park Race Track** is the home of the Florida Derby, one of
the Southeast's foremost horse-racing events. The park greatly improved
its facilities during the past two years: Admission costs have been lowered, time between races shortened, and the paddock ring elevated for
better viewing by fans. Racing is held January through mid-March. ⊠
*901 S. Federal Hwy., Hallandale,* ☎ *954/454–7000.* ☜ *$3, including
parking and program, clubhouse $5 plus $2 for reserved seat or $1.75
for grandstand.* ⊙ *Racing daily at 1.*

**Pompano Harness Track,** Florida's only harness track, was sold in early
1995 to Casino America. However, since Florida doesn't allow casino
gambling, this 327-acre facility continues to operate as a harness track
11 months of the year. The Top O' the Park restaurant overlooks the
finish line. ⊠ *1800 S.W. 3rd St., Pompano Beach,* ☎ *954/972–2000.*
☜ *Grandstand $1, clubhouse $2.* ⊙ *Racing Mon. and Wed.–Sat. 7:30.*

### Jai Alai

**Dania Jai-Alai Palace** has one of the fastest games on the planet. Games
are held year-round. ⊠ *301 E. Dania Beach Blvd., Dania,* ☎ *954/428–
7766.* ☜ *$1, reserved seats $1.50–$7. Games Tues., Thurs., and Sat.
noon and 7:15; Wed. and Fri. 7:15; closed Wed. in June.*

### Rugby

The **Fort Lauderdale Knights** play September through April on the green
at Croissant Park. ⊠ *S.W. 17th St. at 2nd Ave., Fort Lauderdale,* ☎
*954/561–5263.* ☜ *Free.* ⊙ *Games Sat. at 2.*

### Soccer

In their 12th season of play, the **Fort Lauderdale Strikers** will host 12
games, April–September, at 9,500-seat Lockhart Stadium (next door
to the team's office). The Strikers play against U.S. and Canadian
squads in the eight-team American Professional Soccer League. ⊠
*5301 N.W. 12th Ave., Fort Lauderdale,* ☎ *954/771–5677.* ☜ *$8.* ⊙
*Most games at 7 or 7:30; occasional day games.*

# SHOPPING

### Malls

**Galleria Mall** (⊠ 2414 E. Sunrise Blvd., west of Intracoastal Waterway, Fort Lauderdale) occupies more than 1 million square feet and
includes Neiman-Marcus, Lord & Taylor, Saks Fifth Avenue, and
Brooks Brothers. **Pompano Square** (⊠ 2001 N. Federal Hwy., Pompano Beach) has 110 shops with three department stores and food stalls.
**Sawgrass Mills Mall** (⊠ Flamingo Rd. and Sunrise Blvd., Sunrise) is a
2 million-square-foot, candy-colored, Disney-style discount mall containing restaurants and entertainment activities in addition to 250
stores that include Loehmann's, JC Penney, Ann Taylor, Alfred Angelo
Bridal, Levi's, TJ Maxx, and Donna Karan, Saks, and Spiegel's out-

lets. On weekdays, two shuttle buses run: One calls at major beach hotels between 8:55 and 9:30 AM, arrives at the huge mall around 10, and returns at 2:30, while the other leaves between 11:30 and 12:15 and returns just past 5. To schedule a pickup, call 954/846–2350 or 800/356–4557. The charge is $4 each way and includes a coupon book for use at the mall.

## Specialty Stores

ANTIQUES

More than 75 dealers line **Federal Highway** (U.S. 1) in Dania, ½ mile south of the Fort Lauderdale airport and ½ mile north of Hollywood. Take the Stirling Road or Griffin Road East exits off I–95.

UPSCALE BOUTIQUES

If only for a stroll and some window-shopping, don't miss the **Shops of Las Olas** (⊠ 1 block off New River east of U.S. 1, Fort Lauderdale). The city's best boutiques plus top restaurants (many affordable) and art galleries line a beautifully landscaped street.

# FORT LAUDERDALE A TO Z

## Arriving and Departing

### By Bus

Greyhound Lines (☎ 800/231–2222) buses stop in Fort Lauderdale (⊠ 515 N.E. 3rd St., ☎ 954/764–6551).

### By Car

Access to Broward County from the north or south is via Florida's Turnpike, I–95, U.S. 1, or U.S. 441. I–75 (Alligator Alley) connects Broward with Florida's west coast and runs parallel to Route 84 within the county.

### By Plane

**Fort Lauderdale–Hollywood International Airport** (FLHIA) (☎ 954/359–6100), 4 miles south of downtown Fort Lauderdale and just off U.S. 1, is Broward County's major airline terminal and becoming one of Florida's busiest—more than 10 million arrivals and departures a year, a figure that's expected to triple within 20 years. FLHIA is especially favored by new low-cost carriers. Scheduled airlines include **Airways International** (☎ 954/887–2794), **American** (☎ 800/433–7300), **Bahamasair** (☎ 800/562–7661), **Carnival Air Lines** (☎ 954/359–7886), **Chalk's International** (☎ 800/424–2557), **Comair** (☎ 800/354–9822), **Continental** (☎ 800/525–0280), **Delta** (☎ 800/221–1212), **Eagle Air** (☎ 800/332–4533), **Icelandair** (☎ 954/359–2735), **Martinair** (☎ 800/366–4655), **Midwest Express** (☎ 800/452–2022), **Northwest** (☎ 800/225–2525), **Paradise Island** (☎ 800/432–8807), **TWA** (☎ 800/221–2000), **United** (☎ 800/241–6522), **USAir** (☎ 800/842–5374), and **Valujet** (☎ 800/825–8538).

BETWEEN THE AIRPORT AND CENTER CITY

**Broward Transit** (☎ 954/357–8400) operates bus route No. 1 between the airport and its main terminal at Broward Boulevard and N.W 1st Avenue in the center of Fort Lauderdale. Service from the airport begins daily at 5:40 AM; the last bus from the downtown terminal to the airport leaves at 9:30 PM. The fare is 85¢. **Gray Line** (☎ 954/561–8886) provides limousine service to all parts of Broward County. Fares to most Fort Lauderdale beach hotels are in the $6–$10 range.

Rental-car agencies located in the airport include **Avis** (☎ 954/359–3255), **Budget** (☎ 954/359–4700), Dollar (☎ 954/359–7800), **Hertz** (☎ 954/359–5281), and **National** (☎ 954/359–8303). In season you'll pay about $120–$130 by the week; the collision-damage waiver adds about $11 per day.

### By Train

**Amtrak** (☎ 800/872–7245) provides daily service to the Fort Lauderdale station (✉ 200 S.W. 21st Terr., ☎ 954/463–8251) as well as to the other Broward County stops, Hollywood and Deerfield Beach.

**Tri-Rail** (☎ 954/728–8445) operates train service daily, 5 AM–11 PM (more limited on weekends) through coastal Broward, Dade, and Palm Beach counties. There are six stations in Broward County, all of them west of I–95.

## Getting Around

### By Boat

**Water Taxi** (☎ 954/565–5507) provides service along the Intracoastal Waterway between Port Everglades and Commercial Boulevard 10 AM–1 AM and between Atlantic Boulevard and Hillsboro Boulevard in Pompano Beach noon–midnight. The boats stop at more than 30 restaurants, hotels, shops, and nightclubs; the fare is $6 one-way, $14 ($8 for children under 12) for an all-day pass, and $45 ($25 for children) weekly.

### By Bus and Trolley

**Broward County Mass Transit** (☎ 954/357–8400) serves the entire county. The fare is 85¢, plus 10¢ for a transfer. Service on all beach routes starts before 6 AM and continues past 10 PM except on Sunday. Call for route information. Special seven-day tourist passes, which cost $8, are good for unlimited use on all county buses. These are available at some hotels, at Broward County libraries, and at the main bus terminal (✉ Broward Blvd. at N.W. 1st Ave.).

Supplementary bus and trolley services include the expanding free **Downtown Trolley,** which operates weekdays 7:30–5:30 on the Red Line (Courthouse Line) and 11:30–2:30 on the Green (Arts & Science to Las Olas) and Blue (Las Olas to Courthouse) lines. The wait is rarely more than 10 minutes. The lines connect major tourist sites in the Arts and Science District, offices, banks, and government and academic buildings to water taxi stops along the Riverwalk and to the main bus terminal. Along the beach, the **Wave Line Trolley** (☎ 954/527–5600) costs $1 and operates daily every hour 10:15–8:15 except half-hourly 4:45–6:15. It runs along Route A1A from the Galleria Mall on Sunrise Boulevard in the north to close by the Hyatt Regency Pier Sixty-Six in the south.

### By Car

Except during rush hour, Broward County is a fairly easy place to drive. East–west I–595 runs from westernmost Broward County and links I–75 with I–95 and U.S. 1, providing handy access to Fort Lauderdale–Hollywood International Airport. The scenic but slow Route A1A generally parallels the beach.

### By Taxi

It's difficult to hail a cab on the street. Sometimes you can pick one up at a major hotel. Otherwise, phone ahead. Fares are not cheap; meters run at a rate of $2.45 for the first mile and $1.75 for each additional mile; waiting time is 25¢ per minute. The major company serving the area is **Yellow Cab** (☎ 954/565–5400).

## Contacts and Resources

### Emergencies
Dial **911** for police or ambulance.

Florida Poison Information Center (☎ 800/282–3171).

### Guided Tours
**Carrie B.** (✉ Riverwalk at S.E. 5th Ave., ☎ 954/768–9920), a 300-passenger day cruiser, gives 90-minute tours up the New River and Intracoastal Waterway.

**Jungle Queen III and IV** (✉ Radisson Bahia Mar Beach Resort, 801 Seabreeze Blvd., ☎ 954/462–5596) are 155-passenger and 578-passenger tour boats that take day and night cruises up the New River, through the heart of Fort Lauderdale.

**Las Olas Horse and Carriage** (✉ 600 S.E. 4th St., ☎ 954/763–7393) operates in-town tours and transportation to and from the performing arts center.

**Marine Sciences Under Sails School of Environmental Education** (✉ 2514 Hollywood Blvd., Suite 400, Box 222145, Hollywood 33020-2145, ☎ 954/983–7015, FAX 954/923–2585), a not-for-profit organization, conducts dry-land field trips throughout south Florida and one-day, overnight, and longer boat tours as part of its Science & Sailing program. Sailing trips can accommodate as few as two people (about $100 per person for a day, $114 overnight) or families for customized itineraries in the coastal zone. Unaccompanied children can sometimes be accommodated at lower cost in under-subscribed school trips, on both land and water. Call in advance for availability.

**Professional Diving Charters** (✉ Radisson Bahia Mar Beach Resort, 801 Seabreeze Blvd., ☎ 954/467–6030) operates the 60-foot glass-bottom boat *Pro Diver II*. On Tuesday through Saturday mornings and Sunday afternoon, two-hour sightseeing trips take in offshore reefs, and snorkeling can be arranged.

**River and Walking Tours** (✉ 219 S.W. 2nd Ave., ☎ 954/463–4431), cosponsored by the Fort Lauderdale Historical Society, trace the New River by foot and by boat.

**Waterway Tours** (✉ Intracoastal Waterway north of International Swimming Hall of Fame, ☎ 954/943–8738) operates daily 90-minute tours of Millionaires' Row and various waterways on a 26-foot, Bimini-topped catamaran that carries up to six passengers.

### Hospitals
The following hospitals have a 24-hour emergency room: **Broward General Medical Center** (✉ 1600 S. Andrews Ave., Fort Lauderdale, ☎ 954/355–4400; physician referral, ☎ 954/355–4888), **Coral Springs Medical Center** (✉ 3999 Coral Hills Dr., Coral Springs, ☎ 350/344–3000; physician referral, ☎ 954/355–4888), **Hollywood Medical Center** (✉ 3600 Washington St., Hollywood, ☎ 954/985–6274; physician referral, ☎ 800/237–8701), **Holy Cross Hospital** (✉ 4725 N. Federal Hwy., Fort Lauderdale, ☎ 954/492–5753; physician referral, ☎ 954/776–3223), **Imperial Point Medical Center** (✉ 6401 N. Federal Hwy., Fort Lauderdale, ☎ 954/776–8500; physician referral, ☎ 954/355–4888), **North Broward Medical Center** (✉ 201 E. Sample Rd., Pompano Beach, ☎ 954/941–8300; physician referral, ☎ 954/355–4888), **Plantation General Hospital** (✉ 401 N.W. 42nd Ave., Plantation 33317, ☎ 954/797–6470; physician referral, ☎ 954/472–8879),

and **Universal Medical Center in Plantation** (⊠ 6701 W. Sunrise Blvd., Plantation, ☎ 954/581–7800; physician referral, ☎ 954/581–0448).

## Late-Night Pharmacies

**Eckerd Drug** (⊠ 1385 S.E. 17th St., Fort Lauderdale, ☎ 954/525–8173; 1701 E. Commercial Blvd., Fort Lauderdale, ☎ 954/771–0660; 154 University Dr., Pembroke Pines, ☎ 954/432–5510). **Medical Associates Plaza Pharmacy** (⊠ 3700 Washington St., Hollywood, ☎ 954/963–2008 or 800/793–2008). **Walgreen** (⊠ 2855 Stirling Rd., Fort Lauderdale, ☎ 954/981–1104; 5001 N. Dixie Hwy., Oakland Park, ☎ 954/772–4206; 289 S. Federal Hwy., Deerfield Beach, ☎ 954/481–2993).

## Visitor Information

**Chamber of Commerce of Greater Fort Lauderdale** (⊠ 512 N.E. 3rd Ave., Fort Lauderdale 33301, ☎ 954/462–6000). **Visitors Information Center** (⊠ 600 Seabreeze Blvd.), on the beach three blocks south of Las Olas Boulevard.

**Dania Chamber of Commerce** (⊠ 100 W. Dania Beach Blvd., Dania 33004, ☎ 954/927–3377). **Greater Deerfield Beach/North Broward Chamber of Commerce** (⊠ 1601 E. Hillsboro Blvd., Deerfield Beach 33441, ☎ 954/427–1050). **Greater Fort Lauderdale Convention & Visitors Bureau** (⊠ 200 E. Las Olas Blvd., Suite 1500, Fort Lauderdale 33301, ☎ 954/765–4466 or 800/227–8669). **Hollywood Chamber of Commerce** (⊠ 2410 Hollywood Blvd., Hollywood 33019, ☎ 954/923–4000). **Latin Chamber of Commerce of Broward County** (⊠ 4000 Hollywood Blvd., Hollywood 33021, P 954/966–0767). **Lauderdale-by-the-Sea Chamber of Commerce** (⊠ 4201 N. Ocean Dr., Lauderdale-by-the-Sea 33308, ☎ 954/776–1000). **Pompano Beach Chamber of Commerce** (⊠ 2200 E. Atlantic Blvd., Pompano Beach 33062, ☎ 954/941–2940).

# 6 Palm Beach and the Treasure Coast

*Golden beaches are a standard feature of the shoreline of this part of Florida, from the Gold Coast of wealthy Palm Beach, the land of power shopping, to the Treasure Coast of rustic Martin, St. Lucie, and Indian River counties, dotted with nature preserves and small towns with thriving arts communities.*

Herb Hiller

Updated by
Rowland
Stiteler

**P**ALMS AND BEACHES aren't the attractions of Palm
Beach, despite the name. It's not that this island paradise, an hour north of Miami, doesn't have com-
pelling, golden beaches bordered with luxuriant palms—it's just that
every community to the north and south offers the same thing. Collectively, they form a region that Florida marketing strategists have
dubbed the Gold Coast, a reference to the champagne hue of the miles
of beaches between Boca Raton and Vero Beach. The town of Palm
Beach, however, gives its own definition to the region's nickname. The
gold on this particular little stretch of coast is the kind you put in a
vault. Palm Beach is the richest city, per capita, of any city in Florida,
and would easily compete for honors as the most affluent community
in the world with places like Monaco and Malibu.

And while tourists may go to Delray Beach or Jupiter Island or any of
the scores of other towns along the Gold Coast to catch some rays and
feel sand between their toes, most stop in Palm Beach for a completely
different pastime: gawking. For a century now, this island town has
been a capital of conspicuous consumption. Palm Beach has been the
summer address for families with names like Rockefeller, Vanderbilt,
Kennedy, and Trump, and the town has always risen to the occasion.
After you've refreshed yourself with a très-chic snack from one of the
bistros along Worth Avenue, the principal shopping artery, head for
that other must-see on even the shortest of itineraries: Whitehall, the
summer home of Standard Oil Company co-founder Henry Flagler.

When Flagler brought the railroad to Florida in the 1890s, he brought
his own view of civilization. The poor and middle-class fishermen and
laborers who inhabited the place in the pre-Flagler era were moved a
mile west or so to West Palm Beach, still a proletariat cousin, home to
those who serve those with the seven-figure incomes of Flagler's suc-
cessors on the island today.

Nowadays, the town of Palm Beach represents only one percent of the
land area in Palm Beach County. The rest of the area is given over to
classic Florida beach towns, citrus farms, malls, and to the west, Lake
Okeechobee, the largest lake in Florida and one of the country's
hotspots for bass fishing devotees. Elsewhere in Palm Beach County,
the arts also flourish. From Boca Raton in the south to Jupiter in the
north, there's a profusion of museums, galleries, theaters, and towns
committed to historic preservation.

Also worth exploring is the region just north of Palm Beach County;
called the Treasure Coast, it encompasses Martin, St. Lucie, and Indian River counties. Remote and sparsely populated as recently as the
late 1970s, the Treasure Coast lost its relative seclusion in 1987, when
I–95's missing link from Palm Beach Gardens to Fort Pierce was completed. Now malls crowd corridors between I–95 and the beaches
from Palm Beach north to Vero Beach. Martin and Indian River counties are known for their high environmental standards (though not St.
Lucie County in between).

Inland, the Treasure Coast is largely devoted to citrus production,
with cattle ranching in rangelands of pine-and-palmetto scrub. Along
the coast, the broad tidal lagoon called the Indian River separates the
barrier islands from the mainland. In addition to sheltering boaters on
the Intracoastal Waterway and playing nursery for many saltwater game
fish, it's a natural radiator, keeping frost away from the tender orange

and grapefruit trees that grow near its banks. Sea turtles come ashore at night from April to August to lay their eggs on the beaches.

# Pleasures and Pastimes

## Baseball

If you like to watch major league baseball teams in action, spring is your season, with four teams training here. The Atlanta Braves and the Montreal Expos both train at West Palm Beach's Municipal Stadium (also home of the Class A Palm Beach Expos of the Florida State League). The Los Angeles Dodgers train at Dodgertown (actually in Vero Beach), and the New York Mets train at the St. Lucie County Sport Complex in Port St. Lucie.

## Beaches

Half the towns in the area include the word "beach" in their name, for good reason. There are miles of golden strands—some relatively remote and uncrowded, some buzzing with activity, and all blessed with the kind of blue-green waters you just won't find farther north. Among the least crowded are those at Hobe Sound National Wildlife Refuge and Fort Pierce Inlet State Park, north of Palm Beach. Boca Raton's three beaches are among the most popular: South Beach Park, Red Reef Park, and Spanish River Park.

## Biking

A bicycle is an excellent vehicle to use for getting a good look at the Palm Beach area. The town of Palm Beach itself is as small and flat as the top of a billiard table (and just as green). A wonderful, 10-mile-long path runs along the back of many palatial mansions and the edge of Lake Worth. Other bike paths can be found in West Palm Beach, Boynton Beach, Delray Beach, and Hypoluxo.

## Canoeing

Plenty of good canoeing opportunities are available in this area, including organized trips down the Sebastian River, through the Pelican Island Wildlife Refuge, and through the Arthur R. Marshall Loxahatchee National Wildlife Refuge.

## Croquet

With croquet becoming the sport of choice for the highest echelons of American aristocracy, it's no surprise that the blue-blood Palm Beach is a mecca for mallet swingers. The national headquarters of the United States Croquet Association, the largest croquet facility in North America and site of an annual championship in April, is at the Professional Golfing Association (PGA) National Resport & Spa in Palm Beach Gardens. No fewer than half a dozen hotels in and around Palm Beach offer finely manicured, grass croquet courts. The Breakers, long a favorite lodging for the rich and ultrarich, is a good place to watch croquet aficionados in action.

## Dining

Establishments such as Café L'Europe on Worth Avenue or the elegant Florentine Dining Room at the Breakers hotel offer Continental and nouvelle cuisine that stack up well among foodies. But there's also good casual dining in waterfront watering holes that also serve up a mean fried grouper on the side. And just an hour west in Lake Okeechobee, you can dine on panfried catfish, served just a few hundred yards from where it was caught. "Early-bird" menus (lower-priced menus served early in the evening) have become a Florida hallmark, and are offered by most restaurants.

## Dog Racing

The hounds have been racing year-round since 1932 at the Palm Beach Kennel Club. A dollar buys you a seat on the terrace level of the 4,300-seat stadium. There's also television simulcasts of jai alai and horse racing, as well as wagering on both live and televised sports.

## Fishing

Within a 50-mile radius of Palm Beach, you'll find every form of fishing known to man except ice fishing. If it involves a hook and a line, you can do it here—year-round. Charter a boat for deep-sea fishing out of towns from Boca Raton to Sebastian Inlet. West of Vero Beach, there's tremendous marsh fishing for catfish, bass, and perch. Lake Okeechobee is one of the world's bass fishing capitals.

## Golf

Palm Beach County is to golf as Saudi Arabia is to oil. For openers, there's the Professional Golfing Associaton (PGA) headquarters at the PGA National Resort & Spa in Palm Beach Gardens (a mere five golf courses are located there). In all, there are more than 150 public, private, and semiprivate golf courses in Palm Beach County. A Golf-A-Round program, in which more than 100 hotels participate, lets you play at one of ten courses each day, with no green fees.

## Hiking and Walking

You'll never find a wider variety of hiking environments than in the Palm Beach County area. If you want to go uptown, don your high heels and try a walking tour of Worth Avenue. At the other end of the spectrum, venture west to Lake Okeechobee and take a walk through the Everglades. Numerous hiking trails can also be found at wildlife preserves dotting the Gold Coast's barrier islands.

## Jai Alai

Fort Pierce and West Palm Beach both have frontons offering seasonal, live jai-alai games at which you can place your bets and watch them smack that little white ball.

## Lodging

Palm Beach County deserves the nickname "the Gold Coast"—hotel prices hover at the high end of the scale, and it's tough to find a bargain, especially among the glitzy establishments in Palm Beach and Boca Raton. However, surrounding towns generally offer a greater range of reasonably priced, more casual establishments where the owners don't mind a little sand on the floor; prices drop even lower as you move inland toward Lake Okeechobee. To get the best for less you should book far in advance.

## Polo

Polo, a sport for the ultrarich, has an egalitarian side. Many matches are free and open to the public. Palm Beach County is home to four polo organizations, and offers a good chance to catch a match or two at places such as the 1920s-era Gulfstream Polo Club in Lake Worth or the Royal Palm Polo Club in Boca Raton, with seven polo fields and two stadiums.

## Scuba Diving

The 47 miles of Atlantic shoreline in Palm Beach County offer some great opportunities for both scuba diving and snorkeling. Drift diving, in which the gentle Gulf Stream carries divers over dive sites, is particularly popular around Boynton Beach, where the ocean current runs close to shore. Just off Fort Pierce and Vero Beach, sunken ships become divers' playgrounds. Dive shops offering equipment and charter-boat trips can be found throughout the area.

## Shopping

A quarter-mile of the best stores in America cluster here under the Moorish architecture of Worth Avenue. It compares to Rodeo Drive in Beverly Hills as an upscale shopper's nirvana. But there's also plenty of middle-American shopping, including the likes of the Palm Beach Mall and the Manufacturers Outlet Center with 41 stores. There are art galleries and antique shops in Vero Beach along Ocean Boulevard, and in Boca Raton, among the green spaces of a 30-acre shopping village called Mizner Park, are three dozen more retailers.

## Tennis

Tennis is extremely popular in Palm Beach County, with more than 1,000 public and private courts being used daily. Most major hotels offer courts and instruction, usually lighted, along with tennis getaway packages. Among the bigger tennis complexes are the 34 courts at the Boca Raton Resort & Club, the 20 courts at The Breakers in Palm Beach, and the 19 courts at the Professional Golf Association's National Resort & Spa in Palm Beach Gardens.

## Water Sports

Virtually every type of craft imaginable is available for rent, with or without a licensed captain. Options range from sailboards, which you can rent at the Sailboard School in Sebastian (which also offers lessons), to the 170-foot *Lady Windridge,* available for group charters from Windridge Yacht Charters in Boca Raton. Numerous vendors along the Intracoastal Waterway rent jet skis, as well as outboard-powered runabouts where you can be your own captain.

# Exploring Palm Beach and the Treasure Coast

Palm Beach proper (and it certainly is!) is all tucked into an island 12 miles long and about one-quarter mile wide, so it's easy to cover the territory thoroughly in a couple of days. With that done, you've got a couple of good options, exploring the coast and the subtropical delights found to the west of Palm Beach or doing what a lot of visitors like—lazing around soaking up the rays and the atmosphere.

## Great Itineraries

*Numbers in the text below correspond to numbers in the margin and on the maps.*

Since most of what there is to see in and around the Gold Coast and the neighboring Treasure Coast region is within an hour's drive of downtown Palm Beach, it's a good idea to start there. Because of its Gatsby-era architecture, its stunning mansions, and its highbrow shopping, Palm Beach is unlike any other place on the Florida coast. If you have only a short time, go there first.

If you have three or four days, however, you can take in a lot of varied sights, exploring everything from galleries to subtropical wildlife preserves. With a week, you'll be able to see the area, with half-days here and there given over to seasonal pleasures like spring-training baseball games, deep-sea fishing, and canoe trips up the area's cypress-fringed creeks, with egrets and alligators as your companions.

### IF YOU HAVE 3 DAYS

With a short amount of time, you might want to make ⛳ **Palm Beach** ④ your base. On the first day, start in the middle of the downtown area, **Worth Avenue** ⑭. Window shop along the ¼-mile boulevard; dine at one of the numerous cafés; visit some of the galleries. Stop by **Whitehall** ⑬, the mansion built by oil magnate and railroad king Henry Flagler. Spend another day going to the beach; two good options are

**Lantana Public Beach,** which has great food concessions, and **Ocean-front Park.** Finally, spend the better part of a day exploring attractions you wouldn't expect to find in South Florida such as the **Morikami Museum and Japanese Gardens** in nearby Delray Beach that is, trite as it may sound, like a one-day visit to Japan.

IF YOU HAVE 5 DAYS

With five days you can be more contemplative at the galleries and museums, more leisured at the beaches, and have time for more serendipitous exploring. While staying in ⊞ **Palm Beach** ④ you'll have time to visit **The Breakers** ⑥, the luxury hotel build by Flagler in 1895 and rebuilt by his descendants after it was destroyed by fire in 1925. This Italian Renaissance palace is an expensive place to stay, but worth a stop: Have a meal in one of the restaurants or just take a peek at the lavish interior. Take a cultural quantum leap by visiting West Palm Beach and the **Norton Gallery of Art** ㉑, which has an extensive collection of 19th-century French Impressionist paintings. For a change of pace, make a side trip to **Lake Okeechobee,** the bass-fishing capital of the world; you can find a good place to spend the night in many of the small towns surrounding the lake, such as ⊞ Clewiston or ⊞ Indiantown. You could also explore the 221-square-mile **Arthur R. Marshall Loxahatchee National Wildlife Refuge.** Children will probably enjoy the Gumbo Limbo Nature Center in ⊞ **Boca Raton** ①; in the spring and early summer, the staff leads periodic turtle walks, when you can see nesting female ocean turtles come ashore. Boca also has an excellent new shopping village, Mizner Park, with more than three dozen retail stores, plus restaurants, sidewalk cafés, and movie houses.

IF YOU HAVE 7 DAYS

With an entire week, you can see the Gold and Treasure coasts thoroughly, with time left over for learning adventures like sailboard or croquet lessons, or outdoor explorations like deep-sea fishing and jet skiing. Starting once again in ⊞ **Palm Beach** ④, you might want to rent a bicycle and explore the island on two wheels. Two good rides are the 10-mile path along Lake Worth, which gives you a great look into the backyards of many big mansions in Palm Beach, and a five-mile bike path along Flagler Drive in West Palm Beach, just across the Intracoastal Waterway from Palm Beach. While on your bike, you may want to ride over to West Palm's renewed downtown district, **Clematis Street,** now full of lively shops, water-view parks, and outdoor performing areas. Venturing north to Riviera Beach and then across the Jerry Thomas Bridge to Singer Island, you'll find the **John D. McArthur State Park,** with two miles of beach and interpretive walks to a mangrove estuary along the inland shores of the island. Going farther north, you'll find the town of ⊞ **Stuart** ㉘, with a lovely historic downtown area. Farther north still, in ⊞ **Sebastian** ㉜ and **Sebastian Inlet** ㉝, there's excellent fishing at **Sebastian Inlet State Park**—and you don't need a boat: A strong current brings in bluefish, flounder, and mackerel with the changing of the tides. You can learn to sailboard or polish your skills with one- and two-day courses at the Sailboard School in Sebastian. If you choose to venture south from Palm Beach (and there's plenty of time to explore both north and south of the city in a seven-day visit), be sure and spend a day or so in ⊞ **Boca Raton** ①. The town is home of one of the two top resort hotels in the area, the **Boca Raton Resort & Club,** originally built by Addison Mizner in 1926.

## When to Tour Palm Beach and the Treasure Coast

The weather is optimum in November through May. The tradeoff is that most facilities are more crowded then and prices somewhat higher. In summer you'll need a tolerance for heat and humidity if you want to spend time outdoors; you should also watch for frequent afternoon downpours. If you're set on watching the sea turtles come ashore to nest, make sure to visit between late April and August; remember that nesting occurs at night. No matter when you visit, bring insect repellent if you plan outdoor outings.

# PALM BEACH COUNTY

Palm Beach County is easily one of the most diverse counties in Florida, with everything from mansions to mangrove swamps. You can sleep in a five-star hotel, camp among the alligators, or spend days on uncrowded beaches. One of the best aspects of visiting Palm Beach County is the availability of such varied communities—do your best to take advantage of them.

## Boca Raton

*Numbers in the margin correspond to points of interest on the Gold Coast and Treasure Coast map.*

This upscale town at the south end of Palm Beach County, 30 minutes south of Palm Beach, has a lot in common with its ritzy cousin: Both reflect the unmistakable architectural presence of Addison Mizner. In the mid-1920s, he was the principal developer of most of **Boca Raton;** Mizner Park, an important shopping district, bears his name.

### Sights to See

**Boca Raton Museum of Art.** With its whimsical metal sculptures on the lawn, this museum is a must. The permanent collection includes works by Picasso, Degas, Matisse, Klee, and Modigliani as well as notable pre-Columbian art. Along Dixie Highway, on your right, notice the distinctive Boca look: buildings in pink and burnt siena, all with barrel tile roofs, many with canopies and iron balconies. ⊠ *801 W. Palmetto Park Rd.,* ☎ *561/392–2500.* ☞ *Free.* ☉ *Weekdays 10–4, weekends noon–4.*

**Gumbo Limbo Nature Center.** The center is a big draw for kids, with its four huge saltwater sea tanks; there's also a long boardwalk through dense forest, with a 50-foot tower you can climb to overlook the tree canopy. In the spring and early summer, staff members lead nighttime guided turtle walks to the beach to see nesting females come ashore and lay their eggs. ⊠ *1801 N. Ocean Blvd.,* ☎ *561/338–1473.* ☞ *Donations welcome; turtle tours $3 (tickets must be obtained in advance).* ☉ *Mon.–Sat. 9–4, Sun. noon–4; turtle tours late May–mid-July, Mon.–Thurs. 9 PM–midnight.*

**International Museum of Cartoon Art.** Championed by *Beetle Bailey* cartoonist Mort Walker, this museum was transplanted to Boca Raton from New York State. One half of the exhibition space opened in March 1996; it showcases thousands of pieces of cartoon art from more than 50 countries, covering everything from turn-of-the-century Buster Brown cartoons to Charles Schulz's *Peanuts.* ⊠ *201 Plaza Real,* ☎ *561/391–2200.* ☞ *$6.* ☉ *Tues.–Sat. 11–5, Sun. noon–5.*

**Old Floresta.** The residential area behind the Boca Raton Museum of Art is known as Old Floresta. Developed by Addison Mizner starting in 1925 and landscaped with many varieties of palms and cycads, it includes houses that are mainly Mediterranean style, many with upper balconies supported by exposed wood columns.

**2 E. El Camino Real.** Built in 1925 as the headquarters of the Mizner Development Corporation, this structure is a good example of Mizner's

# Gold Coast and Treasure Coast

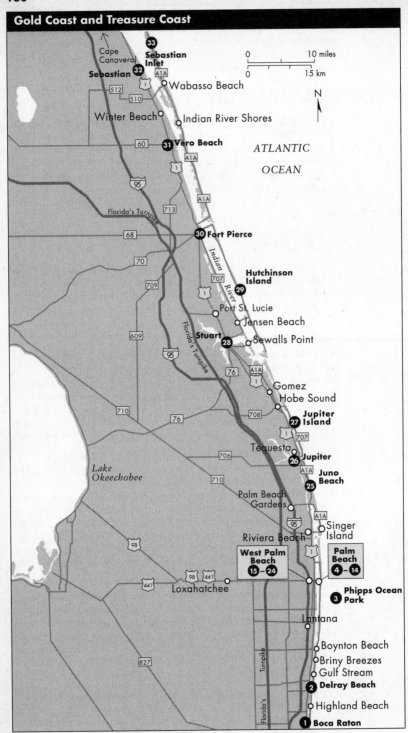

characteristic Spanish-revival architectural style, with its wrought-iron grills and handmade tiles. It now houses an excellent Italian restaurant, **Addison's Flavors of Italy.** ⊠ 2 E. El Camino Real, ☎ 561/391–9800.

## Beaches

Three of the most popular beaches in Boca Raton are **South Beach Park** (⊠ 400 N. Rte. A1A), which has no picnic facilities, and **Red Reef Park** (⊠ 1400 N. Rte. A1A) and **Spanish River Park** (⊠ 3001 N. Rte. A1A), both with picnic tables, grills, and playgrounds.

## Dining and Lodging

$$$–$$$$ ✕ **Addison's Flavors of Italy.** Architecture buffs would be sated just by the building, which is a painstakingly restored old office building designed and built by Addison Mizner in 1925 to house the Mizner Development Corporation. But there are plenty of culinary attractions in this northern Italian restaurant, most notably veal piccata and rigatoni with salmon, tomatoes, and cream. Locals love the courtyard, shaded by massive banyan trees, as a setting for wedding receptions and other galas. The rich and extensive Sunday brunch is a tradition. ⊠ 2 E. Camino Real, ☎ 561/391–9800. AE, D, DC, MC, V.

$$$–$$$$ ✕ **La Vieille Maison.** This French restaurant remains one of the tem-
★ ples of haute cuisine along the Gold Coast. It occupies a 1920s-era, two-story dwelling (hence the name, which translates "old house") believed to be an Addison Mizner design. Closets and cubbyholes have been transformed into intimate private dining rooms. Fixed-price, à la carte, Temptations, and Grand menus are available (the last, with more traditional French cuisine, is the highest priced); an additional fixed-price menu available between Sunday and Thursday in summer offers a a modestly priced sampling of the other three. All menus currently feature many Provençal dishes, including soupe au pistou (vegetable soup with basil and Parmesan cheese), and roast rabbit with artichokes, green olives, and walnut gnocchi. Dessert choices include flourless chocolate cake, a napoleon with candied walnuts, and cinnamon-poached pears. ⊠ 770 E. Palmetto Park Rd., ☎ 561/391–6701 or 561/737–5677. AE, D, DC, MC, V.

$$$ ✕ **Gazebo Cafe.** The locals who patronize this popular restaurant know where it is, even though there is no sign. You'll have to look a little harder. The Boca Raton location is near the Barnett Bank Hyde Park Plaza, a block north of Spanish River Boulevard. Once you find the place, take your seat near the open kitchen, where chef Paul Sellas (co-owner with his mother, Kathleen) and his staff perform a gastronomic ballet. The main dining room can be noisy; you may prefer the smaller back dining room. Specialties include fresh lump crabmeat glazed with excellent Mornay sauce on a marinated artichoke bottom; a robust bouillabaisse that includes Maine lobster; and raspberries with a Grand Marnier–sabayon sauce. ⊠ 4199 N. Federal Hwy., ☎ 561/395–6033; ⊠ 287 E. Indiantown Rd., Jupiter, ☎ 561/744–0605. AE, D, DC, MC, V. Closed Sun. mid-May–Dec.

$$$ ✕ **Maxaluna Tuscan Grill.** Virtually the neighborhood restaurant of choice
★ for affluent Bocans, this 150-seat shrine to nuovo Italian gastronomy is as hard to find as the **Gazebo Café.** With its beautiful landscaping, the setting—the courtyard of Crocker Center, an office park and shopping mall—is as artful as the modern art hanging from the walls. Inside, orchids rise from slender bud vases, and halogen lights drop from colorful ceiling panels suspended from a black roof. Tables zigzag across natural wood floors—and at the rear, past the polished aluminum bar and brick walls, chefs in the open kitchen work in Italian bicycle caps. Lighthearted in style, Maxaluna's is serious about food. Diners exult in chef Pierre Viau's pastas and risottos, as well as such notable

specials as lemon-thyme tagliatelle with shrimp, scallops, and calamari or the risotto of Maine lobster, Vidalia onions, white corn, and escarole. There's also a large selection of wines by the glass. ⊠ *Crocker Center, 5050 Town Center Circle,* ☎ *561/391–7177. AE, D, DC, MC, V. No lunch weekends.*

**$**   ✕ **Tom's Place.** "This place is a blessing from God," says the sign over the fireplace, and after braving the long lines and sampling the superb menu you will add an "Amen!" That's in between mouthfuls of Tom Wright's soul food—sauce-slathered ribs, pork-chop sandwiches, chicken cooked in peppery mustard sauce over hickory and oak, sweet-potato pie. You'll want to leave with a bottle or two of Tom's barbecue sauce ($2.25 a pint) just as Lou Rawls, Ben Vereen, Sugar Ray Leonard, and a rush of NFL players have before you. ⊠ *7251 N. Federal Hwy.,* ☎ *561/997–0920. MC, V. Closed Sun. and sometimes 1 month around Sept; also Mon. May–mid-Nov.*

**$$$$**   🏨 **Boca Raton Resort & Club.** Architect-socialite Addison Mizner de-
**★**   signed and built the Mediterranean-style Cloister Inn here in 1926; it has been added to and renovated several times since then to create this sprawling, elegant resort, which numbers a golf school run by Dave Pelz among its facilities. Rooms in the Cloister tend to be small and warmly traditional; those in the 27-story Tower are in a similar style but larger, while rooms in the Beach Club are light, airy, and contemporary in color schemes and furnishings. The concierge staff speaks at least 12 languages. Rates during the winter season don't include meals, but you can pay extra for MAP (including breakfast and dinner). ⊠ *501 E. Camino Real, 33431-0825,* ☎ *561/395–3000 or 800/327–0101. 963 rooms, suites, studio rooms, and golf villas. 7 restaurants, 3 lounges, 5 pools, 2 championship golf courses, 34 tennis courts, basketball, 3 fitness centers, beach, boating, fishing. AE, DC, MC, V.*

## Nightlife and the Arts

**Caldwell Theatre Company** (⊠ 7873 N. Federal Hwy., Boca Raton 33429, ☎ 561/241–7432, 561/832–2989, or 305/462–5433), a professional Equity regional theater, hosts the multimedia Mizner Festival each April and May and stages four productions each winter.

**Jan McArt's Royal Palm Dinner Theatre** (⊠ 303 S.E. Mizner Blvd., Royal Palm Plaza, ☎ 561/392–3755 or 800/841–6765), an Equity theater, presents five or six musicals a year.

## Outdoor Activities and Sports

### BIKING

Plenty of bike trails and quiet streets make for pleasant pedaling in the area; for current information, contact the city of Boca Raton's Bicycle Coordinator (☎ 561/393–7797).

### BOATING

If you ever wanted the thrill of blasting along across the waters at up to 80 mph, hold on to your life vest aboard an 800 horsepower offshore racing boat at **Air and Sea Charters** (⊠ 490 E. Palmetto Park Rd., Suite 330, ☎ 561/368–3566). For $50 for a half hour or $80 for an hour per person, you and a friend can get the experience that wild-eyed offshore power racers thrive upon. For a more leisurely trip, go for Air and Sea's 55-foot catamaran ($30 a person).

### GOLF

Two championship courses and a golf school are available at **Boca Raton Resort & Club** (⊠ 501 E. Camino Real, ☎ 561/395–3000 or 800/327–0101).

POLO

**Royal Palm Polo,** founded in 1959 by Oklahoma oilman John T. Oxley and now home to the $100,000 International Gold Cup Tournament, has seven polo fields within two stadiums. ⊠ *6300 Old Clint Moore Rd., Boca Raton 33496,* ☎ *561/994–1876.* ☞ *$6, box seats $10–$25.* ⊙ *Games Jan.–Apr., Sun. 1 and 3.*

SCUBA DIVING

Information about dive trips, as well as rental scuba and snorkeling equipment, can be obtained at **Force E** (⊠ 877 E. Palmetto Park Rd., Boca Raton, ☎ 561/368–0555).

## Shopping

**Mizner Park** (⊠ Federal Hwy. between Palmetto Park Rd. and Glades Rd.) is a distinctive 30-acre shopping village with apartments and town houses among the gardenlike spaces. The some three dozen retail stores include the excellent **Liberties Fine Books & Music,** a Jacobson's specialty department store, seven restaurants with sidewalk cafés, and eight movie screens. **Town Center** (⊠ 6000 W. Glades Rd.) combines a business park with ritzy shopping and some of the city's best restaurants. Major retailers include **Bloomingdale's, Burdines, Lord & Taylor, Saks Fifth Avenue,** and **Sears**—187 stores and restaurants in all.

# Delray Beach

❷ **Delray Beach,** which began as an artists' retreat and a small settlement of Japanese farmers, works hard to perfect its "All-American" atmosphere. The local historic preservation movement has yielded great results along Atlantic Avenue, the main drag, which runs about a mile in an east–west direction, ending at the beach; almost entirely lined with stores, it's pleasant for strolling. A lovely pedestrian way begins at the edge of town, across NE 8th Street (⊠ George Bush Blvd.), along the big broad swimming beach that extends north and south of Atlantic Avenue.

## Sights to See

**Cason Cottage.** One street north of the town's cultural center, off Atlantic Avenue, is this restored Victorian-style home, which dates from about 1915 and now serves as offices of the Delray Beach Historical Society. The house is filled with relics of the Victorian era, including an old pipe organ donated by descendants of one of the original families to settle Delray Beach. Periodic displays at the cottage celebrate the town's architectural evolution. ⊠ *5 N.E. 1st St.,* ☎ *561/243–0223.*

**Colony Hotel.** The chief landmark along Atlantic Avenue is this Mediterranean-revival structure, still open only for the winter season as it has been for more than 60 years. ⊠ *525 E. Atlantic Ave.,* ☎ *561/276–4123.*

★ **Morikami Museum and Japanese Gardens.** Florida seems an odd place for this 200-acre cultural and recreational facility, which recalls the Yamato Colony, an agricultural community of Japanese settlers who originally came to Florida in 1905. The gardens include the only known collection of bonsai Florida plants. There are also programs and exhibits in a lakeside museum and theater as well as a permanent display devoted to the colony's history in a building modeled after a Japanese imperial villa. Also on the grounds are a nature trail, picnic pavilions, a library and audiovisual center, and snack bar. ⊠ *4000 Morikami Park Rd.,* ☎ *561/495–0233.* ☞ *$4.25, free Sun. 10–noon.* ⊙ *Park daily sunrise–sunset, museum, Tues.–Sun. 10–5.*

**Old School Square Cultural Arts Center.** This institution just off Atlantic Avenue houses several museums, most notably the **Cornell Museum of Art & History,** plus a performing arts center in restored school buildings dating from 1913 and 1926. ☒ *51 N. Swinton Ave.,* ☎ *561/243–7922.*

NEED A
BREAK?

In addition to selling antiques and gifts, the charmingly old-fashioned **Sundy House** (☒ 106 S. Swinton Ave., ☎ 561/278–2163 or 561/272–3270) has a restaurant that serves lunch and a traditional afternoon tea. Flagler foreman John Shaw Sundy, who became the first mayor of Delray, lived here with his family. The structure's beautiful gardens and five gingerbread gables complement Delray's finest wraparound porch.

## Beaches

The **Municipal Beach** (☒ Atlantic Ave. and Rte. A1A) has a boat ramp and volleyball court.

## Dining and Lodging

$–$$ ★ ✕ **Arcade Pasta Grill.** After 45 years in the restaurant business in New York and New Jersey, William Kontos came here for dinner, got to talking, learned that this Delray landmark was for sale, and bought it. Exceptional cooking, affordable prices, and an unusual setting put it at the top of any south Palm Beach County itinerary. The hexagonal room with a peaked ceiling is either tacky or smart, with its blue-green Tanqueray umbrellas, butcher paper tablecloth covers, and fan-back chairs. The menu may be standard Italian, but the preparations stand out. Penne may come with pressed fresh garlic flecking steamed broccoli, glistening with olive oil. More than 20 other pastas can be ordered with a half dozen toppings such as meatballs, eggplant, or chicken for just $11. ☒ 411 E. Atlantic Ave., ☎ 561/274–0099. AE, D, DC, MC, V.

$–$$ ★ ✕ **Boston's on the Beach.** Often a restaurant that's right on the beach will rely on its location to fill the place up, and not worry too much about the food. Not so with Boston's, just across the street from Delray Public Beach, where you'll find good New England clam chowder and several lobster dishes, as well as fresh fish grilled, fried, or prepared just about any other way. All this is presented in an ultra-informal setting; tables are old and wooden tables and walls are decorated with traffic signs and other conversation-stoppers, most notably Boston Red Sox, Boston Bruins, and New England Patriots paraphernalia—and the entire place is a veritable shrine to Ted Williams. After dark the place is a casual club with live music. ☒ 40 S. Ocean Blvd. (A1A) ☎ 561/278–3364. AE, MC, V.

$$$–$$$$ 🏨 **Seagate Hotel & Beach Club.** The best garden hotel in Palm Beach County, this property offers value, comfort, style, and personal attention. You can dress up and dine in a smart little mahogany- and lattice-trimmed beachfront salon or have the same Continental fare in casual attire in the equally stylish bar. The deluxe one-bedroom suite is all chintz and rattan, with many upholstered pieces. All suites have at least kitchenettes, even the least expensive studios (although here the facilities are compact and behind foldaway doors). Guests enjoy privileges at the private beach club. ☒ 400 S. Ocean Blvd., 33483, ☎ 561/276–2421 or 800/233–3581. 70 1- and 2-bedroom suites. Restaurant, lounge, heated freshwater and heated saltwater pools, beach. AE, DC, MC, V.

$$–$$$$ 🏨 **Harbor House.** The exceptional feature of these white, two-story, 1950s buildings is their privileged location in a quiet residential enclave three blocks east of U.S. 1 and across from the Delray Marina.

In addition to two tiny motel rooms, there are 23 efficiencies and one- and two-bedroom apartments with kitchens and a mix of seating generally done in white, beige, tan, and blue. Everything retains a 1950s look, but carpets and upholstery are replaced before they look tired. In a nice touch, the matching bedroom fabrics are changed by the season: solid blue in summer, blue florals in winter. ⊠ *124 Marine Way, 33483,* ☎ *561/276–4221. 25 units. Pool, shuffleboard, coin laundry. MC, V.*

**$$–$$$$** ☒ **Sea Breeze of Delray Beach.** Considering its prime location—opposite the Gulfstream Bath & Tennis Club, across from the beach—this is an exceptional buy. The one- and two-story buildings are set around beautiful lawns. Each of the studios and one- or two-bedroom apartments has a full kitchen; the updated ones have microwaves. Furnishings include lots of floral prints, brocaded pieces, and French provincial reproductions, which create a comfortable, beachy look. Though the place dates from the 1950s and the kitchenware is mismatched, the place remains beautifully maintained and clean. There is twice-weekly maid service off-season. ⊠ *820 N. Ocean Blvd., 33483,* ☎ *561/276–7496. 23 units. Pool, shuffleboard, coin laundry. MC, V.*

## Nightlife

**Back Room Blues Lounge** (⊠ 303 W. Atlantic Blvd., ☎ 561/276–6492), behind Westside Liquors) has live blues bands Wednesday through Friday. **Boston's on the Beach** (⊠ 40 S. Ocean Blvd., ☎ 561/278–3364) presents live reggae music Monday and rock and roll Tuesday through Sunday. **Cafe Mocha** (⊠ 44 E. Atlantic Ave., ☎ 561/274–0084), a coffee shop and art gallery, brings in live music most nights.

## Outdoor Activities and Sports

### BIKING
There is a bicycle path in Barwick Park and a special oceanfront lane along Route A1A. **Rich Wagn's Bicycle Shop** (⊠ 217 E. Atlantic Ave., ☎ 561/276–4234) has bicycles available for rent.

### SCUBA DIVING
Scuba and snorkeling equipment can be rented from long-time, family-owned **Force E** (⊠ 660 Linton Blvd., Delray Beach, ☎ 561/276–0666). All Force E stores have PADI affiliation and provide instruction at all skill levels; dive-boat charters are also available.

### TENNIS
The **Delray Beach Tennis Center** (⊠ 201 W. Atlantic Ave., ☎ 561/243–7380) hosts an annual winter professional women's tournament that attracts players like Gabriela Sabatini and Steffi Graf. The center is also a great place to practice or take lessons; it has 14 clay courts and five hard courts and offers individual lessons and clinics.

### WATER SPORTS
**Lake Ida Park** (⊠ 2929 Lake Ida Rd., ☎ 561/964–4420) is an excellent place to water ski, whether you're a beginner or a veteran. The park has a boat ramp, slalom course, and trick ski course.

## Shopping

Unlike many cities along this resort coast, Delray Beach has a thriving old-fashioned downtown with hundreds of shops and restaurants, most along **Atlantic Avenue.**

# North of Boca Raton

The towns between Boca Raton and Palm Beach, strung together by Route A1A, run the gamut of modest and unpretentious to high and mighty. The glamour of Palm Beach infiltrates many of the towns to the south, as the Ritz-Carlton Hotel in Manalapan can attest—on the other hand, nearby Lake Worth is a budget traveler's paradise. North of Boca Raton you'll pass through Highland Beach, a town that despite its high rises and mansions is still wet behind the ears, as it was built on bare dunes within the past 25 years. Past Delray Beach is the Mizner-touched Gulf Stream—here you might see a private police officer stopping traffic for a golfer near the bougainvillea-topped walls of the Gulfstream Club—and beyond that is the old blue-collar town of Briny Breezes.

## Sights to See

**Knollwood Groves.** This orange grove dates from the 1930s, when it was planted by the partners of the "Amos & Andy" radio show. You can take a 30-acre tram tour through the groves and a processing plant and visit the Hallpatee Seminole Indian Village, where there's an alligator exhibit and crafts shop. During the busy season, special guest Martin Twofeather gives a lecture and an alligator handling exhibition. ⊠ 8053 Lawrence Rd., Boynton Beach, ☎ 561/734–4800. ☑ $5. ⊙ Daily 8:30–5:30.

❸ **Phipps Ocean Park.** Besides the ubiquitous beautiful beach, Phipps Ocean Park has a Palm Beach County landmark in the Little Red Schoolhouse. Dating from 1886, it was the first schoolhouse in what was then Dade County. ⊠ Rte. A1A, Palm Beach. ☑ Parking 25¢ for 20 min. ⊙ Mon.–Sat. 8–6.

## Beaches

**Oceanfront Park** (⊠ Ocean Ave. at Rte. A1A, Boynton Beach) has boardwalk, concessions, grills, jogging trail, and playground; parking is expensive if you're not a Boynton resident ($10 in winter, $5 the rest of the year). **Lantana Public Beach** (⊠ 100 N. Ocean Ave., Lantana), has one of the best food concessions around; you'll find fresh fish on weekends and breakfast and lunch specials every day outdoors under beach umbrellas. **Lake Worth Municipal Beach** (⊠ Rte. A1A at end of Lake Worth Bridge) has an Olympic-size swimming pool, fishing pier, picnic areas, shuffleboard, restaurants, and shops. ☑ Pool $2.

## Dining and Lodging

$$   ✕ **Old House.** Dating from 1889, the waterfront Lyman House has grown in spurts over the years and it's now a patchwork of shedlike spaces. Partners Wayne Cordero and Captain Bob Hoddinott have turned it into an informal Old-Florida seafood house with a menu of local seafood with Baltimore steamed crab, incongruously, as its specialty. Although there's air-conditioning, dining is still open-air most evenings and in cooler weather. ⊠ 300 E. Ocean Ave., Lantana, ☎ 561/533–5220. AE, MC, V.

$   ✕ **John G's.** About the only time the line lets up at John G's is when the restaurant closes at 3 PM. The menu is as big as the crowd: big fruit platters, sandwich-board superstars, grilled burgers, seafood, and eggs every which way, including a United Nations of ethnic omelets. ⊠ Lake Worth Casino, ☎ 561/585–9860. No credit cards.

$$$$   🏨 **The Ritz-Carlton, Palm Beach.** Despite its name, the Ritz-Carlton, Palm Beach is actually in Manalapan, roughly halfway between Palm Beach and Boca Raton. The bisque-colored, triple-tower landmark hotel may look like the work of '20s architect Addison Mizner, but in fact the property was built in 1991. Dominating the lobby area is a huge, double-sided marble fireplace—an assertion of luxury that foreshadows the marble bathtubs and overstuffed furniture in the guest rooms. Most bedrooms have an ocean view, and the oceanfront rooms have

balconies as well. Not to be outdone by the fabulous beaches, there is a large pool and courtyard area landscaped with more than 100 coconut palms. Bicycles and scuba and snorkeling equipment can be rented. ⊠ *100 S. Ocean Blvd., Manalapan, 33462,* ☎ *561/533–6000 or 800/241–3333,* 🅵🅰🅇 *561/588–4555. 5 restaurants, pool, beauty salon, massage, sauna, spa with steam room, 7 tennis courts. AE, D, DC, MC, V.*

**$$** 🏨 **Riviera Palms Motel.** Hans and Herter Grannemann have owned this small, two-story motel dating from the 1950s since 1978. It has two primary virtues: It's clean. And it's well located, across Route A1A from mid-rise apartment houses on the water, with three wings surrounding a grassy front yard and heated pool. Rooms are done in Danish modern and a blue, brown, and tan color scheme; all have at least a fridge but no phone. ⊠ *3960 N. Ocean Blvd., Gulf Stream 33483,* ☎ *561/276–3032. 17 rooms, efficiencies, and suites. Pool. No credit cards.*

**$–$$** 🏨 **Holiday House.** Standing out from its motel strip, a five-minute walk
**★** from the heart of Lake Worth, is this uncommercial-looking lodging with bougainvillea-entwined balconies and rich tropical gardens. The motel rooms, efficiencies, and one-bedroom apartments here live up to expectations. Located in two adjacent two-story buildings dating from the late 1940s, but kept up nicely, each is warmly furnished, clean, and fitted out with fridge, microwave, phone, and air-conditioning. The owners are thoughtful enough to keep windows open when rooms are vacant. Maid service is provided daily for motel rooms, weekly for efficiencies and apartments. ⊠ *320 N. Federal Hwy., Lake Worth 33460,* ☎ *561/582–3561,* 🅵🅰🅇 *561/582–3561, Ext. 314. 30 units. Pool, coin laundry. MC, V.*

## Nightlife and the Arts

**Demetrius Klein Dance Company** (⊠ 3208 2nd Ave. N, #10, Lake Worth 33461, ☎ 561/964–9779) is a nationally acclaimed, world-touring, professional troupe.

## Outdoor Activities and Sports

### FISHING

For deep-sea fishing in the southern part of the region, try **B-Love Fleet** (⊠ 314 E. Ocean Ave., Lantana, ☎ 561/588–7612); a half day costs $20 per person.

### GOLF

**Boynton Beach Municipal Golf Course** (⊠ 8020 Jog Rd., Boynton Beach, ☎ 561/969–2200) has 27 holes.

### POLO

**Gulfstream Polo Club,** the oldest club in the Palm Beach area, began in the 1920s and plays medium-goal polo (for teams with handicaps of 8–16 goals). There are six polo fields. ⊠ *4550 Polo Rd., Lake Worth 33467,* ☎ *561/965–2057.* 🎟 *Free.* ⊙ *Games Dec.–Apr., Fri. 3, Sun. 1.*

# Palm Beach

Setting the tone in this incredibly wealthy town is the baroque architecture of developer Addison Mizner, who began building homes, stores, and public buildings here in the 1920s, and whose Moorish-gothic style has influenced virtually all the landmarks of the community. Thanks to Mizner and those influenced by him, **Palm Beach** has a kind of neo-Camelot look. On Worth Avenue, you can get a taste of what the town is all about when you squeeze into a parking place among the Mercedes and the Bentleys and rub Versace-covered shoulders in the boutiques with shoppers whose credit card limits likely exceed the gross national product of Liechtenstein. You can see a lot of Palm Beach on a driving tour that can take as little as an hour, depending on how much time you want to spend gawking.

County Road runs south along a row of mansions fronted by thick stands of palm trees and high hedges, some hedge rows higher than 20 feet. Barrel tile roofs seem to be de rigueur in these parts. After a mile, County Road joins Ocean Boulevard to become the shore road (here officially designated Route A1A). A low wall separates the road from the sea and hides the badly eroded beach. Here and there where the seaside strand deepens a bit, homes have been built directly on the beach. Rather than cross the bridge to the mainland, continue to South Ocean Boulevard/Route A1A, heading south along one of Florida's most scenic drives. The road follows the dune top, with some of Palm Beach's most opulent mansions on your left. As you approach Worth Avenue, the public beach begins. Parking meters along Ocean Boulevard between Worth Avenue and Royal Palm Way signify the only stretch of beach in Palm Beach with convenient public access.

## Sights to See

*Numbers in the margin correspond to points of interest on the Palm Beach and West Palm Beach map.*

**⑤ Bethesda-by-the-Sea.** This house of worship was built in 1927 by the first Protestant congregation in southeast Florida. Spanish-Gothic in design, it has ornamental gardens on site. ⊠ *141 S. County Rd.,* ☎ *561/655–4554.* ☉ *Gardens daily 8–5; services Sept.–May, Sun. 8, 9, and 11, and June–Aug., Sun. 8 and 10; call for weekday schedule.*

★ **⑥ The Breakers.** One of the starting points of Florida tourism, this ornate Italian renaissance hotel built in 1926 by Henry M. Flagler's widow replaces an earlier hotel, which had burned twice. About $150 million was spent on a renovation not long ago, which did not disturb items like the 15th-century Flemish tapestries in the Florentine Dining Room.

**⑦ Canyon of Palm Beach.** This road is cut about 25 feet deep through a ridge of sandstone and oolite limestone. The reddish-brown rock gives you a brief feeling of being in the desert Southwest. But the feeling doesn't last long; the canyon is small.

**⑧ East Inlet Drive.** This is at the northern tip of the island, where a dock offers a view of Lake Worth Inlet. Observe the no-parking signs; Palm Beach police issue tickets.

**El Solano.** Perhaps no Palm Beach mansion represents the town's ongoing generations of flashbulb fame better than El Solano, at 720 South Ocean Boulevard. The Spanish-style home was originally built by Addison Mizner for himself in 1925. Mizner then sold it to Harold Vanderbilt, and the property made the rounds of socialites, photo shoots, and expansions until it was bought by John Lennon and Yoko Ono 10 months before Lennon's death. Now owned by a banking executive, El Solano is not open to the public.

**⑨ Mar-A-Lago.** Grandest of homes along Ocean Boulevard is this property with Italianate towers silhouetted against the sky. The former estate of breakfast-food heiress Marjorie Meriweather Post, it has more recently been owned by real-estate magnate Donald Trump, who has turned it into a membership club. The property curves for ⅓ mile along the road. ⊠ *1100 S. Ocean Blvd.*

# Palm Beach and West Palm Beach

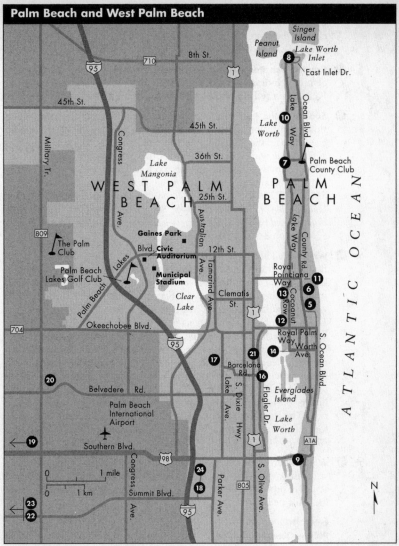

⑩ **Palm Beach Bicycle Trail.** This palm-fringed path skirts the backyards of some of the world's priciest homes and parallels Lake Way. Bicycles can be rented at the Palm Beach Trail Bicycle Shop. ⊠ *223 Sunrise Ave.,* ☎ *561/659–4583.*

⑪ **Palm Beach Post Office.** Art meets function with murals depicting Seminole Indians in the Everglades and royal and coconut palms. ⊠ *95 N. County Rd.,* ☎ *561/832–0633 or 561/832–1867.*

⑫ **Society of the Four Arts.** This privately endowed cultural and educational institution incorporates an exhibition hall, a library, 13 distinct gardens, and the Philip Hulitar Sculpture Garden. The schedule offers concerts, film, art shows, and more. Concert and lecture tickets for nonmembers may be purchased one week in advance; tickets for Friday films are available at the time of showing. ⊠ *Four Arts Plaza,* ☎ *561/655–7226.* ◫ *Suggested donation $3.* ◷ *Exhibitions and programs Dec.–mid-Apr., Mon.–Sat. 10–5, Sun. 2–5; library and children's library weekdays 10–5, also Sat. 9–1 Nov.–Apr.; gardens Mon.–Sat. 10–5, also Sun. 2:30–5 Jan.–Apr. 15.*

★ ⑬ **Whitehall.** This opulent palace is like Texas' Alamo—a historic shrine fundamental to the culture that grew out of a bygone era. The opulence of the Gilded Age in Florida is still apparent at this palatial 73-room mansion, which Henry M. Flagler had built in 1901 for his third wife, Mary Lily Kenan. Then-famous architects John Carrère and Thomas Hastings were instructed to spare no expense in creating the finest home they could imagine. They did as they were told, and Whitehall rivals some of the fine palaces of Europe. In 1960, Flagler's granddaughter, Jean Flagler Matthews, bought the building and made it a museum, with many of the original furnishings on display. In addition to an art collection, you'll find a 1,200-pipe organ and exhibits on the history of the Florida East Coast Railroad. Flagler's personal railroad car, "The Rambler," is parked behind the building. A tour by well-informed guides takes about an hour. ⊠ *Cocoanut Row at Whitehall Way,* ☎ *561/655–2833.* ◷ *$7.* ◷ *Tues.–Sat. 10–5, Sun. noon–5.*

★ ⑭ **Worth Avenue.** It's synonymous with posh, pricey shopping and a stroll among the shops—**Cartier, Charles Jourdan, Giorgio Armani,** and scores of other top-drawer retailers—gives you a taste of what the good life must be like.

## Beaches

**Phipps Ocean Park** (⊠ Rte. A1A) offers picnic tables. Meters are 25¢ per quarter hour.

## Dining and Lodging

$$$–$$$$ ✕ **Café L'Europe.** Sumptuous oak paneling, shirred curtains over fan-
★ light windows, elaborate dried-flower bouquets, and lots of etched and leaded glass set the mood, along with the vintage Sinatra in the background. Even the bar habitués are elegant here. Under chef Joseph Eisenbuchner, ladies-who-lunch can enjoy spa cuisine, while evening guests dine expensively on specialty pastas, such as spinach, shiitake mushroom, and mascarpone ravioli with pignoli-hazelnut butter; seafood dishes such as the potato-crusted Florida snapper with shaved baby fennel and beurre blanc; or Cornish hen, double lamb chops, or black Angus steak. Apple pancake with lingonberries is the signature dessert. ⊠ *150 Worth Ave., Esplanade,* ☎ *561/655–4020. Reservations essential. Jacket required. AE, DC, MC, V. No lunch Sun.*

$$$ ✕ **Bice Ristorante.** This offshoot of an Italian landmark dining establishment, whose brilliant flower arrangements and lots of brass accent a dark beige-and-yellow color scheme, is so thoroughly Italian that it's easy to be disappointed when the parking attendant speaks to you in

English as you leave. Aromas of basil, chive, and oregano fill the air as waiters bring out the divine home-baked focaccia—a Tuscan-style bread—that accompanies such house favorites as *Robespierre alla moda della bice* (sliced steak topped with arugula salad) and *costoletta di vitello impanata alla milanese* (breaded veal cutlet with a tomato salad). The name is short for Beatrice, mother of Roberto Ruggeri, who founded the original in Milan in 1926 and has opened branches here in Palm Beach and other smart places since then. ⊠ *313¼ Worth Ave.,* ☎ *561/835–1600. Jacket required. AE, DC, MC, V.*

$$$ ✕ **The Breakers.** The main hotel dining area at this famous resort hotel consists of the elegant **Florentine Dining Room,** decorated with fine 15th-century Flemish tapestries; the adjoining **Celebrity Aisle,** where the maître d' seats his most honored guests; and the **Circle Dining Room,** where a huge circular skylight frames a bronze-and-crystal Venetian chandelier. Continental specialties such as herb-crusted rack of lamb and sautéed tournedos of beef are still available, but the menu also offers lighter dishes such as poached chicken breast and grilled papaya-marinated swordfish. Desserts are rich, among them *vacherin glacé* (praline-flavored ice cream encased in whipped cream on a meringue base). ⊠ *1 S. County Rd.,* ☎ *561/655–6611 or 800/833–3141. Reservations essential. AE, D, DC, MC, V.*

$$$ ✕ **Jo's.** This pastel, latticed, and mirrored French restaurant, long tucked away behind a thrift shop, now occupies a prominent corner on South County Road, seats 150, and offers a full bar. Chef Richard Kline, son of the owner Jo, holds sway in the kitchen. Look for the three-soup sampler (lobster bisque, green pea soup, and beef consommé) as well as osso buco and boned half roast duckling with orange–always moist but never rare. For dessert try the *tarte tatin* (upside-down apple pie) or fresh raspberries. The restaurant is one of the few open for lunch and dinner seven days a week. ⊠ *375 S. County Rd.,* ☎ *561/659–6776. AE, MC, V.*

$$ ✕ **Chuck & Harold's.** Ivana Trump, Larry Holmes, Brooke Shields, and Michael Bolton are among the celebrities who frequent this combination power-lunch bar, sidewalk café, and jazz/big band garden. Locals who want to be part of the scenery linger in the front-porch area, next to pots of red and white begonias mounted on the sidewalk rail. Specialties include conch chowder, an onion-crunchy gazpacho, and tangy Key lime pie. A big blackboard lists daily specials and celebrity birthdays. ⊠ *207 Royal Poinciana Way,* ☎ *561/659–1440. AE, DC, MC, V.*

$$ ✕ **Dempsey's.** A New York-style Irish pub under the palms, this one is complete with paisley table covers, plaid café curtains, burgundy banquettes, horse prints, and antique coach lanterns. When major sports events are on the big TV, this place is always packed, noisy, and as electric as a frenzied Friday at the stock exchange. Along with much socializing, people enjoy Maine lobster, fresh seafood, chicken hash Dempsey (with a dash of Scotch), followed by hot apple pie. ⊠ *50 Cocoanut Row,* ☎ *561/835–0400. AE, MC, V.*

$$ ✕ **Ta-boo.** Real estate investor Franklyn P. deMarco, Jr., has teamed up with Maryland restaurateur Nancy Sharigan to successfully re-create the legendary Worth Avenue bistro that debuted in 1941. Dressed in gorgeous pinks, greens, and florals, the space is divided into discreet salons: One resembles a courtyard, another an elegant living room with a fireplace, and a third a skylit gazebo. The Tiki Tiki bar makes an elegant salon for the neighborhood crowd. Appetizers range from a very proletariat nachos grande with chili to Beluga caviar; dinners include chicken and arugula from the grill, prime rib and steaks, and main course salads (for instance, grilled strips of filet mignon tossed with greens, mushrooms, tomato, and onion). White pizza, with goat and

mozzarella cheeses, pesto, and sweet roasted red peppers is a favorite. ✉ *221 Worth Ave.,* ☎ *561/835–3500. AE, MC, V.*

**$** ✕ **TooJay's.** New York deli food served in a bright California-style setting—what could be more Florida? The menu at this spot, one of nine TooJay's in the Sunshine State, includes matzoh ball soup, corned beef on rye, and a killer cake made with five kinds of chocolate and topped with whipped cream. A salami-on-rye sandwich layered with onions, Munster cheese, coleslaw, and Russian dressing is a house favorite. On the High Holidays look for carrot *tzimmes* (a sweet vegetable compote), brisket, and roast chicken. Wisecracking waitresses keep the pace fast. ✉ *313 Royal Poinciana Plaza,* ☎ *561/659–7232. AE, DC, MC, V. Beer and wine only.*

**$$$$** 🏨 **Brazilian Court.** With its courtyard rooms and suites, this hotel re-
★ mains the pick of Palm Beach. Spread out over half a block, the yellow-stucco facade with gardens and a red tile roof helps you imagine what the place must have been like at its birth in 1931. Rooms are brilliantly floral—yellows, blues, greens—with theatrical bed canopies, signature white-lattice patterns on carpets, and sunshiny pane windows; the palette captures the magic of the bright Florida sun. Bathroom shelf space is tight, but at least you can line up your toiletries on marble, and the closets will remind you that people once came with trunks enough for the entire season. (Some still do.) French doors, polished wood floors, bay windows, loggias, cherub fountains, and chintz garden umbrellas beneath royal palms are just some of the elements that compose the lyrical style. Rooms are stocked with Evian water, and classical music plays as you enter. ✉ *301 Australian Ave., 33480,* ☎ *561/655–7740 or 800/552–0335; in Canada, 800/228–6852;* 🖷 *561/655–0801. 128 rooms, 6 suites. 2 restaurants, bar, pool. AE, D, DC, MC, V.*

**$$$$** 🏨 **The Breakers.** This opulent seven-story hotel in Italian Renaissance
★ style is more than a Buckingham Palace of a resort: It's part of the very foundation of old Palm Beach. Dating from 1926 and enlarged in 1969, it sprawls over 140 splendid acres in the heart of some of the most expensive real estate in the world. Cupids wrestle alligators in the Florentine fountain in front of the main entrance; inside the lofty lobby are majestic ceiling vaults and frescoes. The hotel still balances formality and a certain casualness typical of tropical resorts, although, in a concession to the times, men and boys are no longer *required* to wear jackets and ties after 7 PM. Rooms come in 15 different sizes and shapes; all have white plantation shutters, Chinese porcelain table lamps, and restored 1920s furniture and are either done in an English chintz colored cool green and soft pink, or in a floral and ribbon chintz in shades of blues. If you prefer more space, request quarters in the addition. ✉ *1 S. County Rd., 33480,* ☎ *561/655–6611 or 800/833– 3141,* 🖷 *561/659–8403. 567 rooms, 48 suites. 4 restaurants, lounge, pool, saunas, 2 golf courses, 20 tennis courts, croquet, fitness center, jogging, shuffleboard, beach, boating, children's programs. AE, D, DC, MC, V.*

**$$$$** 🏨 **The Colony.** An attentive staff that is youthful yet experienced dis-
★ tinguishes this legendary yellow Georgian-style hotel only steps from Worth Avenue. Always "the scene" for the glitterati to make after charity balls at The Breakers, this is where Roxanne Pulitzer retreated after her infamous seven-week marriage in 1992. There's a buzz of competence and true desire to please among the staff—evinced by the policy of relaxing the dress code in summer. The cool and classical guest rooms have fluted blond cabinetry and matching draperies and bed-covers in deep pink, beige, and blue stripes. The only complaint is that the bathrooms are looking tired; at least the lack of shelf space has been partly alleviated by cabinets above the sink. ✉ *155 Hammon Ave.,*

33480, ☎ 561/655–5430 or 800/521–5525, FAX 561/832–7318. *63 rooms, 36 suites and apartments, 7 villas, 3 penthouses. Restaurant, pool, spa. AE, D, DC, MC, V.*

$$$$ ★ 🏨 **Four Seasons Ocean Grand.** This 6-acre property at the south end of Palm Beach is coolly elegant but warm in detail and generous in amenities. Marble, art, fanlight windows, swagged drapes, chintz, and palms create a serene atmosphere throughout. Piano music accompanies cocktails daily in the living room, with jazz on weekend evenings and classical recitals on Sunday afternoon. Although the hotel's name suggests grandeur, it's more like a small jewel, with only four stories and a long beach. All rooms are spacious—equivalent to suites in other hotels—and each has a private balcony and is furnished in typical Palm Beach finery. Muted natural tones prevail in guest rooms, with teal, mauve, and salmon accents. ⊠ *2800 S. Ocean Blvd., 33480,* ☎ *561/582–2800 or 800/432–2335,* FAX *561/547–1557. 210 rooms and suites. 2 restaurants, lounge, pool, saunas, 3 tennis courts, health club, beach. AE, D, DC, MC, V.*

$$$–$$$$ ★ 🏨 **Plaza Inn.** This three-story hotel operates B&B style; a full breakfast is included. The hotel is deco-designed from the 1930s, with pool and gardens and a bar with the intimate charm of a trysting place for the likes of Cary Grant and Katharine Hepburn. Inn owner Ajit Asrani is a retired Indian Army officer who raises show horses and polo ponies. The courteous staff and location in the heart of Palm Beach are pluses. And the uncluttered rooms, all with phone and fridge, provide a welcome change of pace from other B&Bs. ⊠ *215 Brazilian Ave., 33480,* ☎ *561/832–8666 or 800/233–2632,* FAX *561/835–8776. 50 rooms and suites. Pool. AE, MC, V.*

$$$ 🏨 **Palm Beach Historic Inn.** Longtime hoteliers Harry and Barbara Kehr manage this delightfully unexpected inn in the heart of downtown Palm Beach. The setting nicely combines town and vacationland, as it's tucked between Town Hall and a seaside residential block. B&B touches include fresh flowers, wine and fruit, snacks, seasonal turndown, tea and cookies in rooms, and an expanded Continental breakfast. Guest rooms tend to the frilly with lots of lace, ribbons, and scalloped edges. Most are furnished with Victorian antiques and reproductions (some out of old Palm Beach mansions, others looking more secondhand than authentic) and chiffon wall drapings above the bed. With typical B&B whimsy, a 1944 Coke machine on the second floor still supplies an 8-ounce bottle for a dime. Bath towels are as thick as parkas. ⊠ *365 S. County Rd., 33480,* ☎ *561/832–4009,* FAX *561/832–6255. 13 rooms and suites. Library. AE, D, DC, MC, V.*

$$–$$$ 🏨 **Sea Lord Hotel.** If you don't need glamour or brand names, and you're not the B&B type, this garden-style hideaway is for you. Choose from accommodations that overlook Lake Worth, the pool, or the ocean; the reasonably priced café adds to the at-home, comfy feeling and attracts repeat customers. Rooms are plain but not cheap and come with carpet, at least one comfortable chair, small or large fridge, and tropical print fabrics. ⊠ *2315 S. Ocean Blvd., 33480,* ☎ FAX *561/582–1461. 19 rooms, 11 apartments, 6 efficiencies. Restaurant, pool, beach. D, MC, V.*

## Nightlife and the Arts

The **Royal Poinciana Playhouse** (⊠ 70 Royal Poinciana Plaza, Palm Beach 33480, ☎ 561/659–3310) presents seven productions each year between December and April.

**Au Bar** (⊠ 336 Royal Poinciana Way, ☎ 561/832–4800) rocketed to national fame a few years ago with the William Kennedy Smith scandal, and it's still crowded with curiosity seekers. But with its live music, it remains an in spot for locals, and the dance floor is so crowded on weekends that you'll feel like you're in a rugby match.

## Outdoor Activities and Sports

DOG RACING

**Palm Beach Kennel Club** opened in 1932 and has 4,300 seats. ⊠ *1111 N. Congress Ave., Palm Beach 33409,* ☎ *561/683–2222.* ⛄ *50¢, terrace level $1, parking free.* ☉ *Racing Mon. 12:30; Wed., Thurs., and Sat. 12:30 and 7:30; Fri. 7:30; Sun. 1; simulcasts Mon. and Fri. noon and Tues. 12:30.*

GOLF

**Breakers Hotel Golf Club** (⊠ 1 S. County Rd., Palm Beach 33480, ☎ 561/655–6611 or 800/833–3141) has 36 holes.

JAI ALAI

**Palm Beach Jai Alai** reopened under new owners in late 1994 after being closed a year. A five-week re-inaugural season may be lengthened in future years if more players can be contracted, so double-check dates and prices. ⊠ *1415 W. 45th St., West Palm Beach,* ☎ *561/844–2444.* ⛄ *50¢.* ☉ *Games late Nov.–Dec., Fri. and Sat. 12:15 and 7:15; Sun., Mon., Wed., and Thurs. 12:15.*

## Shopping

One of the world's showcases for high-quality shopping, **Worth Avenue** runs ¼-mile east–west across Palm Beach, from the beach to Lake Worth. The street has more than 250 shops, and many upscale stores (**Cartier, Gucci, Hermès, Pierre Deux, Saks Fifth Avenue, and Van Cleef & Arpels**) are represented, their merchandise appealing to the discerning tastes of the Palm Beach clientele. Most merchants open at 9:30 or 10 and close at 5:30 or 6. The six blocks of **South County Road** north of Worth Avenue also have appealing stores. For specialty items (out-of-town newspapers and health foods), try the shops along the north side of **Royal Poinciana Way.**

---

# Palm Beach Gardens and Palm Beach Shores

Palm Beach Gardens, a relaxed, upscale residential community about 20 minutes northwest of Palm Beach, is widely known for its high-profile golf complex, the PGA National Resort & Spa. Although the town is not exactly on the beach, the ocean is just a 15-minute drive away. Palm Beach Shores, a residential town rimmed by mom-and-pop motels, is at the southern tip of Singer Island, across Lake Worth Inlet from Palm Beach. By staying here you get Palm Beach weather and Palm Beach views without the pretense and price of Palm Beach.

## Dining and Lodging

$$  ✕ **Arezzo.** The pungent smell of fresh garlic and olive oil tips you off
★    that the food's the thing at this outstanding Tuscan grill at the PGA National Resort & Spa, but art and service equally rate. In this unusually relaxed, upscale resort setting, you can dine in shorts or in jacket and tie. Families are attracted by the affordable prices (as well as the food), so romantics might be tempted to pass Arezzo up. Their loss. Dishes include the usual variety of chicken, veal, fish, and steaks, but there are a dozen different pastas and an almost equal number of pizzas. Examples are rigatoni *alla Bolognese* (with ground veal, marinara sauce, and Parmesan) and linguine *alla Catalana* (with eggplant, garlic, onions, marinara sauce, and Parmesan). The decor, too, has the right idea: an herb garden in the center of the room, slate floors, upholstered banquettes to satisfy the upscale mood, and butcher paper over yellow table covers to establish the light side. ⊠ *400 Ave. of the Champions,* ☎ *561/627–2000. AE, MC, V. No lunch.*

$$ ✕ **River House.** Much of what South Florida dining is all about can be found at this dinner-only, waterfront restaurant. People keep returning for the large portions of straightforward American fare, the big salad bar and fresh, slice-it-yourself breads, the competent service and, thanks to the animated buzz of a rewarded local clientele, the feeling that you've come to the right place. Choices include seafoods (always with a daily catch), steaks, chops, and seafood/steak combo platters. Booths and freestanding tables are surrounded by lots of blond wood, high ceilings, and nautical art under glass. The wait on Saturday nights in season can be up to 45 minutes. Reserve one of the 20 upstairs tables, available weekends only; the upstairs is a little more formal and doesn't have a salad bar (bread comes from below), but it does possess a cathedral ceiling. ⊠ *2373 PGA Blvd.,* ☎ *561/694–1198. AE, MC, V. No lunch.*

$$-$$$ ✕🏨 **Sailfish Marina.** This long-established, one-story motel has a marina with 94 deep-water slips and 15 rooms and efficiencies that open
★ to landscaped grounds. None are directly on the water, but units 9–11 have ocean views across the blacktop drive. Rooms have peaked ceilings, carpeting, king or twin beds, and stall showers; many have ceiling fans. Much of the art is original, traded with artists who display in an informal show on the dock every Thursday night. From the seawall, you can see fish through the clear inlet water. Don't overlook the open-air waterfront restaurant **The Galley**; after a hot day of mansion-gawking, there's no better place to chill out. The blender seems to run nonstop, churning out tropical drinks like piña coladas and goombay smashes. Mainstays of the menu are old Florida favorites like grouper and conch chowder. But if you want to go upscale (this, after all, Palm Beach County), there are a few highbrow entré es such as lobster tail or baby sea scallops sauteed in garlic and lemon butter. The Marina's staff is informed and helpful, the proprietors as promotional as they are friendly. There are no in-room phones, but several pay phones are on the property and messages are taken. ⊠ *98 Lake Dr., 33404,* ☎ *561/844–1724 or 800/446–4577,* 𝖥𝖠𝖷 *561/848–9684. 15 units. Restaurant, bar, grocery, pool. AE, MC, V.*

$$$$ 🏨 **PGA National Resort & Spa.** Outstanding mission-style rooms are decorated in deep, almost somber florals that evoke a thoughtful and settled-in feel. Facilities throughout the resort are equally richly detailed, from the lavish landscaping to the limitless sports facilities and excellent dining (☞ *Arezzo, above*). The spa, opened in 1992, is housed in a building styled after a Mediterranean fishing village. Its six outdoor therapy pools, dubbed "Waters of the World," are joined by a collection of imported mineral salt pools, as well as men's and women's Jacuzzis and saunas; there are 22 private treatments. Championship golf courses and croquet courts are adorned with 25,000 flowering plants amid a 240-acre nature preserve. Two-bedroom, two-bath cottages with fully equipped kitchens are available, too. ⊠ *400 Ave. of the Champions, 33418,* ☎ *561/627–2000 or 800/633–9150. 275 rooms, 60 suites, 85 cottages. 6 restaurants, no-smoking rooms, lake, pool, sauna, spa, 5 golf courses, 19 tennis courts, croquet, racquetball, boating. AE, D, DC, MC, V.*

## Nightlife and the Arts

**Irish Times** (⊠ 9920 Alternate A1A, Promenade Shopping Plaza, ☎ 561/624–1504) is a four-leaf-clover find, featuring a microbrewery and live Irish acts.

## Outdoor Activities and Sports

AUTO RACING

Weekly ¼-mile drag racing, monthly 2¼-mile, 10-turn road racing, and monthly AMA motorcycle road racing take place year-round at the **Moroso Motorsports Park** (⊠ 17047 Beeline Hwy., Box 31907, Palm Beach Gardens 33420, ☎ 561/622–1400).

GOLF

**PGA National Resort & Spa** (⊠ 1000 Ave. of the Champions, Palm Beach Gardens 33418, ☎ 561/627–1800) offers a reputedly tough 90 holes.

## Shopping

**The Gardens** mall (⊠ 3101 PGA Blvd.) contains the standards if you want to make sure you're not missing out on anything at home: Bloomingdale's, Burdines, Macy's, Saks Fifth Avenue, and Sears.

# West Palm Beach

**⓯** Long considered Palm Beach's impoverished cousin, **West Palm Beach** is economically vibrant in its own right. Far larger than its upper-crust neighbor to the east, it has become the cultural, entertainment, and business center of the county and of the region to the north of Palm Beach. While sparkling new buildings like the mammoth $124 million Palm Beach County Judicial Center and Courthouse and the State Administrative Building exemplify the health of the city's corporate life, facilities such as the $60 million Kravis Center for the Performing Arts attest to the strength of the arts and entertainment community. The historic preservation movement has yielded an attractive downtown area. Along beautifully landscaped Clematis Street, you'll find boutiques, good restaurants, and exuberant nightlife that mimics that of South Beach. There's a free downtown shuttle by day and free on-street parking at night and on weekends.

## Sights to See

**⓰** **Ann Norton Sculpture Gardens.** A monument to the late American sculptor Ann Weaver Norton, second wife of Norton Gallery founder Ralph H. Norton, these gardens consist of charming 3-acre grounds displaying seven granite figures and six brick megaliths. Plantings were designed by Norton, an environmentalist, to attract native bird life. ⊠ 253 Barcelona Rd., ☎ 561/832–5328. ☜ $3. ⊙ Tues.–Sat. 10–4 (call ahead; schedule is not always observed) or by appointment.

**⓱** **Armory Arts Center.** Built by the WPA in 1939, the armory is now a complete visual arts center. Its gallery hosts rotating exhibitions, and classes are held throughout the year. ⊠ 1703 S. Lake Ave., ☎ 561/832–1776. ☜ Free. ⊙ Weekdays 9–5.

**⓲** **Dreher Park Zoo.** This wild kingdom is a 22-acre complex with more than 500 animals representing more than 100 species, including an endangered Florida panther. ⊠ 1301 Summit Blvd., ☎ 561/533–0887 or 561/547–9453. ☜ $5.50, boat rides $1. ⊙ Daily 9–5 (until 7 on spring and summer weekends), boat rides every 15 min.

**⓳** **Lion Country Safari.** Here you drive (with car windows closed) on 8 miles of paved roads through a 500-acre cageless zoo where 1,000 wild animals roam. Lions, elephants, white rhinoceroses, giraffes, zebras, antelopes, chimpanzees, and ostriches are among the species in residence. ⊠ Southern Blvd. W, ☎ 561/793–1084. ☜ $11.95, car rental $5 per hour. ⊙ Daily 9:30–5:30.

**⓴** **Mounts Horticultural Learning Center.** Take advantage of the balmy weather here, where you can walk among displays of tropical and subtropical plants. Free guided tours are given. ⊠ *531 N. Military Trail,* ☎ *561/233–1749.* ⊡ *Free.* ⊙ *Mon.–Sat. 8:30–5, Sun. 1–5; tours Sat. 11, Sun. 2:30.*

★ ㉑ **Norton Gallery of Art.** Constructed in 1941 by steel magnate Ralph H. Norton, this musuem boasts an extensive permanent collection of 19th- and 20th-century American and European paintings with special emphasis on 19th-century French Impressionists. There are also Chinese bronze and jade sculptures, a sublime outdoor patio with sculptures on display in a tropical garden, and a library housing more than 3,000 art books and periodicals. A new wing should open in 1997. ⊠ *1451 S. Olive Ave.,* ☎ *561/832–5194.* ⊡ *Suggested donation $5.* ⊙ *Tues.–Sat. 10–5, Sun. 1–5.*

㉒ **Okeeheelee Nature Center.** At this popular local environmental center you can explore 5 miles of trails through 90 acres of native pine flatwoods and wetlands. A spacious visitor center/gift shop has hands-on exhibits. ⊠ *7715 Forest Hill Blvd.,* ☎ *561/233–1400.* ⊡ *Free.* ⊙ *Visitor center Tues.–Fri. 1–4:45, Sat. 8:15–4:45; trails open daily.*

**Old Northwood Historic District.** This 1920s-era historic district, located just north of downtown and west of Flagler Drive, is on the National Register of Historic Places and hosts special events much of the year. Two-hour walking tours that include visits to historic home interiors are available on Sunday year-round through **Old Northwood Historic District Tours.** ⊠ *501 30th St.,* ☎ *561/863–5633.* ⊡ *$5 donation requested.* ⊙ *Tours: Sundays at 2.*

㉓ **Pine Jog Environmental Education Center.** This 150-acre site encompasses mostly undisturbed Florida pine flatwoods. There are now two self-guided ½-mile trails, and formal landscaping around the five one-story buildings features an array of native plants. Dioramas and displays show native ecosystems. ⊠ *6301 Summit Blvd.,* ☎ *561/686–6600.* ⊡ *Free.* ⊙ *Weekdays 9–5, weekends 1–4.*

☾ **Puppetry Arts Center.** Provides shows and educational programs from the home of the Gold Coast Puppet Guild. ⊠ *Cross County Mall, 4356 Okeechobee Blvd. and Military Trail,* ☎ *561/687–3280.* ⊡ *Shows $2.50.* ⊙ *Fri. evening, Sat. morning (call for schedule).*

☾ ㉔ **South Florida Science Museum.** Here you'll find hands-on exhibits, aquarium displays with touch-tank demonstrations, planetarium shows, and a chance to observe the heavens Friday night through the most powerful telescope in south Florida (weather permitting). ⊠ *4801 Dreher Trail N,* ☎ *561/832–1988.* ⊡ *$5; planetarium $1.75 extra, laser show $2 extra.* ⊙ *Sat.–Thurs. 10–5, Fri. 10–10.*

## Dining and Lodging

$$–$$$ ✕ **Basil's Neighborhood Café.** This informal restaurant is named for a fictitious gentleman who is more or less the establishment's mascot—man and restaurant are named after the herb, which the chef uses frequently and adroitly. Start with the swamp cabbage salad (hearts of palm with an oil-and-basil sauce) before tackling the basil-touched main dishes. (Try chicken breasts stuffed with cheese, walnuts, and spinach and covered with lemon-basil sauce.) Basil mania stops short of dessert, but the chocolate-topped hazelnut cake does fine on its own. ⊠ *771 Village Blvd.,* ☎ *561/687–3801. AE, DC, MC, V.*

$–$$ ✕ **Comeau Bar & Grill.** Everybody still calls it Roxy's (including the staff), its name from 1934 until it moved into an art deco downtown high rise's lobby in 1989. Outside there are tables under the canopy; inside, behind the authentic old saloon, is a clubby, pecky cypress-paneled room that serves no-surprise, all-American food: steaks, shrimp, chicken, duck, some pastas, and Caesar and Greek salads. Try the Roxy Burger—a combination of veal and beef herbed and spiced. ⊠ *319– 323 Clematis St.,* ☎ *561/833–2402 or 561/833–1003. AE, MC, V. No dinner Sun.*

**$$$$** ☷ **Palm Beach Polo and Country Club.** Privately owned and spacious studios, one- and two-bedroom villas, and condominiums are available for daily, weekly, or monthly rental in this exclusive 2,200-acre resort, where World Cup and USPA Gold Cup tournaments are hosted. Each residence is furnished by its owner according to quality standards set by the resort. Still, styles can range from stagily backlit and modern to Ozzie and Harriet plaids and bulky rattan. Be specific about your preferences when reserving. You might also want to request a dwelling closest to the sports activity that interests you: polo, tennis, or golf. All units have kitchens and a wide range of amenities. ⊠ *11809 Polo Club Rd., 33414,* ☎ *561/798–7000 or 800/327–4204. 100 villas and condominiums. 5 dining rooms, 10 pools, sauna, 2 18-hole and 1 9-hole golf courses, 24 tennis courts, croquet, horseback riding, racquetball, squash. AE, DC, MC, V.*

**$$–$$$** ☷ **Royal Palm House Bed & Breakfast.** This Dutch colonial-revival house with a gambrel roof and shed dormers was built in 1925. Of the three second-floor units with wickery interiors, one is a two-room suite and two share a bath. Best of all are innkeeper Anne Walker's wealth of stories about behind-the-scenes Washington, where in 1994 she retired as director of food for the U.S. House of Representatives. Guests get a big Southern breakfast with helpings of tales and can sometimes talk Anne into a North Carolina barbecue in the evening. ⊠ *3215 Spruce Ave., 33407,* ☎ *561/863–9836. 3 units. Pool. No credit cards.*

**$$** ☷ **Hibiscus House.** Few B&B hosts in Florida work harder at hospi-
★    tality and at looking after their neighborhood than Raleigh Hill and Colin Rayner. As proof, since the inn opened in the late 1980s, 11 sets of guests have bought houses in Old Northwood, which is listed on the National Register of Historic Places thanks to Hill and Rayner's efforts. Their Cape Cod-style bed-and-breakfast is full of the antiques Hill has collected during decades of in-demand interior designing: a 150-year-old four-square piano, a gorgeous green and cane planter chair beside an Oriental fan and bamboo poles, and Louis XV pieces in the living room. Outstanding, too, is the landscaped, tropical pool-patio area behind a high privacy fence. Both Hill and Rayner are informed about the best—as well as the most affordable—dining in the area. This is an excellent value. ⊠ *501 30th St., 33407,* ☎ *561/863–5633 or 800/203–4927. 8 rooms. Pool. AE, DC, MC, V.*

**$$** ☷ **West Palm Beach Bed & Breakfast.** Found in Old Northwood, but more informal and Key West–like in atmosphere, this cottage-style B&B has a clump of rare paroutis palms out front. All rooms are vividly colored. However, the splashy poolside carriage house and the new, brightly striped cottage with the fruity fabrics and Peter Max-style posters are where you want to be. The parlor has a delightful montage of work by Florida's favorite painter of hotel art, Eileen Seitz. ⊠ *419 32nd St., 33407,* ☎ *561/848–4064 or 800/736–4064,* FAX *561/842–1688. 2 rooms, carriage house, cottage. Pool. AE, MC, V.*

## Nightlife and the Arts

THE ARTS

Part of the treasury of arts attractions here is the **Raymond F. Kravis Center for the Performing Arts** (⊠ 701 Okeechobee Blvd., ☎ 561/832– 7469), a $55 million, 2,200-seat, glass, copper, and marble showcase occupying the highest ground in West Palm Beach. The 250-seat Rinker Playhouse includes a space for children's programming, family productions, and other special events. Some 300 performances of drama, dance, and music—everything from gospel and bluegrass to jazz and classical—are scheduled each year. **Quest Theatre** (⊠ 444 24th St., 33407, ☎ 561/832–9328) showcases African-American productions in its own performance hall and on tour throughout the county. **Palm Beach Opera** (⊠ 415 S. Olive Ave., West Palm Beach 33401, ☎ 561/833–7888) stages three productions each winter at the Kravis Center.

**Carefree Theatre** (⊠ 2000 S. Dixie Hwy., 33401, ☎ 561/833–7305) is Palm Beach County's premier showcase of foreign and art films.

NIGHTLIFE

**Underground Coffeeworks** (⊠ 105 Narcissus Ave., ☎ 561/835–4792), a retro '60s spot, has "something different going on" (usually live music) several nights a week. **Respectable Street Cafe** (⊠ 518 Clematis St., ☎ 561/832–9999) explodes in high energy like an indoor Woodstock.

## Outdoor Activities and Sports

GOLF

The plush **Emerald Dunes Golf Club** (⊠ 2100 Emerald Dunes Dr., 33411, ☎ 561/684–4653) has 18 holes of golf; **Palm Beach Polo and Country Club** (⊠ 13198 Forest Hill Blvd., 33414, ☎ 561/798–7000 or 800/327–4204) has 45 holes with an excellent overall layout.

## Shopping

Good as the malls are, they're sterile compared to the in-the-midst-of-things excitement—the mix of food, art, performance, landscaping, and retailing—that has renewed downtown West Palm around **Clematis Street**. Shopping per se is still the weakest part of the mix, but new water-view parks, outdoor performing areas, and attractive plantings and lighting—including fanciful palm tree sculptures—add to the pleasure of browsing and window shopping. For those single-mindedly bent on mall shopping, West Palm offers the **Palm Beach Mall** (⊠ Palm Beach Lakes Blvd. at I–95), with Burdines, JCPenney, Lord & Taylor, and Sears.

# THE TREASURE COAST

The Treasure Coast encompasses Martin, St. Lucie, and Indian River counties. Between I–95 and the shoreline from Palm Beach north to Vero Beach, the mall is king; the environment takes precedence further inland, in Martin and Indian River counties. You'll find lots of restaurants and shops in Stuart, the Martin County seat, and lively arts in Vero Beach. Farther inland, it's largely citrus and cattle, with the Indian River between barrier islands and mainland. Boaters ply these sheltered waters, part of the Intracoastal Waterway. You can also join locally organized turtle-watches, which go out to view sea turtles laying eggs in the sand between April and August.

## Around Jupiter

*Numbers in the margin correspond to points of interest on the Gold Coast and Treasure Coast map.*

㉕  You'll have your pick of wildlife centers in this neck of the woods. **Juno Beach** has a special marine park focusing on sea turtles. Heading north
㉖  from Juno Beach toward **Jupiter**, Route A1A runs for almost 4 miles along the beachfront dunes offering a great ocean view. Across the Lox-
㉗  ahatchee River is **Jupiter Island**, a carefully planned community whose estates often retreat from the road behind screens of vegetation; at the north end of town is a wildlife refuge where turtles come to nest.

## Sights to See

**Blowing Rocks Preserve.** Within this 73-acre Nature Conservancy holding, you'll find plant communities native to beachfront dune, coastal strand (the landward side of the dunes), mangrove, and hammock (tropical hardwood forest). The best time to visit is when high tides and strong offshore winds coincide, causing the sea to blow spectacularly through holes in the eroded outcropping. Park in the lot; Jupiter Island police ticket cars parked along the road. ⊠ *Rte. 707,* ☎ *561/575–2297 or 561/747–3113.* ☞ *$3 donation requested.* ☉ *Daily 6–5.*

**Burt Reynolds Ranch and Film Studio Tours.** On this 160-acre working horse ranch owned by the famous actor, you can take a 1½-hour tour by air-conditioned bus, with stops that include movie sets, a chapel, tree house, petting farm, and wherever filming may be in progress. ⊠ *16133 Jupiter Farms Rd. (2 mi west of I–95 at Exit 59-B), Jupiter,* ☎ *561/747–5390.* ☞ *Tour $10, petting farm free.* ☉ *Daily 10–4:30.*

**Dubois Home.** Take a look at how life once was in a modest pioneer home dating from 1898. The house, with design features that include Cape Cod as well as "cracker," sits atop an ancient Jeaga Indian mound 20 feet high, looking onto Jupiter Inlet. Even if you arrive when the house is closed, the surrounding **Dubois Park** is worth the visit for its lovely beaches and swimming lagoons. ⊠ *Dubois Rd., Jupiter,* ☎ *561/747–6639.* ☞ *Donations welcome.* ☉ *Sun. 1–4.*

**Elizabeth W. Kirby Interpretive Center.** To visit this center you must pass through the town of **Hobe Sound,** turn left on U.S. 1, and travel approximately 2½ miles. An adjacent ½-mile trail winds through a forest of sand pine and scrub oak—one of Florida's most unusual and endangered plant communities. ⊠ *13640 SE Federal Hwy., Hobe Sound,* ☎ *561/546–6141.* ☞ *Free.* ☉ *Trail daily sunrise–sunset, nature center weekdays 9–11 and 1–3, call for Sat. hours; group tours by appointment.*

**Florida History Center and Museum.** Permanent exhibits review not only modern-day development along the Loxahatchee River, but also shipwrecks, railroads, and Seminole, steamboat-era, and pioneer history. ⊠ *805 N. U.S. 1, Burt Reynolds Park, Jupiter* ☎ *561/747–6639.* ☞ *$3.* ☉ *Tues.–Sat. 10–4, Sun. 1–5.*

**Hobe Sound National Wildlife Refuge.** Another turtle haven, this refuge has a 3½-mile beach where turtles nest and shells wash ashore. High tides and strong winds have severely eroded the beach; during winter high tides only a sliver of beach remains. ⊠ *Beach Rd. off Rte. 707, Hobe Sound,* ☎ *561/546–6141.* ☞ *$4 per vehicle.* ☉ *Daily sunrise–sunset, generally.*

**Jonathan Dickinson State Park.** Once inside this park, follow signs to Hobe Mountain, an ancient dune topped with a tower. Here you have a panoramic view across the park's 10,285 acres of varied terrain, as well as the Intracoastal Canal. The Loxahatchee River, which cuts through the park, is part of the federal government's wild and scenic rivers program, and harbors manatees in winter and alligators all year round. The park has a fair share of amenities: bicycle and hiking trails, a campground, and a snack bar. **Jonathan Dickinson's River Tour** (☎ 561/746–1466) rents canoes and also has a guided riverboat tour. ⊠ *16450 S.E. Federal Hwy.,* ☎ *561/546–2771.* ☞ *$3.25 per vehicle with up to 8 people.* ☉ *Daily 8–sunset.*

**Jupiter Inlet Light Station.** This redbrick Coast Guard navigational beacon has operated here since 1866. Tours of the 105-foot-tall structure are given regularly, and there is also a small museum. ✉ *Rte. 707, Jupiter Island,* ☎ *Tour $5.* ☉ *Sun.–Wed. 10–4.*

## Beaches

**Carlin Park** (✉ 400 Rte. A1A) provides beachfront picnic pavilions, hiking trails, a baseball diamond, playground, six tennis courts, and fishing sites. The Park Galley, serving snacks and burgers, is usually open daily 9–5.

## Dining and Lodging

**$$–$$$** ✕ **Charley's Crab.** The grand view across the Jupiter River comple-
★ ments the soaring ceiling and striking interior architecture of this ma-
rina-side restaurant—a favorite of affluent retirees. Between November
and Easter, weather generally allows outdoor seating. Otherwise, tiered
seating and a second level of window seats on an indoor balcony provide good water views, and if you come after dark, you can watch the
searching beam of historic Jupiter Light House. Ultimately, though, the
best reason to eat here is the expertly prepared seafood, including outstanding pasta choices: *pagliara* with scallops, fish, shrimp, mussels,
spinach, garlic, and olive oil; fettuccine *verde* with lobster, sun-dried
tomatoes, fresh basil, and goat cheese; and shrimp and tortellini boursin
with cream sauce and tomatoes. Consider also such fresh fish as cit-
rus-marinated halibut with black-bean basmati rice and pineapple relish. Other branches of Charley's are in Boca Raton, Deerfield, Fort
Lauderdale, Palm Beach, and Stuart. ✉ *1000 N. U.S. 1, Jupiter,* ☎
*561/744–4710. AE, D, DC, MC, V.*

**$–$$** ✕ **Log Cabin Restaurant.** "Too much!" exclaim first-timers, respond-
★ ing to the decor and whopping portions of American food at this rustic roadhouse (very easy to miss driving past). Everybody takes home
a doggie bag, unless you've ordered the nightly all-you-can-eat special.
Many also tote home an antique because everything hung on the walls
and from the rafters—old bikes, sleds, clocks, and quilts—is for sale.
The surprising menu starts with the big early-bird breakfast (7–8 AM)
for $1.99 and continues with old-fashioned plates such as pit barbe-
cue, steak and fresh seafood. Dine indoors or on the enclosed and air-
conditioned front porch. There's a full bar and happy hour. ✉ *631 N.
Rte. A1A, Jupiter,* ☎ *561/746–6877. AE, D, DC, MC, V.*

**$** ✕ **Lighthouse Restaurant.** Amsterdam-born brothers John and Bill
Verehoeven bought this long-established place late in 1991 and have
since spruced the place up by bringing in the former chef of the Jupiter
Island Club and Old Port Cove Yacht Club. Though the prices are still
low, you can get items such as chicken breast stuffed with sausage and
fresh vegetables, burgundy beef stew, and king crab cakes. A full-time
pastry chef is at work, too. The restaurant still has the same people-
pleasing formula of more than 60 years: round-the-clock service (except 10 PM on Sunday–6 AM on Monday) and daily menu changes taking
advantage of the best market buys. For those looking for something
less "stick-to-the-ribs," affordable "lite dinners" are served nightly. ✉
*1510 U.S. 1,* ☎ *561/746–4811. D, DC, MC, V.*

**$$$$** 🏨 **Jupiter Beach Resort.** Management can say without equivocation
that this is the best beachfront resort in Jupiter—of course, it's also
the only beachfront resort in Jupiter. But this unpretentious, elegant
hotel would bear itself well even if it were among the Palm Beach properties. Most guest rooms have balconies, and the hotel restaurant is
worth staying in for. The resort takes full advantage of its location; in
season, sign up for the turtle watch, when you can see newly hatched
turtles make their way to the water for the first time. Snorkeling and
scuba equipment are available for rent. ✉ *5 N. Florida A1A, Jupiter*

*33477 ☎ 561/746–2511 or 800/228–8810, FAX 561/747–3304. 194 rooms, 28 suites. Restaurant, 4 bars, pool, tennis court, beach, dive shop, recreation room, children's programs, coin laundry, business services.*

## Outdoor Activities and Sports

### CANOEING

**Canoe Outfitters of Florida** (⊠ 4100 W. Indiantown Rd., Jupiter, ☎ 561/746–7053) runs trips along the Loxahatchee River, Florida's only designated wild and scenic river. Canoe rental for 2 people, with drop off and pickup, cost $25 plus tax.

### GOLF

The **Indian Creek Golf Club,** (⊠ 1800 Central Blvd., Jupiter, ☎ 561/747–6262) has 18 holes of varying difficulty. **Jupiter Dunes Golf Club,** (⊠ 401 Route A1A, Jupiter, ☎ 561/746–6654) also has 18 holes.

# Stuart and Hutchinson Island

**㉘** Restaurants and shops have revived downtown **Stuart,** the Martin County seat. Quality of life is important in Stuart—a onetime fishing village that has become a magnet for sophisticates who want to live **㉙** and work in a small-town atmosphere. North of Stuart is **Hutchinson Island** where unusual care limits development and prevents the commercial crowding found to the north and south. Also nearby is Jensen Beach, a small town that stretches across both sides of the Indian River onto the central part of Hutchinson Island. Citrus farmers and fishermen still play a big role in the community, giving the area a down-to-earth feel. Its most notable population is that of the sea turtles; in summer more than 6,000 turtles come to nest along the town's Atlantic Beach.

## Sights to See

**Coastal Science Center.** This dynamic property of the Florida Oceanographic Society combines a coastal hardwood hammock and mangrove forest. Recent expansion has yielded a visitor center and the beginnings of an interpretive boardwalk which will eventually be 2 miles long. There are also plans for an aquarium, an auditorium, research laboratory, and permanent library. Guided nature walks are offered on Wednesday or Saturday. ⊠ *890 N.E. Ocean Blvd., Stuart, ☎ 561/225–0505 ⊡ $3. ☉ Mon.–Sat. 10–5.*

**Elliott Museum.** This pastel-pink building was built in 1961 in honor of Sterling Elliott, inventor of an early automated addressing machine and a four-wheel bicycle. The museum features antique automobiles, dolls and toys, and fixtures from an early general store, blacksmith shop, and apothecary shop. ⊠ *825 N.E. Ocean Blvd., Hutchinson Island, ☎ 561/225–1961. ⊡ $4. ☉ Daily 11–4.*

★ **Historic downtown Stuart.** Strict architectural and zoning standards guide civic renewal projects in downtown Stuart, which now claims eight antiques shops, nine restaurants, and more than 50 specialty shops within a two-block area. The old courthouse has become the **Court House Cultural Center** (⊠ 80 E. Ocean Blvd., ☎ 561/288–2542), which features art exhibits. The Old Stuart Feed Store has become the **Stuart Heritage Museum** (⊠ 161 S.W. Flagler Ave., ☎ 561/220–4600). The **Lyric Theatre** (⊠ 59 S.W. Flagler Ave., ☎ 561/220–1942) has been revived for performing and community events, and was recently added to the National Register of Historic Places, and a new gazebo features free music performances. For information on downtown, contact the **Stuart Main Street Office** (⊠ 151 S.W. Flagler Ave., 34994, ☎ 561/286–2848).

In an old historic-district bank building sits the **Jolly Sailor Pub** (✉ 1 S.W. Osceola St., Stuart, ☎ 561/221–1111), owned by a retired 27-year British Merchant Navy veteran, which may account for the endless ship paraphernalia. A veritable Cunard museum, it has a model of the *Brittania*, prints of 19th-century side-wheelers, and a big bar painting of the *QE2*. There's a wonderful brass-railed wood bar, a dartboard, and such pub grub as fish-and-chips, cottage pie, and bangers (sausage) and mash, with Guinness and Double Diamond ales on tap.

**House of Refuge Museum.** Built in 1875, this museum is the only one remaining building of nine such structures erected by the U.S. Life Saving Service (a predecessor of the Coast Guard) to aid stranded sailors. Exhibits include antique lifesaving equipment, maps, artifacts from nearby wrecks, and boat-making tools. ✉ *301 S.E. MacArthur Blvd., Hutchinson Island,* ☎ *561/225–1875.* ✄ *$2.* ☉ *Tues.–Sun. 11–4.*

## Beaches

ⓒ **Bathtub Beach** (✉ MacArthur Blvd., off Rte. A1A, Hutchinson Island), at the north end of the Indian River Plantation Beach Resort, is ideal for children because the waters are shallow for about 300 feet offshore and usually calm. At low tide, bathers can walk to the reef. Facilities include rest rooms and showers.

## Dining and Lodging

$$–$$$   ✕ **11 Maple Street.** This 16-table restaurant is as good as it gets on
★   the Treasure Coast. Run by Margee and Mike Perrin, 11 Maple Street offers a Continental menu that changes nightly. The soft recorded jazz and the earnest, friendly staff satisfy as fully as the brilliant food served in ample portions. Appetizers might include walnut bread with melted fontina cheese or sautéed conch with balsamic vinegar; among entrées are salmon with leeks, lobster, and blue-crab cake, or porcini mushroom risotto. For dessert, look out for cherry clafouti (like a bread pudding) and white-chocolate custard with blackberry sauce. ✉ *3224 Maple Ave., Jensen Beach,* ☎ *561/334–7714. Reservations essential. MC, V. Closed Mon. and Tues. No lunch.*

$$   ✕ **The Ashley.** Since expanding in late 1993, this restaurant has more tables, more art, and more plants than before. However, it still has elements of the old bank that was robbed three times early in the century by the Ashley Gang (hence the name). The big outdoor mural in the French Impressionist style was paid for by downtown revivalists, whose names are duly inscribed on wall plaques inside. The Continental menu appeals with lots of salads, fresh fish, and pastas. ✉ *61 S.W. Osceola St., Stuart,* ☎ *561/221–9476. AE, MC, V. Closed Mon. in off-season.*

$$   ✕ **Conchy Joe's.** This classic Florida stilt house full of antique fish mounts, gator hides, and snakeskins dates from the late 1920s—but Conchy Joe's, like a hermit crab sliding into a new shell, only moved up from West Palm Beach in 1983. Under a huge Seminole-built chickee (raised wood platform) with a palm through the roof, you get the freshest Florida seafoods from a menu that changes daily. Staples, however, are the grouper Marsala, broiled sea scallop, and fried cracked conch. Try the rum drinks with names like Goombay Smash and Bahama Mama, while listening to steel-band calypsos Thursday–Sunday. Happy hour is 3–6 daily and during all NFL games. ✉ *3945 N. Indian River Dr., Jensen Beach,* ☎ *561/334–1131. AE, D, MC, V.*

$$   ✕ **Scalawags.** The look is plantation tropical—coach lanterns, gingerbread, wicker, slow-motion paddle fans—but the top-notch buffets are aimed at today's resort guests. Standouts are the all-you-can-eat Wednesday evening seafood buffet, with jumbo shrimp, Alaskan crab

legs, clams on the half shell, marinated salmon, and fresh catch. As if that weren't enough, there's also the Friday prime rib buffet with traditional Yorkshire pudding and baked potato station. A regular menu with a big selection of fish, shellfish, and grills, plus a big salad bar, is also offered. The main dining room overlooks the Indian River; there is also a private 20-seat wine room and a terrace that looks out on the marina. ⊠ *555 N.E. Ocean Blvd., Hutchinson Island,* ☎ *561/225– 3700. AE, DC, MC, V.*

$ ✕ **The Emporium.** Indian River Plantation's coffee shop is an old-fashioned soda fountain and grill that also serves hearty breakfasts. Specialties include eggs Benedict, omelets, deli sandwiches, and salads. ⊠ *555 N.E. Ocean Blvd., Hutchinson Island,* ☎ *561/225–3700. AE, DC, MC, V.*

$$$$ 🏨 **Indian River Plantation Beach Resort.** Long-time Florida visitors rec-
★ ognize this residential-sports complex as one of a kind among full-service resorts. Its oceanfront setting in the assuredly warm subtropics is just the beginning; with an unpretentious style, the resort fits well on Hutchinson Island. Three buildings have rooms and suites available for shorter stays, and there are also rentals available in new condominiums, mostly designed with bright island themes with abundant latticework and balconies. ⊠ *555 N.E. Ocean Blvd., Hutchinson Island 34996,* ☎ *561/225–6990 or 800/947–2148. 326 rooms and suites, 150 condominiums. 5 restaurants, bar, 4 pools, spa, 2 golf courses, 13 tennis courts, boating. AE, DC, MC, V.*

$$–$$$ 🏨 **HarborFront.** On a quiet site that slopes to the St. Lucie River, this B&B combines an unusual mix of accommodations and imaginative extras—a Friday fresh-fish grill, picnic baskets, and conciergelike custom planning. Rooms and cottages are cozy and eclectic. Choose from a spacious chintz-covered suite or apartment or maybe the 33-foot moored sailboat (small rowing dinghy provided). Rooms include wicker and antiques, some airy and bright with private deck, others tweedy and dark. From hammocks in the yard you can watch pelicans and herons. ⊠ *310 Atlanta Ave., 34994,* ☎ *561/288–7289. 8 apartments, cottages, suites, rooms, boat. Lounge. MC, V.*

$$–$$$ 🏨 **Hutchinson Inn.** Sandwiched among the high rises, this modest and affordable two-story motel from the mid-1970s has the feel of a B&B thanks to pretty canopies and bracketing. You get an expanded Continental breakfast in the well-appointed lobby and you can also borrow a book or a stack of magazines to take to your room, where homemade cookies are served in the evenings. On Saturday there's a noon barbecue. Rooms range from small but comfortable, to fully equipped efficiencies and seafront suites with private balconies. ⊠ *9750 S. Ocean Dr., Hutchinson Island 34957,* ☎ *561/229–2000,* ℻ *561/229–8875. 21 units. Pool, tennis court, beach. MC, V.*

$$ 🏨 **The Homeplace.** The house was built in 1913 by pioneer Sam Matthews, who contracted much of the early town construction for railroad developer Henry Flagler. Jean Bell has restored the house to its early look, from hardwood floors to fluffy pillows. Fern-filled dining and sunrooms, full of chintz-covered cushioned wicker, overlook a pool and patio. A full breakfast is included. ⊠ *501 Akron Ave., 34994,* ☎ *561/220–9148. 3 rooms. Pool, hot tub. MC, V.*

## Outdoor Activities and Sports

FISHING

Deep-sea charters are available at the **Sailfish Marina** (⊠ 3565 S.E. St. Lucie Blvd., Stuart, ☎ 561/283–1122).

GOLF

**Indian River Plantation Beach Resort** (⊠ 555 N.E. Ocean Blvd., Hutchinson Island, Stuart 34996, ☎ 561/225–3700 or 800/444–3389) has 18 holes.

## Shopping

More than 60 shops and restaurants featuring antiques, art, and fashions have opened along **Osceola Street** in restored downtown Stuart, with hardly a vacancy.

# Fort Pierce

③⓪ **Fort Pierce,** about an hour north of Palm Beach, has a distinctive rural feel. Rooted in ranching and citrus farming country, the city focuses on these influences rather than on tourism. It has several worthwhile stops for visitors, including those easily seen by following Route 707.

## Sights to See

**A. E. "Bean" Backus Gallery.** As the home of the Treasure Coast Art Association, this gallery displays the works of Florida's foremost landscape artist. The gallery also mounts changing exhibits and offers exceptional buys on work by local artists. ⊠ *500 N. Indian River Dr.,* ☎ *561/465–0630.* ⌑ *Donations welcome.* ☉ *Tues.–Sun. 1–5.*

**Fort Pierce Inlet State Recreation Area.** This section of the park offers swimming, surfing, and a self-guiding nature trail. ⊠ *905 Shorewinds Dr.,* ☎ *561/468–3985.* ⌑ *$3.25 per vehicle with up to 8 people.* ☉ *Daily 8–sunset.*

**Heathcote Botanical Gardens.** A self-guided tour takes in a palm walk, Japanese garden, and subtropical foliage. ⊠ *210 Savannah Rd.,* ☎ *561/464–4672.* ⌑ *$2.50.* ☉ *Tues.–Sat. 9–5, also Sun. 1–5 Nov.–Apr.*

**Jack Island Wildlife Refuge.** This refuge is accessible only by footbridge. The 1½-mile Marsh Rabbit Trail across the island traverses a mangrove swamp to a 30-foot observation tower overlooking the Indian River. Trails cover 4⅓ miles altogether. ⊠ *Rte. A1A,* ☎ *561/468–3985.* ⌑ *Free.* ☉ *Daily 8–sunset.*

**St. Lucie County Historical Museum.** Highlights here include historic photos, early 20th-century memorabilia, vintage farm tools, a restored 1919 American La France fire engine, replicas of a general store and the old Fort Pierce railroad station, and the restored 1905 Gardner House. ⊠ *414 Seaway Dr.,* ☎ *561/468–1795.* ⌑ *$2.* ☉ *Tues.–Sat. 10–4, Sun. noon–4.*

**Savannahs Recreation Area.** This 550-acre site was once a reservoir but has been returned to its natural state. Today it's semi-wilderness with campsites, a petting zoo, botanical garden, boat ramps, and trails. ⊠ *1400 E. Midway Rd.,* ☎ *561/464–7855.* ⌑ *$1 per vehicle.* ☉ *Daily 8 AM–9 PM.*

**UDT-Seal Museum.** This attraction commemorates the site where more than 3,000 Navy frogmen trained during World War II. In 1993 exhibit space was tripled, and further expansions are planned through the decade. Numerous patrol boats and vehicles are displayed outdoors. ⊠ *3300 N. Rte. A1A,* ☎ *561/595–1570.* ⌑ *$2.* ☉ *Tues.–Sat. 10–4, Sun. noon–4.*

## Dining and Lodging

$$ ✕ **Mangrove Mattie's.** Since its opening in the late 1980s this upscale but rustic spot on Fort Pierce Inlet has provided dazzling waterfront views and imaginative nautical decor with delicious seafood. Try the coconut-fried shrimp or the chicken and scampi, or come by during

happy hour for a free buffet (weekdays 5–8). ⊠ *1640 Seaway Dr.,* ☎ *561/466–1044. AE, D, DC, MC, V.*

$ ✕ **Theo Thudpucker's Raw Bar.** Business people dressed for work mingle here with people fresh from the beach wearing shorts. On squally days everyone piles in off the jetty. Specialties include oyster stew, smoked fish spread, conch salad and conch fritters, fresh catfish, and alligator tail. ⊠ *2025 Seaway Dr. (South Jetty),* ☎ *561/465–1078. No credit cards.*

$$–$$$ ⊞ **Harbor Light Inn.** The pick of the pack of lodgings lining the Fort Pierce Inlet along Seaway Drive is this modern, nautical, blue-trimmed motel. Spacious units on two floors feature kitchen or wet bar, and routine but well-cared-for furnishings. Most rooms have a waterfront porch or balcony. In addition to the motel units there is a set of four apartments across the street (off the water), where in-season weekly rates are $350. ⊠ *1156–1160 Seaway Dr., 34949,* ☎ *561/468–3555 or 800/433–0004. 25 units. Pool, fishing, coin laundry. AE, D, DC, MC, V.*

$$ ⊞ **Mellon Patch Inn.** This new B&B has an excellent location—across the shore road from a beach park, at the end of a canal leading to the Indian River Lagoon. One side of the canal has a bank of attractive new homes; the other has the Jack Island Wildlife Refuge. Images of split-open melons permeate the house—on pillows, crafts, in candies on night tables. Each of the four guest rooms has imaginative accessories, art, and upholstery appropriate to its individual theme. The cathedral-ceilinged living room features a wood-burning fireplace and "Howie," a Native American in effigy who will surprise you every time you enter. Full breakfast is included. ⊠ *3601 N. Rte. A1A, North Hutchinson Island 34949,* ☎ *561/461–5231. 4 rooms. MC, V.*

## Outdoor Activities and Sports

### DIVING

Some 200 yards from shore and a quarter mile north of the UDT-Seal Museum on North Hutchinson Island in Fort Pierce lies the **Urca de Lima Underwater Archaeological Preserve.** Here you can dive to the remnant of a flat-bottom, round-bellied storeship once part of a treasure fleet bound for Spain but destroyed by hurricane.

### FISHING

For charter boats and fishing guides try the **Fort Pierce Yachting Center** (⊠ 1 Ave. A, Fort Pierce, ☎ 561/264–1245).

### JAI ALAI

**Fort Pierce Jai Alai** operates seasonally for live jai alai and year-round for off-track betting on horse-racing simulcasts. ⊠ *1750 S. Kings Hwy., off Okeechobee Rd., Fort Pierce,* ☎ *561/464–7500 or 800/524–2524.* 🎫 *$1.* ☉ *Games Jan.–Apr., Wed. and Sat. 12:30 and 7, Thurs. and Fri. 7, Sun. 1; call to double-check schedule; simulcasts Wed.–Mon. noon and 7.*

## Shopping

One of Florida's best discount malls, the **Manufacturer's Outlet Center** (⊠ Rte. 70, off I–95 at Exit 65) contains 41 stores offering such brand names as American Tourister, Jonathan Logan, Aileen, Polly Flinders, Van Heusen, London Fog, Levi Strauss, and Geoffrey Beene.

# Vero Beach

③ The seat of Indian River County, **Vero Beach** has an active arts scene. Coming up to the city along Route 605 (often called Old Dixie Highway), you'll pass through an ungussied landscaped of small farms and residential areas; Vero Beach itself maintains a similar tranquility. In the exclusive Riomar Bay area of town, "canopy roads" are shaded by massive live oaks.

## Sights to See

**Harbor Branch Oceanographic Institution.** This internationally recognized, diversified research and teaching facility offers a glimpse into the high-tech world of marine research. Its fleet of research vessels—particularly its two submersibles—operates around the world for NASA, NOAA, and NATO, among other contractors. Visitors can take a 90-minute tour of the 500-acre facility, including aquariums of sea life indigenous to the Indian River Lagoon, exhibits of marine technology, and other learning facilities. There are also lifelike and whimsical bronze sculptures created by founder J. Seward Johnson, Jr. and a gift shop with imaginative, sea-related items. ⊠ *5600 Old Dixie Hwy.,* ☎ *561/465–2400.* ☒ *$5.* ☉ *Tours Mon.–Sat. 10, noon, and 2.*

**Indian River Citrus Museum.** Photos, farm tools, and videos tell about when oxen hauled the citrus crop to the railroads, when family fruit stands dotted the roadsides, and when gorgeous packing labels made every crate arriving up north an enticement to visit the Sunshine State. You can also book free citrus tours in actual groves. ⊠ *2140 14th Ave., Vero Beach,* ☎ *561/770–2263.* ☒ *Donations welcome.* ☉ *Tues.–Sat. 10–4, Sun. 1–4.*

★ **Jungle Trail.** From Route A1A turn left onto Old Winter Beach Road, where the pavement turns to hard-packed dirt as the road curves north—you've arrived at the old Jungle Trail. For nearly 9 miles the trail meanders through largely undeveloped forest land along the Indian River across from Pelican Island, which harbors the first national wildlife refuge established in the United States, dating from 1903. State agencies are creating a buffer for the trail to shield it from sight of further development and are stabilizing its surface for improved recreational use.

**Riverside Park.** Here you'll find the **Civic Arts Center,** a cluster of cultural facilities that includes the **Center for the Arts** (⊠ 3001 Riverside Park Dr., ☎ 561/231–0707). The center presents a full schedule of exhibitions, art movies, lectures, workshops, and other events, with a focus on Florida artists.

## Beaches

All through town there are beach-access parks with boardwalks and steps bridging the foredune. Admission is free, and the parks are open daily 7 AM–10 PM. **Humiston Park** (⊠ Ocean Dr. below Beachland Blvd.) has a large children's play area and picnic tables and is across the street from shops.

## Dining and Lodging

$$ ✕ **Black Pearl.** This intimate restaurant with pink and green art deco furnishings offers entrées that emphasize fresh local ingredients. Specialties include chilled leek-and-watercress soup, local fish in parchment paper, and panfried veal with local shrimp and vermouth. **Pearl's Bistro** (⊠ 54 Royal Palm Blvd., ☎ 561/778–2950), a more casual and less expensive sister restaurant, serves Caribbean-style food for lunch and dinner. ⊠ *1409 Rte. A1A,* ☎ *561/234–4426. AE, MC, V. No lunch.*

$$ ✕ **Ocean Grill.** Opened by Waldo Sexton as a hamburger shack in 1938, the Ocean Grill is now furnished with Tiffany lamps, wrought-iron chandeliers, and Beanie Backus paintings of pirates and Seminole Indians. The menu includes black-bean soup, jumbo lump crabmeat salad, and at least three kinds of fish every day. The bar looks out on the remains of the *Breconshire,* an 1894 near-shore wreck, from which 34 British

sailors escaped. The event is commemorated by the Leaping Limey, a curious blend of vodka, blue curaçao, and lemon. ⊠ *1050 Sexton Plaza (Beachland Blvd. east of Ocean Dr.),* ☎ *561/231–5409. AE, D, DC, MC, V. Closed Super Bowl Sun., 2 weeks following Labor Day, and Thanksgiving. No lunch weekends.*

**$$$$**    🖬 **Guest Quarters Suite Hotel.** Built in 1986 and completely refurbished in 1993, this five-story rose-color stucco hotel on Ocean Drive provides easy access to Vero Beach's specialty shops and boutiques. One- and two-bedroom suites have patios opening onto the pool or balconies and ocean views. ⊠ *3500 Ocean Dr., 32963,* ☎ *561/231–5666 or 800/841–5666. 55 suites. Bar, pool, wading pool, hot tub. AE, D, DC, MC, V.*

**$$–$$$**    🖬 **Islander Resort.** The aqua-and-white-trim Islander has a snoozy Key West style that contrasts stylishly with the smart shops across from the beach along Ocean Drive. Jigsaw-cut brackets and balusters and beach umbrellas dress up the pool. All rooms feature white wicker, paddle fans hung from vaulted ceilings, and fresh flowers. It's just right for beachside Vero. ⊠ *3101 Ocean Dr., 32963,* ☎ *561/231–4431 or 800/952–5886. 16 rooms, 1 efficiency. Pool. AE, DC, MC, V.*

### Nightlife and the Arts

**Riverside Theatre** (⊠ 3250 Riverside Park Dr., Vero Beach 32963, ☎ 561/231–6990) stages six productions each season in its 633-seat performance hall. Children's productions are mounted in the compound at the **Agnes Wahlstrom Youth Playhouse** (☎ 561/234–8052). **Riverside Children's Theatre** (⊠ 3280 Riverside Park Dr., ☎ 561/234–8052) offers series of professional touring and local productions, as well as acting workshops at the Agnes Wahlstrom Youth Playhouse.

### Shopping

Along **Ocean Drive** near Beachland Boulevard, a specialty shopping area includes art galleries, antiques shops, and upscale clothing stores.

## Around Sebastian

**❸❷** The town of **Sebastian** is one of only a few sparsely populated areas on Florida's east coast and has as remote a feeling as you'll find anywhere between Jacksonville and Miami Beach. That remoteness adds
**❸❸** to the appeal of the recreation area in **Sebastian Inlet,** where you can walk for miles along quiet beaches—the inlet is the antithesis of Daytona and Palm Beach. Among surfers these beaches are known for having the best waves in the state.

### Sights to See

**Mel Fisher's Treasure Museum.** You've really come upon hidden loot as you can view some of the recovery from the treasure ship *Atocha* and its sister ships of the 1715 fleet. Fisher operates a similar museum in Key West. ⊠ *1322 U.S. 1,* ☎ *561/589–9874.* 🎟 *$5.* ☉ *Mon.–Sat. 10–5, Sun. noon–5.*

**McLarty Museum.** A National Historical Landmark site features displays dedicated to the 1715 hurricane that sank a fleet of Spanish treasure ships. ⊠ *13180 N. Rte. A1A, Sebastian,* ☎ *561/589–2147.* 🎟 *$1.* ☉ *Daily 10–4:30.*

**❸❸** **Sebastian Inlet.** At the northern end of Orchid Island is a high bridge that offers spectacular views. Along the sea is a dune area that's part of the **Archie Carr National Wildlife Refuge,** a haven for sea turtles and other protected Florida wildlife. The 587-acre **Sebastian Inlet State Recreation Area,** on both sides of the bridge, is the best-attended park in the Florida state system because of the inlet's highly productive fish-

# It helps to be pushy in airports.

Introducing the revolutionary new TransPorter™ from American Tourister®. It's the first suitcase you can push around without a fight. TransPorter's™ exclusive four-wheel design lets you push it in front of you with almost no effort—the wheels take the weight. Or pull it on two wheels if you choose. You can even stack on other bags and use it like a luggage cart.

Stable 4-wheel design.

TransPorter™ is designed like a dresser, with built-in shelves to organize your belongings. Or collapse the shelves and pack it like a traditional suitcase. Inside, there's a suiter feature to help keep suits and dresses from wrinkling. When push comes to shove, you can't beat a TransPorter™. For more information on how you can be this pushy, call 1-800-542-1300.

Shelves collapse on command.

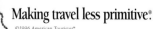

**Use your MCI Card®**

**for the easy way to**

**call when traveling.**

MCI ✶ Calling Card

415 555 1234 2244
J.D. SMITH

### Convenience on the road

- Your MCI Card® number is your home number, guaranteed.
- Pre-programmed to speed dial to your home.
- Call from any phone in the U.S.

1 - 8 0 0 - 7 5 4 - 8 9 4 1

http://www.mci.com

ing waters. ⊠ *9700 S. Rte. A1A, Melbourne Beach,* ☎ *561/984–4852 or 561/589–9659.* ☉ *Bait and tackle shop daily 7:30–6, concession stand daily 8–5.*

## Beaches

South and north of **Sebastian Inlet** and inland of the bridge are fine sandy beaches, which are reputedly excellent territory for surfing. A concession stand on the north side of the inlet, open 8–5 (bait and tackle available 7:30–6), sells short-order food, rents canoes, kayaks, and paddleboats and has an apparel and surf shop.

## Dining and Lodging

**$–$$** ✕ **Capt. Hiram's.** This family-friendly restaurant on the Indian River Lagoon is easygoing, fanciful and fun—and definitely not purposefully hip. "Neckties," as the sign says, "are prohibited." Other than molded-plastic tables, the place is "real"—full of wood booths, stained glass, umbrellas on the open deck, and ceiling fans. Don't miss Capt. Hiram's Sandbar, where kids can play while parents enjoy a drink at stools set in an outdoor shower or a beached boat. Choose from among seafood brochette, New York strip steak, fresh catch, and lots of other seafood dishes as well as raw-bar items. The full bar has a weekday happy hour and free hot hors d'oeuvres Fridays 5–6. There's nightly entertainment in season. ⊠ *1606 N. Indian River Dr.,* ☎ *561/589–1345. AE, D, MC, V.*

**$–$$** ✕ **Hurricane Harbor.** Built in 1927 as a garage and used during Prohibition as a smugglers' den, Hurricane Harbor now draws a year-round crowd of retirees and locals. Guests love the waterfront window seats on stormy nights, when sizable waves break outside in the Indian River Lagoon. The menu features seafood, steaks, and grills, along with lighter fare. On Friday and Saturday nights the Antique Dining Room is opened, with its linen, stained glass, and a huge antique breakfront. There's also live music nightly. ⊠ *1540 Indian River Dr.,* ☎ *561/589–1773. AE, D, MC, V. Closed Mon.*

**$–$$** ⌷ **Captain's Quarters.** The four units—three overlooking the Indian River Lagoon and the marina at Capt. Hiram's restaurant and one two-room suite—are all Key-West cute. Painted in bright colors with matching fabrics, the rooms have pine and white wicker furniture and pine plank floors with grass rugs. The adequate bathrooms have large stall showers. Glass doors open to a plank porch, but the porches are all within sight of each other. ⊠ *1606 Indian River Dr., 32958,* ☎ *561/589–4345. 3 rooms, 1 suite. Restaurant. AE, D, MC, V.*

**$–$$** ⌷ **Davis House Inn.** Vero native Steve Wild modeled his two-story inn after the clubhouse at Augusta National. Wide overhung roofs shade wraparound porches. In a companion house that Steve calls the Gathering Room, he serves a complimentary expanded Continental breakfast. Though the inn is a newcomer, having opened in 1992, it looks established, fitting right in with the fishing-town look of Sebastian. Rooms are huge—virtual suites, with large sitting areas—though somewhat underfurnished. Overall, it's a terrific value. ⊠ *607 Davis St., 32958,* ☎ *561/589–4114. 12 efficiencies. Bicycles. MC, V.*

## Outdoor Activities and Sports

CANOEING

**Bill Rogers Outdoor Adventures** (⊠ *1541 DeWitt La., Sebastian,* ☎ *561/388–2331*) outfits canoe trips down the Sebastian River, along Indian River Lagoon, through Pelican Island Wildlife Refuge, as well as more distant locations.

FISHING

The best inlet fishing in the region is at **Sebastian Inlet State Recreation Area,** where the catch includes bluefish, flounder, jack, redfish, sea trout, snapper, snook, and Spanish mackerel. For deep-sea fishing try **Miss Sebastian** (⌧ Sembler Dock, ½ block north of Capt. Hiram's restaurant, Sebastian, ☎ 561/589–3275); $25 for a half day covers rod, reel, and bait. Another option is the charters offered at **Sebastian Inlet Marina at Capt. Hiram's** (⌧ 1606 Indian River Dr., Sebastian, ☎ 561/589–4345).

SAILING

The **Sailboard School** (⌧ 9125 U.S. 1, Sebastian, ☎ 561/589–2671 or 800/253–6573, ⅻⅫ 561/589–7963) provides year-round one-day, weekend, and five-day programs of sailboarding instruction, including boards, for $120 a day, $575 for five days.

# LAKE OKEECHOBEE

Rimming the western shore of Palm Beach County, this second-largest freshwater lake in the United States is girdled by 120 miles of roads; yet for almost its entire circumference, it remains hidden from sight. It is Lake Okeechobee—the Seminole's Big Water—heart of the great Everglades watershed.

All the headlines about the troubled Everglades have their source in the flood-control system that for half a century has contained Lake Okeechobee within a 30-foot-high levee, a great grassy berm officially called the Herbert Hoover Dike and locally known as "the wall." Outside the wall, small towns depend for their livelihoods on raising the sugarcane, beef and dairy cows, and, more recently, citrus that flood control makes possible. Inside the wall, on the big lake itself, fisherfolk come from everywhere for reputably best bass fishing in North America. However, by curtailing the natural water flow Lake Okeechobee does serious damage to the Everglades ecosystem. Water pollution due to fertilizer runoff from nearby farms is also a constant concern.

As the bass fishing capital of the world, the lake region is the antithesis of Palm Beach, and as important a place to blue collar culture as Palm Beach is to the starched-collar group. While Palm Beach is alive with polo and croquet matches, bass fishing zealots fill up the trailer camps along the lake shores.

This propensity for fish naturally shows up on local menus. In particular, no menu's without catfish, and not just any catfish—fried catfish. You can try to get it broiled or steamed, but waitresses may let you know they'd rather not pass that order on to the kitchen. If you're lucky they will, and you might find yourself eating one of Florida's succulent delicacies, rather than something that's gray and fallen apart.

The Okeechobee region makes for one-of-a-kind touring and outdoor recreation that can occupy days at a time for anyone interested in exploring an unadvertised Florida. Or you can tour the region in a single (but exhausting) day.

## Between Belle Glade and Lake Harbor

The motto of **Belle Glade** is "Her soil is her fortune," for Belle Glade is the eastern hub of the 700,000-acre Everglades Agricultural Area, the crescent of farmlands lying south and east of the lake. Belle Glade is easily reached from the Palm Beach area by taking U.S. 98/441 west; on the way, you'll pass the **Arthur R. Marshall–Loxahatchee National**

**Wildlife Refuge,** the healthiest part of the Everglades. Moving westward around the lake on U.S. 27, you'll come to **Lake Harbor,** a tiny town with massive locks, where you can see water-flow control for the Miami Canal at work. You can also see Lock No. 1, a restored lock that dates from 1919.

## Sights to See

**Arthur R. Marshall–Loxahatchee National Wildlife Refuge.** The most robust part of the Everglades, this refuge is one of three huge water-retention areas that account for much of the Everglades outside of the national park. These areas are managed less to protect natural resources, however, than to prevent flooding to the south. Start from the visitor center, where there are two walking trails—a boardwalk through a dense cypress swamp and a marsh trail to a 20-foot-high observation tower overlooking a pond. There is also a 5½-mile canoe trail, recommended for more experienced canoers since it's rather overgrown. Wildlife viewing is good year-round, and you can fish for bass and panfish. ⊠ *10119 Lee Rd., off U.S. 441 between Boynton Beach Blvd. (Rte. 804) and Atlantic Ave. (Rte. 806), west of Boynton Beach,* ☎ *561/734–8303.* ☞ *$4 per vehicle, $1 per pedestrian.* ☉ *Daily 6–sunset.*

**Municipal Complex.** Grouped together here are Belle Glade's public library and the Lawrence E. Will Museum, both with materials on the town's history. Out front on the lawn is a Ferenc Verga sculpture of a family fleeing from the wall of water that poured from the lake in the catastrophic hurricane of 1928. More than 2,000 people lost their lives and 15,000 families were left homeless by the torrential flood. ⊠ *530 Main St.,* ☎ *561/996–3453.*

**Torry Island.** To get to Torry Island, you'll cross the last remaining swing bridge in Florida. Brothers Charles and Gordon Corbin, who operate Slim's Fish Camp (☎ 561/996–3844), also operate the bridge, which is cranked open and closed by hand, swinging at right angles to the road. Also on the island are the Belle Glade Municipal Campground and Marina (☎ 561/996–6322) and J-Mark Fish Camp (☎ 561/996–5357).

**Zora Neale Hurston Roof Garden Museum.** One of Hurston's best-known works, *Their Eyes Were Watching God,* includes a fictional account of the terrible hurricane that struck the area in 1928. At this museum you can view a collection of Hurston's research and writings, as well as a history of the African-American experience around Lake Okeechobee. ⊠ *Glades Pioneer Park, 866 Rte. 715,* ☎ *561/996–2161,* FAX *561/996–0894.*

## Dining

$ ✕ **Dino's Restaurant.** Downtown Belle Glade's best, this faux-Tudor pizza house with Leatherette booths and lyre-back chairs features subs, steaks, dogs, burgers, pastas, and salads. It's open for three meals a day. ⊠ *1100 N. Main St., Belle Glade,* ☎ *561/996–1901. AE, D, DC, MC, V.*

$ ✕ **Drawbridge Cafe.** A big-windowed country-club dining room is to one side; the Rusty Anchor Lounge, with pool table, jukebox, and TV, is to the other. There are buffets for midweek luncheons and weekend breakfasts plus nightly specials: If you haven't had your fill of catfish yet, come on Wednesday. ⊠ *Torry Island Rd., Belle Glade,* ☎ *561/992–9370.*

$ ✕ **Old South Bar-B-Q Ranch.** Curiosity about the piles of cornball signs that lead here ("Y'all be shore'n stop in t'help pay for theez dern signs") pull in half a million visitors a year. Displays of pioneer home and farm relics, Confederate money, and stagey versions of legendary

moments in Western lore make it a great spot for kids. There are
wagon wheels behind the picnic tables, and servers sport western wear.
The chow is lots of barbecue, catfish, hush puppies, and corn on the
cob. ⊠ *602 E. Sugarland Hwy.,* ☎ *941/983–7756. D, MC, V.*

### Nightlife and the Arts
The **Dolly Hand Cultural Arts Center** (⊠ 1977 College Dr., ☎ 561/992–
6160) on the Palm Beach Community College Glades Campus presents
a winter series of seven or eight various productions.

### Outdoor Activities and Sports
FISHING
You can fish the canal at the **Arthur R. Marshall–Loxahatchee National Wildlife Refuge** (☎ 561/734–8303); there's a boat-launching ramp,
and the waters are decently productive—but be sure to bring your own
equipment.

GOLF
**Belle Glade Municipal Country Club** (⊠ Torry Island Rd., ☎ 561/996–
6605) has an 18-hole golf course and restaurant open to the public.

## Clewiston

"The sweetest town in America" is also the most prosperous lake
town thanks to the resident headquarters of the United States Sugar
Corporation (☎ 941/983–8121), on the west side of the crescent-shaped
Civic Park. As largest employer and tax-revenue source, the company
effectively governs **Clewiston.** Its style reflects an enlightened paternalism
that dates from 1931, when an investment group of General Motors
principals took over the Southern Sugar Company, which had failed
with the onset of the Depression. To the park's north is the Public Library (☎ 941/983–1493), and to the east is the Clewiston Inn, a local
landmark for its antebellum architecture, restaurant, and lounge. As
you enter town on the U.S. 27, otherwise known as the Sugarland Highway, you'll come to several marinas, stores offering every type of freshwater fishing equipment, and modern condominium-motels extending
along a canal in the lee of the dike.

### Sights to See
**Clewiston Museum.** A history of the city details stories not only of sugar
and of the Herbert Hoover Dike construction, but also of a ramie crop
grown here once to make rayon, of RAF pilots who trained at the Clewiston airfield during World War II, and of a German POW camp. ⊠ *112
S. Commercio St.,* ☎ *941/983–1493.*

### Dining and Lodging
$     ✕ **Colonial Dining Room.** This dining room in the Clewiston Inn has
ladder-back chairs, chandeliers, and fanlight windows, and though the
food is good, the attitude's not fancy. Southern regional and Continental dishes—chicken, pork, steak, and the ubiquitous catfish—are
served. ⊠ *108 Royal Palm Ave. at U.S. 27,* ☎ *941/983–8151.*

$–$$    🔟 **Clewiston Inn.** This classic antebellum-style country hotel in the heart
of town was built in 1938. Its cypress-paneled lobby, wood-burning
fireplace, Colonial Dining Room, and Everglades Lounge with the
wraparound Everglades mural are standouts. Rooms are pleasant but
basic, with reproduction furniture. Still it's worth a stay to soak up
the lore and take advantage of the excellent value (full breakfast included). A pool is across the street in the park, and an 18-hole golf
course is in town. ⊠ *108 Royal Palm Ave. at U.S. 27, Clewiston
33440,* ☎ *941/983–8151 or 800/749–4466,* 🄵🄰🄷 *941/983–4602. 48*

*rooms, 5 suites. Restaurant, lounge, lighted tennis courts, jogging.*
*AE, D, DC, MC, V.*

# Moore Haven

With a population under 2,000, **Moore Haven** is the seat of the pro-
portionally small Glades County. Sugar-cane farming and cattle ranching account for most private-sector jobs here. On the U.S. 27, just before
town, the four-laner narrows and crosses a drawbridge over the
Caloosahatchee River, which along with the St. Lucie Canal (on the
opposite side of the lake) and the lake constitute the fully navigable,
152-mile Okeechobee Waterway, linking the Atlantic Ocean with the
Gulf of Mexico. (A six-lane bridge over the river is under construction.) The prominent downtown landmark is the Lone Cypress, a tree
that has guided explorers to this spot on the lake since early Seminole
times.

## Shopping

**Lundy's Hardware** (35 Ave. J, ☎ 941/946–0833) is the genuine arti-
cle—in business since 1919, it's a catchall general store, although the
only food it carries is for livestock.

# Between Lakeport and Okeechobee

Route 78 curves along most of the western shore of Lake Okeechobee,
passing Lakeport and the **Brighton Seminole Indian Reservation** before ending near the town of **Okeechobee,** perched near the top of the
lake. Long before the town was settled, the vicinity was immortalized
by the Battle of Okeechobee. On Christmas day, 1837, General Zachary
Taylor's forces defeated a Seminole force led by Chiefs Alligator, Sam
Jones, and Wildcat, effectively ending large-scale Seminole conflict,
though resistance continued for almost 20 more years. The region
came to prominence more peacefully in 1915, when the Florida East
Coast Railway arrived and the town was formally laid out as an agricultural center. Citrus production has outgrown cattle ranching as the
principal economy, while dairying, though still important, is diminishing
as the state acquires land in its efforts to reduce water pollution.

Okeechobee's downtown is distinctive for its wide, grass-malled,
east–west main street. Make sure you see the graceful, Mediterranean
revival **Okeechobee County Courthouse,** which sits on N.W. 2nd Street
(☎ 941/763–6441). U.S. 441 branches off from Okeechobee and follows the eastern shore of the lake; near the town, it is an especially
beautiful rural road. About 6½ miles down the pike is a historical marker
commemorating the Battle of Okeechobee, and there are also several
unforgettable views.

## Sights to See

**Brighton Seminole Indian Reservation.** One of the region's largest
ranches with 35,000 acres, this reservation is off of Route 721. Get
your chips ready—Brighton features bingo Monday–Friday nights.
For information, contact the Seminole Tribe of Florida, Inc. (✉ Culture Educational Center, Rte. 6, Box 585, Okeechobee 34974, ☎
941/763–7501, 941/467–6857, or 941/467–9998).

## Beaches

A modest **public beach** rims the north shore of the lake near Okeechobee,
where Route 78 meets U.S. 441, a pivotal corner of the lake. Access
to the beach and a fishing pier is via a short cutoff over the dike.

## Dining and Lodging

**$–$$** ✕ **Lightsey's.** The pick of the lake, this beautiful lodgelike restaurant
★ at the Okee-Tantie Recreation Area started closer to town as a fish company with four tables in a corner. Now everybody comes out here. You can get most items fried, steamed, broiled, or grilled. The freshest are the catfish, cooter (freshwater turtle), frogs' legs, and gator. ✉ *10430 Rte. 78 W, Okeechobee* ☎ *941/763–4276. MC, V. Beer and wine only.*

**$** ✕ **Calusa Lodge Restaurant.** Some places call themselves rustic, but this is the real thing. Everybody's here, from locals griping about the Corps of Engineers' plan to remove part of the dike to Seminoles to cyclists. Weekend breakfast buffets and all-you-can-eat catfish dinners are popular. There's live entertainment in the lounge on weekends. You gotta be here if you're in town. ✉ *Rtes. 78 and 721, Lakeport,* ☎ *941/946–0544. MC, V.*

**$** 🏨 **Okeechobee Days Inn.** Locals know this modern two-story motel
★ on the rim canal with a five-story observation tower for looking over the levee to the lake as the Motel Pier II. (It took on the Days Inn franchise in 1994.) Large, clean, motel-plain rooms are well maintained. Out back there's a 600-foot fishing pier and Oyster Bar, one of the best hangouts on the lake for shooting a game of pool or watching a game on TV. It attracts a good mix of locals and out-of-towners. ✉ *2200 SE U.S. 441, 34974,* ☎ *941/763–8003 or 800/874–3744,* 🗚 *941/763–2245. 89 rooms. Lounge, fishing. AE, D, DC, MC, V.*

## Outdoor Activities and Sports

CYCLING

**Euler's Cycling & Fitness** (✉ 50 SE U.S. 441, Okeechobee, ☎ 941/357–0458) is the only professional source for bicycle rentals and repairs on the lake.

FISHING

**Okee–Tantie Recreation Area** (✉ 10430 Rte. 78 W, Okeechobee, ☎ 941/763–2622) has plenty of campsites, plus direct access to the lake. The park offers 215 RV sites, 38 tent sites, two public boat ramps, fish-cleaning stations, a marina, picnic areas, a playground, rest rooms, showers, Lightsey's (☞ Dining, *above*), and a bait and tackle shop (☎ 941/763–9645), which supplies groceries and sandwiches.

# Between Indiantown and Pahokee

Somewhat set back from the lake on Route 710 is **Indiantown,** a good place to stop when visiting the nearby Barley Barber Swamp—400 acres of cypress wetlands. Route 76 will take you back toward the lake and U.S. 441, ending up near the ghost town of Port Mayaca. Going south on U.S. 441 toward **Canal Point,** you'll find yourself in serious sugar country; almost 80% of Florida's sugarcane production takes place in this area. Canal Point itself is just a sliver of a town along a bend in the road between sugar fields and a rim canal edging the omnipresent levee. The canal is one of six that allow the high waters of the lake to run off and drain the surrounding lowlands. Maintained jointly by a state flood-control agency and the U.S. Army Corps of Engineers, this system of drainage canals dates from the late 19th century, when a bankrupt Florida contracted with a wealthy Philadelphian, Hamilton Disston, to drain the Everglades for agriculture.

Farther south, U.S. 441 turns into East Main Street in **Pahokee,** which means "grassy waters" in the Seminole language. Pahokee may share a county with Palm Beach, but its rural style twangs a world away. The town of nearly 7,000 depends almost entirely on sugar. Two giant mills are located here and the **Bank of Pahokee** (☒ 800 S. Main St., ☎ 561/924–5272), has a series of Everglades murals. For a look back into the sugar-centric past, check out the **Pahokee Historical Museum,** located in the chamber of commerce. It's also possible to drive up onto the levee and look across the lake, which spreads out like an ocean.

## Sights to See

**Barley Barber Swamp.** This 400-acre freshwater cypress swamp preserve on Route 710 is maintained by the Florida Power and Light Company's Martin Power Plant. A 5,800-foot-long boardwalk enables you to walk through this vestige of what near-coastal Florida was largely like before the vast water-control efforts began in the 19th century. Dozens of birds, reptiles, and mammals inhabit these wetlands and lowlands with an outstanding reserve of bald cypress trees, land and swamp growth, and slow-flowing, coffee-colored water. Reservations are required at least one week in advance. ☒ *Rte. 710,* ☎ *800/552–8440.* ☒ *Free.* ☉ *Tours Fri.–Wed. 8:30 and 12:30.*

**Lake Okeechobee Scenic Trail.** Stretching north and south atop the levee near Pahokee, this coarse track has been integrated into the Florida National Scenic Trail. The dike trail is the focus of one of the most ambitious recreational trail developments in the United States. Although the route can be hiked or ridden on mountain bikes, some $8 million in improvements, to be completed before 2000, will smooth the surface and provide shelters and interpretive materials.

## Dining and Lodging

$ ✕ **Pam's Seafood & Deli.** This longtime downtown favorite is run by Jimmy and Georgia Jones, whose motto is "You buy. We fry." Their rationale: "The kitchen isn't big enough anyway for a grill." A block from city hall, the place is bright with vinyl and a lot of shell art. Anybody you want to meet shows up. ☒ *149 S. Lake Ave., Pahokee,* ☎ *561/924–7231. No credit cards. Closed Sun.*

$ ▣ **Seminole Country Inn.** This two-story, Mediterranean revival inn,
★ once the southern headquarters of the Seaboard Airline Railroad, was restored by longtime Indiantown patriarch, the late Holman Wall. It's now being run for the second time (other innkeepers didn't get it right) by his daughter, Jonnie Wall Williams, a fifth-generation native, who is devoted to the inn's restoration. Rooms are done in country ruffles and prints, with full carpeting and comfy beds. There are rocking chairs on the porch, Indiantown memorabilia in the lobby, a sitting area on the second floor, and good local art throughout. ☒ *15885 S.W. Warfield Blvd., Indiantown 34956,* ☎ *561/597–3777. 28 rooms. 2 restaurants, pool. AE, D, MC, V.*

## Nightlife and the Arts

The **Prince Theater,** a restored 1939 art deco movie house in downtown Pahokee (☒ 231 E. Main St., ☎ 561/924–5534), is now used as a performance center.

## Outdoor Activities and Sports

FISHING

After seeing them in all the local restaurants, try to catch your own catfish at the **Pahokee Marina & Campground** (☒ 171 N. Lake Ave., Panhokee ☎ 561/924–7832).

# PALM BEACH AND THE TREASURE COAST A TO Z

## Arriving and Departing

### By Bus
**Greyhound Lines** (☎ 800/231–2222) buses arrive at the station in West Palm Beach (✉ 100 Banyan Blvd., ☎ 561/833–8534).

### By Car
I–95 runs north–south, linking West Palm Beach with Miami and Fort Lauderdale to the south and with Daytona, Jacksonville, and the rest of the Atlantic Coast to the north. To get to central Palm Beach, exit at Belvedere Road or Okeechobee Boulevard. Florida's Turnpike runs up from Miami through West Palm Beach before angling northwest to reach Orlando.

The best way to get to Lake Okeechobee from West Palm is to drive west on Southern Boulevard from I–95, past the cutoff road to Lion Country Safari. From here, the boulevard is designated U.S. 98/441.

### By Plane
**Palm Beach International Airport (PBIA)** (✉ Congress Ave. and Belvedere Rd., West Palm Beach, ☎ 561/471–7400) is served by **Air Canada** (☎ 800/776–3000), **American/American Eagle** (☎ 800/433–7300), **American Trans-Air** (☎ 800/225–2995), **Canadian Holidays** (☎ 800/661–8881), **Carnival Airlines** (☎ 800/824–7386), **Comair** (☎ 800/354–9822), **Continental** (☎ 800/525–0280), **Delta** (☎ 800/221–1212), **KIWI Intl. Airlines** (☎ 800/538–5494), **Northwest** (☎ 800/225–2525), **Paradise Island** (☎ 800/432–8807), **Republic Air Travel** (☎ 800/233–0225), **TWA** (☎ 800/221–2000), **United** (☎ 800/241–6522), and **USAir/USAir Express** (☎ 800/428–4322).

**Rte. 10 of Tri-Rail Commuter Bus Service** (☎ 800/874–7245) runs from the airport to Tri-Rail's nearby Palm Beach Airport station daily. **CoTran** (☞ Getting Around by Bus, *below*) Rte. 4-S operates from the airport to downtown West Palm Beach every two hours at 35 minutes after the hour from 7:35 AM until 5:35 PM. The fare is $1.

**Palm Beach Transportation** (☎ 561/689–4222) provides taxi and limousine service from PBIA. Reserve at least a day in advance for a limousine. The lowest fares are $1.50 per mile, with the meter starting at $1.25. Depending on your destination, a flat rate (from PBIA only) may save money. Wheelchair-accessible vehicles are available.

### By Train
**Amtrak** (☎ 800/872–7245) connects West Palm Beach (✉ 201 S. Tamarind Ave., ☎ 561/832–6169) with cities along Florida's east coast and the Northeast daily and via the *Sunset Limited* to New Orleans and Los Angeles three times weekly. Included in Amtrak's service is transport from West Palm Beach to Okeechobee (✉ 801 N. Parrott Ave.; station unmanned).

## Getting Around

A new Downtown Transfer Facility is to open in 1996 at Banyan Boulevard and Clearlake Drive, off Australian Avenue at the western entrance to downtown. It links the downtown shuttle, Amtrak, Tri-Rail (the commuter line of Dade, Broward, and Palm Beach counties), CoTran (the county bus system), and taxis. Greyhound is also expected to tie in.

## By Bus

**CoTran** (Palm Beach County Transportation Authority) buses require exact change. The cost is $1.50 for students, seniors, and people with disabilities (with $1 reduced-fare ID); transfers are 20¢. Service operates between 5 AM and 8:30 PM, though pickups on most routes are 5:30 AM to 7 PM. For details, call 561/233–1111 (Palm Beach) or 561/930–5123 (Boca Raton–Delray Beach).

**Palmtran** (☎ 561/833–8873) is a shuttle system that provides free transportation around downtown West Palm Beach from 6:30 AM to 7:30 PM weekdays.

## By Car

U.S. 1 threads north–south along the coast, connecting most coastal communities, while the more scenic Route A1A ventures out onto the barrier islands. The interstate, I–95, runs parallel to U.S. 1 a bit farther inland. Southern Boulevard (U.S. 98) runs east–west from West Palm Beach to Lake Okeechobee.

In 1995 a new nonstop four-lane route, Okeechobee Boulevard, began carrying traffic from west of downtown West Palm Beach, near the Amtrak station in the airport district, directly to the Flagler Memorial Bridge and into Palm Beach. Flagler Drive will be turned over for pedestrian use only before the end of the decade.

## By Taxi

**Palm Beach Transportation** (☎ 561/689–4222) has a single number serving several cab companies. Meters start at $1.25, and the charge is $1.25 per mile within West Palm Beach city limits; if the trip at any point leaves the city limits, the fare is $1.50 per mile. Some cabs may charge more. Waiting time is 25¢ per 75 seconds.

## By Train

**Tri-Rail** (☎ 305/728–8445 or 800/874–7245), the commuter rail system, has six stations in Palm Beach County (13 stops altogether between West Palm Beach and Miami). The round-trip fare is $5, $2.50 for students and seniors.

# Contacts and Resources

## Emergencies

Dial **911** for **police** or **ambulance.**

### HOSPITALS

The following hospitals have a 24-hour emergency room: **Good Samaritan Hospital** (⊠ Flagler Dr. and Palm Beach Lakes Blvd., West Palm Beach, ☎ 561/655–5511; physician referral, ☎ 561/650–6240), **JFK Medical Center** (⊠ 5301 S. Congress Ave., Atlantis, ☎ 561/965–7300; physician referral, ☎ 561/642–3628), **Palm Beaches Medical Center** (⊠ 2201 45th St., West Palm Beach, ☎ 561/881–2670; physician referral, ☎ 561/881–2661), **Palm Beach Regional Hospital** (⊠ 2829 10th Ave. N, Lake Worth, ☎ 561/967–7800; physician referral, ☎ 800/237–6644), and **St. Mary's Hospital** (⊠ 901 45th St., West Palm Beach, ☎ 561/844–6300; physician referral, ☎ 561/881–2929).

### LATE-NIGHT PHARMACIES

**Eckerd Drug** (⊠ 3343 S. Congress Ave., Palm Springs, ☎ 561/965–3367). **Walgreen Drugs** (⊠ 1688 S. Congress Ave., Palm Springs, ☎ 561/968–8211; ⊠ 7561 N. Federal Hwy., Boca Raton, ☎ 561/241–9802; ⊠ 1634 S. Federal Hwy., Boynton Beach, ☎ 561/737–1260; ⊠ 1208 Royal Palm Beach Blvd., Royal Palm Beach, ☎ 561/798–9048;

✉ 6370 Indiantown Rd., Jupiter, ☎ 561/744–6822; ✉ 20 E. 30th St., Riviera Beach, ☎ 561/848–6464).

## Guided Tours

### AIRBOAT TOURS

**Loxahatchee Everglades Tours** (☎ 561/482–6107) operates year-round from west of Boca Raton through the marshes between the built-up coast and Lake Okeechobee. **J-Mark Fish Camp** (☎ 561/996–5357) in Belle Glade offers 45- to 60-minute airboat rides for $20 per person, with a minimum of two people and a maximum of six; 90- to 120-minute rides for $30 per person include a look at an active eagle's nest.

### BOAT TOURS

**Water Taxi Scenic Cruises** (☎ 561/775–2628) in Palm Beach offers several different daily tours designed to let you get a close-up look at the mansions of the rich and famous. The southern tour includes the mansions of Palm Beach, while the northern tour includes the North Palm Beach Canal. There's also a one-hour BYOB sunset cruise. Departures are from Sailfish Marina and Riviera Beach Marina. Capt. Doug's (☎ 561/589–2329) offers three-hour lunch and dinner cruises from Sebastian along the Indian River on board a 35-foot sloop. Cost is $100 per couple including meal, tips, beer, and wine. **Jonathan Dickinson's River Tours** (☎ 561/746–1466) runs two-hour cruises from Jonathan Dickinson State Park in Hobe Sound daily at 9, 11, 1, and 3 and once a month, at the full moon, at 7. Cost is $10. **Louie's Lady** (☎ 561/744–5550) gives steamboat-style sightseeing and luncheon tours of Jupiter Island and the Intracoastal Waterway, departing from the docks behind Harpoon Louie's Restaurant on the Jupiter River. **The Manatee Queen** (☎ 561/744–2191), a 49-passenger catamaran, offers day and evening cruises on the Intracoastal Waterway and into the cypress swamps of Jonathan Dickinson State Park, November to May. **Ramblin' Rose Riverboat** (☎ 561/243–0686) operates luncheon, dinner-dance, and Sunday brunch cruises from Delray Beach along the Intracoastal Waterway. **The Spirit of St. Joseph** (☎ 561/467–2628) offers seven lunch and dinner cruises weekly on the Indian River, leaving from alongside the St. Lucie County Historical Museum, November through April. **Star of Palm Beach** (☎ 561/842–0882) runs year-round from Singer Island, each day offering one dinner-dance and three sightseeing cruises on the Intracoastal Waterway. In the Okeechobee area, **Capt. JP Boat Cruises** (☎ 941/946–3306), based at the Moore Haven marina, operates tours on the lake and rim canal from mid-November to mid-April.

### ENVIRONMENTAL TOURS

Contact the **Audubon Society of the Everglades** (☎ 561/588–6908) for field trips and nature walks. **Swampland Tours** (☎ 941/467–4411) on Lake Okeechobee operates interpretive boat tours through the National Audubon Society Wildlife Sanctuary.

### HISTORICAL TOURS

The **Boca Raton Historical Society** (☎ 561/395–6766) offers afternoon tours of the Boca Raton Resort & Club on Tuesday year-round and to other south Florida sites. The **Indian River County Historical Society** (✉ 2336 14th Ave., Vero Beach, ☎ 561/778–3435) has walking tours of downtown Vero on Wednesday at 11 and 1 (by reservation) and occasional driving tours of the Jungle Trail.

## Visitor Information

**Belle Glade Chamber of Commerce** (✉ 540 S. Main St., Belle Glade 33430, ☎ 561/996–2745). **Clewiston Chamber of Commerce** (✉ 544 W. Sugarland Hwy., Clewiston 33440, ☎ 941/983–7979). **Glades**

County Chamber of Commerce (✉ U.S. 27 and 10th St., Moore Haven 33471, ☎ 941/946–0440). **Indian River County Tourist Council** (✉ 1216 21st St., Box 2947, Vero Beach 32961, ☎ 561/567–3491). **Indiantown Chamber of Commerce** (✉ 15518 S.W. Osceola St., Indiantown 34956, ☎ 561/597–2184). **Okeechobee County Chamber of Commerce** (✉ 55 S. Parrott Ave., Okeechobee 34974, ☎ 941/763–6464). **Pahokee Chamber of Commerce** (✉ 115 E. Main St., Pahokee 33476, ☎ 561/924–5579). **Palm Beach County Convention & Visitors Bureau** (✉ 1555 Palm Beach Lakes Blvd., Suite 204, West Palm Beach 33401, ☎ 561/471–3995). **Chamber of Commerce of the Palm Beaches** (✉ 401 N. Flagler Dr., West Palm Beach 33401, ☎ 561/833–3711). **Palm Beach Chamber of Commerce** (✉ 45 Cocoanut Row, Palm Beach 33480, ☎ 561/655–3282). **St. Lucie County Tourist Development Council** (✉ 2300 Virginia Ave., Fort Pierce 34982, ☎ 561/462–1535 or 800/344–8443). **Stuart/Martin County Chamber of Commerce** (✉ 1650 S. Kanner Hwy., Stuart 34994, ☎ 561/287–1088). For more information on the Okeechobee area, contact the **U.S. Army Corps of Engineers** (✉ South Florida Operations Office, 525 Ridgelawn Rd., Clewiston 33440-5399, ☎ 941/983–8101).

# 7 The Florida Keys

*This slender necklace of landfalls off the southern tip of Florida is strung together by a 110-mile-long highway. The Keys have two faces: one, a wilderness of flowering jungles and shimmering seas amid mangrove-fringed islands dangling toward the tropics; the other, a traffic jam with a view of billboards, shopping centers, and trailer courts. Embrace the best of the Keys by enjoying the deep-sea fishing, the first-class snorkeling and diving, and the colorful community of Key West.*

By Herb Hiller

Updated by
Mike Radigan

**T**HE FLORIDA KEYS ARE A WILDERNESS of flowering jungles and shimmering seas, a jade necklace of mangrove-fringed islands dangling toward the tropics. The Florida Keys are also a 110-mile traffic jam lined with garish billboards, hamburger stands, shopping centers, motels, and trailer courts. Unfortunately, in the Keys you can't have one without the other. A river of tourist traffic gushes along U.S. 1 (also called the Overseas Highway), the only road to Key West. Residents of Monroe County live by diverting that river's flow of green dollars to their own pockets. In the process, the fragile beauty of the Keys—or at least the 45 that are inhabited and linked to the mainland by 43 bridges—has paid the environmental price.

Despite a state-mandated development slowdown, the Keys' natural resources are still in peril. Since 1992, new building has been severely restricted, with an eye to protecting the environment as well as improving hurricane evacuation procedures. In 1990, Congress designated the Florida Keys National Marine Sanctuary, covering 2,800 square nautical miles of coastal waters off the Florida Keys. Adjacent to the Keys landmass are spectacular, unique, and nationally significant marine environments including sea grass meadows, mangrove islands, and extensive living coral reefs. These marine environments support rich biological communities possessing extensive conservation, recreational, commercial, ecological, historical, research, educational, and aesthetic values. This ecosystem is the marine equivalent of tropical rain forests, supporting high levels of biological diversity. They are fragile and easily susceptible to damage while possessing a high value to humans if properly conserved. In late 1996, a comprehensive management plan designed to protect the 200-mile-long reef and surrounding waters was put into place. The Florida Keys National Marine Sanctuary and Protection Act, which includes a new marine zoning concept that would reserve 6% of the waters as "no harvest" zones, is intended to protect the coral reefs and restore worsening water quality. But the problem continues. Increased salinity in Florida Bay has continued to cause large areas of sea grass to die and drift in mats out of the bay. These mats then block the sunlight from reaching the corals reefs, stifling their growth, and threatening both the Keys' significant recreational diving economy and tourism in general.

For now, however, take pleasure as you drive down U.S. 1 along the islands. Most days you can gaze over the silvery blue and green Atlantic and its still-living reef; Florida Bay, the Gulf of Mexico, and the backcountry on your right. (The Keys extend east–west from the mainland.) At some points, the ocean and the Gulf are as much as 10 miles apart. On the narrowest landfill islands, they are separated only by the road.

The Overseas Highway varies from a frustrating traffic-clogged trap to a mystical pathway skimming the sea. More islands than you can remember appear. Follow the green mile markers by the side of the road, and even if you lose track of the names of the islands, you won't get lost.

Things to do and see are everywhere, but first you have to remind yourself to get off the highway. Once you do, rent a boat and find a secluded anchorage and fish, swim, and marvel at the sun, sea, and sky. In the Atlantic, you can dive to spectacular coral reefs or pursue dolphin, blue marlin, and other deep-water game fish. Along the Florida Bay coastline you can seek out the bonefish, snapper, snook, and tarpon that lurk in the grass flats and in the shallow, winding channels of the backcountry.

Along the reefs and among the islands are more than 600 kinds of fish. Diminutive deer and pale raccoons, related to but distinct from their mainland cousins, inhabit the Lower Keys. And throughout the islands you'll find such exotic West Indian plants as Jamaica dogwood, pigeon plum, poisonwood, satinwood, and silver and thatch palms, as well as tropical birds, including the great white heron, mangrove cuckoo, roseate spoonbill, and white-crowned pigeon.

Another Keys attraction is the weather: In the winter it's typically 10° warmer than on the mainland; in the summer it's usually 10° cooler. The Keys also get substantially less rain, around 30 inches annually compared to 55–60 inches in Miami and the Everglades. Most of the rain falls in quick downpours on summer afternoons. In winter, continental cold fronts occasionally stall over the Keys, dragging overnight temperatures down to the 40s.

The Keys were only sparsely populated until the early 20th century. In 1905, however, railroad magnate Henry Flagler began building the extension of his Florida railroad south from Homestead to Key West. His goal was to establish a rail link to the steamships that sailed between Key West and Havana, just 90 miles across the Straits of Florida. The railroad arrived at Key West in 1912 and remained a lifeline of commerce until the Labor Day hurricane of 1935 washed out much of its roadbed. For three years thereafter, the only way in and out of Key West was by boat. The Overseas Highway, built over the railroad's old roadbeds and bridges, was completed in 1938, and many sections and bridges have recently been widened or replaced.

## Pleasures and Pastimes

### The Arts
The Keys are more than warm weather and luminous scenery—a vigorous and sophisticated artistic community flourishes here. Key West alone currently claims among its residents several dozen full-time writers and hundreds of painters and craftspeople. Arts organizations in the Keys sponsor many special events—some lasting only a weekend, others spanning an entire season.

### Boating and Fishing
Fishing is popular throughout the Keys, and particularly in Key Largo, Islamorada, and Key West. You have a choice of deep-sea fishing on the ocean or the Gulf or flat-water fishing in the mangrove-fringed shallows of the backcountry. Charter-boat captains can take you where the right kind of fish are biting. Many motor yacht and sailboat captains will also take paying passengers on day, sunset, or night cruises on the Atlantic, Florida Bay, and the shimmering Gulf of Mexico; glass-bottom boats, which depart daily (weather permitting) from docks throughout the Keys, are popular with visitors who want to admire the reefs without getting wet. (If you're prone to seasickness, don't try to look through the glass bottom in rough seas.) Motor yachts, sailboats, Hobie Cats, Windsurfers, and canoes are all available for rent by the day or on a long-term basis. (Some hotels have their own rental services; others will refer you to a separate vendor.)

### Dining
A number of talented, young chefs have settled in the Keys, contributing to the area's image as one of the nation's points of culinary interest. The restaurant menus, the rum-based fruit beverages, and even the restaurant's music reflect the Keys' tropical climate and their prox-

imity to Cuba and other Caribbean islands. The better American and Cuban restaurants serve imaginative and tantalizing fusion cuisine that draws on food traditions from all over the world; Florida citrus, seafood, and tropical fruits figure prominently.

Since 1985, the U.S. government has protected the queen conch as an endangered species, so be aware that any conch you order in the Keys has come fresh-frozen from the Bahamas, Belize, or the Caribbean. However, Florida lobster and stone crab should be local and fresh from August to March. You should also keep an eye out for authentic Key lime pie. While many restaurants now serve a green version made with white-pastry crust and whipped cream, the real McCoy has a yellow custard in a graham-cracker crust with a meringue top and tastes like nothing else.

Remember: The laid-back atmosphere of the Keys is reflected in the casual hours kept by some smaller restaurants. Hours change, and lunch may be canceled on a whim: Dial ahead, especially if driving any distance.

### Diving and Snorkeling

Although there are reefs and wrecks all along the east coast of Florida, the state's most extensive diving grounds are in the Keys. Divers come for the quantity and quality of living coral reefs within 6 or 7 miles of shore, the kaleidoscopic beauty of 650 species of tropical fish, and the adventure of probing wrecked ships that foundered in these seemingly tranquil seas as long as four centuries ago. Although the majority of diving outfitters are based in Key Largo and the Lower Keys, many of them offer snorkel trips and dives region-wide. South Florida residents fill dive boats on weekends, so plan to dive Monday through Thursday, when the boats and reefs are less crowded.

### Lodging

Historic cottages, restored turn-of-the-century Conch (pronounced "conk") houses, and lodges nestled in the mangroves here attract tourists and celebrities alike. Key West offers the greatest variety, from large resorts to guest homes in wonderful old ship-carpentered houses. (When registering, keep in mind that salty winds and soil play havoc with anything man-made, and constant maintenance is a must; inspect your accommodations before checking in.)

## Exploring the Keys

Finding your way around the Keys isn't hard once you understand the unique address system. The only address many people have is a mile marker (MM) number. The markers themselves are small green rectangular signs along the side of the Overseas Highway (U.S. 1). They begin with MM 126 a mile south of Florida City and end with MM 0 on the corner of Fleming and Whitehead streets in Key West. Keys residents use the abbreviation BS for the bay side of U.S. 1 and OS for the ocean side.

The Keys are usually divided into three areas: the Upper Keys, from Key Largo to Long Key Channel (MM 126 to 67); the Middle Keys, from Conch Key through Marathon to Pigeon Key (MM 63 to 47); and the Lower Keys, from Bahia Honda Key down to Key West (MM 37 to 0). The sections below cover each of these three areas, in addition to a section devoted solely to Key West.

### Great Itineraries

*Numbers in the text below correspond to numbers in the margin and on the maps.*

IF YOU HAVE 3 DAYS

One of the pleasures of the Keys is the unique, scenic drive on the Overseas Highway between Key Largo and Key West. Be sure to get an early start so you will have plenty of daylight to savor the breathtaking views of the oceans, bays, and gulfs that lap against the roadway. For lunch, try one of the roadside stands along the way. At **Bahia Honda State Park** you can stretch your legs on one of the park's forest trails, or go snorkeling at the site of an offshore reef. From here, it is less than an hour's drive to ⬚ **Key West.** Spend the next day and night exploring beaches or taking a walking tour of Old Town. On the third day, wake up early, and drive back to the mainland, stopping at **John Pennekamp Coral Reef State Park,** for its aquarium, trails, beaches, or snorkeling.

IF YOU HAVE 4 DAYS

An extra day allows for a more leisurely pace than 3 days afford. Coast on the Overseas Highway, stopping at **Bahia Honda State Park,** before heading to ⬚ **Key West** for the night. Spend the next day and night in Key West, touring the town. On the third day, have lunch in Key West, and then set off on U.S. 1 back to ⬚ **Key Largo.** The whole of day four can be spent at **John Pennekamp Coral Reef State Park,** just minutes from Key Largo, and only a half hour from the mainland.

IF YOU HAVE 7 DAYS

Visit **Bahia Honda State Park** and tour ⬚ **Key West** on days one and two. After lunch on day three, travel to the destination of your choice where you can devote days four, five, and six to one of the Keys' special pleasures, whether it's fishing, boating, snorkeling, or enjoying Key West's colorful atmosphere. Allow enough time at the end of day six to drive to ⬚ **Key Largo** for dinner and the night. On day seven, see **John Pennekamp Coral Reef State Park** before heading back to the mainland.

## When to Tour the Keys

From November to the middle of December, the crowds are thinner and the weather is superlative. High season is January through March, when traffic on the Overseas Highway is inevitably heavy and sometimes bumper-to-bumper on weekends. Key West's annual **Fantasy Festival** is the last week in October; if you plan to visit Key West for this increasingly popular event, reserve at least 6 months ahead of time.

# THE UPPER KEYS

Although overdevelopment has spoiled some of the natural beauty of the region, these Keys of ancient coral rock still have many areas of pristine wilderness to offer, as well as top-rate opportunities for diving and snorkeling and charter fishing.

## Key Largo and Vicinity

*Numbers in the margin correspond to points of interest on the Florida Keys map.*

❶ From Mile Marker 126 to 95, the landscape is disappointingly suburban, with shopping centers and chain restaurants abounding. **North Key Largo,** however, still contains a wide tract of virgin forest, and is also sanctuary to the largest concentration of crocodiles in North ❷ America. The great number of dive shops in **Key Largo** attests to the spectacular, accessible, and irreplaceable coral reef just off the coast in the Key Largo Marine Sanctuary and John Pennekamp Coral Reef State Park.

## The Florida Keys

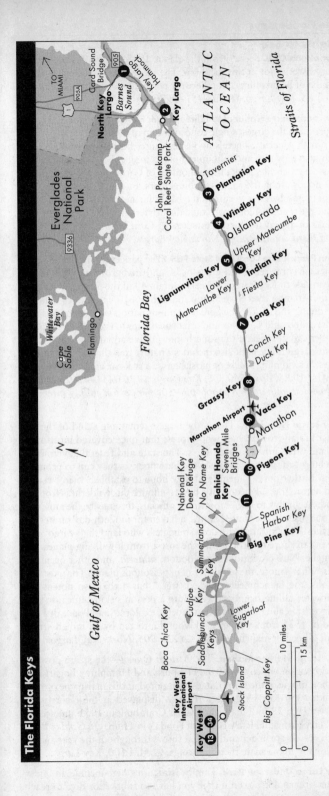

## Sights to See

**Caribbean Club.** Scenes from the classic 1948 Bogart-Bacall flick *Key Largo* were shot in this local bar. The place is plastered with memorabilia of Bogart films. Stop here for postcard–perfect sunsets. ⊠ *MM 104, BS, Key Largo,* ☎ *305/451–9970.*

**Crocodile Lakes National Wildlife Refuge.** Here dwell some 300 to 500 crocodiles, the largest single concentration of these shy, elusive reptiles in North America. There's no visitor center here—just 6,800 acres of mangrove swamp and adjoining upland jungle. For your best chance to see a crocodile, park on the shoulder of Card Sound Road and scan the ponds along the road with binoculars. In winter, crocodiles often haul themselves out to sun on the banks farthest from the road. Don't leave the road shoulder; you could disturb tern nests on the nearby spoil banks or aggravate the rattlesnakes. ⊠ *Card Sound Rd. (Rte. 905A), over Card Sound Bridge, North Key Largo.*

★ **John Pennekamp Coral Reef State Park.** The park encompasses 78 square miles of coral reefs, sea-grass beds, and mangrove swamps on the ocean side of Key Largo. Its reefs contain 40 of the 52 species of coral in the Atlantic Reef System and more than 650 varieties of fish, and the diving and snorkeling here are famous nationwide. A concessioner rents canoes and sailboats and offers boat trips to the reef. Even a landlubber can appreciate the superb interpretive aquarium in the park's visitor center. The park also includes a nature trail through a mangrove forest, a swimming beach, picnic shelters, a snack bar, and a campground. ⊠ *MM 102.5, Box 1560, OS, Key Largo,* ☎ *305/451–1202.* 🖾 *$3.25 per vehicle with up to 8 people plus 50¢ per person county surcharge.* ☉ *Daily 8–sunset.*

**Key Largo Hammock.** This is the largest remaining stand of the vast West Indian tropical hardwood forest that once covered most of the upland areas in the Florida Keys. The state and federal governments are busy acquiring as much of the hammock as they can to protect it from further development, and they hope to establish visitor centers and nature trails. For now, it's best to admire this wilderness from the road. According to law-enforcement officials, this may be the most dangerous place in the United States, a haven for modern-day pirates and witches. The "pirates" are drug smugglers who land their cargo along the ocean shore or drop it into the forest from low-flying planes. The "witches" are practitioners of voodoo, *santeria,* and other occult rituals. What's more, the jungle is full of poisonous plants. The most dangerous, the manchineel or "devil tree," has a toxin so potent that rainwater falling from its leaves onto a person's skin can cause sores that resist healing. Florida's first tourist, explorer Juan Ponce de León, died in 1521 from a superficial wound inflicted by an Indian arrowhead dipped in manchineel sap. ⊠ *Rte. 905, North Key Largo.*

**Key Largo Harbor Marina.** The *African Queen*—the steam-powered workboat on which Katharine Hepburn and Humphrey Bogart rode in their movie of the same name—is moored at this marina next to the Holiday Inn Key Largo Resort. Also displayed at the resort is the *Thayer IV,* a 22-foot mahogany Chris Craft built in 1951 and used by Ms. Hepburn and Henry Fonda in Fonda's last film, *On Golden Pond.* Both vessels are in demand at boat shows throughout the year and occasionally may vacate their moorings. ⊠ *MM 100, Key Largo.*

**Key Largo Undersea Park.** Family attractions here include an underwater archaeology exhibit that you have to snorkel or dive to reach, and comes complete with underwater music. Also at the site are the **Scott Carpenter Man in the Sea** program established by the former astronaut in 1995; a pilot submarine, which gives three-hour tours for up to six people; and Jules' Undersea Lodge, an offbeat underwater inn. ⊠ *51 Shoreland Dr., Key Largo,* ☎ *305/451–2353.* ⊡ *Aquarium theater free; scuba fee, including tanks and gear, $20–$30; snorkel fee, including gear, $10, $35 for family of 4; submarine tour $199.* ⊙ *Daily 9–3.*

**Maritime Museum of the Florida Keys.** This small but earnest museum depicts the history of shipwrecks and salvage efforts along the Keys: retrieved treasures, reconstructed wreck sites, and artifacts in various stages of preservation. Some of the more notable exhibits have come from a fleet of treasure ships wrecked in 1715 by a hurricane. ⊠ *MM 102.5, BS, Key Largo,* ☎ *305/451–6444.* ⊡ *$5.* ⊙ *Fri.–Wed. 10–5.*

**St. Justin Martyr Catholic Church.** This church is notable for its architecture, which evokes the colors and materials of the Keys. Among its art are a beautiful fresco of the Last Supper and an altar table formed of a 5,000-pound mass of Carrara marble quarried in Tuscany. ⊠ *MM 105.5, BS, North Key Largo,* ☎ *305/451–1316.*

## Dining and Lodging

$$ ✕ **The Fish House.** Behind the screened, diner-style facade are a gor-
★ geous and amusing mural of the Keys and display cases filled with the freshest catches, which are then baked, blackened, broiled, fried, sautéed, steamed, or stewed as if every night were the finals in some Keys seafood competition. (In fact, there are many such competitions, and the Fish House often comes up the winner.) The dining room is as redolent of the Keys as a Bogart movie—festooned with nets and every imaginable fishy Christmas ornament. You can sit in captain's chairs or banquettes. Servers wear shorts, and the place is relaxed about everything except the food. Everything comes in generous portions with corn, new potatoes, and coleslaw. Key lime pie is homemade, and there are a few wines and beers. You can't beat the fast service and great eats. ⊠ *MM 102.4, OS,* ☎ *305/451–4665. AE, D, MC, V.*

$–$$ ✕ **Crack'd Conch.** Behind the white clapboard and lattice facade with the green and violet trim is a dining room festooned with foreign money and patrons' business cards, where vertical bamboo stakes support the bar. There's also a screened porch and an outdoor garden. This was originally a fish camp from the 1930s. Specialties include conch (cracked and in chowder, fritters, and salad), a great lobster taco, fried alligator, smoked chicken, and 115 kinds of beer. Portions are big; they do take-out. ⊠ *MM 105, OS, 105045 Overseas Hwy.,* ☎ *305/451–0732. AE, D, MC, V. Closed Wed. and holidays.*

$ ✕ **Alabama Jack's.** In 1953 Alabama Jack Stratham opened his restaurant on two barges at the end of Card Sound Road, 13 miles southeast of Homestead in an old fishing community between Card and Barnes sounds. The spot, something of a no-man's-land, belongs to the Keys in spirit thanks to the Card Sound toll bridge, which joined the mainland to upper Key Largo in 1969. (You may avoid the bridge toll if you drive down from the North.) Regular customers include Keys fixtures such as balladeer Jimmy Buffett, Sunday cyclists, local retirees, boaters who tie up at the restaurant's dock, and anyone else fond of dancing to country-western music and clapping for cloggers. There's a live band on weekends. You can also admire the tropical birds cavorting in the nearby mangroves and the occasional crocodile swimming up the canal. Though Jack has been gone since the early 1980s, owner Phyllis Sague has kept the favorites, including peppery homemade crab cakes, crispy-chewy conch fritters, crunchy breaded shrimp, homemade tartar sauce, and tangy cocktail sauce with horseradish. The completely open-air place closes early because that's when the skeeters come out. ⊠ *58000 Card Sound Rd.,* ☎ *305/248–8741. No credit cards. Closes weekdays at 7, weekends at 7:30 (unless it's busy).*

$ ✕ **Harriette's Restaurant.** Typical of roadside places where the Coke signs outrank the restaurants', this eatery is thick with down-home personality. Owner Harriette Mattson makes it her business to know many of her guests by name and even takes the trouble to remember what they eat. Wisecracking waitresses, perfectly styled for this joint, will tell you that the three-egg omelet is usually a six-egg omelet because Harriette has a heavy hand. Harriette's is famous for its breakfasts: steak and eggs with hash browns or grits and toast and jelly for $6.95, or old-fashioned hotcakes with whipped butter and syrup and sausage or bacon for $3.75. A new Keys mural, a little paneling, some carpet, and acoustic ceiling tiles touch things up, but you can still count on a homey style punctuated with local crafts and photos on consignment. ⊠ *MM 95.7, BS, 95710 Overseas Hwy.,* ☎ *305/852–8689. No credit cards. No dinner.*

$ ✕ **Mrs. Mac's Kitchen.** Hundreds of beer cans, beer bottles, and expired auto license plates from all over the world decorate the walls of this wood-paneled, open-air restaurant. At breakfast and lunch, the counter and booths fill up early with locals. Regular nightly specials are worth the stop: meat loaf on Mon., Italian on Wed., and seafood Thurs.– Sat. The chili is always good, and the beer of the month is $1.50 a bottle. ⊠ *MM 99.4, BS,* ☎ *305/451–3722. No credit cards. Closed Sun. and holidays.*

$$$$ ▦ **Jules' Undersea Lodge.** This, the world's first and only underwater hotel, consists of 720 square feet of space anchored at 30 feet. It has two bedrooms, one bath, and a dining-living room with radio and TV that can accommodate a cramped six. The lodge takes reservations from divers throughout the year and offers a PADI resort course for new divers. Rates include breakfast, snacks and beverages, a light dinner, and unlimited diving in a lagoon of limited visibility. Novelty is what this is all about. ⊠ *MM 103.2, OS, 51 Shoreland Dr., 33037,* ☎ *305/451–2353,* ₣₳ₓ *305/451–4789. 2 rooms. Dining room. AE, D, MC, V.*

$$$$ ▦ **Marriott's Key Largo Bay Beach Resort.** At this 17-acre bayside resort, Marriott reimagines Key Largo as if it hadn't become one more sense-dulling suburb of Miami. Proximity to the mainland does, however, make this the easiest to reach by car of the Keys' glamour resorts. Its five lemon-yellow, grill-balconied, and spire-topped stories are sliced between highway and bay and give off an air of warm indolent days. The facilities are as good as the guest rooms, which are joyfully styled with chintz, rattan, and paddle fans, and feature balconies (from some of which you can watch the sunset sweep across the bay). The resort creates its own virtual reality. You might even end up believing it's real. ⊠ *MM 103.8, BS, 103800 Overseas Hwy.,* ☎ *305/453–0000 or 800/932–9332,* ₣₳ₓ *305/453–0093. 122 rooms, 14 2-bedroom suites, 6 3-bedroom suites, 1 penthouse suite. 3 restaurants, bar, pool, beach, fishing, game room. AE, D, DC, MC, V.*

$$$$ ▦ **Sheraton Key Largo Resort.** Of all the large resort enclaves in the Keys, this is the original, and it's imaginatively done considering it's part of a chain. A big bushy buffer between hotel and highway makes you feel you're a million miles from tumult. The building is long and lean; a three-story atrium fit into the trees has windowpane and coral-rock walls. Service is good and sometimes outstanding. All units are small suites or larger, and all are spacious and comfortable, even if the decor's not exciting. The least desirable rooms are the 230, 330, and 430 series, which overlook the parking lot. Nature trails and board-

walks lead through hammocks to mangrove overlooks by the shore. (Bring bug spray.) Both restaurants guarantee grand views three stories above the bay. ⊠ MM 96.9, BS, 97000 Overseas Hwy., 33037, ☎ 305/852–5553, 800/826–1006, or 800/325–3535, FAX 305/852–8669. 190 rooms, 10 suites. 2 restaurants, 3 lounges, 2 pools, whirlpool, 2 lighted tennis courts, dock, windsurfing, boating, fishing. AE, D, DC, MC, V.

$$$ 🏨 **Holiday Inn Key Largo Resort and Marina.** New owners have been busy refurbishing, so that even though this place, the closest resort to Pennekamp Reef, *is* a Holiday Inn, it's outfitted with Keys pride. New chintz and Keys-themed art accent guest rooms, while good sense has brought a new kids' playroom with an imaginative mural and convenient buffet meal service off the lobby to accommodate families. Former owner James W. Hendricks still docks the *African Queen* at the adjacent Key Largo Harbor Marina much of the time. ⊠ MM 100, OS, 99701 Overseas Hwy., 33037, ☎ 305/451–2121, 800/465–4329, or 800/843–5397, FAX 305/451–5592. 32 rooms. Restaurants, 2 pools, hot tub, boating. AE, D, DC, MC, V.

$$$ 🏨 **Marina Del Mar Resort and Marina.** This two-to-four-story resort on a deep-water marina caters to sailors and divers. Heavy use doesn't show, as owner Scott Marr renovates rooms year-round. Units have original watercolors by Keys artist Mary Boggs, as well as refrigerators. Suites 502, 503, and 504 have full kitchens and plenty of room for groups. There's live entertainment nightly in the restaurant and bar, a free Continental breakfast in the lobby, and spectacular sunrise and sunset views from the fourth-floor observation deck. ⊠ MM 100, OS, Box 1050, 33037, ☎ 305/451–4107 or 800/451–3483, FAX 305/451–1891. 52 rooms, 8 suites, 16 studios with kitchen. Restaurant, bar, heated pool, 2 tennis courts, exercise room, boating, fishing. AE, D, DC, MC, V.

$$–$$$ 🏨 **Largo Lodge.** No two rooms are the same in this vintage 1950s re-
★ sort, but all are cozy, with rattan furniture and screened porches with Cuban tile floors. The prettiest palm alley you've ever seen sets the mood. Tropical gardens with more palms, sea grapes, and orchids surround the guest cottages. There's 200 feet of bay frontage, and late in the day, wild ducks, pelicans, herons, and other birds come looking for a handout from longtime owner Harriet "Hat" Stokes. If you want a top-value tropical hideaway not too far down the Keys, this is it. ⊠ MM 101.5, BS, 101740 Overseas Hwy., 33037, ☎ 305/451–0424 or 800/468–4378. 6 apartments with kitchen, 1 efficiency. MC, V.

$–$$ 🏨 **Bay Harbor Lodge.** Owner Laszlo Simoga speaks German, Hungarian, and Russian and caters to an international clientele. Situated on two heavily landscaped acres, his little resort offers a rustic wood lodge, tiki huts, and concrete block cottages; every room has either a small fridge or full kitchen, cable TV, and a phone. Unit 14, a large efficiency apartment with a deck, has a wood ceiling, original oil paintings, and a dining table made from the hatch cover of a World War II Liberty Ship. Laszlo and his wife, Sandra, are the kind of caring hosts who make mom-and-pop lodges such as this worthy of your patronage. The rates and the waterfront setting make this place especially good. ⊠ MM 97.7, BS, 97702 Overseas Hwy., 33037, ☎ 305/852–5695. 16 rooms. Pool, hot tub, exercise room, boating, 2 docks. D, MC, V.

## Guided Tours

**Florida Bay Outfitters** (⊠ MM 104, BS, Key Largo 33037, ☎ 305/451–3018) operates a year-round schedule of sea kayak tours from half-day to weeklong tours in the backcountry.

## Nightlife

The best source of information for entertainment and nightlife in the area is the semiweekly *Keynoter* (⊠ 3015 Overseas Hwy., Marathon 33050, ☎ 305/743–5551).

**Breezers Tiki Bar** (⊠ MM 103.8, BS, ☎ 305/453–0000), in Marriott's Key Largo Bay Beach Resort, is popular with the smartly coiffed crowd. **Caribbean Club** (⊠ MM 104, BS, ☎ 305/451–9970) draws a hairy-faced, down-home group to shoot the breeze while shooting pool; it's friendlier than you might imagine. **Coconuts** (⊠ MM 100, OS, ☎ 305/453–9794), in the Marina Del Mar Resort, has nightly entertainment year-round. **Holiday Casino Cruises** (⊠ MM 100, OS,☎ 305/451–0000 or 800/843–5397) operates cruises out beyond the 3-mile limit from 2 PM aboard the 92-foot custom yacht *Pair-A-Dice*.

## Outdoor Activities and Sports

### BIKING

Cyclists are now able to ride all but 2 of the next 20 miles south from MM 106 on Key Largo on a combination of bike paths and old roads separate from the Overseas Highway. **Key Largo Bikes** (⊠ MM 99.5, BS, 105 Laguna Ave., ☎ 305/451–1910), just east of the Overseas Highway behind Blockbuster Video, rents adult, children's, and tandem bikes—single-speed bicycles with coaster brakes and multispeed mountain bikes.

### BOATING

**Florida Bay Outfitters** (⊠ MM 104, BS, Key Largo, ☎ 305/451–3018) arranges camping, canoeing, and kayaking in the Upper Keys and beyond, from one to seven days. It also rents equipment, such as one- and two-person sea kayaks, by the hour, half day, or day. **Coral Reef Park Co.** (⊠ John Pennekamp Coral Reef State Park, MM 102.5, OS, Key Largo, ☎ 305/451–1621) runs sailing trips on a 38-foot catamaran as well as glass-bottom boat tours. It also rents boats and equipment for sailing, canoeing, and windsurfing. **Key Largo Princess** (⊠ MM 100, OS, Key Largo, ☎ 305/451–4655) offers glass-bottom boat trips and sunset cruises on a luxury 70-foot motor yacht with a 280-square-foot glass viewing area, departing from the Holiday Inn docks. **Sailors Choice** (⊠ MM 100, OS, Key Largo, ☎ 305/451–1802 or 305/451–0041) operates daily charters, including a nighttime trip, on an ultra-modern 60-foot, 49-passenger boat with an air-conditioned cabin, from the Holiday Inn docks. **Everglades Safari Tours** (Box 3343, Key Largo 33037, ☎ 305/451–4540 or 800/959–0742), departing from the Quay Restaurant docks (⊠ MM 102, BS, Key Largo), operates daily 60-minute champagne sunset tours year-round on a 30-passenger pontoon boat ($15 per person); two-hour mangrove tunnel, skiff tours ($35 per person); and a variety of custom tours.

### DIVING AND SNORKELING

The **Key Largo National Marine Sanctuary** (Box 1083, Key Largo 33037, ☎ 305/451–1644) protects 103 square miles of coral reefs from the eastern boundary of John Pennekamp Coral Reef State Park, 3 miles off Key Largo, to a depth of 300 feet some 8 miles offshore. Managed by NOAA (The National Oceanic and Atmospheric Administration), the sanctuary includes Elbow, French, and Molasses reefs; the 1852 Carysfort Lighthouse and its surrounding reefs; Grecian Rocks; Key Largo Rocks; the torpedoed World War II freighter *Benwood*; and the 9-foot **Christ of the Deep** statue. A popular dive destination, the statue, a gift to the Underwater Society of America from an Italian dive equipment manufacturer, is a smaller copy of the 50-foot Christ of the Abysses off Genoa, Italy. It is about 6 miles east–northeast of Key Largo's

South Cut in about 25 feet of water. The ☞ **John Pennekamp Coral Reef State Park** also contains a wealth of diving and snorkeling.

**Captain Slate's Atlantis Dive Center** (✉ MM 106.5, OS, 51 Garden Cove Dr., Key Largo 33037, ☎ 305/451–3020 or 800/331–3483) is a full-service dive shop (NAUI, PADI, and YMCA certified) that also offers underwater weddings. **American Diving Headquarters** (✉ MM 105.5, BS, Key Largo 33037, ☎ 305/451–0037 or 800/634–8464) is the oldest dive shop in the Keys (since 1962) and operates a complete photographic department. **Coral Reef Park Co.** offers scuba and snorkeling tours of John Pennekamp Coral Reef State Park. **Quiescence Diving Service, Inc.** (✉ MM 103.5, BS, 103680 Overseas Hwy., Key Largo 33037, ☎ 305/451–2440) takes groups of up to six people per boat and provides transport to John Pennekamp.

# Plantation Key to Long Key

From Mile Marker 95 to 67, U.S. 1 skirts through a number of coral rock-made Keys. To the north are the waters of Florida Bay—the "backcountry," populated with colorful birds and the endangered manatee. The area around Islamorada, known for its concentration of restaurants, accommodations, and charter fishing boats, proclaims it-

❸ self "Sport Fishing Capital of the World." **Plantation Key,** named for the plantings of limes, pineapples, and tomatoes cultivated here at the turn of the century, is home to the Wild Bird Rehabilitation Center.

❹ You'll find one of the oldest marine parks in the world on **Windley Key,**

❺ at Theater of the Sea. **Lignumvitae Key** is an unpopulated island that has escaped development and contains well over 100 varieties of trees.

❻ Another uninhabited island, **Indian Key,** was the site of a flourishing

❼ town in the 1830s. On **Long Key** you'll find opportunities for nature walks and swimming at the State Recreation Area.

## Sights to See

**Florida Keys Wild Bird Rehabilitation Center.** Woodcarver and teacher Laura Quinn brought this sanctuary here in 1991; nowhere else in the Keys can you see bird life so close up. Many are kept for life because of injuries that can't be healed. Others are brought for rehabilitation, and then set free. At any time the resident population can include ospreys, hawks, pelicans, cormorants, terns, and herons of various types. A short nature trail has been built into the mangrove forest (bring bug spray), and a small office showcases a video explaining the center's mission. A helpful notice explains that wild animals *do* feel pain when injured but don't scream because screaming would attract predators. ✉ *MM 93.6, BS, 93600 Overseas Hwy., Tavernier,* ☎ *305/852–4486.* 🎟 *Donations welcome.* ☉ *Daily sunrise–sunset.*

**Hurricane Memorial.** Beside the highway stands this marker for the mass grave of 423 victims of the 1935 Labor Day hurricane. Many of those who perished were veterans who had been working on the Overseas Highway; they died when a tidal surge overturned a train sent to evacuate them. The art deco–style monument depicts wind-driven waves and palms bowing before the storm's fury. ✉ *MM 81.6.*

**Indian Key State Historic Site.** Small as it is—only 11½ acres—this islet near Windley Key was a county-seat town and base for early 19th-century shipwreck salvagers, known as wreckers, until an Indian attack wiped out the settlement in 1840. Dr. Henry Perrine, a noted botanist, was killed in the raid. Today you can see his plants overgrowing the town's ruins. Though no guide is available, trails are marked and sites labeled. As the site is accessible only by water, you will need your own boat or a rental. The nearest boat source is Robbie's Boat Rentals and Charters (☞ *below*). ⊠ *Indian Key.*

**Layton Trail.** By a historical marker partially obscured by foliage is this trail, named after Del Layton, who incorporated the city of Layton in 1963 and served as its mayor until his death in 1987. The clearly marked trail, which should take 20–30 minutes to walk, leads through tropical hardwood forest to a rocky Florida Bay shoreline overlooking shallow grass flats offshore. The marker relates the history of the Long Key Viaduct, the first major bridge on the rail line, and the Long Key Fishing Club, which Henry Flagler established nearby in 1906. Zane Grey, the noted western novelist, was president of the club. It consisted of a lodge, guest cottages, and storehouses—all obliterated by the 1935 hurricane. ⊠ *Just below MM 67, Long Key.*

**Lignumvitae Key State Botanical Site.** A virgin hardwood forest still cloaks the area, punctuated only by the home and gardens that chemical magnate William Matheson built as a private retreat in 1919. As the key is only accessible by water, you will need your own boat or a rental. Even with your own boat, you need to reserve a guided ranger tour, given Thurs.–Mon. at 10 and 2. You can request a list of native and well-naturalized plants from the ranger. To make a reservation, contact Long Key State Recreation Area (☞ *below*). ⊠ *Lignumvitae Key,* ☜ *$1.*

**Long Key State Recreation Area.** This park features the Golden Orb Trail, which leads onto a boardwalk through a mangrove swamp alongside a lagoon where a great number of herons and other waterbirds congregate in winter. The park also has a campground, a picnic area, a canoe trail through a tidal lagoon, and a not-very-sandy beach fronting on a broad expanse of shallow grass flats. Bring a mask and snorkel to observe the marine life in this rich nursery area. ⊠ *MM 67.5, OS, Box 776, Long Key 33001,* ☎ *305/664–4815.* ☜ *$3.25 per vehicle with up to 8 people plus 50¢ per person county surcharge; canoe rental $10 deposit plus $2.14 per hour, including tax.* ☉ *Daily 8–sunset.*

**Theater of the Sea.** 12 dolphins, two sea lions, and an extensive collection of tropical fish swim at this Windley Key attraction in the pits of a 1907 railroad quarry. Allow at least two hours to attend the dolphin and sea-lion shows and visit all the exhibits, which include an injured birds of prey display, a "bottomless" boat ride, touch tank, a pool where sharks are fed by a trainer, and a 300-gallon "living reef" aquarium with invertebrates and small reef fishes. For an additional fee, you can even swim with dolphins for 30 minutes, after a 30-minute orientation. ⊠ *MM 84.5, OS, Box 407, Islamorada 33036,* ☎ *305/664–2431.* ☜ *$14 adults.* ☜ *Swim with dolphins $80, reservations required with 50% deposit; video or still photos $70 (inquire at concession).* ☉ *Daily 9:30–4.*

## Dining and Lodging

$$ ✕ **Green Turtle Inn.** Once upon a time, around 1947, this was Sid and Roxie's Green Turtle Inn, and women in Betty Grable hairdos and guys in crew cuts would drive from miles around to socialize over dinner and dancing. Third owner Henry Rosenthal is still devoted to the era. Photographs of locals and famous visitors line the walls, and stuffed turtle dolls dangle from the ceiling over the bar. The background music is "Speak Low" and "In the Mood" in wood-paneled rooms kept on the dark side. Specialties remain from the old days, including a turtle chowder; conch fritters, nicely browned outside, light and fluffy inside; conch salad; alligator steak (tail meat) sautéed in an egg batter; and

Key lime pie. Whole pies are available for carryout. ⊠ *MM 81.5, OS,* ☎ *305/664–9031. AE, D, DC, MC, V. Closed Mon.*

**$$** ✕ **Marker 88.** The best seats in chef-owner Andre Mueller's main dining room catch the last glimmers of sunset. After that, the lighting gets
★ a little dim (romantic, some might contend). Hostesses recite a lengthy list of daily specials and offer you a wine list with more than 200 entries. You can get a good steak or veal chop here, but seafood is the specialty. Try the robust conch chowder, banana blueberry bisque, salad Trevisana (radicchio, leaf lettuce, Belgian endive, watercress, and sweet-and-sour dill dressing—former President Bush's favorite), sautéed conch, and grouper Rangoon (with papaya, banana, and pineapple in a cinnamon and currant jelly sauce), Key lime pie and Key lime baked Alaska. ⊠ *MM 88, BS, Plantation Key,* ☎ *305/852–9315. AE, D, DC, MC, V. Closed Mon. No lunch.*

**$$** ✕ **Papa Joe's Landmark Restaurant.** The look: captain's chairs, mounted fish, fish buoys, and driftwood strung year-round with Christmas lights. The decor never gets ahead of the food, which is first-rate. You can savor succulent dolphin and fresh green beans and carrots al dente. An early-bird menu served from 4 to 6 is priced at $7.95–$9.95. For dessert dive into the Key lime cake or Key lime pie, or the peanut-butter pie. Here, they will still cook but not clean your own catch: $8.95 up to 1 pound per person fried, broiled, or sautéed; $10.95 any other style, which includes meunière, blackened, coconut-dipped, Cajun, amandine, or Oscar (sautéed, topped with béarnaise sauce, crabmeat, and asparagus). Joe's—which dates from 1937—includes an upper-level, over-the-water tiki bar. ⊠ *MM 79.7, BS, 798786 Overseas Hwy.,* ☎ *305/664–8756. AE, MC, V. Closed Tues.*

**$$** ✕ **Squid Row.** This roadside eatery may look like just another cute,
★ affordable food stop on the way to Key West, but it's attitude-free and serves the freshest fish you haven't caught yourself, courtesy of the seafood wholesalers who own it. Grouper comes grilled, divinely flaky, or in bread crumbs and sautéed, served with citrus butter. Service is friendly and prompt, and the wait staff can talk about the specials without theatrics. They'll brew a fresh pot of coffee and volunteer to wrap what's left of the flavorful, airy banana bread that comes at the start of the meal but is best as dessert. There's also a bar with happy hour 4–7. ⊠ *MM 81.9, OS,* ☎ *305/664–9865. AE, D, DC, MC, V. Closed Sun. Aug. 15–Dec. 24.*

**$$** ✕ **Whale Harbor Inn.** This coral-rock building has oyster shells cemented onto the walls, an old Keys bottle collection, and a watermark at 7 feet, a reminder of Hurricane Donna's fury in 1960. Several employees rode out the storm in the lighthouse tower. The main attraction is the 50-foot-long, all-you-can-eat buffet, which includes a stir-fry area and a plentiful shrimp, mussels, crayfish, and snow crab legs. The adjoining Dockside Restaurant and Lounge are open for breakfast, while the upstairs raw bar and grill and the open-air bar, at eye level with the flying bridges of the marina charter fleet, stay open until midnight. ⊠ *MM 83.5, OS, Upper Matecumbe Key,* ☎ *305/664–4959. AE, D, DC, MC, V.*

**$$$$** 🏨 **Cheeca Lodge.** Winner of many awards for environmental responsibility, this 27-acre, low-rise resort on Upper Matecumbe key is the longstanding leader in green activism in the Keys' hospitality industry. Biodegradable products are used, almost everything is recycled, and the resort has banned jet skis and other noisemakers. Camp Cheeca, for children ages 6–12, employs marine-science counselors to make learning about the fragile Keys environment fun. The beachfront pioneer burial ground of the Matecumbe United Methodist Church is preserved on the grounds, and tranquil fish-filled lagoons and gardens surround. Guest rooms feature periwinkle blue/strawberry and green/hot orange color schemes; all have British colonial–style furniture of tightly woven wicker, cane, and bamboo. Touches include intriguing hand-painted mirror frames, faintly surreal art prints and romantic waterscapes, and natural shell soap dishes. Suites have full kitchens and private screened balconies; fourth-floor rooms in the main lodge open onto terraces with ocean or bay views. ⊠ *MM 82, OS, Upper Matecumbe Key, Box 527, 33036,* ☎ *305/664–4651 or 800/327–2888,* FAX *305/664–2893. 139 rooms, 64 suites. 2 restaurants, lounge, 2 pools, saltwater tidal pool, 9-hole golf course, 6 lighted tennis courts, boating, parasailing, fishing. AE, D, DC, MC, V.*

$$$$ ⚟ **The Moorings.** If the facts don't convince you this is one of the finest
★ places to stay in the Keys, your first glimpse will. This one-time coconut plantation has one-, two-, and three-bedroom cottages on 17 acres that even today remain luxuriously free of cluttering "profit centers." The beach has 1,000 feet of sea frontage, a scattering of Adirondack chairs and hammocks, a dock you can swim from (no Jet Skis allowed), a pool, and a tennis court. Cottages are tucked in the tropical forest and furnished with wicker and artistic African fabrics, and have pristine white kitchens. Peaked roofs rise behind French doors, lighting is soft, and there are many exquisite touches from towels thick as conspiracy to extra-deep cushiony bedcovers. The word "paradise" forms easily in your mouth. ⊠ *MM 81.6, OS, 123 Beach Rd., 33036,* ☎ *305/664–4708,* FAX *305/664–4242. 18 cottages. Pool, tennis court, beach, dock. MC, V.*

$$–$$$ ⚟ **Ragged Edge Resort.** Most downstairs units now have screened porches at this unusually spacious, grassy little oceanside establishment, ¼ mile off the Overseas Highway. The two-story buildings are covered with rustic planks outside; inside, rooms are decorated with pine paneling, tile, carpet, and chintz. Each unit has a large tiled bath suite. Most units have full kitchens with island counters, chopping blocks, lots of cabinets, and irons and boards. Upper units have more windows and light and open-beam ceilings. The place feels expensive, though it's surprisingly affordable because there's no staff to speak of and there aren't a lot of extras (like in-room phones). Amenities take the form of a two-story thatch-roof observation tower, picnic areas with barbecue pits, and free coaster-brake bikes. Though there's not much of a beach, you can swim off the large dock—a virtual rookery when boating activity isn't disturbing the pelicans, herons, anhingas, and terns. Look north and south, and only mangroves cluster the near distance. ⊠ *MM 86.5, OS, 243 Treasure Harbor Rd., 33036,* ☎ *305/852–5389. 10 units. Pool, shuffleboard, bicycles. MC, V.*

## Nightlife

Back behind the big plaster mermaid on the highway sits the Keys-easy, over-the-water cabana bar **The Lorelei** (⊠ MM 82, BS, ☎ 305/664–4656). Live nightly sounds are mostly reggae and light rock.

## Outdoor Activities and Sports

BOATING AND FISHING

**Treasure Harbor Marine** (⊠ MM 86.5, OS, 200 Treasure Harbor Dr., Islamorada, ☎ 305/852–2458 or 800/352–2628, FAX 305/852–5743) rents bareboat and crewed sailboats, from a 19-foot Cape Dory to a 41-foot custom-built ketch, plus a 43-foot Carver luxury cruising yacht. **Caloosa** (⊠ MM 83.5, OS, Whale Harbor Marina, ☎ 305/852–3200) is a 65-foot party fishing boat captained by Ray and David Jensen. **Gulf Lady** (⊠ MM 79.8, OS, Islamorada, ☎ 305/664–2628 or 305/664–2451), a 65-foot deluxe party boat, operates full day and night fishing trips from Bud 'n' Mary's Marina. **Robbie's Boat Rentals &**

**Charters** (⊠ MM 77.5, Islamorada, ☎ 305/664–9814) rents a 14-foot skiff with a 25-horsepower outboard (the smallest you can charter) for $25 an hour, $60 for four hours, and $80 for the day. Boats up to 27 feet are also available. At a second location (⊠ MM 84.5, OS, Holiday Isle, ☎ 305/664–8070), Robbie's operates deep-sea- and reef-fishing boats. **Captain Kevin** (⊠ MM 68.5, BS, Long Key, ☎ 305/664–0750) arranges for backcountry fishing guides and operates recreational watercraft from Lime Tree Bay Resort.

### DIVING AND SNORKELING

**San Pedro Underwater Archaeological Preserve** is an underwater park in 18 feet of water about 1 mile off the western tip of Indian Key (☞ Sights to See, *above*). The *San Pedro* was part of a Spanish treasure fleet wrecked by a hurricane in 1733. You can get there only by boat.

**Captain Corky's Diver's World** (⊠ MM 92.5, OS, Box 1663, Key Largo 33037, ☎ 305/451–3200 or 305/852–5176) offers reef and wreck-diving packages, exploring the *Benwood,* Coast Guard cutters *Bibb* and *Duane,* and French Molasses reefs. **Florida Keys Dive Center** (⊠ MM 90.5, OS, 90500 Overseas Hwy., Box 391, Tavernier 33070, ☎ 305/852–4599 or 800/433-8946) organizes dives from John Pennekamp Coral Reef State Park to Alligator Light. This center has two Coast Guard-approved dive boats and offers scuba training. **Lady Cyana Divers** (⊠ MM 85.9, BS, Box 1157, Islamorada 33036, ☎ 305/664–8717 or 800/221–8717), a PADI training center, operates 40-, 45- and 50-foot dive boats.

## Shopping

**Rain Barrel** (⊠ MM 86.7, BS, 86700 Overseas Hwy.), a 3-acre crafts village attended by free-running cats, represents 450 local and national artists and has eight resident artists. During the third weekend of March each year, the largest arts show of the Keys takes place here, when some 20,000 visitors view the work of 100 artists. A tearoom and bakery were recently added. Where salvage master Art McKee ran McKee's Treasure Museum in the 1950s and an enormous fabricated crustacean now stands, a dozen crafts and specialty shops plus the excellent little Made to Order eat-in and carryout restaurant operate as **Treasure Village** (⊠ MM 86.7, OS).

# THE MIDDLE AND LOWER KEYS

Here, the Keys become more rustic; fishing dominates the economy, and many residents are descendents of the earlier immigrants from the mainland South.

## The Middle Keys—Conch Key to Pigeon Key

The journey on U.S. 1 is most impressive at this stretch between Mile Marker 63 and 40, for the three longest bridges of the Keys are here. **⑧** Next to Duck Key, site of an upscale residential community, is **Grassy ⑨ Key,** the home of the Dolphin Research Center. **Vaca Key** contains the town of Marathon, the commercial hub of the Middle Keys. A National **⑩** Historic District reachable by the Old Seven Mile Bridge, **Pigeon Key** showcases a number of Keys artifacts.

## Sights to See

**Dolphin Research Center.** A 35-foot-long concrete sculpture of the dolphin Theresa and her offspring Nat stands outside this former home of Milton Santini, creator of the original *Flipper* movie, now home to 14 dolphins on Grassy Key. The dolphins here today frequently leave the fenced area that protects them from boaters and predators and return later. A half-day program called Dolph*Insight* teaches about dolphin biology and human–dolphin communications, and allows you to touch the dolphins out of the water. A 2½-hour instruction-education program aptly called Swim with Dolphins enables you to do just that for 20 minutes. ⊠ *MM 59, BS, Box 522875, Marathon Shores 33052, Grassy Key,* ☎ *305/289–1121.* 🖾 *$9.50, DolphInsight $75, swim with dolphins $90.* ☉ *Tues. noon–4, Wed.–Sun. 9–4; DolphInsight Wed. and weekends 9:15; walking tours Wed.–Sun. 10, 11, 12:30, 2, and 3:30. Children 5–12 must swim with accompanying, paying adult. Reserve for dolphin swim after 1st day of any month for next month (for example, Mar. 1 for Apr.).*

★ **Museums of Crane Point Hammock.** This group of museums—part of a 63-acre tract that includes the last known undisturbed thatch-palm hammock—is owned by the Florida Keys Land Trust, a private, nonprofit conservation group. In the **Museum of Natural History of the Florida Keys,** behind a stunning bronze-and-copper door crafted by Roy Butler of Plantation, Florida, are dioramas and displays on the Keys' geology, wildlife, and cultural history. Also here is the **Florida Keys Children's Museum.** Outside, on the 1-mile indigenous loop trail, you can visit the remnants of a Bahamian village, site of the restored **George Adderly House,** the oldest surviving example of Conch-style architecture outside Key West. From Nov.–Easter, weekly docent-led hammock tours may be available; bring good walking shoes and bug repellent. ⊠ *MM 50, BS, 5550 Overseas Hwy., Box 536, Marathon 33050, Vaca Key,* ☎ *305/743–9100.* 🖾 *$7.50 including tour.* ☉ *Mon.–Sat. 9–5, Sun. noon–5.*

**New Seven Mile Bridge.** Actually 6.79 miles long, this bridge is believed to be the world's longest segmental bridge, with 39 expansion joints separating its cement sections. It was built between 1980 and 1982 at a cost of $45 million. Each April, runners gather in Marathon for the annual Seven Mile Bridge Run.

★ **Pigeon Key.** This small patch of land was once the site of a railroad work camp, and later, of a bar and restaurant, a park, and government administration building. In 1993 the nonprofit Pigeon Key Foundation leased this National Historic District from Monroe County and started developing it as a center focusing on the encompassing culture of the Florida Keys. Its first project is the restoration of the old railroad work-camp buildings, the earliest of which date from 1908, and a museum recalling the history of the railroad and the Keys is taking shape, too. Among its first exhibits are two old Cuban fishing boats. To reach the island, you can either take the shuttle (which departs from the depot on Knight's Key at MM 47), or walk across a 2-mile stretch of the **Old Seven Mile Bridge** (no private cars are allowed). Listed on the National Register of Historic Places, the old bridge was an engineering marvel in its day, resting on a record 546 concrete piers that spanned the broad expanse of water separating the Middle and Lower Keys. ⊠ *Box 500130, Pigeon Key 33050,* ☎ *305/289–0025,* 🅵🅰🆇 *305/289–1065.* 🖾 *Shuttle $1.50 each way, Key admission and tour $2.* ☉ *Shuttle Tues.–Sun. 9–5.*

## Dining and Lodging

$$ ✕ **Kelsey's.**The walls in this restaurant at the Faro Blanco Marine Resort are hung with boat paddles inscribed by charter boat captains and other frequent diners. All entrées here are served with fresh-toasted baguettes prepared daily in the kitchen by a professional baker. You can bring your own cleaned and filleted catch for the chef to prepare. Dessert offerings may include banana pecan pie, white chocolate mousse, or macadamia pie and Key lime cheesecake. ✕ *MM 48.5, BS,*

1996 Overseas Hwy., ☎ 305/743–9018. AE, D, MC, V. Closed Mon. No lunch.

**$$** ✕ **WatersEdge.** A collection of historic photos on the walls depicts the railroad era, the development of Duck Key (which later became Hawk's Cay), and many of the notables who have visited this eatery at the Hawk's Cay Resort (☞ Lodging, below). You can dine indoors or under the dockside canopy. Dinners include soup and a 40-item salad bar. Specialties range from homemade garlic bread, Swiss onion soup, Florida stone crab claws (in season), and steaks to mud pie and coffee ice-cream pie. ✉ MM 61, OS, ☎ 305/743-3816. No credit cards. Closed Sun. and Mon. No lunch Sat.

**$** ✕ **Grassy Key Dairy Bar.** Tables, counters, and even white shirts in the kitchen are now found at this ever-improving little landmark that dates from 1959 and is marked by the Dairy Queen–style concrete ice-cream cones near the road. Locals and construction workers stop here for quick lunches. Owners-chefs George and Johnny Eigner are proud of their fresh-daily homemade bread, soups and chowders, and fresh seafood and fresh-cut beef. ✉ MM 58.5, OS, ☎ 305/743-3816. No credit cards. Closed Sun. and Mon. No lunch Sat.

**$** ✕ **Herbie's.** A local favorite for lunch and dinner since the 1940s, Herbie's has three small rooms, including a screened outdoor room, with two counters. Specialties include spicy conch chowder with chunks of tomato and crisp conch fritters with homemade horseradish sauce. ✉ MM 50.5, BS, 6350 Overseas Hwy., ☎ 305/743-6373. No credit cards. Closed Sun. and 1 month in fall (usually Sept.).

**$** ✕ **7 Mile Grill.** The walls of this open-air diner built in 1954 at the
★ Marathon end of Seven Mile Bridge are lined with beer cans, mounted fish, sponges, and signs describing individual menu items. The prompt, friendly service rivals the great food at breakfast, lunch, and dinner. Favorites include fresh-squeezed orange juice, a cauliflower and broccoli omelet, conch chowder, fresh fish sandwiches, and foot-long chili dogs. The daily special could be a Caesar salad with marinated chicken, popcorn shrimp, chicken almondine, grouper, or snapper. Don't pass up the authentic Key lime pie or, for a change, the peanut-butter pie, served near frozen in a chocolatey shell. ✉ MM 47, BS, 1240 Overseas Hwy., ☎ 305/743-4481. No credit cards. Closed Wed., Thurs., and at owner's discretion Aug.–Sept.

**$$$$** 🏨 **Hawk's Cay Resort.** Morris Lapidus, architect of the Fontainebleau Hilton hotel in Miami Beach, designed this rambling West Indies–style resort, which opened in 1959 as the Indies Inn and Marina. Over the years it has entertained a steady stream of film stars and politicians (including Harry Truman, Dwight Eisenhower, and Lyndon Johnson), who come to relax and be pampered by a friendly, low-key staff. Decor in guest rooms and public areas features wicker rattan, a sea-green-and-salmon color scheme, and original contemporary artwork. Many rooms face the water. Two-bedroom marina villas, 22 in all, are available. Guests can use the Sombrero Golf Course in nearby Marathon. Dive trips are offered. Also on site is a Chicago Zoological Society dolphin research facility. ✉ MM 61, OS, 33050, ☎ 305/743-7000 or 800/432-2242, FAX 305/743-5215. 160 rooms, 16 suites. 4 restaurants, 2 lounges, pool, 8 tennis courts, fitness center, boating, fishing, video games, summer children's program. AE, D, DC, MC, V.

**$$$–$$$$** 🏨 **Conch Key Cottages.** It's getting kind of trendy, this happy hideout on its own little island slightly larger than a tot's sandbox and bridged by a pebbly causeway. The look is castaway, hidden; the mood live-and-let-live. Allamanda, bougainvillea, and hibiscus jiggle colorfully, and the beach curves around a little mangrove-edged cove. Lattice-trimmed cottages with kitchens rise up on pilings, old-fashioned in Dade County pine; try to get one of the three that directly face the beach. Owners Wayne Byrnes and Ron Wilson have lately replaced pine floors with cool tile, and pine doors with glass, unfortunately somewhat mucking up the authentic look. Furnishings are reed, rattan, and wicker, with hammocks out front. People are meant to live comfortably here. ⊠ *MM 62.3, OS, R.R. 1, Box 424, 33050,* ☎ *305/289–1377 or 800/330–1577,* FAX *305/743–8207. 12 cottages, including 2 with 2 bedrooms. Pool, beach. D, MC, V.*

**$$–$$$**   🏨 **Lime Tree Bay Resort Motel.** Attractive wicker- and rattan-furnished
★   guest rooms, tropical art, and cottages with kitchens are part of the deal at this long-popular 2½-acre hideaway on Long Key. A boat-rental hut, little sandy beach, nice landscaping, beautiful pool deck, hammocks, a gazebo, and covered walkway complete the look. The best units are the cottages out back (no bay views, unfortunately) and the four deluxe rooms upstairs, which have high cathedral ceilings and skylights. The upstairs Tree House is the best bet for two couples traveling together; it has a palm tree growing through its private deck and a divine canvas sling chair with a separately strung footrest. You can swim and snorkel in the shallow grass flats just offshore. ⊠ *MM 68.5, BS, Box 839, Layton 33001,* ☎ *305/664–4740 or 800/723–4519,* FAX *305/664–0750. 29 rooms. Restaurant, picnic area, pool, hot tub, tennis court, horseshoes, shuffleboard, beach, boating. AE, D, DC, MC, V.*

**$–$$**   🏨 **Bonefish Resort.** A caring, competent pair of nurses, Jackie and Paula,
★   know how to make guests comfortable at their little oceanfront motel resort, providing the hospitality of a B&B yet without being intrusive. All the rooms and efficiencies are different—some have futons, some tub-showers, some director's chairs with tropical covers, some daybeds, some fishnets strung on walls, and others original art sent by former guests—but all are clean and well maintained. If you sleep lightly, ask for one of the rooms set back from the highway. On the small waterfront, you have free use of canoes, a Windsurfer, pedal boat, rowboat, shore pavilion, and fishing poles; there's also a Jacuzzi under a thatch hut and a potbellied pig named Willie. It's a wonderfully tropical spot, utterly informal and perfect for slowing down. A two-night minimum stay is required Dec. 15–March 31. ⊠ *MM 58, OS, Grassy Key 33050,* ☎ *305/743–7107. 12 units. Hot tub, boating. AE, D, MC, V.*

**$–$$**   🏨 **Valhalla Beach Resort Motel.** Guests come back year after year to this unpretentious motel with the waterfront location of a posh resort. There's a sandy beach and plenty of peace and quiet. Bruce Schofield is the second-generation proprietor of this 1950s-era plain-Jane place. Clean and straightforward, with rattan and laminate furniture and refrigerators in the rooms, it's excellent for families because of the safe, shallow beaches. It's also far off the highway, so don't miss the sign. ⊠ *MM 56.5, OS, Crawl Key, Rte. 2, Box 115, 33050,* ☎ *305/289–0616. 4 rooms, 8 efficiencies. Beach, dock, canoes. No credit cards.*

**$**   🏨 **Sea Cove Motel.** "So un-Sea Cove," is how one of the owners of this cheapest-of-the-cheap, yet not uncharming, motel described the considerable improvements lately made here. Next to the motel rooms and efficiencies, which poke down a partially paved road are three houseboats at a plain but private dockside. One has multiple rooms on upper and lower decks, the other two are self-contained units. Rooms on the larger houseboat now have bathrooms with makeup lights, tile, and pretty floral papers, though the ceilings and floors are on the "to do" list. Low lighting over the beds gives the tiny rooms an intimate feel. Televisions and telephones have been added to all rooms and air-conditioning is now in all but one. Otherwise the motel has zero amenities. Expect savings. Pets are allowed for an extra $5 a day. ⊠

*MM 54, OS, 12685 Overseas Hwy., 33050, ☎ 305/289–0800 or
800/653–0800. 23 rooms (8 with shared baths), 4 efficiencies. Picnic
area, fishing. AE, D, MC, V.*

## Nightlife

Nightly, four-hour, offshore casino gambling cruises operate on the **Mr.
Lucky** (✉ Marathon Marina, MM 47.5, ☎ 305/289–9700), with day
cruises on weekends. There's also gourmet dinner service.

## Outdoor Activities and Sports

### BIKING

The Marathon area is popular with cyclists. Some of the best paths include those along Aviation Boulevard on the bay side of Marathon Airport, the four-lane section of the Overseas Highway through Marathon,
Sadowski Causeway to Key Colony Beach, Sombrero Beach Road
from the Overseas Highway to the Marathon public beach, and the
roads on Boot Key (✉ across a bridge from Vaca Key on 20th St., OS).
There's easy cycling at the south end of Marathon, where a 1-mile off-
road path connects to the 2 remaining miles of the Old Seven Mile Bridge
to Pigeon Key, where locals like to ride to watch the sunset.

**Equipment Locker Sport & Cycle** (✉ MM 53, BS, 11518 Overseas
Hwy., ☎ 305/289–1670) rents mountain bikes, and single-speed adult
and children's bikes.

### BOATING AND FISHING

**Marathon Lady** and **Marathon Lady III** (✉ MM 53, OS, Marathon, ☎
305/743–5580), a pair of 65-footers, provides half- and full-day fishing charters from the Vaca Cut Bridge, north of Marathon.

**Captain Pip's** (✉ MM 47.5, BS, ¼ mi east of Seven Mile Bridge,
Marathon, ☎ 305/743–4403) lets you rent your own 20-foot or larger
motor-equipped boat.

### DIVING AND SNORKELING

**Marathon Marine Sanctuary,** in Hawk Channel opposite MM 50, OS,
runs from Washerwoman Shoal on the west to navigation marker 48
on the east. The 2-square-mile underwater park contains a dozen patch
reefs ranging from the size of a house to about an acre. For more detailed dive information, contact the Marathon Chamber of Commerce
(☞ Contacts and Resources, *below*).

**Hall's Diving Center and Career Institute** (✉ MM 48.5, BS, 1994 Overseas Hwy., Marathon 33050, ☎ 305/743–5929 or 800/331–4255) offers trips to Looe Key, Sombrero Reef, Delta Shoal, Content Key,
Coffins Patch, and the 110-foot wreck *Thunderbolt*.

### GOLF

**Key Colony Beach Par 3** (MM 53.5, OS, 8th St., Key Colony Beach,
☎ 305/289–1533), a nine-hole course near Marathon, charges $6.50
for nine holes, $4.50 for each additional nine and $2 per person for
club rental.

## Shopping

In season, supermarkets and roadside stands sell tropical fruits. Look
for Key limes (Apr.–Jan.), guavas (Aug.–Oct.) litchi nuts (June), and
sapodillas (Feb.–Mar.).

In the Gulfside Village, **Food For Thought** (MM 51, BS, 5800 Overseas
Hwy., ☎ 305/743–3297) is a bookstore and natural-foods store with
a good selection of Florida titles—including *The Monroe County Environmental Story,* "must" reading for anyone who wants the big picture on the Keys ($35—not cheap, but worth it).

**T.L.C. Nursery & Botanical Garden** (7455 Overseas Hwy., ☎ 305/743–6428) lets you browse through a fairyland of brilliant plantings, indoors and out, all for sale, The displays make up one of the Keys' best attractions.

## The Lower Keys—Bahia Honda Key to Stock Island

From Mile Marker 37 to 5, U.S. 1 passes by a number of limestone keys of varying size. **Bahia Honda Key** contains a lovely park with a fine beach for swimming. **Big Pine Key** is best known for its concentration of Key deer. Other islets between here and Key West include: Big Torch, Middle Torch, and Little Torch keys (named for the torchwood tree, which settlers used for kindling because it burns easily even when green); Ramrod Key, a base for divers headed to the Looe Key National Marine Sanctuary; the Saddlebunch Keys, Big Coppitt Key, and finally, Stock Island—the gateway to Key West.

### Sights to See

★ **Bahia Honda State Park.** The park's Silver Palm Trail leads through a dense tropical forest where you can see rare West Indian plants, including the Geiger tree, sea lavender, Key spider lily, bay cedar, thatch and silver palms, and several species found nowhere else in the Florida Keys: the West Indies yellow satinwood, Catesbaea, Jamaica morning glory, and wild dilly. The park also contains a beath that's sandy most of the time. Lateral drift builds up in summer; storms whisk away much of the sand in winter. The park includes a campground, cabins, snack bar, marina, and dive shop offering offshore-reef snorkel trips, scuba trips, and boat rentals. ⊠ *MM 37, OS, Box 782, Bahia Honda Key, 33043,* ☎ *305/872–2353. ☞ $3.25 per vehicle with up to 8 people plus 50¢ per person county surcharge. ☉ Daily 8–sunset.*

**National Key Deer Refuge.** This sanctuary was established in 1954 to protect the dwindling population of Key deer. A subspecies of the Virginia white-tailed deer, the Key deer once ranged throughout the Lower and Middle keys, but hunting and habitat destruction reduced the population to fewer than 50 in 1947. Due to the efforts of the refuge, the deer herd grew to about 600 by the early 1970s. But the government owns only about a third of Big Pine Key, and as the human population on the remaining land grew during the 1980s, the deer herd declined again until today only 250 to 300 remain. The best place to see Key deer in the refuge is along Key Deer Boulevard (Rte. 940), which leads onto No Name Key, a sparsely populated island just east of Big Pine Key. You can get out of your car to walk around, but close all doors and windows to keep raccoons from wandering in. Deer may turn up along the road at any time of day—especially in early morning and late afternoon. Admire their beauty, but don't try to feed them—it's against the law. ⊠ *Key Deer Refuge Headquarters, MM 30, Big Pine Key,* ☎ *305/872–2239.*

### Dining and Lodging

$ ✕ **Island Reef Restaurant.** This Keys-perfect cottage-style foodery was built in the Flagler era and has six counter seats, 15 tables covered with bright beneath-the-sea-blue prints, and outdoor tables—outdoor rest rooms, too. Nightly dinner specials, which start at $9 and don't run much higher, all come with soup or salad; potato; vegetable; rolls and scones; homemade pie, pudding, or ice cream; and tea or coffee. Entrées include seafood, steaks, veal, frogs' legs, and vegetarian stir-fry. ⊠ *MM 31.25, BS, Big Pine Key* ☎ *305/872–2170. MC, V. Closed Sun.*

$$$$ ✕▦ **Little Palm Island.** The lobby sits blandly beside the Overseas High-
★ way on Little Torch Key, but the resort itself—sybaritic and secluded—

# In case you want to see the world.

At American Express, we're here to make your journey a smooth one. So we have over 1,700 travel service locations in over 120 countries ready to help. What else would you expect from the world's largest travel agency?

## do more™

http://www.americanexpress.com/travel

**Travel**

# In case you want to be welcomed there.

We're here to see that you're always welcomed at establishments everywhere. That's why millions of people carry the American Express® Card – for peace of mind, confidence, and security, around the world or just around the corner.

do more®

Cards

# In case you're running low.

We're here to help with more than 118,000 Express Cash locations around the world. In order to enroll, just call American Express before you start your vacation.

*do more*

**Express Cash**

# And just in case.

We're here with American Express® Travelers Cheques and Cheques *for Two*® They're the safest way to carry money on your vacation and the surest way to get a refund, practically anywhere, anytime.
Another way we help you...

do more ®

**Travelers Cheques**

dazzles 3 miles off by launch on a palm-fringed island at the western edge of the Newfound Harbor Keys. There guests lodge in 14 thatch-roof villas, each close by the water, each up on stilts, and each with two suites. Even guests to the manor born find the spaces well detailed—Mexican-tile bath and dressing areas, Jacuzzis, beds draped with mosquito netting, Mexican and Guatemalan wicker and rattan furniture, wet bars, minibars, and safes. A suite on the third floor of a stationary houseboat was added to the mix not long ago. The only phone sits in a dolled-up former outhouse, and there is no TV. Instead, a fountain-fed pool beguiles, and the crescent of beach beckons you to some of the best snorkeling, diving, and fishing waters in the continental United States. The island is in the middle of Coupon Bight State Aquatic Preserve and is the closest land to the Looe Key National Marine Sanctuary. The food rates many stars. Yachtfolk from up and down the Keys know their way into the Little Palm Marina and sooner or later at dinner time tie up. ⊠ MM 28.5, OS, 28500 Overseas Hwy., 33042, ☎ 305/872–2524 or 800/343–8567, FAX 305/872–4843. 30 suites. Restaurant, bar, pool, sauna, exercise room, fishing, boating. AE, D, DC, MC, V.

$$–$$$ ★ 🏠 **The Barnacle.** This bed-and-breakfast is one of three under separate ownership within a mile of each other, all built on stilts. Tim and Jane Marquis, owners of a dive shop in Louisiana, bought The Barnacle and moved down to run it in 1995. There are two rooms in the main house, both on the second floor, and two in the Cottage, one upstairs and one down but each with its own kitchen. Guest rooms are large, and those in the main house open to an atrium, where a hot tub sits in a beautiful garden screened so it overlooks the sea and sky. Furnishings, collected from around the world, are colorful and whimsical. The stained-glass windows are very impressive. ⊠ Long Beach Dr., east off Overseas Hwy. south of MM 33, Rte. 1, Box 780 A, 33043, ☎ 305/872–3298. 4 rooms. Hot tub, beach, dock, boating, bicycles. MC, V.

$$–$$$ ★ 🏠 **Casa Grande.** This B&B next to the Barnacle is run by Jon and Kathleen Threlkeld. Since the sea deepens very gradually here, the shore is often covered with seaweed. Casa Grande is markedly Mediterranean, with a massive Spanish door and mainly Mexican furnishings. The spacious guest rooms have color TVs, small refrigerators, air-conditioning, carpeting, and high open-beam ceilings with paddle fans. Here, too, there is a screened, second-story atrium facing the sea. Guests cozy up to the sitting room fireplace and get to know one another on cool nights. ⊠ Long Beach Dr., east of Overseas Hwy., south of MM 33, Box 378, 33043, ☎ 305/872–2878. 3 rooms. Beach, hot tub, dock, boating, bicycles. No credit cards.

$$–$$$ 🏠 **Deer Run.** The most casual of the three B&Bs in the area, this lodging is populated by lots of animals: cats, caged birds, and a herd of deer, which forages along the beach and lush seafront gardens. The inn is run by burned-out real-estate operator and 35-year Big Pine resident Sue Abbott, who, like her fellow innkeepers, is caring and informed, well settled and generously hospitable. Two downstairs units (one with a sea view) occupy part of a onetime garage area. There is one unit upstairs, which has a view of the sea through the trees and mulched pathways. Guests have use of a living room and screened porch. Like its neighbors, this offers some of the best value for the money in the Keys. ⊠ Long Beach Dr., east of Overseas Hwy., south of MM 33, Box 431, 33043, ☎ 305/872–2015. 3 rooms. Beach. No credit cards.

## Guided Tours

### BOAT TOURS

**Gale Force Eco-tours** (⊠ Rte. 2, Box 669-F, Summerland Key 33042, ☎ 305/745–2868) runs tours into the Great White Heron National Wildlife refuge aboard *The Gale Force,* a 24-foot skiff with a viewing tower. Departing from T.J.'s Sugarshack Marina (⊠ MM 17, BS, next to Sugar Loaf Lodge), four-hour trips cost $45 per person for two to six people; seven-hour tours for two people cost $175, $50 each additional person. All tours include free snorkel gear, instruction, snacks, beverages, and sometimes walking tours and beach time.

### KAYAK TOURS

With the easily identifiable Parmer's Place Bed and Breakfast in Little Torch Key as its base, **Reflections Kayak Nature Tours** (⊠ MM 28.5, OS/BS, Box 430861, Big Pine Key 33043, ☎ 305/872–2896) operates daily trips into the Great White Heron National Wildlife Refuge and Everglades National Park from the Upper and Lower Keys. Tours last about three hours, and $45 per person covers granola bars, fresh fruit, raisins, spring water, a bird-identification sheet, and the use of water-proof binoculars; snorkling gear (if you want it) is extra. Six-hour tours ($80) also include lunch.

## Outdoor Activities and Sports

### BIKING

Opportunities in the Lower Keys are mostly for off-road bikes. On Big Pine Key, a good 10 miles of paved and unpaved roads run from MM 30.3, BS, along Wilder Road across the bridge to No Name Key and along Key Deer Boulevard into the National Key Deer Refuge. You might see some Key deer. Stay off the trails that lead into wetlands, where fat tires can do damage. A mile of Big Coppitt Key has a separated path along the highway. Farther south, on Sugarloaf Key, are another 10 miles of roads with little traffic; Routes 939 and 939A leave the Overseas Highway on the ocean side at MM 20 (Mangrove Mama's) and loop back at MM 17 (Sugar Loaf Lodge). The nearest bike rental shop is Equipment Locker Sport & Cycle near Marathon (☞ Middle Keys, Biking, *above*).

### BOATING AND FISHING

*Scandia-Tomi* (⊠ MM 25, BS, Summerland Chevron Station, Summerland Key, ☎ 305/745–8633 or 800/257–0978), under Capt. Bill Hjorth, takes up to six passengers on varied fishing trips; he also takes divers and snorkelers to Looe Key.

**Strike Zone Charters** (⊠ MM 29.5, BS, Big Pine Key, ☎ 305/872–9863 or 800/654–9560), run by Lower Keys native Capt. Larry Threlkeld, offers fishing and sightseeing excursions into the backcountry as well as Looe Key and offshore snorkeling, diving, and deep-sea-fishing outings.

### DIVING AND SNORKELING

**Great White Heron National Wildlife Refuge** (⊠ Box 430510, Big Pine Key 33043-0510, ☎ 305/872–2239) and the adjacent **National Key Deer Refuge** contain reefs where the Keys' northern margin drops off into the Gulf; these parks attract fewer divers than the better-known Atlantic reefs. A favorite Gulf spot for local divers is the **Content Key** (⊠ MM 30), 5 miles off Big Pine Key. **Looe Key National Marine Sanctuary** (⊠ 216 Ann St., Key West 33040, ☎ 305/292–0311) contains a reef 5 miles off Ramrod Key (MM 27.5), perhaps the most beautiful and diverse coral community in the entire region. It has large stands of elkhorn coral on its eastern margin, immense purple sea fans, and abundant populations of sponges and sea urchins. On its seaward side, it has an almost-vertical drop-off to a depth of 50–90 feet. The reef is named for H.M.S. *Looe*, a British warship wrecked there in 1744.

NEED A
BREAK?
Enjoy outstanding Keys cooking at **Mangrove Mama's** (MM 20, BS, Sugarloaf Key, ☎ 305/745–3030), a lattice-front Conch house, a remnant from around 1919, when trains outnumbered cars in the Keys. Fresh fish, seafood, some decent beers, and rave-worthy Key lime pie are served. Concrete floors, Keys art, a Tennessee oak bar, and lights twinkling at night in the banana trees all contribute to the romantic ambience here.

**Bahia Honda Dive Shop** (✉ MM 37, OS, Bahia Honda Key 33043, ☎ 305/872–1127), the concessioner at Bahia Honda State Park, operates snorkel trips daily at 10 and 2. Included in the cost are instruction and 90 to 120 minutes in the water. For nonsnorkelers, 90-minute sunset eco tours are offered Wednesday, Friday, and Saturday for $12.50 per person.

**Looe Key Dive Center** (✉ MM 27.5, OS, Box 509, Ramrod Key 33042, ☎ 305/872–2215 or 800/942–5397), the dive shop closest to Looe Key National Marine Sanctuary, offers overnight dive packages.

# KEY WEST

In April 1982 the U.S. Border Patrol threw a roadblock across the Overseas Highway just south of Florida City to catch drug runners and illegal aliens. Traffic backed up for miles as Border Patrol agents searched vehicles and demanded that the occupants prove U.S. citizenship. City officials in Key West, outraged at being treated like foreigners by the federal government, staged a mock secession and formed their own "nation," the so-called Conch Republic. They hoisted a flag and distributed mock border passes, visas, and Conch currency. The embarrassed Border Patrol dismantled its roadblock, and now an annual festival recalls the secessionists' victory.

The episode exemplifies Key West's odd station in Florida affairs. Situated 150 miles from Miami and just 90 miles from Havana, this tropical island city has always maintained its strong sense of detachment, even after it was connected to the rest of the United States—by the railroad in 1912 and by the Overseas Highway in 1938.

The U.S. government acquired Key West from Spain in 1821 along with the rest of Florida. The Spanish had named the island Cayo Hueso (Bone Key) after the Native American skeletons they found on its shores. In 1823 Uncle Sam sent Commodore David S. Porter to the Keys to chase pirates away.

For three decades, the primary industry in Key West was "wrecking"—rescuing people and salvaging cargo from ships that foundered on the nearby reefs. According to some reports, when pickings were lean, the wreckers hung out lights to lure ships aground. Their business declined after 1849, when the federal government began building lighthouses.

In 1845 the Army started construction of Fort Taylor, which held Key West for the Union during the Civil War. After the war, an influx of Cuban dissidents unhappy with Spain's rule brought the cigar industry to Key West. Fishing, shrimping, and sponge gathering became important industries, and a pineapple-canning factory opened. Major military installations were established during the Spanish-American War and World War I. Through much of the 19th century and into the second decade of the 20th, Key West was Florida's wealthiest city in per-capita terms.

In 1929 the local economy began to unravel. Modern ships no longer needed to provision in Key West, cigar making moved to Tampa, Hawaii dominated the pineapple industry, and the sponges succumbed to a blight. Then the Depression hit, and the military moved out. By 1934 half the population was on relief. The city defaulted on its bond payments, and the Federal Emergency Relief Administration took over the city and county governments.

Federal officials began promoting Key West as a tourist destination. They attracted 40,000 visitors during the 1934–35 winter season. Then the 1935 Labor Day hurricane struck the Middle Keys, sparing Key West but wiping out the railroad and the tourist trade. For three years, until the Overseas Highway opened, the only way in and out of town was by boat.

Ever since, Key West's fortunes have waxed and waned with the vagaries of world affairs. An important naval center during World War II and the Korean conflict, the island remains a strategic listening post on the doorstep of Fidel Castro's Cuba. It was during the '60s that the fringes of society began moving here and in the mid '70s that gay guest houses began opening in rapid succession. Whatever tensions between gays and straights existed during these years, nearly none is apparent today.

Key West reflects a diverse and refreshingly harmonious population: native "Conchs" (white Key Westers, many of whom trace their ancestry to the Bahamas), freshwater Conchs (longtime residents who migrated from somewhere else years ago), gays (who now make up at least 20% of Key West's citizenry), Bahamians, Hispanics (primarily Cubans), recent refugees from Miami and Fort Lauderdale, transient Navy and Air Force personnel, students waiting tables, and a miscellaneous assortment of vagabonds, drifters, and dropouts in search of refuge at the end of the road.

As a tourist destination, Key West has a lot to sell—superb frost-free weather with an average temperature of 79°F, quaint 19th-century architecture, and a laid-back lifestyle. Promoters have fostered fine restaurants, galleries, and shops, and new museums to interpret the city's intriguing past. There's also a growing calendar of artistic and cultural events and a lengthening list of annual festivals—including the Conch Republic celebration in April, Hemingway Days in July, and a Halloween Fantasy Fest that rivals the New Orleans Mardi Gras (big with both gays and straights alike). Few cities of its size—a mere 2 miles by 4 miles—offer the joie de vivre of this one.

Yet as elsewhere when preservation has successfully revived once tired towns, next have come those unmindful of style, eager for a buck. Duval Street is becoming show biz—an open-air mall of T-shirt shops and tour shills. Mass marketers directing the town's tourism have attracted cruise ships, which dwarf the town's skyline and flood Duval Street with day-trippers who gawk at the earringed hippies with dogs in their bike baskets and the otherwise oddball lot of locals. You can still find fun, but the best advice is to come sooner rather than later.

## Sights to See

*Numbers in the margin correspond to points of interest on the Key West map.*

**16** **Audubon House and Gardens.** This three-story dwelling built in the mid-1840s commemorates ornithologist John James Audubon's 1832 visit to Key West. On display are several rooms of period antiques, a children's room, and a large collection of Audubon engravings. Admission includes an audiotape for the self-guided tour of the first floor; then proceed on your own through the upper stories. The self-guided tour continues through the tropical gardens, complemented by an informational booklet and signs that identify the rare indigenous plants and trees you'll see. ⊠ *205 Whitehead St.,* ☎ *305/294–2116.* ⊡ *$7.50.* ⊙ *Daily 9:30–5.*

| | |
|---|---|
| NEED A BREAK? | Pause for a libation at the open-air **Green Parrot Bar** (⊠ 601 Whitehead St. at Southard St., ☎ 305/294–6133). Built in 1890, the bar is said to be Key West's oldest, a sometimes-rowdy saloon where locals outnumber the tourists, especially on weekends when bands play. |

★ **27** **City Cemetery.** Clustered near a flagpole resembling a ship's mast are the graves of 22 sailors killed in the sinking of the battleship U.S.S. *Maine.* Volunteers from the Historic Florida Keys Foundation lead three guided tours a week from the sexton's office. Brochures are available at the sexton's office. ⊠ *Margaret and Angela St.,* ☎ *305/292–6718.* ⊡ *Free, tour donation $5.* ⊙ *Sunrise–6 PM; 90-min. tours Tues., Wed., and Thurs 9:30.*

**18** **Curry Mansion.** This 22-room home built in 1899 for Milton Curry, the son of Florida's first millionaire, is an adaptation of a Parisian town house. It has Key West's only widow's walk open to the public. Owners Edith and Al Amsterdam have restored and redecorated most of the house and turned it into a winning B&B. Take an unhurried self-guided tour with its brochure, which includes floor plans and is full of details about the history and contents of the house. ⊠ *511 Caroline St.,* ☎ *305/294–5349.* ⊡ *$5.* ⊙ *Daily 10–5.*

**21** **Donkey Milk House.** This classic Key West revival house was built around 1866 by prominent businessman and U.S. marshal Peter "Dynamite" Williams, a hero of the great fire of 1886. Antiques and artifacts fill its two balconied floors. The house, with a veranda off every room, won a 1992 restoration award. ⊠ *613 Eaton St.,* ☎ *305/296–1866.* ⊡ *$5.* ⊙ *Daily 10–5.*

**20** **Duval Street Wreckers Museum.** Built in 1829 and alleged to be the oldest house in South Florida, the museum was originally the home of Francis Watlington, a sea captain and wrecker. He was also a Florida state senator but resigned to serve in the Confederate Navy during the Civil War. Six of the home's eight rooms are now open, furnished with 18th- and 19th-century antiques and providing information and exhibits on the wrecking industry of the 1800s. In an upstairs bedroom is an eight-room dollhouse of Conch design, outfitted with tiny early 19th-century furniture. ⊠ *322 Duval St.,* ☎ *305/294–9502.* ⊡ *$4 adults.* ⊙ *Daily 10–4.*

★ **34** **East Martello Tower.** Just past the entrance to Key West International Airport stands one of two Civil War forts of similar design overlooking the Atlantic Ocean. Housed here are relics of the battleship U.S.S. *Maine,* which was blown up in Havana Harbor in 1898. In addition, the Key West Art and Historical Society operates a museum in East Martello's vaulted casemates. The collection includes Stanley Papio's "junk art" sculptures, Cuban primitive artist Mario Sanchez's chiseled and painted wood carvings of historic Key West street scenes, memorabilia from movies shot on location in the Keys, a Cuban refugee raft, and books by many of the 60-some famous writers (including seven

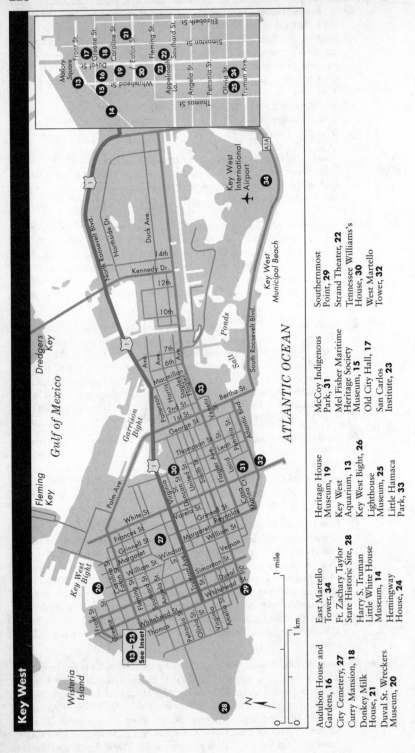

**Key West**

226

Audubon House and Gardens, **16**
City Cemetery, **27**
Curry Mansion, **18**
Duval St. Wreckers Museum, **20**
East Martello Tower, **34**
Ft. Zachary Taylor State Historic Site, **28**
Harry S. Truman Little White House Museum, **14**
Hemingway House, **24**
Heritage House Museum, **19**
Key West Aquarium, **13**
Key West Bight, **26**
Lighthouse Museum, **25**
Little Hamaca Park, **33**
McCoy Indigenous Park, **31**
Mel Fisher Maritime Heritage Society Museum, **15**
Old City Hall, **17**
San Carlos Institute, **23**
Southernmost Point, **29**
Strand Theater, **22**
Tennessee Williams's House, **30**
West Martello Tower, **32**

Donkey Milk House, **21**

Pulitzer Prize winners) who have lived in Key West. Historical exhibits present a chronological history of the Florida Keys. A circular 48-step staircase in the central tower leads to a platform overlooking the airport and surrounding waters. ⊠ *3501 S. Roosevelt Blvd.*, ☎ *305/296–6206 or 305/296–3913.* 🎟 *$5.* ⊙ *Daily 9:30–5, last admission 4 PM.*

**㉘ Ft. Zachary Taylor State Historic Site.** Built between 1845 and 1866, this fort served as a base for the Union blockade of Confederate shipping during the Civil War. More than 1,500 Confederate vessels captured while trying to run the blockade were brought to Key West's harbor and detained under the fort's guns. What you will see at Ft. Taylor today is a fort within a fort (and a small museum inside of that); a new moat suggests how the fort originally looked when it was surrounded by water. Because of an artificial reef, snorkeling is excellent here, except when the wind blows south–southwest and muddies the water. ⊠ *Southard St.*, ☎ *305/292–6713.* 🎟 *$3.25 per vehicle, 50¢ per person up to 8 people, $1.50 per pedestrian or bicyclist.* ⊙ *Park daily 8–sunset, fort 9–5, free 50-min tour daily noon and 2.*

**⑭ Harry S. Truman Little White House Museum.** The president's former vacation home contains Truman family memorabilia on display. The museum is located on the grounds of **Truman Annex**, a 103-acre former military parade grounds and barracks. During World War II, Truman Annex housed some 18,000 military and civilian employees. Pritam Singh, a Key West hippie-turned-millionaire has been developing this site, successfully transforming it into a suburban community of pastel, picket, and lattice charm—a mix of affordable condominiums and grassy-yard family homes surrounded by colorful bougainvillea and allamanda vines. Recent additions have included three-story town houses in the old brick machine shop. The whole community, set behind high black wrought-iron gates, is designed in the Victorian style that knits Old Town together. Pedestrians and cyclists are welcome on the grounds daily between 8 AM and sunset. ⊠ *111 Front St.*, ☎ *305/294–9911.* 🎟 *$7.50.* ⊙ *Daily 9–5.*

**★ ㉔ Hemingway House.** Hemingway bought this house in 1931 and wrote about 70% of his life's work here, including *For Whom the Bell Tolls* and *The Old Man and the Sea*. It is now a museum dedicated to the novelist's life and work. Built in 1851, this two-story Spanish colonial dwelling was the first house in Key West to have running water and a fireplace. Three months after Hemingway died in 1961, local jeweler Bernice Dickson bought the house and its contents from Hemingway's estate and two years later opened it as a museum. Of special interest are the huge bed with a headboard made from a 17th-century Spanish monastery gate, a ceramic cat by Pablo Picasso (a gift to Hemingway from the artist), the hand-blown Venetian glass chandelier in the dining room, and the swimming pool. The museum staff gives guided tours rich with anecdotes about Hemingway and his family and feeds the more than 50 feline habitants, descendants of Hemingway's own 50 cats. Tours begin every 10 minutes and take 25–30 minutes; then you're free to explore on your own. ⊠ *907 Whitehead St.*, ☎ *305/294–1575.* 🎟 *$6.50.* ⊙ *Daily 9–5.*

**⑲ Heritage House Museum.** The former residence of Jessie Porter Newton, grand dame of Old Town restoration, this Caribbean-colonial house dates from the 1830s, when it was home to ship's captain George Carey. It includes among its original furnishings antiques and seafaring artifacts from 19th-century China. Out back in beautiful gardens is a cottage that was often occupied by the late poet Robert Frost, and where recordings of his poetry can be heard. ⊠ *410 Caroline St.*, ☎ *305/296–3573.* 🎟 *$6.* ⊙ *Mon.–Sat. 10–5, Sun. 1–5.*

**❸ Key West Aquarium.** Hundreds of brightly colored tropical fish and other fascinating sea creatures from the waters around Key West make their home here. A touch tank enables you to handle starfish, sea cucumbers, horseshoe and hermit crabs, even horse and queen conchs—living totems of the Conch Republic. Built in 1934 by the Works Progress Administration as the world's first open-air aquarium, the building has been enclosed for all-weather viewing, though an outdoor area with a small Atlantic shores exhibit, including red mangroves, remains. ⊠ *1 Whitehead St.,* ☎ *305/296–2051.* 🎫 *$6.50.* ☉ *Daily 10–6; guided tours with shark feeding 11, 1, 3, and 4:30.*

NEED A
BREAK?

For $4.50 you can get six (a dozen for $7.50) of what may be the Keys' most authentic conch fritters at the strictly stand-up **Original Conch Fritters** (⊠ 1 Whitehead St., ☎ 305/294–4849), previously a Cuban snack stand from the '30s. Current owners flaunt their buttermilk and peanut oil recipe. Aficionados say it's the conch that counts.

**㉖ Key West Bight.** Also known as Harbor Walk, this site was formerly the Singleton Shrimp Fleet and Ice & Fish House. It is the last funky area of Old Key West. In the area are numerous charter boats, classic old yachts, and the Waterfront Market. Also nearby is the **Reef Relief Environmental Center** (⊠ 201 William St., ☎ 305/394–3100), a public facility that has videos, displays, and free information about the coral reef. Proceeds from the gift shop go right back into preservation efforts. The center is open weekdays (and most weekends in season) 9–5.

NEED A
BREAK?

**Schooner Wharf Bar** (⊠ 202 William St., ☎ 305/292–9520), a laid-back tiki hut called "the last little piece of Old Key West." It's where the town's waiters and waitresses hang out. You can hear live music weekends (and sometimes at other times) in the warehouse space next door.

**㉕ Lighthouse Museum.** Behind a spic-and-span white picket fence is this a 92-foot lighthouse built in 1847 and an adjacent 1887 clapboard house, where the keeper lived. You can climb 88 steps to the top of the lighthouse for a glimpse of the sizable Fresnel lens, installed at a cost of $1 million in the 1860s; a spectacular view of the island town awaits you as well. On display in the keeper's quarters are vintage photographs, ship models, nautical charts, and lighthouse artifacts from all along the Key reefs. ⊠ *938 Whitehead St.,* ☎ *305/294–0012.* 🎫 *$5.* ☉ *Daily 9:30–5, last admission 4:30.*

**㉝ Little Hamaca Park.** This area, a vestige of the old Key West and for years a wildlife sanctuary, was saved from condo development in 1991 and turned into a park. A boardwalk leads into the natural area. Nearby is Smathers Beach (☞ Beaches, *below*) and the salt ponds where early residents evaporated seawater to collect salt. (Although the sign says that the park is open 7 AM to dusk, the gates are not necessarily open. Cyclists lift their bikes over.) ⊠ *Government Rd. off Flagler Ave.*

**㉛ McCoy Indigenous Park.** The park contains more than 100 species of trees and shrubs; the largest collection of native tropical plants in the Florida Keys, including many fruit-bearing trees; migrating songbirds spring and fall; and many species of colorful butterflies. ⊠ *Atlantic Blvd. and White St.,* ☎ *305/292–8157.* 🎫 *Free.* ☉ *Weekdays 7–4.*

**❶❺ Mel Fisher Maritime Heritage Society Museum.** Gold and silver bars, coins, jewelry, and other artifacts recovered in 1985 from the Spanish treasure ships *Nuestra Señora de Atocha* and *Santa Margarita* are displayed here. The two galleons foundered in a hurricane in 1622 near the Marquesas Keys, 40 miles west of Key West. In the museum you can lift a gold bar weighing 6.3 Troy pounds and see a 77.76-carat natural emerald crystal worth almost $250,000. ⊠ *200 Greene St.,* ☎ *305/294–2633.* ☜ *$6.* ☉ *Daily 9:30–5, last video showing 4:30.*

**🟢17 Old City Hall.** The City Commission still has its meetings in this 1891 edifice, designed by William Kerr, the architect responsible for the Custom House. It has a rectangular tower with four clock faces and a fire bell. The ground floor was used as a city market for many years. Inside Old City Hall is a permanent exhibition of old Key West photographs, including an 1845 daguerreotype, the oldest known photographic image of Key West. ⊠ *510 Greene St.*

**🟢23 San Carlos Institute.** This Cuban-American heritage center houses a museum and research library focusing on the history of Key West and of 19th- and 20th-century Cuban exiles. The San Carlos Institute was founded in 1871 by Cuban immigrants who wanted to preserve their language, customs, and heritage while organizing the struggle for Cuba's independence from Spain. Cuban patriot Jose Martí delivered many famous speeches from the balcony of the auditorium. Opera star Enrico Caruso sang in the 400-seat hall of the Opera House, which reportedly has the best acoustics of any concert hall in the South. The original building (built in 1871) burned in the Key West fire of 1886, in which two-thirds of the city was destroyed, and a second version succumbed to the hurricane of 1919. The current building was completed in 1924, but after Cuba and the United States broke off diplomatic relations in 1961, it deteriorated. It was saved from demolition when Miami attorney Rafael A. Peñalver, Jr. secured a $3 million state grant for its restoration. The building reopened Jan. 3, 1992, exactly 100 years after Martí founded the Cuban Revolutionary Party here. A self-guided tour takes close to an hour; on weekends you can top it off by watching the almost hour-long documentary *Nostalgia Cubano,* about Cuba in the 1930s to 1950s. ⊠ *516 Duval St.,* ☎ *305/294–3887.* ☜ *$3.* ☉ *Tues.–Fri. 11–5, Sat. 11–9, Sun. 11–6.*

**🟢29 Southernmost House.** Two houses jockey for the title of southernmost domicile: the cream-brick Queen Anne mansion at 1400 Duvall Street and the Spanish-style home at 400 South Street; the latter was built in the 1940s by Thelma Strabel, author of *Reap the Wild Wind,* a novel about the wreckers who salvaged ships that ran aground on the reef in Key West's early days. Neither is open to the public.

**🟢29 Southernmost Point.** A huge concrete marker wrongly proclaims this spot to be the southernmost point in the United States. Most tourists snapping pictures of each other in front of the marker are oblivious to Key West's real southernmost point, on a nearby Navy base off limits to civilians but visible through the fence to your right.

**☝ 🟢22 Strand Theater.** Pause to admire the colorful marquee and ornamental facade of this edifice, built in 1918 by Cuban craftsmen. After a period as a movie theater and a music hall, the Strand is now the Odditorium, one of a chain of Ripley's Believe It or Not museums, displaying weird and eccentric artifacts. ⊠ *527 Duval St.,* ☎ *305/293–9686.* ☜ *$8.95.* ☉ *Sun.–Thurs. 10–11, Fri. and Sat. 10–midnight.*

**🟢30 Tennessee Williams's House.** This modest two-story, red-shuttered Bahamian-style cottage behind a white picket fence was the playwright's home from 1949 until his death in 1983. After years of neglect, the house was purchased in 1992 and fixed up by a couple named Paradise. The house is not open to the public, nor is there any historical marker. ⊠ *1431 Duncan St.*

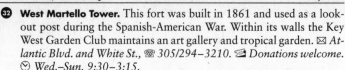 **West Martello Tower.** This fort was built in 1861 and used as a lookout post during the Spanish-American War. Within its walls the Key West Garden Club maintains an art gallery and tropical garden. ⊠ *Atlantic Blvd. and White St.,* ☎ *305/294–3210.* ✉ *Donations welcome.* ⊙ *Wed.–Sun. 9:30–3:15.*

## Beaches

**Atlantic Shores Resort** (⊠ 510 South St.) has a beach where women can go topless. **Dog Beach,** at Vernon and Waddell streets, is the only beach in Key West where dogs are allowed. **Fort Zachary Taylor State Historic Site** has several hundred yards of beach near the western end of Key West, and an adjoining picnic area has barbecue grills in a stand of Australian pines. Snorkeling is good except when winds blow from the south–southwest. This beach is relatively uncrowded and attracts more locals than tourists; nude bathing is not allowed. **Higgs Memorial Beach,** a Monroe County park near the end of White Street, is a popular sunbathing spot. A nearby grove of Australian pines provides shade, and the West Martello Tower provides shelter should a storm suddenly sweep in. **Simonton Street Beach,** at the north end of Simonton Street, faces the Gulf of Mexico and is a great place to watch boat traffic in the harbor. Parking, however, is difficult. **Smathers Beach** features almost 2 miles of sand beside South Roosevelt Boulevard. Trucks along the road will rent you rafts, Windsurfers, and other beach "toys." **Southernmost Beach,** on the Atlantic Ocean at the foot of Duval Street, is popular with tourists at nearby motels. It has limited parking and a nearby buffet-type restaurant, the **South Beach Seafood and Raw Bar.**

Almost all of the beaches are man-made, with sand imported from the U.S. mainland or the Bahamas. Public beaches are open daily 7 AM–11 PM, and admission is free. Tip: If you go out swimming, wear an old pair of tennis shoes to protect your feet against the coral strewn along the ocean floor.

## Dining and Lodging

$$$     ✕ **Cafe des Artistes.** The classic Key West dining at this intimate
  ★     restaurant is so good that guests in T-shirts and shorts don't even blanch at a $100 dinner check for two. It was once part of a hotel building constructed in 1935 by C.E. Alfeld, Al Capone's bookkeeper. The look is studiously unhip with its rough stucco walls, old-fashioned lights, and a knotty-pine ceiling. Haitian paintings and Keys scenes by local artists dress the walls. You dine in two indoor rooms or on a rooftop deck beneath a sapodilla tree. Chef Andrew Berman presents a French interpretation of tropical cuisine, using fresh local seafood and produce and light sauces. Specialties include Lobster Tango Mango (served with shrimp in a mango-saffron beurre blanc), half roast duckling with raspberry sauce, and yellowtail Atocha (sautéed with shrimp and scallops in lemon butter with basil). The wine list is strong on both French and California labels. ⊠ *1007 Simonton St.,* ☎ *305/294–7100. AE, MC, V. No lunch.*

$$$     ✕ **Cafe Marquesa.** This intimate restaurant with attentive service and
  ★     superb food is a felicitous counterpart of the excellent small Marquesa Hotel of which it's a part. It's a mellow place with bluesy ballads in the background and an open kitchen viewed through a trompe l'oeil pantry mural. Ten or so entrées are featured nightly, and all star regional ingredients—mango relish with grilled boneless quail and veal and pork *boudin* sausage, coconut milk in the Caribbean shrimp chowder with sweet potatoes, and perhaps a little tropical fruit chutney with the grilled tamarind-glazed pork tenderloin. Some low-fat options are

featured. Desserts are quite the contrary: a plum cardamom cake with fresh whipped cream, crème brûlée, and warm apple crisp with caramel sauce. There's also a fine selection of wines and a choice of microbrewery beers. ✉ *600 Fleming St.,* ☎ *305/292–1244. AE, DC, MC, V. No lunch.*

$$$  ✕ **Louie's Backyard.** Key West paintings and pastels adorn this ocean-front institution, where you dine outside under the mahoe tree. Chef de cuisine Doug Shook shares Louie's limelight with lunch chef Annette Foley and sous chef Rich DesRoches. The menu changes regularly but might include venison with port, wild mushrooms, and goat-cheese strudel; grouper with Thai peanut sauce; and stir-fried Asian vegetables. Top off the meal with Louie's lime tart or the irresistible chocolate terrine Grand Marnier with crème anglais. ✉ *700 Waddell Ave.,* ☎ *305/294–1061. AE, DC, MC, V.*

$$$  ✕ **Pier House Restaurant.** The brick in this elegant dining room hints at the North, but guests in T-shirts and shorts are emphatically in the tropics. Steamships from Havana once docked at the pier jutting into the Gulf of Mexico. Now guests watch pleasure boats glide by in the harbor, while at night the restaurant shines lights into the water, attracting schools of brightly colored parrot fish. The menu highlights American and Caribbean cuisine, featuring such dishes as Caesar salad with smoked shrimp; yellowtail snapper with avocado, papaya, and a Key lime butter sauce; rack of lamb with macadamia nut, coconut and mint breading; and chocolate decadence with raspberry coulis. Even simple food becomes art. ✉ *1 Duval St.,* ☎ *305/296–4600, Ext. 555. AE, D, DC, MC, V. No lunch.*

$$  ✕ **Dim Sum.** In a sophisticated little Oriental kiosk set in a garden square
★  off Duval Street, Far Eastern cookery notable for its variety if not always its subtlety is turned out splendidly. Ask for dishes light on the sauces, and you'll enjoy the food as well as the captivating atmosphere. The intimate 15-table restaurant has a high-peaked bamboo roof, bamboo dividers, batik covers under glass, and Oriental art in lacquer frames. The culinary mix includes vegetarian dishes (vegetable vindaloo or a three-curry platter served with leavened nan and crackly papadum breads, and chutney), noodles including pad Thai with roast pork, Chinese sausage or shrimp, and entrées such as the so-called Delights Exotica (sweet and sour grouper, cashew chicken, and roast duck stir-fried with lily flowers and black mushrooms). There's a good selection of beer and wine. ✉ *613½ Duval St.,* ☎ *305/294–6230. AE, D, DC, MC, V.*

$$  ✕ **Pepe's Cafe and Steak House.** Judges, police officers, carpenters, and anglers rub elbows every morning in their habitual breakfast seats, at tables or dark pine booths under a jumbo paddle fan. Face the street or dine outdoors under a huge rubber tree if you're put off by the naked-lady art on the back wall. Pepe's was established downtown in 1909 (which makes it the oldest eating house in the Keys) and moved to the current site in 1962. The specials change nightly: barbecued chicken, pork tenderloin, ribs, steak, at least one fresh fish item, potato salad, red or black beans, and corn bread on Sunday; meat loaf on Monday; seafood Tuesday and Wednesday; a full traditional Thanksgiving dinner every Thursday; filet mignon on Friday; and prime rib on Saturday. ✉ *806 Caroline St.,* ☎ *305/294–7192. D, MC, V.*

$–$$  ✕ **Mangia Mangia.** Fresh homemade pasta comes alfredo, marinara,
★  meaty, or with pesto, either in the twinkly brick garden with its specimen palms or in the nicely dressed-up old-house dining room. One of the best restaurants in Key West—and one of its best values—Mangia Mangia is run by Elliot and Naomi Baron, ex–Chicago restaurateurs who found Key West's warmth and laid-back style irresistible. Everything that comes out of the open kitchen is outstanding, especially the pasta, made-on-the-premises Key lime pie, and Mississippi mud pie.

The wine list with over 350 selections, the largest in Monroe County, contains a good selection under $20. ✉ *900 Southard St.,* ☎ *305/294–2469. MC, V. No lunch.*

$    ✕ **Blue Heaven.** The inspired remake of an old blue-on-blue clapboard,
★    Greek revival house with peach and yellow trim was, not too long ago, a bordello where Ernest Hemingway refereed boxing matches and customers watched cockfights. There's still a rooster graveyard out back, as well as a water tower hauled here from Little Torch Key in the 1920s. Upstairs is an art gallery (check out the zebra-stripe bikes), and downstairs are affordable fresh eats, both in the old house and in the big leafy yard. There are five nightly specials, and a good mix of natural foods (carrot and curry soup, Caribbean tofu stir-fry) and West Indian favorites (pork tenderloin pan-seared with sweet potato, Jamaican jerk chicken). Top it off with Banana Heaven (banana bread, bananas flamed with spiced rum, and homemade vanilla ice cream). Three meals are served six days a week; on Sunday, there's a to-die-for Sunday brunch accompanied by hammered dulcimer music. Expect a line; everybody knows how good this is. ✉ *729 Thomas St.,* ☎ *305/296–8666. D, MC, V.* ☼ *Schedule may change in summer.*

$    ✕ **El Siboney.** This sprawling, three-room, family-style restaurant serves traditional Cuban food, including a well-seasoned black-bean soup. Specials include beef stew Monday, pepper steak Tuesday, chicken fricassee Wednesday, chicken and rice Friday, and oxtail stew on Saturday. Always available are roast pork, cassava, paella, and *palomilla* steak. Popular with locals, sí, but enough tourists pass through that you'll fit right in even if you have to ask what a "Siboney" is. (Answer: A Cuban Indian tribe.) ✉ *900 Catherine St.,* ☎ *305/296–4184. No credit cards. Closed 2 wks in June.*

$    ✕ **Half Shell Raw Bar.** "Eat It Raw" is the motto, and even off-season the oyster bar keeps shucking. You eat at shellacked picnic tables in a shed, with ship models, life buoys, a mounted dolphin, and old license plates overhead and a view of the deep-sea fishing fleet outside. Classic signs offer homage to Keys' passions. Reads one: "Fishing is not a matter of life and death. It's more important than that." Specials, chalked on the blackboard, may include broiled dolphin sandwich or linguine seafood marinara. Whatever it is, it's fresh. ✉ *Land's End Marina,* ☎ *305/294–7496. D, MC, V.*

$    ✕ **Sunset Pier Bar.** When the crowds get too thick on the Mallory Dock at sunset, you can thin your way out 200 feet offshore behind the Ocean Key House. A limited menu offers crispy conch fritters, potato salad, shrimp, and jumbo Hebrew National hot dogs. Live island music is featured nightly. If you prefer your sunsets with a dash of serenity, better look elsewhere. ✉ *0 Duval St.,* ☎ *305/296–7701. AE, D, DC, MC, V.*

$$$$    ▦ **Banyan Resort.** Guests sitting on their porches reading the morning paper over coffee exude a wonderful feeling of proprietorship at this tropical-Victorian-style time-share resort across the street from the Truman Annex. The five houses that make up this jungle-landscaped compound include a former cigar factory and bottling works, both on the National Register of Historic Places, and three modern buildings in the Victorian style. The colorful, palmy gardens are a jumble of avocado, banyans, bromeliads, caladiums, crotons, cycads, eggfruit, elephant ears, ferns, papaya, Persian lime, sapodilla, and who knows what else. Living spaces vary widely—some of them have two stories with circular stairs and stunning high ceilings, while others have palms growing up through holes cut in porch decks. All are furnished in wicker and rattan. Pools, an outdoor bar, lovely walkways, and fountains com-

plete the picture. ⊠ *323 Whitehead St., 33040,* ☎ *305/296–7786 or 800/225–0639,* ℻ *305/294–1107. 38 suites. Bar, 2 pools, hot tub. AE, D, DC, MC, V.*

**$$$$** ⊞ **Curry Mansion Inn.** Here, careful dedication to detail by Key West
★ architect Thomas Pope and much care by owners Al and Edith Amsterdam have made the annex rooms exceptionally comfortable, even if not as detailed as the now rarely used rooms in the main house, which dates from 1899 and was the first of the island's millionaire mansions. Each room has a different tropical pastel color scheme; all have carpeting, wicker furnishings, and quilts from the Cotton Gin Store in Tavernier. Rooms 1 and 8, honeymoon suites, feature canopy beds and balconies. Eight suites are at the restored James House across the street; 306 and 308 face south and have beautiful morning light. There's complimentary Continental breakfast and happy hour with an open bar and live piano music; guests also enjoy beach privileges at Pier House Beach Club and Casa Marina. A wheelchair lift is available. ⊠ *511–512 Caroline St., 33040,* ☎ *305/294–5349 or 800/253–3466,* ℻ *305/294–4093. 15 rooms, 8 suites. Pool. AE, D, DC, MC, V.*

**$$$$** ⊞ **Gardens Hotel.** In the 1930s, the celebrated gardener Peggy Mills
★ planted this site with orchids, bromeliads, palms, and other tropical exotica, making her gardens a work of art. In 1992, Bill and Corinna Hettinger rescued this property and these gardens from a long decline. The inn has the character of an English country home in the tropics. The rooms contain distinctive furniture of yew and mahogany, overstuffed floral chintz, and marble baths (most with Jacuzzi tubs). Original Key West art by Peter Williams deserves your attention. A Continental breakfast, Nina Ricci bathroom amenities, and bottle of champagne on arrival are included. ⊠ *526 Angela St., 33040,* ☎ *305/294–2661 or 800/526–2664,* ℻ *305/292–1007. 14 rooms, 2 suites, 1 cottage. Bar, pool, spa. AE, MC, V.*

**$$$$** ⊞ **Hyatt Key West.** Given the imaginative adaptation of traditional Old Town architecture carried out here, this compound comes off a winner, with its three four-story buildings shoehorned into a tight waterfront site. Rooms have Hyatt flair, many with irregular shapes, high tongue-in-groove wainscoting, and generally a good blend of muted and bold colors. In a city where water pressure is notoriously low, the showers at the Hyatt flow with knock-down force. ⊠ *601 Front St., 33040,* ☎ *305/296–9900 or 800/233–1234,* ℻ *305/292–1038. 116 rooms, 4 full suites, 4 minisuites. 2 restaurants, 2 bars, pool, hot tub, massage, fitness room, beach, boating, fishing, bicycles. AE, D, DC, MC, V.*

**$$$$** ⊞ **Island City House.** This guest house is actually three buildings: the vintage-1880s Island City House, Arch House (a former carriage house), and a 1970s reconstruction of an old cigar factory that once stood on the site. Arch House features a dramatic carriage entry that opens into a lush courtyard, and though all its suites (most old Key West in character) front on busy Eaton Street, only the bedrooms numbers 5 and 6 actually face it. Units in Cigar House are largest, those in the original Island City House the best decorated. Floors are pine, ceiling fans abound, and suites (with parlor and kitchen) contain antiques. Guests share a private tropical garden and are given free Continental breakfasts. Children are welcome here—something of a rarity in adult-oriented Old Town guest houses. A widow's walk atop the three-story Island House building is like a visit to the top of a tropical jungle—only treetops and scattered residential rooftops are visible under the sky. ⊠ *411 William St., 33040,* ☎ *305/294–5702 or*

*800/634–8230, FAX 305/294–1289. 24 suites. Pool, hot tub, bicycles. D, DC, MC, V.*

$$$$ 🏨 **La Concha Holiday Inn.** This seven-story Art Deco hotel in the heart of downtown, the city's tallest building, dates from 1926, and the louvered room doors, the light fixtures, and the floral trim on the archways are all original. The lobby's polished floor of pink, mauve, and green marble and a conversation pit with comfortable chairs are among the details beloved by La Concha's guests. Large rooms are fitted out with 1920's-era antiques, lace curtains, and big closets. You can enjoy the sunset from The Top, a lounge that overlooks the entire island. No-smoking rooms are available. ✉ *430 Duval St., 33040,* ☎ *305/296–2991, 800/745–2191, or 800/465–4329,* FAX *305/294–3283. 158 rooms, 2 suites. 2 restaurants, 4 bars, pool, bicycles. AE, D, DC, MC, V.*

$$$$ 🏨 **Marquesa Hotel.** Guests of this coolly elegant, restored 1884 home
★ (typically shoeless in Marquesa robes), appear almost like models as they relax in among richly landscaped pools and gardens against a backdrop of brick steps rising to the villalike suites on the property's perimeter. Elegant rooms are detailed with eclectic antique and reproduction furnishings, dotted Swiss curtains, and botanical print fabrics. The newer units are larger but equally well thought out—with well-organized closets, fans and air-conditioning as silent as can be, and lighting that's bright in the bathrooms and soft and golden in the bedchambers. The lobby resembles a Victorian parlor, with its antique furniture, Audubon prints, fresh flowers, and wonderful photos of early Key West, (including one of Harry Truman driving by in a convertible). Tea is offered poolside from 11:30 until 6. Also of note—although the clientele is mostly straight, the hotel is very gay-friendly as well. You'll find here the finest lodging experience in Key West. On-site parking is available. ✉ *600 Fleming St., 33040,* ☎ *305/292–1919 or 800/869–4631,* FAX *305/294–2121. 27 rooms. Restaurant, 2 heated pools. AE, DC, MC, V.*

$$$$ 🏨 **Marriott's Casa Marina Resort.** Flagler's heirs built 13-acre La Casa Marina in 1921 at the end of the Florida East Coast Railway line. The entire resort revolves around an outdoor patio and lawn facing the ocean. The rich, luxurious lobby has a beam ceiling, polished Dade County pine floor, and wicker furniture; guest rooms are decorated in mauve and green pastels and Key West scenes. Among the best rooms are the two-bedroom loft suites with balconies facing the ocean and the lanai rooms on the ground floor of the main building, which have French doors opening onto the lawn. Rooms for nonsmokers are available. ✉ *1500 Reynolds St., 33040,* ☎ *305/296–3535 or 800/228–9290; in FL, 800/235–4837;* FAX *305/296–4633. 248 rooms, 63 suites. 2 restaurants, bar, 2 pools, massage, sauna, 3 tennis courts, exercise room, health club, boating, jet skiing, fishing, bicycles, children's programs. AE, D, DC, MC, V.*

$$$$ 🏨 **Pier House.** This is Key West's catbird seat—just off the intersection of Duval and Front streets and an easy walk from Mallory Square
★ and downtown. It's the action here that makes the Pier House so desirable. Since the 1930s, when David Wolkowsky began restoring and expanding this once-modest lodging, the Pier House has defined Key West's festive ambience for many visitors. Weathered-gray buildings, including an original Conch house, flank a courtyard of tall coconut palms and hibiscus blossoms. Most rooms are smaller than in newer hotels, except in the Caribbean Spa section, where you'll find hardwood floors, two-poster plantation beds, and some baths that convert to steam rooms or have whirlpool tubs. One-bedroom suites come supplied with VCRs with movies and CD players with compact discs. Gather with the locals around the thatch-roof tiki bar at the Beach Club or

have a loofa rub, massage, aromatherapy, or facial in the fitness center. ✉ *1 Duval St., 33040,* ☎ *305/296–4600 or 800/327–8340,* FAX *305/296–7569. 129 rooms, 13 suites. 5 restaurants, 4 bars, pool, beach. AE, D, DC, MC, V.*

$$$–$$$$ ★ 🏨 **Best Western Key Ambassador Inn.** Even though the rooms are decorated in a typical motel style, there is a cheerful spirit with bright appointments and ample room. The grounds are well cared for, and the pool looks over the Atlantic a couple of hundred feet away across Roosevelt Boulevard. Each room has a balcony and most offer ocean and pool views. The motel is on seven acres bordered in the rear by the salt ponds. A complimentary Continental breakfast is included and a complimentary newspaper is delivered to each room on weekdays. ✉ *3755 S. Roosevelt Blvd., 33040,* ☎ *305/296–3500 or 800/432–4315,* FAX *305/296–9961. 100 rooms. Bar, snack bar, pool, outdoor fitness course, shuffleboard, laundry. AE, D, DC, MC, V.*

$$$–$$$$ 🏨 **Heron House.** With four separate buildings centered on a pool, all slightly different but all Key West-style, Heron House feels like an old town within Old Town. A high coral fence, brilliantly splashed with spotlights at night, surrounds the compound (just a block off Duval Street but quieter by a mile). Owner Fred Geibelt doesn't keep his place up just to stay in business; he simply can't resist showing how good he can make it. Neither antiques nor frills are Fred's thing. Superb detailing is. Most units feature a complete wall of exquisitely laid wood (parquet, chevron pattern, herringbone), entries with French doors, and bathrooms of polished granite. Some have floor-to-ceiling panels of mirrored glass and/or an oversized whirlpool bathtub. A Continental breakfast is included. ✉ *512 Simonton St., 33040,* ☎ *305/294–9227,* FAX *305/394–5692. 22 rooms. Pool. AE, MC, V.*

$$$–$$$$ ★ 🏨 **Watson House.** This small guest house with many amenities provides utmost privacy with Duval Street convenience: It's a block from the bustle but light years from the hassle. Ed Czaplicki, with partner Joe Beres, has restored the house to its 1860s Bahamian look, which guests find caressingly soothing once they get past the busy lobby doubling as Ed's real estate office. French doors and gingerbread trim dress up the pristine yellow-and-white exterior. The deco Cabana Suite, by the two-tier pool gardens, and the contemporary second-floor William Suite, have full kitchens. The Susan Room is charmingly furnished in white wicker. ✉ *525 Simonton St., 33040,* ☎ *305/294–6712 or 800/621–9405,* FAX *305/294–7501. 1 room, 2 suites. Pool, whirlpool. AE, MC, V.*

$$–$$$$ ★ 🏨 **Popular House/Key West Bed & Breakfast.** Unlike so many prissy hotels that wall the world out, Jody Carlson brings Key West in. Doors stay open all day. Local art—large splashy canvases, a mural in the style of Gauguin—hangs on the walls, and tropical gardens and music set the mood. Jody offers inexpensive rooms with shared bath and luxury rooms in the same house, reasoning that budget travelers deserve the same good local style as the rich. Low-end rooms burst with bright yellows and reds; the hand-painted dressers will make you laugh out loud. Spacious third-floor rooms, though, are best (and most expensive), decorated with a paler palette and brilliantly original furniture: a bench made of newel posts from the old Key West City Hall, another piece crafted of attic I-beams. Terra-cotta tiles, rockers with cane insets, and arched windows overlooking Key West rooftops provide added pleasures. The Continental breakfast is lavish. ✉ *415 William St., 33040,* ☎ *305/296–7274 or 800/438-6155. 10 rooms (5 with shared baths). Hot tub, dry sauna. AE, D, DC, MC, V*

$$$ 🏨 **Harborside Motel & Marina.** The appeal of this ordinary motel is its affordability and its safe, pleasant location between a quiet street and Garrison Bight (the charter boat harbor), between Old Town and

New Town. Units (all efficiencies) are boxy, clean, and basic with little patios and ceramic tile floors, phones, and basic color cable TV. A stationary houseboat sleeps five. ⊠ *903 Eisenhower Dr., 33040,* ☎ *305/294–2780,* 𝔽𝔸𝕏 *305/292–1473. 12 efficiencies. Pool, laundry. AE, D, DC, MC, V.*

**$$$**  🏨 **Southwinds.** A short walk from Old Town, this pastel, 1940s-style motel has mature tropical plantings, all nicely set back from the street a block from the beach. Rooms have basic furnishings. It's as good as you'll find at the price, and though rates have gone up, they drop if demand gets slack. ⊠ *1321 Simonton St., 33040,* ☎ *305/296–2215. 13 rooms, 5 efficiencies. Pool, laundry. AE, D, DC, MC, V.*

**$$–$$$**  🏨 **The Colony Exclusive Cottages.** Separating this romantic hideaway
**★**   from the chaos of Duval Street two blocks away is an authentic Conch-style residential neighborhood. The Colony's owners—Didier Moritz and Irwin Mayer—converted two ramshackle Conch homes in 1985 into the first of what is now nine luxury units. Guests enjoy large suites, many with cathedral ceilings and sunlights. Most units have a living room, dining area, kitchen, and a wooden deck—all in a secluded tropical garden. Big on what's best for the guest, Didier and Irwin see to it that every new arrival is greeted with a large welcome basket. ⊠ *714 Olivia St., 33040,* ☎ *305/294–6691. 9 units. Heated pool. MC, V.*

**$$–$$$**  🏨 **Frances Street Bottle Inn.** With established inns going more and more for the luxury trade, this wonderful B&B is a refreshing change. Owners Bob and Katy Elkins look after guests as if they were all favorite cousins. The two-story Conch house dates from the 1890s, and the clean and tidy rooms are all pale, with carpet and plain furniture, paddle fans, and air-conditioning that's virtually silent. Dedicated to conservation, the Elkins have installed low-flow toilets and shower heads, and they compost and recycle. There is one bedroom downstairs, which is open to a porch-patio, and three rooms are upstairs with a balcony; even the two least-expensive rooms have two exposures. In the courtyard is a Jacuzzi. The house's name comes from the antique bottles that Bob, a commercial spear fisherman, collects. Continental breakfast is included. ⊠ *535 Frances St., 33040,* ☎ *305/294–8530 or 800/294–8530. 6 rooms. MC, V.*

## Guided Tours

### Air Tours

**Island Aeroplane Tours** (⊠ 3469 S. Roosevelt Blvd., Key West Airport 33040, ☎ 305/294–8687) fly up to two passengers in an open cockpit biplane. Tours range from a quick six- to eight-minute overview of Key West ($50 for two) to a 50-minute look at the offshore reefs ($200 for two).

**Key West Seaplane Service** (⊠ 5603 College Rd., Key West 33040, ☎ 305/294–6978) operates half-day and full-day tours of the Dry Tortugas in single-engine seaplanes, departing from Stock Island (last island before Key West). The capacity is five passengers per plane, and the cost is $159 per person for a half day, $275 for a full day (including refreshments and snorkeling gear). Round-trip transportation for those wishing to camp for up to two weeks costs $299.

### Bike Tours

The **Key West Nature Bike Tour** (⊠ Truman Ave. and Simonton St., ☎ 305/296–3344) departs from Moped Hospital on Sunday at 10:30 and Tuesday–Saturday at 9 and 3. The cost is $15 per person with your own bike, $3 more if you rent one.

## Boat Tours

**Adventure Charters** (✉ 6810 Front St., Key West 33040, ☎ 305/296–0362) operates tours on the 42-foot catamaran *Island Fantasea* for a maximum of six passengers. Trips range from a half day into the backcountry to daylong and overnight sojourns.

**M/V Discovery** (✉ Land's End Marina, 251 Margaret St., Key West 33040) and the 65-foot **Pride of Key West** (✉ 2 Duval St., Key West 33040, ☎ 305/296–6293 or 305/294–8704) are glass-bottom boats.

**M/V Miss Key West** (✉ Ocean Key House, 0 Duval St., Key West 33040, ☎ 305/296–8865) offers a one-hour, narrated cruise of the harbor. The sundown cruise includes live music.

**Vicki Impallomeni** (✉ 23 Key Haven Terr., Key West 33040, ☎ 305/294–9731), an authority on the colony of Florida Bay, features half-day ($275) and full-day ($375) charters in her 22-foot Aquasport open fisherman, *The Imp II.* Families especially like exploring with Captain Vicki because of her ability to teach youngsters. Tours depart from Murray's Marina (✉ MM 5, Stock Island).

**Wolf** (✉ Schooner Wharf, Key West Seaport, end of Greene St., Key West 33040, ☎ 305/296–9653) is Key West's tall ship and the flagship of the Conch Republic. The 74-foot, 44-passenger topsail schooner operates day cruises as well as sunset and starlight cruises with live music.

## Kayak Tours

**Mosquito Coast Island Outfitters and Kayak Guides** (✉ 1107 Duval St., Key West 33040, ☎ 305/294–7178) runs full-day, guided sea kayak natural history tours around the mangrove islands just east of Key West. The $45-a-day charge covers transportation and supplies, including snorkeling gear.

## Orientation Tours

The **Conch Tour Train** (☎ 305/294–5161) is a 90-minute, narrated tour of Key West, traveling 14 miles through Old Town and around the island, daily 9:30–3:30. Board at Mallory Square Depot every half hour, or at Roosevelt Boulevard Depot (just north of the Quality Inn) every half hour. The cost is $14.

**Old Town Trolley** (✉ 1910 N. Roosevelt Blvd., Key West, ☎ 305/296–6688) operates 12 trackless trolley-style buses, departing every 30 minutes daily 9–4:30, for 90-minute, narrated tours of Key West. The trolleys are smaller than the Conch Tour Train and go places the train won't fit. You may disembark at any of 14 stops and reboard a later trolley. The cost is $14.

## Walking Tours

The **Cuban Heritage Trail,** whose 36 sites demonstrate Key West's close connection to Cuba, is detailed in a free pamphlet and map published by the Historic Florida Keys Preservation Board and is available at the Chamber of Commerce.

**"Pelican Path"** is a free walking guide to Key West published by the Old Island Restoration Foundation. The tour discusses the history and architecture of 43 structures along 25 blocks of 12 Old Town streets. Pick up a copy at the Chamber of Commerce.

**"Solares Hill's Walking and Biking Guide to Old Key West,"** by historian Sharon Wells, contains eight walking tours, covering the city as well as the Key West cemetery. Free copies are available from the Chamber of Commerce and many hotels and stores.

**Writers' Walk** is a one-hour guided tour past the residences of prominent authors who have lived in Key West (Elizabeth Bishop, Robert Frost, Ernest Hemingway, Wallace Stevens, Tennessee Williams, among others). Tours depart at 10:30 AM, on Saturday from the Heritage House Museum (✉ 410 Caroline St.) and on Sunday from in front of Hemingway House (✉ 907 Whitehead St.). Tickets, which are $10, can be purchased from the museum and Key West Island Bookstore (✉ 513 Fleming St.) or at the time of departure if the tour isn't full.

## Nightlife and the Arts

The best of the Keys publications is **Solares Hill,** (✉ 330-B Julia St., Key West 33040, ☎ 305/294–3602, FAX 305/294–1699). The monthly is witty, controversial, and tough on environmental issues and gets the best arts and entertainment advertising. The best monthly for the rest of the Keys is the equally controversial libertarian organ **Island Navigator** (✉ 81549 Overseas Hwy., Islamorada 33036, ☎ 305/664–2266 or 800/926–8412, FAX 305/664–8411). It's free at banks, campgrounds, and stores, and its monthly community calendar lists cultural and sports events. A sister publication, the **Free Press,** fills in by the week. The best weekday source of information is the **Key West Citizen** (✉ 3420 Northside Dr., Key West 33040, ☎ 305/294–6641), which also publishes a Sunday edition. The **Miami Herald** publishes a Keys edition with good daily listings of local events. The monthly **Southern Exposure** is a good source for gay and lesbian travelers.

### The Arts

**Red Barn Theater** (✉ 319 Duval St. [rear], ☎ 305/296–9911), a professional, small theater performs dramas, comedies, and musicals, including plays by new playwrights.

**Tennessee Williams Fine Arts Center** (✉ Florida Keys Community College, 5901 College Rd., ☎ 305/296–9081, Ext. 336) presents chamber music, dance, jazz concerts, and dramatic and musical plays with national and international stars, as well as other performing-arts events, November–April.

**Waterfront Playhouse** (✉ Mallory Sq., ☎ 305/294–5015) is a mid-1850s wrecker's warehouse that was converted into a 185-seat, non-Equity community theater presenting comedy and drama November–May.

### Nightlife

**Capt. Tony's Saloon** (✉ 428 Greene St., ☎ 305/294–1838) is a landmark bar, owned until 1988 by a legend in his own right, Capt. Tony Tarracino—a former bootlegger, smuggler, mercenary, gunrunner, gambler, raconteur—and former Key West mayor. The building dates from 1851, when it was first used as a morgue and ice house; later it was Key West's first telegraph station. The bar was the original Sloppy Joe's from 1933 to 1937. Hemingway was a regular, and Jimmy Buffett got his start here. Live country and rhythm and blues set the scene nowadays, and the rum-based house drink, the Pirates' Punch, still wows those brave enough to try it. **Havana Docks Lounge** (✉ 1 Duval St., ☎ 305/296–4600), a high-energy disco, is popular with young locals and visitors. The deck is a good place to watch the sun set when Mallory Square gets too crowded. **Margaritaville Cafe** (✉ 500 Duval St., ☎ 305/292–1435) is owned by Key West resident and recording star Jimmy Buffett, who has been known to perform here but more often just has lunch. The drink of choice is, of course, a margarita. There's live music nightly. **Sloppy Joe's** (✉ 201 Duval St., ☎ 305/294–5717) is the successor to a famous speakeasy named for its founder, Capt.

Joe Russell. Ernest Hemingway liked to gamble in a partitioned club room in back. Decorated with Hemingway memorabilia and marine flags, the bar is popular with tourists and is full and noisy all the time. Live entertainment plays daily, noon to 2 AM. The **Top Lounge** (⌧ 430 Duval St., ☎ 305/296–2991) is on the seventh floor of the La Concha Holiday Inn, Key West's tallest building, and is one of the best places to view the sunset. (**Celebrities,** on the ground floor, presents nightly entertainment and serves food.)

## Outdoor Activities and Sports

### Biking

Key West is a cycling town, but if you aren't accustomed to driving with so many bikes around, ride carefully. Paved road surfaces are poor, so it's best to ride a fat-tired Conch cruiser. Some hotels rent bikes to guests; others will refer you to a nearby shop and reserve a bike for you.

**Keys Moped & Scooter** (⌧ 523 Truman Ave., ☎ 305/294–0399) rents beach cruisers with large baskets as well as mopeds and scooters and rates are the lowest in Key West. Look for the huge American flag on the roof. **Moped Hospital** (⌧ 601 Truman Ave., ☎ 305/296–3344) supplies balloon-tire bikes with yellow safety baskets, as well as mopeds, tandem mopeds, and scooters for adults and children.

### Diving

**Captain's Corner** (⌧ 511-A Greene St., Key West 30040, ☎ 305/296–8865), a PADI five star–rated shop, provides dive classes in English, French, German, Italian, Swedish, and Japanese. All captains are licensed dive masters. Reservations are accepted for regular reef and wreck diving, spear and lobster fishing, and archaeological and treasure hunting. The shop also runs fishing charters and a 60-foot dive boat—*Sea Eagle*—which departs twice daily.

### Fishing

*Linda D III* and *IV* (⌧ Dock 19, Amberjack Pier, City Marina, Garrison Bight, Key West, ☎ 305/296–9798), captained by Billy Wickers III and his father, Bill Wickers, Jr., offers half-day, full-day, and night sportfishing. With Billy III, the family business enters the fourth generation of Wickers to lead fishermen to sea.

### Golf

**Key West Resort Golf Course** (⌧ 6450 E. College Rd., Key West, ☎ 305/294–5232) is an 18-hole course on the bay side of Stock Island. Visitor fees are $58 for 18 holes (cart included) in season.

## Shopping

Key West contains dozens of characterless T-shirt shops, but some art galleries and curiosity shops have lots worth toting home.

Like a parody of Duval Street T-shirt shops, the hole-in-the-wall **Art Attack** (⌧ 606 Duval St., ☎ 305/294–7131) throws in every icon and trinket anyone nostalgic for the days of peace and love might fancy: beads, necklaces, medallions, yin-yang banners, harmony bells, and of course Dead and psychedelic T-shirts.

Take time, even if you're not buying, to enjoy the smells at **Baby's Place Espresso Bar** (⌧ 1111 Duval St., ☎ 305/292–3739 or 800/523–2326), the "southernmost coffee roasters." Dozens of varieties of beans plus fresh-baked pastries are for sale.

Several interesting shops, including one of the best bookstores in town, **Caroline Street Books** (⌧ 800 Caroline St., ☎ 305/294–3931), occupies the Red Doors Building, a restored 1868 house that was once a brothel. The bookstore has one of the largest selections of books by or about local authors (Hemingway, Tennessee Williams, Robert Frost, etc.), as well as a range of gay and lesbian books and magazines.

**Fast Buck Freddie's** (⌧ 500 Duval St., ☎ 305/294–2007) sells imaginative items you'd never dream of, including battery-operated alligators that eat Muenster cheese, banana leaf-shape furniture, fish-shape flatwear, and every flamingo item anyone's ever come up with.

**Fausto's Food Palace** (⌧ 522 Fleming St., ☎ 305/296–5663; ⌧ 1105 White St., ☎ 305/294–5221) may be under a roof, but it's a market in the traditional town-square style. Since 1926, Fausto's has been the spot to catch up on the week's gossip, and to chill out in summer—it's got the heaviest air-conditioning in town.

The oldest private art gallery in Key West, **Gingerbread Square Gallery** (⌧ 1207 Duval St., ☎ 305/296–8900) represents mainly Keys artists who have attained national and international prominence.

**Haitian Art Co.** (⌧ 600 Frances St., ☎ 305/296–8932) sells the original colorful iron, wood, and ceramic works of 200 or more Haitian artists.

**H. T. Chittum & Co.** (⌧ 725 Duval St., ☎ 305/292–9002) features informal clothing from Timberland and Nautica, specialty knives, and smart ready-to-wear. There's also a branch in Islamorada (⌧ MM 82.7, OS, ☎ 305/664–4421).

**Inter Arts** (⌧ 506 Southard St., ☎ 305/296–4081) is stocked with textiles to wear, display, walk on, and keep you cool in bed.

**Key West Aloe** (⌧ 524 Front St., ☎ 305/294–5592 or 800/445–2563) was founded in a garage in 1971; today it produces some 300 perfume, sunscreen, and skin-care products for men and women. You can also visit the factory store (⌧ Greene and Simonton Sts.), open seven days a week, where you can watch the staff measure and blend ingredients, then fill and seal the containers.

**Key West Hand Print Fashions and Fabrics** (⌧ 201 Simonton St., ☎ 305/294–9535 or 800/866–0333), in business since 1964, is noted for the vibrant tropical prints, yard goods, and resort wear for men, women, and children it offers for sale in the Curry Warehouse—a brick building erected in 1878 to store tobacco.

**Key West Island Bookstore** (⌧ 513 Fleming St., ☎ 305/294–2904) is the literary bookstore of the large Key West writers' community.

In a town with a gazillion T-shirt shops, **Last Flight Out** (⌧ 710 Duval St., ☎ 305/294–8008) stands out for its selection of classic namesake T's that recall the pre–World War II heyday of tourist flights between Key West and Havana.

**Lazy Way Shops** (⌧ Elizabeth and Greene Sts., ☎ 305/294–3003) sells a constantly changing sampling of local arts and crafts in an old shrimpers' net shop.

**Lucky Street Gallery** (⌧ 919 Duval St., ☎ 305/294–3973) shows tropical contemporary crafts, blown glass, wood carvings, and other art for hanging and mounting.

**L. Valladares & Son** (⊠ 1200 Duval St., ☎ 305/296–5032), a fourth-generation newsstand, sells more than 4,000 periodicals and 3,000 paperback books along with state, national, and international newspapers.

**Pelican Poop** (⊠ 314 Simonton St., ☎ 305/296–3887) sells Haitian and Ecuadorean art around a lush, tropical courtyard garden with its gorgeous aqua pool. (Hemingway once lived here, in the apartments out back called Casa Antigua.)

A survivor of Key West's seafaring days, **Perkins & Son Chandlery** (⊠ 901 Fleming St., ☎ 305/294–7635), redolent of pine tar and kerosene, offers one of the largest selections of used marine gear in the Keys, as well as nautical antiques, books, outdoor clothing, and collectibles.

**Plantation Pottery** (⊠ 521 Fleming St., ☎ 305/294–3143) is not to be missed for its original, never-commercial pottery.

**Tikal Trading Co.** (⊠ 129 Duval St., ☎ 305/296–4463) sells its own line of women's clothing of hand-woven Guatemalan cotton and knit tropical prints.

**Waterfront Market** (⊠ 201 William St., ☎ 305/294–8418 or 305/296–0778) purveys health and gourmet foods, deli items, produce, salads, cold beer, and wine. If you're there, be sure to check out the bulletin board. In the same building are a fish market (☎ 305/296–0778) and bait and tackle shop (☎ 305/292–1961).

Potters Charles Pearson and Timothy Roeder are **Whitehead St. Pottery** (⊠ 1011 Whitehead St., ☎ 305/294–5067), where they display their porcelain stoneware and raku-fired vessels.

| | |
|---|---|
| Off the Beaten Path | DRY TORTUGAS NATIONAL PARK — 70 miles off the shores of Key West, this sanctuary for thousands of birds consists of seven small islands, whose main facility is the long-deactivated Fort Jefferson, where Dr. Samuel Mudd was imprisoned for his alleged role in Lincoln's assassination. For information, contact Everglades National Park (⊠ 40001 Rte. 9336, Homestead 33034-6733, ☎ 305/242–7700). |

# THE FLORIDA KEYS A TO Z

## Arriving and Departing

### By Boat
Boaters can travel to Key West either along the Intracoastal Waterway through Florida Bay or along the Atlantic Coast. The Keys are full of marinas that welcome transient visitors, but they don't have enough slips for everyone who wants to visit the area. Make reservations in advance, and ask about channel and dockage depth—many marinas are quite shallow.

**Coast Guard Group Key West** (⊠ Key West 33040, ☎ 305/292–8727) provides 24-hour monitoring of VHF-FM Channel 16. Safety and weather information is broadcast at 7 AM and 5 PM Eastern Standard Time on VHF-FM Channel 16 and 22A. There are three stations in the Keys: Islamorada (☎ 305/664–4404), Marathon (☎ 305/743–6778), and Key West (☎ 305/292–8856).

### By Bus
**Greyhound Lines** (☎ 305/871–1810 or 800/231–2222) serves the Keys from downtown Miami, MIA, and Homestead to Key Largo (⊠ MM 92, BS, ☎ 305/296–9072), Islamorada (⊠ Burger King, MM 83.5,

BS), Marathon (⊠ Kingsail Resort, MM 50, BS), Looe Key (⊠ Ramrod Resort, MM 27.5, OS), and Key West (⊠ 615½ Duval St.).

## By Car

If you want to avoid Miami traffic on the mainland en route to the Keys, take the Homestead Extension of Florida's Turnpike; although it's a toll road and carries a lot of commuter traffic, it's still the fastest way to go. If you prefer traffic to tolls, take U.S. 1.

Just south of Florida City, the turnpike joins U.S. 1, and the Overseas Highway begins. Eighteen miles farther on, you cross the Jewfish Creek bridge at the north end of Key Largo, and you're officially in the Keys.

Work is underway on improving U.S. 1 from Card Sound to Key Largo, which includes widening a large section of road to four lanes and replacing the Jewfish Creek bridge, and will continue through the decade. In all likelihood, delays will increase. You can save time by taking Card Sound Road (Rte. 905A) from Florida City 13 miles southeast to the Card Sound Bridge (toll $1.75), across to North Key Largo. Continue until you reach the only stop sign and turn right onto Rte. 905, which cuts through some of the Keys' last remaining jungle and rejoins U.S. 1, 31 miles from Florida City.

Try to avoid flying into Key West and driving back to Miami; there are substantial drop-off charges for leaving a Key West car in Miami.

## By Plane

Continuous improvements in service now link airports in Miami, Fort Lauderdale/Hollywood, Naples, Orlando, and Tampa directly with Key West International Airport (⊠ S. Roosevelt Blvd., ☎ 305/296–5439 or 305/296–7223). Service is provided by **Airways International Airlines** (☎ 305/292–7777), **American Eagle** (☎ 800/433–7300), **Cape Air** (☎ 800/352–0714), **Comair** (☎ 800/354–9822), **Gulfstream International Airlines** (☎ 800/992–8532), and **USAir/USAir Express** (☎ 800/428–4322).

Direct service between Miami and Marathon Airport (⊠ MM 52, BS, 9000 Overseas Hwy., ☎ 305/743–2155) is provided by American Eagle and Gulfstream International. USAir Express connects Marathon with Tampa.

Another option is to fly into Miami International Airport (MIA) and take a van or taxi. **Airporter** (☎ 305/852–3413 or 800/830–3413) operates scheduled van and bus service from MIA's baggage areas to wherever you want to go in Key Largo and Islamorada. Drivers post Airporter signs with the names of clients they are to meet. The cost is $30 per person to Key Largo and $33 per person to Islamorada. Reservations are required. **Upper Keys Transportation** (☎ 305/453–0100 or 800/749–5397) meets arriving flights at MIA. Reservations are required 24 hours in advance for arrivals, one hour for departures. Fares to Key Largo from 8AM–6PM for one person is $40 ($25 per person additional service charge outside that time frame) or $75 for two people 8AM–6PM with a $20 per person service charge from about 6PM–8AM; fare to Marathon is $115 for one person, $125 for two. **Keys Super Shuttle** (☎ 305/871–2000 or 800/874–8885) charges $77 to Key Largo for the first person, $15 each additional person; fare to Islamorada is $88 and $22. To go farther into the Keys, you must book an entire van (up to 11 passengers), which costs $250 to Marathon, $350 to Key West. Super Shuttle requests 24-hour advance notice for transportation back to the airport.

# Getting Around

## By Bus
**The City of Key West Department of Transportation** (☎ 305/292–8165) operates two bus routes: Mallory Square (counterclockwise around the island) and Old Town (clockwise around the island). The fare is 75¢, which must be paid in exact change. (☞ Arriving and Departing by Bus, *above.*)

## By Car
In Key West's Old Town, parking is scarce and costly ($1.50 per hour at Mallory Square). Use a taxi, bicycle, or moped to get around, or walk. Elsewhere in the Keys, however, a car is crucial. Gas prices are higher here than on the mainland, so fill your tank in Miami and top it off in Florida City.

Except for four-lane sections through Key Largo, Marathon, Boca Chica Key and Stock Island (just north of Key West), Tavernier and Bahia Honda State Park, the Overseas Highway is narrow and crowded (especially on weekends). Expect delays behind large tractor-trailer trucks, cars towing boats, and rubbernecking tourists. Fortunately, recent highway improvements, including replacement of almost all bridges and new four-lane sections, have reduced the driving time between Florida City and Key West to between 3½ and 4 hours on a good day, where five hours used to be standard. After midnight, you can make the trip in three hours—but then, of course, you'll miss all the scenery.

The best road map for the Florida Keys is published by the Homestead/Florida City Chamber of Commerce. You can obtain a copy for $2 from the **Tropical Everglades Visitor Center** (✉ 160 U.S. 1, Florida City 33034, ☎ 305/245–9180 or 800/388–9669).

Throughout the Keys, local chambers of commerce, marinas, and dive shops offer you the local **Teall's Guide**—a land and nautical map—free or for $1. Before you leave home for the Keys, it makes good sense to purchase the whole set, which pinpoints the most popular fishing and diving areas for the entire Keys, John Pennekamp Coral Reef State Park, Everglades National Park, and Miami to Key Largo; cost of the set is $7.95, postage included (✉ 111 Saguaro La., Marathon 33050, ☎ 305/743–3942).

## By Limousine
One service operates in Key West: **Paradise Transportation Service, Inc.** (✉ 3134 Northside Dr., ☎ 305/293–3010).

## By Taxi
Two companies named **Island Taxi** serve the Keys, one for the Upper Keys (☎ 305/664–8181) between MM 94 and MM 74, the other (☎ 305/743–0077) from MM 74 to MM 0 in Key West. Both taxi companies offer 24-hour service and calculate fares at $4 for the first 2 miles and $1.50 for each additional mile for up to two adults and any accompanying children; extra adults pay $1 per mile.

Four cab companies operate around the clock in Key West: **Florida Keys Taxi Dispatch** (☎ 305/296–1800), **Maxi-Taxi Sun Cab System** (☎ 305/296–7777), **Five Sixes Cabs** (☎ 305/296–6666), and **Yellow Cabs of Key West** (☎ 305/294–2227). The fare from the airport for two or more to New Town is $5 per person with a cap of $15; to Old Town it's $6 and $20. Otherwise meters register $1.40 to start, 35¢ for each ⅕ mile, and 35¢ for every 50 seconds of waiting time.

# Contacts and Resources

## Camping

The State of Florida operates recreational-vehicle and tent campgrounds in **John Pennekamp Coral Reef State Park** (✉ MM 102.5, Box 1560, Key Largo 33037, ☎ 305/451–1202), Long Key State Recreation Area (✉ MM 67.5, Box 776, Long Key 33001, ☎ 305/664–4815), and Bahia Honda State Park (✉ MM 37, 36850 Overseas Hwy., Big Pine Key 33043, ☎ 305/872–2353). Bahia Honda also has duplex rental cabins. The best bet to reserve one is to call at 8 AM 60 calendar days before your planned visit.

## Car Rentals

If you don't have your own car, you can rent one at several places in the Keys. **Avis** (☎ 305/743–5428 or 800/331–1212) and **Budget** (☎ 305/743–3998 or 800/527–0700) serve Marathon Airport. Key West International Airport has booths for **Avis** (☎ 305/296–8744 or 800/831–2847), **Budget** (☎ 305/294–8868), **Dollar** (☎ 305/296–9921 or 800/800–4000), **Hertz** (☎ 305/294–1039 or 800/654–3131), and **Value** (☎ 305/296–7733 or 800/468–2583). **Tropical Rent-A-Car** (✉ 1300 Duval St., ☎ 305/294–8136) is based in the center of Key West. **Enterprise Rent-A-Car** (☎ 305/292–0220 or 800/325–8007) has several Keys locations.

## Emergencies

Dial **911** for police or ambulance. **Florida Marine Patrol** (✉ MM 48, BS, 2796 Overseas Hwy., Suite 100, State Regional Service Center, Marathon 33050, ☎ 305/289–2320), maintains a 24-hour telephone service to handle reports of boating emergencies and natural resource violations. **Coast Guard Group Key West** (☞ Arriving and Departing by Boat, *above*) responds to local marine emergencies and reports of navigation hazards.

### HOSPITALS

The following hospitals have 24-hour emergency rooms: **Fishermen's Hospital** (✉ MM 48.7, OS, 3301 Overseas Hwy., Marathon, ☎ 305/743–5533), **Lower Florida Keys Health System** (✉ MM 5, BS, 5900 College Rd., Stock Island, ☎ 305/294–5531), and **Mariners Hospital** (✉ MM 88.5, BS, 50 High Point Rd., Tavernier, Plantation Key, ☎ 305/852–4418).

### LATE-NIGHT PHARMACIES

The Keys have no 24-hour pharmacies. Hospital pharmacists will help with emergencies after regular retail business hours.

## Lodging Reservations

In Key West, three services can help arrange for accommodations. **Key West Reservation Service** (✉ 628 Fleming St., Drawer 1689, 33040, ☎ 305/294–8850 or 800/327–4831, FAX 305/296–6291) makes hotel reservations and helps locate rental properties (hotels, motels, bed-and-breakfasts, oceanfront condominiums, and luxury vacation homes). **Key West Vacation Rentals** (✉ 525 Simonton St., 33040, ☎ 305/292–7997 or 800/621–9405, FAX 305/294–7501) lists historic cottages, homes, and condominiums for rent. **Property Management of Key West, Inc.** (✉ 1213 Truman Ave., 33040, ☎ 305/296–7744) offers lease and rental service for condominiums, town houses, and private homes.

## Visitor Information

**Florida Keys & Key West Visitors Bureau** (✉ Box 1147, Key West 33041, ☎ 800/352–5397). **Greater Key West Chamber of Commerce (mainstream)** (✉ 402 Wall St., Key West 33040, ☎ 305/294–2587 or 800/527–8539, FAX 305/294–7806). **Key West Business Guild (gay)** (✉

Box 1208, 33041, ☎ 305/294–4603). **Islamorada Chamber of Commerce** (✉ MM 82.5, BS, Box 915, Islamorada 33036, ☎ 305/664–4503 or 800/322–5397). **Key Largo Chamber of Commerce** (✉ MM 106, BS, 105950 Overseas Hwy., Key Largo 33037, ☎ 305/451–4747 or 800/822–1088). **Lower Keys Chamber of Commerce** (✉ MM 31, OS, Box 430511, Big Pine Key 33043, ☎ 305/872–2411 or 800/872–3722). **Marathon Chamber of Commerce & Visitor Center** (✉ MM 53.5, BS, 12222 Overseas Hwy., Marathon 33050, ☎ 305/743–5417 or 800/842–9580).

# 8 Walt Disney World® and the Orlando Area

*When Walt Disney chose 28,000 acres in central Florida as the site of his eastern Disneyland, he forever changed the face of a cattle-and-citrus town called Orlando. Over the years those who followed Walt have expanded his empire. But today there is plenty of competition as the big companies play the corporate equivalent of keeping up with the Joneses. Universal Studios, Sea World, Church Street Station, and Splendid China all give Mickey a run for his money. It's easy to spend weeks here—and there isn't an ocean-pounded beach in sight.*

**L**ONG BEFORE "IT'S A SMALL WORLD" echoed through the palmetto scrub, other theme parks tempted visitors away from the beaches into the scruffy interior of central Florida. I–4 hadn't even been built when Dick and Julie Pope created Cypress Gardens, celebrating 60 years in 1997, which holds the record as the region's oldest continuously running attraction. But when Walt Disney World (WDW) opened with the Magic Kingdom as its centerpiece on October 1, 1971, and was immediately successful, the central Florida theme-park scene became big business. Sea World filled its tanks two years later. WDW debuted Epcot Center in 1982 and Disney–MGM Studios Theme Park in 1989; Universal Studios answered the latter's challenge one year later. Things continue to evolve as Disney looks to opening Wild Kingdom, an animal-themed park in 1998, and Universal targets the evening crowd with the E-Zone.

The problem for visitors with tight schedules or slim wallets is that each park is worth a visit. The Magic Kingdom, Epcot Center, and Sea World are not to be missed. Of the two movie parks, Universal Studios and Disney–MGM Studios, the former is probably more spectacular. Cypress Gardens is a 60-minute drive through the dusty remnants of the region's citrus groves.

It is easy to forget that this ever-expanding fantasy world grew up around a sleepy farming town founded as a military outpost, Fort Gatlin, in 1838. Though not on any major waterway, Orlando was surrounded by small spring-fed lakes, and transplanted northerners planted sprawling oak trees to vary the landscape of palmetto scrub and citrus groves. Most of the tourist development is in southwest Orlando, along the I–4 corridor south of Florida's Turnpike. Orlando itself has become a center of international business, and north of downtown are several handsome, prosperous suburbs, most notably Winter Park, which retains its white-gloves-at-tea Southern charm.

## Pleasures and Pastimes

### The Arts
From the Bob Carr Center for the Performing Arts to the Tiffany glass at the Morse Museum, Orlando's arts scene is thriving. All those theme park shows have brought lots of talent to town, and because of this, the local theater scene showcases a better-than-average bunch of actors and musicians. The internationally known Bach Festival at Rollins College is just one manifestation of the very un-Disney culture found beyond the kingdom of the Mouse.

### Boating
With a lagoon at its heart, Walt Disney World offers lots of it. Boat tours in Winter Park are decidedly pleasant as well, a nice way to absorb the area's old-fashioned charm.

### Dining
If they batter it, fry it, microwave it, torture it under a heat lamp until it's ready to sign a confession, and serve it with a side of fries, you can find it in central Florida. Cruise down International Drive or U. S. 192 and you'll probably be convinced that some obscure federal law mandates that any franchise restaurant company doing business in the United States has to have at least one outlet in Orlando. Not all the franchises are burger barns, however, and even those that are try to put their best foot forward in Orlando, where food is consumed by millions of international visitors. The McDonald's on International Drive,

for example, is the largest in the nation. Restaurateurs build monuments here, so you'll ask "Hey, why don't they have one of these in our town?" This fiercely competitive dining market even brings out the best from the hometown eateries that predate Disney. The result is that dining choices in Orlando are like entertainment choices. There's simply more than you can sample on any one trip.

And because of the large, international tourist trade and the community's own increasing sophistication, Orlando eateries don't end with fast food. The whole spectrum is available, from the very simplest mom-and-pops to basic ethnic eateries to elaborate restaurants serving excellent food, beautifully presented in lovely surroundings.

### Learning Vacations

The Disney Institute (☞ Contacts and Resources, *below*), opening in 1996, should offer great packages, packed with classes, seminars, lectures, and other activities. Unlike many other American learning vacations centers, Disney Institute has plenty of of activities for participants' traveling companions.

### Lodging

From Disney's themed palaces to reasonably priced family hotels—if you want it, Orlando has it. Moreover, most of these properties have programs and facilities for children that range from good to fabulous—from baby-sitting and children's programs to onsite rentals of VCRs and videos and rooms full of state-of-the-art videos.

### Museums

The Charles Morse Museum in Winter Park, which specializes in Tiffany glass, and the Orange County Historical Museum and the Orlando Science Center, which share a complex in Orlando with the Orlando Museum of Art, are all well worth a day away from the theme park crowds.

## Exploring the Orlando Area

### Great Itineraries

*Numbers in the text below correspond to numbers in the margin and on the maps.*

#### IF YOU HAVE 3 DAYS

A day in the area wouldn't be complete without a trip to the **Magic Kingdom.** A full three-day trip would include that bit of Disney magic, plus a trip to **Epcot Center.** Catch the fireworks one night and spend the other night at one of the local dinner show extravaganzas. Finish out your stay with a day up the road at **Universal Studios.** Choose lodging inside 🏨 **Walt Disney World** to make the most of your short stay.

#### IF YOU HAVE 5 DAYS

Spend the first two days at **Walt Disney World**, visiting the **Magic Kingdom** and **Epcot Center,** followed by evenings at **Pleasure Island** and **Church Street Station.** The third day should be at **Universal Studios,** the fourth at **Sea World..** End your day at Universal by dining at the **Hard Rock Cafe,** then spend the rest of the night around your hotel pool. On your fourth evening, take in a dinner show extravaganza, perhaps Sea World's luau. A slow-paced final day will give everyone a chance to unwind before heading home, so, on the fifth day, venture into Winter Park and take a leisurely boat tour, visit the **Charles Morse Museum** ②, and stop by the **Orlando Museum of Art.** If you have younger children, consider the **Orlando Science Center** near **Loch Haven Park,** for its great interactive activities. Lodging at 🏨 **Walt Disney World** or on 🏨 **International Drive** in Orlando is most convenient.

IF YOU HAVE 10 DAYS

You'll have time to see *all* the theme parks, but pacing is key. So that go-go Orlando tourism scene doesn't wear you down, intersperse theme park outings with some low-key sightseeing or shopping. Start in **Walt Disney World** with the **Magic Kingdom,** staying late the first night for the fireworks. The second day, tackle WDW's **Epcot Center,** and that evening hit **Pleasure Island.** Set aside the third day for a visit to slower-paced **Sea World,** making luau reservations when you enter the park. Head back to Disney on your fourth day, to **Blizzard Beach** or **Typhoon Lagoon.** Return to the Magic Kingdom and the other WDW parks on your fifth and sixth days, hitting every attraction you've missed or taking one more spin on those you loved. Have dinner one night at **Planet Hollywood,** maybe taking in a late movie at the Pleasure Island cinemas or, instead, strolling along International Drive. On Day 7, a day of (relative) rest, head into Orlando to take a boat tour through Winter Park and visit the **Orlando Science Center** and **Orlando Museum of Art** on **Loch Haven Park,** which has lovely grassy areas good for a picnic. In late afternoon, walk around **Church Street Station,** visiting **Terror on Church Street** and having dinner before heading back to the hotel. On Day 8, drive out to **Cypress Gardens** or **Splendid China,** catching a dinner show in the evening. Reserve Day 9 for **Universal Studios** and dinner at the **Hard Rock Cafe.** On Day 10, head to the mall or the outlet mall for some last-minute shopping, or revisit your favorite theme park. Leave time to clean up back at the hotel and have a bon voyage dinner at a restaurant outside Walt Disney World, to ease your return to real life. Since you'll be jumping around the area on this one, no lodging is more convenient than any other; if money is an object, go for the U.S. 192 area and if you want total immersion in Disney, go for lodgings that are both on-site and Disney-owned.

## When to Tour the Orlando Area

That the Orlando area is an obvious destination for vacationing families has a few important corollaries. If you're traveling without youngsters, try to avoid school holiday periods. If you have preschoolers, follow the same course; crowds can overwhelm small fry. If you're traveling with children of varying ages and those in school are good students, consider taking the kids out of school so that you can visit during a less-congested period. If your children cannot afford to miss school, try to vacation in late May or early June, as soon as the school year ends. Or visit at Thanksgiving, which is not as busy as other holidays. Especially if you're bringing small children, you may want to avoid the period around July 4 and the Christmas season—despite the many special activities and beautiful decorations: Although the parks are completely staffed up, the crowds can be more wearing than staying at home.

# THE DISNEY THEME PARKS

# The Magic Kingdom, Disney–MGM Studios, Epcot Center, and Blizzard Beach, Discovery Island, River Country, and Typhoon Lagoon

No doubt about it, the Disney parks have a special magic. You probably know lots about the three major layouts—the Magic Kingdom (which is something like California's Disneyland), Epcot Center, and Disney–MGM Studios (discussed below in alphabetical order). But there are also three wonderful water parks—River Country (the oldest), Typhoon Lagoon, and Blizzard Beach. Discovery Island, in the middle of one of the several lakes on the Disney property, displays birds and other

small animals and makes a pleasant break during a day in the larger
theme parks.

## Ratings

Every visitor leaves the Magic Kingdom, Epcot Center, and Disney–MGM Studios with a different opinion about what was "the
best." Some attractions get raves from all visitors, while others are enjoyed most by young children or older travelers. To take this into account, our descriptions rate each attraction with ★, ★★, or ★★★,
depending on the strength of its appeal to the visitor group noted by
the italics.

# Disney–MGM Studios Theme Park

*Take the Epcot Center–Disney Village exit off I–4.*

Here, in "the Hollywood that never was and always will be," the Disney organizations showcases its own knack for colorful detail combined
with MGM's motion-picture expertise. The amalgamation blends
theme park with fully functioning movie and television production center (Star Search is filmed here), breathtaking rides with instructional
tours, and nostalgia with high-tech wonders.

Although some attractions will interest young children, Disney–MGM
is best for teenagers old enough to catch all the cinematic references.

When the lines are minimal, the park can be easily visited in a day with
time for repeat rides. The **Crossroads of the World** kiosk in the Entrance
Plaza dispenses maps, brochures, and entertainment schedules; the
**Production Information Window,** also in the Entrance Plaza, can tell
you what's being taped when and how to sit in the audience. Tapings
are interesting, especially when you watch the results at home months
later. Be warned, however, that tapings last several hours and you are
not allowed to leave until the end.

## Hollywood Boulevard

With its palm trees, pastel buildings, and flashy neon, Hollywood
Boulevard paints a rosy picture of Tinseltown in the 1930s. The sense
of having walked right onto a movie set is enhanced by the Art Deco
storefronts, strolling brass bands, and roving actors dressed in costume
and playing everything from would-be starlets to nefarious agents. Hollywood Boulevard is crammed with souvenir shops and memorabilia
collections, including **Oscar's Classic Car Souvenirs & Super Service Station; Sid Cahuenga's One-of-a-Kind** antiques and curios, where you might
find (and acquire) Brenda Vaccaro's shawl, Liberace's table napkins,
or autographed stars photos; and **Cover Story,** where you can have your
picture put on the front cover of a major magazine.

**Great Movie Ride.** Housed in a fire-engine red pagoda replica of Grau-
man's Chinese Theatre, this 22-minute tour of great moments in film
is packed with action and special effects. After waiting successively in
a lobby filled with movie memorabilia and a preshow area that screens
film clips, you ride open trams through numerous scenes depicting cli-
mactic moments of famous films, replete with Audio-Animatronic
characters, scrim, smoke, and Disney magic. *Audience: All but young
children (for whom it may be too intense). Rating:* ★★★

## Sunset Boulevard

This newest of Disney–MGM's theme avenues pays tribute to famous
Hollywood monuments.

**Theater of the Stars.** This 1,500-seat amphitheater recalls the Hollywood Bowl; rather than hosting rock acts, however, it is home to a mu-

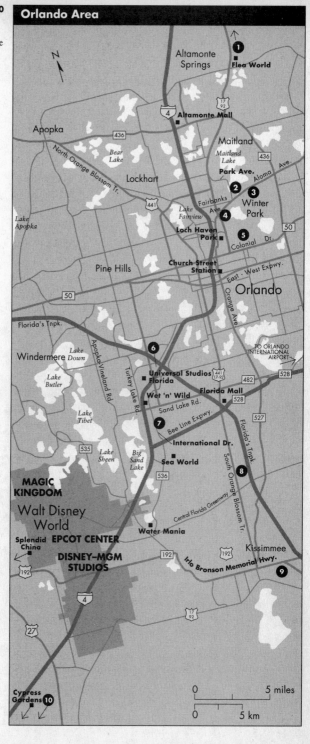

# Walt Disney World

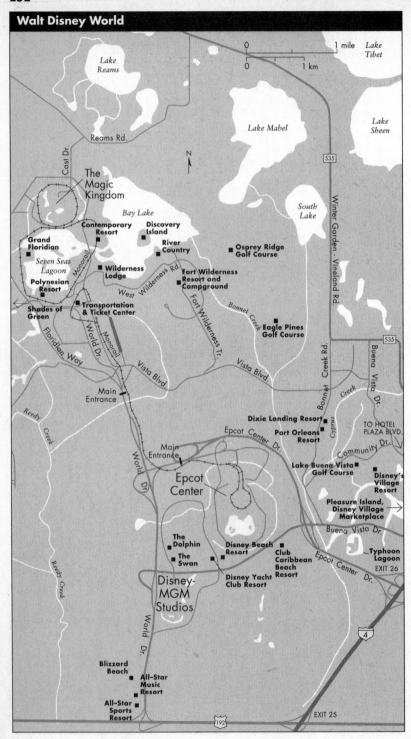

0 _____ 1 mile
0 _____ 1 km

Lake Tibet

Lake Reams

Reams Rd.

Lake Mabel

Lake Sheen

535

N

Cast Dr.

The Magic Kingdom

Bay Lake

South Lake

Winter Garden - Vineland Rd.

Contemporary Resort

Discovery Island

River Country

Osprey Ridge Golf Course

Grand Floridian

Seven Seas Lagoon

Wilderness Lodge

Fort Wilderness Resort and Campground

Monorail

Wilderness Rd.

Polynesian Resort

West

Bonnet Creek

Eagle Pines Golf Course

Shades of Green

Transportation & Ticket Center

Fort Wilderness Tr.

535

Floridian Way

World Dr.

Monorail

Vista Blvd.

Vista Blvd.

Bonnet Creek Rd.

Buena Vista Dr.

Main Entrance

Reedy Creek

Dixie Landing Resort

Cyprus Creek

TO HOTEL PLAZA BLVD.

Epcot Center Dr.

Port Orleans Resort

Community Dr.

World Dr.

Main Entrance

Lake Buena Vista Golf Course

Disney's Village Resort

Epcot Center

Pleasure Island, Disney Village Marketplace

Buena Vista Dr.

The Dolphin

Disney Beach Resort

The Swan

Club Caribbean Beach Resort

Typhoon Lagoon

Reedy Creek

Disney-MGM Studios

Disney Yacht Club Resort

Epcot Center Dr.

EXIT 26

4

Blizzard Beach

All-Star Music Resort

All-Star Sports Resort

World Dr.

EXIT 25

192

sical production called *Beauty and the Beast—Live on Stage. Audience: All ages. Rating:* ★★

**Twilight Zone Tower of Terror.** All the crowds on Sunset Boulevard are most likely looking for the park's newest excuse for an adrenaline rush: the 13-story Twilight Zone Tower of Terror, which ominously over-looks the street and is reputedly the now-deserted Hollywood Tower Hotel. Once inside, you take an eerie stroll before boarding a giant "el-evator," which takes you upward past seemingly deserted hallways where ghostly former residents appear around you, until suddenly—faster than you can say "where's Rod Serling?"—the creaking vehicle abruptly plunges downward in a terrifying, 130-foot free-fall drop! Adjusted to be even scarier after its initial tests with the public, this is hands down the best thrill ride in any Disney Park (sorry, Space Mountain Lovers). *Audience: Adults and older children. No pregnant women or guests with back, neck, or heart problems; minimum height 42". Rating:* ★★★

## Studio Courtyard

**Backstage Studio Tour.** This combination tram ride and walking tour takes you on a 25-minute tour of the back-lot building blocks of movies: set design, costumes, props, lighting, and special effects. You literally ride through working offices, peering through windows as Foley artists mix sound, as lighting crews sort cables, as costumers stitch seams, and so on. At Catastrophe Canyon, the tram bounces up and down in a simulated earthquake, an oil tanker explodes in gobs of smoke and flame, and a water tower crashes to the ground, touching off a flash flood. *Audience: All but young children. Rating:* ★★★

**Inside the Magic Special Effects and Production Tour.** This one-hour walk-ing tour explains how clever camera operators make illusion seem like reality through camera angles, miniaturization, matte backgrounds, and a host of other magic tricks. You visit the soundstages used for filming the *Mickey Mouse Club, Ed McMahon's Star Search,* and assorted movies. In the **Post-Production** area, *Star Wars* director George Lucas, aided by the robots R2D2 and C3PO, explains how computers are used for edit-ing, and Mel Gibson and PeeWee Herman switch voices in a lecture on sound tracks. *Audience: Adults and older children. Rating:* ★★★

**The Magic of Disney Animation.** This 30-minute self-guided tour through the Disney animation process is one of the funniest and most engaging attractions at the park. You'll watch a hilarious eight-minute film in which Walter Cronkite and Robin Williams explain the basics of animation. You then follow walkways with windows overlooking working anima-tion studios, where you see actual salaried Disney artists at their draft-ing tables doing everything you just learned about. Once you get over the feeling that you are in a zoo watching human animals, this is better than magic—this is real. *Audience: All but toddlers. Rating:* ★★★

**Studio Showcase.** A continually updated exhibit of film and television memorabilia. You can also follow Roger Rabbit's pink footsteps to the **Loony Bin,** where kids can have their picture taken in front of the di-rectional signs indicating Thisaway and Thataway. *Audience: Adults and older children. Rating:* ★★

**Voyage of the Little Mermaid.** Here you're invited to join Ariel, Sebastian, and the underwater gang in a stage show that condenses the movie into a 15-minute presentation of its best numbers. The black light effects make for an unusual show. One of the better shows for parents, who will be amazed by the puppeteers. *Audience: All ages. Rating:* ★★

**Walt Disney Theater.** At half-hour intervals, this screens *The Making of The Lion King,* a fascinating behind-the-scenes look at Disney's smash hit that was originally produced for the Disney Channel. Narrated by Robert Guillaume (the voice of Rafiki, the film's psychic baboon), the film traces the creation of the animated classic from concept to final scenes. *Audience: All ages. Rating:* ★★★

## The Backlot

In this rather amorphous area, you can tour the New York Street sets on foot as long as crews aren't filming—and it's worth it for the wealth of detail to be seen in the store windows.

***Honey, I Shrunk the Kids*** **Movie Set Adventure.** Take a left at Mickey Avenue and New York Street and let the kids run free in this state-of-the-art playground based on the movie about lilliputian children in a larger-than-life world. *Audience: Children. Rating:* ★★★

**Jim Henson's Muppet*Vision 3-D.** A spectacular combination of 3-D movie and musical revue, this is lots of fun—and air-conditioned. The theater was constructed especially for this 30-minute show, with special effects literally built into the walls. All of the most beloved Muppet characters make an appearance. *Audience: All ages. Rating:* ★★★

## Backlot Annex

**Indiana Jones Epic Stunt Spectacular.** Don't leave Disney–MGM Studios without seeing this 30-minute show featuring the stunt choreography of veteran coordinator Glenn Randall. (*Raiders of the Lost Ark, Indiana Jones and the Temple of Doom, E. T.,* and *Jewel of the Nile* are among his credits.) Presented in a 2,200-seat amphitheater, it teaches how the most breathtaking movie stunts are pulled off, with the help of 10 audience participants (go ahead, volunteer!). Arrive early because the theater does fill to capacity. *Audience: All but young children. Rating:* ★★★

**Star Tours.** This flight simulator inspired by the *Star Wars* films is a real show stopper. Piloted by Star Wars characters R2D2 and C3PO, 40-passenger vehicles called StarSpeeders take a seven-minute flight that's fraught with misadventures: You shoot into deep space, dodge giant ice crystals and comet debris, innocently bumble into an intergalactic battle, and whiz through the canyons of some planetary city before coming to a heart-stopping halt. *Audience: Adults and older children. Rating:* ★★★

## Lakeside Circle

**Monster Sound Show.** Despite its name, it's anything but scary. Rather, it's a delightful, multifaceted demonstration of the use of movie sound effects. Volunteer sound-effects specialists dash around trying to coordinate their sound effects with the short movie being shown simultaneously, where a hilariously klutzy Chevy Chase plays an insurance man on a visit to a haunted house. *Audience: All ages. Rating:* ★★★

**SuperStar Television.** Here, 28 volunteers are chosen from the audience to "play" the starring roles on everything from *I Love Lucy* to *Gilligan's Island.* While the volunteers are led off to makeup and costume, the audience files into a 1,000-seat theater reminiscent of the days of live television broadcasting. On 6-foot-wide monitors, the onstage action appears merged with clips from classic shows. *Audience: All but young children. Rating:* ★★

# Epcot Center

*Take the Epcot Center–Disney Village exit off I-4.*

WDW was created because of Walt Disney's dream of EPCOT, an "Experimental Prototype Community of Tomorrow." He envisioned a future in which nations coexisted in peace and harmony, reaping the miraculous harvest of technological achievement. He suggested the idea as early as October 1966. But with Disneyland hemmed in by development, Disney had to search for new land. He found it in Florida. The permanent community that he envisioned has not yet come to be, but instead we have Epcot Center (which opened in 1982, years after Disney's death), a showcase, ostensibly, for the concepts that would be incorporated into the EPCOTs of the future. Then, as now, it was composed of two parts: Future World, where the majority of its 10 pavilions are sponsored by major American corporations, and World Showcase, whose 11 exhibition areas each represent a different country.

Epcot is that rare paradox—an educational theme park—and a very successful one, too. Although rides have been added over the years to try to amuse the young-uns, the thrills are mostly in the mind. Consequently, Epcot is best suited for older children and adults. A dedicated visitor really needs two days to explore it all; to cram it into one day, arrive early. Don't waste time at sit-down meals, see the shows when the park is empty, and slow down and enjoy the shops and the live entertainment when the crowds thicken.

Epcot Center is divided into two distinct areas, **Future World** and **World Showcase,** separated by the 40-acre **World Showcase Lagoon.** The monorail drops you off at the official entrance, in Future World; trams from the WDW Dolphin and Swan hotels and Disney's Yacht Club and Beach Club resorts drop you off at International Gateway, the entrance to World Showcase.

## Future World
Future World's inner core is composed of the Spaceship Earth geosphere and, just beyond it, the Innoventions exhibit and Innoventions Plaza. Seven pavilions make up the outer ring of the circle, containing both rides and interactive displays.

Balanced like a giant golf ball waiting for some celestial being to tee off, the multifaceted silver geosphere known as **Spaceship Earth** is to Epcot what the Cinderella Castle is to the Magic Kingdom. It weighs 1 million pounds, measures 164 feet in diameter and 180 feet in height, and encompasses more than 2 million cubic feet of space. The anodized aluminum sheath is composed of 954 triangular panels, not all of equal size or shape. Since it is not a geodesic dome (which is only a half sphere), the name "geosphere" was invented for it.

**Earth Station.** Inside the **Spaceship Earth** geosphere is the principal Epcot information center, the place to pick up schedules of live entertainment, park brochures, and the like. The computerized World Key Information System kiosks, most located in Earth Station, let you obtain detailed information about every pavilion, leave messages for companions, and most important of all, make reservations for meals in Epcot Center restaurants.

**Horizons.** Here General Electric sponsors a relentlessly optimistic look at the once and future future. After being enjoined to "live your dreams," you ride a tram for 15 minutes past dioramas of the future, depicting what great minds have imagined that the world would be like in a hundred years or so. The tram then moves past a series of tableaux of life in a future space colony. The Omega Centuri tableau, portraying a free-floating space colony, prefigures virtual reality with its games of zero-gravity basketball and simulated outdoor sports. *Audience: Adults and older children. Rating:* ★★

**Innoventions.** Disney's latest addition to Future World is this two-building, 100,000-square-foot attraction at the center of the complex. Live stage demonstrations, interactive hands-on displays, and exhibits highlight new technology that affects daily living. Innoventions visitors get a first look at new electronic games and toys, computers, home appliances, televisions, and other major innovations of the near future. Each of 15 major exhibit areas is presented by a leading manufacturer. This is a great place for both adults and children to play. A nice change from the non-interactive feel of much of the park. *Audience: Adults and older children. Rating:* ★★

**Journey Into Imagination.** One of the big three pavilions on the west side of Future World, Eastman Kodak's sets your mind spinning. The **Journey into Imagination Ride** is a dreamy exploration of how creativity works. Laser beams zing back and forth, lightning crackles, letters leap out of a giant typewriter, and an iridescent painting unfolds across a wall. *Audience: All ages. Rating:* ★★★

The **Image Works** is an electronic fun house crammed with interactive games and wizardry. *Audience: All ages. Rating:* ★★★

The 3-D film *Honey, I Shrunk the Audience* has quickly become one of Epcot Center's most popular attractions. Like the two hit films on which it's based, the adventure stars Rick Moranis as Dr. Wayne Szalinski. While he's demonstrating his latest shrinking machine, things go really, really wrong. It's just too much fun to give anything else away, but be prepared to laugh your head off, courtesy of special in-theater effects such as moving seats and 3-D film technology developed by Walt Disney Studios. *Audience: All ages. Rating:* ★★★

**The Land.** Shaped like an intergalactic greenhouse, this enormous skylighted pavilion dedicates 6 acres and a host of different attractions to everyone's favorite topic: food. You can easily spend two hours here.

The main event is a 14-minute boat ride called **Listen to the Land,** where you cruise through three biomes (rain forest, desert, and prairie ecological communities) and into an experimental greenhouse that demonstrates how food sources may be grown in the future, not only on earth but also in outer space. *Audience: Adults and older children. Rating:* ★★★

The terminally cute singing fruits and vegetables of the Kitchen Kabaret revue have been replaced with **Food Rocks,** a rowdy concert in which rock musicians taking the shape of favorite foods (the Peach Boys, Chubby Cheddar, and Neil Moussaka, among others) wail about the joys of nutrition. *Audience: All ages. Rating:* ★

The **Harvest Theater** is home to a 20-minute, National Geographic-like film called *Symbiosis,* an intelligent look at how we can profit from the earth's natural resources while ensuring that the earth benefits, too. *Audience: Adults and teenagers. Rating:* ★★

**Living Seas.** The United Technologies pavilion is a favorite among children. An imaginative fountain flings surf in a never-ending wave against a rock garden beneath the stylized marquee. Smack in the center is a 5.7-million-gallon aquarium walled in acrylic. The three-minute **Caribbean Coral Reef ride** encircles the tank. Sometimes you'll catch sight of a diver testing out the latest scuba equipment, surrounded by a cloud of parrot fish as he scatters food for the tank's denizens. After the ride, you can circumnavigate the tank at your own speed on an upper level, pointing out barracudas, stingrays, parrot fish, sea turtles, and even sharks, before exploring the two levels of **Sea Base Alpha,** which is supposed to look like an undersea research facility. Actually, it is made up of six modules, each dedicated to a specific subject and fitted out with interactive devices that help you explore the history of robotics, ocean exploration, ocean ecosystems, dolphins, porpoises, and sea lions. *Audience: Adults and older children. Rating:* ★★★

**Spaceship Earth ride.** Hands down, this is the most popular ride at Epcot Center. Scripted by science-fiction writer Ray Bradbury and narrated by actor Jeremy Irons, the 15-minute journey begins in the darkest tunnels of time, proceeds through history as we know it, and ends poised on the edge of the future, including a dramatic look at a "virtual reality" classroom. Audio-Animatronic figures present history in astonishing detail. Toward the conclusion of the ride, visitors arrive in a "Global Neighborhood" that ties all the peoples of the earth together through an interactive global network. Special effects, animated sets, and audience-enclosing laser beams are used to create the experience. *Audience: Adults and older children. Rating:* ★★★

**Universe of Energy.** Two large topiary dinosaurs stand guard at this attraction, which occupies a large, lopsided pyramid, sheathed in thousands of mirrors, which serve as solar collectors to power the ride and films within. One of the most technologically complex shows at Epcot Center, this Exxon-sponsored exhibit combines a half-hour ride, two films, the largest Audio-Animatronic animals ever built, 250 prehistoric trees, and enough cold, damp fog to make you think you've been transported to the inside of a defrosting icebox.★★★

**Wonders of Life.** A towering statue of a DNA double helix stands outside the gold-crowned dome of Metropolitan Life's popular pavilion, which takes an amusing but serious and educational look at health, fitness, and modern lifestyles via several attractions. One improvisational theater revue, two films, and dozens of interactive gadgets that whiz, bleep, and blink make up the **Fitness Fairground.** *Audience: Adults and older children. Rating:* ★★

The biggest attraction in the Wonders of Life pavilion may be **Body Wars,** Walt Disney World's first flight simulator attraction, which takes visitors on a five-minute bumpy platelet-to-platelet ride through the human circulatory system. *Audience: Adults and older children. Rating:* ★★★

A 20-minute multimedia presentation, **Cranium Command** reveals the workings of the mind of a typical 12-year-old boy during the course of an ordinary day. *Audience: Adults and older children. Rating:* ★★★

NEED A BREAK? Met Life practices its preaching at **Pure & Simple,** a food stall offering healthful snacks and full meals, and proves that nutritious can also be delicious. The prices won't give you a heart attack either.

**World of Motion.** This General Motors pavilion is shaped like a wheel. The main attraction is the 15-minute **World of Motion ride,** which is essentially a dippy, feel-good frolic through scenarios depicting the history of human attempts to get somewhere else faster. *Audience: Adults and older children. Rating:* ★★

At the exit of the World of Motion ride is the **Trans-Center,** a 33,000-square-foot exhibit and auto showroom displaying new and experimental car models. It's dark, cool, and pleasant on a hot day. *Audience: Adults and older children. Rating:* ★

## World Showcase

The World Showcase Lagoon is just 1⅓ miles around, but in that space, you circumnavigate the globe.

**The American Adventure.** Housed in a scrupulous reproduction of Philadelphia's Liberty Hall, this multimedia blockbuster presents a 100-yard dash through history, a pageant that uses evocative sets, the world's largest rear-projection screen (72 feet in width), enormous movable stages, and 35 Audio-Animatronic players. Beginning with the arrival of the Pilgrims at Plymouth Rock, Ben Franklin and a wry, pipe-smoking Mark Twain narrate 30 minutes of episodes—both praiseworthy and shameful—that have shaped the American spirit. *Audience: Adults and older children. Rating:* ★★★

**American Gardens Theatre.** Directly opposite the **American Adventure,** on the edge of the lagoon, this amphitheater is currently host to the *Magical World of Barbie,* a high-spirited song-and-dance review about the world's most famous doll and her adventures around the world (aha! the Epcot connection!). *Audience: All ages. Rating:* ★

**Canada.** A striking rocky chasm and tumbling waterfall make just one of the high points here. Like the Rocky Mountains and the Great Canadian North, the scale of the structures seems immense, thanks to a trick called forced perspective, which exaggerates the smallness of the distant parts to make the entire thing look humongous. The top attraction is the 17-minute CircleVision film *O Canada! Audience: All but toddlers. Rating:* ★★★

**China.** This shimmering red-and-gold, three-tier replica of Beijing's Temple of Heaven towers over a serene Chinese garden, an art gallery displaying treasures from the People's Republic, a spacious emporium crammed with Chinese goods, and two restaurants. The garden, planted with rosebushes native to China, a 100-year-old mulberry tree, and water oaks (whose twisted branches look Asian but are actually Florida homegrown), is one of the most peaceful spots in Epcot Center. The 19-minute film *Wonders of China* is dramatically portrayed on a 360° CircleVision screen. *Audience: All but toddlers. Rating:* ★★★

**France.** You don't need the scaled-down model of the Eiffel Tower to tell you what country you're in—or what city. There's the poignant accordion music wafting out of concealed speakers, solid mansard-roof mansions crowned with iron filigree, and delicious aromas surrounding the **Boulangerie Pâtisserie** bakeshop. The intimate **Palais du Cinema,** inspired by the royal theater at Fontainebleau, screens the 18-minute film *Impressions de France,* a five-screen homage to the glories of the country. *Audience: All but toddlers. Rating:* ★★★

**Germany.** This jovial make-believe village distills the best folk architecture from all over that country. Don't miss the chimes from the specially designed glockenspiel on the clock tower, which plays hourly; you'll also hear many musical toots and tweets from multitudinous cuckoo clocks, folk tunes from the spinning dolls and lambs sold at Der Teddybär, and the satisfied grunts of hungry visitors chowing down on hearty German cooking. Other than the four-times-a-day oom-pah band show in the **Biergarten** restaurant, Germany doesn't offer any specific entertainment—just more shops than any other pavilion. *Audience: Adults and older children. Rating:* ★★

NEED A BREAK?    The **Sommerfest** pretzel-and-bratwurst cart is one of the rare options for snacks in this part of the World.

**Italy.** The feature here is the Piazza San Marco, complete with a reproduction of Venice's Doges Palace that's true right down to the gold leaf on the angel perched 100 feet atop the Campanile, gondolas tethered to a seawall stained with age, and Romanesque columns, Byzantine mosaics, Gothic arches, and stone walls carefully "antiqued" to look historic. Inside, shops sell Venetian beads and glasswork, leather purses and belts, and Perugina chocolate "kisses." *Audience: Adults and older children. Rating:* ★★

**Japan.** A brilliant vermillion torii gate epitomizes the striking yet serene mood here. Disney horticulturists deserve a hand for their achievement in constructing a very Japanese landscape, complete with rocks, pebbled streams, pools, and hills, out of all-American plants and boulders. The heart of the pavilion is a brilliant blue winged pagoda, based on the 8th-century Horyuji Temple in Nara. Entertainment takes the form of Japanese musicians and demonstrations of exotic, traditional Japanese crafts—a lot more amusing than they sound. *Audience: Adults and older children. Rating:* ★★★

| | |
|---|---|
| NEED A BREAK? | Westerners with a yen for the flavors of Japan will be satisfied at the **Yakitori House,** which serves broiled chicken and beef (a sort of Japanese shish kebab) and batter-fried seafood and vegetables, as well as such Japanese specialties as clear soup and pickled ginger. |

**Mexico.** Housed in a spectacular Mayan pyramid surrounded by a tangle of tropical vegetation, this pavilion contains an exhibit of pre-Columbian art, a restaurant, a delightfully cool, dim shopping plaza, and the **El Rio del Tiempo boat ride.** This nine-minute journey from the jungles of the Yucatán to modern-day Mexico City is enlivened (somewhat) by video images of feathered Toltec dancers, by Spanish-colonial Audio-Animatronic dancing puppets, and by film clips of the cliff divers in Acapulco, the speedboats in Manzanillo, and snorkeling around Isla Mujeres. However, the boat ride is not the best part, and if there's a line, skip it and go right on through the doors to stroll around the plaza and its shops. *Audience: Adults and older children. Rating:* ★

**Morocco.** After entering through the pointed arches of the Bab Boujouloud gate, ornamented with beautiful wood carvings and encrusted with intricate mosaics, you can take a guided tour (inquire of any cast member), check out the exhibit in the **Gallery of Arts and History,** and entertain yourself examining the wares at such shops as **Casablanca Carpets, Jewels of the Sahara, the Brass Bazaar,** and **Berber Oasis.** The belly dancing in the restaurant **Marrakesh,** is tame, but youngsters like it. *Audience: Adults and older children. Rating:* ★★

**Norway.** Here you'll see rough-hewn timbers and sharply pitched roofs (so the snow will slip right off), bloom-stuffed window boxes, figured shutters, and lots of smiling, blond and blue-eyed young Norwegians. The pavilion complex contains a 14th-century stone fortress that mimics Oslo's Akershus, cobbled streets, rocky waterfalls, and a wood stave church with dragons glaring from the eaves. The church houses an exhibit called "To the Ends of the Earth," which tells the story of two early 20th-century polar expeditions with vintage artifacts. Norway also has a dandy boat ride, **Maelstrom** (★★), in which dragon-headed longboats take a 10-minute voyage through time. *Audience: All but toddlers. Rating:* ★★

**United Kingdom.** A pastiche of there-will-always-be-an-England architecture, this pavilion rambles from the elegant mansions lining a London square and the bustling, half-timbered shops of a village High Street to the thatch-roof cottages of the countryside (their thatch made of plastic broom bristles). The pavilion has no single major attraction. Instead, you can wander through shops selling tea and tea accessories, Welsh handicrafts, Royal Doulton figurines, and woolens and tartans from

Pringle of Scotland. Outside, the strolling Old Globe Players coax audience members into participating in their lowbrow versions of Shakespeare. *Audience: Adults and older children. Rating:* ★★★

### Entertainment

Above the lagoon every night, about a half hour before closing, don't miss the spectacular **IllumiNations** sound-and-light show, with fireworks, lasers, and lots of special effects to the accompaniment of a terrific score. Best viewing spots are on the bridge between France and the United Kingdom, the promenade in front of Canada and Norway, and the bridge between China and Germany.

## Magic Kingdom

*Take the Magic Kingdom–U.S. 192 exit off I–4; from there it's 4 miles along Disney's main entrance road and another mile to the parking lot; be prepared for serious traffic.*

For most people, the Magic Kingdom is Walt Disney World. Certainly it is both the heart and soul of the Walt Disney World empire; it was the first theme park on property when WDW opened in 1971, and it is the park that traveled, with modifications, to France and Japan. For a park that has demonstrated such worldwide appeal, it is surprisingly small, just 98 acres. However, it packs in six different themed areas known as "lands," with nearly 50 major crowd pleasers, and that's not counting all the ancillary attractions: shops, eateries, live entertainment, strolling cartoon characters, fireworks, and parades.

The park is laid out on a north–south axis, with Cinderella Castle at the epicenter and the various lands surrounding it in a broad circle. Upon passing through the entrance gates, you immediately discover yourself in Town Square, a central area containing City Hall, the principal information center. Here you can pick up park brochures and a schedule of daily events, search for misplaced belongings or companions, and ask questions of the omniscient staffers behind the desk.

Town Square gives onto Main Street, a boulevard filled with Victorian-style stores and dining spots. Main Street runs due north and ends at The Hub, a large tree-lined circle in front of Cinderella Castle. Moving clockwise from The Hub, the Magic Kingdom's different lands include Adventureland, Frontierland, Liberty Square, Fantasyland (directly behind Cinderella Castle), and Tomorrowland.

### Main Street

On this charming thoroughfare, there are plenty of inducements to spend more than the 40 minutes allowed by most visitors. Most of the structures house stores; these range from the **House of Magic,** complete with trick-showing proprietors, and the **Harmony Barber Shop,** where you can have yourself shorn, to the milliner's emporium, stocking Cat-in-the-Hat fantasies, and all sorts of snackeries and souvenir shops. The best time to shop is mid-afternoon, when the lines at the rides are long and slow; things are mobbed beginning around 5 PM, when parents with small fry are heading home, and just before park closing.

**Main Street Cinema.** Six screens run continuous vintage Disney cartoons in the cool, air-conditioned quiet here. It's a great opportunity to see the genius of Walt Disney and to see Steamboat Willie, Mickey Mouse's debut cartoon. *Audience: All ages. Rating:* ★★

**Penny Arcade.** Vintage coin-operated games and kinescopes charm adults on this corner of Main Street; kids go for the battalions of more modern diversions.

**Walt Disney World Railroad.** In Town Square, you can step right up to the elevated platform above the Magic Kingdom's entrance for a ride. The 1½-mile track runs along the perimeter of the Magic Kingdom, through the woods and past Tom Sawyer Island and other attractions; stops are in Frontierland and Mickey's Starland. It's a great introduction to the layout of the park if you ride just after you arrive and a welcome relief for tired feet if you travel in the afternoon. Four trains run at five- to seven-minute intervals; a complete circuit takes 21 minutes. *Audience: All ages. Rating:* ★

## Adventureland

From the manicured lawns and meticulously pruned trees of the Hub, an artfully dilapidated wooden bridge leads to this land, Disney's attempt to inspire jungle fever. Landscape artists went wild here: South African Cape honeysuckle droops, Brazilian bougainvillea drapes, Mexican flame vines cling, spider plants clone, and three different varieties of palm trees sway, all creating a seemingly spontaneous mess.

**Enchanted Tiki Birds.** Inside this blessedly air-conditioned Polynesian longhouse, the "Tropical Serenade" is sung and whistled by hundreds of Audio-Animatronic figures: exotic birds, swaying flowers, and Tiki god statues with blinking red eyes. This was Disney's first Audio-Animatronics attraction; the animatronics still hold up fine but the audio could use an update. *Audience: All ages. Rating:* ★

**Jungle Cruise.** This ride has you gliding through three continents along four rivers: the Congo, the Nile, the Mekong, and the Amazon. The canopied launches pack in visitors tighter than sardines, the safari-suited guide makes a point of checking his pistol, and the Irrawady Irma or Mongala Millie is off for another "perilous" journey. The guide's spiel is surprisingly funny, with just the right blend of cornball humor and gently snide asides. *Audience: All ages. Rating:* ★★★

**Pirates of the Caribbean.** "Avast, ye scurvy scum!" is the sort of greeting your kids will proclaim for the next week—which gives you an idea of the impact of this stellar 10-minute boat ride. Here is Disney at its best, with memorable vignettes, incredible detail, and catchy music. Emerging from a pitch-black tunnel of time, you're literally in the middle of a furious battle as a pirate ship, cannons blazing, attacks a stone fortress. Audio-Animatronic pirates hoist the Jolly Roger while brave soldiers scurry to defend the fort. The wild antics of the pirates result in a conflagration, the town goes up in flames, and everyone goes to their just reward. *Audience: All ages, although scary to young children. Rating:* ★★★

**Swiss Family Treehouse.** Based on the classic novel by Johann Wyss about the adventures of a family shipwrecked on the way to America, this tree house shows what you can do with a big banyan and a lot of imagination: The kitchen sink is made of a giant clamshell; the boys' room, strewn with clothing, has two hammocks instead of beds; and an ingenious system of rain barrels and bamboo pipes provides running water in every room (German visitors seem especially fascinated by this). It's recognizable from the camouflaged entrance and the tree looming overhead. *Audience: All ages; toddlers unsteady on their feet and some senior citizens may have trouble with stairs. Rating:* ★★

## Frontierland

In the northwest quadrant of the Magic Kingdom, Frontierland invokes the spirit of the American frontier, with staffers dressed in checked shirts, leather vests, cowboy hats, and brightly colored neckerchiefs. Banjo and fiddle music twangs from tree to tree.

**Country Bear Jamboree.** In this cornpone stage show in a miniature opry barn, wisecracking Audio-Animatronic bears joke, sing, and play country music and 1950s rock and roll. *Audience: All ages. Rating:* ★★★

**Diamond Horseshoe Jamboree.** The rip-roaring, raucous, corny, high-kicking dance-hall show here features a sextet of beruffled girls and high-spirited cowboys, among them Sam, the stagestruck and lovelorn saloon keeper, and Lily, a shimmying, feather-boa-toting Mae West. Seating begins half an hour before curtain time and snacks and light refreshments may be purchased at your table. *Show times: 10:45, 12:15, 1:45, 3:30, and 4:45; reservations essential. Book in early morning at booth in front of Disneyana Collectibles on Main Street (12:15 show fills up first) or show up 30 min before show time to wait for cancellations. Audience: All but young children. Rating:* ★★

**Splash Mountain.** As soon as the park opens in the morning, hordes in the know hoof it to this thriller. Based on the animated sequences in Disney's 1946 film, *Song of the South,* it features Audio-Animatronic creations of Brer Rabbit, Brer Bear, Brer Fox, and a menagerie of other brer beasts. An eight-person hollowed-out log carries you through a lily pond and up the mountain. You get one heart-stopping pause at the top—just long enough to grab the safety bar—and then the boat plummets down the world's longest and sharpest flume drop right into a gigantic briar patch. Whoosh. You will get wet. *Audience: All but young children. No pregnant women or guests wearing back, neck, or leg braces; minimum height 44". Rating:* ★★★

**Big Thunder Mountain.** As any true roller-coaster lover can tell you, this three-minute ride is a tame one, but the thrills are there, thanks to the intricate details and stunning scenery. Set in Gold Rush days, the runaway railroad train rushes and rattles past 20 Audio-Animatronic figures—including donkeys, chickens, a goat, and a grizzled old miner surprised in his bathtub—a derelict mining town, hot springs, and a flash flood. (It's especially fun at night.) Note that because of the lack of shade, the line here is one of Disney's worst on hot summer days. *Audience: All but young children. No pregnant women or guests in back, neck, or leg braces; minimum height 40". Rating:* ★★★

**Tom Sawyer Island.** Although it's actually two islands connected by an old-fashioned swing bridge, most of what you'll want to see are on the main island: the mystery cave, a pitch-black (almost) labyrinth where the wind wails in a truly spooky fashion; Injun Joe's cave, all pointy stalactites and stalagmites; Harpers Mill, an old-fashioned grist mill (nothing scary here); and, in a clearing at the top of the hill, a rustic playground for younger kids. On the other island is Fort Sam Clemens, a log fortress from which you can fire air guns (with great booms and cracks) at the soporific passengers on the Liberty Square Riverboat. *Audience: All ages. Rating:* ★★

## Liberty Square
The weathered siding of WDW's Frontierland gives way to neat clapboard and solid brick, the mesquite and cactus are replaced by stately oaks and masses of azalea, and the rough-and-tumble western frontier gently slides into colonial America. Shops tend to sell more arts than kitsch, and the **Liberty Tree Tavern,** an institutional but fairly charming table-service restaurant that could have been airlifted from Colonial Williamsburg, is one of the best at the Magic Kingdom (reservations essential).

**Hall of Presidents.** This 30-minute multimedia tribute to the Constitution is another marvel of Audio-Animatronics. The two-part show starts with a film, narrated by writer Maya Angelou, that discusses the importance of the Constitution. The second half is a roll call of all 42 American presidents, including William Jefferson Clinton, who, unlike other contemporary presidential robots, has a speaking part—the voice-over done by Bill Clinton himself. The detail is lifelike right down to the brace on Franklin Delano Roosevelt's leg, and the robots can't resist nodding, fidgeting, and even whispering to each other while waiting for their names to come up. *Audience: Adults and older children. Rating:* ★★

**Haunted Mansion.** Part walk-through, part ride on a "doom buggy," this eight-minute buggy ride is scary but not terrifying, and the special effects are phenomenal. Catch the glowing bats' eyes on the wallpaper; the strategically placed gusts of damp, cold air; the wacky inscriptions on the tombstones; and the spectral xylophone player. One of the all-time best. *Audience: All but young children. Rating:* ★★★

**Liberty Square Riverboat.** A real old-fashioned steamboat, the Richard F. Irvine (named for a key Disney designer) is authentic from the big rear paddle wheel to the gingerbread trim on its three decks to its calliope whistle. The 15-minute trip is slow and certainly not thrilling, but it makes a relaxing break for all concerned. *Audience: All but young children (they'll be bored). Rating:* ★

**Mike Fink Keel Boats.** Plying the same waters as the Liberty Square Riverboat, these craft are short and dumpy and you have to listen to a heavy-handed, noisy spiel about those roistering, roustabout days along the Missouri. Skip this one on your first visit. *Audience: All ages. Rating:* ★

## Fantasyland
Many of the rides here are for children, and the lines move slowly. If you're traveling without young kids, skip this area, with the possible exception of Cinderella's Golden Carrousel.

**Cinderella Castle.** At 180 feet, this castle is more than 100 feet taller than Disneyland's Sleeping Beauty Castle, and, with its elongated towers and lacy fretwork, immeasurably more graceful.

**Cinderella's Golden Carrousel.** The whirling, musical heart of Fantasyland—and maybe even of the entire Magic Kingdom—is the antique Cinderella's Golden Carrousel. It has 90 prancing horses, each one completely different. The rich notes of the band organ—no calliope here—play favorite tunes from Disney movies. *Audience: All but young children. Rating:* ★★★

**Dumbo, the Flying Elephant.** Jolly Dumbos fly around a central column, each pachyderm packing a couple of kids and a parent. A joystick controls each Dumbo's vertical motion, making him ascend or descend at will. Doesn't sound like much? It's one of Fantasyland's best rides. Just ask any mom or dad towing a toddler, or the littl'uns themselves. Alas, the ears do not flap. *Audience: Young children and the young at heart. Rating:* ★

**It's a Small World.** Visiting Walt Disney World and not stopping here—why, the idea is practically un-American. Moving somewhat slower than a snail, barges inch through several barnlike rooms, each crammed with musical moppets dressed in various national costumes and madly singing the theme song, "It's a Small World After All." But somehow by the time you reach the end of the 11-minute ride, you're grinning and humming, too—as has been the case with almost everyone who's ever heard them since it debuted at the 1964–65 New York World's Fair. *Audience: All ages. Rating:* ★★

**Legend of the Lion King.** Unlike many of Magic Kingdom stage shows, this one showcases "humanimals," Disneyspeak for bigger-than-life-size figures that are manipulated by human "animateers" hidden from audience view. (The adult Simba, for instance, is nearly 8 feet tall.) The preshow consists of the "Circle of Life" overture from the film. *Audience: All ages. Rating:* ★★★

**Mad Tea Party.** In this ride based on the 1951 Disney film about a girl named Alice in Wonderland, you hop into oversize, pastel-color teacups and whirl for two minutes around a giant platter. If the centrifugal force hasn't shaken you up too much, check out the soused mouse that pops out of the teapot centerpiece. *Audience: All ages. Rating:* ★

**Mickey's Starland.** This 3-acre niche in Fantasyland, built in 1988 to celebrate Mickey Mouse's 60th birthday, is rarely crowded, perhaps because its appeal is mostly to small fry. The attractions are located in the imaginary town of Duckburg (yes, Donald and Huey, Dewey, and Louie are all here, along with a cast of other Disney characters), whose pastel-color houses are positively lilliputian, with miniature driveways and toy-size picket fences and signs scribbled with finger paint. **Mickey's Starland Show,** held under a yellow-and-white stripe big top, presents the television stars of *The Disney Afternoon* in a cheerful sing-along musical comedy that kids adore. Afterward, all the kids dash around backstage to **Mickey's Dressing Room,** where the star graciously signs autographs and poses for pictures with his adoring public. Kids can climb, jump, slide, explore, and have a plain good time in **Mickey's Treehouse** and **Minnie's Doll House.** For toddlers and preschoolers, there's the **Mouse-Ka-Maze,** a scaled-down version of the maze from Alice in Wonderland. Nearby there's a petting zoo with live animals at **Grandma Duck's Farm.** *Audience: Mainly young children. Rating:* ★★

**Mr. Toad's Wild Ride.** Based on the 1949 Disney release *The Adventures of Ichabod and Mr. Toad,* itself derived from Kenneth Grahame's classic children's novel, *The Wind in the Willows,* this attraction puts you in the jump seat of the speed-loving amphibian's flivver for a jolting, jarring three-minute jaunt through the English countryside. *Audience: All ages. Rating:* ★★

**Peter Pan's Flight.** Here you board two-person magic sailing ships with brightly striped sails that catch the wind and soar into the skies above London en route to Never-Never-Land. Adults will especially enjoy the dreamy views of London by moonlight. *Audience: All ages. Rating:* ★★

**Skyway to Tomorrowland.** This cable car takes off on its one-way aerial trip to Tomorrowland from an enchanted attic perched above the trees in a far corner of Fantasyland not far from **It's a Small World.** Can anyone say "photo opportunity"? *Audience: All ages. Rating:* ★

**Snow White's Adventures.** What was for many years an unremittingly scary, three-minute, indoor spook-house ride, whose dwarfs might as well have been named Anxious and Fearful, has reopened as a kinder, gentler attraction. Now with six-passenger cars and more like a miniversion of the movie, the ride has been tempered. There's still the evil queen, her nose wart, and her cackle, and the trip is still packed with scary moments, but the Prince and Snow White have joined the cast, and there's an honest-to-goodness kiss followed by a happily ever-after ending, which might even have you heigh-ho-ing on your way out. *Audience: All ages; toddlers may be scared. Rating:* ★★

## Tomorrowland

The stark, antiseptic future that Disney Imagineers seemed to be forecasting with their original design had become embarrassingly inaccurate: Its huge expanses of concrete, its plain white walls trying so hard to be sleek, and its outdated rides said more about Eisenhower-era aesthetics (or lack thereof) than third-millennium progress.

Disney artists and architects learned their lesson, and in the recently debuted Tomorrowland redesign, they gave up on predicting tomorrow and focused instead on "the future that never was"—the future envisioned by sci-fi writers and moviemakers in the 1920s and 1930s, when space flight, laser beams, and home computers belonged in the world of fiction, not fact.

**Alien Encounter.** The story here is that you've entered a convention center of the future to watch a test of a new teleportation system, when an attempt to transport the CEO of the devices manufacturer, an alien corporation called XS-Tech, fails. The catastrophic result is a close encounter with a frightening alien creature. Despite a disappointing lack of truly special effects, this is still certain to become one of the Magic Kingdom's most popular new attractions. *Audience: All but young children. Rating:* ★★

**AstroOrbiter.** The superstructure of revolving planets is gleaming and will most likely come to symbolize the new Tomorrowland, just as Dumbo has long represented Fantasyland. Despite the spiffy new look, though, the ride is still the old Starjets ride, something like Dumbo for grown-ups but with Buck Rogers-style vehicles rather than elephants to ride in. You control the altitude if not the velocity. *Audience: All ages. Rating:* ★★

**Carousel of Progress.** This 20-minute show in a revolving theater, first seen at the 1964–65 World's Fair and updated many times since then, traces the impact of technological progress from the turn of this century into the near future. In each decade, an Audio-Animatronic family sings the praises of the new gadgets that technology has wrought. The preshow, on overhead video monitors, details the design of the original carousel and features Walt Disney himself singing the theme song, "There's a Great Big Beautiful Tomorrow"—very fitting for the new Tomorrowland. *Audience: All ages. Rating:* ★

**Delta Dreamflight.** That there's almost never a wait here should put your suspicions on red alert. It's in the same building complex as the Transportarium, and, in fact, the entrances can be easily confused—Dreamflight is farther along and to the right. Sponsored by Delta Airlines, this ride takes a look at the adventure and romance of flying. The idea is cute, but the execution—surprising given Disney's experience with special effects—falls far short of thrilling. *Audience: All ages. Rating:* ★

**Grand Prix Raceway.** Be prepared for instant addiction among kids: brightly colored Mark VII model gasoline-powered cars swerve around the four 2,260-foot tracks with much vroom-vroom-vrooming. But there's way too much waiting. *Audience: Older children (minimum height 52" to drive; be sure to check your youngster's height before lining up). Rating:* ★

**Skyway to Fantasyland.** You can pick up the brightly colored cable cars right outside of **Space Mountain** for the commute to the far western end of Fantasyland. The silence aloft is quite pleasant after the hubbub on the ground. *Audience: All ages. Rating:* ★

**Space Mountain.** Its needlelike spires and 180-foot-high, gleaming white concrete cone are a Magic Kingdom icon. Inside you'll find a roller coaster that may well be the world's most imaginative. The ride only lasts two minutes and 38 seconds and attains a top speed of a mere 28 mph, but the devious twists and drops, and the fact that it's all in the dark so that you can never see where you're going, make it seem twice as long and four times as thrilling. Try and grab the very front car. *Audience: All but young children; minimum height 44". Rating:* ★★★

**Tomorrowland Transit Authority (TTA).** All aboard for a nice, leisurely ride around the perimeter of Tomorrowland, circling the **AstroOrbiter** and eventually gliding through the middle of **Space Mountain.** Like the old WEDway People Mover, of which this is a redo, the TTA is smooth and noiseless, thanks to an electromagnetic linear induction motor that has no moving parts, uses little power, and emits no pollutants. It's Disney's look at the future of mass transit. Audience: All ages. Rating:★

**Transportarium.** Disney Imagineers have pulled out the stops for this attraction in the Metropolis Science Centre, which replaces the **Circle-vision 360** American Journeys. Combining CircleVision 360 filmmaking with Audio-Animatronic figures, it takes you on a time-traveling adventure to the past and into the future. Don't plan on a relaxing voyage, however; there are no seats in the theater—only lean rails, which veterans of the Epcot film circuit can tell you all about. Hosted by Time Keeper, a C3PO clone whose frenetic personality is provided by Robin Williams, and Nine-Eye, a slightly frazzled droid, the trip introduces you to famous inventors and visionaries of the machine age. *Audience: All ages. Rating:* ★★

## Entertainment

Beginning at 3 every day, the 30-minute-long **Daily Parade** proceeds down Main Street through Frontierland; there are floats, balloons, cartoon characters, dancers, singers (usually lip-synching to music played over the PA system), and much waving and cheering. It's pleasant and young children love it. Really thrilling is **SpectroMagic,** an incredible 30-minute nighttime extravaganza of twinkle-lighted floats, sequined costumes, sparkling decorations, and sparkling trees. **Fantasy in the Sky** is the Magic Kingdom fireworks display. Heralded by a dimming of all the lights along Main Street, a single spotlight illuminates the top turret of the Cinderella Castle and—poof!—Tinkerbell emerges in a shower of pixie dust to fly over the treetops and the crowds. Her disappearance signals the start of the fireworks. It's a great show and well worth waiting around for.

# The Disney Water Parks

## Blizzard Beach

Blizzard Beach promises the seemingly impossible—a seaside playground with an Alpine theme. The Disney Imagineers have gone all out to create a ski resort in the midst of a tropical lagoon. Playing with the snow-in-Florida motif, there are lots of puns and sight gags. The park centers on **Mt. Gushmore,** a 90-foot "snowcapped" mountain. After riding a chairlift to the top, "skiers" slide down the face of the mountain, tackling moguls, slalom courses, and toboggan and sled runs. At the base of the mountain, there's a sandy beach featuring the de rigueur wave pool, a lazy river, and play areas for both young children and preteens.

Mt. Gushmore's big gun is **Summit Plummet,** which Disney bills as "the world's tallest, fastest free-fall speed slide." From the top, it's a wild

55-mph plunge straight down to a splash landing at the base of the mountain. **Teamboat Springs** is a "white-water raft ride" in which six-passenger rafts zip along a twisting series of rushing waterfalls. No water park would be complete without a flume ride. Enter **Snow Stormers**—actually three flumes that descend from the top of Mt. Gushmore. Riders follow a switchback course through ski-type slalom gates. Slightly less adventurous swimmers take note: There are also rides for you, too.

## River Country

Imagine a mountain in Utah's red-rock country. Put a lake at the bottom, and add a verdant fuzz of maples and pines here and there up the sides. Then plant some water slides among the greenery, and call it a "good ol' fashioned swimmin' hole." Then you'll have River Country, adjoining the Fort Wilderness Campground Resort.

It was the first of Walt Disney World's water parks. Whereas larger, glitzier **Typhoon Lagoon** is balmy and tropical, this is rustic and rugged. Walking from the dressing rooms brings you to the 330,000-gallon swimming pool, bright blue and concrete-paved, like something out of a more modern Midwest; there are a couple of short, steep water slides here. Beyond that is **Bay Cove,** the roped-off corner of Bay Lake that's the main section of River Country. Rope swings hang from a rustic boom, and there are various other woody contraptions from which kids dive and cannonball. Two big water slides, 100 and 260 feet long respectively, descend the side of the mountain, while **White Water Rapids,** a series of short chutes and swirling pools that you descend in jumbo inner tubes, provides a more leisurely trip. In summer, come first thing in the morning or in late afternoon to avoid crowds.

## Typhoon Lagoon

Four times the size of River Country, Typhoon Lagoon offers a full day of activities: bobbing in 4-foot waves in a surf lagoon the size of two football fields; speeding down arrow-straight water slides and around twisty storm slides; bumping through white-water rapids; and snorkeling in **Shark Reef,** a 360,000-gallon snorkeling tank (closed Nov.–Apr.) containing an artificial coral reef and 4,000 real tropical fish. More mellow folks can float in inner tubes along the 2,100-foot **Castaway Creek,** which circles the entire park (it takes about 30 minutes to do the whole circuit; you can stop as you please along the way). A children's area, **Ketchakiddie Creek,** replicates adult rides on a smaller scale (all children must be accompanied by an adult). It's Disney's version of a day at the beach—complete with lifeguards in spiffy red-and-white stripe fisherman T-shirts.

Typhoon Lagoon is popular—in summer and on weekends, the park often reaches capacity (7,200) by midmorning. If you must go in summer, head out for a few hours during the dreamy late afternoons or when the weather clears up after a thundershower. (Typically, rainstorms drive away the crowds, and lots of people simply don't come back.) If you plan to make a whole day of it, avoid weekends—Typhoon Lagoon is big among locals as well as tourists.

# Discovery Island

Originally conceived as a re-creation of the setting of Robert Louis Stevenson's Treasure Island, complete with wrecked ship and Jolly Roger, this island in Bay Lake evolved gradually into its contemporary status as an animal preserve where visitors can see and learn about some 100 different species of exotic birds and animals amid 11½ lushly landscaped acres. Although it's possible to "do" Discovery Island in less than an hour, anything faster than a stop-and-start saunter would do it injustice. You can wander along the shady boardwalks at your own pace, stopping to inspect the bougainvillea or visit with a rhinoceros hornbill. You can picnic on the beach or on one of the benches in the shade and watch trumpeter swans glide by. The only thing you may not do is go swimming—the Water Sprites and motor launches come just too close for safety.

**Discovery Island Bird Show.** These aviary "Animal Encounters" shows are presented in an open amphitheater equipped with benches and numerous perches. There's usually a show every hour from 11 to 4; most last about 15 minutes. *Audience: All ages. Rating:* ★★

---

## Tips for Making the Most of Your Visit

- Line up for star attractions either first thing in the morning, during a parade, or at the end of the day.

- Whenever possible, eat in a restaurant that takes reservations, or have meals before or after mealtime rush hours (from 11 AM to 2 PM and again from 6 to 8 PM). Or leave the theme parks altogether for a meal in one of the hotels.

- Spend afternoons in high-capacity sit-down shows or catching live entertainment—or leave the park for a swim in your hotel pool.

- If you plan to take in Typhoon Lagoon, Blizzard Beach, or River Country, go early in your visit (but not a weekend). You may like it so much you'll want to go again.

- If a meal with the characters is in your plans, save it for the end of your trip, when your youngsters will have become accustomed to these large, looming figures.

- Familiarize yourself with all age and height restrictions to avoid having younger children get excited about rides they're too short or too young to experience.

- Call ahead to check on operating hours and parade times, which vary greatly throughout the year.

---

## Walt Disney World Essentials

### Admission Fees

Visiting Walt Disney World is not cheap, especially if you have a child or two along. Everyone 10 and older pays adult prices; reductions are available for children three through nine. Children under three get in free. No discounted family tickets are available.

TICKETS

In Disneyspeak, "ticket" refers to a single day's admission to the Magic Kingdom, Epcot Center, or the Disney–MGM Studios. A ticket is good in the park for which you buy it only on the day you buy it; if you buy a one-day ticket and later decide to extend your visit, you can apply the cost of it toward the purchase of any pass (but only before you leave the park). Exchanges can be made at City Hall in the Magic Kingdom, at Earth Station in Epcot Center, or at Guest Relations at Disney–MGM.

PASSES

A number of options can save you money. The **Four-Day Value Pass** allows you to visit each of the three parks on any three days and then one of the parks again on one more day. You cannot visit more than one park on any day. To avoid this restriction, you can get the **Four-Day Park Hopper Pass,** a personalized photo-ID pass that allows unlimited admission to the three parks on any four days. The **Five-Day**

**World Hopper Pass** is also a photo ID; it includes unlimited visits to the three theme parks over five days, plus seven days admission to WDW's minor parks—Pleasure Island, Typhoon Lagoon, River Country, Blizzard Beach, and Discovery Island. Walt Disney World says it introduced the new park-hopping passes as photo IDs to prevent counterfeiting and the illegal resale of passes. (First, however, there was quite a controversy over an earlier decision to allow park hopping only to guests at hotels on WDW property.) Each time you use a pass the entry date is stamped on it; remaining days may be used years in the future. A variety of annual passes are also available, at a cost only slightly more than a World Hopper; if you plan to visit twice in a year, these are a good deal.

Guests at Disney resorts can also purchase **Length of Stay Passes,** which are good from the time of arrival until midnight of the departure day. Passes may be purchased at the front desks of all resorts as well as in Guest Services at the three theme parks. Prices (not including tax) are based upon the number of room nights and range from $80 for a one-night/two-day adult pass to $262 for nine nights/10 days. The pass is good for all three theme parks, as well as the three water parks, Pleasure Island, and Discovery Island.

PRICES

WDW changes its prices at least once a year and without any notice. At press time, the following rates were in effect (including 6% tax). For current information, call ahead.

**One-day ticket:** $39.22 adults, $31.80 children.
**Four-Day Value Pass:** $130.95 adults, $102.45 children.
**Four-Day Park Hopper:** $145.22 adults, $112.54 children.
**Value Pass:** $131.44 adults, $103.82 children.
**Five-Day World Hopper:** $197.16 adults, $156.88 children.
**River Country:** $15.64 adults, $12.19 children.
**Combined River Country/Discovery Island:** $19.61 adults, $14.05 children.
**Discovery Island:** $10.60 adults, $5.83 children.
**Typhoon Lagoon:** $23.85 adults, $18.00 children.
**Blizzard Beach:** $23.85 adults, $18.02 children.
**Pleasure Island:** $16.91 for all.

Tickets and passes to Walt Disney World, Epcot Center, and Disney–MGM Studios can be purchased at admission booths at the TTC, in all on-site resorts (if you're a registered guest), and at the Walt Disney World kiosk at Orlando International Airport (second floor, main terminal). American Express, Visa, and MasterCard are accepted, as are cash, personal checks (with ID), and travelers checks. Many offices of the American Automobile Association (AAA) sell discounted tickets. Check with your local office.

## Operating Hours

Operating hours for the Magic Kingdom, Epcot Center, and Disney–MGM Studios Theme Park vary widely throughout the year and change for school and legal holidays. In general, the parks stay open longest during prime summer months and over the year-end holidays. During these peak seasons, the Magic Kingdom is open to midnight (later on New Year's Eve), Epcot Center is open to 11 PM, and Disney–MGM Studios is open until 9 PM. At other times, Epcot Center and Disney–MGM are open until 8 and the Magic Kingdom until 7. Always call ahead to make sure of closing time.

Note that though the Magic Kingdom, Epcot Center's Future World, and Disney–MGM officially open at 9 AM, visitors may enter at 8:30

and sometimes at 8. The parking lots open at least an hour earlier. Arriving at the Magic Kingdom turnstiles before "rope drop," the official opening time, you can breakfast in a restaurant on Main Street, which opens before the rest of the park, and be ready to dash to one of the popular attractions in other areas as soon as officially possible. Arriving in Epcot Center or Disney–MGM studios, you can make dinner reservations before the crowds arrive and take in some of the attractions and pavilions well before the major crowds descend, at about 10.

### Parking

Every theme park has a parking lot—and all are huge. Always write down exactly where you park your car and take the number with you. (Repeating "Goofy, Goofy, Goofy" or something similar as a reminder of your Disney-themed locations doesn't always help; by the end of the day, you'll be so goofy with eating and shopping and riding that you'll be thinking "Sleepy, Sleepy, Sleepy.") Parking area trams deliver you to the park entrance. For each lot, the cost is $5 for cars and $6 for RVs and campers (free to WDW resort guests with ID). At Typhoon Lagoon and River Country, parking is free.

### Transportation

Walt Disney World has its own transportation system, which can get you wherever you want to go. It's fairly simple once you get the hang of it.

**The monorail** serves many important destinations. It has two loops: one linking the Magic Kingdom, an area known as the Transportation and Ticket Center (TTC), and a handful of resorts, including the Contemporary, the Grand Floridian, and Polynesian Village; and the other looping from the TTC direct to Epcot Center.

**Motor launches** connect WDW destinations on lakes and waterways. Specifically, they operate between the Epcot Center resorts (except the Caribbean Beach) and Disney–MGM Studios; and between Discovery Island and the Magic Kingdom, Wilderness Lodge, Grand Floridian, and the Fort Wilderness Campground, Polynesian, and Contemporary resorts (Discovery Island admission ticket, WDW resort ID, or multi-day admission ticket required).

**Buses** provide direct service from every on-site resort to both major and minor theme parks, and express buses go direct between the major theme parks. To Typhoon Lagoon, you can go direct from (or make connections at) the Disney Village Marketplace, Epcot Center, and the Epcot Center resorts (the Beach and Yacht clubs, the Caribbean Beach Resort, the Swan, and the Dolphin).

Monorails, launches, buses, and trams all operate from early in the morning until at least midnight. (Hours are shorter when the park closes earlier.) All transportation is free if you are staying at an on-site resort or if you hold a three-park ticket. If not, you can buy unlimited transportation within WDW for $2.50 a day.

# SEA WORLD, UNIVERSAL STUDIOS, AND BEYOND

Theme parks grow so well in the sandy central Florida soil that you might almost imagine a handful of seeds, scattered across the fertile I–4 belt, waiting for the right combination of money and vision. Growth engendered more growth. Whereas it used to be that you could do a whole park—any park—in about six hours, a thorough visit now can barely be contained in a day. As competition sharpened and tastes grew more sophisticated, a sort of me-too mentality became prevalent. If one park has a flight simulator attraction, then all parks must have one (the best are Disney–MGM's Star Tours and Universal Studios' Back to the Future . . . The Ride). Ditto Broadway-style music-and-dance shows. A blessing for parents is that every park now has a sophisticated children's play area, with ball crawls, bouncing rooms, and the like.

## Sea World

*Near the intersection of I–4 and the Bee Line Expressway; take I–4 to Exit 28 and follow signs.*

Aptly named, 1,200-acre Sea World is the world's largest zoological park and is devoted entirely to the mammals, birds, fish, and reptiles living in the ocean and its tributaries. Every attraction is designed to demonstrate the beauty of the marine world and how it is threatened by human thoughtlessness. Yet the presentations are rarely dogmatic, never pedantic, and almost always memorable as well as enjoyable. The park rivals Disney properties for squeaky-cleanliness, courteous staff, and its clever attention to details.

Sea World is organized around a 17-acre central lake. As you enter, the lake is to your right. You can orient yourself by the Sky Tower, whose revolving viewing platform is generally visible even above the trees; it's directly opposite Shamu Stadium.

**Clydesdale Hamlet.** Stop by to visit the hulking Clydesdale horses, the trademark of park owner Anheuser-Busch. It's around the corner from **Terrors of the Deep.**

**Key West.** The region made famous by artists from Jimmy Buffett to Ernest Hemingway has been re-created here. Don't miss the up-close view of the dolphins and stingrays in the attached exhibits. Be a part of the fun by tossing a few smelt to the snack-happy stars that are the heart of these exhibits.

**Manatees: The Last Generation?** After a short film, you can watch manatees splash about in their 300,000-gallon tank (there's also a 30,000-gallon nursing lagoon for manatee moms and their babies).

**Pacific Point Preserve.** The fun-loving California sea lions and harbor and fur seals on these 2½ acres will literally sing for their supper.

**Penguin Encounter.** Whip into this one early, to visit one of the most spectacular attractions at its least crowded time. This refrigerated recreation of Antarctica is home to 17 species of penguins; a Plexiglas wall on the viewers side of the tank lets you see that the penguins are as graceful in the water as they are awkward on land.

**Sea World Theatre.** Early in the day, stop here to see the 20-minute *Window to the Sea.* It'll help you get oriented and get a sense of the larger vision of the park. After 5, the theater is turned into a giant wading pool for the **Water Fantasy,** with 36 revolving nozzles spraying water into fountains, waving plumes, and helices, all set to music and colored lights. It's great late in the afternoon.

**Shamu: Close Up.** This is a high point of every visitor's Sea World experience. Go as much as 45 minutes early to get a seat—even the wait is fun, with a camera playing along with the audience as you watch each other while watching the whales swim around their tank.

**Shamu Research and Breeding Pool.** Don't miss this for an opportunity to glimpse one of these big mothers nursing her young.

**Shamu's Happy Harbor.** If you've got kids, find the time to let them unwind at this 3-acre, state-of-the-art playground.

**Terrors of the Deep.** Videos and walk-through Plexiglas tunnels let you get acquainted with the world's largest collection of such dangerous sea creatures as eels, barracuda, venomous and poisonous fish, and sharks.

**Tropical Reef.** More than 1,000 tropical fish swim around a 160,000-gallon man-made coral reef in this soothing indoor attraction built around a cylindrical mega-aquarium.

**Wild Arctic.** The park's most ambitious attraction is a unique hybrid of a thrill ride and training center about the Arctic's most deceptively cuddly predators. It provides a chilly encounter with polar bears and some interesting interactive displays. To see it, follow the crowds across the bridge to **Shamu Stadium;** while they're watching Sea World's orca mascot perform, you can sneak in without a wait.

## Admission Fees
**One day:** $39.95 adults, $32.80 children 3–9.
**Two days:** $44.95 adults, $37.80 children 3–9.
**Parking:** $5 per car, $7 per RV or camper.

## Entertainment
Pick up an entertainment schedule when you come into the park, and as you wander through the exhibits, keep an eye on the time: You'll want to make sure to catch the delightful shows at the **Whale & Dolphin Stadium** (20 minutes) and the **Sea Lion & Otter Stadium** (40 minutes). At **Bay Watch at Sea World,** the mixture of power boats and pretty folks that made the showcase for beauty and the beach is on display in this water ski show narrated by star David Hasselhoff.

## Operating Hours
Sea World is open daily 9–7 (until 9 during July, Aug., and Thanksgiving and Christmas holidays).

# Universal Studios Florida

*Near the intersection of I–4 and Florida's Turnpike. Take I–4 to Exit 29; turn onto Sand Lake Rd. (to the right if you've traveled west on I–4, to the left if you've traveled east) then turn right onto Turkey Lake Rd.*

Far from being a "me-too" version of Disney–MGM Studios, Universal Studios Florida, which opened in 1990, is a theme park with plenty of personality of its own. It's saucy, sassy, and hip—and doesn't hesitate to invite comparisons with the competition. Disney–MGM's strolling actors are pablum compared to the Blues Brothers peeling rubber in the Bluesmobile. And let's face it, even Disney–MGM's Muppets are matched by E.T., Tickli Moot, and other inventions of Steven Spielberg, Universal's genius on call. They've even figured out a way to keep people entertained while they wait in line; from arcade games at Nickelodeon to news shows on overhead screens in the Jaws line, Universal makes the most of its video connection.

The lofty adult ticket prices raise expectations very high indeed. They are met most of the time, but resentment can set in if you're confronted by too many long lines and the price gouging at ubiquitous concession stands and snackeries. With Disney–MGM just down the road, is Universal worth the visit? The answer is an unqualified yes. Actually, Universal Studios and Disney–MGM dovetail rather than replicate each other. Universal's attractions are geared more to older children than to the stroller set.

The 444 acres of Universal Studios are a bewildering conglomeration of stage sets, shops, reproductions of New York and San Francisco, and anonymous soundstages housing theme attractions as well as genuine moviemaking paraphernalia. On the map, these sets are neatly divided into six neighborhoods, surrounding a huge blue lagoon. As you walk around the park, however, expect to get lost, and if you do, just ask directions of the nearest staffer.

## The Front Lot
This is essentially a scene setter, and the place to find many services. The main drag, the Plaza of the Stars, stretches from the marble-arch entrance gateway straight down to the other end of the lot.

## Hollywood
Angling off to the right of Plaza of the Stars, Rodeo Drive forms the backbone of Hollywood.

**AT&T at the Movies.** You can play high-tech computer games here.

**The Gory, Gruesome & Grotesque Horror Make-Up Show.** Although young children may be frightened, older kids and teens love this production, showing as it does what goes into and oozes out of the most mangled monsters in movie history.

**Jurassic Park: Behind the Scenes.** Although surprisingly small considering this movie was the largest-grossing in history, it's worth dropping by, if only to see the triceratops lying in the entryway.

**Lucy: A Tribute.** This walk-through collection of Lucille Ball's costumes, accessories, and other memorabilia is best for real fans of the ditzy redhead.

**Termimator 2/3-D.** Arnold is back in this 3-D adventure based on the popular movies. Lots of fun because the film features not only the muscle man himself but his original co-stars from the cinematic version.

## Production Central
This area is comprised of six huge warehouses containing working soundstages, as well as several attractions. Follow Nickelodeon Way left from the Plaza of the Stars to the embarkation point for the main event, the Production Tram Tour.

**The Adventures of Rocky & Bullwinkle.** A musical revue starring Bullwinkle the Moose, his faithful friend Rocky Squirrel, and those two Russian no-goodniks, Boris Badenov and his slinky sidekick, Natasha, it's staged hourly on an animated set at the edge of Universal's New York back lot.

**Alfred Hitchcock's 3-D Theatre.** This is a dandy 40-minute multimedia tribute to the master of suspense (young children may be frightened).

**The Funtastic World of Hanna-Barbera.** This combination ride–video–interactive display at the corner of Nickelodeon Way and Plaza of the Stars is one of the most popular attractions at Universal Studios and always crowded. Using Hanna-Barbera animated characters (Yogi Bear, the Jetsons, the Flintstones), it shows how cartoons are made and gives you eight minutes of thrills in the process. (It may be too much for toddlers.)

***Murder, She Wrote Mystery Theatre.*** Based on the popular TV series starring Angela Lansbury as senior-citizen sleuth Jessica Fletcher, this show is presented in a large sit-down theater. The audience is placed in the role of executive producer, racing the clock to put together an episode of the show.

**Nickelodeon Studios.** The Green Slime Geyser entices visitors into the home of the world's only television network designed for kids. A 30-minute tour shows how a television show is produced. The banks of lights, concrete floors, and general warehouse feel go a long way toward demystifying movie magic, but it's exactly that behind-the-scenes perspective that makes the tour interesting. About 90% of the Nickelodeon shows are made on Nick's pair of soundstages, so you can always expect to see some action. Lines are often long, so you may want to skip it if no shows are taping.

**Production Tram Tour.** This 20-minute nonstop narrated ride around the park neither orients you nor takes you inside any of the soundstages. It lets you off right back where you started, at **Nickelodeon Studios.**

## The New York Back Lot
Here the Big Apple is rendered with surprising detail, right down to the cracked concrete and slightly stained cobblestones. The **Blues Brothers Bluesmobile** regularly cruises the neighborhood, and musicians hop out to give impromptu performances at 70 Delancey.

**Ghostbusters.** Part special-effects demonstration, part high-tech haunted house, it lasts 15 minutes.

**Kongfrontation.** A thriller, this very popular five-minute ride is just down the street from Ghostbusters.

## San Francisco/Amity
This area combines two sets. One part is the wharves and warehouses of San Francisco's Embarcadero and Fisherman's Wharf district, with cable-car tracks and the distinctive redbrick Ghirardelli chocolate factory; the other is the New England fishing village terrorized by the shark in *Jaws.*

**Beetlejuice's Graveyard Revue.** A live 15-minute sound-and-light spectacle, this stars the ghoul of the same name, from the 1991 movie starring Michael Keaton. Its theme is rock and roll and monsters, and it's carried off with lots of noise, smoke, and wit.

**Earthquake—The Big One.** Located next to **Beetlejuice's Graveyard Revue,** this starts off with a preshow that reproduces choice scenes from the movie *Earthquake,* then takes you onto San Francisco Bay Area Rapid Transit subway cars to ride out an 8.3 Richter-scale tremor and its consequences: fire, flood, blackouts. Unlike Disney–MGM Studios' Disaster Canyon, this ride has no "safe" seats; it's not for younger children. It lasts 20 minutes, and lines are always long.

**Jaws: The Ride.** Stagger out of San Francisco into Amity and you can stand in line for the revamped Jaws: The Ride, a terror-filled boat trip with concomitant explosions, noise, shaking, and gnashing of sharp shark teeth.

**The Wild, Wild, Wild West Stunt Show.** Presented in a covered amphitheater at the very end of Amity Avenue, this extravaganza involves trapdoors, fistfights, bullwhips, water gags, explosions, shoot-outs, horseback riding, and jokes that skewer every other theme park in central Florida.

## Expo Center
The southeastern corner of the park contains a treasure trove of attractions.

**Back to the Future . . . The Ride.** Universal's flight simulator ride is a flight simulator ride to beat all others, even (probably) those yet to be built. A seven-story, one-of-a-kind Omnimax screen surrounds your Delorean-shape simulator so that you lose all sense of perspective as you rush backward and forward in the space-time continuum—and there are no seat belts. You may have to wait up to two hours for this five-minute ride unless you make a beeline here first thing in the morning.

**A Day in the Park with Barney.** America's most famous purple dinosaur presides over a host of activities for children here.

**E.T. Adventure.** This trip aboard bicycles mounted on a movable platform takes you through fantastic forests and across the moon in an attempt to help the endearing extraterrestrial find his way back to his home planet. You can wait hours to ride and (almost) be glad you did.

**Fievel's Playland.** For younger children, this is a true gift. Based on the adventures of Steven Spielberg's mighty-if-miniature mouse, this gigantic playground incorporates a four-story net climb, tunnel slides, water play areas, ball crawls, a 200-foot water slide, and a harmonica slide that plays music when you slide along the openings. Around the corner from **E.T. Adventure.**

## Admission Fees
Tickets are available at the entrance, by mail from the park, and by mail through Ticketmaster (☎ 800/745–5000); discounted tickets available at Orlando/Orange County Convention and Visitors Bureau ticket office (✉ 8445 International Dr.).

**One day:** $37 adults, $30 children 3–9.
**Two days:** $55 adults, $44 children 3–9.
**Parking:** $5 cars, $7 campers.

## Other Entertainment
The lake at the center of Universal Studios is the setting for the **Dynamite Nights Stunt Spectacular,** a shoot-'em-up stunt show (performed on water skis, no less!). It's presented nightly at 7.

## Operating Hours
The park is open daily 9–7 (extended as late as 10 in summer and during holiday periods).

# Cypress Gardens

*Take I–4 to U.S. 27S exit and follow signs.*

A botanical garden, amusement park, and waterskiing circus rolled into one, Cypress Gardens is a uniquely Floridian combination of natural beauty and utter kitsch. A 45-minute drive from Walt Disney World, the park now encompasses more than 200 acres and contains more than 8,000 varieties of plants gathered from 75 countries. More than half of the grounds are devoted to flora, ranging from natural landscaping to cutesy-poo topiary to chrysanthemum cascades. Even at a sedate pace, you can see just about everything in six hours.

**Botanical Gardens Cruise.** This float through cypress-hung canals passes hoop-skirted southern belles, flowering shrubs, 27 different species of palm, and the occasional baby alligator. Doing this as soon as you arrive in Cypress Gardens gives you a sense of the place.

**Carousel Cove.** Cypress Gardens' playground, at **Southern Crossroads,** has lots of ball rooms and bouncing pads plus a lovely old carousel.

**Crossroads Arena.** Here, in **Southern Crossroads,** you'll find a rotating collection of circus-theme acts, from acrobats to trained birds.

**Exhibition Gardens.** The path leading from the ski stadiums to the amusement-park area meanders through this expanse of landscaping, whose philosophy is heroic in intent and hilariously vulgar in execution.

**Southern Crossroads.** Many of the park's attractions are here: the bird show at the **Cypress Theatre;** a huge walk-through **butterfly conservatory;** a **museum of antique radios;** **Cypress Junction,** the nation's most elaborate model railroad exhibit; and **Cypress Roots,** a clapboard shack chock-full of fascinating memorabilia about the Gardens' founders, Dick and Julie Pope. **Kodak's Island in the Sky,** a 153-foot-high revolving platform, provides aerial views of the park. **Carousel Cove** is also here.

**Water Ski Stadiums.** The souvenir shop shamelessly sited at the main entrance funnels visitors right on in for a stunt-filled half-hour water-skiing revue, presented every two hours.

## Admission Fees
**One day:** $26.91 for adults, $16.45 children 6–12.
**Parking:** Free.

## Operating Hours
The park is open daily 9:30–5:30 (later in summer).

# Splendid China

*12 mi from Orlando, on U.S. 192 approximately 2½ mi west of I-4 (exit 25B).*

Splendid China is more a superlative open-air museum than a theme park. Here you can stroll among painstakingly re-created versions of China's greatest landmarks and watch artisans demonstrate traditional Chinese woodworking, weaving, and other crafts, while tinkling, meditative music plays in the background. It took $100 million and 120 Chinese craftspeople working for two years and using, whenever possible, historically accurate building materials and techniques to create the 60-plus replicas. Both man-made structures and natural phenomena are represented—some life-size, others greatly reduced in scale. (The bricks in the Great Wall, for example, are only 2 inches long.) To appeal to theme-park savvy western visitors, live entertainment and a playground are also on the grounds.

The park is at its most magical at night. Evenings kick off at 6:30 with a parade, so try to arrive after noon. As you come through the turnstile, you enter Splendid China's version of Main Street: Suzhou Gardens, a re-creation of a 14th-century Chinese village. Inside are most of the park's shops and restaurants, all a cut above those at typical theme parks. Check with Guest Services, inside the main entrance and to the right, for show times and any special events.

Before touring the park, stop at Harmony Hall to see the 15-minute film *This Is Splendid China,* which explains the park's history and construction. Then, when you're ready to see the monuments, head clockwise (rather than counterclockwise, as the exhibits are numbered), in order to save the best for last. Along the way you'll pass replicated stone grottoes, the originals of which are used as temples, and more.

**Golden Peacock Theater.** The acrobat shows here are better than those in the **Temple of Light Amphitheater.**

**Great Wall.** Although it can't compare to the original—the 1,500-mile-long behemoth that is the only man-made structure visible from space—it's nonetheless impressive, especially when you realize that the 6.5 million tiny bricks used to make the wall were mortared by hand.

**Imperial Palace.** A reproduction of the centerpiece of Beijing's Forbidden City is one of Splendid China's most impressive sights. The compound in Beijing, built in the early 1400s as the home of the royal family, was constructed with materials from all over China and decorated with centuries worth of loot. It housed so many people that as many as 6,000 cooks were needed to feed them. Even the scale model gives a feeling of its immense size and artistry.

**Mongolia.** As in China, on the other side of the **Great Wall** lies Mongolia, and Mongolian wrestling demonstrations are scheduled in the Mongolian Yurt.

**Potala Palace.** In the far back corner of the park is this reproduction of the traditional home of the Dalai Lama, Tibet's spiritual and political leader. The dusty rose-and-white structure seems even taller than it is, since the walls lean inward, creating a false perspective.

**Stone Forest.** The odd obelisks arranged mazelike here are replicas of limestone pillars whittled by aeons of erosion.

**Temple of Light Amphitheater.** This is Splendid China's live-action venue. A costume show and a demonstration of folk dances and music are presented on alternating hours. Both are slow-moving affairs (though the latter is considerably more interesting) and not improved by the mumbling Chinese announcer.

**Terra Cotta Warriors.** These figures, not far from the **1,000 Eyes and 1,000 Hands Guanyin Buddha Statue,** are modeled after 7,000 life-size clay figurines unearthed in 1974; the originals, realistic portraits of servants, soldiers, and cavalry in the employ of Emperor Ch'in Shih Huang Ti, were buried with the emperor on his death 2,000 years ago.

**1,000 Eyes and 1,000 Hands Guanyin Buddha Statue.** After the acrobat show in the **Temple of Light Amphitheater,** stop here. The Buddha's many hands are said to ease the troubles of the world.

## Admission Fees
**One day:** $23.55 adults, $13.90 children 5–12, $21.50 senior citizens, 10% discount AAA members and senior citizens.

## Operating Hours
⊙ Daily 9:30–7 (later in peak seasons); Suzhou Gardens shops and restaurants until 9.

# Orlando and Kissimmee Water Parks

Given Orlando's steamy summers, it's no surprise that the area has no fewer than five major water parks, three of which are on Disney property (Blizzard Beach, River Country, and Typhoon Lagoon). A fourth is in Kissimmee on U.S. 192 and the fifth is on International Drive: at these, children under three are admitted at no charge, and there's only a small reduction for older youngsters.

## Water Mania
All the requisite rides and slides are here in this park—without the highly developed aesthetics you'll find at Walt Disney World. However, it's the only water park around with **Wipe Out,** a surfing simulator, where you grab a body board and ride a continuous wave form. The giant **Pirate Ship** in the **Rain Forest,** one of two children's play areas, is

equipped with water slides and water cannons. The **Abyss** is an enclosed tube slide through which you twist and turn on a one- or two-person raft for 300 feet—in deep blue darkness. The park also offers miniature golf, a sandy beach, snack bars, gift shops, and periodic concerts. ⊠ 6073 W. Irlo Bronson Memorial Hwy., Kissimmee, ☎ 407/239–8448, 407/396–2626, or 800/527–3092. ⌨ $20.95 adults, $17.95 children 3–12. ☉ Daily 11–5 (until about 8 in summer).

### Wet 'n' Wild

This park, in Orlando, is best known for its outrageous water slides, most notably the **Black Hole**—a 30-second, 500-foot, twisting, turning ride on a two-person raft through total darkness propelled by a 1,000-gallon-a-minute blast of water. There's also an elaborate **Kids' Park,** for those 4 feet tall and under, full of miniature versions of the bigger rides. The latest addition is the **Bubba Tub,** a six-story, triple-dip slide with a tube big enough for the entire family to ride in together. The park has snack stands, but visitors are allowed to bring their own food and picnic around the pool or on the lakeside beach. ⊠ 6200 International Dr., Orlando, ☎ 407/351–3200. ⌨ $20.95 adults, $17.95 children 3–9. ☉ Daily 10–5 (until about 9 in summer) except for Orlando's few really cold days.

## Winter Park and North

Once the winter refuge of some wealthy Northerners, the tony community of Winter Park, though part of Orlando's metro area, maintains a proud, independent identity. To the north, you'll find the local zoo.

### Sights to See

*Numbers in the margin correspond to points of interest on the Orlando Area map.*

**❶ Central Florida Zoological Park.** If you're expecting a grand metro zoo, you'll be disappointed. However, this display of about 230 animals on 110 acres, tucked under pine trees in a natural setting, is more than respectable, and, like Orlando, it continues to grow. Although a boardwalk shows off wetlands and there are elephants and tortoises, the specialty is becoming small- and medium-size exotic cats such as jaguars. Kids like the petting area and pony rides. ⊠ 3755 N. U.S. 17–92, Sanford, ☎ 407/323–4450. ⌨ $5. ☉ Daily 9–5.

**❷ Charles Hosmer Morse Museum of American Art.** An outstanding collection of stained-glass windows, blown glass, and lamps by Louis Tiffany (who, incidentally, was the son of Charles Tiffany of New York jewelry fame). There's also a collection of paintings by 19th- and 20th-century American artists, as well as jewelry and pottery. A major expansion has made it possible to display many treasures that have long been in storage. ⊠ 445 Park Ave., Winter Park, ☎ 407/645–5311. ⌨ $2.50. ☉ Tues.–Sat. 9:30–4, Sun. 1–4.

**❺ Leu Botanical Gardens.** Orlando's 56-acre horticultural extravaganza, formerly the estate of the late industrialist and citrus industry entrepreneur Harry P. Leu, displays a collection of historical blooms, many varieties of which were established before 1900. You'll see ancient oaks, a 50-foot floral clock, an orchid conservatory, and one of the largest camellia collections in eastern North America (in bloom October through March). **Mary Jane's Rose Garden** is the largest formal rose garden south of Atlanta. The simple 19th-century **Leu House Museum,** once the Leu family home, preserves the furnishings and appointments of a well-to-do, turn-of-the-century Florida family. A newly expanded shop and hall adds a more modern air without diminishing the property's natural charm. ⊠ *1730 N. Forest Ave., Orlando,* ☎ *407/246–2620.* 🖼 *$4.* ⊙ *Daily 9–5; museum Tues.–Sat. 10–3:30, Sun. and Mon. 1–3:30.*

**Loch Haven Park.** Three of the city's museums encircle this grassy field: the **Orange County Historical Museum,** the **Orlando Museum of Art,** and the **Orlando Science Center.**

❹ **Mead Gardens.** These 55 acres have been left wild as a natural preserve. A boardwalk through the property provides a good view of the delicate wetlands. ⊠ *S. Denning Ave., Winter Park,* ☎ *407/623–3334.* 🖼 *Free.* ⊙ *Daily 8–sunset.*

**Orange County Historical Museum.** In this storehouse of Orlando memorabilia, photographs, and antiques, permanent exhibits explore the culture of local Native Americans and crackers (native Floridians) and show off a country store, a Victorian parlor, a print shop, and an actual 1926 brick firehouse. On Loch Haven Park. ⊠ *812 E. Rollins St., Orlando,* ☎ *407/897–6350.* 🖼 *$2.* ⊙ *Mon.–Sat. 9–5, Sun. noon–5.*

**Orlando Museum of Art.** Displays include 19th- and 20th-century American art and a permanent exhibit of pre-Columbian artifacts from a Mayan excavation. Young children enjoy the first-class Art Encounter, created with the help of Walt Disney World Imagineers. On Loch Haven Park. ⊠ *2416 N. Mills Ave., Orlando,* ☎ *407/896–4231.* 🖼 *Suggested donation $4.* ⊙ *Tues.–Sat. 9–5, Sun. noon–5; tours Sept.–May, Wed. and Sun. 2; Art Encounter Tues.–Fri. and Sun. noon–5, Sat. 10–5.*

**Orlando Science Center.** One of the largest museums of its type in the Southeast, this newly expanded museum is full of hands-on and interactive exhibits, including a special water play area for preschoolers and a planetarium. Cosmic Concerts are held on weekend evenings. On Loch Haven Park. ⊠ *Entrances on Rollins and Princeton Sts. (1 mi east of I–4 at Exit 43), 810 E. Rollins St., Orlando,* ☎ *407/896–7151.* 🖼 *$6.50.* ⊙ *Mon.–Thurs. and Sat. 9–5, Fri. 9–9, Sun. noon–5; Cosmic Concerts Fri. and Sat. 9, 10, 11, and midnight.*

**Park Avenue.** This charming street, the heart of Winter Park, is lined with trendy boutiques and restaurants; long and narrow Central Park stretches through the heart of the shopping district, and benches under the ancient trees offer a respite from the hustle and bustle.

❸ **Rollins College.** A private liberal arts school, at the south end of Park Avenue. Take time to look at the Spanish-style architecture, especially **Knowles Memorial Chapel,** home to the Bach Festival Society. Also on campus is the **Cornell Fine Arts Museum,** which has the largest collection of American and European art in central Florida. ⊠ *1000 Holt Ave., Winter Park,* ☎ *407/646–2526.* 🖼 *Free.* ⊙ *Tues.–Fri. 10–5, weekends 1–5.*

## Other Orlando Area Points of Interest

If you are spending as long as a week in the Orlando area, try to find time to take in some of these attractions, some showcasing Orlando's deep Southern charm.

❿ **Bok Tower Gardens.** This sanctuary of plants, flowers, trees, and wildlife native to subtropical Florida is a peaceful world of silvery moats, mockingbirds and swans, blooming thickets, hidden sundials, and shady paths in forests of pine. There is a quirky appeal to the majestic 200-foot **Bok Tower,** constructed of coquina (limestone made from seashells) and pink, white, and gray marble. The tower is carved with symbolic designs, and reliefs on the bronze doors tell the complete story of Genesis. The tower's carillon, made up of 57 bronze bells, plays every half hour after 10 AM. Also on the grounds is the 230-room, Mediterranean revival–style **Pinewood House,** built in 1930. To get to Bok Tower Gardens, take I–4 to U.S. 27 South, and about 5 miles past the Cypress Gardens turnoff, turn right on Rte. 17A to Alternate U.S. 27; past the orange groves, turn left on Burns Avenue and follow it about 1½ miles to the gardens; allow about an hour. ⊠ *Burns Ave. and Tower Blvd., Lake Wales,* ☎ *813/676–1408.* ☞ *$4; house tour suggested donation $5.* ☉ *Daily 8–5; house tour Sept. 15–May 15, Tues. and Thurs. 12:30 and 2, Sun. 2.*

**❾ Flying Tigers Warbird Air Museum.** The hangar of this working aircraft restoration facility also houses a museum displaying about 30 vintage planes; there are a few big ones outside on the tarmac. Tour guides are full of facts and personality and have an infectious passion for the planes. ⊠ *231 Hoagland Blvd., Kissimmee,* ☎ *407/933–1942.* ☞ *$6.* ☉ *Mon.–Sat. 9–5:30, Sun. 9–5 (later in peak seasons).*

**❽ Gatorland.** Long before Walt Disney World, there was Gatorland, a kitschy attraction south of Orlando on U. S. 441 that has endured since 1949. Through the monstrous aqua gator-jaw doorway lie thrills and chills in the form of thousands of alligators and crocodiles, swimming and basking in the Florida sun as well as many other reptiles, mammals, and birds. A free train ride provides a park overview, and a three-story observation tower overlooks the gator breeding marsh. Don't miss the **Gator Jumparoo** show, the **Gator Wrestling** show, and the educational **Snakes Alive** show, with 30–40 rattlesnakes in the pit around the speaker. Children's admissions are just slightly lower than adults'. ⊠ *14501 S. Orange Blossom Trail between Orlando and Kissimmee,* ☎ *407/855–5496 or 800/393–5297.* ☞ *$10.95.* ☉ *Daily 8–sunset.*

**❻ Mystery Fun House.** This attraction, which includes an 18-chamber maze that comes with the warning that it is "90% dark," is also full of gory and distorted images. Outside are an 18-hole **Mystery Mini-Golf,** a video arcade, and the high-tech **Starbase Omega** laser game, in which you are suited up and outfitted with a reflector gun and badge for a game of laser tag. ⊠ *5767 Major Blvd., Orlando,* ☎ *407/351–3355.* ☞ *Maze $7.95, miniature golf $4.95, laser game $6.95, all 3 $13.85.* ☉ *Daily 10 AM–11 PM (until midnight in peak seasons).*

**❼ Ripley's Believe It or Not!** You won't believe this museum in the heart of tourist territory, part of a national chain displaying all sorts of weird and amazing artifacts. The fertility sculpture in the collection has been rumored to account for several pregnancies among the museum staff. Children's admission fees approach those for adults. ⊠ *8201 International Dr., Orlando,* ☎ *407/363–4418.* ☞ *$8.95.* ☉ *Daily 10 AM–11 PM (later in peak seasons).*

**Terror on Church Street.** A haunted house you can visit year-round. Don't miss the gift shop, stocked with all kinds of creepy things. Children's discounts are negligible. At Church Street Station. ⊠ *Church St. and Orange Ave., Orlando,* ☎ *407/649–3327.* ☞ *$12 nonresidents.* ☉ *Sun.–Thurs. 7 PM–midnight, Fri. and Sat. 7 PM–1 AM.*

# DINING

Because tourism is king here, casual dress is the rule, and few restaurants require fancier attire. Reservations are always a good idea in a city where the phrase "Bus drivers eat free" is emblazoned on the coat of arms. If you don't have reservations, the entire Ecuadorean soccer team or the Platt City High School senior class may arrive moments before you and keep you waiting a long, long time. Save that experience for the attractions.

Orlando is not big, but getting to places is frequently complicated, so always call for directions. Some of the smaller, hungrier restaurant operators may offer to come get you. The other benefit of the competitive restaurant market is that prices have remained cheaper than elsewhere in Florida. For this chapter only, the following ranges apply:

| CATEGORY | COST* |
|---|---|
| $$$$ | over $40 |
| $$$ | $30–$40 |
| $$ | $20–$30 |
| $ | under $20 |

*per person for a three-course meal, excluding drinks, service, and 6% sales tax

# In and Around Walt Disney World

## American

$$$$ ✕ **Victoria and Albert's.** All the servers work in boy-girl pairs, call themselves Victoria and Albert, and recite the day's specials in tandem, like something out of a Lewis Carroll fantasy. Despite the gimmick, this lavish, romantic dining room is a real treat. The intimate dome-ceilinged room, in the Grand Floridian, fits the Victorian theme, with fabric-covered walls, lots of fresh flowers, and marbleized columns. A harpist adds an ethereal touch. Orlando's most popular mystery meal, a seven-course, prix-fixe menu ($65), changes substantially each day; you can also get it with four glasses of wine chosen to complement the food. Chef Scott Hunnel loves creating exotic dishes but always offers something for proletarian palates. Appetizers might include velvety veal sweetbreads and rare New Zealand venison or artichokes in a lusty duxelles (mushroom-based) sauce. Entrées range from sautéed duck breast or veal tournedos on braised onions to well-prepared sirloin. Two seatings are offered nightly (6 and 9). Expect to spend about $100 a person with drinks; prix-fixe for children 2 through 11 is $45 (doesn't that baby-sitter sound better by the minute?). Kosher and vegetarian meals are available on advance order. ⊠ *Grand Floridian, Magic Kingdom resort area,* ☎ *407/824–1089. Reservations essential. AE, MC, V.*

$$–$$$ ✕ **White Horse Saloon.** Improbable as it sounds, this western-theme saloon is in the Hyatt Regency Grand Cypress. You can get a barbecued half chicken for $20 or pay $1 more for prime rib. If you want to go for the 28-ounce beef-worshipper's cut—that's more than 1½ pounds of corn-fed beef—it's $46. All entrées come with sourdough bread, baked or mashed potatoes, and your choice of creamed spinach or corn on the cob. A hearty hot apple pie with cinnamon-raisin sauce awaits desperadoes who can still handle dessert. There's live music with your vittles. ⊠ *Hyatt Regency Grand Cypress, 1 Grand Cypress Blvd., Orlando,* ☎ *407/239–1234. AE, DC, MC, V.*

$$ ✕ **Artist Point.** This excellent restaurant offers those not booked at the
★ Wilderness Lodge a good excuse to see the huge hunting lodge–style hotel. The northwestern salmon sampler is one good option; you might also try the smoked duck breast, maple-glazed steak, or sautéed elk sausage. Most meats are hardwood grilled. The house specialty is Trail Dust Shortcake, a buttermilk biscuit with strawberries, vanilla ice cream, and whipped cream. To fully get that Pacific Northwest feeling, try a Washington State or Oregon wine. ⊠ *Wilderness Lodge, Magic Kingdom resort area,* ☎ *407/939–3463. AE, MC, V.*

$$   ✗ **Austin's.** Stephen F. Austin, founder of the Republic of Texas, was the inspiration for this Floridian fantasy of what a Texas beef palace should be. It's a good fantasy. The barbecued ribs and chicken are tasty, and the Galveston Bay—half a pound of ribs and a skewer of hickory-grilled shrimp—should satisfy buckaroos who can't decide between surf and turf. The hickory-grilled fish is quite good, especially when Norwegian salmon is available. ✉ *8633 International Dr., Orlando,* ☎ *407/363–9575. AE, D, DC, MC, V.*

$$   ✗ **Beeline Diner.** This slick 24-hour 1950s-style diner in the Peabody Hotel is not cheap, but the salads, sandwiches, and griddle foods are tops. Though very busy at times, this joint can be fun for breakfast or a late-night snack, and for just a little silver, you can play a lot of old tunes on the jukebox. ✉ *9801 International Dr., Orlando,* ☎ *407/352–4000. Reservations not accepted. AE, DC, MC, V.*

$$   ✗ **Cafe Tu Tango.** Artists work at easels in this très-chic bistro, and the
★   menu gives the International Drive address a new meaning—witness the Cajun chicken egg rolls, stuffed with blackened chicken, Greek goat cheese, Creole mustard, and tomato salsa; trendy sun-dried tomato pizza and smoked chicken quesadillas add a hip spin. Most people order just appetizers, to accompany drinks like the Matisse margarita and the Renoir rum runner. A children's menu offers nonfancy burgers and pizza. Even though nothing costs more than $8, it's easy to spend $50 on lunch for two, especially if you order sangria early and often, as the servers suggest. ✉ *8625 International Dr., Orlando,* ☎ *407/248–2222. AE, D, MC, V.*

$$   ✗ **Pebbles.** Offering just the right mix of elegance and informality, this has become one of the most popular local dining spots, perennially voted best in the city by the readers of the *Orlando Sentinel.* On tap is California cuisine, dude, with the Florida cracker touch of grouper and other regional favorites. Good entrées include angel-hair pasta smothered with Asian-spiced smoked duck and scallops, and Mediterranean salad, where sun-dried tomatoes put in the obligatory appearance. The Caesar salad, tossed tableside, is unusually memorable. Desserts are worth the calories, and the wine list is intelligent without being a wallet breaker. ✉ *Crossroads Shopping Center, at the Lake Buena Vista entrance to Walt Disney World, Orlando,* ☎ *407/827–1111;* ✉ *17 W. Church St., Orlando,* ☎ *407/839–0892;* ✉ *2516 Aloma Ave., Winter Park,* ☎ *407/678–7001;* ✉ *2100 Rte. 434, Longwood,* ☎ *407/774–7111. AE, D, DC, MC, V.*

$$   ✗ **Planet Hollywood.** On weekend nights, when nearby clubs are jumping, the line approaching this place in WDW's **Pleasure Island** rivals the one outside Lenin's Tomb during the Soviet era. The rationale for queuing here is similar: You want to see a piece of history—in this case, movie history, as assembled by club owners Demi Moore, Bruce Willis, Arnold Schwarzenegger, Sylvester Stallone, and the biggest showman of all, restaurateur Robert Earl. Memorabilia, like the bus that was used in the movie *Speed,* rotate between the Orlando Planet and the sister restaurants around the world. At the souvenir shop, you can buy T-shirts while you ponder which day you'll get inside. In actuality, the wait is about two hours. If you want to minimize it, go mid-afternoon. The menu doesn't change—you'll find fresh, healthful dishes like turkey burgers, smoked and grilled meats, and unusual pastas and salads. The 110-foot-tall, 20,000-square-foot building, complete with indoor waterfall, cost $15 million, about as much as a theme park attraction. If someone else is driving, try a Comet, the $13 gargantuan souvenir-glass drink with vodka, rum, tequila, and orange and pineapple juice. ✉ *Pleasure Island, Walt Disney World Village,* ☎ *407/363–7827. AE, DC, MC, V.*

**$–$$** ✕ **Hard Rock Café Orlando.** The motto at this place is "Save the planet," but that was before founder Robert Earl jumped ship and moved on to Planet Hollywood. Both chains purvey a similar fantasy: a few hours of being cool for the price of a wait in line. The huge, guitar-shape Hard Rock, loaded down with memorabilia, adjoins **Universal Studios Florida.** In addition to Universal visitors, it draws members of the NBA Orlando Magic, and, oh yes, it even serves food. Both menu and prices could be a lot worse, considering the location. Best bets are the pig sandwich, made of pork shoulder hickory smoked for 14 hours, and the old reliable, a ⅓-pound charbroiled cheeseburger with all the trimmings. There's also an extensive collection of beers. Don't go if you can't tolerate noise that would drown out a 747; this place is a rock club and proud of it. ⊠ *Universal Studios Florida, 5800 Kirkman Rd., Orlando,* ☎ *407/351–7625. AE, MC, V.*

## Chinese

**$$** ✕ **Ming Court.** The building is as important as the cooking here, and both the architect and the chef get high marks. Even on International Drive, the wall that looks like a dragon's back provides serenity in an enclosed courtyard. Diners look out through glass walls over a beautiful series of floating gardens. Inside, touches like rosewood chopsticks and linen tablecloths add to the classy feel. If you eat Chinese a lot, you probably won't see any dishes you haven't heard of, but the versions here are expertly prepared. The jumbo shrimp in lobster sauce, flavored with crushed black beans, may cost more than you're used to ($15), but they're worth the money. Also popular is the Hunan kung pao chicken, with red and green peppers, cashews, and walnuts. Within walking distance of the Orange County Convention Center. ⊠ *9188 International Dr., Orlando,* ☎ *407/351–9988. AE, DC, MC, V.*

## Continental

**$$$$** ✕ **Arthur's 27.** The view from the 27th floor of the **Buena Vista Palace Hotel,** overlooking all of WDW and its environs, is breathtaking, but you may be even more light-headed when you get your check. Handle the fiscal traumas up front with one of two prix-fixe dinner options, $60 (not including drinks and gratuities) for a six-course meal or $45 for a four-course special. What you get for your money is a well-prepared meal and a formal dining experience that will last two to three hours. All entrées come with some kind of heavenly sauce, like the rich, creamy cognac-based mixture spooned over the beef tenderloin or the herbed garlic sauce that accompanies the roast lamb. Lobster bisque, a house specialty, is served in a flaky puff pastry shell. Desserts include a credible crème brûlée with raspberries and a chocolate cake to die for. The wine selection is extensive. Service can be pretentious, with waiters making the changing of plates seem like a ritual at the Tomb of the Unknown Soldier. Because there's only one seating a night, reserve as early as a month in advance. ⊠ *Buena Vista Palace Hotel, Walt Disney World Village, Lake Buena Vista,* ☎ *407/827–3450. Reservations essential. Jacket required. AE, D, DC, MC, V.*

## French

**$$$–$$$$** ✕ **La Coquina.** Pheasant and truffle wonton with foie gras and chives is a wonderful example of the French cuisine with Asian flavors that's the specialty here. The high point, though, is Sunday brunch, which stars a generous selection of waffles, omelets, tropical fruits, poached salmon, quartered duck, and pastries against a backdrop of harp music, with a view of black swans on the lake outside. For dinner, arrange in advance and your party can eat in the kitchen—you get lots of special attention and it's loads of fun. Half portions at half price are available for kids 12 and under. ⊠ *Hyatt Regency Grand Cypress,*

*1 Grand Cypress Blvd., Orlando,* ☎ *407/239–1234. Jacket required. AE, DC, MC, V.*

## Italian

**$$$**  ✗ **Portobello Yacht Club.** Operated by Chicago's famed Levy brothers, this eatery has a much better pedigree than the one the Disney brain trust made up for the building, which is in **Pleasure Island.** Supposedly, it was the home of Merriweather Adam Pleasure, the man for whom this nightlife park was named. Start with something simple like the chewy, tasty sourdough bread, served with roast garlic. Then move on to bigger and better things like the stick-to-your-ribs spaghettini alla Portobello, with scallops, clams, shrimp, mussels, tomatoes, garlic, and herbs over copious amounts of pasta. There's always a catch of the day, and servers are attentive and knowledgeable. Since party animals are a protected species in Pleasure Island, the people-watching can be interesting, especially after a little sangria. This is a good spot for a late meal. ✉ *Pleasure Island, Walt Disney World Village,* ☎ *407/934–8888. AE, DC, MC, V.*

**$–$$**  ✗ **Enzo's at the Marketplace.** This pizzeria and deli combines the Italian flavor of its sister in Longwood with a more casual atmosphere and a location convenient for tourists. Owner Enzo Perlini, a food purist, imported the pizza ovens from Italy to ensure that his pizza napoli would have the proper thin, crispy crust. It does. The toppings are Italian style—fresh tomatoes and mozzarella, seafood, or grilled vegetables. If you don't feel like pizza, order the chicken cacciatore or a pasta dish like chicken ravioli. The deli has takeout. ✉ *7600 Dr. Phillips Blvd., Orlando,* ☎ *407/351–1187. AE, D, DC, MC, V.*

## Middle Eastern

**$**  ✗ **Phoenician.** The menu at this member of the rich culinary clique at the **Marketplace** is topped by hummus, babaganoush (roasted eggplant purée), and lebneh (soft, seasoned, yogurt-based cheese). The best bet is to order a tableful of mezes and sample as many as possible. ✉ *7600 Dr. Phillips Blvd., Orlando,* ☎ *407/345–1001. AE, MC, V.*

## Seafood

**$$$**  ✗ **Ariel's.** The centerpiece of this restaurant (named for the main character in *The Little Mermaid*) in the **Disney Beach Club Resort,** a favorite dining spot for Disney executives, is a 2,500-gallon saltwater tank. The fare comes from Florida, the Northeast, and the Northwest, and it's most often simply grilled over a hardwood fire. Want something more exotic? Start with the shellfish gumbo with andouille sausage and then tuck into Ariel's strudel—chicken and ricotta wrapped in a flaky basil-perfumed pastry. ✉ *Disney Beach Club Resort, Lake Buena Vista,* ☎ *407/939–3463. AE, MC, V.*

**$$–$$$**  ✗ **Hemingway's.** There's usually a wait at this popular, elegant eatery
   ★  that overlooks the huge pool at the **Hyatt Regency Grand Cypress,** but when you taste the seafood, you'll forget about the delay. Try the Old Man and the Sea special—grouper, swordfish, tuna, mahimahi, red snapper, pompano, or salmon, charbroiled or blackened, and served with Cajun tartar or béarnaise. You can sample dishes inspired by all phases of Hemingway's life, like paella, which he might have eaten in Madrid before writing *For Whom the Bell Tolls,* and it's assumed that you have a Papa-size appetite. Beer-battered coconut shrimp with orange marmalade–horseradish sauce is a house specialty, and Florida stone crabs are available October through March. There's a good variety of tropical drinks. ✉ *Hyatt Regency Grand Cypress, 1 Grand Cypress Blvd., Orlando,* ☎ *407/239–1234. AE, DC, MC, V.*

### Thai

**$$** ✕ **Siam Orchid.** One of Orlando's several elegant Asian restaurants, this one occupies a gorgeous structure a bit off I-Drive. Waitresses, who wear costumes from their homeland, serve such authentic fare as Siam wings (a chicken wing stuffed to look like a drumstick) and *pla lad prig* (a whole, deep-fried fish covered with a sauce flavored with red chili, bell peppers, and garlic). If you like your food spicy, say "Thai hot" and grab a fire extinguisher. Otherwise, a request to make a dish spicy will be answered with a smile, and your food will come merely mild. ⊠ *7575 Republic Dr., Orlando,* ☎ *407/351–0821. AE, DC, MC, V.*

# Epcot Center

### British

**$$** ✕ **Rose and Crown.** If you love British street culture and a good thick beer, you'll love this friendly pub in the **United Kingdom,** on World Showcase Lagoon. As in all World Showcase restaurants, natives staff the dining room, so you can get a great foreign-affairs lesson with your meal. You'll also get simple pub fare, such as steak-and-kidney pie and fish-and-chips. Dark wood floors, sturdy pub chairs, and brass lamps create a warm, homey atmosphere. At 4, a traditional tea is served, and at day's end, visitors mingle with Disney employees over pints of Bass Ale and Guinness Stout with Stilton cheese. The food is relatively inexpensive, especially at lunch, and the terrace has a splendid view of IllumiNations. It's one of the best bets in Epcot.

### French

**$$$** ✕ **Les Chefs de France.** To create this sparkling café-restaurant in France, three of France's most famous culinary artists came together: Paul Bocuse, who operates one restaurant north of Lyon and two in Tokyo; Gaston Lenôtre, noted for his pastries and ice creams; and Roger Vergé, proprietor of the celebrated Mougins, near Cannes. Although the trio doesn't actually prepare each meal, they did develop the menu, trained the chefs, and look in frequently to make sure the food and service stay up to snuff, which they do. Start with a chicken-and-duck pâté in a pastry crust, follow up with a classic coq au vin or broiled salmon with sorrel sauce, and end up with chocolate-doused ice cream–filled pastry shells.

**$$–$$$** ✕ **Bistro de Paris.** One of the best-kept secrets of the **France** pavilion—
★ and, indeed, in all of Epcot Center—is this bistro upstairs and around the back from **Les Chefs de France.** The sophisticated menu changes regularly and reflects the cutting edge of French cooking. The dining salon is serene—and often filled with well-dressed French people. Come late, ask for a window seat, and watch IllumiNations. French wines are moderately priced and available by the glass.

### German

**$$** ✕ **Biergarten.** Oktoberfest runs 365 days a year in this spot. The cheerful—some would say raucous—atmosphere is what you would expect in a place with an oompah band. Waitresses in typical Bavarian garb serve hot pretzels, hearty German fare such as sauerbraten and bratwurst, and stout pitchers of beer and wine, which patrons pound on their long communal tables—even when the yodelers, singers, and dancers aren't egging them on.

### Italian

**$$$** ✕ **L'Originale Alfredo di Roma Ristorante.** The most popular restaurant at Epcot Center, this one in **Italy** was created, with the help of Disney, by the descendants of Alfredo de Lelio, who invented the now-classic fettuccine sauced with cream, butter, and Parmesan. The true secret to the dish here is butter flown in from Italy. A very good variation is the fettuccine *alla carbonara,* which contains enough bacon to make your cardiologist scream. Stick with pasta, for other menu items are undistinguished, or try the chef's selection—a spaghetti or fettuccine appetizer, a mixed green salad, and a chicken or veal entrée. At dinner, Italian waiters skip around belting out Italian songs and arias.

## Japanese

$$–$$$    ✕ **Mitsukoshi.** This complex of dining areas overlooking tranquil gar-
★    dens of **Japan** in World Showcase is actually three restaurants: the **Yakitori,** which specializes in grilled and skewered fare; the **Tempura Kiku,** where you can sit around a central counter and watch chefs prepare sushi, sashimi, and tempura; and a series of five **Teppanyaki Rooms,** where chefs chop vegetables, meat, and fish at lightning speed and then stir-fry them at grills set into communal dining tables. The **Matsunoma Lounge** pours Japanese sake, plum wine, and saketinis (martinis made with sake rather than vermouth). Food is authentic and tasty—witness the number of Japanese diners. If you just want sushi, go to the lounge and you'll avoid a wait.

## Mexican

$$    ✕ **San Angel Inn.** The lush, tropical surroundings—cool, dark, and almost surreal—make this restaurant in the courtyard of World Showcase's **Mexico** perhaps the most exotic in Walt Disney World. It's popular among Disney execs and tourists who treasure a respite, especially when the humid weather outside makes central Florida feel like Africa in August. The restaurant is open to the "sky" and filled with the music of folk singers, guitars, and marimbas. Above looms an Aztec pyramid, whose soft, fiery light evokes a sense of the distant past. The best seats are along the outer edge, directly alongside the "river," where boatloads of sightseers stream by. On the roster of authentic dishes, one specialty is mole poblano (chicken simmered in a rich sauce of different chilies, green tomatoes, cumin, spices, and cocoa). Fresh tortillas are made each day and served filled with beef, chicken, and cheese and fresh green salsa. You probably won't see a Disney employee, even off duty, ordering one of the margaritas; they're so bad as to be legendary.

## Moroccan

$$–$$$    ✕ **Marrakesh.** This restaurant in **Morocco** is the least popular of the World Showcase restaurants and relatively easy to get into, despite its belly dancers, three-piece Moroccan band, and stunning building, painstakingly constructed with extensive carving and tile work by Moroccan artisans and an attraction itself. That's possibly because the average American hasn't heard much about that nation's cuisine. The food is mildly spicy and delicious. Try the couscous, the national dish, served with vegetables, or bastila (an appetizer made of alternating layers of sweet-and-spicy pork and a thin pastry, redolent of almonds, saffron, and cinnamon).

## Norwegian

$$    ✕ **Restaurant Akershus.** In these four dining rooms in a copy of Oslo's Akershus Castle in World Showcase's **Norway,** the national tradition of seafood and cold-meat dishes is highlighted at a wonderful *koldtboard* (Norwegian buffet). Hosts and hostesses explain the dishes and suggest which ones go together, then send you off to the groaning board. There is no need to shovel everything onto your plate at one time; it's traditional to make several trips. Start with appetizers (usually herring, which comes several ways); then move on to cold seafood like gravlax; next to cold salads and meats; and finally hot lamb, veal, or venison.

Desserts, offered à la carte, include cloudberries (in season)—delicate fruits that grow on the tundra.

---

# Elsewhere Around Orlando

## American

$$$–$$$$ ✕ **Manuel's on the 28th.** How's this for one-upmanship? In 1994 this
★ restaurant on the 28th floor of the downtown Barnett Bank Building replaced the 27th-floor Arthur's 27 as Orlando's loftiest. Unlike the many dining rooms where only the view is exceptional, this one serves excellent food. Try the seared loin of lamb in cayenne–Scotch whiskey sauce, wood-roast chicken and lobster in a coconut-lime sauce, or hickory-grilled Muscovy duck breast with plum-ginger sauce. Manuel's offers an extensive wine list, several tasting packages, and even wines by the half glass. If it's not mealtime, check in at the door and gawk at the view across the flat, green landscape. ✉ *390 N. Orange Ave., Orlando,* ☎ *407/246–6580. Reservations essential. AE, D, DC, MC, V. No lunch.*

$$–$$$ ✕ **Chatham's Place.** The Chatham brothers, Culinary Institute of
★ America graduates, prepare everything to order here, and the staff is genuinely concerned that each patron has a perfect experience. The office building that the restaurant calls home, across from the Marketplace, lends nothing in the way of atmosphere; nor is the decor anything to get excited about—hanging plants, glass-topped paisley tablecloths, and a view of the kitchen. But the meticulously prepared food rises above the setting. Try the black grouper with pecan butter, the rosemary-infused rack of lamb, or the duck breast, grilled to crispy perfection. ✉ *7575 Dr. Phillips Blvd., Orlando,* ☎ *407/345–2992. MC, V. No lunch.*

$$–$$$ ✕ **Moorefield's.** Erudite but not snobby, this downtown restaurant at-
★ tracts an after-theater crowd. The trendy menu and fresh, sophisticated fare make you think Martha Stewart might be in the kitchen, but it's really owner-chef Elizabeth Moorefield. Though the menu changes constantly, you can always find some variation of grilled salmon and roast pork, as well as the very popular pasta with artichoke hearts, hearts of palm, chèvre, sun-dried tomatoes, and Parmesan. A favorite appetizer is minipizza topped with mushrooms and roasted garlic. About 20 carefully selected wines by the glass are served. ✉ *123 S. Orange Ave., Orlando,* ☎ *407/872–6960. AE, MC, V.*

## Chinese

$–$$ ✕ **Forbidden City.** You're in for a treat if you can get past this former gas station's decor, or lack thereof, to the terrific Hunan-style food. Diced chicken with pine seeds in a package (icy lettuce cups wrapped around spicy chicken) is a delightful mix of cold and hot. The sesame chicken goes perfectly with bright-green broccoli in a subtle garlic sauce, and the 10-ingredient lo mein is full of fresh shrimp, chicken, beef, and pork. ✉ *948 N. Mills Ave., Orlando,* ☎ *407/894–5005. MC, V. Closed Sun. No lunch Sat.*

## Continental

$$$$ ✕ **Chalet Suzanne.** If you like to drive or are returning from a day at
★ Cypress Gardens or Bok Tower Gardens, consider stopping here at this unlikely family-owned country inn. Expanded bit by quirky bit since it opened in the 1930s, it looks like a small Swiss village in the middle of the orange groves. In the restaurant, the china, glasses, chairs, and even the tables are of different sizes, shapes, and origins, yet somehow they all work together as the expression of a single sensibility. As an appetizer, try the broiled grapefruit, basted with a butter, cinnamon, and sugar mixture and served with a grilled chicken liver; then move

on to shrimp curry, lobster Newburg, or filet mignon. Crêpes Suzanne are a good bet for dessert. All meals are prix fixe, with seven courses; prices begin at $40 and are determined by the cost of your entrée. The wine list offers many excellent choices at reasonable prices. Guests may step into the cellar to taste some of the wines being featured that night. Or you can spend the night. ⊠ *3800 Chalet Suzanne Dr., Lake Wales,* ☎ *813/676–6011. Jacket required. AE, DC, MC, V. Closed Mon. in summer.*

## Cuban

$ ★ ✕ **Numero Uno.** To the followers of this long-popular Latin restaurant, the name is quite appropriate. The place calls itself "the home of paella," and that's probably the best dish. If you have time and a good appetite, try the paella Valenciana, made to order an hour and 15 minutes in advance, with yellow rice, sausage, chicken, fish, Spanish spices, and a side of plantains. If you don't have that long, go for traditional Cuban fare like shredded flank steak or arroz con pollo. Good homemade lemonade, worthwhile flan, and a selection of sodas from south of the border are available. ⊠ *2499 S. Orange Ave., Orlando,* ☎ *407/841–3840. AE, D, MC, V.*

## French

$$ ★ ✕ **Le Coq au Vin.** Louis Perrotte could run a stuffed-shirt kind of place, because his traditional French cuisine is as expertly prepared as any you'll find in the area. Instead, he chooses to run a modest little kitchen in a small but charming house in south Orlando. Perrotte and his wife, Magdalena, who acts as hostess, make the place feel warm and homey, and it's usually filled with friendly Orlando residents. The menu changes quarterly, reflecting the cooking of various regions of Perrotte's native France, but the fare is always first class. Try homemade chicken liver pâté, fresh rainbow trout with champagne sauce, or Long Island duck with green peppercorns. For dessert, sample the crème brûlée, and pat yourself on the back for discovering a place that few tourists know about. Ask to be seated in the main dining room—it's the center of action. ⊠ *4800 S. Orange Ave., Orlando,* ☎ *407/851–6980. AE, DC, MC, V.*

$$ ✕ **Le Provence Bistro Français.** This charming two-story restaurant in the heart of downtown does a fine imitation of an out-of-the-way bistro on Paris's Left Bank. Reasonable prices and first-rate service add to the delightful surroundings and excellent food. For lunch, try the *salade niçoise* with fresh grilled tuna, French string beans, and hard-boiled eggs, or the *cassoulet toulousain,* a hearty mix of white beans, lamb, pork, and sausage. At dinner you can choose among a six-course prix-fixe menu, a less pricey four-course version, or à la carte options. ⊠ *50 E. Pine St., Orlando,* ☎ *407/843–1320. AE, DC, MC, V. Closed Sun. No lunch Sat.*

## Italian

$$–$$$ ✕ **Antonio's La Fiamma.** The wood-burning grill and oven, used expertly to turn out great grilled fish dishes, gourmet pizzas, and homemade bread, are definitely the ticket to this restaurant's success. In the main section upstairs, diners can watch the chef working his magic. The *linguine alla cine di rapa* (with sautéed bitter greens, sausage, and slivered garlic) is a tantalizing marriage of tastes and textures, and the deboned roast duck with a sweet-sour sauce of balsamic vinegar, rosemary, and honey is heavenly. On weekends the restaurant can be noisy and the service slow, but the interesting wine choices ease the wait. ⊠ *611 S. Orlando Ave., Maitland,* ☎ *407/645–1035. AE, MC, V. Closed Sun.*

**$$–$$$** ✕ **Enzo's on the Lake.** Enzo's is one of Orlando's most popular restau-
★ rants, even though it's on a tacky stretch of highway filled with used-
car lots. The Roman charmer who owns the place, Enzo Perlini, has
turned a rather ordinary lakefront house in suburban Longwood,
about 30 minutes from I-Drive, into a delightful Italian villa. A wall
in front shields it from its shabby surroundings and makes the grounds
look bucolic. It's worth the trip to sample the antipasto (a huge array
of fresh grilled vegetables), homemade frittatas and pâtés, bean salad,
and marinated seafood salad—tiny whole squid, tender calamari, and
shrimp. Daily specials are well done, particularly the fish. The electricity
in the air is such that even people with reservations don't mind waiting at the bar (as is often necessary); they simply get into the party.
Once you've adjusted to the clamor, your only problem will be decid-
ing what to eat. ✉ *1130 S. U.S. 17–92, Longwood,* ☎ *407/834–9872.*
*Reservations essential. AE, DC, MC, V. Closed Sun.*

**$–$$** ✕ **Gargi's Italian Restaurant.** You can feel this delightful ma-and-pa
pasta place vibrate when Amtrak trains roll by only feet away, but that
just adds to the charm. If you crave old-fashioned spaghetti and meat-
balls, lasagna, or manicotti made with sauces that you know have been
simmering all day, this storefront hole-in-the-wall in Orlando's antiques
district, just a little north of downtown, is the place. Well-heeled Or-
landoans eat here before Magic games; it's also a favorite of water-skiers
from Lake Ivanhoe across the street. Only a few hundred yards from
I-4, it's worlds away from touristy I-Drive. ✉ *1421 N. Orange Ave.,*
*Orlando,* ☎ *407/894–7907. MC, V. Beer and wine only. Closed Sun.*

## Mexican

**$** ✕ **Amigos.** Orlando is not exactly a hotbed of Mexican restaurants,
but the best is this one, run by a family of transplanted Texans. The
cuisine is built on good basics, like refried beans that would play well
in San Antonio. Go for the Santa Fe dinner, so big it almost takes a
burro to bring it to your table; you can sample tamales, enchiladas,
chilies rellenos, and those heavenly frijoles and wash it all down with
Mexican beer. ✉ *120 Westmoreland, Altamonte Springs,* ☎ *407/774–*
*4334;* ✉ *494 N. Semoran, Winter Park,* ☎ *407/657–8111. AE, MC,*
*V.*

## Seafood

**$$** ✕ **Straub's Seafood.** Generally, the farther you drive from Walt Dis-
ney World, the less you pay, and Straub's exemplifies the rule. Escar-
gots cost $6—less than you'd pay for a burger on U.S. 192 in Kissimmee.
This is one of those minimalist restaurants that emphasizes food, not
atmosphere (tablecloths are covered with Plexiglas). But owner Robert
Straub, a fishmonger of many years, knows how to prepare a mighty
mean mesquite-grilled Atlantic salmon with a little béarnaise on the
side. He fillets his own fish and won't serve anything that's not fresh.
Blackened dolphin Cajun style (the fish, not the Sea World inhabitant)
is quite good. The menu lists the calorie count and fat content of every
fish item, but for the coconut-banana cream pie, made on premises,
you just don't want to know. ✉ *5101 E. Colonial Dr., Orlando,* ☎
*407/273–9330;* ✉ *512 E. Altamonte Dr., Altamonte Springs,* ☎
*407/831–2250. AE, D, DC, MC, V.*

## Vietnamese

**$** ✕ **Little Saigon.** As Orlando flourishes, so do its ethnic restaurants, in-
★ cluding some Vietnamese eateries about 1½ miles east of I-4's U. S. 50
exit. The folks here are friendly and love to introduce novices to their
healthy and delicious national cuisine. Sample the spring rolls or the
summer rolls (spring roll filling in a soft wrapper). Then move on to
the grilled pork and egg, served atop rice and noodles, or the tradi-

tional soup, filled with noodles, rice, vegetables, and either chicken or seafood; ask to have extra meat in the soup if you're hungry, and be sure they bring you the mint and bean sprouts to sprinkle in. Request an English-speaking waiter if you're unfamiliar with the cuisine. ⌧ *1106 E. Colonial Dr., Orlando,* ☎ *407/423–8539. MC, V. Beer and wine only.*

### West Indian

$ ✕ **Spicy Pot.** One taste of the food in this luncheonette in a rather dingy shopping center will take you straight to Trinidad. The roti sandwich is wrapped around a delicately spiced and curried filling—vegetable, potato, beef, or chicken. Be sure to drink sorrel or mauby, nonalcoholic beverages made from the bark of trees and the perfect accompaniment to the hot food. The traditional entrée is spicy Jamaican jerk chicken. On weekends there's music and dancing in a back room. The neighborhood is not appealing, but it's safe. ⌧ *6203 Silver Star Rd., Orlando,* ☎ *407/297–8255. No credit cards. Beer and wine only. Closed Sun. and Mon.*

# LODGING

Your basic options come down to properties that are (1) owned and operated by Disney on WDW grounds, (2) not owned or operated by Disney but located on Disney property, and (3) not located on WDW property. There are advantages to each. If you are coming to Orlando for only a few days and are interested solely in the Magic Kingdom, Epcot Center, and the other Disney attractions, the resorts on Disney property—whether or not they're owned by Disney—are the most convenient. But if you plan to spend time sightseeing in and around Orlando, it makes sense to look into the alternatives. On-site hotels are generally more expensive, though there are now some moderately priced establishments on Disney property. But Orlando is not huge, and even apparently distant properties are only a half hour's drive from Disney entrance gates. As a rule, the greater the distance from Walt Disney World, the lower the room rates.

Reservations should be made several months in advance—as much as a year in advance for the best rooms during high season (historically, Christmas vacation, summer, and from mid-February through the week after Easter). Many hotels and attractions offer discounts up to 40% from September to mid-December.

Orlando lodging prices tend to be a little higher than elsewhere in Florida, but in all but the smallest motels there is little or no charge for children under 18 who share a room with an adult. Consequently, for this chapter only, the following ranges (for two adults with up to two children in high season, unless otherwise noted) apply.

| CATEGORY | COST* |
| --- | --- |
| $$$$ | over $180 |
| $$$ | $120–$180 |
| $$ | $65–$120 |
| $ | under $65 |

*All prices are for a standard double room, excluding 10% tax.*

## Inside Walt Disney World

For locations of these hotels and resorts, *see* the Walt Disney World map, except for the resorts on or near Hotel Plaza Boulevard, which are shown on the Orlando Lodging map. For these properties, all reservations may be booked through **Disney Central Reservations** (☞ Contacts and Resources, *below*).

## Disney-Owned Properties

The **Magic Kingdom Resort Area** has ritzy hotels, all of which lie on the Magic Kingdom monorail route and are only minutes away from the park. **Fort Wilderness Campground Resort,** with trailers and RV and tent sites, is just southeast of this area. The **Epcot Resort Area,** south of the park, includes the luxurious Beach and Yacht Club resorts, as well as the popular Caribbean Beach Resort. The **Disney Village Resort Area,** east of Epcot Center, is conveniently located near Pleasure Island and the Disney Village Marketplace. Accommodations include two mid-priced, southern-theme resorts, as well as Disney's Village Resort, which has town houses and villas equipped with kitchens. The newest complex, the All-Star Village, lies near the intersection of World Drive and U.S. 192, south of Epcot and the Magic Kingdom.

**$$$$** 🏨 **Contemporary Resort.** This modern 15-story A-frame in the Magic Kingdom resort area has a slick, space-age impersonality. It seems to be crowded with children and conventioneers, yet it is also the center of action, with entertainment, shops, and restaurants. Tower rooms are the most expensive because of their spectacular views out toward the Cinderella Castle or onto Bay Lake, though they can be somewhat noisy at night—sounds rise through the busy atrium. Rooms in the North and South gardens overlook the pool and gardens; the best are on the shore of Bay Lake. (Note that units described as having a view of the Magic Kingdom really look onto the parking lot.) Regardless of location, all rooms have a small terrace and most have two queen-size beds and a small daybed, though you can request a room with a king-size bed and double sofa bed. Many recreational facilities are right on the property, including one of WDW's largest swimming pools and the World's major tennis facility. Kids will be happy to disappear into the Fiesta Fun Center, one of the biggest game rooms known to childkind. ☎ 407/824–1000, FAX 407/824–3539. *961 rooms, 80 suites. 3 restaurants, 3 lounges, snack bar, lake, 3 pools, 6 lighted tennis courts, shuffleboard, volleyball, beach, boating, waterskiing, children's programs. AE, MC, V.*

**$$$$** 🏨 **Disney Beach and Yacht Club Resorts.** Set on a 25-acre lake and accessible from Epcot Center via a romantic water taxi, these two properties are New England inns on a grand Disney scale. The five-story **Yacht Club** recalls the turn-of-the-century New England seacoast with its hardwood floors, gleaming brass, oyster gray clapboard facade, and evergreen landscaping; there's even a lighthouse on its pier. Equally impressive is the blue-and-white, three- to five-story **Beach Club,** where a croquet lawn, cabana-dotted white-sand beach, and staffers' 19th-century "jams" and T-shirts set the scene. Both establishments are refreshingly unstuffy, just right for families. *Beach,* ☎ 407/934–8000; *Yacht* 407/934–7000. *1,188 rooms, 30 suites. 6 restaurants, 3 lounges, 3 pools, beauty salon, golf, 2 lighted tennis courts, croquet, health club, volleyball, boating, baby-sitting. AE, MC, V.*

**$$$$** 🏨 **Grand Floridian.** Set on the shores of the Seven Seas Lagoon, this
★ looks like a turn-of-the-century summer resort, with its gabled red roof, brick chimneys, rambling verandas, and delicate gingerbread. Although equipped with every modern convenience, the softly colored rooms have real vintage charm, especially the attic nooks, up under the eaves. Even the resort's monorail station carries the elegant Victorian theme. Deluxe suites are available in the smaller lodge. ☎ 407/824–3000, FAX 407/824–3186. *834 rooms, 71 suites. 5 restaurants, 4 lounges, pool,*

**292**

**Note:** For locations of
Disney-owned
accommodations, see the
Walt Disney World map.

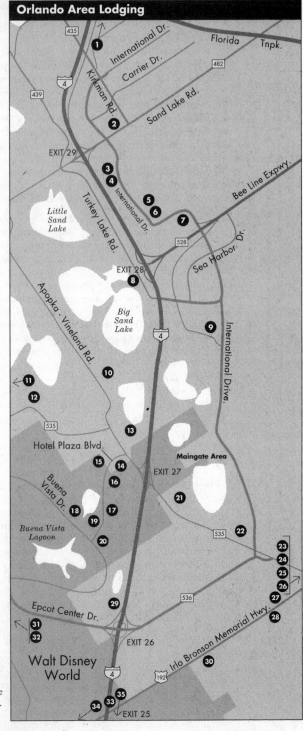

## Orlando Area Lodging

*health club, 2 lighted tennis courts, beach, boating, children's programs, playground. AE, MC, V.*

**$$$$** ▦ **Polynesian Resort.** This resort is one of the most popular of all owned by Disney. An atrium full of orchids, coconut palms, and volcanic rock fountains is the centerpiece; guest rooms are in 11 two- and three-story "longhouses" stretching from this main building. All offer two queen-size beds and a smaller daybed to accommodate up to five, and except for some second-floor rooms, all have a balcony or patio. Lagoon-view rooms—the priciest—include a host of upgraded amenities and services. The least expensive rooms overlook the other buildings, the monorail, and the parking lot across the street. One of the two pools is an extravagantly landscaped free-form affair with rocks and caverns. The Neverland Club, the hotel's child-care center, even offers its guests a dinner show. ☎ 407/824–2000, ℻ 407/824–3174. *763 rooms, 12 suites. 3 restaurants, lounge, snack bar, lake, 2 pools, health club, volleyball, beach, game room, children's programs, playground. AE, MC, V.*

**$$$–$$$$** ▦ **Disney's Village Resort.** The secret's out: You don't have to stay at a hotel at WDW. Though villas are not quite as plush and aren't on the monorail, they are more spacious. And free shuttle buses operate every 20 minutes to take you anywhere on the property. A choice of layouts is available. ☎ 407/934–7639 or 407/827–1100, ℻ 407/934–2741. *4 restaurants, 4 lounges, kitchenettes, 5 outdoor pools (3 heated), 84 hot tubs, health club, boating, video games, baby-sitting, playground, guest laundry. AE, MC, V.*

**$$$** ▦ **Walt Disney World Wilderness Lodge.** This mammoth, rustic, six-story lodge, located on the southwest shore of Bay Lake in the Magic Kingdom resort area, is modeled after the early 20th-century structures in America's national parks, but guests won't exactly rough it. Its massive lobby features a huge, three-sided stone fireplace constructed of rocks from the Grand Canyon, enormous iron chandeliers with Native American and buffalo motifs, and two authentic 50-foot totem poles. Rooms all have western decor: hard-back leather chairs, patchwork quilts, and cowboy art. The large swimming-pool area begins as a hot spring in the main lobby, flows under a window wall to an upper courtyard, and widens into a rushing waterfall. ☎ 407/934–7639, ℻ 407/824–3232. *697 rooms, 29 suites. 3 restaurants, lounge, pool, wading pool, golf, game room, children's programs. AE, MC, V.*

**$$** ▦ **All-Star Sports and All-Star Music Resorts.** This large complex, at the northwest quadrant of the World Drive/U.S. 192 interchange and southwest of Disney–MGM Studios and Epcot Center, is the first phase of a project that is rumored to include a fourth major theme park. Meanwhile, guests can enjoy the zany design of the resorts themselves, whose architecture, landscaping, and lighting display positively over-the-top devotion to their themes: The five three-story buildings at each represent a different sport (baseball, football, tennis, surfing, and basketball) or type of music (Broadway, country and western, calypso, jazz, and rock and roll). So you'll see such eye-catching features as stairwells in the shape of soda cups, a courtyard that looks like a football field, a three-story silhouette of a sax player, and a pool shaped like a guitar. The rooms, which have two double beds, are intended to accommodate four. ☎ 407/934–7639. *1,920 rooms at each. 2 bars, 2 food courts.*

**$$** ▦ **Caribbean Beach Resort.** This immensely popular 200-acre prop-
**★** erty surrounding a 42-acre lake, just east of Epcot Center and Disney–MGM Studios, comprises five palm-studded island "villages" awash with the bright colors of the Caribbean, each with its own pool and white-sand beach. Bridges over the lake connect the mainland with 1-acre Parrot Cay, where there's a play area for children. A mile-long

promenade circles the lake and is favored by joggers, bikers, and strollers. Attractive, pastel-hued guest rooms are equipped with mini-bars and coffeemakers. The only drawbacks compared to other on-site properties are somewhat smaller rooms, limited dining options, and the lack of a supervised children's program. ☎ 407/934–7639, FAX 407/934–3288. *2,106 rooms. Food court, lounge, 7 pools, wading pool, jogging, beach, boating, bicycles, game room, baby-sitting, playground. AE, MC, V.*

**$$** 🏨 **Dixie Landings Resort.** Disney's dream engineers drew inspiration from the architecture of the Old South for this sprawling resort complex. Rooms, which accommodate four in two double beds, are in three-story plantation-style mansions and two-story rustic bayou dwellings. The well-designed food court, Colonels Cotton Mill and Market, offers burgers, sandwiches, breakfast items, and pizza (which can be delivered to your room upon request), plus one full-service restaurant. The pool, a 3½-acre old-fashioned swimming hole complex called Ol' Man Island, looks like something out of a Mark Twain novel; it has slides, rope swings, and an adjacent play area. ☎ 407/934–7639, FAX 407/934–5777. *2,048 rooms. Restaurant, food court, pools, wading pools, golf, boating, game room, playground, laundry. AE, MC, V.*

**$$** 🏨 **Port Orleans Resort.** Disney's version of New Orleans's French Quarter consists of ornate row-house buildings, with overgrown wrought-iron balconies and hanging plants, clustered around squares with stone fountains and lush plantings. Lamp-lit sidewalks edge the streets, which are named after authentic French Quarter thoroughfares. New Orleans specialties, such as jambalaya, Cajun chicken, and beignets, are served (along with the usual burgers, deli sandwiches, and pizza) at the Sassagoula Floatworks Factory, the hotel's food court; the restaurant offers Creole and other Louisiana-style fare. The large, free-form pool ("Doubloon Lagoon") is one of the most exotic of all Disney hotel pools. Note that most rooms here have two double beds and accommodate four; for quarters with one king-size bed, book early. ☎ 407/934–5502, FAX 407/934–5353. *1,008 rooms. Restaurant, food court, pool, wading pool, boating, bicycles, game room, baby-sitting, laundry, concierge. AE, MC, V.*

## Other Walt Disney World Hotels

**$$$$** 🏨 **Buena Vista Palace and Palace Suite Resort at Walt Disney World Village.** This bold, modern hotel, the largest at Lake Buena Vista, seems small and quiet when you enter its lobby. Don't be fooled—it's huge. Upper-floor rooms are more expensive; the best look out toward Epcot Center. Ask for a room in the 27-story main tower, to avoid the late-night noise that reverberates through the atrium from the Kookaburra nightclub. All bedrooms have a small balcony and come with one king- or two queen-size beds. At the top of the hotel, the **Top of the Palace Lounge** offers a ringside seat on the local sunsets and Epcot Center's nightly laser-and-fireworks show. Suites in the adjacent **Palace Suite Resort** accommodate up to eight people; most have private balconies or patios, and all come with living rooms with sleeper sofas and dining areas (sink, coffeemaker, microwave, and refrigerator). Rooms have VCRs. ✉ *1900 Lake Buena Vista Dr., Lake Buena Vista 32830,* ☎ *407/827–2727 or 800/327–2990. 1,028 rooms. 5 restaurants, 4 lounges, snack bar, indoor-outdoor pool, 2 outdoor pools, sauna, 3 lighted tennis courts, health club, volleyball, summer children's programs, playground, business services. AE, D, DC, MC, V.*

**$$$$** 🏨 **Hilton at Walt Disney World Village.** Don't be put off by the unim-
★  pressive facade; you'll find a pleasant interior with tasteful carpeting, lots of gleaming brass and glass, and a decor softly hued in peach, mauve, and green. The lobby is rich with tile and latticework, and the pool

area has an attractive deck and gazebo. Each guest room has a king-size bed or two double beds. The most expensive have views of Disney Village Marketplace and Pleasure Island, but pool-view rooms are a better value. Parents are particularly enthusiastic about the **Vacation Station,** a supervised playroom with large-screen TV, video arcade, and a six-bed dormitory that operates every evening; meals are served on schedule, and the cost is $4 an hour. A Continental breakfast is served. ⊠ *1751 Hotel Plaza Blvd., Lake Buena Vista 32830,* ☎ *407/827–4000 or 800/782–4414,* FAX *407/827–3890. 787 rooms, 27 suites. 7 restaurants, 2 lounges, 2 pools, 2 lighted tennis courts, health club, business services. AE, D, DC, MC, V.*

**$$$$** 🏨 **Walt Disney World Dolphin.** This Disney landmark features two myth-
**★** ical 56-foot sea creatures—labeled dolphins by the hotel's noted architect, Michael Graves—perched atop each end of the building; between them soars a 27-story pyramid, one of the highest structures in Walt Disney World. A waterfall cascades down the coral-and-turquoise facade, which displays a mural of giant banana leaves. Inside, chandeliers are shaped like monkeys, and brightly painted wooden benches sprout wooden palm trees. Rooms are decorated in equally jocular fashion, with palm tree–shape lamps and wildly colorful bedspreads; the best overlook Epcot Center and have a stunning view of its nightly fireworks-and-laser show. The 12th–20th Tower floors are concierge levels. With its emphasis on the convention trade, this hotel is more urban and adult than many other on-site properties. ⊠ *1500 Epcot Resort Blvd., Lake Buena Vista 32830,* ☎ *407/934–4000 or 800/227–1500,* FAX *407/934–4884. 1,510 rooms (140 suites and 185 Tower rooms). 8 restaurants, 3 lounges, 4 pools, 8 lighted tennis courts, health club, beach, boating, game room, children's programs. AE, D, DC, MC, V.*

**$$$$** 🏨 **Walt Disney World Swan.** Two 45-foot swans, each weighing more than 25,000 pounds, grace the rooftop of this coral-and-aquamarine hotel, which is connected by a covered causeway to the Dolphin. Inside, architect Michael Graves has canopied the ceiling with tall, gathered papyrus reeds and lined up a regiment of columns with palm-frond capitals. Rooms are decorated in coral, peach, teal, and yellow floral and geometric patterns; each has an in-room safe, stocked refrigerator, and daily newspaper delivery. As at the Dolphin, the atmosphere is less family-oriented than at many other on-site properties. ⊠ *1200 Epcot Resorts Blvd., Lake Buena Vista 32830,* ☎ *407/934–3000, 800/248–7926, or 800/228–3000,* FAX *407/934–4499. 758 rooms (45 concierge level rooms). 3 restaurants, 2 lounges, pool, 8 lighted tennis courts, health club, beach, baby-sitting, children's programs. AE, D, DC, MC, V.*

**$$$** 🏨 **Courtyard Marriott.** Though somewhat charmless, with its lobby-ful of white Formica and nondescript 14-story atrium, this chain hotel is undeniably one of the most reasonably priced places on WDW property, and it's popular with young couples and seniors. The restaurant, open until midnight, is better than average. Rooms have coffeemakers. ⊠ *1805 Hotel Plaza Blvd., Lake Buena Vista 32830,* ☎ *407/828–8888 or 800/223–9930,* FAX *407/827–4623. 323 rooms. Restaurant, lounge, 2 pools, wading pool, exercise room, game room, baby-sitting, playground, laundry. AE, D, DC, MC, V.*

**$$$** 🏨 **Grosvenor Resort.** Offering a wealth of facilities and comfortable rooms for a fair price, this attractive member of the Best Western chain is the best deal in the neighborhood. Rooms are average in size, but they're colorfully decorated in lilacs and pinks and have two double beds, their own safes, refrigerators, minibars, and coffeemakers, plus cable TV and a VCR (the lobby rents movies as well as video cameras). Public areas are spacious, with white columns, high ceilings, wicker furniture, cheerful colors, and plenty of natural light. ⊠ *1850 Hotel Plaza Blvd., Lake Buena Vista 32830,* ☎ *407/828–4444 or 800/624– 4109,* ⨳ *407/828–8192. 624 rooms, 6 suites. 2 restaurants, lounge, 2 pools, wading pool, 2 lighted tennis courts, basketball, shuffleboard, volleyball, game room, baby-sitting, playground. AE, D, DC, MC, V.*

**\$\$–\$\$\$**  🔲 **Royal Plaza.** Though dated in comparison to the slick hotels in the neighborhood, this casual, lively establishment with an arty 1960s exterior of white and blue tiles is quite popular among families. Each of the generously proportioned rooms has a terrace or balcony; the best quarters overlook the pool. Lower-floor rooms can be noisy—the **Giraffe,** the hotel's Top 40 nightclub, hops until the wee, wee hours. Burt Reynolds and Barbara Mandrell theme rooms are available. ⊠ *1905 Hotel Plaza Blvd., Lake Buena Vista 32830,* ☎ *407/828–2828 or 800/248–7890,* ⨳ *407/827–3977. 386 rooms, 10 suites. 2 restaurants, 2 lounges, pool, sauna, 4 lighted tennis courts. AE, D, DC, MC, V.*

**\$\$–\$\$\$**  ✕🔲 **Travelodge Hotel.** Although unexceptionally furnished, the amenities make this 18-story, periwinkle blue and pink lodging a good choice for families. All guest rooms are done in pastels with touches of brass and attractive furniture. There's nightly entertainment in the 18th-floor Topper's Nightclub, which overlooks Epcot Center. ⊠ *2000 Hotel Plaza Boulevard, Lake Buena Vista 32830,* ☎ *407/828–2424 or in FL, 800/423–1022; outside FL, 800/348–3765,* ⨳ *407/828–8933. 325 rooms. Restaurant, lounge, 2 snack bars, heated pool, playground, game room, guest laundry, baby-sitting. AE, DC, MC, V.*

**\$\$**  🔲 **Guest Quarters Suite Resort.** This all-suite hotel attracts a quiet family crowd and few of the noisy conventioneers often found at larger, splashier properties. Each bedroom in the one- or two-bedroom units has two double beds or a king-size bed, and the separate living area is equipped with a sofa bed; each can accommodate up to six (if not particularly comfortably). There's a television in each room (including a small one in the bathroom), refrigerator, wet bar, and coffeemaker; microwave ovens are available on request. ⊠ *2305 Hotel Plaza Blvd., Lake Buena Vista 32830,* ☎ *407/934–1000 or 800/424–2900,* ⨳ *407/934–1011. 229 units. Restaurant, bar, ice cream parlor, lounge, pool, wading pool, 2 lighted tennis courts, exercise room, jogging, baby-sitting. AE, D, DC, MC, V.*

**\$–\$\$**  🔲 **Shades of Green on Walt Disney World Resort.** Formerly the Disney Inn, this quiet resort only two minutes by car from the Magic Kingdom and a short walk from the Polynesian Village Resort is now operated by the U.S. Armed Forces Recreation Center. Vacationing active-duty and retired personnel from all branches of the armed forces—including the reserves, National Guard, and Department of Defense—are eligible to stay here; rates are on a sliding scale based on rank. Situated at the junction of three world-class golf courses, the hotel offers spacious, country-style rooms that accommodate up to five in two queen-size beds and a comfortable sleeper sofa. Choose between views of the fairways, the gardens, or pools. ☎ *407/824–3600. 288 rooms. 2 restaurants, lounge, 2 pools, wading pool, golf, 2 lighted tennis courts, health club, game room, laundry. AE, MC, V.*

## Around Walt Disney World

Hotels off Disney property are clustered in several principal areas near Walt Disney World: along International Drive, a few minutes south of downtown Orlando; along U.S. 192 in Kissimmee, the town that is actually closest to Walt Disney World, where hotels tend to be small and cheap; and in the Disney Maingate area. Nearly every hotel in these areas provides frequent transportation to and from Walt Disney World.

## International Drive

I-Drive, as it's known, is a cheek-by-jowl jumble of good-size hotels and franchised fast-food spots, including the world's largest McDonald's—themed, of course. It's a bit farther from WDW than the other areas, although not that far, and it's quite convenient to other area theme parks and to downtown Orlando nightlife.

**$$$$** ⊞ **Peabody Orlando.** From afar, this 27-story structure looks like three high-rise office buildings, but don't be put off. Inside, the place is very impressive and handsomely designed, from the lobby's rich marble floors and fountains to the sweeping views and the modern art throughout. Like its parent property in Memphis, Tennessee, the Orlando Peabody has a resident flock of ducks splashing in the lobby fountain. The most panoramic of the oversize beige and cream rooms have views of Walt Disney World. The restaurants are noteworthy. Located across the street from the Orange County Convention Center, the hotel attracts rock stars and other performers as well as conventioneers. ⊠ *9801 International Dr., Orlando 32819,* ☎ *407/352–4000 or 800/732–2639,* FAX *407/351–9177. 891 rooms. 3 restaurants, 2 lounges, pool, wading pool, spa, concierge level, golf privileges, 4 lighted tennis courts, health club, children's programs. AE, D, DC, MC, V.*

**$$$–$$$$** ⊞ **Westgate Lakes.** Formerly the Sonesta Villa Resort, this collection of one- and two-bedroom lakefront town houses comprises homey, comfortable apartments. Each is small but fully equipped with a kitchenette, dining area, living room, small patio, bedroom, and one or two bathrooms. The conveniently located outdoor facilities, including a lake and sandy beach, are equally attractive. If you want to cook at "home" but are too busy to shop, the hotel will pick up groceries for you and deliver them while you're out. ⊠ *10000 Turkey Lake Rd., Orlando 32819,* ☎ *407/352–8051 or 800/766–3782,* FAX *407/345–5384. 369 units. 2 restaurants, bar and grill, ice cream parlor, lounge, pool, wading pool, 2 lighted tennis courts, health club, jogging, shuffleboard, volleyball, boating, jet skiing, waterskiing, children's program. AE, D, DC, MC, V.*

**$$$** ⊞ **Embassy Suites International Drive South.** This all-suites hotel serves a free buffet breakfast with cooked-to-order items as well as complimentary cocktails, yet room rates are less than a single room in the top-notch hotels. Each unit has both a bedroom and a full living room equipped with wet bar, refrigerator, pullout sofa, and two TVs. With its marble floors, pillars, hanging lamps, and ceiling fans, the lobby has an expansive, old-fashioned feel. Tropical gardens with mossy rock fountains, 20-foot palm trees, and wrought-iron railings give the atrium a distinctive taste of the humid Deep South. ⊠ *8978 International Dr., Orlando 32819,* ☎ *407/352–1400 or 800/432–7272,* FAX *407/363–1120. 245 suites. Restaurant, lounge, indoor pool, sauna, steam room, children's programs. AE, D, DC, MC, V.*

**$$$** ⊞ **Parc Corniche Resort.** Framed by an 18-hole Joe Lee–designed golf course called the International Golf Club, this all-suites resort is ideal for golf enthusiasts. Each of the one- and two-bedroom suites is decked out in pastels and tropical patterns and has a patio or balcony with a golf course view as well as a kitchen. The largest accommodations, a two-bedroom, two-bath unit, can sleep up to six. The resort serves a complimentary Continental breakfast daily, and Sea World is only a few blocks away. ⊠ *6300 Parc Corniche Dr., Orlando 32821,* ☎ *407/239–7100 or 800/446–2721,* FAX *407/239–8501. 210 suites. Restaurant, lounge, pool, wading pool, golf, playground. AE, D, MC, V.*

$$$    🛏 **Summerfield Suites Hotel.** A great option for big families, the all-suites Summerfield is small enough that guests get plenty of personal attention, but accommodations are quite roomy. Two-bedroom units, the most popular, have fully equipped kitchens (complete with stove, coffeemaker, microwave, jumbo refrigerator, dishes, and pots and pans), plus a living room with TV and VCR. All bedrooms have their own bathroom. The courtyard shelters a small but pretty pool. If you don't want to hassle with whipping up eggs in the morning, you can sample a free Continental buffet. ✉ *8480 International Dr., Orlando 32819,* ☎ *407/352–2400 or 800/833–4353,* 📠 *407/352–4631. 42 1-bedroom suites, 104 2-bedroom suites. Lounge, pool, wading pool, exercise room. AE, D, DC, MC, V.*

$$–$$$    🛏 **Enclave Suites at Orlando.** With three 10-story, step-shape buildings surrounding an office, restaurant, and recreation area, this all-suites lodging is less a hotel than a condominium complex. You get a complete apartment, with significantly more space than in other all-suites hotels. Accommodating up to six, the units have full kitchens, living rooms, two bedrooms, and small terraces. ✉ *6165 Carrier Dr., Orlando 32819,* ☎ *407/351–1155 or 800/457–0077,* 📠 *407/351–2001. 321 suites. Restaurant, lounge, indoor pool, 2 outdoor pools, sauna, lighted tennis court, exercise room, playground. AE, D, DC, MC, V.*

$$    🛏 **Orlando Heritage Inn.** Smaller hotels do have more charm. The ex-
★    terior of this two-story structure—pale pink clapboard and white railings—was inspired by *Gone with the Wind,* the interior modeled on Victorian-era Florida, with lots of reproduction turn-of-the-century furnishings, French windows, patterned tin ceilings, and brass lamps, and even a few 19th-century antiques. In the guest rooms, folk art hangs on the walls and lace curtains on the double French doors, and quilted spreads cover the beds. Dinner shows are presented in the rotunda several nights weekly. In-room safes are provided. ✉ *9861 International Dr., Orlando 32819,* ☎ *407/352–0008 or 800/447–1890,* 📠 *407/352–5449. 150 rooms. Restaurant, lounge, pool, baby-sitting, laundry. AE, D, DC, MC, V.*

$–$$    🛏 **Wynfield Inn–Westwood.** This three-story motel is a find. Its cheerful, contemporary rooms, large enough to accommodate four, are smartly appointed with colorful, floral-print bedspreads and understated wall hangings. Complimentary fruit, coffee, and tea are served in the lobby daily. The staff is friendly and helpful. In-room movies are available. ✉ *6263 Westwood Blvd., Orlando 32821,* ☎ *407/345–8000 or 800/346–1551,* 📠 *407/345–1508. 300 rooms. Bar, 2 pools, game room, laundry. AE, D, MC, V.*

## Maingate

These properties are clustered around WDW's northernmost entrance, just off I–4.

$$$$    🛏 **Hyatt Regency Grand Cypress.** Part of what is perhaps the Orlando
★    area's most spectacular resort, this hotel offers virtually every resort amenity and then some. Golf facilities are world-class, with 45 Jack Nicklaus–designed holes (making up four courses) and the high-tech Academy of Golf. The huge, three-level, 800,000-gallon, free-form pool is fed by 12 cascading waterfalls, and there's a 45-acre Audubon nature preserve. Rooms are not memorable but spacious; those with the best views overlook the pool and Lake Windsong. Service is attentive, and the restaurants excellent. The hotel has just one drawback: the king-size conventions that it commonly attracts. Also at the 1,500-acre resort complex are 146 villas. ✉ *1 Grand Cypress Blvd., Orlando 32836,* ☎ *407/239–1234 or 800/233–1234,* 📠 *407/239–3800. 676 rooms.*

5 restaurants, 4 lounges, 2 pools, 45-hole golf complex, 12 tennis courts (6 lighted), health club, horseback riding, jogging, boating, bicycles, children's programs. AE, D, DC, MC, V.

**$$$$** ⊞ **Marriott's Orlando World Center.** This 27-story titan towers over even the giants among Orlando's hotels, and the lineup of amenities seems endless; one of the four swimming pools is the largest in the state. The lobby is a huge, opulent atrium, and rooms are clean and comfortable. Luxurious villas, the Royal Palms and Sabal Palms, are available for daily and weekly rentals. If you like your hostelries cozy, you'll consider the size of this place a definite negative; otherwise, its only unappealing aspect is the horde of conventioneers who sweep across the main lobby area. ⊠ 8701 World Center Dr., Orlando 32821, ☎ 407/239–4200 or 800/228–9290, ℻ 407/238–8777. 1,504 rooms. 7 restaurants, 2 lounges, indoor pool, 3 outdoor pools, wading pool, 18-hole golf course, miniature golf, 8 lighted tennis courts, health club, volleyball, children's programs. AE, D, DC, MC, V.

**$$$$** ⊞ **Vistana Resort.** Consider this peaceful resort if you're interested in tennis: You can play on its clay and all-weather courts without charge; private or semiprivate lessons are available for a fee. A good bet for families or a group of friends, its spacious, tastefully decorated villas and town houses are spread over 95 landscaped acres and have two bedrooms each, plus a living room, full kitchen, washer/dryer, and so on. The price may seem high, but considering that each unit can sleep six or eight, it's a bargain. ⊠ 13500 Rte. 535, Orlando 32821, ☎ 407/239–3100 or 800/877–8787, ℻ 407/239–3111. 722 units. 2 restaurants, lounge, 5 outdoor pools, 5 wading pools, miniature golf, basketball, health club, shuffleboard, children's programs. AE, D, DC, MC, V.

**$$$–$$$$** ⊞ **Embassy Suites Resort Lake Buena Vista.** Some local folks have been shocked by this all-suites hotel's wild turquoise, pink, and yellow facade, clearly visible from I–4. But it's an attractive option—just 1 mile from Walt Disney World, 3 miles from Sea World, and 7 miles from Universal Studios Florida. The central atrium lobby, loaded with tropical vegetation and soothed by a rushing fountain, is a great place to enjoy the complimentary breakfast and evening cocktails. ⊠ 8100 Lake Ave., Lake Buena Vista 32830, ☎ 407/239–1144 or 800/362–2779, ℻ 407/238–0230. 280 suites. Restaurant, deli, lounge, indoor-outdoor pool, wading pool, lighted tennis court, basketball, fitness room, shuffleboard, volleyball, children's programs, playground. AE, D, DC, MC, V.

**$$–$$$** ⊞ **Holiday Inn Sunspree Resort Lake Buena Vista.** You might first notice the striking, terra-cotta–colored facade, but what really earns the kudos at this place is the way it seems to be built around family fun. **Camp Holiday**—a free children's program of magic shows, arts and crafts, movies, cartoons, and other supervised activities, day and night—is the finest program of its kind. Children even have their own restaurant, the **Kids' Kottage,** where they eat for free if a parent is dining in the main restaurant, and the hotel rents beepers so that parents can have some time to themselves without worrying about their offspring. Furnished with two queen-size beds or one king-size bed and a sleeper, all rooms have a TV and VCR plus a kitchenette equipped with refrigerator, electronic safe, microwave, and coffeemaker. In the hotel courtyard is a large free-form pool, plus a whirlpool and a wading pool. ⊠ 3351 Rte. 535, Lake Buena Vista 32821, ☎ 407/239–4500, 800/366–6299, or 800/465–4329, ℻ 407/239–8463. 507 rooms. Restaurant, lounge, pool, wading pool, health club, children's programs. AE, D, DC, MC, V.

$$-$$$   ⬚ **Ramada Plaza Resort Maingate at the Parkway.** With its attractive
★   setting, good facilities, and competitive prices, this bright, spacious Ramada may offer the best deal in the neighborhood. Its delicatessen comes in handy when you want to assemble a picnic. Generously proportioned rooms are decked out with tropical patterns, pastel colors, and white wooden furniture carved with pineapples; units with the best view and light face the pool. ✉ *2900 Parkway Blvd., Kissimmee 34746,* ☎ *407/396–7000 or 800/634–4774; in FL, 800/225–3939;* ⨳ *407/396– 6792. 712 rooms, 6 suites. Restaurant, deli, 2 lounges, snack bar, 2 pools, sauna, 2 lighted tennis courts, fitness center, volleyball. AE, D, DC, MC, V.*

$$   ⬚ **Perri House.** Exactly 1 mile from the Magic Kingdom as the crow flies and situated at the top of a sheltered side road, this modern, B&B-style country inn, set amid 20 acres of serenity, is a truly unique lodging in "build it bigger and they will come" Orlando. Nick and Angi Perretti and their three grown children planned and built the clever circular house so that each neatly furnished room has an outside entrance. What really sets Perri House apart, however, is that it is in the process of becoming an Audubon Society–recognized bird sanctuary, including walking paths, gazebos, a pond, feeding station, and so on. A Continental breakfast is included. ✉ *10417 Rte. 535, Lake Buena Vista 32830,* ☎ *407/876–4830 or 800/780–4830,* ⨳ *407/876–0241. 6 rooms. Pool. AE, D, MC, V.*

$$   ⬚ **Wyndham Garden Hotel.** Formerly the Doubletree Club Hotel, this
★   six-story complex looks like an office building from the outside. Don't let that put you off. Inside it's full of homey touches, including the 5,000-square-foot club area with loads of big comfy couches and a giant-screen TV. ✉ *8688 Palm Pkwy., Lake Buena Vista 32830,* ☎ *407/239–8500 or 800/996–3426,* ⨳ *407/239–8591. 167 rooms. Restaurant, lounge, pool, health club. AE, D, DC, MC, V.*

## U.S. 192 Area

For real bargains and basic accommodations, head for this strip—also known as the Irlo Bronson Memorial Highway—crammed with mom-and-pop motels and bargain basement hotels, cheap restaurants, fast-food spots, nickel-and-dime attractions, gas stations, and minimarts. Room rates start at $20 a night—lower at the right time of year, if you can cut the right deal.

$$$   ⬚ **Sol Orlando Resort.** The brochure of this resort hotel complex stretches a point when it says it has the charm of a small village in Andalusia. While the red tile and stucco villas and palm-studded grounds are attractive, it's the spacious accommodations that are truly noteworthy. Each of the one-, two-, and three-bedroom units has a living and dining area, a kitchen, and two TVs; the three-bedroom villa sleeps up to eight comfortably. Complimentary breakfast is also included. ✉ *4787 W. Irlo Bronson Memorial Hwy., Kissimmee 34746,* ☎ *407/397–0555,* ⨳ *407/397–0553. 150 villas. Restaurant, lounge, pool, wading pool, lighted tennis court, health club, racquetball, squash. AE, D, DC, MC, V.*

$$–$$$   ⬚ **Quality Suites Maingate East.** Ideal for large families, the spacious rooms are designed to sleep six or 10, and come equipped with a microwave, refrigerator, and dishwasher. Suites have two bedrooms with two double beds each and a living room with a double pullout couch. A complimentary Continental breakfast is offered each morning, and free beer and wine are served every day at the tropical poolside **Kokomo's** bar. Children will enjoy the restaurant: A toy train chugs along overhead. ✉ *5876 W. Irlo Bronson Memorial Hwy., Kissimmee*

34746, ☎ 407/396–8040 or 800/848–4148, FAX 407/393–6766. *225 units. Restaurant, bar, lounge, pool, playground. AE, D, DC, MC, V.*

**$$–$$$** 🏨 **Residence Inn by Marriott on Lake Cecile.** Of the all-suites hotels on U.S. 192, this complex of town houses is probably the best. One side of the complex faces the highway, the other overlooks an attractive lake, and a free water shuttle takes you to a dock from which you can sail, waterski, jet ski, and fish. Penthouse units accommodate four, with complete kitchens, small living rooms, loft bedrooms, and fireplaces. All others accommodate two and are like studio apartments but still have full kitchens and fireplaces. Each suite has a private entrance. While the price may seem high considering the location, there is no charge for additional guests, so you can squeeze in the whole family; both Continental breakfast and a grocery-shopping service are complimentary. ⊠ *4786 W. Irlo Bronson Memorial Hwy., Kissimmee 34746,* ☎ *407/396–2056 or 800/468–3027, FAX 407/396–2296. 159 units. Pool, tennis court, basketball, playground. AE, D, DC, MC, V.*

**$$** 🏨 **Best Western Kissimmee.** Overlooking a nine-hole, par-3 executive golf course, this three-story hotel is a hit with golf-loving seniors as well as with families. The two swimming pools in the garden courtyard are amply shaded. The spacious rooms are done in soft pastels, with light wood furniture and attractive wall hangings. Units with king-size beds and kitchenettes are available. ⊠ *2261 E. Irlo Bronson Memorial Hwy., Kissimmee 34744,* ☎ *407/846–2221 or 800/944–0662, FAX 407/846–1095. 282 rooms. Restaurant, lounge, picnic area, 2 pools, playground. AE, D, MC, V.*

**$$** 🏨 **Sheraton Lakeside Inn.** This complex of 15 two-story buildings with balconies is spread over 27 acres with a small man-made lake. Comfortable though undistinguished, the resort offers quite a few recreational facilities for the money. The nondescript beige rooms have either two double beds or one king-size bed as well as a refrigerator and safe. ⊠ *7769 W. Irlo Bronson Memorial Hwy., Kissimmee 34746,* ☎ *407/239–2650 or 800/848–0801, FAX 407/396–2222. 651 rooms. 2 restaurants, deli, lounge, 3 pools, wading pool, miniature golf, 4 lighted tennis courts, boating, fishing, children's programs. AE, D, DC, MC, V.*

**$** 🏨 **Park Inn International.** The Mediterranean-style architecture is not likely to charm you off your feet, but the staff is friendly and the property has all the facilities you're likely to want—and it's on Cedar Lake. Ask for a room as close to the water as possible. There is a restaurant, but for an extra $10 you can get a room with a kitchenette. ⊠ *4960 W. Irlo Bronson Memorial Hwy., Kissimmee 34741,* ☎ *407/396–1376 or 800/327–0072, FAX 407/396–0716. 197 rooms. Restaurant, pool, game room. AE, D, DC, MC, V.*

**$** 🏨 **Record Motel.** This simple property is the kind of few-frills, rock-bottom-rates, mom-and-pop operation that made U.S. 192 famous. Clean rooms with free HBO, complimentary morning coffee, and a solar-heated pool are the major amenities. What the place lacks in luxuries and ambience, it more than makes up for with its friendly staff. ⊠ *4651 W. Irlo Bronson Memorial Hwy., Kissimmee 34746,* ☎ *407/396–8400, FAX 407/396–8415. 57 rooms. Pool, baby-sitting. AE, D, MC, V.*

**$** 🏨 **Sevilla Inn.** This classy, family-operated motel is one of the best buys
★ in the Orlando area. Stucco and wood on the outside, the three-story building has up-to-date rooms inside, with colorful bedspreads, tasteful wall hangings, a fresh mauve or green paint job, and cable TV. The pool area, encircled by palm trees and tropical flowers, feels like something you'd find in a much fancier resort. ⊠ *4640 W. Irlo Bronson Memorial Hwy., Kissimmee 34746,* ☎ *407/396–4135 or 800/367–1363, FAX 407/396–4992. 46 rooms. Pool. AE, D, MC, V.*

## Orlando Suburbs

### Winter Park

$$–$$$  🏨 **Park Plaza Hotel.** Small and intimate, this old-fashioned, 1922-vintage establishment feels almost like a private home, but there are nice touches: A newspaper is slid under your door each morning, and the complimentary breakfast is also brought to your room. Key to a special stay here is getting one of the front garden suites (with living room), which open onto one long balcony. Affectionately called "the garden in the sky" by locals, the balcony is abloom with ferns and flowers; it's punctuated by wicker chairs and tables and has views of Park Avenue or Central Park. All rooms have either a double, queen-size, or king-size bed; units in the back can be small and cramped. Definitely not for people who want recreational facilities or have young children. ⊠ *307 Park Ave. S, Winter Park 32789,* ☎ *407/647–1072 or 800/228–7220,* ℻ *407/647–4081. 27 rooms. Restaurant, lounge. AE, DC, MC, V.*

### Lake Wales

$$–$$$  🏨 **Chalet Suzanne.** You'll find this friendly, homespun mom-and-pop
★  operation in orange-grove territory next to Lake Suzanne, some 60 miles southwest of Orlando and about a half hour from Walt Disney World. A homemade billboard directs you down a country road that turns into a palm-lined drive; then cobblestone paths lead to a balconied chalet-style house and cabins with thatch roofs. Fields and gardens extend to one side, a lake on the other. The happily quirky grounds are decorated with colorful tile work from Portugal, ironwork from Spain, pottery from Italy, and porcelain from England and Germany. In the rooms and public spaces, furnishings vary wildly from the rare and valuable to the garage-sale one-of-a-kind. Each room has its own personality; all have eccentrically tiled bathrooms with old-fashioned tubs and washbasins. The most charming rooms face the lake. The eponymous restaurant made its fame serving Continental fare back in the days that that was unusual; a complimentary breakfast is served. ⊠ *3800 Chalet Suzanne Dr., Lake Wales 33853,* ☎ *813/676–6011,* ℻ *813/676–1814. 30 rooms. Restaurant, lounge, pool, badminton, fishing, game room, laundry. AE, D, DC, MC, V.*

# NIGHTLIFE AND THE ARTS

Disneyesque street signs with bright colors and engaging graphics are not the only new things in downtown Orlando. Nightspots have sprung up and are thriving in an area that used to be deserted after office workers went home. Orlando's club owners have figured out that there's big money to be made by luring tourists into the city center. The result is a diverse collection of nighttime activities offering everything from cutting-edge palaces and quiet coffeehouses to jousting tournaments and murder-mystery buffets. Even locals who haven't ventured out in a few years are surprised. And there's also a reasonably lively arts scene.

## The Arts

Check out the local fine arts scene in *The Orlando Weekly,* a local entertainment magazine, or "Calendar," which is printed every Friday in the *Orlando Sentinel.* They are available at most newsstands. Ticket prices for performing-arts events in the Orlando area rarely exceed $12 and are often half that.

**Carr Performing Arts Centre.** Orlando has an active agenda of dance, classical music, opera, and theater, much of it taking place here. ⊠ *401 W. Livingston St., Orlando,* ☎ *407/849–2020.*

**Civic Theater of Central Florida.** Here you can catch a variety of shows, with evening performances Wed.–Sat. and Sun. matinees. ⊠ *1001 E. Princeton St., Orlando,* ☎ *407/896–7365.*

**Orange County Convention and Civic Center.** On the south end of International Drive, it sometimes is the venue for local concerts by top artists. ☎ *407/345–9800.*

**Orlando Arena.** Downtown on West Amelia Street, it plays host to many big-name performers. ☎ *407/849–2020.*

**Rollins College.** During the school year, this Winter Park institution (☎ 407/646–2233) has a choral concert series that is open to the public and usually free. The last week in February there is a **Bach Music Festival** (☎ 407/646–2182) that has been a Winter Park tradition for nearly 60 years. Also at the college, the **Annie Russell Theater** (☎ 407/646–2145) has a regular series of productions.

# Nightlife

## Bars and Discos

Inside Walt Disney World, every hotel has its quota of bars and lounges. Jazz trios and bluegrass bands, DJs and rockers tune up and turn on their amps after dinner's done. Many are at **Pleasure Island**—but not all. Fancy drinks with even more fanciful names are a staple. And you can drink later here than off-property—clubs on Disney property will serve you a drink as late as 2:45 AM.

Outside Walt Disney World, there's plenty going on as well, lots of it at **Church Street Station** but plenty in freestanding clubs as well.

AROUND ORLANDO

Nightclubs in Orlando proper have significantly more character than those in the areas around Walt Disney World, but close earlier.

**Baja Beach Club.** This two-story inland answer to a beach party plays hits from the 1960s to the 1990s. It has a sand volleyball court and an open deck that serves sandwiches and just-grilled burgers. ⊠ *8510 Palm Pkwy., Lake Buena Vista,* ☎ *407/239–9629.*

**Bennigan's.** Crowds of young singles make this scene in the early evening and during happy hours: 2–7 PM and 11 PM–midnight. ⊠ *6324 International Dr., Orlando,* ☎ *407/351–4436.*

**Coach's Locker Room.** A two-level sports palace, it boasts six big-screen TVs and 12 smaller monitors and shows every pro football game, plus every other kind of sport imaginable. The food is not the major attraction, but the Buffalo wings are worth trying. It's in the strip mall behind the T.G.I.Fridays at the intersection of I–4 and Rte. 436. ⊠ *269 W. Rte. 436, Altamonte Springs,* ☎ *407/869–4446.*

**Dad's Road Kill Cafe.** In this tiny bar-and-restaurant with an eclectic menu, the bar area is littered with things to keep you busy as you drink your beer and wine: games, puzzles, a computer, plus the obligatory pool table and dart boards. On Friday and Saturday nights, there's low-key live entertainment. In a strip mall on the corner of Lake and Orlando avenues. ⊠ *106 Lake Ave., Maitland,* ☎ *407/647–5288.*

**The Edge.** The current hot dance spot in downtown Orlando is a multilevel converted warehouse with light shows and smoke machines; the pounding dance music is played just below the pain threshold. Cover charges are $4–$5. Nationally known alternative and rock groups often play in an adjoining concert field. ⊠ *100 W. Livingston, Orlando,* ☎ *407/426–9166.*

**Howl at the Moon.** What's the perfect solution to the problem of the rowdy barfly who insists on crooning loudly with the band? Orlando's only sing-along bar encourages its patrons to warble the pop classics of yesteryear or campy favorites like the Time Warp and Hokey Pokey (turn yourself around). Piano players keep the music rolling in the evening, and the World's Most Dangerous Wait Staff adds to the entertainment. No food is served, but the management encourages you to bring your own or order out; several nearby restaurants deliver. There's a cover charge of $2–$4 Wed.–Sat., Sun–Tues. free. ⊠ *55 W. Church St., 2nd floor of Church St. Marketplace, Orlando,* ☎ *407/841–4695.*

**Jani Lane's Sunset Strip.** Spacious and woody, this rock-and-roll club attracts acts in the Mötley Crüe vein. For a breather, stand out on the balcony and watch downtown Orlando's nightlife pass below. ⊠ *26 S. Orange Ave., Orlando,* ☎ *407/649–4803.*

**Mulvaney's Irish Pub.** There are seven imported beers on tap here, including Guinness, and traditional Irish music Wed.–Sat. It's packed on weekends and on Orlando Magic game nights. The kitchen serves mostly sandwiches but also has such British staples as shepherd's pie, fish-and-chips, and bangers and mash. ⊠ *27 W. Church St., Orlando,* ☎ *407/872–3296.*

**Pinkie Lee's.** A jazz club with a gourmet menu, this is among Orlando's most grown-up nightspots. The entertainment is usually top-notch, reflected in the $7.50 minimum and $11–$17 cover charge on weekends. ⊠ *380 W. Amelia Ave., Orlando,* ☎ *407/872–7393.*

**Sullivan's Entertainment Complex.** People of all ages come to Orlando's only country-and-western dance hall to strut their stuff. Big-name performers entertain on occasion; a house band plays Tues.–Sat. The cover charge runs $2 and up. ⊠ *1108 S. Orange Blossom Trail [U.S. 441], Orlando,* ☎ *407/843–2934.*

**Yab Yum.** In this bohemian refuge from downtown's hustle and bustle, the crowd is heavy with aspiring-poet types hunched over espresso while giving form to their latest angst, but you don't have to be tormented to enjoy a sandwich, specialty coffee, or a hunk of fresh carrot cake along with the music of local bands. ⊠ *25 Wall St. Plaza, Orlando,* ☎ *407/422–3322.*

**Zuma Beach.** The sound system at this art deco, beach-party dance club is a real rainmaker; there's also an extensive light show. It draws a 30ish crowd most nights. The cover is $6. ⊠ *46 N. Orange Ave., Orlando,* ☎ *407/648–8727.*

## Church Street Station

In this entertainment complex, the old-fashioned saloons, dance halls, dining rooms, and shopping arcades are almost Disneyesque in their attention to detail. Unlike much of what you see in Walt Disney World, however, this place doesn't just look authentic—it is. The train on the tracks is an actual 19th-century steam engine; the whistling calliope was specially rebuilt to blow its original tunes. Just about everything down to the cobblestones that clatter under the horse-drawn carriages is the real McCoy. For a single admission, you can wander freely and stay as long as you wish. Food and drink cost extra and are not cheap. Parts of the complex are open during the day, but the place is usually quiet then; the pace picks up at night, especially on weekends, with crowds thickest from 10 to 11.

**Rosie O'Grady's Good Time Emporium.** The original bar on Church Street is a turn-of-the-century saloon with dark wood, brass trim, a full Dixieland band, banjo shows, tap dancers, and vaudeville singers.

**Apple Annie's Courtyard.** This quiet spot offers recorded easy-listening music from Jimmy Buffett to James Taylor.

**Cheyenne Saloon and Opera House.** Immensely popular, this trilevel former opera house is now full of moose racks, steer horns, buffalo heads, and Remington rifles; the seven-piece country-and-western band that plays here darn near brings the house down, and an upstairs restaurant serves chicken-and-ribs fare.

**Crackers Oyster Bar.** This spot behind the Orchid Garden is a good place to get a meal of fresh Florida seafood and pasta; it also has one of the largest wine cellars in Florida.

**Lili Marlene's Aviators Pub and Restaurant.** Relaxed and wood-paneled, it feels like an English pub; here you'll find the best food on Church Street—hearty, upscale, and very American steaks, ribs, and seafood.

**Orchid Garden Ballroom.** Iron latticework, arch ceilings, and stained-glass windows create a striking Victorian setting here, where visitors sit, drink, and listen to a first-rate band pounding out popular tunes from the 1950s to the present.

**Phineas Phogg's Balloon Works.** This Top 40 club plays tunes on a sound system that will blow your socks off. It draws a good-looking yuppie tourist crowd and a few local young singles; the place is jammed by midnight. ⊠ *129 W. Church St., Orlando,* ☎ *407/422–2434.* ⊠ *$15.95.*

## Dinner Shows

For a single price, these hybrid eatery-entertainment complexes deliver a theatrical production and a multicourse dinner. Performances run the gamut from jousting to jamboree tunes, and tend to be better than the rather forgettable meal; unlimited beer, wine, and soda are usually included, but mixed drinks will cost you extra. What the shows lack in substance and depth they make up for in color and enthusiasm; children often love them. Most shows have seatings at 7 and 9:30, and at most you sit with strangers at long tables. Always call and make reservations in advance, especially for weekends and shows at Walt Disney World.

WALT DISNEY WORLD
The evening of song, dance, and food on Disney property goes for a fairly steep price, somewhere in the range of $30–$45 for adults, $15–$25 for children.

**Hoop-Dee-Doo Revue.** Staged at **Fort Wilderness Campground Resort's** rustic Pioneer Hall, this may be corny, but it is also the liveliest show in Walt Disney World. A troupe of jokers called the Pioneer Hall Players stomp their feet, wisecrack, and otherwise make merry while the audience chows down on barbecued ribs, fried chicken, corn on the cob, strawberry shortcake, and all the fixin's. There are three shows nightly; prime times sell out months in advance for busy seasons. *In advance,* ☎ *407/934–7639; day of show, 407/824–2748.*

**Polynesian Luau.** At this outdoor barbecue, the entertainment is in keeping with the colorful, South Pacific setting at the **Polynesian Resort.** There are two shows nightly, plus an earlier wingding for children called Mickey's Tropical Luau, wherein Disney characters do a few numbers decked out in South Seas garb. ☎ *407/934–7639.*

Dinner shows are as immensely popular around Orlando as in Walt Disney World. Adult prices range from $32–$39, fees for children $18–$28, depending on their ages.

**Arabian Nights.** An elaborate palace outside, it's more like an arena within, with seating for more than 1,200. The show features some 25 acts with more than 80 performing horses, music, special effects, and a chariot race; keep your eyes open for a unicorn. The three-course dinners are of prime rib or vegetarian lasagna. ⊠ *6225 W. Irlo Bronson Memorial Hwy., Kissimmee,* ☎ *407/396–7400, 407/239–9223, or 800/553–6116; in Canada, 800/533–3615.* ☜ *$34.95. AE, D, DC, MC, V.*

**Capone's Dinner and Show.** Returning to the gangland Chicago of 1931, this one comes complete with mobsters and their dames. The evening begins in an old-fashioned ice-cream parlor; say the secret password and you'll be ushered inside Al Capone's private Underworld Cabaret and Speakeasy. Dinner is an unlimited Italian buffet heavy on pasta. Beer and sangria are included. ⊠ *4740 W. Irlo Bronson Memorial Hwy., Kissimmee,* ☎ *407/397–2378.* ☜ *$36.99. AE, D, MC, V.*

**King Henry's Feast.** Jesters, jugglers, dancers, magicians, and singers ostensibly fête Henry VIII as he celebrates his birthday in this Tudor-style building. Saucy wenches serve forth potato-leek soup, salad, and chicken and ribs. ⊠ *8984 International Dr., Orlando,* ☎ *407/351–5151 or 800/883–8181.* ☜ *$31.95. AE, D, DC, MC, V.*

**Mark Two.** Broadway musicals—such as *Oklahoma!, My Fair Lady, West Side Story,* and *South Pacific*—are performed here throughout the year except during the Yuletide holidays, when there are musical revues chockablock with Broadway tunes. For about two hours before curtain, you can order from the bar and help yourself at buffet tables laden with institutional seafood Newburg, baked whitefish, meats, and salad; dessert arrives during intermission. Unlike other dinner theaters, the Mark Two offers only tables for two and four. ⊠ *Edgewater Center, 3376 Edgewater Dr., drive west from I–4 Exit 44, Orlando,* ☎ *407/843–6275 or 800/726–6275.* ☜ *$29–$33. AE, D, MC, V.*

**Medieval Times.** No fewer than 30 charging horses and a cast of 75 knights, nobles, and maidens perform in this huge, medieval-style manor house, in a two-hour tournament of sword fights, jousting matches, and other games. The bill of fare is heavy on meat and potatoes. ⊠ *4510 W. lrlo Bronson Memorial Hwy., Kissimmee,* ☎ *407/239–0214 or 800/229–8300.* ☜ *$32. AE, D, MC, V.*

**Wild Bill's Wild West Dinner Show.** Held in the 22-acre Fort Liberty complex, this is a mixed bag of Indian dances, foot-stompin' sing-alongs, and acrobatics. The chow, served by a rowdy chorus of cavalry recruits, is beef soup, fried chicken, corn on the cob, and pork and beans. No smoking in the showroom. ⊠ *5260 W. Irlo Bronson Memorial Hwy., Kissimmee,* ☎ *407/351–5151.* ☜ *$31.95. AE, DC, MC, V.*

## Pleasure Island

This 6-acre after-dark entertainment complex, connected to Disney Village Marketplace and the mainland by three footbridges, is better than you might expect—despite its location on Disney property, the entertainment has real grit and life. In addition to seven clubs, you'll find a few restaurants, shops, and a 10-screen AMC cinema that starts showing movies at 1:30 PM. The pay-one-price admission gets you into all the clubs and shows except the movie house.

**Adventurer's Club.** This whimsically re-creates a private club of the 1930s. Strange things happen, thanks to Disney wizardry and some clever scripting for a group of talented actors and actresses, who mingle with patrons.

**Comedy Warehouse.** There's an improvisational setup here, with five shows nightly. And not everything has been sanitized for your protection.

**8trax.** Groove to the recorded music of Donna Summer or the Village People while light reflects from disco balls.

**Planet Hollywood.** You may not see movie stars, but you can see plenty of movie memorabilia, much of it with a central Florida connection. Check out the motorcycle from Wesley Snipes's *Passenger 57,* which was filmed north of Orlando in Sanford. Food is available.

**Rock & Roll Beach Club.** This throbs with live rock music of the 1950s and 1960s. ☎ *407/934–7781.* ✑ *$16.91.*

# OUTDOOR ACTIVITIES AND SPORTS

## Basketball

The NBA **Orlando Magic** (✉ Box 76, 600 W. Amelia St., 2 blocks west of I–4 Amelia St. exit, Orlando, ☎ 407/839–3900) plays in the 15,077-seat Orlando Arena.

## Bicycling

The Orlando area does have a collection of city-constructed **bike paths** through downtown and there are a few places suitable for cycling in the Winter Park area. Serious cyclists head to the rolling hills of nearby **Lake County.**

## Boating

Marinas at the Caribbean Beach Resort, Contemporary Resort, Disney Village Marketplace, Fort Wilderness Campground, Grand Floridian, Polynesian Village, and Yacht and Beach Club rent Sunfish, catamarans, motor-powered pontoon boats, pedal boats, and tiny two-passenger Water Sprites—a hit with kids—for use on their nearby waters: Bay Lake, Seven Seas Lagoon, Lake Buena Vista, Club Lake, or Buena Vista Lagoon. The Polynesian Village marina also rents outrigger canoes, and Fort Wilderness rents canoes for paddling along the placid canals in the area. For waterskiing reservations ($65 per hour), call 407/824–1000.

## Dog Racing

**Sanford Orlando Kennel Club** (✉ 301 Dog Track Rd., Longwood, ☎ 407/831–1600) has dog racing as well as south Florida horse-racing simulcasts, Nov–May. **Seminole Greyhound Park** (✉ 2000 Seminola Blvd., Casselberry, ☎ 407/699–4510), open May–October, is a newer track.

## Golf

Golf is extremely popular in central Florida. **Golfpac** (✉ Box 162366, Altamonte Springs 32701, ☎ 407/260–2288 or 800/327–0878) packages golf vacations and prearranges tee times at more than 40 courses around Orlando. Rates vary based on hotel and course, and 60–90 days advance notice is recommended to set up a vacation.

Be sure to reserve tee times well in advance.

### In Walt Disney World

Walt Disney World has five championship 18-hole courses—all on the PGA Tour route: **Eagle Pines** (Bonnet Creek Golf Club, 6,722 yds), Lake Buena Vista (Lake Buena Vista, 6,829 yds), **Magnolia** (Shades of Green, 7,190 yds), **Osprey Ridge** (Bonnet Creek Golf Club, 7,101 yds), and **The Palm** (Shades of Green, 6,957 yds). Except for **Oak Trail,** a nine-hole layout for novice and preteen golfers, these courses are among the busiest and most expensive in the region.

The three older Disney courses have the same fees and discount policies: $85 for guests at WDW, $95 for all others regardless of season. Prices at the newer course, Eagle Pines and Osprey Ridge, go up to $100 and $115 between January and April. A twilight discount rate, $45 for all, goes into effect at 2 PM in winter and peak seasons, at 3 PM in summer and off-seasons. For tee times and private lessons on any of the five, call 407/824–2270.

### Elsewhere in the Area

Greens fees usually vary by season—the highest and lowest figures are listed, all including mandatory cart rental. (For more area courses, *see* Chapter 2.)

**Cypress Creek Country Club** (⊠ 5353 Vineland Rd., Orlando, ☎ 407/351–2187) is a demanding 6,955-yard, 18-hole course with 16 water holes and lots of trees; greens fees run $25–$38.

**Grand Cypress Golf Resort** (⊠ 1 N. Jacaranda, Orlando, ☎ 407/239–4700) has 45 holes designed by Jack Nicklaus, including the New Course, a re-creation of the famed Old Course in St. Andrews, Scotland. Greens fees are high, in the over-$75 range.

**Grenelefe Golf & Tennis Resort** (⊠ 3200 Rte. 546, Haines City, ☎ 813/422–7511 or 800/237–9549), about 45 minutes from Orlando, has three excellent 18-hole courses, of which the toughest is the 7,325-yard West Course. Greens fees run $39–$110.

## Horseback Riding

**Fort Wilderness Campground** (☎ 407/824–2832) offers tame trail rides through backwoods. Children must be over nine, and adults must be under 250 pounds. Trail rides cost $17 for 45 minutes. Rides are daily at 9, 10:30, noon, and 2.

## Jai Alai

**Orlando-Seminole Jai-Alai** (⊠ 6405 S. U.S. 17–92, Fern Park, ☎ 407/331–9191), about 20 minutes north of Orlando off I–4, offers south Florida horse-racing simulcasts and betting in addition to jai alai at the fronton (closed May).

## Jogging

Walt Disney World has several scenic jogging trails. Pick up jogging maps at any Disney resort. **Fort Wilderness Campground** (☎ 407/824–2900) has a 2.3-mile course with plenty of fresh air and woods as well as numerous exercise stations along the way.

# SHOPPING

## Flea Market

**Flea World** (✉ 3 mi east of I–4 Exit 50 on Lake Mary Blvd., then 1 mi south on U.S. 17–92, between Orlando and Sanford) claims to be America's largest flea market under one roof. More than 1,600 booths sell only new merchandise—everything from car tires and pet tarantulas to gourmet coffee, leather lingerie, and beaded evening gowns. Kids love **Fun World** next door, which offers miniature golf, arcade games, go-carts, bumper cars, bumper boats, kiddie rides, and batting cages.

## Outlet Stores

The International Drive area is filled with factory outlet stores.

**Belz Factory Outlet World** (✉ 5401 W. Oakridge Rd., Orlando), with nearly 170 stores.

**Kissimmee Manufacturers Outlet Mall** (✉ 1 mi east of Rte. 535 on U.S. 192, Kissimmee) contains approximately 20 stores.

## Shopping Areas and Malls

### In and Around WDW

**Crossroads of Lake Buena Vista** (✉ Rte. 535 and I–4, Lake Buena Vista), across the street from the entrance to the hotels at Lake Buena Vista, contains restaurants and nearly 20 shops that are convenient for tourists. The necessities, such as a 24-hour grocery and pharmacy, post office, bank, and cleaners, are all here, and while you shop, your offspring can entertain themselves at Pirates Cove Adventure Golf.

**Disney Village Marketplace,** nestled along the shores of Buena Vista Lagoon in Walt Disney World, is a complex of shops packed with art, fashions, crafts, and more. If you are looking for one-stop shopping for Disney collectibles and souvenirs, this is the place. Stores are open to 10.

**Florida Mall** (✉ 8001 S. Orange Blossom Trail, 4½ mi east of I–4 and International Dr., Orlando), the largest mall in central Florida, includes Sears, JCPenney, Belk Lindsey, Gayfers, Dillards, 200 specialty shops, seven theaters, and one of the better food courts around.

**Mercado Mediterranean Village** (✉ 8445 International Dr., Orlando) houses more than 60 specialty shops, with a Spanish-style setting. A walkway circles the courtyard, where live entertainment can be enjoyed throughout the day. The clean, quick, and large food court offers a selection of cuisines from around the world.

**Old Town** (✉ 5770 Irlo Bronson Memorial Hwy., Kissimmee) is a shopping-entertainment complex featuring a 1928 wheel, a 1909 carousel, and more than 70 specialty shops in a re-creation of a turn-of-the-century Florida village.

### Elsewhere in the Area

**Altamonte Mall** (✉ 451 Altamonte Ave., ½ mi east of I–4 on Rte. 436, Altamonte Springs) is an airy, spacious two-level mall containing Sears, Gayfers, Burdines, and JCPenney department stores and 165 specialty shops.

**Church Street Exchange** (✉ Church St. Station, 129 W. Church St., Orlando) is a decorative, brassy, Victorian-theme marketplace with more than 50 specialty shops. Perhaps the best demonstration is at **Augusta**

**Janssen,** where free candy samples are distributed during a lighthearted look at the process of making fudge. Across the street from the complex is **Bumby Emporium,** a souvenir shop, and across the railroad tracks is yet another collection of unusual shops and pushcarts, the **Historic Railroad Depot.**

**Orlando Fashion Square** (✉ 3201 E. Colonial Dr., 3 mi east of I–4 Exit 41, Orlando) has 130 shops including Burdines, JCPenney, Sears, Camelot Music, the Disney Store, the Gap, and Lerner.

**Sanford Towne Centre** (✉ I–4, Exit 52, north of Orlando), the area's newest mall, has some interesting specialty shops and several department stores.

# WALT DISNEY WORLD AND THE ORLANDO AREA A TO Z

## Arriving and Departing

### By Bus
**Greyhound Lines** (☎ 800/231–2222) buses stop in Orlando (✉ 555 N. Magruder Ave., ☎ 407/843–7720).

### By Car
From I–95, which runs down Florida's east coast, you can turn off onto I–4 just below Daytona; it's about 50 miles from there to Orlando. If you're taking I–75 down through the middle of the state, get off at Wildwood and take Florida's Turnpike for about 50 miles. The scenic Beeline Expressway, a toll road, links Orlando and Cocoa Beach, about an hour away.

### By Plane
More than 20 scheduled airlines and more than 30 charter firms operate in and out of Orlando International Airport, providing direct service to more than 100 cities in the United States and overseas. The most active carriers are **Delta** and **United.** Other airlines include **America West, American, Bahamasair, British Airways, Continental, Icelandair, KLM, Mexicana, Northwest, TransBrasil, TWA,** and **USAir.**

BETWEEN THE AIRPORT AND THE HOTELS

Find out in advance whether your hotel offers a free airport shuttle; if not, ask for a recommendation.

Public buses operate between the airport and the main terminal of the **Tri-County Transit Authority** (✉ 1200 W. South St., Orlando, ☎ 407/841–8240). Though the cost is 75¢, other options are preferable since downtown is far from most of the hotels used by theme-park vacationers.

**Mears Transportation Group** (☎ 407/423–5566) has a meet-and-greet service—they'll meet you at the gate, help you with your luggage, and whisk you away, either in an 11-passenger van, a town car, or a limo. Vans run to Walt Disney World and along U.S. 192 every 30 minutes; prices range from $12.50 one-way to $22 round-trip for adults. Limo rates run around $50–$60 for a town car that accommodates three or four and $90 for a stretch limo that will seat six. **Town & Country Limo** (☎ 407/828–3035) charges $30 to $40 one-way for up to seven, depending on the hotel; **First Class Transportation** (☎ 407/578–0022) charges $45 one-way for up to four people.

Taxis take only a half hour to get from the airport to most hotels used by WDW visitors, and charge about $25 plus tip to the International Drive area, about $10 more to the U.S. 192 area.

## By Train

**Amtrak** (☎ 800/872–7245) operates the Silver Star and the Silver Meteor to Florida. Both stop in Winter Park (✉ 150 Morse Blvd.), Orlando (✉ 1400 Sligh Blvd.), and Kissimmee (✉ 416 Pleasant St.).

If you want to have your car in Florida without driving it there, it'll cost you more than flying but it can be done—just board the **Auto-Train** in Lorton, Virginia, near Washington, D.C. Its southern terminus is Sanford, Florida, some 23 miles north of Orlando.

# Getting Around

Although the public transportation in Orlando could use some work and taxis are expensive because of the distances involved, it is by no means absolutely necessary to rent a car in Orlando.

If you are staying at a Walt Disney World hotel, or if you buy a four- or five-day pass instead of buying daily admission tickets to the Disney parks, your transportation within WDW is free.

Outside Walt Disney World, just about every hotel, and even many motels, are linked to one of several private transportation systems that shuttle travelers back and forth to most of the area attractions for only a few dollars. However, if you want to visit the major theme parks outside Walt Disney World, venture off the beaten track, or eat where most tourists don't, a rental car is essential. And if you are traveling with your family, you may spend more on these shuttles, which charge by the head, than on a rental car: Orlando offers some of the lowest rental-car rates in the entire United States.

## By Bus

If you are staying along International Drive, in Kissimmee, or in Orlando proper, you can ride public buses to get around the immediate area. To find out which bus to take, ask your hotel clerk or call the **Tri-County Transit Authority Information Office** (☎ 407/841–8240) during business hours. Fares are 75¢, 10¢ extra for transfers.

## By Car

The most important artery in the Orlando area is **I-4.** This interstate highway, which links the Atlantic Coast to Florida's Gulf of Mexico, ties everything together, and you'll invariably receive directions in reference to it. The problem is that I–4, though considered an east–west expressway in our national road system (where even numbers signify an east–west orientation and odd numbers a north–south orientation), actually runs north and south in the Orlando area. So when the signs say east, you are usually going north, and when the signs say west, you are usually going south.

Another main drag is **International Drive,** a.k.a. I-Drive, which has many major hotels, restaurants, and shopping centers. You can get onto International Drive from I–4 Exits 28, 29, and 30B. The other main road, **U.S. 192,** cuts across I–4 at Exits 25A and 25B. This highway goes through the Kissimmee area and crosses WDW property, taking you to the Magic Kingdom's main entrance. U.S. 192 is sometimes called by its former names, Spacecoast Parkway and Irlo Bronson Memorial Highway.

## By Shuttle

Scheduled service and charters linking just about every hotel and major attraction in the area are available from **Mears Transportation Group** (☎ 407/423–5566), **Gray Line of Orlando** (☎ 407/422–0744), **Rabbit Bus Lines** (☎ 407/291–2424), and **Phoenix Tours** (☎ 407/859–4211). In addition, many hotels run their own shuttles especially for guests; to arrange a ride, ask your hotel concierge, inquire at the front desk, or phone the company directly.

One-way fares are usually $6–$7 per adult, a couple of dollars less for children 4–11, between major hotel areas and the WDW parks. Round-trip excursion fares to Cypress Gardens are $27 per person, including admission.

## By Taxi

Taxi fares start at $2.45 and cost $1.40 for each mile thereafter. Call **Yellow Cab** (☎ 407/699–9999) or Town and Country Cab (☎ 407/828–3035). Sample fares are: to WDW's Magic Kingdom, about $20 from International Drive, $11–$15 from U.S. 192; to Universal Studios, $6–$11 from International Drive, $25–$30 from U.S. 192; to downtown Orlando's Church Street Station, $20–$25 from International Drive, $30–$40 from U.S. 192.

# Guided Tours

## Orientation Tours

In Walt Disney World, there are 3½- to 4-hour **Magic Kingdom tours** ($5 plus park admission). Tours include visits to some of the rides, but don't allow you to skip to the head of the line—you still have to wait your turn. For schedules, ask at City Hall.

Reserve up to three weeks in advance for the two four-hour **behind-the-scenes Epcot Center tours** (☎ 407/345–5860), which cost $20 plus park admission and are open to guests 16 and up; Hidden Treasures of the World Showcase (Sun., Wed., and Fri. at varying times); and Gardens of the World (Mon., Tues., and Thurs. at varying times).

**Sea World's Animal Lover's Adventures** are among many other educational programs there. These guided, 90-minute excursions ($5.95) provide a close-up look at the park's breeding, research, and training facilities and are as interesting to children as to adults, as is **Sea World's Let's Talk Training** ($5.95), which lasts 45 minutes and introduces guests to the park's animal-behavior and training techniques.

## Special-Interest Tours

### BALLOON RIDES

**Balloons by Terry** (✉ 3529 Edgewater Dr., Orlando, ☎ 407/422–3529) meets you at Church Street Station, transports you to the launch site, takes you floating above the city for an hour, and returns you to Church Street for a champagne breakfast. The fare is $150 per adult, $100 for children.

**Rise & Float Balloon Tours** (✉ 5767 Major Blvd., opposite Universal Studios at Mystery Fun House, Orlando, ☎ 407/352–8191) takes you up in a craft decorated with two hot-pink flamingoes and a giant palm tree. There's a regular **Champagne Balloon Excursion** ($150 per adult, $280 per couple) and a romantic **For Lovers Only** trip, which goes aloft with one couple at a time, with a picnic basket laden with champagne, fruits, cheeses, crackers, and pastries ($350 per couple).

BOAT TOUR

**Scenic Boat Tour** (⊠ 312 E. Morse Blvd., Winter Park, ☎ 407/644–4056) is a relaxing, hour-long cruise past 12 miles of fine old homes and through the grounds of Rollins College, on one of Winter Park's three main lakes, which are connected by 100-year-old canals.

HELICOPTER RIDES

Seven different area tours, ranging from $20 to $399, are available from the **Falcon Helicopter Service** (⊠ 8990 International Dr., next to Caruso's Palace, Orlando, ☎ 407/352–1753; ⊠ Hyatt Hotel, I–4 and U.S. 192, ☎ 407/396–7222; ⊠ Howard Johnson, 5071 W. Irlo Bronson Memorial Hwy., Kissimmee, ☎ 407/397–0228).

# Contacts and Resources

## Dining Reservations

It's now easy to get dining reservations at Walt Disney World; there's a single phone number, ☎ 407/939–3463. No longer can you make reservations only on the day of the meal and only in person for Epcot Center restaurants.

## Emergencies

Dial **911** for police or ambulance. All the area's major theme parks (and some of the minor ones) have first-aid centers.

DENTISTS

**Emergency dental referral** (☎ 407/847–7474).

HOSPITALS

Hospital emergency rooms are open 24 hours a day. The most accessible hospital, located in the International Drive area, is the **Orlando Regional Medical Center/Sand Lake Hospital** (⊠ 9400 Turkey Lake Rd., ☎ 407/351–8500).

LATE-NIGHT PHARMACIES

**Eckerd Drugs** (⊠ 908 Lee Rd., off I–4 at Lee Rd. exit, Orlando, ☎ 407/644–6908) and **Walgreens** (⊠ 6201 International Dr., opposite Wet 'n' Wild, Orlando, ☎ 407/345–8311 or 407/345–8402; ⊠ 4578 S. Kirkman Rd., north of Universal Studios, ☎ 407/293–8458).

## Learning Vacations

The new **Disney Institute** (☎ 800/746–5858) offers lectures, seminars, panel discussions, and classes of varying lengths and intensity.

## Visitor Information

DISNEY WORLD

**Production Information** (☎ 407/560–4651) can tell you how to be a member of the audience at a show being taped at Disney–MGM Studios.

**Walt Disney World Information** (⊠ Box 10040, Lake Buena Vista 32830, ☎ 407/824–4321, TDD 407/827–5141) can send general information.

**Walt Disney World Central Reservations** (☎ 407/934–7639, 407/345–5984) can book meal seatings, entertainment, and lodging; people with disabilities can call WDW Special Request Reservations (☎ 407/939–7807, TDD 407/939–7670) to get information or book rooms.

**Walt Disney Travel Co.** (⊠ 1675 Buena Vista Dr., Lake Buena Vista 32830, ☎ 800/828–0228) can arrange packages, including cruises, car rentals, and hotels both on and off Disney property. Or contact your travel agent.

OTHER ATTRACTIONS

**Cypress Gardens** (⊠ Box 1, Cypress Gardens 33884, ☎ 813/324–2111 or 800/237–4826; in FL, 800/282–2123).

**Sea World** (⊠ 7007 Sea World Dr., Orlando 32821, ☎ 407/351–3600).

**Splendid China** (⊠ 3000 Splendid China Blvd., Kissimmee 34747, ☎ 407/397–8800 or 800/244–6226).

**Universal Studios** (⊠ 1000 Universal Studios Plaza, Orlando 32819-7610, ☎ 407/363–8000, TTY 407/363–8265).

VISITOR BUREAUS

**Kissimmee/St. Cloud Convention and Visitor's Bureau** (⊠ 1925 E. Irlo Bronson Memorial Hwy., Kissimmee 34744, ☎ 407/847–5000 or 800/327–9159).

**Orlando/Orange County Convention and Visitor's Bureau** (⊠ 8445 International Dr., Orlando 32819, ☎ 407/363–5871).

**Winter Park Chamber of Commerce** (⊠ Box 280, Winter Park 32790, ☎ 407/644–8281).

# 9 The Tampa Bay Area

*Tampa and St. Petersburg, on Florida's west coast, are eclectic and busy. Inland is typical suburban sprawl. To the north are extensive nature preserves and parks. Tarpon Springs has been known for its Greek population for decades, Ybor City for its Cuban flavor. Although Sarasota stands out with its thriving arts community, all the cities south of Tampa Bay—including Bradenton and the offshore keys lining the Gulf Coast—are restful, more like resort towns.*

**W**HILE GLITZY MIAMI and Mickey Mouse in Orlando grab most of the Florida tourism headlines, the rapidly growing Tampa Bay area has quietly become a favorite spot for pleasure-seeking visitors from the U.S. and around the world. The region offers astoundingly diverse terrain—from the rolling, pine-dotted northern reaches to the coast's white-sand beaches and barrier islands.

Updated by
Pamela
Acheson

Over the last 25 years the region has become fully developed, but at a much slower pace and with a less commercial atmosphere than the east coast. The resulting community has a varied economic base that is not entirely dependent upon tourism as well as excellent beaches and superior hotels and resorts. Many hotels offer supervised children's programs in addition to reasonably priced two-bedroom, two-bath suites with full kitchens and facilities ranging from golf and tennis to boating to deep-sea fishing.

As for cities, Tampa is now a major metropolis, the crown jewel and entertainment hub of the west coast region, with the greatest concentration of restaurants, stores, and nightlife. Tampa's semitropical climate and access to the Gulf of Mexico make it an ideal port for the cruise industry. Currently, Carnival and Holland America depart from the Port of Tampa. Tampa does not have a Gulf beach, however. For more than a dip, head to neighboring St. Petersburg, which sits on a peninsula bordered on three sides by bays and the Gulf of Mexico—all often filled with pleasure and commercial craft.

It's fitting that an area with a thriving international port should also be populated by a wealth of nationalities. The center of the Cuban community is the east Tampa suburb of Ybor City, and north of St. Petersburg, in Dunedin, the heritage is Scottish. North of Dunedin, Tarpon Springs has supported a large Greek population for decades and is the largest producer of natural sponges in the world.

Native Americans were the sole inhabitants of the region for many years. The Spanish explorers Juan Ponce de León, Pánfilo de Narváez, and Hernando de Soto passed through in the mid-1500s, and the U.S. Army and civilian settlers arrived in 1824. A military presence remains in Tampa at MacDill Air Force Base, the U.S. Operations Command.

Inland, to the east of Tampa, it's all suburban sprawl, freeways, shopping malls, and—the main draw—Busch Gardens.

The coastal area north of Tampa, from Weeki Wachee to Crystal River, can aptly be called the Manatee Coast. Of these gentle vegetarian water mammals, distantly related to elephants, only 1,200 are alive today, and they are threatened by development and speeding motor boats. Extensive nature preserves and parks have been created to protect them and other wildlife indigenous to the area and are among the best spots to view manatees in the wild. Although they are far from mythical beauties, it is believed that manatees inspired ancient mariners' tales of mermaids.

The southern end of Tampa Bay is anchored by Bradenton and Sarasota, two cities that also have their string of barrier islands with fine beaches. Sarasota is very much a resort town—Sarasota County has no less than 35 miles of Gulf beaches, as well as two state parks, 22 municipal parks, and more than 30 golf courses, many open to the public. But Sarasota also has a thriving cultural scene, thanks mostly to John Ringling, founder of the Ringling Brothers Barnum & Bailey Circus, who chose this area for the winter home of his circus and his family. Bradenton maintains a lower profile than Sarasota, though it has its share of sugar-sand beaches, golf courses, and historic sites dating back to the mid-1800s. Some of Sarasota County's beaches are located around Venice, a few miles south on the Gulf Coast, which claims the world's only clown college.

## Pleasures and Pastimes

### Beaches

Conditions on the Gulf of Mexico, which is fed by rivers and streams originating "up North," vary according to tides and storms. Though not all beaches are pristine, you'll find some great ones with excellent swimming water on almost every barrier island, from Clearwater all the way to Venice. Don't swim in the bays, which boaters, marinas, and industry have polluted.

### Biking

There aren't many designated bike paths in this part of Florida, but there are many lovely rural areas to bike through and plenty of places to rent bikes, should you want to pedal along the streets. Be wary of traffic in downtown Tampa.

### Canoeing

Several inland rivers are good for canoeing, and several outfits rent canoes and provide guided tours.

### Dining

Fresh seafood is plentiful. Raw bars serving fresh oysters, clams, and mussels are everywhere. The region's ethnic diversity is also well represented. Tarpon Springs adds a hearty helping of such classic Greek specialties as moussaka and baklava. In Tampa, the ethnic cuisine is Cuban, so you'll find black beans and rice and plenty of paella. In Sarasota, the emphasis is Continental, both in food and service.

Many restaurants, from family neighborhood spots to very expensive places, offer extra cheap early-bird menus with seating before 6 PM. These are even more prevalent off-season, from May to October.

### Fishing

Anglers flock to southwest Florida's coastal water to catch tarpon, kingfish, speckled trout, snapper, grouper, sea trout, snook, sheepshead, and shark. You can charter a fishing boat or join a group on a party boat for full- or half-day outings. Avoid fishing in polluted Tampa Bay.

### Golf

There are dozens of good and even great golf courses, in this part of Florida, most near Sarasota and Tampa/St. Petersburg.

### Lodging

Historic hotels and ultramodern chrome-and-glass high rises, sprawling resorts and cozy inns, and luxurious waterfront lodges and just-off-the-highway budget motels are among the options. In general, you'll pay more for a water view. Rates are highest between mid-December and mid-April; the lowest prices are available from May through November.

### Shopping

Special souvenirs from this area include local natural sponges, which can be bought at reasonable prices along Dodecanese Boulevard, the main street in Tarpon Springs. In Tampa's Ybor City, many small shops sell hand-rolled cigars unlike any others north of Havana. Sarasota's upscale boutiques sell everything from antiques to resort wear. There are also flea markets throughout the region.

## Spectator Sports

The baseball season comes early to Florida with the annual convergence of the Grapefruit League and spring training. These major-league teams offer exhibitions in March and April, and tickets are usually easily available and reasonably priced. Dog races are held somewhere in the region all year. Spectator sports in Tampa include NFL football (Tampa Bay Buccaneers), Thoroughbred racing, NHL hockey (Tampa Bay Lightning), and jai alai.

# Exploring the Tampa Bay Area

Whether you feel like walking on white-sand beaches, watching sponge fishermen, or wandering through the upscale shopping districts, you'll find something to your liking in the remarkably diverse Tampa Bay area. Tampa is the area's commercial center, a bright, modern city. Peninsular St. Petersburg lies across the bay with a variety of attractions, including some good beach life and Tarpon Springs, settled by Greek mariners and still Greek in flavor. The Manatee Coast to the north is quite rural with extensive nature preserves. To the south is Bradenton, with several museums; Sarasota, a sophisticated resort town; and small, canal-crossed Venice.

## Great Itineraries

*Numbers in the text below correspond to numbers in the margin and on the maps.*

### IF YOU HAVE 2 OR 3 DAYS

**Florida Aquarium** ① in downtown ⌖ **Tampa** and **Busch Gardens** ④, 8 miles northeast of the city, are probably the two most popular attractions in the area. You'll need a half day for the Florida Aquarium and a full day for Busch Gardens. Then it's on to ⌖ **Sarasota,** whose highlights include both the **Ringling Museums** ㉕, with its ornate mansion, extensive art collection, and statue garden, and **Bellm's Cars and Music of Yesterday** ㉖, an outstanding collection of antique automobiles and music-making machines.

### IF YOU HAVE 4 DAYS

Spend a half day in downtown ⌖ **Tampa.** Start with a walk through the **Florida Aquarium** ①, where you'll want to spend a half day. Then it's just a short drive to **Ybor City** ②, where you can rest your feet over lunch before an hour or two of strolling through the shops. **Busch Gardens** ④ takes a full day and is worth a visit whether your preference is thrilling rides or seeing animals in their natural settings. One of the best spots for a full day at the beach is pristine **Fort De Soto Park** ⑫, a perfect spot for a picnic. Art lovers and circus buffs can spend a morning in **Sarasota** traipsing through the **Ringling Museums** ㉕, and **Bellm's Cars and Music of Yesterday** ㉖ is a delight if you love antique cars or music boxes.

### IF YOU HAVE 10 DAYS

If you have this much time, stay in ⌖ **Sarasota** for the first five days and then base yourself in ⌖ **St. Petersburg** for the remainder of the trip. **St. Petersburg** is centrally located for several engaging half- and full-day trips. You could easily spend a full day in downtown **Tampa.** Start with a morning visit to the spectacular **Florida Aquarium** ①. Then head to **Ybor City** ② for a bit of exploring and lunch. End the day with a visit to the **Tampa Museum of Art** ③. The next three attractions are clustered together northeast of Tampa and can be reached in about 45 minutes to an hour by car from St. Petersburg. Spend a day at **Busch**

**Gardens** ④, getting there early if you plan to see it all. Another day, plan a day of water fun at **Adventure Island** ⑤, Busch Gardens' water-park cousin. The **Museum of Science and Industry** ⑥ is the perfect diversion for a long rainy morning or afternoon. You can also spend a day in the **Tarpon Springs** ⑮ area, the sponge capital of the world. **Salvador Dali Museum** ⑧, the **Museum of Fine Arts** ⑨, **Great Explorations!** ⑦, and **Sunken Gardens** ⑩ are all in downtown St. Petersburg. **Fort De Soto Park** ⑫ and **Caladesi Island State Park** ⑭ are both excellent for a day of relaxing at the beach.

Sarasota is a convenient base for the second part of your stay. One day, drive up to Bradenton and visit the **Gamble Plantation and Confederate Memorial** ㉑, the **Manatee Village Historical Park** ㉒, and the **South Florida Museum and Bishop Planetarium** ㉓. If you feel like a boat ride, begin or end the day with a trip to **Egmont Key** ㉔. Another morning, in Sarasota, visit both the **Ringling Museums** ㉕ and **Bellm's Cars and Music of Yesterday** ㉖; allow about three hours to cover everything. In the afternoon, you might stop by the **Sarasota Jungle Gardens** ㉗. Children especially enjoy the petting zoo and the exhibits of snakes and turtles. Another day, visit **Marie Selby's Botanical Gardens** ㉙, quieter but still tropical. **Venice** ㉚ makes an enjoyable half- or full-day trip. Give yourself a couple of hours to shop at **St. Armand's Circle** on Lido Key and to spend some time on the beach.

## When to Tour the Tampa Bay Area

Winter and spring are high season here; in summer there are huge, showy thunderstorms on many afternoons, and the temperatures are uniformly torrid, with humidity almost as high.

# TAMPA

Tampa is the business and commercial hub of this part of the state, with numerous high-rise buildings and heavy traffic. But amid the bustle are all the delights—restaurants, nightlife, and cultural events—you'd expect to find in a major city, with some appealing extras. The historic and very lively Ybor City district is great for a spicy meal or some lively Latin music.

One good way to get around is via the **Tampa-Ybor Trolley** (50¢), which runs from 7:30 until 5:30; it makes 17 stops between Ybor City, the Florida Aquarium, and Harbour Island.

## Sights to See

*Numbers in the margin correspond to points of interest on the Tampa/St. Petersburg map.*

❺ **Adventure Island.** Water slides, pools, and artificial wave pools create a 36-acre water wonderland at this water park, a corporate cousin of Busch Gardens. Along with a championship volleyball complex, you'll find cafés, snack bars, changing rooms, and video games. The complex is less than a mile north of Busch Gardens. ⊠ *4500 Bougainvillea Ave.,* ☎ *813/987–5660.* 🎫 *$16.95.* ☺ *Mar.–Oct., daily 10–5.*

★ ❹ **Busch Gardens.** More than 3,400 animals are just part of the attraction of this regional favorite, a sprawling, immaculately manicured site combining a zoolike setting with a theme park, where ten themed sections attempt to capture the spirit of turn-of-the-century Africa. In addition to a monorail ride that simulates an African safari—taking in free-roaming zebras, giraffes, rhinos, lions, and other exotic animals—the 335-acre park has live entertainment, animal exhibits, shops, restaurants, games, and thrill rides. The heart-stopping Kumba and

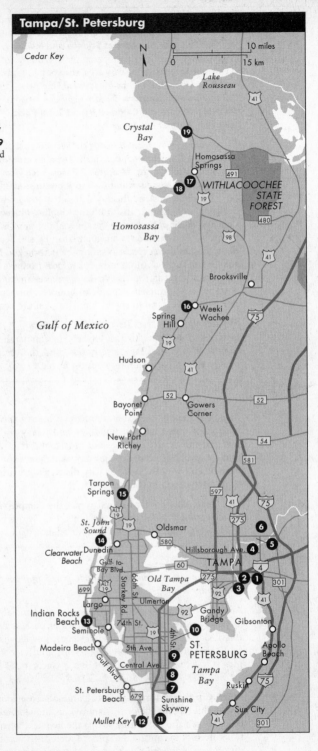

Tampa/St. Petersburg

Montu are among the largest and fastest roller coasters in the southeastern United States, both reaching speeds of more than 60 mph. You can also tour a brewery and sample the fresh-brewed product. Allow six to eight hours. Parents take note: Although there's a small area of rides for littl'uns and the animals hold universal appeal, major rides are too wild for toddlers and young grade-schoolers—and the admission price for kids from 3 through 9 approaches the cost of adult tickets. Busch Gardens is 18 miles northeast of downtown Tampa and 2 miles east of I–275. ⊠ *3000 Busch Blvd*, ☎ *813/987–5082.* ⊠ *$34.60, parking $3.* ☉ *Daily 9:30–6.*

★ ❶ **Florida Aquarium.** This $84 million complex opened on the waterfront not far from downtown in spring 1995, its 83-foot-high multitier glass dome a dazzling landmark. Included are more than 4,300 specimens of fish, other animals, and plants representing 550 species native to Florida. When visiting, you follow the path of a drop of water from the freshwater springs and limestone caves of an aquifer through rivers and wetlands to beaches and open seas. Four major exhibit areas reflect the variety of Florida's natural habitats—springs and wetlands, bay and barrier beach, coral reef, and the Gulf Stream and open ocean. Perhaps the most spectacular is the full-scale replica of a Florida coral reef in a 500,000-gallon tank ringed with viewing windows, including an awesome 43-foot-wide panoramic opening; part of the tank is an acrylic tunnel through an underwater thicket of elk horn coral teeming with tropical fish, where a dark cave reveals sea life you can ordinarily glimpse only on night dives. ⊠ *300 S. 13th St.*, ☎ *813/273–4020.* ⊠ *$13.95.* ☉ *Fri.–Wed. 9–6, Thurs. 9–8.*

❻ **Museum of Science and Industry.** In this thrilling scientific playground, you learn by doing as well as by seeing. The Gulf Coast Hurricane Exhibit re-creates the force of high-speed winds; the Butterfly Encounter is an interactive garden inhabited by free-flying butterflies; the GTE Challenger Learning Center offers simulated flights; and the 100-seat Saunders Planetarium, Tampa Bay's only planetarium, has afternoon and evening shows daily, one of them a trek through the universe. There's also a spiffy IMAX theater. The museum is a mile north of Busch Gardens. ⊠ *4801 E. Fowler Ave.*, ☎ *813/987–6300.* ⊠ *Florida residents $4.50, nonresidents $5, planetarium show $1.50; Mon. admission optional.* ☉ *Daily 9–5, longer in peak season.*

❸ **Tampa Museum of Art.** The permanent collection of more than 7,000 works in this 35,000-square-foot institution includes the most comprehensive collection of Greek, Roman, and Etruscan antiquities in the southeastern United States as well as an excellent collection of 20th-century American art. In addition, it presents more than a dozen special exhibitions annually. The latest additions include the Florida Gallery, which showcases the state's well-known and emerging artists, and a sculpture garden and seven-acre park. ⊠ *600 N. Ashley Dr.*, ☎ *813/274–8130.* ⊠ *$5.* ☉ *Thurs. and Tues. 10–5, Wed. 10–9, Sun. 1–5.*

★ ❷ **Ybor City.** With cobblestone streets and wrought-iron balconies, Tampa's Cuban enclave is one of only three national historic landmark districts in Florida. The Cubans brought their cigar-making industry to Ybor (pronounced *Ee*-bore) City in 1866, and this east Tampa area is still primarily Cuban. The smell of cigars—hand rolled by Cuban immigrants—still drifts through the heart of Ybor City. These days the area is emerging as Tampa's hot spot as empty cigar factories are transformed into trendy boutiques, art galleries, restaurants, and nightclubs. There's even a new microbrewery. Take a stroll past the ornately tiled **Columbia** restaurant and the stores lining **7th Avenue,** or step back to the past at **Ybor Square** (⊠ 1901 13th St.), a restored cigar factory listed in the National Register of Historic Places that now houses boutiques, offices, and restaurants. (Free guided walking tours are given at 1:30 PM Tues., Thurs., and Sat.) You can watch as artisans hand-roll cigars following time-honored methods. ⊠ *Between Nuccio Pkwy. and 22nd St. from 7th to 9th Aves.*

## Dining and Lodging

**$$$$** ✕ **Armani's.** Located at the top of the Hyatt Regency Westshore, this
★ award-winning northern Italian restaurant offers a great view of Old Tampa Bay and the city. Romantic lighting highlights the sophisticated almond and black decor. Service is impeccable and the food incredible. The antipasto bar, which changes nightly, is a feast in itself. Pasta dishes are excellent, and someone at your table should order the tasty veal Armani (with mushrooms, cream, and cognac in black and white truffle sauce). ⊠ *6200 Courtney Campbell Causeway,* ☎ *813/281–9165. Jacket and tie. AE, DC, MC, V. Closed Sun. No lunch.*

**$$$$** ✕ **Bern's Steak House.** Known well beyond the state line as perhaps
★ the best steak house in Florida, Bern's uses only finely aged prime beef. In fact, chef-owner Bern Lexer ages his own beef, grows his own organic vegetables, roasts his own coffee, and even maintains his own saltwater fish tanks. The wine list offers some 7,000 selections ranging in price from $10 to $10,000 a bottle. The sumptuous desserts are served upstairs in small, glass-enclosed rooms equipped with a control panel that lets you tune in to TV, radio, or the live entertainment in the lounge. ⊠ *1208 S. Howard Ave.,* ☎ *813/251–2421. AE, DC, MC, V. No lunch.*

**$$$** ✕ **Donatello.** Superb service and exquisite classic northern Italian cui-
★ sine make this elegant restaurant one of Tampa's most enjoyable. The veal can be prepared with ham and truffles, brandy and mushrooms, or however you prefer. There are also great pasta, seafood, chicken, and duck entrées. ⊠ *231 N. Dale Mabry Hwy.,* ☎ *813/875–6660. Reservations essential. AE, DC, MC, V. No lunch weekends.*

**$$** ✕ **Colonnade.** The nautical decor suits the wharfside location of this popular family restaurant. Seafood—particularly grouper, red snapper, and lobster—is a specialty, but steak and chicken are also well prepared. ⊠ *3401 Bayshore Blvd.,* ☎ *813/839–7558. AE, DC, MC, V.*

**$$** ✕ **Columbia.** A Spanish fixture in Ybor City since 1905, this magnif-
★ icent structure with ceramic murals, high archways, and ornate railings occupies an entire city block and contains several airy, spacious dining rooms and a sunny atrium. Specialties include paella, black bean soup, and the Columbia 1905 salad (with ham, olives, cheese, and garlic). There's also flamenco dancing. ⊠ *2117 E. 7th Ave.,* ☎ *813/248–4961. AE, DC, MC, V.*

**$$** ✕ **Selena's.** This antiques-filled restaurant serves New Orleans Creole food and some Sicilian dishes, including shrimp scampi and other fresh seafood. ⊠ *1623 Snow Ave.,* ☎ *813/251–2116. AE, DC, MC, V.*

**$** ✕ **Cactus Club.** Fajitas and other southwestern dishes make up the bill of fare at this casual, fashionable restaurant. Or try the tasty pizza with its thin crispy crust. ⊠ *1601 Snow Ave., Old Hyde Park Mall,* ☎ *813/251–4089. AE, DC, MC, V.*

**$$$$** ▥ **Hyatt Regency Westshore.** This large, business-oriented luxury hotel with a marble-accented lobby and a scattering of villas is convenient to downtown. It also has a view of a waterfront bird sanctuary and Tampa Bay. ⊠ *6200 Courtney Campbell Causeway, 33607,*

☎ 813/874–1234, ℻ 813/281–9168. *445 rooms. 3 restaurants, 4 lounges, pool, tennis, jogging, racquetball. AE, D, DC, MC, V.*

**$$$$** ⚏ **Saddlebrook Golf and Tennis Resort.** With its 45 tennis courts and 36 holes of golf, this is arguably one of Florida's premier resorts of its type. Its heavily wooded grounds sprawl just 15 miles north of Tampa, offering varied accommodations, including two-bedroom, two-bath suites with kitchens. ⊠ *5700 Saddlebrook Way, Wesley Chapel 33543,* ☎ *813/973–1111 or 800/729–8383,* ℻ *813/773–4504. 542 rooms. 3 restaurants, 2 lounges, pools, wading pools, saunas, golf, 45 tennis courts, health club, fishing, bicycles. AE, DC, MC, V.*

**$$$$** ⚏ **Wyndham Harbour Island Hotel.** With its dark wood paneling, substantial furniture, and attentive service, this place is an elegant spot. The tennis facilities are excellent and the location is convenient to downtown and the Convention Center. ⊠ *725 S. Harbour Island Blvd., 33602,* ☎ *813/229–5000,* ℻ *813/229–5322. 300 rooms. Restaurant, lounge, pool, tennis, health club, dock, boating. AE, DC, MC, V.*

**$$$** ⚏ **Embassy Suites Hotel–Tampa Airport/Westshore.** In this modern hotel midway between Tampa International Airport and downtown, all rooms are suites and each has a kitchen. A complimentary breakfast is served. Pets are allowed. ⊠ *555 N. Westshore Blvd., 33609,* ☎ *813/875–1555,* ℻ *813/287–3664. 221 suites. Restaurant, lounge, pool, health club, airport shuttle. AE, DC, MC, V.*

**$$** ⚏ **Holiday Inn Busch Gardens.** This well-maintained family-oriented motor inn is a mile west of Busch Gardens, across the street from the University Square Mall, Tampa's largest. ⊠ *2701 E. Fowler Ave., 33612,* ☎ *813/971–4710,* ℻ *813/977–0155. 398 rooms, 7 suites. Restaurant, lounge, pool, exercise room. AE, DC, MC, V.*

**$** ⚏ **Tahitian Inn.** Comfortable rooms and budget prices are the draws at this family-run motel. It's five minutes from Tampa Stadium and 20 minutes from Busch Gardens. ⊠ *601 S. Dale Mabry Hwy., 33609,* ☎ *813/877–6721,* ℻ *813/877–6218. 79 rooms. Restaurant, pool. AE, DC, MC, V.*

# Nightlife and the Arts

## The Arts

The **Tampa Bay Performing Arts Center** (⊠ 1010 W. C. MacInnes Pl., Box 2877, Tampa, ☎ 813/221–1045 or 800/955–1045) occupies 9 acres along the Hillsborough River and is one of the largest such complexes south of the Kennedy Center in Washington, D.C. The 290,000-square-foot complex, which includes a 2,400-seat festival hall, 900-seat playhouse, and 300-seat theater, houses opera, ballet, drama, and concerts; the **Tampa Ballet** (☎ 813/229–7827) performs here. The **Tampa Theater** (⊠ 711 N. Franklin St., Tampa, ☎ 813/223–8981) presents shows, musical performances, and films. The **Tampa Convention Center** (⊠ 333 S. Franklin St., ☎ 813/223–8511) hosts concerts throughout the year.

## Nightlife

The bar at the **Harbour Island Hotel** (⊠ Harbour Island, ☎ 813/229–5000) has a great view of the bay and large-screen TV. **Skippers Smokehouse** (⊠ 910 Skipper Rd., ☎ 813/971–0666), a restaurant and oyster bar, has live reggae and blues.

On Friday and Saturday nights, crowds head to the noisy, boisterous **Dallas Bull** (⊠ 8222 N. U.S. 301, ☎ 813/985–6877) to stomp to down-home country sounds. For cry-in-your-cabernet blues, sail down to the **Blue Ships Cafe** (⊠ 1910 E. 7th Ave., Ybor City, ☎ 813/248–6097) any Wednesday.

# Outdoor Activities and Sports

### Canoeing

Just south of Tampa, **Canoe Outpost** (⊠ 18001 U.S. 301S, Wimauma, ☎ 813/634–2228) offers half-day, full-day, and overnight canoe trips on several southwest Florida waters, including the Little Manatee River.

### Dog Races

**Tampa Greyhound Track** holds dog races from July to December (⊠ 8300 N. Nebraska Ave., ☎ 813/932–4313).

### Football

At press time, NFL football currently comes in the form of the **Tampa Bay Buccaneers,** at Tampa Stadium (⊠ 4201 N. Dale Mabry Hwy., ☎ 813/461–2700 or 800/282–0683).

### Golf

**Apollo Beach Golf & Sea Club** (☎ 813/645–6212): 18-hole, public course. **Babe Zaharias Golf Course** (☎ 813/932–8932): 18-hole public course. **Bloomingdale Golfers Club** (⊠ Valrico, ☎ 813/685–4105): 18 holes and a driving range. **Rocky Point Golf Course** (☎ 813/884–5141): 18 holes. **Saddlebrook Golf and Tennis Resort** (⊠ Wesley Chapel, ☎ 913/973–1111): a 36-hole course.

### Horse Racing

**Tampa Bay Downs** (⊠ Race Track Rd., off Rte. 580, Oldsmar, ☎ 813/855–4401) holds Thoroughbred races from mid-December to early May.

### Ice Hockey

The **NHL Tampa Bay Lightning** team plays at the Ice Palace (⊠ 401 Channelside Dr., 33602, ☎ 813/229–2658), a new $153 million downtown waterfront arena.

### Jai Alai

**Tampa Jai-Alai Fronton** (⊠ S. Dale Mabry Hwy. and Gandy Blvd., ☎ 813/837–2441) is open year-round.

### Tennis

The **City of Tampa Tennis Complex** (⊠ Hillsborough Community College, ☎ 813/348–1173), across from Tampa Stadium, has 12 clay courts and 16 hard courts.

## Shopping

**Old Hyde Park Village** (⊠ Swan Ave. near Bayshore Blvd.) is an elegant outdoor shopping center stretching over several blocks. The five-story bayfront **Pier** (⊠ 800 2nd Ave. NE), near the Museum of Fine Arts, looks like an inverted pyramid; inside are numerous shops and eating spots. **The Shops on Harbour Island** (⊠ 601 S. Harbour Island Blvd.) is a waterfront marketplace with shops, restaurants, and a food court. For bargains, stop at the **Big Top** (⊠ 9250 Fowler Ave.), open weekends 8–5, where vendors hawk new and used items at more than 600 booths.

# ST. PETERSBURG

St. Petersburg and the Pinellas Suncoast form the thumb of the hand jutting out of Florida's west coast, holding in Tampa Bay. There are two distinct parts of St. Petersburg—the downtown and cultural area, centered on the bay, and the beach area, on a string of barrier islands facing onto the Gulf. Causeways link the beach communities to the mainland.

## Sights to See

**⑭ Caladesi Island State Park.** One of Florida's few undeveloped barrier islands, this 600-acre preserve lies 3 miles off the coast, across Hurricane Pass, and is accessible only by boat. There's a beach on the Gulf side, mangroves on the bay side, and a self-guided nature trail winding through the island's interior. Park rangers are available to answer questions. A good spot for swimming, fishing, shelling, boating, and nature study, its facilities include boardwalks, picnic shelters, bathhouses, and a concession stand. ⊠ *Dunedin Causeway to Honeymoon Island, then board ferry.* ☎ *813/734–5263.* 🎫 *Parking $3.25, ferry $4.* ☉ *Daily 8–sunset, ferry hourly 10–5 in fair weather.*

**⑫ Fort De Soto Park.** Actually spread over six small islands, or keys, this 900-acre park lies at the mouth of Tampa Bay. It has seven miles of beaches, two fishing piers, picnic and camping grounds, and a historic fort. The fort for which it's named was built on the southern end of Mullet Key to protect sea lanes in the Gulf during the Spanish-American War. Roam the fort (admission is free) or wander the beaches of any of the islands within the park. ⊠ *Rte. 682 (54th Ave. S).*

**❼ Great Explorations!** In this museum, you'll never hear, "Don't touch." It's hands-on in every room: The Body Shop, where you can explore health; the Think Tank, featuring mind-stretching puzzles; the Touch Tunnel, a 90-foot-long, pitch-black, crawl-through maze; and Phenomenal Arts, where you can play a Moog music synthesizer and explore neon-filled tubes that glow vividly when touched. ⊠ *1120 4th St. S,* ☎ *813/821–8885.* 🎫 *$5.* ☉ *Mon.–Sat. 10–5, Sun. noon–5.*

**❾ Museum of Fine Arts.** Outstanding examples of European, American, pre-Columbian, and Far Eastern art line the walls of this museum. There are also photographic exhibits. ⊠ *255 Beach Dr. NE,* ☎ *813/896–2667.* 🎫 *$5.* ☉ *Tues.–Sat. 10–5, Sun. 1–5.*

**❽ Salvador Dali Museum.** The world's most extensive collection of originals by famous Spanish surrealist Salvador Dali can be found here. Valued at more than $125 million, it includes 94 original oils, more than 100 watercolors and drawings, and 1,300 graphics, sculptures, photographs, and objets d'art, including floor-to-ceiling murals. ⊠ *1000 3rd St. S,* ☎ *813/823–3767.* 🎫 *$5.* ☉ *Tues.–Sat. 10–5, Sun. and Mon. noon–5.*

**⑬ Suncoast Seabird Sanctuary.** When pelicans become entangled in fishing lines, locals sometimes carry them here. The sanctuary, which backs up to the beach, is a nonprofit center dedicated to the rescue, repair, recuperation, and release of sick and injured birds. At times, there are 500 to 600 land and seabirds in residence, including pelicans, egrets, herons, gulls, terns, cranes, ducks, owls, and cormorants. Many of them are kept in open-air pens while they recover. ⊠ *18328 Gulf Blvd., Indian Shores,* ☎ *813/391–6211.* 🎫 *Donations welcome.* ☉ *Daily sunrise–sunset.* ☉ *Guided tour Wed. and Sun. 2.*

**❿ Sunken Gardens.** This is one of Florida's most colorful attractions. Walk through an aviary full of tropical birds, stroll among more than 50,000 exotic flowers and other plants, stop to smell the rare, fragrant orchids, and take a peek into the antiques store. You'll also find gator wrestling and macaw bird shows several times a day. ⊠ *1825 4th St. N,* ☎ *813/896–3186.* 🎫 *$14.* ☉ *Daily 10–5.*

★ ⓫ **Sunshine Skyway.** It costs $1 to travel southbound on this 4.1-mile-long bridge connecting Pinellas and Manatee counties, a section of I–275. But it's money well spent. The roadway is 183 feet above Tampa Bay at its highest point and the view out over the bay is spectacular. You'll see the several small islands that dot the bay if you're heading southeast, St. Petersburg Beach if you're going northwest.

⓯ **Tarpon Springs.** Decades ago, sponge divers from Greece moved to Tarpon Springs and continued to pull riches from the sea, and by the 1930s it was the world's largest sponge center. Although a bacterial blight wiped out the sponge beds in the 1940s, the Greeks held on, and though it's not as strong as it once was the sponge industry has returned. Today, the Greek influence remains evident in the churches, the restaurants, and, often, the language spoken on the streets. Don't miss the **St. Nicholas Greek Orthodox Church,** a replica of St. Sophia's in Constantinople and an excellent example of New Byzantine architecture, and **Spongeorama,** an exhibit and film about the history of the sponge industry. You'll come away converted to (and loaded up with) natural sponges and loofas. ✉ *Rte. 19 north of Dunedin Causeway.*

## Beaches

**Bay Beach** (✉ North Shore Dr. and 13th Ave. NE), on Tampa Bay, has showers and picnic shelters. **Clearwater Beach,** on a narrow island between Clearwater Harbor and the Gulf, is connected to downtown Clearwater by Memorial Causeway and is a popular hangout for teens and college students. Facilities include a marina, concessions, showers, rest rooms, and lifeguards. On five islands totaling some 900 acres, **Fort De Soto Park** has St. Petersburg's southernmost beaches. Facilities include two fishing piers, picnic sites overlooking lagoons, a waterskiing and boating area, and miles of beaches for swimming. It's open daily until dark. To get there, take the Pinellas Bayway through three toll gates (85¢). **Indian Rocks Beach** (✉ off Rte. 8 south of Clearwater Beach) attracts mostly couples. **Maximo Park Beach** (✉ 34th St. and Pinellas Point Dr. S, Madeira Beach) is on Boca Ciega Bay. It's unguarded, but there is a picnic area with grills, tables, shelters, and a boat ramp. **North Shore Beach** (✉ 901 North Shore Dr. NE, Belleair Beach) charges $1 admission and has a pool, beach umbrellas, cabanas, windbreaks, and lounges. **Pass-A-Grille Beach,** the southern part of St. Petersburg Beach, has parking meters, a snack bar, rest rooms, and showers. **St. Petersburg Municipal Beach** (✉ 11260 Gulf Blvd.) is a free beach on Treasure Island. There are dressing rooms, metered parking, and a snack bar. **Tarpon Springs** has two public beaches: **Howard Park Beach** (✉ Sunset Dr.) and **Sunset Beach** (✉ Gulf Rd.), both guarded in spring and summer; the latter has rest rooms, picnic tables, grills, and a boat ramp.

## Dining and Lodging

### Clearwater

$$–$$$ ✗ **Bob Heilman's Beachcomber.** Southern-fried chicken and mashed potatoes with gravy have long been the Sunday staple at this 40-year-old restaurant otherwise known for its seafood, homemade desserts, and hearty portions. ✉ *447 Mandalay Ave., Clearwater Beach,* ☎ *813/442–4144. AE, DC, MC, V.*

$$$$ ▦ **Belleview Mido Resort Hotel.** This charming 21-acre Victorian re-
★ sort was built in 1896 and is on the National Register of Historic Places. Overlooking Clearwater Bay, the units are luxuriously decorated, and there are recreational opportunities aplenty. ✉ *25 Belleview Blvd.,*

34616, ☎ 813/442–6171, ℻ 813/441–4173. *292 rooms. 2 restaurants, 5 lounges, 2 pools, saunas, spa, golf, tennis, fitness center, boating, bicycles, playground, shopping. AE, D, DC, MC, V.*

$$$ ⊞ **Sheraton Sand Key Resort.** This is a supreme spot for those searching for sun, sand, and surf. Balconies and patios overlook the Gulf and well-manicured grounds. ⊠ *1160 Gulf Blvd., Clearwater Beach 33515,* ☎ *813/595–1611,* ℻ *813/596–8488. 390 rooms. Restaurant, lounge, pool, wading pool, tennis, beach, windsurfing, boating, playground. AE, DC, MC, V.*

$$ ⊞ **Comfort Inn/Clearwater.** A comfortable, unpretentious motor inn centrally located near St. Petersburg and Tampa Bay. It is built around an atrium courtyard and pool. ⊠ *3580 Ulmerton Rd. (Rte. 688), 34622,* ☎ *813/573–1171,* ℻ *813/572–8736. 119 rooms. Restaurant, pool, fitness center. AE, DC, MC, V.*

## Dunedin

$$ ✕ **Bon Appetit.** This restaurant with views of the Intracoastal Water-
★ way and the Gulf used to be known for its elegance and Continental cuisine. Then European-trained chef-owners Peter Kreuziger and Karl Heinz Riedl decided to go casual. The menu now changes twice a month and offers salads and light entrées as well as fresh seafood and more ambitious fare such as peppered quail and scallops with figs and raisins on fettuccine. ⊠ *148 Marina Plaza,* ☎ *813/733–2151. AE, MC, V.*

$$ ⊞ **Inn on the Bay.** A good value, this modest four-story motel has comfortable rooms and a small number of two-bedroom units. Check to see if you can get one with excellent Gulf views. The inn has a fishing pier and rents bicycles, and good beaches and water sports rentals are nearby, as is the ferry to Caladesi State Park. ⊠ *1420 Bayshore Blvd., 34698,* ☎ *813/734–7689. 41 rooms. Pool, fishing, lounge. AE, MC, V.*

## St. Petersburg

$–$$ ✕ **Apropos.** Sit indoors or out at this little harbor-front café open all day. For breakfast try the delicious blueberry pancakes. For lunch, choose a light salad or one of the appealing sandwiches—filet mignon, tarragon chicken club, or ginger-marinated pork loin. Dinner entrées include salads, grilled meats, and pastas. ⊠ *2nd Ave. at beginning of pier,* ☎ *813/823–8934. MC, V. Closed Mon.*

$–$$ ✕ **Nick's on the Water.** Sitting at the end of the St. Petersburg Pier is this peaceful place with pretty water views. Wood-burning-oven-baked pizzas are a specialty, with toppings ranging from barbecued chicken to Philly cheese steak. Rigatoni à la vodka, the signature dish, headlines the pastas. ⊠ *800 2nd Ave. NE,* ☎ *813/898–5800. AE, MC, V.*

$ ✕ **Hurricane Seafood Restaurant.** Everyone loves this seafood joint on historic Pass-A-Grille Beach for its steamed shrimp, homemade crab cakes, and grilled, broiled, or blackened grouper. One of the few places in St. Petersburg with live jazz (Wednesday to Sunday), it also has a disco next door, Stormy's at the Hurricane. Crowds descend on the third-floor sundeck to see those gorgeous sunsets. ⊠ *807 Gulf Way,* ☎ *813/360–9558. MC, V.*

$ ✕ **Ted Peters Famous Smoked Fish.** The menu is limited to mackerel, mullet, and salmon, but all are smoked and seasoned to perfection and served with heaping helpings of German potato salad. All meals are served outdoors. ⊠ *1350 Pasadena Ave. S, Pasadena,* ☎ *813/381–7931. No credit cards. Closed Tues. No dinner.*

$$$$   🏨 **Don CeSar Beach Resort.** Still echoing with the ghosts of Scott and Zelda Fitzgerald, this sprawling, sybaritic, beachfront "Pink Palace" has long been a Gulf Shore landmark because of its remarkable architecture. It is steeped in turn-of-the-century elegance. ⊠ *3400 Gulf Blvd., St. Petersburg Beach 33706,* ☎ *813/360–1881,* FAX *813/367–3609. 277 rooms, 3 restaurants, 3 bars, 2 pools, 2 spas, tennis courts, exercise room, beach, boating, jet skiing, parasailing, children's programs, meeting rooms. AE, DC, MC, V.*

$$$$   🏨 **Stouffer Vinoy Resort.** More than $100 million was spent to renovate this bayfront hotel, built in 1925 and listed on the National Register of Historic Places, and it shows. The spacious rooms have three phones, two televisions, minibars, hair dryers, and bathrobes. Ron Garl designed the 18-hole, par-70 golf course. And though a tiny beach adjoins the property, transportation is provided to ocean beaches 20 minutes away. Rooms in the original building have more character but all are comfortable and stylish. Be sure to check out the frescoed ceilings in the dining room. ⊠ *501 5th Ave. NE, 33701,* ☎ *813/894–1000,* FAX *813/822–2785. 360 rooms. 4 restaurants, 2 lounges, 2 pools, golf, tennis, croquet, fitness center, business services. AE, DC, MC, V.*

$$$$   🏨 **Tradewinds on St. Petersburg Beach.** This elegant beachfront complex feels a little like old Florida. Rooms and suites (some with kitchens) are scattered among six buildings on exquisitely manicured grounds. White gazebos, gondolas on canals, and swaying hammocks set the mood. ⊠ *5500 Gulf Blvd., St. Petersburg Beach 33706,* ☎ *813/367–6461,* FAX *813/367–4567. 577 rooms. 3 restaurants, ice cream parlor, lounge, pools, wading pool, sauna, tennis, putting green, exercise room, racquetball, beach, dock, windsurfing, boating, waterskiing, fishing, bicycles, playground. AE, DC, MC, V.*

$$   🏨 **Colonial Gateway Resort Inn.** This well-maintained Gulf-front hotel is family oriented. Half of the rooms are equipped with kitchenettes, and all are nicely decorated with light green floral prints. ⊠ *6300 Gulf Blvd., St. Petersburg Beach 33706,* ☎ *813/367–2711 or 800/237–8918,* FAX *813/362–7068. 20 rooms. restaurant, lounge, bar, pool, water sports. AE, DC, MC, V.*

## Tarpon Springs

$$   ✕ **La Brasserie.** A bit of French cuisine in this highly Greek area makes this little place noteworthy. Appetizers include escargot, frogs' legs, and quiche, while entrées range from veal in a white sauce and veal cordon bleu to coq au vin and fondue. Onion soup is the house specialty. ⊠ *200 E. Tarpon Ave.,* ☎ *813/942–3011. AE, MC, V.*

$$   ✕ **Louis Pappas' Riverside Restaurant.** The decor consists mainly of
★   wall-to-wall people who pour into this waterfront landmark for all manner of Greek fare, especially the Greek salad (lettuce, feta cheese chunks, onions, and olive oil). ⊠ *10 W. Dodecanese Blvd.,* ☎ *813/937–5101. AE, DC, MC, V. Closed Sun. lunch.*

$$$$   🏨 **Innisbrook Hilton Resort.** This 1,000-acre resort is a pleasure.
★   Grounds are beautifully maintained, and the three golf courses are highly rated and of championship caliber. All units are all suites, all are roomy, and all have kitchens; some have balconies or patios as well. A good mix of restaurants and lounges compensates for the resort's isolation. ⊠ *U.S. 19, Box 1088, 34689,* ☎ *813/942–2000,* FAX *813/942–5576. 1,200 rooms. 4 restaurants, pools, saunas, golf, miniature golf, tennis, health club, racquetball, nightclub, children's programs, playground. AE, DC, MC, V.*

$$   🏨 **Inness Manor.** Originally built in the late 1800s, this charming building, now a B&B, was home to the well-known American painter George Inness, Jr. Highlights of the house are natural cypress beams,

a magnificent staircase, and burled yellow-pine panels. There are currently five guest rooms—four with balconies, three with private bath. Picnic lunches are available. ⊠ 34 W. Orange St., 34689, ☎ 813/938–2900. 5 rooms. No smoking. AE, MC, V.

# Nightlife and the Arts

### The Arts
**Ruth Eckerd Hall** (⊠ 1111 McMullen Booth Rd., Clearwater, ☎ 813/791–7400) hosts many national performers of ballet, opera, and music—pop, classical, or jazz. The **St. Petersburg Concert Ballet** (☎ 813/892–5767) performs periodically throughout the year, mostly at the Bayfront Center in St. Petersburg.

### Nightlife
**Harp & Thistle** (⊠ 650 Corey Ave., St. Petersburg Beach, ☎ 813/360–4104) presents live Irish music Wednesday through Sunday. **Carlie's** (⊠ 5641 49th St., ☎ 813/527–5214) is hopping on Friday and Saturday nights, with plenty of dancing. Weekend crowds pack the noisy, boisterous **Joyland Country Night Club** (⊠ 11225 U.S. 19, ☎ 813/573–1919). At the popular **Cha Cha Coconuts** (⊠ City Pier, ☎ 813/822–6655), there is live contemporary music several nights a week and reggae on Sundays. **Hurricane Lounge** (⊠ 807 Gulf Way, Pass-A-Grille Beach, ☎ 813/360–9558) is a nice place to watch the sun going down and listen to jazz. **Coliseum Ballroom** (⊠ 535 4th Ave. N, ☎ 813/892–5202) offers ballroom dancing Wednesday and Saturday nights.

# Outdoor Activities and Sports

### Baseball
St. Pete's Lang Stadium (⊠ 1st St. and 2nd Ave., ☎ 813/822–3384) is home to spring training camps for the **Baltimore Orioles** and the **St. Louis Cardinals.** The **Toronto Blue Jays** hold spring training at Grant Field (⊠ 373 Douglas Ave., north of Rte. 88, Dunedin, ☎ 813/733–9302). The **Philadelphia Phillies** get ready for the season at Jack Russell Stadium (⊠ Seminole St. and Greenwood Ave., Clearwater, ☎ 813/442–8496).

### Biking
**Beach Cyclist** (⊠ 7517 Blindpass Rd., St. Petersburg, ☎ 813/367–5001) rents bicycles.

### Dog Racing
Dog races are held January–June at **Derby Lane** (⊠ 10490 Gandy Blvd., St. Petersburg, ☎ 813/576–1361).

### Golf
**Clearwater Golf Park** (⊠ Clearwater, ☎ 813/447–5272): 18 holes and a driving range. **Dunedin Country Club** (⊠ Dunedin, ☎ 813/733–7836): 18 holes and a driving range. **Innisbrook Hilton Resort** (⊠ Tarpon Springs, ☎ 813/942–2000): 63 holes of golf, driving ranges, and putting greens. **Largo Golf Course** (⊠ Largo, ☎ 813/587–6724): 18 holes. **Mangrove Bay Golf Course** (⊠ St. Petersburg, ☎ 813/893–7797): driving range and 18 holes. **Twin Brooks Golf Course** (⊠ St. Petersburg, ☎ 813/893–7445): 18 holes and a driving range.

### Tennis
**McMullen Park** (⊠ 1000 Edenville Ave., Clearwater, ☎ 813/462–6144) has 17 hard-surface courts.

### Water Sports
**Florida Charter** (⊠ 1740 Liebman La., St. Petersburg, ☎ 941/347–7245) has power- and sailboats for rent, bareboat or captained. You can take

sailing lessons and rent boats at **M & M Beach Service & Boat Rental** (⊠ 5300 Gulf Blvd. St. Petersburg Beach, ☎ 941/360–8295).

## Shopping

**Hamlin's Landing** (⊠ 401 2nd St. E, Indian Rocks Beach) has several shops and restaurants along the Intracoastal Waterway, in a Victorian-style setting. **John's Pass Village and Boardwalk** (⊠ 12901 Gulf Blvd., Madeira Beach) features a collection of shops and restaurants in an old-style fishing village near St. Petersburg where you can pass the time watching the pelicans cavorting and dive-bombing for food. At the **Wagonwheel** flea market (⊠ 7801 Park Blvd., Pinellas Park), some 2,000 vendors set up shop on 100 acres weekends between 8 and 4.

# THE MANATEE COAST

U.S. 19 is the prime route through rural manatee country, and traffic flows freely once you've left the congestion of St. Petersburg. Since most of the sights are outdoors, plan for a picnic lunch by picking up provisions before you leave the city.

## Sights to See

**㉑ Cedar Key Historical Society Museum.** Up in the area known as the Big Bend, Florida's long, curving coastline north of Tampa, you won't find many beaches. But you will find an idyllic collection of small cays and a little island village tucked in among the marshes and scenic streams feeding the Gulf of Mexico. Once a strategic port for the Confederate States of America, remote **Cedar Key** today is a commercial fishing center. Its museum displays historical photographs and exhibits that focus on the development of the area. From U.S. 19, take Route 24 until the highway ends at Cedar Key. (Don't be surprised if you don't see another car, despite the fact that this is the only route to the island.) ⊠ *Rte. 24 and 2nd St.,* ☎ *904/543–5549.* ☞ *$1.* ☉ *Daily 11–4.*

**㉑ Crystal River Wildlife Refuge.** Here, in this U.S. Fish and Wildlife Service sanctuary for the endangered manatee, wide stretches of the river are designated for people to watch and swim with the peaceful giants. The main spring feeds crystal-clear water into the river at 72° year-round, and in winter, manatees congregate around the spring. In warmer months, when manatees scatter, the main spring is still fun for a swim. Though accessible only by boat, the refuge provides neither tours nor boat rentals. For these, contact marinas in town. ⊠ *1502 S. Kings Bay Dr., Crystal River,* ☎ *904/563–2088.* ☞ *Free.* ☉ *Daily 9–4, office weekdays 7:30–4.*

**㉑ Homosassa Springs State Wildlife Park.** Here you may see manatees, but the main attraction is the "Spring of 10,000 Fish," a clear spring with many species of fish that can be easily watched through a floating glass observatory. A walk along the park's paths will lead you to alligator, other reptile, and exotic bird shows. Jungle boat cruises on the Homosassa River are available across Fish Bowl Drive from the entrance. ⊠ *1 mi west of U.S. 19 on Fish Bowl Dr., Homosassa Springs,* ☎ *904/628–2311.* ☞ *$7.95.* ☉ *Daily 9–5:30.*

**㉑ Weeki Wachee Spring.** The spring here, which flows at the remarkable rate of 170 million gallons a day with a constant temperature of 74°, has long been famous for its live mermaids. Nowadays, clever breathing makes possible performances of *Pocahontas* and *The Little Mermaid* in the underwater theater. A nature trail threads through the subtropical wilderness and a jungle boat cruises to view local wildlife.

You'll need at least four hours to see everything. ✉ *U.S. 19 and Rte. 50, Weeki Wachee,* ☎ *904/596–2062.* ≋ *$16.95.* ☉ *Daily 9:30–5:30.*

**⑱ Yulee Sugar Mill State Historic Site.** The ruined remains of a 5,100-acre sugar plantation owned by Florida's first U.S. Senator, David Levy Yulee, make for pleasant picnicking. ✉ *County Rte. 490-A, Homosassa Springs,* ☎ *904/795–3817.* ≋ *Free.* ☉ *Daily sunrise–sunset.*

## Dining and Lodging

### Cedar Key

$$ 🏨 **Park Place Motel.** Views of the Gulf are lovely from the private balconies off many units at this three-story motel within walking distance of stores and restaurants. On the top floor are bi-level units with sleeping lofts, but there's no elevator. ✉ *2nd St. at A St., 32625,* ☎ *904/543–5575. 34 rooms. MC, V.*

### Crystal River

$ ✗ **Charlie's Fish House Restaurant.** This popular, no-frills seafood spot serves fish caught locally as well as oysters, crab claws, and lobster. ✉ *224 U.S. 19 N, Crystal River,* ☎ *904/795–3949. MC, V.*

$$ 🏨 **Plantation Inn & Golf Resort.** Set on the banks of Kings Bay, this rustic two-story plantation-style resort sits on 175 acres near several nature preserves and rivers. Pets are permitted. ✉ *9301 W. Fort Island Trail, 34423,* ☎ *904/795–4211 or 800/632–6262,* FAX *904/795–1368. 136 rooms. Restaurant, lounge, pools, saunas, golf, tennis, boating, fishing. AE, DC, MC, V.*

$ 🏨 **Best Western Crystal River Resort.** This cinder-block roadside motel is close to Kings Bay and its manatee population. A marina is steps away, with dive boats departing for scuba and snorkeling excursions. Only two rooms view the water: 114 and 128. ✉ *614 N.W. U.S. 19, 34428,* ☎ *904/795–3171,* FAX *813/795–3179. 96 rooms, 18 efficiencies. Restaurant, lounge, pool. AE, DC, MC, V.*

### Homosassa Springs

$$$ ✗ **K. C. Crump.** This 1870 Old Florida residence on the Homosassa River was restored in 1986 and opened as a restaurant serving meat and seafood in 1987. In addition to the large, airy dining rooms, there's outdoor dining, a lounge, and a marina on the river. ✉ *11210 Halls River Rd.,* ☎ *904/628–1500. AE, MC, V.*

$$ ✗🏨 **Riverside Inn.** This rustic little inn is intimately set beside the Homosassa River and across from Monkey Island—residence of six such mammals. Though it has its own restaurant and lounge, the Riverside is within walking distance of three local restaurants, and two others are accessible by boat. Rent bicycles to get a feel for the lovely surroundings. ✉ *Box 258, 32687,* ☎ *904/628–2474,* FAX *904/628–5208. 76 rooms. Restaurant, lounge, pool, tennis courts, bicycles. AE, MC, V.*

$$ 🏨 **Ramada Inn Downtown.** This is a simple motor inn with queen-size beds in most rooms. It accepts pets. ✉ *U.S. 19 at Rte. 490A, 34448,* ☎ *904/628–4311,* FAX *904/628–4311. 104 rooms. Restaurant, lounge, pool, tennis courts, playground. AE, D, DC, MC, V.*

$ 🏨 **Homosassa River Retreat.** Located right on the banks of the Homosassa River, with two boat docks and nearby boat and pontoon rentals, this resort of one- and two-bedroom cottages with kitchens is well situated for outdoor adventuring. ✉ *10605 Hall's River Rd., 32646,* ☎ *904/628–7072. 9 cottages. Docks, laundry. MC, V.*

# Golf

**Plantation Inn & Golf Resort** (⊠ Crystal River, ☎ 813/795–7211): 27 holes and a putting green.

# BRADENTON

This city on the Manatee River is the site of some 20 miles of beaches and is well sited for access to fishing, both fresh- and saltwater.

## Sights to See

*Numbers in the margin correspond to points of interest on the Bradenton/Sarasota map.*

**㉔ Egmont Key.** Just off the northern tip of Anna Maria Island, Bradenton's barrier island to the west, lies Egmont Key. On it is Fort Dade, a military installation built in 1900 during the Spanish-American War, and Florida's sixth-brightest lighthouse. The primary inhabitant of the 2-mile-long island is the threatened gopher tortoise. The only way to get here is by the *Miss Cortez,* an excursion boat (☞ Guided Tours *in* Tampa Bay Area A to Z). Shellers, in particular, will find the trip rewarding.

**㉑ Gamble Plantation and Confederate Memorial.** Built in 1850, this is the only pre–Civil War plantation house in south Florida, and original furnishings are on display. The Confederate secretary of state took refuge here when the Confederacy fell to Union forces. ⊠ *3708 Patten Ave., Ellenton,* ☎ *813/723–4536.* 🎫 *$2.* ☉ *Thurs.–Mon. 8–5; tours 9:30, 10:30, 1, 2, 3, and 4.*

**㉒ Manatee Village Historical Park.** This is the real thing—an 1860 courthouse, 1887 church, 1903 general store and museum, a circa 1908 one-room schoolhouse, and a settler's home dating from 1912. The Old Manatee Cemetery, which dates back to 1850, contains the graves of early settlers. An appointment is required for the cemetery tour. ⊠ *Rte. 64,* ☎ *813/749–7165.* 🎫 *Free.* ☉ *Sept.–June, weekdays 9–4:30, Sun. 1:30–4:30; July and Aug., weekdays 9–4:30.*

**㉓ South Florida Museum and Bishop Planetarium.** Showcased here are Florida artifacts, including displays relating to Native American culture and an excellent collection of Civil War objects. The museum is also home to Snooty, the oldest living manatee in captivity, who likes to shake hands and perform other tricks at feeding time in his new 60,000-gallon home. At the domed Bishop Planetarium, you can see star shows and laser-light displays. ⊠ *201 10th St.,* ☎ *813/746–4132.* 🎫 *$6.* ☉ *Tues.–Sat. 10–5, Sun. noon–5, star show Tues.–Sun. 1:30 and 3.*

## Beaches

**Anna Maria Island,** just west of the Sunshine Skyway Bridge, has four public beaches. **Anna Maria Bayfront Park,** adjacent to the municipal pier, is a secluded beach fronting both the Intracoastal Waterway and the Gulf of Mexico. Facilities include picnic grounds, a playground, rest rooms, showers, and lifeguards. At mid-island, in the town of Holmes Beach, is **Manatee County Beach,** popular with all ages. It has picnic facilities, a snack bar, showers, rest rooms, and lifeguards. **Cortez Beach** (⊠ Gulf Blvd., Bradenton Beach) is for those who like their beaches without facilities—nothing but sand, water, and trees. At the southern end is **Coquina Beach,** popular with singles and families. Facilities here

## Bradenton/Sarasota

Bellm's Cars & Music of Yesterday, **26**

Cedar Key Historical Society Museum, **20**

Egmont Key, **24**

Gamble Plantation and Confederate Memorial, **21**

Manatee Village Historical Park, **22**

Marie Selby Botanical Gardens, **29**

Mote Marine Aquarium, **28**

Ringling Museums, **25**

Sarasota Jungle Gardens, **27**

South Florida Museum and Bishop Planetarium, **23**

Venice, **30**

include a picnic area, boat ramp, playground, refreshment stand, rest rooms, showers, and lifeguards.

**Greer Island Beach** is at the northern tip of the next barrier island south—Longboat Key—and is accessible by boat or via North Shore Boulevard. This secluded peninsula has a wide beach and excellent shelling, but no facilities. **Palma Sola Causeway,** which takes Manatee Avenue on the mainland to Anna Maria Island, has a long, sandy beach fronting Palma Sola Bay, with boat ramps, a dock, and picnic tables.

## Dining and Lodging

$$ ✕ **Crab Trap.** Rustic decor, ultrafresh seafood, gator tail, and wild pig are among the trademarks of this restaurant. ⊠ *U.S. 19 at Terra Ceia Bridge, Palmetto,* ☎ *813/722–6255;* ⊠ *4814 Memphis Rd., Ellenton,* ☎ *813/729–7777. D, MC, V.*

$$$ 🏨 **Holiday Inn Riverfront.** This Spanish Mediterranean–style motor inn near the Manatee River is easily accessible from I–75 and U.S. 41. One-third of the rooms are suites. ⊠ *100 Riverfront Dr. W, 34205,* ☎ *813/747–3727,* FAX *813/746–4289. 153 rooms. Restaurant, lounge, pool. AE, DC, MC, V.*

## Outdoor Activities and Sports

### Baseball
The **Pittsburgh Pirates** have spring training in Bradenton at McKechnie Field (⊠ 17th Ave. W and 9th St., ☎ 941/747–3031).

### Biking
**Bicycle Center** (⊠ 2610 Cortez Rd., Bradenton, ☎ 941/756–5480) rents bicycles by the hour and by the day.

### Golf
**Buffalo Creek** (⊠ Palmetto, ☎ 813/776–2611): 18 holes and a driving range. **Manatee County Golf Course** (⊠ Bradenton, ☎ 813/792–6773): a driving range and 18 holes.

## Shopping

Some vendors at the **Red Barn** (⊠ 1707 1st St. E, Bradenton), a flea market in a big red barn, do business during the week (often Tuesday through Sunday from 10 to 4), but the number of vendors skyrockets to 1,000 on weekends (when many are open beginning at 8).

# SARASOTA AND VENICE

Despite the clown-college reputation, Sarasota, where Ringling began his famous circus, is a sophisticated resort town with cultural events scheduled year-round, not to mention the 30 golf courses and a long expanse of white beach. Venice, south of Sarasota, is still a small town, now known mostly for the ancient shark teeth you can find on its beach.

## Sights to See

㉖ **Bellm's Cars & Music of Yesterday.** You could say they are rocking and rolling here with both 175 restored antique automobiles—including Rolls-Royces, Pierce Arrows, and Auburns—and more than 1,200 old-time music makers, such as hurdy-gurdies, calliopes, and music boxes. ⊠ *5500 N. Tamiami Trail,* ☎ *941/355–6228.* 🎫 *$8.* ☯ *Mon.–Sat. 8:30–6, Sun. 9:30–6.*

**㉙ Marie Selby Botanical Gardens.** Stroll through a world-class display of orchids, see air plants and colorful bromeliads, and wander through 14 garden areas along Sarasota Bay when you visit these nine-acre gardens. There is also a small museum of botany and art in a gracious restored mansion. ⊠ *800 S. Palm Ave.,* ☎ *941/366–5730.* ⊑ *$6.* ☉ *Daily 10–5.*

**Myakka River State Park.** With 28,900 acres, this outstanding wildlife area is absolutely lovely and great for bird watching and gator sighting. Tram tours explore the natural hammocks, air boat tours whiz over the lake, and there are hiking trails and bike rentals. ⊠ *17 mi E of Sarasota on Hwy. 72,* ☎ *941/361–6511.* ⊑ *$3.25 per vehicle.* ☉ *Daily 8–sunset.*

**㉘ Mote Marine Aquarium.** The 135,000-gallon shark tank here lets you see its inhabitants from above and below the water's surface. Other tanks show off sharks, rays, and various marine creatures native to the area. A neat touch-tank lets you handle rays, guitar fish, horseshoe crabs, and sea urchins. ⊠ *1600 City Island Park,* ☎ *941/388–2451.* ⊑ *$6.* ☉ *Daily 10–5.*

★ **㉕ Ringling Museums.** Decades ago, circus tycoon John Ringling found Sarasota an ideal winter spot for his clowns and performers to recuperate from their months of travel while preparing for the next journey. Along Sarasota Bay, Ringling also built himself a fancy home, patterned after the Palace of the Doges in Venice, Italy. Today, the Ringling Museums include that mansion, as well as his art museum (with a world-renowned collection of Rubens paintings and 17th-century tapestries) and a museum of circus memorabilia. ⊠ *½ mi south of Sarasota-Bradenton Airport on U.S. 41,* ☎ *941/355–5101.* ⊑ *$8.50 (good for mansion and museums).* ☉ *Daily 10–5:30.*

**㉗ Sarasota Jungle Gardens.** There's a 10-acre spread of tropical plants here—it takes a couple of hours to stroll through it all. Also on site are a petting zoo and playground, a shell and butterfly museum, and reptile and bird shows. ⊠ *3701 Bayshore Rd.,* ☎ *941/355–5305.* ⊑ *$9.* ☉ *Daily 9–5, show daily 10, noon, 2, and 4.*

**㉚ Venice.** This town is crisscrossed with even more canals than the city for which it was named. Venice beaches are quite good for shell collecting, but they're best known for their wealth of sharks' teeth and fossils. ⊠ *U.S. 41 south of Sarasota.*

## Beaches

### Sarasota

**Siesta Beach** (⊠ Beach Rd., Siesta Key) and its 40-acre park contain nature trails, a concession stand, soccer and softball fields, picnicking facilities, a playground, rest rooms, and tennis and volleyball courts. **South Lido Park,** at the southern tip of Lido Key, has one of the largest and best beaches in the region. The sugar-sand beach offers little for shell collectors, but the interests of virtually all other beach lovers are served on its 130 acres, attracting a diverse mix of people. Facilities include nature trails, a volleyball court, playground, horseshoe pits, rest rooms, and picnic grounds. Only 14 acres, **Turtle Beach** (⊠ Midnight Pass Rd., Siesta Key) includes boat ramps, horseshoe pits, picnic and play facilities, a recreation building, rest rooms, and a volleyball court.

### Venice Area

**Caspersen Beach** (⊠ Beach Dr., South Venice) is the county's largest park. It has a nature trail, fishing, picnicking, rest rooms, and lots of beach for those who prefer space to a wealth of amenities. Along with a plentiful mix of shells, observant beachcombers are likely to find sharks' teeth on Venice beaches, washed up from the ancient shark burial grounds just offshore. **Manasota Key** spans much of the county's southern coast, from south of Venice to Englewood. It has two choice beaches: **Manasota,** with a boat ramp, picnic area, and rest rooms, and **Blind Pass** (⊠ both on Manasota Beach Rd.), where you can fish and swim but will find no amenities. **Nokomis Beach** (⊠ Albee Rd.), just north of North Jetty Park, offers rest rooms, a concession, picnic equipment, play areas, two boat ramps, a volleyball court, and fishing. **North Jetty Park** (⊠ Albee Rd.) is at the south end of Casey Key. It's a favorite for family outings, and fossil hunters may get lucky here. Facilities include rest rooms, a concession stand, play and picnic equipment, horseshoes, and a volleyball court.

## Dining and Lodging

### Sarasota

$$$ ✕ **Bijou Cafe.** Wood, brass, and sumptuous green carpeting surround
★ diners in this 1920 gas station-turned-restaurant. Chef-owner Jean Pierre Knaggs's Continental specialties include superb crab cakes with rémoulade sauce, crispy roast duckling with tangerine brandy sauce or cassis and blackberry sauce, rack of lamb for two, and crème brûlée. ⊠ 1287 1st St., ☎ 941/366–8111. DC, MC, V.

$$$ ✕ **Cafe L'Europe.** Located on fashionable St. Armand's Circle, this green-
★ ery- and art-filled café specializes in fresh veal and seafood. Menus change frequently but might include fillet of sole Picasso, Dover sole served with a choice of fruits, or Wiener schnitzel sautéed in butter and topped with anchovies, olives, and capers. ⊠ 431 St. Armand's Circle, ☎ 941/388–4415. AE, DC, MC, V.

$$$ ✕ **Marina Jack.** Eat in the restaurant overlooking Sarasota Bay or, Wednesday through Sunday, take a dinner cruise on the *Marina Jack II,* a paddle wheeler that cruises for two romantic hours with entertainment. Either place, fresh seafood prevails. ⊠ 2 Marina Plaza, ☎ 941/365–4232. MC, V.

$$–$$$ ✕ **Michael's on East.** Prices are reasonable despite the elegant setting of this favorite in downtown Sarasota. The cuisine is contemporary, ranging from penne with grilled summer vegetables and black olives to grilled fillet of beef served with a house specialty—mashed potatoes. A light menu is served in the intimate bar, where there's often piano music or jazz in the evening. The lunch menu includes unusual sandwiches—grilled portobello mushrooms with gouda, for example—and an excellent assortment of fresh salads. ⊠ 1212 East Ave. S, ☎ 941/366–0007. AE, MC, V.

$$ ✕ **Ophelia's on the Bay.** Sample mussel soup, eggplant crepes, chicken pot pie, or cioppino, among other things, at this waterfront restaurant. ⊠ 9105 Midnight Pass Rd., Siesta Key, ☎ 941/349–2212. AE, D, DC, MC, V. No lunch.

$ ✕ **Trolley Station.** Not surprisingly, this popular spot looks and feels a lot like a trolley station, inside and out. Long benches frame the entrance, the cashier sits behind an old-fashioned ticket counter, and people line up for dinner as for the trolley. The offerings range from a salad and baked-potato bar to roast beef, fish, chicken, and pastas. Prices are remarkably low. ⊠ 1941 Stickney Point Rd., ☎ 941/923–2721. AE, MC, V.

$$$$ ✕🏨 **Colony Beach and Tennis Resort.** If tennis is your game, this is the
★ place to stay—such tennis greats as Björn Borg make the Colony their home court, and for good reason. Ten of the resort's 21 courts are clay

hydro-surfaced (the others are hard). And all professionals are USPTA-certified; they run clinics and camps for all levels of players, do video analyses of your game, and play with guests when no other guests are available. They even have scaled-down rackets for children. For those who want more workout, the fitness center provides StairMasters, free weights, yoga, and aerobics classes. And to ease aching muscles, you'll appreciate the spa with its seaweed body packs, facials, massages, hot tubs, steam baths, and more. All accommodations are suites, some sleeping up to eight; private beach houses that open onto sand and sea are also available. The formal Colony Restaurant has garnered several Wine Spectator Grand Awards. Many other activities are available, including ecology-oriented trips and deep-sea fishing. ⊠ *1620 Gulf of Mexico Dr., Longboat Key 34228,* ☎ *941/383–6464 or 800/237–9443; in FL, 800/282–1138;* ⨳ *941/383–7549. 25 rooms, 235 suites. 3 restaurants, bar, pool, 21 tennis courts, health club, children's programs. AE, D, MC, V.*

$$$$ ✕⊞ **Resort at Longboat Key.** Not just another luxury hotel, this beautifully landscaped, 1,000-acre property is one of *the* places to golf in the state and one of the top tennis resorts in the country. Some 5,000 palm trees are scattered around the par-72 Islandside Course, designed by Billy Mitchell; like the championship Harbourside Course, designed by Willard Byrd, the real test is the water. Both have excellent pro shops and offer lessons and clinics. All 38 tennis courts are Har-Tru–surfaced. Hobie Cats, kayaks, Sunfish, deep-sea charters, and ecology trips are aso available. Suites, which accommodate four or six, are done with tropical motifs and light woods; huge private balconies overlook the golf course, beaches, or a private lagoon where manatees can be seen from time to time. Some suites have kitchens. ⊠ *301 Gulf of Mexico Dr., Box 15000, Longboat Key 34228,* ☎ *941/383–8821 or 800/237–8821; in FL, 800/282–0113;* ⨳ *941/383–0359. 228 suites. 4 restaurants, pool, golf courses, 38 tennis courts, beach, library, meeting rooms. AE, DC, MC, V.*

$$$$ ⊞ **Hyatt Sarasota.** The Hyatt is contemporary in design and conveniently located in the heart of the city, across from the Van Wezel Performing Arts Hall, a major cultural attraction. All of the spacious rooms overlook Sarasota Bay or the marina. ⊠ *1000 Blvd. of the Arts, 34236,* ☎ *941/953–1234,* ⨳ *914/952–1987. 297 rooms. 2 restaurants, lounge, pool, sauna, health club, dock, boating. AE, DC, MC, V.*

$$$ ⊞ **Half Moon Beach Club.** You get a sense of the elegance of this sleek horseshoe-shape hotel, on Lido Key just minutes from St. Armand's Circle, as soon as you walk into the alabaster-accented lobby, or take a look at the tropical garden surrounding the pool and, beyond it, the spacious beach deck where you can have a drink. The beach is wide, and partially fringed with forest. Although all rooms and suites are asymmetrical and decorated in shades of pink, each is unique. Four have Gulf views and those on the inside of the horseshoe overlook the pool and garden. ⊠ *2050 Ben Franklin Dr., Lido Beach 34236,* ☎ *941/388–3694 or 800/358–3245,* ⨳ *813/388–1938. 85 rooms, 12 suites. Restaurant, bar, pool, beach. AE, DC, MC, V.*

$$ ⊞ **Best Western Midtown Motor Inn.** This three-story motel is clean, comfortable, and very affordable. Set back from U.S. 41 and somewhat removed from traffic noise, it is within walking distance of a shopping center and several restaurants—including one of Sarasota's most popular spots, Michael's on East—and is central to area attractions and downtown. Rooms, which have seating areas, are done in pale pastel fabrics and blond wood. ⊠ *1425 S. Tamiami Trail, 34239,* ☎ *941/955–9841,* ⨳ *941/954–8948. 100 rooms. Pool. AE, DC, MC, V.*

$$ ⊞ **Days Inn Sarasota-Siesta Key.** Good value is the strong point of this modest but comfortable and well-maintained motel on U.S. 41. Rooms are decorated in earth tones. Beaches are a mile away and many restaurants and shopping centers are close by. ⊠ *6600 S. Tamiami Trail, 34231,* ☎ *941/924–4900,* ℻ *941/923–7774. 132 rooms. Pool. AE, DC, MC, V.*

## Venice

$$ ✕ **Sharky's on the Pier.** Gaze out on the beach and sparkling waters while dining on fresh, grilled seafood. ⊠ *1600 S. Harbor Dr.,* ☎ *941/488–1456. MC, V.*

$$ ⊞ **Days Inn.** This simple but well-kept motel is on the main business route through town—but it's only 10 minutes from the beach. Rooms are comfortable, and pets are allowed. ⊠ *1710 S. Tamiami Trail, 34293,* ☎ *941/493–4558,* ℻ *941/493–1593. 73 rooms. Restaurant, lounge, pool. AE, MC, V.*

$$ ⊞ **Veranda Inn-Venice.** A landscaped pool is the focal point of this small but spacious inn on U.S. 41. All rooms look out on the pool and courtyard. ⊠ *625 S. Tamiami Trail, 34285,* ☎ *941/484–9559,* ℻ *941/484–8235. 38 rooms. Restaurant, pool. AE, DC, MC, V.*

# Nightlife and the Arts

## The Arts

### FILM

The **Sarasota Film Society** operates year-round, showing foreign and art films daily at 2, 5:45, and 8 at the Burns Court Cinema (⊠ 506 Burns La., ☎ 813/388–2441).

### MUSIC

**Florida West Coast Symphony Center** (⊠ 709 N. Tamiami Trail, ☎ 813/953–4252) consists of a number of area groups that perform in Manatee and Sarasota counties regularly: the Florida West Coast Symphony, Florida String Quartet, Florida Brass Quintet, Florida Wind Quintet, and New Artists String Quartet. The **Sarasota Concert Band** (⊠ Van Wezel Performing Arts Hall, 777 N. Tamiami Trail, ☎ 813/955–6660) includes 50 players, many of them full-time musicians. The group performs monthly concerts.

### OPERA

The **Sarasota Opera** (⊠ 61 N. Pineapple Ave., ☎ 813/953–7030) performs February through March in a historic theater downtown. Internationally known artists sing the principal roles, supported by a professional chorus of 24 young apprentices.

### THEATER

The $10 million **Asolo Center for the Performing Arts** (⊠ 5555 N. Tamiami Trail, ☎ 813/351–8000) mounts productions nearly year-round. The small, professional **Florida Studio Theatre** (⊠ 1241 N. Palm Ave., ☎ 813/366–9796) presents contemporary dramas, comedies, and musicals. **Golden Apple Dinner Theatre** (⊠ 25 N. Pineapple Ave., ☎ 813/366–5454) serves up both a standard buffet and musicals and comedies. A long-established community theater, the **Players of Sarasota** (⊠ U.S. 41 and 9th St., ☎ 813/365–2494) has launched such performers as Montgomery Clift and Pee-Wee Herman. The troupe performs comedies, thrillers, and musicals. The **Van Wezel Performing Arts Hall** (⊠ 777 N. Tamiami Trail, Sarasota, ☎ 813/953–3366) is easy to find—just look for the purple shell rising along the bay front. It hosts some 200 performances each year, including Broadway plays, ballet, jazz, rock concerts, symphonies, children's shows, and ice skating.

In Venice, **Theatre Works** (⊠ 1247 1st St., ☏ 813/952–9170) presents professional, non-Equity productions at the Palm Tree Playhouse. **Venice Little Theatre** (⊠ Tampa and Nokomis Aves., ☏ 813/488–1115) is a community theater offering comedies, musicals, and a few dramas during its October–May season.

## Nightlife

**The Patio** (⊠ Columbia Restaurant, St. Armand's Circle, Lido Key, ☏ 813/388–3987), a casual lounge, has live music Wednesday through Sunday. **In Extremis** (⊠ Sarasota Quay, Sarasota, ☏ 813/954–2008) has laser-light shows and high-energy disco and alternative music.

# Outdoor Activities and Sports

## Baseball

The **Chicago White Sox** have spring training at the Ed Smith Stadium (⊠ 2700 12th St., Sarasota, ☏ 941/954–7699).

## Biking

**Bicycles International** (⊠ 744 Tamiami Trail S, Venice, ☏ 941/497–1590) rents its varied stock weekly as well as hourly and daily. **D & S Bicycle Shop** (⊠ 12073 Seminole Blvd., Largo, ☏ 941/393–0300) has bikes of all sizes for rent by the hour, day, or week. **Mr. CB's** (⊠ 1249 Stickney Point Rd., Sarasota, ☏ 941/349–4400) rents hourly and daily.

## Canoeing

At **Myakka River State Park** (⊠ 15 mi southeast of Sarasota on Rte. 72, ☏ 813/361–6511), you can rent canoes, paddles, and life vests.

## Dog Racing

The greyhounds run late December through June at the **Sarasota Kennel Club** (⊠ 5400 Bradenton Rd., Sarasota, ☏ 941/355–7744).

## Fishing

**Marina Jack's** (⊠ U.S. 41 on bay front, Sarasota, ☏ 941/366–3373) has several boats that can be chartered for deep-sea fishing and offers scheduled group trips. **Gulfwater Marine** (⊠ 215 Tamiami Trail S, Venice, ☏ 813/484–9044) is also a good place to try for deep-sea fishing.

## Golf

SARASOTA

**Bobby Jones Golf Course** (☏ 941/955–8097): 18 holes and a driving range. **Forest Lake Golf Course** (☏ 941/922–1312): a driving range and 18 holes. **Resort at Longboat Key** (⊠ Longboat Key, ☏ 941/383–8821): 45 holes and several putting greens.

VENICE

**Bird Bay Executive Golf Course** (☏ 914/485–9333): 18 holes. **Plantation Golf & Country Club** (☏ 813/493–2000): 36 holes and a driving range.

## Tennis

If you love tennis, consider staying at the **Colony Beach and Tennis Resort** or the **Resort at Longboat Key** (☞ *above*), which are among the U.S.'s top tennis resorts.

## Water Sports

**Don and Mike's Boat and Jet Ski Rental** (⊠ 520 Blackburn Point Rd., Sarasota, ☏ 941/966–4000) has water skis, Jet Skis, pontoon boats, and instruction for all activities. For sailboard rentals and lessons try **Gulf Water Sports** (⊠ Colony Beach and Tennis Resort, 1620 Gulf of Mexico Dr., Longboat Key, ☏ 941/383–7692).

# Shopping

**St. Armand's Circle** (⊠ Lido Key) is a cluster of oh-so-exclusive shops and restaurants. If you follow the flea market circuit, check out the **Dome** (⊠ Rte. 775 west of U.S. 41, Venice), which has dozens of stalls under sheltered walkways, where you can buy new and recycled wares. It's open October–August, Friday–Sunday 9–4.

# TAMPA BAY AREA A TO Z

## Arriving and Departing

### By Bus

Service to and throughout the state is provided by **Greyhound Lines** (☎ 800/231–2222; in Tampa ☎ 813/229–2112, St. Petersburg ☎ 813/898–1496, and Sarasota ☎ 941/955–5735).

### By Car

I–75 spans the region from north to south. Once you cross the Florida border from Georgia, it should take about three hours to reach Tampa and another hour to reach Sarasota. If coming from Orlando, you're likely to drive west into Tampa on I–4.

### By Plane

SARASOTA

Sarasota's airport, **Sarasota-Bradenton** (☎ 941/359–5200), lies just north of the city. It is served by **American, Continental, Delta, Northwest, TWA, United,** and **USAir.** Transportation to and from the airport is provided by **Airport Shuttle** (☎ 941/355–9645) and **West Coast Executive Sedan** (☎ 941/359–8600).

The average cab fare between airport and downtown is $15–$25.

TAMPA

Several carriers serve **Tampa International** (☎ 813/870–8700), 6 miles from downtown, including **Air Canada, Air Jamaica, American, Bahamasair, British Airways, Canadian Holidays, Cayman Airlines, Continental, Delta, Mexicana, Northwest, TWA, United, USAir,** and **Virgin Atlantic. Central Florida Limousine** (☎ 813/396–3730) provides airport service to and from Hillsborough and Polk counties. **The Limo** (☎ 813/572–1111 or 800/282–6817) serves Pinellas County.

Expect taxi fares from the airport to be about $12–$25 for most of Hillsborough County and about twice that for Pinellas County.

### By Train

**Amtrak** trains run from the Northeast, Midwest, and much of the South to the Tampa station.

## Getting Around

### By Bus

Around Tampa, the **Hillsborough Area Regional Transit (HART;** ☎ 813/254–4278) serves most of the county. In Sarasota, the public transit company is **Sarasota County Area Transit (SCAT;** ☎ 941/951–5850).

### By Car

I–75 and U.S. 41 (which runs concurrently with the Tamiami Trail for much of the way) stretch the length of the region. U.S. 41 links the business districts of many communities, so it's best to avoid it and all bridges during rush hours, 7–9 AM and 4–6 PM. U.S. 19 is St. Petersburg's major north–south artery; traffic can be heavy, and there are many lights, so use a different route when possible.

I–275 heads west from Tampa across Tampa Bay to St. Petersburg, swings south, and crosses the bay again on its way to Terra Ceia, near Bradenton. Along this last leg—the Sunshine Skyway and its bright-yellow suspension bridge—you'll get a bird's-eye view of bustling Tampa Bay.

The Bayshore Boulevard Causeway also yields a spectacular view of Tampa Bay, and Route 679 takes you along two of St. Petersburg's most pristine islands, Cabbage and Mullet keys. Route 64 connects I–75 to Bradenton and Anna Maria Island. Route 789 carries you over several of the coast's slender barrier islands, past miles of green-blue Gulf waters, beaches, and waterfront homes. The road does not connect all the islands, however; it runs from Holmes Beach off the Bradenton coast south to Lido Beach in Sarasota, then begins again on Casey Key south of Osprey and runs south to Nokomis Beach.

# Contacts and Resources

## Emergencies
Dial **911** for **police** and **ambulance.**

## Guided Tours
AIR TOURS
Helicopter tours of the Tampa Bay area and the Gulf Coast are offered by **Suncoast Helicopters** (⊠ Tampa International Airport, ☎ 813/872–6625). **West Florida Helicopters** (⊠ Albert Whitted Airport, ☎ 813/823–5200) also offers air tours of the area.

BOAT TOURS
The *Lady Anderson* (☎ 813/367–7804) combines sightseeing with lunch and dinner cruises from the St. Petersburg Causeway (⊠ 3400 Pasadena Ave., St. Petersburg Beach), operating October–May. The *Miss Cortez* (☎ 941/794–1223) departs from Cortez, just north of Bradenton, every Tuesday, Thursday, and Sunday for Egmont Key. **Myakka Wildlife Tours** (☎ 813/365–0100) is at Myakka River State Park, east of Sarasota on Route 72; there are four daily hour-long tours of this wildlife sanctuary aboard the *Gator Gal,* a large airboat. The *Starlite Princess* (☎ 813/595–1212), an old-fashioned paddle-wheel excursion boat, has sightseeing and dinner cruises from Hamlin's Landing, Indian Rocks Beach.

## Hospitals
There are 24-hour emergency rooms at **Bayfront Medical Center** (⊠ 701 6th St. S, St. Petersburg), **Manatee Memorial Hospital** (⊠ 206 2nd St. E, Bradenton), **Sarasota Memorial Hospital** (⊠ 1700 S. Tamiami Trail, Sarasota), and **University Community Hospital** (⊠ 3100 E. Fletcher Ave., Tampa).

## Late-Night Pharmacy
**Eckerd Drugs** (⊠ 11613 N. Nebraska Ave., Tampa, ☎ 813/978–0775).

## Visitor Information
**Greater Clearwater Chamber of Commerce** (⊠ 128 N. Osceola Ave., Clearwater 34615, ☎ 813/461–0011). **Greater Dunedin Chamber of Commerce** (⊠ 301 Main St., Dunedin 34698, ☎ 813/736–5066). **Greater Tampa Chamber of Commerce** (⊠ Box 420, Tampa 33601, ☎ 813/228–7777). **Visitors Information Department** (☎ 813/223–1111, Tampa). **Gulf Beaches on Sand Key Chamber of Commerce** (⊠ 501 150th Ave., Madeira Beach 33701, ☎ 813/595–4575 or 813/391–7373). **St. Petersburg Chamber of Commerce** (⊠ 100 2nd Ave. N, St. Petersburg

33701, ☎ 813/821–4069). **St. Petersburg/Clearwater Area Convention & Visitors Bureau** (✉ Thunderdome, 1 Stadium Dr., Suite A, St. Petersburg 33705-1706, ☎ 813/582–7892). **Sarasota Convention Visitors Bureau** (✉ 655 N. Tamiami Trail, Sarasota 34236, ☎ 941/957–1877 or 800/522–9799). **Tampa/Hillsborough Convention and Visitors Association** (✉ 111 Madison St., Suite 1010, Tampa 33601-0519, ☎ 800/826–8358; information and hotel reservations, ☎ 800/448–2672; vacation packages, ☎ 800/284–0404). **Tarpon Springs Chamber of Commerce** (✉ 210 S. Pinellas Ave., Suite 120, Tarpon Springs 34689, ☎ 813/937–6109). **Treasure Island Chamber of Commerce** (✉ 108th Ave., Treasure Island 33706, ☎ 813/367–4529).

# 10 Southwest Florida

*Most noted for Sanibel Island, a low-key spot home to world-class shelling, and Naples, a once-sleepy fishing village that's developed fast, this region is subtropical to the core. Unlike the East Coast, much of the development here has been inland of the mangrove swamps, and the area prides itself on the number of access points along its 41 miles of sand.*

T**HE SOUTHWEST FLORIDA COAST** is often called "Florida's Florida" because its natural subtropical environment has made it a favorite vacation spot for

Updated by
Pamela
Acheson

Florida natives as well as visitors from across the United States and abroad. There's lots to do in this small corner of the state and, although much activity centers on sun and surf, there are several distinctly different travel destinations in a relatively compact area.

Fort Myers is a small and pretty inland city built along the Caloosahatchee River. It got its nickname, "the City of Palms," from the hundreds of towering royal palms that inventor Thomas Edison planted along McGregor Boulevard, the main residential street and site of his winter estate. Edison's idea caught on, and there are now more than 2,000 royal palms on McGregor Boulevard alone.

Off the coast west of Fort Myers, more than 100 barrier islands range in length from just a few feet to over 20 miles. Here you'll find Sanibel and Captiva, two thoughtfully developed resort islands. Connected to the mainland by a 3-mile causeway, Sanibel is known for its world-class shelling, fine fishing, luxury hotels and restaurants (at the south end of the island), and its wildlife refuge. You won't be able to see most of the houses, which are shielded by tall Australian pines, but the beaches and tranquil Gulf waters are readily accessible.

Down the coast is Naples, once a small fishing village and now a thriving and sophisticated town—something like a smaller version of Palm Beach. There are a number of fine restaurants and several upscale shopping complexes, including the gracious, tree-lined 3rd Street South area. The number of golf courses per capita in Naples is said to be the highest in the world, a 1,200-seat performing arts hall attracts world-class performers, and the town is the west coast home of the Miami City Ballet. Unlike Palm Beach, the Naples area offers easy access to its many miles of sun-drenched white beach.

East of Naples stretches the wilderness of the Big Cypress National Preserve, and a half hour south is Marco Island, with several large resorts, good beaches, restaurants, and shops. Still farther southeast on U.S. 41 is Everglades City, the western gateway to Everglades National Park (☞ Chapter 4).

## Pleasures and Pastimes

### Beaches
Southwest Florida has beautiful white sand beaches along the coast and on the many barrier islands just offshore. Many beaches are prime shelling spots.

### Biking
There are excellent opportunities for biking in the less populated areas of southwest Florida. Boca Grande, a barrier island about an hour from Fort Myers, has good bike paths. Sanibel Island's well-maintained and extensive bike lanes run throughout the island but away from traffic, providing safe routes and allowing for plenty of opportunity to enjoy the scenic waterways and wildlife.

### Canoeing
Sanibel Island's J.N. "Ding" Darling National Wildlife Refuge is a popular spot for canoeing. There are also many opportunities to canoe inland in the less developed areas of the region; several outfits offer half- and full-day trips and overnighters.

## Dining

In Fort Myers and Naples, seafood reigns supreme. Expect ample fresh fish on the menu. A particular treat is a succulent claw of the native stone crab usually served with drawn butter or a tangy mustard sauce and in season from mid-October through mid-May. Many restaurants offer early-bird menus with seating before 6 PM.

## Fishing

Tarpon, kingfish, speckled trout, snapper, grouper, sea trout, snook, sheepshead, and shark are among the species to be found in coastal waters. You can charter your own boat or join a group for full- or half-day outings.

## Golf

Southwest Florida has one of the highest concentrations of golf courses in the nation. In fact, Naples alone has more than 40 courses (new ones are opening all the time) and *Golf Digest* named it the "Golf Capital of the World."

## Lodging

Generally, inland rooms are considerably cheaper than those on the islands or along the shore, with waterfront accommodations being on the upper end of the price scale. Recent years, however, have seen the creation of many apartment-motels that bring great savings for families or groups, especially if dining costs are cut by cooking some of your own meals. Rates are highest between mid-December and mid-April. The lowest prices are available from May to November.

## Shopping

Prepare to shell out some cash for at least one kitschy crustacean creation. As one of the world's premier shelling grounds, Sanibel Island has numerous shops seriously selling shells (try to say that three times fast)—from lamps to jewelry. Naples has many upscale stores carrying gift items, men's and women's clothing, shoes, linens, and lingerie.

## Spectator Sports

Several major-league baseball teams offer exhibitions during spring training in March and April. For information on all the teams, call the Florida Sports Foundation at ☎ 904/488–8347. There is dog racing outside of Fort Myers.

## Tennis

Most resorts and hotels and many motels in Florida have outdoor tennis courts, and most are lighted. Plus, nearly every town has public tennis facilities.

# Exploring Southwest Florida

Vacationers to southwest Florida tend to spend most of their time outdoors—swimming, sunning, shelling, or playing tennis or golf. Fort Myers is the only inland destination; it is situated along a winding river and has a number of interesting museums. The offshore barrier islands vary from tiny undeveloped islands to popular vacation spots with numerous hotels and restaurants. Sanibel and Captiva, connected to each other and to the mainland by causeways, offer beautiful beaches, some of the best shelling in Florida, and a superb wildlife preserve. Naples is a sophisticated town with art galleries, fine dining, and upscale shopping and rapid development along its north shore. Nearby is Marco Island, where you can take an airboat to see tight clusters of tiny undeveloped islands. While high-rise condominiums and hotels line much of Marco Island's waterfront, many natural areas have been pre-

served, including the tiny fishing village of Goodland, an outpost of
Old Florida.

## Great Itineraries

Visitors to southwest Florida are generally in search of warm sun, white
sand, and an outdoor diversion such as tennis or golf. For those who
want more to do, there are numerous appealing attractions that can
take anywhere from an hour to a full day.

*Numbers in the text below correspond to numbers in the margin and
on the map.*

### IF YOU HAVE 2 OR 3 DAYS

🏠 **Fort Myers** ① is a good base for a short visit; it's not directly on
the beach, but its central location makes day trips easy. In the downtown area visit Thomas Edison's Winter Home, one of the best museums in southwest Florida. To visit **Sanibel Island** ④, follow McGregor
Boulevard out of Fort Myers—it's a beautiful road lined with palm trees.
Once on the island, stop by the new Bailey-Matthews Shell Museum,
which displays more than a million shells from around the world, and
the J. N. "Ding" Darling National Wildlife Refuge. In **Naples** ⑧,
south of Fort Myers on I–95, you'll find the 52-acre Caribbean Gardens, which showcases tropical flora and exotic wildlife, including tigers.
Those with a warm spot in their heart for teddy bears should stop by
the Teddy Bear Museum of Naples.

### IF YOU HAVE 4 OR 5 DAYS

With a little extra time for getting around, you'll be able to stay near
the water. Head into **Fort Myers** ① for a day to see Thomas Edison's
Winter Home and the neighboring Mangoes property, winter home of
automaker Henry Ford. About 11 miles northeast of downtown is **Babcock Wilderness Adventures** ③; here you can ride a swamp buggy and
spot alligators, deer, and bobcats. On 🏠 **Sanibel Island** ④ you can spend
more time at the J. N. "Ding" Darling National Wildlife Refuge—you
could even try an early morning or evening bird-watch. Moving south
to 🏠 **Naples** ⑧, visit the Caribbean Gardens park to see exotic wildlife
and wander through tropical gardens. For even more wildlife, head northeast to the **Corkscrew Swamp Sanctuary** ⑩, where you can walk
along a boardwalk through a nature preserve managed by the National
Audubon Society.

### IF YOU HAVE 10 DAYS

During an extended stay you'll have time to book accommodations in
Sanibel and Fort Myers before heading south to Naples. When exploring
the 🏠 **Fort Myers** ① area, you can get a taste of southern viticulture
at the Eden Vineyards Winery and Park; or, if the Babcock Wilderness
Adventures has whetted your ecological appetite, head to the Calusa
Nature Center and Planetarium. While staying on 🏠 **Sanibel Island**
④ you might want to spend a day on an isolated key, such as **Cabbage
Key** ⑦ or **Boca Grande** ⑥. For the second half of your trip you might
relocate to 🏠 **Naples** ⑧, where you can combine beach activities with
days of wandering through art galleries and shops in Olde Naples. The
Caribbean Gardens and the **Corkscrew Swamp Sanctuary** ⑩ are good
bets for kids; to try your hand at paddling, you can rent a canoe or
kayak at the Naples Nature Center.

## When to Tour Southwest Florida

In winter, this part of Florida is one of the warmest areas of the United
States and is a hugely popular destination. From January through
April you may find it next to impossible to find a hotel room. Although
winter temperatures are likely to be relatively warm, the weather is occasionally cold, even for a visitor from up north. Fewer people visit in

the off season, but there really is no bad time to visit this part of Florida. Ocean breezes keep the coast cool even in summer.

# FORT MYERS AREA

## Fort Myers

*Numbers in the margin correspond to points of interest on the Southwest Florida map.*

❶ **Fort Myers,** a small, inviting inland city, stretches along the southern edge of the Caloosahatchee River. Although the nearest beach is a half hour away, there is still plenty to do here. The town is best known as the winter home of inventors Thomas A. Edison and Henry Ford.

### Sights to See

**Calusa Nature Center and Planetarium.** For a look at frequently changing exhibits on wildlife, fossils, and Florida's native animals and habitats, this tour is a must. Rustic boardwalks lead through subtropical wetlands, an aviary, and a village. There are snake and alligator demonstrations several times daily. The planetarium offers star shows, laser light shows, and Cinema-360 films in its 90-seat theater. ⊠ *3450 Ortiz Ave., Fort Myers,* ☎ *941/275–3435.* ☜ *Nature center $3, planetarium $3, laser light and music shows $5 per person.* ☉ *Nature center Mon.–Sat. 9–5, Sun. 11–5; planetarium Thurs.–Sun. 9–5.*

**ECHO.** The Educational Concerns for Hunger Organization (ECHO) is a small, active group striving to solve the world's hunger problems. The group offers tours of its gardens (which feature the largest collection of tropical food plants in Florida), walks through a simulated rain forest, and looks at crops such as sesame and rice grown without soil. ⊠ *17430 Durrance Rd., North Fort Myers,* ☎ *941/543–3246.* ☜ *Free.* ☉ *Tours Tues., Fri., and Sat. at 10 or by appointment.*

**Fort Myers Historical Museum.** Housed in a restored railroad depot, this collection showcases the area's history dating back to 1200 BC. Displays include prehistoric Calusa artifacts, a reconstructed *chickee* hut, canoes, clothing and photos from Seminole settlements, and the Ethel Cooper collection of decorative glass. A favorite attraction is the **Esperanza,** a 1930s private rail car. ⊠ *2300 Peck St.,* ☎ *941/332–5955.* ☜ *$2.50.* ☉ *Mon.–Sat. 9–4:30, Sun. 1–5.*

**McGregor Boulevard.** One of the most scenic stretches of highway in southeastern Florida is McGregor Boulevard. Lined with majestic palm trees, some planted by Thomas Edison, the street runs from downtown Fort Myers to the Gulf of Mexico.

**Thomas Edison's Winter Home.** The city's premier attraction contains a laboratory, botanical gardens, and a museum. A remarkable showpiece, the house was donated to the city by Edison's widow. As a result, the laboratory is not merely reconstructed but just as Edison left it. The property straddles McGregor Boulevard about a mile west of U.S. 41 near downtown Fort Myers. The inventor spent his winters on the 14-acre estate, developing the phonograph and teletype, experimenting with rubber, and planting some 600 species of plants from those collected throughout the world. Next door is **Mangoes,** the more modest winter home of fellow inventor and longtime friend, automaker Henry Ford. It is said that the V-8 engine was primarily designed on the back porch of this home. ⊠ *2350 McGregor Blvd.,* ☎ *941/334–3614.* ☜ *Edison home and Mangoes (combined) $10.* ☉ *Tours Mon.–Sat. 9–4, Sun. noon–4. Closed Thanksgiving and Dec. 25.*

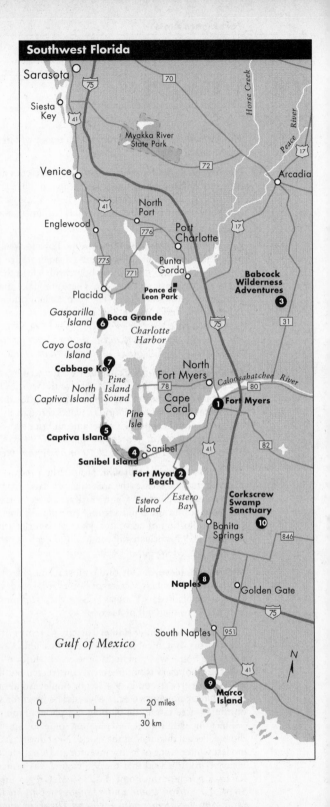

**Southwest Florida**

Sarasota

Siesta Key

75

41

70

Myakka River State Park

Horse Creek

Peace River

17

Venice

41

North Port

72

Arcadia

17

Englewood

776

Port Charlotte

775

771

Punta Gorda

Ponce de Leon Park

Babcock Wilderness Adventures ③

31

Placida

75

Gasparilla Island ⑥ **Boca Grande**

Charlotte Harbor

Cayo Costa Island

⑦ **Cabbage Key**

Pine Island Sound

North Captiva Island

Pine Isle

North Fort Myers

78

Caloosahatchee River

80

① **Fort Myers**

82

Cape Coral

⑤ **Captiva Island**

④ Sanibel

**Sanibel Island**

41

**Fort Myers Beach** ②

Estero Island

Estero Bay

**Corkscrew Swamp Sanctuary**
⑩

Bonita Springs

846

**Naples** ⑧

Golden Gate

75

*Gulf of Mexico*

South Naples

951

N

41

⑨ **Marco Island**

0          20 miles

0          30 km

## Dining and Lodging

**$$$** ✕ **Prawnbroker Restaurant and Fish Market.** This dyed-in-the-wool
★   establishment has ads urging you to scratch and sniff—there is no odor,
says the ad, because truly fresh fish has no odor. The restaurant has
an abundance of seafood seemingly just plucked from Gulf waters, plus
some selections for culinary landlubbers. This place is almost always
crowded, for good reason. ✉ *13451 McGregor Blvd.,* ☎ *941/489–
2226. AE, MC, V. No lunch.*

**$$** ✕ **The Veranda.** An imaginative assortment of American regional cuisine, with an emphasis on Southern cooking, is turned out in this
sprawling turn-of-the-century home. This is a popular place for business and government bigwigs. Courtyard and indoor dining is available. ✉ *2122 2nd St.,* ☎ *941/332–2065. AE, DC, MC, V.*

**$** ✕ **Mel's Diner.** During peak hours you have to wait for a table, but
★   it's worth it at this 1950s-style diner, which serves real mashed potatoes, homemade soups, spicy chili, and blue-plate specials. For dessert,
try their popular mile-high pies. ✉ *4820 Cleveland Ave.,* ☎ *941/275–
7850. No credit cards.*

**$** ✕ **Miami Connection.** If you hunger for choice chopped liver, lean-but-
tender corned beef, and a chewy bagel, this kosher-style deli can fill
the bill. The sandwiches are huge. It is, as the local restaurant critic
aptly said, "the real McCohen." ✉ *11506 Cleveland Ave.,* ☎ *941/936–
3811. No credit cards. No dinner.*

**$** ✕ **Mill Bakery, Eatery, and Brewery.** Homemade beer is just one of the
draws (draughts?) at this popular spot. People flock to dine on freshly
baked breads, pizzas, deli-style stacked sandwiches, and prime rib. ✉
*11491 S. Cleveland Ave.,* ☎ *941/939–2739. AE, MC, V.*

**$$$** 🏨 **Sheraton Harbor Place.** This modern, pink high-rise hotel commands
a dominant spot in the downtown Fort Myers skyline, rising above the
Caloosahatchee River and Fort Myers Yacht Basin. Well-furnished
rooms have panoramic views of the water and surrounding city. An
unusual indoor/outdoor bar is complete with waterfalls. Restaurants,
the Harborside Convention Center, and Thomas Edison's Winter Home
are all within easy walking distance. ✉ *2500 Edwards Dr., 33901,* ☎
*941/337–0300 or 800/325–3535,* 🖷 *941/337–1530. 417 rooms.
Bar, pool, whirlpool, tennis, exercise room, dock, game room. AE, DC,
MC, V.*

## Nightlife and the Arts

THE ARTS

**The Barbara B. Mann Performing Arts Hall** (✉ 8099 College Pkwy. SW,
☎ 941/481–4849) presents plays, concerts, musicals, and dance pro-
grams. **The Broadway Palm Dinner Theater** (✉ 1380 Colonial Blvd.,
☎ 941/278–4422) serves up buffet dinner along with some of Broad-
way's best comedies and musicals. Call for schedules for both.

NIGHTLIFE

**Flashback's Bar and Grill** (✉ 2855 Colonial Blvd., ☎ 941/275–4487)
has country-dancing lessons Tues. and Wed. 7:30–8:30, followed by
open dancing. **Shoeless Joe's Sports Cafe** (✉ Holiday Inn, 13051 Bell
Tower Dr., ☎ 941/482–2900) plays Top 40 tunes, usually with live
bands every night but Monday. Musicians play nightly at **Upstairs at
Peter's** (✉ 2224 Bay St., ☎ 941/332–2228). The music is usually blues,
but about once a week there's jazz.

## Outdoor Activities and Sports

BASEBALL

The **Boston Red Sox** (✉ 2201 Edison Ave., ☎ 941/334–4700) play in
Fort Myers during their spring training sojourn. The **Minnesota Twins**

(⊠ Lee County Sports Complex, 1410 Six Mile Cypress Pkwy., ☎ 941/768–4278) play exhibition games in March and April during spring training.

BIKING

The best choice in Fort Myers is the path along Summerlin Road; for rentals, try **Trikes & Bikes & Mowers** (⊠ 3224 Fowler St., ☎ 941/936–4301).

FISHING

Party-boat and private charters can be arranged at **Deebold's Marina** (⊠ 1071 San Carlos Blvd., ☎ 941/466–3525).

GOLF

The **Eastwood Golf Club** (⊠ 4600 Bruce Herd Ln., ☎ 941/275–4848) has a practice range and an 18-hole course. **The Fort Myers Country Club** (⊠ 3591 McGregor Blvd., ☎ 941/936–2457) offers golf lessons and an 18-hole course.

TENNIS

**Lochmoor Country Club** (⊠ 3911 Orange Grove Blvd., North Fort Myers, ☎ 941/995–0501) has two Har-Tru clay courts; lessons are available.

WATER SPORTS

For sailing lessons or bareboat or captained sail cruises, contact **Fort Myers Yacht Charters** (⊠ Port Sanibel Yacht Club, South Fort Myers, ☎ 941/466–1800) or **Southwest Florida Yachts** (⊠ 3444 Marinatown La. NW, Fort Myers, ☎ 941/656–1339 or 800/262–7939).

## Shopping

Historic downtown **First Street** has been renovated and features charming restaurants and stores as well as street musicians and artists. **Bell Tower** (⊠ U.S 41 and Daniels Rd., South Fort Myers), an outdoor shopping center catering to upscale tastes, has about 50 boutiques and specialty shops, a large department store, and three multiplex cinemas. **Royal Palm Square** (⊠ Colonial Blvd. between McGregor Blvd. and U.S. 41) has more than two dozen shops and restaurants set amid waterways and tropical foliage. **Sanibel Factory Outlets** (⊠ McGregor Blvd. and Summerlin Rd.) has 35 brand-name outlets, including Dexter, Van Heusen, Maidenform, and Corning/Revere. **The Shell Factory** (⊠ 2787 N. Tamiami Trail, North Fort Myers, ☎ 941/995–2141) claims to have the world's largest display of seashells and coral.

# Around Fort Myers

On the north side of the Caloosahatchee River, across from Fort Myers, ❷ is Cape Coral, a relaxed residential town. **Fort Myers Beach,** on an island off the coast southwest of Fort Myers, is a casual, laid-back place lined with motels, hotels, and restaurants. Two other small islands make up the Carl E. Johnson Recreation Area, which is reserved for boating, fishing, and other outdoor activities.

## Sights to See

★ ❸ **Babcock Wilderness Adventures.** See what Florida looked like centuries ago, about 11 miles northeast of downtown Fort Myers. Here swamp buggies take you on 90-minute excursions through the Telegraph Cypress Swamp on the 90,000-acre Babcock Crescent B Ranch, southeast of Punta Gorda. Among the inhabitants you are likely to see are turkey, deer, bobcats, alligators, cows, and a herd of bison. Reservations are essential. ⊠ *Rte. 31, Fort Myers,* ☎ *941/489–3911.* 🖙 *$15.95.* ⊘ *4 tours daily, weather permitting; closed Mon. May–Dec. and Sun.*

**Carl E. Johnson Recreation Area** lies on the two islands between Estero Island and Bonita Beach. Admission covers a round-trip tram ride from the park entrance in Bonita Beach. Shelling, bird-watching, fishing, canoeing, and nature walks in an unspoiled setting are the main attractions here. There are also rest rooms, picnic tables, a snack bar, and showers. ⊠ *Rte. 865, Black Island* ☞ *$1.50.*

★ ☙ ★ **Children's Science Center.** Nature walks, bubblebins, xeriscape displays, mazes, optical tricks, mind-benders, and brain twisters are just some of the attractions here. ⊠ *2915 N.E. Pine Island Rd., Cape Coral,* ☎ *941/997–0012.* ☞ *$4.* ☉ *Weekdays 9:30–4:30, weekends noon–5.*

**Eden Vineyards Winery and Park.** Even connoisseurs can't resist a stop here, reputed to be the southernmost bonded winery in the United States. Besides half a dozen kinds of traditional wine, the vineyard puts its own spin on the trade with carambola (starfruit) wine. The family-owned winery offers tours, tastings, picnics, and tram rides. Reservations are needed for groups of 10 or more. ⊠ *10.2 mi east of I–75 on Rte. 80, Fort Myers,* ☎ *941/728–9463.* ☞ *$2.50; complimentary tasting.* ☉ *Daily 11–5, last tour 3:30.*

**Estero Island.** A bit south of the Pine Island Sound barrier islands and just 18 miles away from Fort Myers is Estero Island. You'll find the marina at the north end of the island, which is the starting point for much boating activity including sunset cruises, sightseeing cruises, and deep-sea fishing.

☙ **Sun Splash Family Waterpark.** This waterpark has more than two dozen wet and dry attractions, including three large water slides, the Lilypad Walk, where you step from one floating "lilypad" to another, an arcade, and Squirtworks, a special play area for very young children. ⊠ *400 Santa Barbara Blvd., Cape Coral,* ☎ *941/574–0558.* ☞ *$8.50.* ☉ *Mid-Mar.–May, Wed.–Fri. 11–5, weekends 10–5; June–Aug., Sun.–Wed. and Fri. 10–6, Thurs. and Sat. 10–9; Aug.–Oct., weekends 10–5.*

## Beaches

**Lynn Hall Memorial Park** is on Estero Boulevard, in the more commercial northern part of Estero Island. The shore slopes gradually into the usually tranquil and warm Gulf waters, providing a safe swimming area for children. Since this beach is, for the most part lined with houses, condominiums, and hotels, you're never far from civilization. A number of nightspots and restaurants are also within easy walking distance. There's a free fishing pier, picnic tables, barbecue grills, playground equipment, and a bathhouse with rest rooms. ☉ *Daily 7 AM–10 PM, lifeguards on duty 10–5:45.*

## Dining and Lodging

$$$ ✕ **Dario's Restaurant and Lounge.** This casual yet quiet and intimate
★ place, with candlelight and tablecloths, serves gourmet northern Italian and Continental cuisine. People head here for the delicious chicken Dario (breast of chicken in a garlic and white wine sauce) and for the wide selection of other excellently prepared entrées, plus several nightly specials. Save room for the desserts, which are all homemade. It's tough to choose between the tiramisù and the Cappuccino Commotion. ⊠ *1805 Del Prado Blvd., Cape Coral,* ☎ *941/574–7798. AE, MC, V. No lunch weekends.*

$$ ✕ **Cape Crab and SteakHouse.** Crabs are served Maryland-style—heaped on a tablecloth of newspaper with a mallet on the side. Don't want to whack out some frustrations on your dinner? A more refined second

dining room has linen tablecloths and a piano player. ⊠ *Coralwood Mall, Del Prado Blvd., Cape Coral,* ☎ *941/574–2722. AE, MC, V.*

**$**    ✕ **Siam Hut.** Thai music pings and twangs in the background while your taste buds do the same. Specialties are pad thai (a mixture of noodles, crushed peanuts, chicken, shrimp, egg, bean sprouts, and scallions) and crispy Siam rolls (spring rolls stuffed with ground chicken, bean thread, and vegetables). Get it fiery hot or extra mild. ⊠ *1873 Del Prado Blvd., Coral Pointe Shopping Center, Cape Coral,* ☎ *941/772–3131. AE, MC, V.*

**$$$**    🏨 **Outrigger Beach Resort.** This informal, family-oriented resort is set on a wide beach overlooking the Gulf of Mexico. Rooms and efficiencies are decorated in bright prints. Views vary so ask when making reservations. The resort also has a broad deck for sunning, tiki huts to sit under when you want to escape from the heat, and a beachfront pool. ⊠ *6200 Estero Blvd., Fort Myers Beach, 33931,* ☎ *941/463–3131 or 800/749–3131. 144 units. Pool, shuffleboard, volleyball, beach, water sports, bicycles, laundry. MC, V.*

**$$–$$$**    🏨 **Best Western Pink Shell Beach Resort.** Set on 12 acres, this beach-
**★**    front and very family-focused resort offers accommodations ranging from cottages on stilts to rooms and apartments in a five-story building. There are children's, social, and recreation programs. ⊠ *275 Estero Blvd., Fort Myers Beach, 33931,* ☎ *941/463–6181,* FAX *941/463–1229. 208 units. 3 pools, tennis courts, shuffleboard, volleyball, water sports, beach, fishing. AE, MC, V.*

**$–$$**    🏨 **Cape Coral Golf & Tennis Resort.** Aimed at golf and tennis enthusiasts, this resort is a good value. In the main clubhouse is a reception area and the restaurant; the 100 comfortably furnished rooms are in a nearby two-story, motel-like building. Understated decor reflects the sporty atmosphere. ⊠ *4003 Palm Tree Blvd., Cape Coral, 33904,* ☎ *941/542–3191 or 941/542–4694. 100 rooms. Restaurant, lounge, pool, driving range, golf, tennis, baby-sitting. AE, DC, MC, V.*

**$–$$**    🏨 **Quality Inn.** Conveniently located in downtown Cape Coral near parks, beaches, restaurants, and malls, this motel offers no-smoking and wheelchair-accessible rooms with complimentary breakfast and newspaper. Pets permitted. ⊠ *1538 Cape Coral Pkwy., Cape Coral, 33904,* ☎ *941/542–2121,* FAX *941/542–6319. 146 rooms. Pool. AE, DC, MC.*

## Outdoor Activities and Sports

### CANOEING

Up the Peace River, about 25 miles northeast of Fort Myers, **Canoe Safari** (⊠ 3020 N.W. Rte. 661, Arcadia, ☎ 941/494–7865) operates half- and full-day trips, plus overnighters including camping equipment.

### GOLF

The **Bay Beach Club Executive Golf Course** (⊠ 7401 Estero Blvd., Fort Myers Beach, ☎ 941/463–2064) has 18 holes and a practice range; golf lessons are also available. **Coral Oaks Golf Course** (⊠ 1800 NW 28th Ave., Cape Coral, ☎ 941/283–4100) has an 18-hole course and a practice range. A practice range and 18-hole course can also be found at the **Cypress Pines Country Club** (⊠ Lehigh Acres, ☎ 941/369–8216).

## Shopping

Just east of Fort Myers, **Fleamasters Fleamarket** (about 1 mile west of I–75 Exit 23 on Rte. 82) features covered walkways and hundreds of vendors selling new and used items. It's open Fri.–Sun. 8–4.

# PORT CHARLOTTE AND PUNTA GORDA

The small town of Port Charlotte and the even smaller town of Punta Gorda are at the mouth of the Peace River, where it empties into Charlotte Harbor. Although both towns are on the water, they are not on the ocean, and the closest beach is about 20 minutes away. This is a good destination if you're interested in canoeing, walking through the Florida wilderness, and most of all, escaping the crowds.

## Sights to See

**Cypress Knee Museum.** You won't just happen upon this attraction; 40 minutes east of Punta Gorda, you'll spy spindly hand-carved signs along U.S. 27 with such sayings as LADY, IF HE WON'T STOP, HIT HIM ON THE HEAD WITH A SHOE. In the museum are hundreds of cypress knees—the knotty, gnarled protuberances that sprout mysteriously from the bases of some cypress trees and grow to resemble all manner of people and things. Specimens resemble dogs, bears, ballet dancers' feet, an ant eater, Joseph Stalin, and Franklin D. Roosevelt. There's also a beautiful ¼-mile walk into a cypress swamp. ⊠ ¼ mi north of Rte. 29 on U.S. 27, Palmdale, ☎ 941/675–2951. ☞ Donations welcome. ◷ Daily 8–sunset.

**Florida Adventure Museum.** This museum features mounted animal specimens from Africa and North America, as well as a rotating exhibit on local artifacts such as fossils. A variety of programs entertain and educate the kids. ⊠ 260 W. Retta Esplanade, Punta Gorda, ☎ 941/639–3777. ☞ Donations welcome. ◷ Weekdays 8:30–5, Sat. 10–3.

**Gatorama.** Take a good long gander at some gators; more than 1,000 alligators and assorted crocodiles await at Gatorama, smiling toothily. A variety of species and sizes cohabit. This is also a commercial gator farm, so you'll see how the "mink" of the leather trade is raised for profit. ⊠ 3 mi south of Rte. 29 on U.S. 27, Palmdale, ☎ 941/675–0623. ☞ $4.50. ◷ Daily 8–6.

## Beaches

**Englewood Beach,** near the Charlotte–Sarasota County line, is popular with teenagers, although beachgoers of all ages frequent it. In addition to a wide and shell-littered beach, there are barbecue grills, picnic facilities, boat ramps, a fishing pier, and a playground.

## Dining and Lodging

$$ ✕ **Salty's Harborside.** Although seafood is the specialty here, including some of the freshest mahimahi and grouper around, you'll also find a menu packed with grilled filet mignon, rosemary chicken, and various salads. The dining room looks out on Burnt Store Marina and Charlotte Harbor. ⊠ Burnt Store Rd., Punta Gorda, ☎ 941/639–3650. AE, DC, MC, V.

$$$ 🏠 **Burnt Store Marina Resort.** For boating, golfing, and getting away from it all, this sprawling resort and marina fills the bill. Modern one- and two-bedroom apartments are situated along a relatively undeveloped stretch of vast Charlotte Harbor. All have kitchens, and some face the water. ⊠ 3150 Matecumbe Key Rd., Punta Gorda 33955, ☎ 941/575–4488 or 800/859–7529. 39 1-bedroom suites, 1 2-bedroom suite. Restaurant, lounge, pool, tennis, boating. AE, DC, MC.

$$ 🏠 **Days Inn of Port Charlotte.** Although this modern three-story motel is on Charlotte County's major business route between Fort Myers and

Sarasota, it's off the highway on oak-shaded grounds and offers free coffee in the lobby, as well as a refrigerator in every room. ⊠ *1941 Tamiami Trail, Port Charlotte 33948* ☎ *813/627–8900,* ℻ *813/743– 8503. 126 rooms. Pool. AE, DC, MC, V.*

## Outdoor Activities and Sports

### Baseball

The **Texas Rangers** (⊠ Charlotte County Stadium, Rte. 776, Port Charlotte, ☎ 941/625–9500) hold exhibition games during spring training.

### Canoeing

With several locations throughout Florida, **Canoe Outpost** (⊠ Rte. 7, Arcadia, ☎ 941/494–1215) conducts all-day and overnight canoe trips; camping equipment is included.

### Fishing

**King Fisher Charter** (⊠ Fishermen's Village, Punta Gorda, ☎ 941/639– 0969) offers deep-sea fishing on half- and full-day trips.

### Golf

The **Burnt Store Marina Resort** (3150 Matecumbe Key Rd., Punta Gorda, ☎ 941/332–7334) has 27 holes of golf and lessons are available. There are 18 holes of golf at the **Deep Creek Golf Club** (⊠ 1260 San Cristobal Ave., Port Charlotte, ☎ 941/625–6911).

### Tennis

**Port Charlotte Tennis Club** (⊠ 22400 Gleneagles Terr., Port Charlotte, ☎ 941/625–7222) features four hard-surface courts lit for night play.

# THE BARRIER ISLANDS

Forming a backwards "J," dozens of islands curve toward Fort Myers and Cape Coral, separated from the mainland by Pine Island Sound. Easily reached by a causeway, Sanibel and Captiva islands are the most-visited spots; to reach many of the other islands (some uninhabited), a short boat trip is necessary. The tourist-pampering hotels on Sanibel and Captiva have counterparts in neighboring islands such as Cabbage Key and Pine Island, which have older properties and a sleepier atmosphere. When exploring the beaches, keep one eye on the sand; shelling is a major pursuit in these parts.

## Sanibel Island and Captiva Island

**④**
**⑤**
About 23 miles from downtown Fort Myers, popular **Sanibel Island** and its quieter northern neighbor, **Captiva Island,** are reached via the Sanibel Causeway. There is a $3 round-trip bridge toll, but avid shell collectors and nature enthusiasts will get their money's worth, for Sanibel's beaches are rated among the best shelling grounds in the world. For the choicest pickings, arrive as the tide is going out or just after a storm—you'll probably see plenty of other shell-seekers with the telltale "Sanibel stoop." Captiva has more private development than Sanibel, and its resorts reflect this sense of seclusion.

### Sights to See

★ **J. N. "Ding" Darling National Wildlife Refuge.** Footpaths, winding canoe routes, and the 5-mile, dirt Wildlife Drive meander through this beautiful refuge on Sanibel Island. Visitors can drive, walk, bicycle, canoe, or ride a specially designed open-air tram with a naturalist on board. With 5,030 acres, the area covers about a third of the island and is home to raccoons, otters, alligators, and numerous exotic birds, such as roseate spoonbills, egrets, ospreys, and herons. Walk among sea grape, wax and salt myrtles, red mangrove, sabal palms, and other flora native to Florida. An observation tower along the road is a prime bird-watching site, especially in the early morning and just before dusk. ⊠ *Refuge: Sanibel-Captiva Rd.,* ☎ *941/472–1100; Tarpon Bay Recreation Center, 941/472–8900.* ⌨ *$4 per car, $1 per pedestrian/bicyclist, $15 duck stamp (which covers all national wildlife refuges), tram $6.75.* ☉ *Wildlife Drive Sat. and Mon.–Thurs. 7–5:45, visitor center daily 9–5, tram weekdays except Fri., Sat. 10:30, 1, 3:15; Sun. 2.*

**Sanibel Lighthouse.** At the southern tip of Sanibel Island stands a historic wooden lighthouse, a frequently photographed landmark. It was built in 1884 when the entire island was a nature preserve. While you can't enter the lighthouse itself, the beach there is especially good for shell collecting. ⊠ *Old Lighthouse Beach, Sanibel Island.*

★ **Bailey-Matthews Shell Museum.** As though to one-up the nearby beaches, this collection contains more than a million shells from around the world. The centerpiece, a 6-foot revolving globe, shows visitors where in the world the museum's shells are found. Novice collectors can identify their beach finds by comparing their own shells with the numerous local specimens displayed. ⊠ *3075 Sanibel-Captiva Rd.,* ☎ *941/395–2233.* ⌨ *$4.* ☉ *Tues.–Sun. 10–4.*

## Beaches

**Bowman's Beach** is mainly a family beach on Sanibel's northwest end. Off of Sanibel-Captiva Road, **Gulfside Park** is a lesser-known and less-populated beach, ideal for those who seek solitude and who do not require facilities. Off Casa Ybel Road at Sanibel's southern end is **Old Lighthouse Beach,** which attracts a mix of families, shellers, and singles; rest rooms are available, and a plus is the historic lighthouse. ⊠ *East end of West Gulf Dr.*

## Dining and Lodging

$$$ ✗ **Bubble Room.** It's hard to say which is more eclectic here, the atmosphere or the menu. Waiters and waitresses wearing Boy Scout uniforms race amid a dizzying array of art deco, while music from the 1940s sets the mood. The aged prime rib is ample enough to satisfy two hearty eaters—at least. Chances are you'll be too full for dessert, but it can be wrapped to go. The Red Velvet cake is an unforgettable meal in itself. ⊠ *Captiva Rd., Captiva,* ☎ *941/472–5558. AE, DC, MC, V.*

$$$ ✗ **The French Corner.** The food here is finely seasoned with everything but the highfalutin attitude often dished up in French establishments. Excellent onion soup, salmon in a creamy dill sauce, veal medallions in a cream sauce with mushrooms, and roast duckling in fruit sauce are among the few but well-prepared choices on the menu. ⊠ *708 Tarpon Bay Rd., Sanibel,* ☎ *941/472–1493. MC, V. Closed Sun. No lunch.*

$$$ ✗ **Greenhouse at Thistle Lodge.** Take a seat at the copper-topped bar
★ to look into the full-view kitchen and try to pick out the day's specials. The menu reflects Continental, Asian, and Southwestern cuisine and includes rack of lamb, red snapper with wild mushrooms, homemade sausage, fresh seafood, and an excellent assortment of desserts. ⊠ *Captiva Rd., Captiva,* ☎ *941/472–6066. DC, MC, V. No lunch.*

$$ ✗ **McT's Shrimphouse and Tavern.** This lively and informal gathering spot features a host of fresh seafood specialties, including numerous oyster and mussel appetizers, shrimp prepared all kinds of ways, and all-you-can-eat shrimp and crab. Landlubbers will enjoy the black-bean soup, prime rib, and blackened chicken. There's always a dessert du jour, but most people end up choosing the Sanibel mud pie, a delicious

concoction heavy on the Oreos. ⊠ *1523 Periwinkle Way, Sanibel,* ☎ *941/472–3161. AE, DC, MC, V.*

$$$$ ✕🖭 **Casa Ybel Resort.** This time-share property faces the Gulf on 23 acres of tropical grounds, complete with palms, ponds, and a footbridge. Contemporary one- and two-bedroom apartments with full kitchens are brightly furnished in tropical prints, and big screened-in porches look out to the beach. There is a well-respected restaurant on site. ⊠ *2255 W. Gulf Dr., Sanibel 33957,* ☎ *941/472–3145 or 800/237–8906,* ℻ *941/472–2109. 40 1-bedroom units, 74 2-bedroom units. Restaurant, lounge, pool, tennis, shuffleboard, boating, water sports, bicycles, game room, baby-sitting, playground. AE, DC, MC, V.*

$$$$ ✕🖭 **South Seas Plantation Resort and Yacht Harbour.** This busy 330-acre property, at the far end of Captiva Island and quite out of the way, is more like a closely clustered neighborhood than a beach resort. Nine different types of accommodations include tennis and harbor-side villas, Gulf cottages, and private homes. Sign up for some of the many outdoor activities, including wave running, sailboarding, waterskiing, tennis, golf, and shelling. From the service in the posh restaurant—the King's Crown Dining Room—to the waterskiing instructors, the staff is five-star. Somehow, even with all the options, the pace is satisfyingly slow and the atmosphere calm and relaxed. Rates can drop as much as 40% off-season. ⊠ *South Seas Plantation Rd., Captiva 33924,* ☎ *941/472–5111 or 800/237–1260,* ℻ *941/472–7541. 620 rooms. 4 restaurants, 2 lounges, pools, beauty salon, golf, putting green, tennis, docks, windsurfing, boating, canoeing, parasailing, waterskiing, fishing, game room, children's programs, playground. AE, DC, MC, V.*

$$$–$$$$ ✕🖭 **Sundial Beach & Tennis Resort.** This resort is a good pick for families; many suites face the Gulf of Mexico, and all have full kitchens and laundry facilities. Of the 400 units, each individually owned, about two-thirds are available for rent. Some are in better condition than others, and there have been reports of bad service and dirty rooms. Among the four on-site restaurants is a Japanese steak and seafood house as well as the justly renowned Windows on the Water. Windows on the Water prepares some of Sanibel's finest food, with interesting Cajun and Caribbean overtones, such as scampi in mandarin-orange tequila butter. The bronzed fish special, a takeoff on blackened fish, is outstanding. ⊠ *1451 Middle Gulf Dr., Sanibel 33957,* ☎ *941/472–4151 or 800/237–4184,* ℻ *941/472–8892. 265 suites in rental pool. 4 restaurants, bar, deli, lounge, 5 pools, tennis, shuffleboard, beach, fishing, boating, bicycles, game room, baby-sitting, children's programs. AE, DC, MC, V.*

$$ 🖭 **Shalimar Motel.** Well-maintained grounds and an inviting beach make this small property very appealing. Efficiencies and one- and two-bedroom units (all with full kitchen) are in small two-story cottages set back from the beach amid tropical greenery. There's a swimming pool in the center of a courtyard, and there are barbecue facilities. ⊠ *2823 West Gulf Dr., Sanibel, 33957,* ☎ *941/472–1353 or 800/645–4092,* ℻ *941/472–6430. 33 units (21 efficiencies, 10 1-bedroom units, 2 2-bedroom units). Pool, shuffleboard, beach. DC, MC, V.*

## Outdoor Activities and Sports

BIKING

On Sanibel, rent bicycles by the hour at **Tarpon Bay Marina** (⊠ 900 Tarpon Bay Rd., Sanibel, ☎ 941/472–8900). On Captiva, rent bicycles by the hour or day from **Jim's Bike & Scooter Rental** (⊠ 11534 Andy Rosse La., Captiva, ☎ 941/472–1296).

CANOEING

**Tarpon Bay Marina** (✉ 900 Tarpon Bay Rd., Sanibel, ☎ 941/472–8900) has canoes and equipment for exploring the waters of Sanibel's J. N. "Ding" Darling National Wildlife Refuge.

GOLF

You can rent golf clubs and take lessons as well as play at **The Dunes** (✉ 949 Sand Castle Rd., Sanibel, ☎ 941/472–2535), which has 18 holes.

TENNIS

At **The Dunes** (✉ 949 Sand Castle Rd., Sanibel, ☎ 941/472–3522) there are seven clay courts and two tennis professionals ready to give lessons.

WATER SPORTS

**Boat House of Sanibel** (✉ Sanibel Marina, Sanibel, ☎ 941/472–2531) rents powerboats.

## Shopping

The largest cluster of shops on Sanibel, **Periwinkle Place** (✉ 2075 Periwinkle Way), has 42 shops and several restaurants. **Aboriginals** (✉ 2340 Periwinkle Way, ☎ 941/395–2200) sells textiles, baskets, pottery, and jewelry from Native Americans, Australians, and Africans. At **She Sells Sea Shells** (✉ 1157 Periwinkle Way, ☎ 941/472–6991), everything imaginable is made out of shells, from decorative mirrors and lamps to Christmas ornaments.

# Around Sanibel Island and Captiva Island

Besides Sanibel and Captiva, there are dozens of barrier islands and keys scattered nearby in Pine Island Sound and the Gulf of Mexico. Quite often you'll have to take a boat between islands, and if you're cutting through Pine Island Sound, you have a good chance of being escorted by bottlenose dolphins. Many of the islands are tiny and uninhabited and are excellent spots for bird-watching and nature walks.

## Sights to See

**6** **Boca Grande.** Before roads to southwest Florida were even talked about, wealthy northerners came by train to spend the winter at the **Gasparilla Inn,** built in 1912 in Boca Grande on Gasparilla Island. While condominiums and modern sprawl creep up on the rest of Gasparilla, much of the town of Boca Grande looks as it has for a century or more. The mood is set by the old Florida homes, many made of wood, with wide, inviting verandas and wicker rocking chairs. The island's relaxed atmosphere is disrupted only in the spring, when tarpon fishermen descend with a vengeance on Boca Grande Pass, considered among the best tarpon-fishing spots in the world.

**7** **Cabbage Key.** You'll have to take a boat from Bokeelia on Pine Island to get to Cabbage Key, which sits at Marker 60 on the Intracoastal Waterway. Here, atop an ancient Calusa Indian shell mound is the friendly, six-room **Cabbage Key Inn,** built by novelist and playwright Mary Roberts Rinehart in 1938. The inn also offers several guest cottages, a marina, and a dining room papered in thousands of dollar bills, signed and posted by patrons over the years.

## Dining and Lodging

$$ ✕ **Mucky Duck.** Yes, there are two restaurants by this name—one on the Captiva Island waterfront, the other a slightly more formal restaurant in Fort Myers Beach. Both concentrate on fresh, well-prepared seafood. A popular dish is the bacon-wrapped barbecued shrimp, and local grouper prepared any number of ways is the house specialty. ✉

*2500 Estero Blvd., Fort Myers Beach,* ☎ *941/463–5519;* ✉ *Andy Rosse La., Captiva,* ☎ *941/472–3434. MC, V.*

$$ ✕ **Snug Harbor.** You can watch boats coming and going whether you sit inside or outside at this dockside restaurant on stilts. The secret of its success is the absolutely fresh seafood, courtesy of the restaurant's private fishing fleet. This place is a favorite of year-round residents and seasonal visitors alike. ✉ *645 San Carlos Blvd., Fort Myers Beach,* ☎ *941/463–4343. MC, V.*

$$$$ ✕🏨 **Sanibel Harbour Resort & Spa.** Take the last mainland exit be-
★ fore the Sanibel causeway to reach this high-rise, waterfront resort with large, well-decorated rooms and apartments—all with sweeping views of island-studded San Carlos Bay. A wooden walkway leads through woods and across a pond to tennis courts, racquetball courts, and an exceptional full-service spa that offers everything from herbal body wraps to personal trainers to a total-body workout room. The beach is only fair, but there is a large free-form pool and free transportation to the beautiful beaches of Sanibel. There is also the Kids Klub to keep children busy. Three restaurants include the elegant Chez le Bear and the Courtside Bar & Grill, a popular sports bar. The staff is exceptionally helpful. ✉ *17260 Harbour Pointe Dr., 33908,* ☎ *941/466–4000 or 800/767–7777,* 📠 *941/466–2150. 320 rooms, 80 2-bedroom condominiums. 3 restaurants, 3 lounges, indoor pool, outdoor pool, tennis, health club, racquetball. AE, DC, MC, V.*

### Outdoor Activities and Sports

TENNIS

You'll find six Har-Tru clay courts plus private and group lessons at the **Bay Beach Racquet Club** (✉ 120 Lenell St., Fort Myers Beach, ☎ 941/463–4473).

WATER SPORTS

**Getaway Bait and Boat Rental** (✉ 1091 San Carlos Blvd., Fort Myers Beach, ☎ 941/466–3200) rents motorboats and fishing equipment and sells bait.

# NAPLES AND MARCO ISLAND

Driving U.S. 41 south from Fort Myers you'll come across the Naples and Marco Island area, sandwiched between the Big Cypress Swamp and the Gulf of Mexico. Over the past few years high-end restaurants and shops have sprouted in Naples, and the city is becoming a major tourist destination. A similar, though not so thorough, change has occurred on Marco Island; once a quiet fishing community, it has also been transformed into a sun-seekers vacation spot.

## Naples

⑧ **Naples** is fast becoming Florida's west-coast version of Palm Beach. Twenty-story condominiums now line the north shore of Naples; there are many sophisticated (and expensive) restaurants and a number of upscale shopping areas, including the tree-lined Third Street South. Golf courses, tennis courts, and miles of beach draw visitors to this area year-round, but the winter months are by far the most crowded.

### Sights to See

★ ☺ **Caribbean Gardens.** Originally a botanical garden planted in the early 1900s, this 52-acre junglelike educational park now houses exotic wildlife including African lions, mandrills, Bengal tigers, lemurs, antelope, and monkeys. The Primate Expedition Cruise takes visitors through islands of monkeys and apes living in natural habitat. There are elephant demonstrations and alligator feedings, and kids will particularly enjoy the petting zoo. ⊠ *1590 Goodlette Rd.,* ☎ *941/262–5409.* ⊞ *$12.95.* ☉ *Daily 9:30–5:30.*

**Naples Nature Center.** Situated on 13 acres bordering a tidal lagoon teeming with wildlife, this center includes an aviary, a wildlife rehabilitation clinic, a natural science museum with a serpentarium, and a 3,000-gallon marine aquarium. Free guided trail walks and miniboat tours are scheduled several times daily and there are canoes and kayaks for rent. ⊠ *1450 Merrihue Dr.,* ☎ *941/262–0304.* ⊞ *Free.* ☉ *Daily 9:30–5:30.*

Ⓒ **Teddy Bear Museum of Naples.** Teddy bear lovers of all ages delight in the more than 2,400 teddy bears on display in this collection. Built by oil heiress and area resident Frances Pew Hayes, the $2 million museum also has a reading library—stocked with books just about bears—and a life-sized Three Bears House. ⊠ *2511 Pine Ridge Rd.,* ☎ *941/598–2711.* ⊞ *$5.* ☉ *Wed.–Sat. 10–5, Sun. 1–5.*

## Beaches

**Clam Pass Park,** on Seagate Drive, is a glistening stretch of particularly pristine white sand. A 3,000-foot boardwalk winds through tropical mangroves to the beach. ⊠ *Seagate Dr.,* ☎ *941/353–0404.* ☉ *8 AM–sunset.*

**Delnor-Wiggins Pass State Recreation Area** is a well-maintained park with 100 acres with sandy beaches, lifeguards, barbecue grills, picnic tables, boat ramp, observation tower, rest rooms with wheelchair access, lots of parking, bathhouses, and showers. Fishing is best in Wiggins Pass at the north end of the park. Alcohol is prohibited in the recreation area. ⊠ *West end of 111th Ave. N.* ⊞ *Florida residents $1 per car plus 50¢ per passenger, all other $2 per car plus $1 per passenger, boat launching $1.*

Stretching along Gulf Shore Boulevard in Naples, **Lowdermilk Park** has over 1,000 feet of beach, volleyball courts, a playground, rest rooms, showers, a pavilion, vending machines, and picnic tables. No alcoholic beverages or fires are permitted. ⊠ *Gulf Shore Dr. at Banyan Blvd.*

## Dining and Lodging

$$$ ✕ **Bistro 821.** The decor for this trendy restaurant is spare but sophisticated. Entrées range from rotisserie chicken to wild-mushroom pasta, vodka penne, risotto, and a seasonal vegetable plate. ⊠ *821 5th Ave. S,* ☎ *941/261–5821. Reservations essential. AE, DC, MC, V. No lunch.*

$$$ ✕ **Chef's Garden.** A focus on new American cuisine has consistently won this restaurant awards over the past decade. House favorites include grilled portobello mushrooms, veal tenderloin, roast duck, seared filet mignon, and whiskey-marinated grilled chicken. Lighter lunch fare includes black-bean soup, chicken and grape salad, and a spinach and fresh mango salad with toasted cashews and honey vinaigrette. The less formal Truffles bistro upstairs features creative sandwiches, pastas, and salads, plus tasty pastries to take out or eat in. The wine list is extensive. ⊠ *1300 3rd St. S,* ☎ *941/262–5500. Jacket required. AE, D, DC, MC, V. No lunch Sun.*

$–$$ ✕ **Busghetti Ristorante.** Despite the cutesy name and the very affordable prices, this eatery serves excellent Italian cuisine in an appealing, upscale setting. The menu includes a wide range of pastas, from traditional lasagna to "busghetti" with everything from Gorgonzola to ratatouille. There are also many veal, steak, chicken, and seafood selections and a good wine list. ⊠ *1181 3rd St. S,* ☎ *941/263–3667. AE, MC, V.*

$    ✕ **Old Naples Pub.** From Robinson Court, walk up a few stairs to this comfortable pub, where from 11 AM until late at night you can sample from 20 kinds of beer and the not-so-traditional pub menu. It encompasses fish-and-chips, burgers, bratwurst, pizza, and chicken Caesar salad as well as a good selection of snacks: nachos, fries smothered in chili, and cheese-stuffed, deep-fried jalapeños. There's piano entertainment Mon.–Sat. ⊠ *255 13th Ave. S,* ☎ *941/649–8200. AE, MC, V.*

$$$$   ✕▥ **Registry Resort.** From the elegant marble and oak lobby to the
★      sumptuously decorated rooms to the exceptional service, this high rise is the essence of luxury. You may never want to leave your room, but if you do, elegant restaurants and bars, upscale shops, and a complete fitness center await you. Sign up for a therapeutic massage, or work out with a beautiful view of the mangroves. Outside are unique, free-form swimming pools with waterfalls. Walk a half mile on a boardwalk through a mangrove forest to 3 miles of glistening white beach, or take an open-air tram. Try paddling around a lagoon in a canoe. For golfers, the Caddymaster service arranges tee times at the area's finest golf clubs months in advance. The tennis program is especially strong here. Sunday brunch is outstanding, with table after table of exquisitely prepared selections. Guests dress up for it, although very neat casual attire is acceptable. ⊠ *475 Seagate Dr., 33940,* ☎ *941/597–3232,* 𝔽𝔸𝕏 *941/566–7919. 395 rooms, 29 suites, 50 tennis villas. 4 restaurants, 2 lounges, 3 pools, golf, tennis, health club, bicycles, children's programs. AE, DC, MC, V.*

$$$$   ▥ **Edgewater Beach Hotel.** At the north end of fashionable Gulf Shore Boulevard stands this compact, high-rise, waterfront resort. The brightly decorated units are either one- or two-bedroom suites and have full kitchens, and patios or balconies. Many have exquisite views of the Gulf. Dine by the pool or in the elegant restaurant, or enjoy piano music in the lounge during happy hour. Shopping, golf, and tennis are close by. ⊠ *1901 Gulf Shore Blvd. N, 33940,* ☎ *941/262–6511 or 800/821–0196; in FL, 800/282–3766;* 𝔽𝔸𝕏 *941/262–1243. 124 units. Restaurant, lounge, pool, bicycles, exercise room, beach. AE, DC, MC, V.*

$$$$   ▥ **Ritz-Carlton.** Equally fabulous hotel rooms can be had elsewhere, but the extensive network of lavishly appointed public rooms is astounding, with a dozen meeting rooms of varying shapes and sizes and an estimable collection of 19th-century European oils. Though you might feel a little uncomfortable traipsing through the lobby in tennis shoes, you will be graciously welcomed. Guests have access to a nearby 27-hole golf course. ⊠ *280 Vanderbilt Beach Rd., 33941,* ☎ *941/598–3300,* 𝔽𝔸𝕏 *941/598–6690. 463 rooms. 4 restaurants, lounge, pool, saunas, 6 tennis courts, fitness center, beach, windsurfing, boating, children's programs. AE, D, DC, MC.*

$$$    ▥ **La Playa Beach & Racquet Inn.** Nestled between a bay and the Gulf, this large hotel stretches along the beach. Rooms and efficiencies are in a three-story low rise, and one- and two-bedroom suites are in a 14-story high rise. Units, furnished in rattan and tropical prints, have plenty of room, and all have patios or balconies overlooking the Gulf, providing excellent views. ⊠ *9891 Gulf Shore Blvd., 33963,* ☎ *941/597–3123,* 𝔽𝔸𝕏 *941/597–6278. 172 units. 2 restaurants, lounge, 2 pools, tennis, shuffleboard, volleyball, beach, kayaks, dock. AE, MC, V.*

$$$ ⊡ **Naples Beach Hotel & Golf Club.** This appealing resort, owned and
★ operated by the same family since it opened in 1946, sprawls along
the Gulf on upscale Gulf Shore Boulevard. Comfortable rooms and suites,
furnished in rattan and tropical prints, are located in several buildings.
Quite a few have spectacular water views, and orchids, grown on site,
are placed in your room daily. The beach and pool stretch along the
western edge of the property, while tennis courts and the 18-hole
championship golf course flank the eastern edge. Among the eateries
is the only beachfront bar and restaurant in Naples, built prior to strict
zoning laws. ⊠ *851 Gulf Shore Blvd. N, 33940,* ☎ *941/261–2222 or
800/237–7600,* FAX *941/261–7380. 315 units. 3 restaurants, 2 bars,
deli, pool, 18-hole golf course, tennis, beach. AE, MC, V.*

$$ ⊡ **Best Western Naples Inn & Suites.** You'd never know you were anywhere near busy U.S. 41 at this two-story spot, which is set back in
lush tropical gardens with waterfalls. It is a half mile walk to Gulf beaches
and an easy walk to shopping and restaurants. ⊠ *2329 9th St. N, 33940,*
☎ *941/261–1148 or 800/528–1234,* FAX *941/262–4684. 80 rooms.
Restaurant, lounge, pools, shuffleboard. AE, D, DC, MC, V.*

## Nightlife and the Arts

### THE ARTS

Naples tends to be the cultural capital of this stretch of the coast. **The
Naples Philharmonic Center for the Arts** (⊠ 5833 Pelican Bay Blvd.,
☎ 941/597–1111) has two theaters and two art galleries offering a
variety of plays, concerts, and exhibits year-round. It's home to the 80-
piece Naples Philharmonic, which presents both classical and pop
concerts; the Miami Ballet Company also performs during its winter
season in town. Halfway between U.S. 41 and I–75, the **Naples Dinner Theatre** (⊠ Immokalee Rd., ☎ 941/597–6031) features professional companies performing mostly musicals and comedies, Oct.–Aug.;
admission includes a candlelight French buffet. **The Naples Players** (⊠
399 Goodlette Rd., ☎ 941/263–7990) has winter and summer seasons—winter shows often sell out well in advance.

### NIGHTLIFE

**Witch's Brew** (⊠ 4836 N. Tamiami Trail, Naples, ☎ 941/261–4261)
is a lively location for nightly entertainment. There's a happy hour weekdays 4–6 and an excellent menu featuring Continental cuisine. The upstairs lounge at Witch's Brew's sister restaurant, **Seawitch** (⊠ 179
Commerce St., Vanderbilt Beach, Naples, ☎ 941/566–1514), overlooks
Vanderbilt Bay and is a relaxing spot for casual dining. Bands play Top
40 music Tues.–Sun. **Club Zanzibar** (⊠ 475 Seagate Dr., North Naples,
☎ 941/597–3232), at the Registry Resort, is a light and airy multilevel nightclub where DJs pump out Top 40 Hits from 9 PM until 2AM.
Stop at the **Silver Dollar Saloon** (⊠ Gulf Gate Shopping Plaza, Naples,
☎ 941/775–7011) for open country dancing and lessons Wed.–Sun.
The extremely casual **Backstage Tap & Grill** (⊠ 5535 U.S. 41 N, Naples
☎ 941/598–1300) has great jazz a few nights each week. **Chef's Garden** (⊠ 1300 3rd St. S, Naples, ☎ 941/262–5500) is a quiet spot for
jazz once or twice a week.

## Outdoor Activities and Sports

### BIKING

In Naples, try the **Bicycle Shop** (⊠ 941 Vanderbilt Beach Rd., ☎
941/566–3646).

### FISHING

If you want to attempt to catch some fish in the Naples area, ask for
Captain Tom at **Deep Sea Charter Fishing** (⊠ Boat Haven, Naples, ☎
941/263–8171).

GOLF

The **Hibiscus Golf Club** (⊠ 175 Doral Circle, ☎ 941/774–3559) has an 18-hole course and a practice range. **Naples Beach Hotel & Golf Club** (⊠ 851 Gulfshore Blvd. N., ☎ 941/261–2222) offers 18 holes and has a golf pro and a putting green. **Naples Golf Center** (⊠ 7700 E. Davis Blvd., ☎ 941/775–3337) has a 300–yard driving range and offers private and group lessons by a PGA teaching staff; it even has computerized swing analysis.

TENNIS

**Cambier Park Tennis Courts** (⊠ 775 8th Ave. S, ☎ 941/434–4694) offers clinics and night play on 14 courts. **Naples Racquet Club** (⊠ 100 Forest Hills Blvd., ☎ 941/774–2442) sports seven Har-Tru clay courts.

WATER SPORTS

**Port-O-Call** (⊠ 550 Port-O-Call Way, ☎ 941/774–0479) rents 16- to 25-foot powerboats.

## Shopping

The largest shopping area is **Olde Naples,** with more than 100 shops and a number of restaurants. Here shoppers stroll along broad, tree-lined walkways in an eight-block area bordered by Broad Avenue on the north and 4th Street South on the east. **Old Marine Market Place** at Tin City (⊠ 1200 5th Ave. S), in a collection of former fishing shacks along Naples Bay, has 40 boutiques, artisans' studios, and souvenir shops with everything from scrimshaw to Haitian art. The **Village on Venetian Bay** (⊠ 4200 Gulf Shore Blvd.) has more than 50 upscale shops built over the bay. The **Waterside Shops** (⊠ Seagate Dr. and U.S. 41) are built around an interior courtyard with a series of waterways. Anchored by a Saks Fifth Avenue boutique and Jacobson's Department Store, Waterside houses 50 shops and several eating places. **Gattle's** (⊠ 1250 3rd St. S, ☎ 941/262–4791) is the place for beautifully made (and very pricey) linens. **Marissa Collections** (⊠ 1167 3rd St. S, ☎ 941/263–4333) showcases fashionable designer women's wear, including Louis Féraud, Donna Karan, and Calvin Klein. Stop at **Mettlers** (⊠ 1258 3rd St. S, ☎ 941/434–2700) for high-fashion men's and women's sportswear, including full lines of clothing by Giorgio Armani and Polo. At the **Mole Hole** (⊠ 1201 3rd St. S, ☎ 941/262–5115), every surface is covered with gift items large and small, from glassware to paperweights to knickknacks.

# Marco Island

⑨ **Marco Island,** about 20 miles south of Naples, is connected to the mainland by causeways. This island stubbornly retains its isolated feeling; although it has its share of modern development, many natural areas have been carefully preserved. There is also the old fishing village of Goodland, which resists tourism-induced change. Surfing, sunning, swimming, golf, and tennis are the primary activities.

## Sights to See

**Ten Thousand Islands.** There aren't really 10,000, but it sure looks as if there could be. The best way to see this cluster of small, undeveloped, protected islands—and the remarkable wildlife that lives on them—is by airboat. Cruises usually last about two hours, and you'll see many birds, including pelicans and hawks. There's also a strong chance you'll see dolphins swimming alongside the boat. ⊠ *1079 Bald Eagle Dr., at Factory Bay Marina,* ☎ *941/642–6717.* ☞ *$20.* ☉ *Departures daily at 10 and 2.*

## Beaches

**Tigertail Beach** is on the southwest side of the island. Facilities include parking, a concession stand, a picnic area, sailboat rentals, volleyball, rest rooms, and showers.⊠ *480 Hernando Ct.,* ☎ *941/642–0818.* ⊙ *Daily sunrise–sunset.*

## Dining and Lodging

$$  ✕ **Marco Lodge Waterfront Restaurant & Lounge.** Built in 1869, this tin-roof, wooden building is Marco's oldest landmark. As you dine along the waterfront, veranda boats, up to 35 feet long, tie up nearby. Fresh local seafood and Cajun entrées are featured. One specialty is a wooden bowl of blue crabs in rich garlic butter. ⊠ *1 Papaya St., Goodland,* ☎ *941/642–7227. AE, DC, MC, V. Closed Mon.*

$$  ✕ **Old Marco Inn.** This turn-of-the-century home is now a beautifully
★  decorated spot for intimate dinners. The menu covers a cross section of cuisines: grilled steaks and chops, Wiener schnitzel, and fresh seafood. The piano bar opens nightly at 8. ⊠ *100 Palm St., Marco Island,* ☎ *941/394–3131. AE, MC, V. No lunch weekends.*

$$$$ ✕🏨 **Marriott's Marco Island Resort and Golf Club.** A circular drive leads up to the reception area of this big beachfront resort hotel and its beautifully manicured grounds. Large rooms are plush, have good to exceptional water views from their balconies, and come with a multitude of amenities, including coffeemaker, small refrigerator, TV with movie channels, minibar, and double-sink vanity. There are also luxurious penthouse suites, beachfront lanais, and private villas. Serious shell seekers will delight in the beachside shell-washing spigot, and golf is not far away. ⊠ *400 S. Collier Blvd., Marco Island, 33937,* ☎ *941/394–2511 or 800/438–4373,* FAX *941/394–4645. 736 rooms, 6 penthouse suites, 30 lanais, 8 private villas. 6 restaurants, lounge, 3 pools, golf, miniature golf, tennis, health club, beach, windsurfing, boating, waterskiing, bicycles, children's programs. AE, DC, MC, V.*

$$  ✕🏨 **Lakeside Inn.** Though it will never win any architectural awards and it's not on the beach (it's about a mile away), this longtime inn is one of Marco Island's best values and does overlook a small lake. Comfortably furnished efficiencies and one-bedroom suites have kitchens and are on the cozy side. An excellent, affordable Italian restaurant, Busghetti Ristorante, is on the premises. ⊠ *155 1st Ave., 33937,* ☎ *941/394–1161. 26 efficiencies, 12 suites. Restaurant, pool, lake, fishing. AE, MC, V.*

$$$$ 🏨 **Marco Beach Hilton.** With fewer than 300 rooms and wisely apportioned public areas, the Hilton is smaller than the other big-name resorts in the area, and facilities tend to be a little less crowded. All of the rooms in this 11-story beachfront hotel are spacious and have private balconies with unobstructed Gulf views, a sitting area, wet bar, and refrigerator. There is golf nearby. ⊠ *560 S. Collier Blvd., Marco Island, 33937,* ☎ *941/394–5000 or 800/443–4550,* FAX *941/394–5251. 298 rooms. 2 restaurants, snack bar, pool, tennis, fitness center, beach, water sports. AE, D, DC, MC, V.*

$$$  🏨 **Radisson Beach Suite Resort.** There's something for everyone at this full-service, beachfront property designed with families in mind. All rooms and one- and two-bedroom suites in this medium high rise are tastefully decorated and contain fully equipped kitchens. Though rooms are a bit tight, suites have plenty of space. Offerings include daily children's programs as well as many scheduled activities for adults. ⊠ *600 S. Collier Blvd., Marco Island, 33937,* ☎ *941/394–4100 or 800/333–3333,* FAX *941/394–0419. 55 rooms, 214 suites. 3 restaurants, 2 lounges, pool, exercise room, beach, water sports, bicycles, game room, children's programs. AE, DC, MC, V.*

### Outdoor Activities and Sports

BIKING

On Marco Island, rentals are available at **Scootertown** (⊠ 855 Bald Eagle Dr., ☎ 941/394–8400).

FISHING

**Sunshine Tours** (⊠ Marco Island, ☎ 941/642–5415) has half- and full-day party boat trips.

WATER SPORTS

For sailing lessons or bareboat or captained sail cruises, contact **Marco Island Sea Excursions** (⊠ 1281 Jamaica Rd., Marco Island, ☎ 941/642–6400).

## Beyond Naples

The land east of Naples is undeveloped all the way to Fort Lauderdale. Most of it is swampland and forms the northern border of the Florida Everglades—making it excellent territory for visiting nature preserves and parks. To the north, between Naples and Bonita Springs, are several sizable, popular beaches.

### Sights to See

★ ➓ **Corkscrew Swamp Sanctuary.** To get a feel for what this part of Florida was like before civil engineers began draining the swamps, drive 20 miles northeast of Naples. The National Audubon Society manages this 11,000-acre sanctuary to help protect 500-year-old trees and endangered birds, such as wood storks, which often nest high in the bald cypress. Visitors taking the 1¾-mile self-guided tour along the boardwalk may glimpse alligators, graceful wading birds, and air plants that cling to the sides of trees. ⊠ *16 mi east of I–75 on Rte. 846,* ☎ *941/657–3771.* ⊠ *$6.50.* ⊙ *Dec.–Apr., daily 7–5; May–Nov., daily 8–5.*

**Everglades Wonder Gardens.** This attraction, one of the first in the state, captures the feral beauty of untamed Florida through zoological gardens containing Florida panthers, black bear, crocodiles and alligators, tame Florida deer, and trained otters and birds. There's also an eclectic natural history museum on site. ⊠ *Old U.S. 41, Bonita Springs,* ☎ *941/992–2591.* ⊠ *$8.* ⊙ *Daily 9–5.*

### Beaches

**Bonita Springs Public Beach** is on Bonita Beach Road, at the southern end of Bonita Beach. There are picnic tables, free parking, and nearby refreshment stands and shopping.

**Barefoot Beach,** between Naples and Bonita, is another very popular spot; it has picnic tables, a nature trail, refreshment stands, and other comforts. ⊠ *Lely Beach Rd.*

### Outdoor Activities and Sports

BIKING

In Bonita Springs, rent bicycles at **Pop's Bicycles** (⊠ 3685 Bonita Beach Rd., ☎ 941/947–4442).

CANOEING

**Estero River Tackle and Canoe Outfitters** (⊠ 20991 Tamiami Trail S, Estero, ☎ 941/992–4050) has canoes and equipment for use on the meandering Estero River.

DOG RACING

There's dog racing year-round at the **Naples/Fort Myers Greyhound Track** (⊠ 10601 Bonita Beach Rd., Bonita Springs, ☎ 941/992–2411).

# SOUTHWEST FLORIDA A TO Z

## Arriving and Departing

### By Bus
**Greyhound Lines** (☎ 800/231–2222) has service to Fort Myers (✉ 2275 Cleveland Ave., ☎ 941/334–1011) and Naples (✉ 2669 Davis Blvd., ☎ 941/774–5660).

### By Car
I–75 spans the region from north to south. Once you cross the border into Florida from Georgia, it should take about five hours to reach Fort Myers and another hour to Naples. Alligator Alley, a section of I–75, is a two-lane toll road (75¢ at each end) that runs from Fort Lauderdale through the Everglades to Naples, bringing travelers from the east coast. Count on two hours between Naples and Fort Lauderdale.

### By Plane
The Fort Myers/Naples area's airport is **Southwest Florida International Airport** (☎ 941/768–1000), about 12 miles southwest of Fort Myers, 25 miles north of Naples. It is served by **Air Canada** (☎ 800/776–3000), **American** (☎ 800/433–7300), **Canadian Holidays** (☎ 800/282–4751), **Continental** (☎ 800/525–0280), **Delta** (☎ 800/221–1212), **Northwest** (☎ 800/225–2525), **TWA** (☎ 800/221–2000), **United** (☎ 800/241–6522), and **USAir** (☎ 800/428–4322). A taxi ride from the airport to downtown Fort Myers or the beaches (Sanibel, Captiva) costs about $30; it's about twice that to Naples. Other transportation companies include **Aristocrat Super Mini-Van Service** (☎ 941/275–7228), **Personal Touch Limousines** (☎ 941/549–3643), and **Sanibel Island Limousine** (☎ 941/472–8888).

The **Naples Airport** (☎ 941/643–6875), a small facility just east of downtown Naples, is served by **American Eagle** (☎ 800/433–7300), **Comair** (☎ 800/282–3424), and **USAir Express** (☎ 800/428–4322). Commercial shuttle service between the airport and Naples is generally $10 to $25 per person. Once arrived, call **Naples Taxi** (☎ 941/643–2148) or, to get to nearby Marco Island, try **Marco Transportation, Inc.** (☎ 941/394–2257).

## Getting Around

### By Bus
**The Lee County Transit System** (☎ 941/939–1303) serves most of the county.

### By Car
I–75 and U.S. 41 run the length of the region. U.S. 41, also known as the Tamiami Trail, goes through downtown Fort Myers and Naples and is also called Cleveland Avenue in the former and 9th Street in the latter. McGregor Boulevard (Rte. 867) is Fort Myers's main road. Lined with thousands of royal palm trees and many large old homes, it passes what were the winter homes of Thomas Edison and Henry Ford and heads southwest toward Sanibel-Captiva. San Carlos Boulevard runs southwest from McGregor Boulevard to Fort Myers Beach, and Pine Island–Bayshore Road (Rte. 78) leads from North Fort Myers through northern Cape Coral onto Pine Island.

## Guided Tours

**Naples Trolley Tours** (☎ 941/262–7300) has five 1¾-hour narrated tours daily, covering more than 100 points of interest. Tickets are $9. The tour lasts approximately one hour and forty–five minutes but you can get off and reboard at no extra cost.

## Special-Interest Tours

### AIR TOURS

**Boca Grande Seaplane Service** (☎ 941/964–0234) operates sightseeing tours in the Charlotte Harbor area, leaving from 4th and Bayou streets, Boca Grande. **Classic Flight** (☎ 941/939–7411) flies an open cockpit biplane for sightseeing tours of the Fort Myers area, leaving from the Fort Myers Jet Center (✉ 501 Danley Rd.).

### BOAT TOURS

**Adventure Sailing Charters** (☎ 941/472–7532) offers captained, half- and full-day sailing cruises and sunset cruises for groups of six or fewer. Boats leave from South Seas Plantation on Captiva. **Estero Bay Boat Tours** (☎ 941/992–2200) takes you on guided boat tours of waterways once inhabited by the Calusa Indians. You'll see birds and other wildlife and may even spot some manatees or dolphins. **Everglades Jungle Cruises** (☎ 941/334–7474) explores the Caloosahatchee and Orange rivers of Lee County. From mid-November through mid-April, there are a variety of cruises along the Caloosahatchee River conducted on the *Capt. J.P.*, a stern paddle wheeler, and there is a manatee-watching cruise on a smaller boat. Brunch, lunch, and dinner cruises are available, departing from the Fort Myers Yacht Basin. **Island Rover** (☎ 941/765–7447), a 72-foot schooner, takes morning, afternoon, and sunset sails in the Gulf of Mexico, leaving from Gulf Star Marina, Fort Myers Beach. **Jammin' Sailboat Cruises** (☎ 941/463–3520) offers day and sunset cruises from Fort Myers Beach. Call for reservations. **King Fisher Cruise Lines** (☎ 941/639–0969) has half-day, full-day, Sunday brunch, and sunset cruises in Charlotte Harbor, the Peace River, and the Intracoastal Waterway. Boats depart from Fishermen's Village, Punta Gorda. **Quest** (☎ 941/334–0670) is a 34-foot classic sloop that runs two-hour morning and afternoon sailing trips and sunset and moonlight champagne cruises out of the Fort Myers Yacht Basin. Call for reservations. **Tarpon Bay Recreation Center** (☎ 941/472–8900) operates guided canoe tours through the J. N. "Ding" Darling Wildlife Refuge's mangroves.

## Contacts and Resources

### Emergencies

Dial **911** for police or ambulance.

#### HOSPITALS

The following hospitals have 24-hour emergency rooms: **Lee Memorial Hospital** (✉ 2776 Cleveland Ave., Fort Myers), **Naples Community Hospital** (✉ 350 7th St. N, Naples), and **North Collier Hospital** (✉ 1501 Imokolee Rd., Naples).

#### LATE-NIGHT PHARMACIES

**Walgreen** (✉ 70703 College Pkwy., Fort Myers, ☎ 941/939–2142; ✉ 8965 Tamiami Trail, North Naples, ☎ 941/597–8196).

### Visitor Information

The following offices are open weekdays 9–5 and closed holidays: **Charlotte County Chamber of Commerce** (✉ 2702 Tamiami Trail, Port Charlotte 33950, ☎ 941/627–2222), **Lee County Visitor and Convention Bureau** (✉ 2180 W. 1st St., Fort Myers 33901, ☎ 941/338–3500 or 800/533–4753), **Naples Area Chamber of Commerce** (✉ 3620 N. Tamiami Trail, Naples 33940, ☎ 941/262–6141), and **Sanibel-Captiva Chamber of Commerce** (✉ Causeway Rd., Sanibel 33957, ☎ 941/472–1080).

# 11 The Panhandle

*With its magnolias, live oaks, and loblolly pines, northwest Florida has more in common with the Deep South than with the Florida of the Everglades. Even the high season is different: Things in the Panhandle are just gearing up by May, as activities are winding down south of Tampa. Fabulous beaches are, however, a Panhandle staple. A recent coastal research study named Grayton Beach, St. Andrews State Recreation Area, St. Joseph Peninsula State Park, and St. George Island among the top 10 beaches in the country.*

**T**HE LITTLE GREEN CORNER of Florida that snuggles up between the Gulf of Mexico and the Alabama and Georgia state lines, just west of Tallahassee, is Florida's long, narrow northwest corner, known as the Panhandle. Some call it "the other Florida"; instead of everglades and palm trees, thriving here are the magnolias, live oaks, and loblolly pines common in the rest of the Deep South. As South Florida's season is winding down in May, action in the northwest is just picking up. The area is even in a different time zone: the Apalachicola River marks the dividing line between eastern and central times.

Updated by
Ann Hughes

Others call this section of the state "Florida's best-kept secret." Until World War II, when activity at the Panhandle air bases took off, it really was. But by the mid-1950s, the 100-mile stretch along the coast between Pensacola and Panama City was dubbed the "Miracle Strip" because of a dramatic rise in property values. In the 1940s this beachfront land sold for less than $100 an acre; today that same acre can yield tens of thousands of dollars. Still, the movers and shakers of the area felt this sobriquet fell short. So to convey the richness of the region, with its white sands and sparkling green waters, swamps, bayous, and flora, they coined the phrase "Emerald Coast."

It's a land of superlatives: It has the biggest military installation in the Western Hemisphere (Eglin Air Force Base), arguably the oldest city in the state (Pensacola, claiming a founding date of 1559), and the most productive fishing waters in the world (off Destin). It has resorts that out-glitz the Gold Coast's, campgrounds where possums invite themselves to lunch, and every kind of lodging in between. Lovers of the past can wander the many historic districts or visit archaeological digs. For sports enthusiasts, there's a different golf course or tennis court for each day of the week, and for those who decide to spend time with nature, there's a world of hunting, canoeing, biking, and hiking. And anything that happens on water happens here: surfing, scuba diving, and plenty of fishing, both from a deep-sea charter boat and the end of a pier.

## Pleasures and Pastimes

### Beaches

Thanks to restrictions against commercial development imposed by Eglin Air Force Base (AFB) and the Gulf Islands National Seashore, the Emerald Coast has been able to maintain several hundred miles of unspoiled beaches. A 1994 study by the University of Maryland's Laboratory for Coastal Research named Grayton Beach, St. Andrews State Recreation Area, St. Joseph Peninsula State Park, and St. George Island among the top 10 beaches in the United States.

### Biking

Some of the nation's best bike paths run through northwest Florida's woods and dunelands, particularly on Santa Rosa Island, where you can pedal for almost 20 miles and never lose sight of the water. Routes through Eglin AFB Reservation present cyclists with tortuous, wooded trails.

### Canoeing

Both beginners and veterans will get a kick out of canoeing the Panhandle's abundance of waterways. The shoals and rapids of the Blackwater River in the Blackwater River State Forest, 40 miles northeast of Pensacola, will challenge even the most seasoned canoeist, while the gentler currents in the sheltered marshes and inlets are much less intimidating.

## Dining

Since the Gulf of Mexico is only an hour's drive from any spot in the Panhandle, restaurants from modest diners to elegant cafés feature seafood, most served the same day it is hauled out of the water. Native fish such as grouper, red snapper, amberjack, catfish, and mullet are the regional staples. Prices are generally reasonable here, but if you visit during the off-season, or during the winter months, watch for dining discounts, such as two-for-one meal deals and early-bird specials.

## Diving

In the Panama City Beach area, you can investigate the wreckage of sunken tanker ships, tugboats, and cargo vessels. For snorkelers and beginning divers, the jetties of St. Andrews State Recreation Area, where there is no boat traffic, are safe.

## Fishing

Northwest Florida's fishing options range from fishing for pompano, snapper, marlin, and grouper in the saltwater of the Gulf of Mexico to angling for bass, catfish, and bluegill in the freshwater of the region. If you're planning a deep-sea fishing excursion, be advised that rates for charter boats are usually quoted by the day (about $575) or half day (about $300). This is an immensely popular pastime on the Emerald Coast, so there are boat charters in plenty.

## Lodging

For the most part, you won't have to worry about far-in-advance reservations in this part of the state; most accommodations accept walk-ins. To be on the safe side, though, you can reserve a spot through a property management service. Note that summer is high season for this part of Florida and you can expect to pay a premium for rooms then; winters are chilly—if you want to get warm, you need to head south.

# Exploring the Panhandle

Pensacola, with its antebellum homes and historic landmarks, is a good place to start your trek through northwest Florida. After exploring the museums and preservation districts, head east on U.S. 98. Don't overlook the deserted beaches along the Gulf of Mexico, where the sugar-white quartz-crystal sand crunches underfoot like snow on a sub-zero night. Farther east are Fort Walton Beach, the Emerald Coast's largest city and the hub of its vacation activity; neighboring Destin, where sport-fishing is king; and the twin cities of Valparaiso and Niceville. An interesting side trip along Route 20—a road that twists along Choctawhatchee Bay past bait shacks and catfish restaurants—allows a glimpse of some of Florida's best-kept secrets.

The next resort center along the coast is Panama City Beach, while to the far southeast is Apalachicola, an important oyster-fishing town. Inland, a number of interesting towns and state parks lie along I–10 on the long eastward drive to the state capital, Tallahassee.

## Great Itineraries

*Numbers in the text below correspond to numbers in the margin and on the map.*

There are sights to see in the Panhandle, but sightseeing is not the principal activity here. The area is better known for its ample opportunities for sports such as fishing and diving, and just plain relaxation. Although Hurricane Opal wore out her welcome when she blew through in October 1995, most of the damage to tourist facilities and the landscape is now repaired.

IF YOU HAVE 2 OR 3 DAYS

History and nature are the two biggest calling cards of this part of the Sunshine State. Visit ⛳ **Fort Walton Beach** ③ or Eglin Air Force Base, depending on whether your heart lies in the skies or on the seas. Kids might enjoy a stop at the Indian Temple Mound Museum. On Day Two visit the capital, ⛳ **Tallahassee** ⑯, and soak up some of Florida's history. Also stop by **Wakulla Springs State Park** ⑲, about 15 miles south of Tallahassee, where you'll find one of the world's deepest springs. It might look familiar as the filming site of those old Tarzan movies.

IF YOU HAVE 4 OR 5 DAYS

Start with a visit to the Palafox Historic District in ⛳ **Pensacola** ① and spend the day enjoying a glimpse of old Florida, as well as visiting the National Museum of Naval Aviation. While staying in ⛳ **Fort Walton Beach** ③, stop by the Eglin Air Force Base and the antebellum mansion at the **Eden State Gardens** ⑦, set amid moss-draped live oaks. Be sure to spend an afternoon at the Grayton Beach State Recreation Area, one of the most scenic spots along the Gulf Coast. Moving inland, go spelunking at the **Florida Caverns State Park** ⑮ before heading to ⛳ **Tallahassee** ⑯. If you have time, make day trips to **Wakulla Springs State Park** ⑲ and **St. Marks Wildlife Refuge and Lighthouse** ⑱, where you can hike, swim, or have a leisurely picnic.

# PENSACOLA

*Numbers in the margin correspond to points of interest on the Panhandle map.*

❶ In the years since its founding, **Pensacola** has come under the control of five nations, earning this fine, old Southern city its nickname, "the City of Five Flags." Spanish conquistadors, under the command of Don Tristan de Luna, landed on the shores of Pensacola Bay in 1559, but discouraged by a succession of destructive tropical storms and dissension in the ranks, De Luna abandoned the settlement two years after its founding. In 1698, the Spanish once again established a fort at the site, and during the early 18th century, control jockeyed back and forth between the Spanish, the French, and the British. Finally, in 1819, Pensacola passed into U.S. hands, though during the Civil War, it was governed by the Confederate States of America and flew yet another flag.

Historic Pensacola consists of three distinct districts—Seville, Palafox, and North Hill—though they are easy to explore as a unit. Stroll down streets mapped out by the British and renamed by the Spanish, such as Cervantes, Palafox, Intendencia, and Tarragona. Be warned, though, that it is best to stick to the beaten path; Pensacola is a port town and can get rough around the edges, especially at night.

The best way to orient yourself is to stop at the **Pensacola Visitor Information Center** (⬛ 1401 E. Gregory St., ☎ 904/434–1234), located at the foot of the Pensacola Bay Bridge. Here you can pick up maps of the self-guided historic district tours.

## Sights to See

**Fort Barrancas.** This Civil War fort's grounds now include picnic areas and a ½-mile woodland nature trail. The fort is part of the Gulf Islands National Seashore, protected by the National Park Service. ⬛ *Navy Blvd.,* ☎ *904/455–5167.* 🎫 *Free.* ☉ *Dec.–Jan., Wed.–Sun. 10:30–4; Feb.–Nov., daily 9:30–5.*

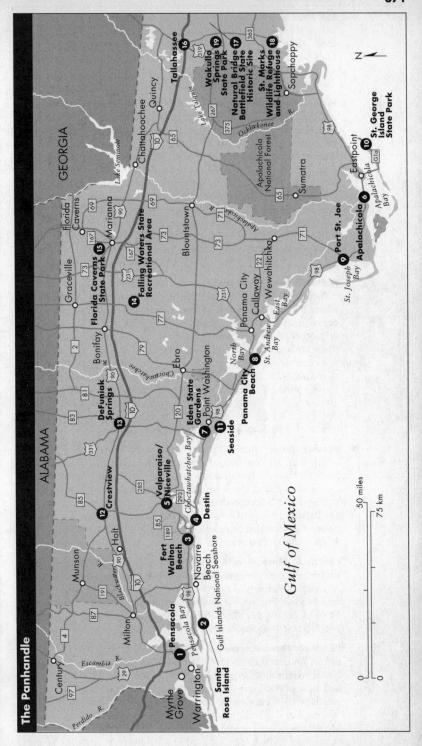

**The Panhandle**

GEORGIA

ALABAMA

Gulf of Mexico

Tallahassee 16

19 Wakulla Springs State Park

17 Natural Bridge Battlefield State Historic Site

18 St. Marks Wildlife Refuge and Lighthouse

Sopchoppy

Apalachicola National Forest

Ochlockonee R.

Eastpoint

10 St. George Island State Park

Apalachicola 6

Apalachicola Bay

9 Port St. Joe

St. Joseph Bay

Wewahitchka

Callaway

Panama City

8 Panama City Beach

St. Andrew Bay

East Bay

North Bay

Blountstown

Apalachicola R.

Sumatra

Marianna

Florida Caverns

15 Florida Caverns State Park

Graceville

Bonifay

14 Falling Waters State Recreational Area

Ebro

Choctawhatchee R.

Point Washington

7 Eden State Gardens

11 Seaside

Chattahoochee

Quincy

Lake Seminole

Lake Talquin

DeFuniak Springs 13

12 Crestview

5 Valparaiso/Niceville

Choctawhatchee Bay

4 Destin

Holt

3 Fort Walton Beach

Navarre Beach

Gulf Islands National Seashore

Santa Rosa Island

Pensacola Bay

1 Pensacola

2

Warrington

Myrtle Grove

Milton

Munson

Century

Escambia R.

Perdido R.

Blackwater R.

Choctawhatchee R.

50 miles

75 km

N

**Fort Pickens.** This fort's most famous resident was imprisoned Apache Indian chief Geronimo, who was reportedly fairly well liked by his captors. Located at the western tip of Santa Rosa Island (now part of the Gulf Islands National Seashore), Fort Pickens has a museum, nature exhibits, aquariums, and a large campground. ⊠ *Ranger station at Ft. Pickens Rd.,* ☎ *904/934–2635.* ⊡ *$4 per car.* ☉ *Daily 8:30–sunset.*

**Historic Pensacola Village.** More than a half dozen historical museums and buildings are clustered together between Adams and Tarragona streets. The **Museum of Industry,** housed in a late-19th-century warehouse, hosts permanent exhibits dedicated to the lumber, maritime, and shipping industries—once mainstays of Pensacola's economy. A reproduction of a 19th-century streetscape is displayed in the **Museum of Commerce,** and the city's historical archives are kept in the **Pensacola Historical Museum**—what was once one of Florida's oldest churches. Also in the village are the **Julee Cottage Museum of Black History, Dorr House, Lavalle House,** and **Quina House.** ⊠ *Historic Pensacola Village, Zaragoza and Tarragona Sts.,* ☎ *904/444–8905.* ⊡ *Free.* ☉ *Mon.–Sat. 10–4.* ⊠ *Pensacola Historical Museum,* ☎ *904/433–1559.* ⊡ *$2.* ☉ *Apr.–Sept., Mon.–Sat. 9–4:30; Oct.–Mar., Mon.–Sat. 10–4:30.*

**North Hill Preservation District.** Pensacola's affluent families, many made rich during the turn-of-the-century timber boom, built their homes here, where British and Spanish fortresses once stood. Today, residents still occasionally unearth cannonballs while digging in their gardens. North Hill occupies 50 blocks with over 500 homes in Queen Anne, neo-classical, Tudor revival, and Mediterranean styles. Take a drive through this community, but remember these are private residences not open to the public. Places of general interest in the district include the 1902 Spanish mission-style Christ Episcopal Church; Lee Square, where a 50-foot obelisk stands as Pensacola's tribute to the Old Confederacy; and Fort George, an undeveloped parcel of land at the site of the largest of three forts built by the British in 1778.

★ **Palafox Historic District.** Palafox Street is the main stem of this area, which was the commercial and government hub of old Pensacola. Note the Spanish Renaissance–style Saenger Theater, Pensacola's old movie palace, and the Bear Block, a former wholesale grocery with wrought-iron balconies that are a legacy from Pensacola's Creole past. On Palafox between Government and Zaragoza streets is a statue of Andrew Jackson that commemorates the formal transfer of Florida from Spain to the United States in 1821.

**Pensacola Museum of Art.** In the days of the horse-drawn paddy wagon, the two-story mission revival building housing the Pensacola Museum of Art served as the city jail. Now it offers a wide range of international fine art, rotating its two exhibits about every six weeks. ⊠ *407 S. Jefferson St.,* ☎ *904/432–5682.* ⊡ *$2, free Tues.* ☉ *Tues.–Fri. 10–5, Sat. 10–4, Sun. 1–4.*

**Pensacola Naval Air Station.** This air base, established in 1914, is the nation's oldest such facility. On display in the **National Museum of Naval Aviation** (☎ *904/452–9304*) are more than 100 aircraft that had an important role in aviation history. Among them are the NC-4, which in 1919 became the first plane to cross the Atlantic by air; the famous World War II fighter, the F6 *Hellcat*; and the *Skylab Command Module.* A recent attraction is a 14-seat flight simulator. ⊠ *190 Radford Blvd.,* ☎ *904/452–2311* ⊡ *Free.* ☉ *Daily 9–5; closed Thanksgiving, Dec. 25, and Jan. 1.*

**❷ Santa Rosa Island.** Since 1971 more than 280 species of birds, from the common loon to the majestic osprey, have been spotted here. Two caveats for visitors: "Leave nothing behind but your footprints," and "Don't pick the sea oats" (natural grasses that help keep the dunes intact). This stop is a must for bird-watchers. To get onto the island by car, take U.S. 98 to the Route 399 bridge.

**Seville.** This historic district is the site of Pensacola's first permanent Spanish colonial settlement. Its center is Seville Square, a live oak-shaded park bounded by Alcaniz, Adams, Zaragoza, and Government streets. Roam these brick streets past honeymoon cottages and bay-front homes. Many of the buildings have been converted into restaurants, commercial offices, and shops where you can buy anything from wind socks to designer clothes.

**T. T. Wentworth, Jr. Florida State Museum.** Pensacola's old City Hall, built in 1908, has been refurbished and reopened to display some 150,000 artifacts ranging from Civil War weaponry to bottle caps. ⊠ *330 S. Jefferson St.,* ☏ *904/444–8905.* ☞ *$5.50.* ⊙ *Mon.–Sat. 10–4.*

NEED A BREAK? The **Napoleon Bakery** (⊠ 101 S. Jefferson St., ☏ 904/434–9701) is French right down to the accents of the waiters. Mingle with town folk over a Continental breakfast of just-baked pastries or a lunch of quiche, croissants, and, of course, napoleons served tearoom-style with fresh-brewed, aromatic coffees.

**The Zoo.** The local zoo is home to plants, animals, and 30 acres of ponds, lakes, and open plains. ⊠ *5701 Gulf Breeze Pkwy., Gulf Breeze,* ☏ *904/932–2229.* ☞ *$5.25* ⊙ *Daily 9–5.*

## Beaches

Dotting the 150-mile stretch between Destin and Gulfport, Mississippi is **Gulf Islands National Seashore** (☏ 904/934–2600), which consists of a number of beach and recreational spots along pristine coastline. Managed by the National Park Service, they include **Fort Pickens,** at the west end of Santa Rosa Island; the **Santa Rosa Day Use Area,** 10 miles east of Pensacola Beach; and **Johnson's Beach** on Perdido Key, about 20 miles southwest of Pensacola's historic districts. Check with the National Park Service for any restrictions that might apply.

**Pensacola Beach** (☏ 904/932–2258) is 5 miles south of Pensacola. Take U.S. 98 to Gulf Breeze, and cross the Bob Sikes Bridge over to Santa Rosa Island. Beachcombers and sunbathers, sailboarders and sailors keep things going at a fever pitch in and out of the water.

## Dining and Lodging

$$ ✕ **Jamie's.** Dining here is like spending the evening in the antiques-
★ filled parlor of a fine old Southern home. If a visit to Florida has you oystered and shrimped out, the chef recommends the Maine lobster. The wine list has more than 200 labels. ⊠ *424 E. Zaragoza St.,* ☏ *904/434–2911. AE, MC, V. Closed Sun. No lunch Mon.*

$ ✕ **McGuire's Irish Pub.** Drink beer brewed right on the premises in copper and oaken casks, and eat your corned beef and cabbage while an Irish tenor croons in the background. Located in an old firehouse, the pub is replete with antiques, moose heads, Irish Tiffany lamps, and Erin-go-bragh memorabilia. More than 100,000 dollar bills signed and dated by the pub's patrons flutter from the ceiling. The waitresses are chatty and aim to please. Menu items run from kosher-style sandwiches to chili con carne to pecan pie. ⊠ *600 E. Gregory St.,* ☏ *904/433–6789. AE, D, DC, MC, V.*

$ ✕ **Mesquite Charlie's.** Stop by for the best gol' darn steaks east (or west) of the Mississippi. You can watch 'em broil over mesquite charcoal in a pit just inside the door. Got a hankerin' for sumpin' else? Try baby-back ribs barbecued with a tangy house sauce. No neckties allowed— "We cut 'em off." ⊠ *5901 North W St., ☎ 904/434–0498. AE, MC, V. No lunch.*

$$$–$$$$ ⌸ **Pensacola Grand Hotel.** The lobby will instantly tip you off that this hotel is actually the renovated Louisville & Nashville train depot. Ticket and baggage counters are still intact, and old railroad signs remind guests of the days when steam locomotives chugged up to these doors. The old train station connects via a canopied two-story galleria to a 15-story tower. Here's where the spittoons and hand trucks give way to upholstered furniture and deep-pile carpet; standard doubles are up-to-date and roomy. Bi-level penthouse suites have snazzy wet bars and whirlpool baths. ⊠ *200 E. Gregory St., 32501, ☎ 904/433–3336, FAX 904/432–7572. 212 rooms. Restaurant, lounge, pool, airport shuttle. AE, D, DC, MC, V.*

$$$–$$$$ ⌸ **Perdido Sun.** This high-rise is the perfect expression of Gulf-side resort living. One-, two-, or three-bedroom decorator-furnished units all have seaside balconies with spectacular views of the water. You can choose to make this your home away from home—accommodations include fully equipped kitchens—or you can pamper yourself with daily maid service. ⊠ *13753 Perdido Key Dr., 32507, ☎ 904/492–2390 or 800/227–2390, FAX 904/492–4135. 93 units. Indoor pool, outdoor pool, spa, health club. D, MC, V.*

$$–$$$ ⌸ **Holiday Inn/Pensacola Beach.** Inside, the lobby is simple, with potted plants, floral arrangements, and a coral-color decor. Outside, there's 1,500 feet of private beach. From the ninth-floor Penthouse Lounge, you can watch the goings-on in the Gulf, which is especially nice when the setting sun turns the western sky to lavender and orange. ⊠ *165 Ft. Pickens Rd., Pensacola Beach 32561, ☎ 904/932–5361 or 800/465–4329, FAX 904/932–7121. 150 rooms. Restaurant, lounge, pool, tennis courts, beach, recreation room. AE, D, DC, MC, V.*

$$ ⌸ **New World Inn.** This is Pensacola's hush-hush hotel, the one where ★ celebrities who visit the city are likely to stay. Photos of dozens of the inn's famous guests (Lucille Ball, Shirley Jones, Charles Kuralt) hang behind the front desk. The guest rooms' exquisite furnishings take their inspiration from the five periods of Pensacola's past: French or Spanish provincial, early American, antebellum, or Queen Anne. The baths are handsomely appointed. ⊠ *600 S. Palafox St., 32501, ☎ 904/432–4111, FAX 904/435–8939. 14 rooms, 2 suites. Restaurant, lounge. AE, DC, MC, V.*

$–$$ ⌸ **Ramada Inn North.** This hotel is close to the airport and a good bet if you've got an early flight. Suites have game tables and entertainment centers; some have whirlpools. ⊠ *6550 Pensacola Blvd., 32505, ☎ 904/477–0711 or 800/272–6232, FAX 904/477–0711, Ext. 602. 106 rooms. Restaurant, lounge, pool, airport shuttle. AE, D, DC, MC, V.*

# Nightlife and the Arts

## The Arts

Productions at the **Saenger Theatre** (⊠ 118 S. Palafox St., ☎ 904/769–1217) include touring Broadway shows and two locally staged operas a year. The **Pensacola Little Theatre** (⊠ 186 N. Palafox St., ☎ 904/432–8621) presents plays and musicals during a season that runs from fall through spring. **Pensacola's Symphony Orchestra** (☎ 904/435–2533) offers a series of five concerts each season at the Saenger Theatre.

### Nightlife

After dark, **McGuire's Irish Pub** (⊠ 600 E. Gregory St., ☎ 904/433–6789) particularly welcomes those of Irish descent. If you don't like crowds, stay away from McGuire's on Friday night and nights when Notre Dame games are televised. **Mesquite Charlie's** (⊠ 5901 North W St., ☎ 905/434–0498) offers country music and all the trappings of a Wild West saloon. The **Seville Quarter** (⊠ 130 E. Government St., ☎ 904/434—0498) has seven fabulous bars and features music from disco to Dixieland; it's Pensacola's equivalent of the New Orleans French Quarter.

## Outdoor Activities and Sports

### Auto Racing

Billed as the fastest ½-mile track in the country, **Five Flags Speedway** features action-packed racing with top-name stock-car drivers. ⊠ 7451 Pine Forest Rd., ☎ 904/944–0466. ⊑ $8. ☉ Racing late Mar.–Sept., Fri. at 8.

### Canoeing

Canoe rentals for the versatile Blackwater River are available from **Blackwater Canoe Rental** (⊠ U.S. 90E, Milton, ☎ 904/623–0235) and **Adventures Unlimited** (⊠ Rte. 87, 12 mi north of Milton, ☎ 904/623–6197).

### Dog Racing

Rain or shine, year-round, there's live racing at the **Pensacola Greyhound Track.** Lounge and grandstand areas are fully enclosed and air-conditioned and have instant-replay televisions throughout. ⊠ U.S. 98 at Dog Track Rd., West Pensacola, ☎ 904/455–8598 or 800/345–3997. ⊑ $1, kennel club $2.50. ☉ Tues.–Sat. nights, weekend afternoons.

### Fishing

For a full- or half-day deep-sea charter, try the **Moorings Marina** (⊠ 655 Pensacola Beach Blvd., Pensacola Beach, ☎ 904/932–0305). Licenses and tackle are available at **Penny's Sporting Goods** (⊠ 1800 Pace Blvd., Pensacola, ☎ 904/438–9633). In a pinch, you can drop a line from **Old Pensacola Bay Bridge.**

### Golf

There are several outstanding golf courses in and around Pensacola. The **Club at Hidden Creek** (⊠ 3070 PGA Blvd., Navarre, ☎ 904/939–4604) has 18 holes. The **Perdido Bay Resort** (⊠ 1 Doug Ford Dr., Pensacola, ☎ 904/492–1223), also has an 18-hole course and **Tiger Point Golf & Country Club** (⊠ 1255 Country Club Rd., Gulf Breeze, ☎ 904/932–1333) has 36 holes.

### Tennis

Tennis courts are available in more than 30 locations in the Pensacola area; among them is the **Pensacola Racquet Club** (⊠ 3450 Wimbledon Dr., Pensacola, ☎ 904/434–2434).

### Water Sports

When you rent a sailboat, Jet Ski, or catamaran from **Bonifay Water Sports** (⊠ 460 Pensacola Beach Blvd., Pensacola Beach, ☎ 904/932–0633) you'll also receive safety and sailing instructions.

## Shopping

**Cordova Mall** (⊠ 5100 N. 9th Ave., Pensacola) is anchored by four department stores, plus specialty shops and a food court. **Harbourtown**

**Shopping Village** (✉ 913 Gulf Breeze Pkwy., Gulf Breeze) has trendy shops and the ambience of a wharfside New England village.

# CHOCTAWHATCHEE BAY

There's a handful of interesting towns around the western end of Choctawhatchee Bay, two of which have had sudden growth spurts, and two of which are on the brink of expansion. Fort Walton Beach got its jump start during World War II; now greater Fort Walton Beach has more than 78,000 residents, making it the largest urban area on the Emerald Coast. Destin, on the southern side of the strait that connects Choctawhatchee Bay to the Gulf of Mexico, boomed in the 1930s, when its rich fishing waters were recognized. The twin cities of Valparaiso and Niceville are still relatively tranquil, although the 1993 opening of the Mid-Bay Bridge, linking the cities with beaches across the bay, may soon alter their quiet status.

## Fort Walton Beach

**❸ Fort Walton Beach** dates from the Civil War but had to wait more than 75 years to come into its own. Patriots loyal to the Confederate cause organized Walton's Guard (named in honor of Colonel George Walton, onetime acting territorial governor of West Florida) and camped at a site on Santa Rosa Sound, later known as Camp Walton. In 1940 fewer than 90 people lived in Fort Walton Beach, but within a decade the city became a boomtown, thanks to New Deal money for roads and bridges and the development of Eglin Field during World War II. The military is now Fort Walton Beach's main source of income, but tourism runs a close second.

### Sights to See

★ **Air Force Armament Museum.** This collection just outside the Eglin Air Force Base's main gate, contains more than 5,000 Air Force armaments from World Wars I and II and the Korean and Vietnam wars. Included are uniforms, engines, weapons, aircraft, and flight simulators; larger craft such as transport planes are exhibited on the grounds outside the museum. A 32-minute movie about Eglin's history and its role in the development of armaments plays continuously throughout the day. ✉ *Rte. 85, Eglin Air Force Base,* ☎ *904/882–4062.* ☞ *Free.* ☉ *Daily 9:30–4:30; closed Thanksgiving, Dec. 25, and Jan. 1.*

**Eglin Air Force Base.** This base encompasses 728 square miles of land including 10 auxiliary fields and a total of 21 runways. Jimmie Doolittle's Tokyo Raiders trained here, as did the Son Tay Raiders, a group that made a daring attempt to rescue American POWs from a North Vietnamese prison camp in 1970. Group tours are given by special arrangement. ✉ *Rte. 85,* ☎ *904/882–3931.*

**Indian Temple Mound Museum.** Kids especially enjoy this museum, where they can learn all about the prehistoric peoples who inhabited northwest Florida up to 10,000 years ago. The funerary masks and weaponry on display are particularly fascinating. The museum is adjacent to the 600-year-old **National Historic Landmark Temple Mound,** a large earthwork built over salt water. ✉ *139 Miracle Strip Pkwy., U.S. 98,* ☎ *904/243–6521.* ☞ *$2.* ☉ *Sept.–May, weekdays 11–4, Sat. 9–4; June–Aug., Mon.–Sat. 9–4.*

### Beaches

**John C. Beasley State Park** (no phone) is Fort Walton Beach's seaside playground on Okaloosa Island. A boardwalk leads to the beach, where you'll find covered picnic tables, changing rooms, and freshwater showers. Lifeguards are on duty during the summer. **Eglin Reservation Beach** (no phone) is on 5 miles of undeveloped military land, about 3 miles west of the Brooks Bridge in Fort Walton Beach. This beach is a favorite haunt of local teenagers.

## Dining and Lodging

$$ ✕ **Staff's.** Sip a Tropical Depression or a rum-laced Squall Line while you peruse a menu tucked into the centerfold of a tabloid-size newspaper filled with snippets of local history, early photographs, and family memorabilia. Since 1931, people have been coming to this garage-turned-eatery for steaks broiled as you like them and seafood dishes like freshly caught Florida lobster and char-grilled amberjack. The grand finale is a trip to the delectable dessert bar; try a generous wedge of cherry cheesecake. ⊠ *24 S.E. Miracle Strip Pkwy,* ☎ *904/243–3482. AE, D, MC, V. No lunch.*

$ ✕ **Pandora's.** On the Emerald Coast the name Pandora's is synony-★ mous with prime rib. On the outside, this waterfront restaurant appears gray and weather-beaten, but inside it's decorated in warm, cozy earth tones and filled with alcoves and tables for four that lend an air of intimacy to dining here. You can order your prime rib regular or extra cut; fish aficionados should try the char-grilled yellowfin tuna, bacon-wrapped and topped with Jamaican sauce. The mood turns a bit more gregarious in the lounge where there is live entertainment several evenings a week. ⊠ *1120 Santa Rosa Blvd.,* ☎ *904/244–8669. AE, D, DC, MC, V. No lunch.*

$$–$$$ 🏨 **Holiday Inn.** This U-shaped hotel consists of a seven-story tower flanked by three-story wings. Rooms have a pastel green-and-peach decor and face either the Gulf or the pool, although even the poolside rooms have some view of the sea. In the contemporary lobby, colored banners hang from the ceiling. ⊠ *1110 Santa Rosa Blvd., 32548,* ☎ *904/243–9181 or 800/732–4853,* 🖷 *904/664–7652. 380 rooms. Restaurants, lounge, 3 pools, tennis courts, exercise room, beach. AE, D, DC, MC, V.*

$$–$$$ 🏨 **Ramada Beach Resort.** The lobby and entrance are slick—black marble and disco lights—and some locals feel it's too much like the Las Vegas strip. Activity here centers on a pool with a grotto and swim-through waterfall; there's also an 800-foot private beach. ⊠ *U.S. 98E, 32548,* ☎ *904/243–9161, 800/874–8962, or 800/447–0010,* 🖷 *904/243–2391. 454 rooms. 3 restaurants, 2 lounges, pools, tennis courts, exercise room, beach. AE, D, DC, MC, V.*

## Nightlife and the Arts

### THE ARTS
The **Okaloosa Symphony Orchestra** (☎ 904/244–3308) performs a series of concerts featuring guest artists at the Fort Walton Beach Civic Auditorium, (⊠ U.S. 98W, Fort Walton Beach). **Stage Crafters Community Theatre** (⊠ U.S. 98W, Fort Walton Beach, ☎ 904/243–1102) stages four first-rate amateur productions a year at the Fort Walton Beach Civic Auditorium. The **Northwest Florida Ballet** (⊠ 101 S.E. Chicago Ave., Fort Walton Beach, ☎ 904/664–7787) has a repertoire of the classics and performs in communities throughout the Panhandle.

### NIGHTLIFE
Catch the action at **Cash's Faux Pas Lounge** (⊠ 106 Santa Rosa Blvd., ☎ 904/244–2274), where anything goes.

## Outdoor Activities and Sports

### BIKING

Routes through Eglin Air Force Base Reservation present cyclists the challenges of tortuous, wooded trails. Biking here requires a $3 permit, which can be obtained from the **Jackson Guard** (⊠ 107 Rte. 85N, Niceville, ☎ 904/882–4164). Rentals are available from **Bob's Bicycle Center** (⊠ 415 Mary Esther Cutoff, Fort Walton Beach, ☎ 904/243–5856).

### DIVING

You can arrange for diving lessons or excursions at the **Scuba Shop** (⊠ 348 Miracle Strip Pkwy., ☎ 904/243–1600).

### FISHING

Get outfitted with a license and tackle at **Stewart's Outdoor Sports** (⊠ 4 S.E. Eglin Pkwy., ☎ 904/243–9443).

### GOLF

**Island Golf Center** (⊠ 1306 Miracle Strip Pkwy., Fort Walton Beach, ☎ 904/244–1612) has 36 holes of miniature golf, a nine-hole par-3 course, and video games. The **Fort Walton Beach Municipal Golf Course** (⊠ Rte. 189, Fort Walton Beach, ☎ 904/862–3314) with 36 holes is rated as one of Florida's best public layouts. **Shalimar Pointe Golf & Country Club** (⊠ 203 Country Club Dr., Shalimar, ☎ 904/651–1416) has an 18-hole course.

### TENNIS

The **Municipal Tennis Center** (⊠ W. Audrey Dr., Fort Walton Beach, ☎ 904/243–8789) has 12 lighted Laykold courts and four practice walls. You can play tennis on seven Rubico and two hard courts at the **Fort Walton Racquet Club** (⊠ 23 Hurlburt Field Rd., Fort Walton Beach, ☎ 904/862–2023).

### WATER SPORTS

Pontoon-boat rentals are available at **Consigned RV's** (⊠ 101 W. Miracle Strip Pkwy., ☎ 904/243–4488).

## Shopping

Stores in the **Manufacturer's Outlet Center** (⊠ 127 and 255 Miracle Strip Pkwy., Fort Walton Beach), offer well-known brands of clothing and housewares at a substantial discount. Near Fort Walton Beach, there are four department stores in the **Santa Rosa Mall** (⊠ 300 Mary Esther Cutoff, Mary Esther), as well as 118 other shops and 15 bistro-style eateries.

## Destin

❹ **Destin,** Fort Walton Beach's neighbor, lies on the other side of the strait that connects Choctawhatchee Bay with the Gulf of Mexico. Destin takes its name from its founder, Leonard A. Destin, a Connecticut sea captain who settled his family here sometime in the 1830s. For the next 100 years, Destin remained a sleepy little fishing village until the strait, or East Pass, was bridged in 1935. Then, recreational anglers discovered its white sands, blue-green waters, and abundance of some of the most sought-after sport fish in the world. More billfish are hauled in around Destin each year than from all other Gulf fishing ports combined. But you don't have to be the rod-and-reel type to love Destin. There's plenty to entertain the sand-pail set as well as senior citizens, and there are many gourmet restaurants.

## Sights to See

**Destin Fishing Museum.** The highlight here is a dry aquarium, where lighting and sound effects create the sensation of being underwater. You can get the feeling of walking on a sandy bottom broken by coral reef and dotted with sponges. It's a good place for the marine enthusiast to get an overview of aquatic life in the Gulf of Mexico. ⊠ *35 U.S. 98E,* ☎ *904/654–1011.* ⊇ *$1.* ☉ *Tues.–Sat. noon–4, Sun. 1–4.*

**Old Destin Post Office Museum.** To get an idea of the rampaging growth that's occurred in the Destin area, visit the Old Destin Post Office Museum. This tiny facility was a working post office until 1954; its display of old photographs and office machines reflects the fishing-hamlet character of Old Destin. ⊠ *Stahlman Ave.,* ☎ *904/837–8572.* ⊡ *Free.* ☉ *Wed. 1:30–4:30.*

## Beaches

**Crystal Beach RV Park** (☎ 904/837–6447) has something to appeal to just about everyone. This sanctuary, located just 5 miles east of Destin, is protected on each side by undeveloped state-owned land.

## Dining and Lodging

$$ ✕ **Marina Cafe.** A harbor-view setting, impeccable service, and uptown
★ ambience have earned this establishment a reputation as one of the finest dining experiences on the Emerald Coast. The decor's oceanic motif is expressed in shades of aqua, green, and sand accented with marine tapestries and sea sculptures. Diners have a choice of classic Creole, Italian, or Pacific Rim cuisine. Try a regional specialty, such as the award-winning black pepper-crusted yellowfin tuna with braised spinach and spicy soy sauce. The wine list is extensive. ⊠ *404 U.S. 98E,* ☎ *904/837–7960. AE, D, DC, MC, V. No lunch.*

$ ✕ **Flamingo Cafe.** This café serves up two different atmospheres. The pink and teal color scheme, carried through to the teal cummerbunds and bow ties on the waiters, creates a tropical ambience the proprietor calls "Floribbean," while the panoramic view of Destin harbor seen from every seat in the house lends an airy, seaside feel. Chef's specialties include a delicious Floribbean grilled swordfish with papaya chutney butter, wilted spinach, black beans, and roasted sweet peppers. ⊠ *414 U.S. 98E,* ☎ *904/837–0961. AE, D, DC, MC, V.*

$ ✕ **Harbor Docks.** An unimposing gray clapboard building in front fans out into a series of dining areas behind, all within the sights and sounds of the fishing boats and jet skis in Destin Harbor. Char-grilled, sautéed, or poached fish include such regional favorites as snapper, cobia, and triggerfish, fresh from the restaurant's own wholesale market. ⊠ *538 U.S. 98E,* ☎ *904/837–2506. AE, D, DC, MC, V.*

$$–$$$$ ⊞ **Sandestin Beach Resort.** This 2,600-acre resort of villas, cottages,
★ condominiums, and an inn seems to be a town unto itself. All rooms have a view, either of the Gulf, Choctawhatchee Bay, a golf course, lagoon, or bird sanctuary. This resort provides something for an assortment of tastes, from simple to extravagant, and offers special rates September through March. ⊠ *9300 U.S. 98W, 32541,* ☎ *904/267–8000 or 800/277–0800,* FAX *904/267–8222. 175 rooms, 375 villas. 4 restaurants, 11 pools, 3 golf courses, 14 tennis courts, health club, beach, pro shops. AE, D, DC, MC, V.*

$$–$$$ ⊞ **Summer Breeze.** White picket fences and porches or patios outside each unit make this condominium complex look like a summer place out of the Gay '90s. One-bedroom suites have fully equipped kitchens and can sleep up to six people in queen-size beds, sleeper sofas, or bunks. It's halfway between Destin and the Sandestin Beach Resort area and is across from a roadside park, which gives it a private and secluded

feel. ✉ *2384 Old Hwy. 98, 32541,* ☎ *904/837–4853, 800/874–8914, or 800/336–4853,* FAX *904/837–5390. 36 units. Pool, hot tub. AE, D, MC, V.*

**$–$$**   🏨 **Village Inn of Destin.** This property, only minutes away from the Gulf, was built in 1983 with families in mind. A variety of amenities, including entertainment, is provided to occupy each member of the family. Rooms have serviceable dressers and queen- or king-size beds. ✉ *215 U.S. 98E, 32541,* ☎ *904/837–7413,* FAX *904/654–3394. 100 rooms. Pool. AE, D, DC, MC, V.*

### Nightlife
**Nightown** (✉ 140 Palmetto St., ☎ 904/837–6448) has a dance floor with laser lights and a New Orleans–style bar with a live band.

### Outdoor Activities and Sports

#### DIVING
Diving instruction and outings are available through **Aquanaut Scuba Center, Inc.** (✉ 24 U.S. 98W, ☎ 904/837–0359).

#### FISHING
If you're planning a deep-sea fishing excursion, be advised that rates for charter boats are usually quoted by the day (about $575) or half day (about $300). This is an immensely popular pastime, especially in this acclaimed fishing area. Among the charters are **Miller's Charter Services** (off U.S. 98 on the docks next to A.J.'s Restaurant, Destin, ☎ 904/837–6059) and **East Pass Charters** (East Pass Marina, U.S. 98E, Destin, ☎ 904/654–2022). Also, you can always pier fish from the 3,000-foot-long **Destin Catwalk,** along the East Pass Bridge.

#### GOLF
For sheer numbers of holes, the **Sandestin Beach Resort** (✉ 300 U.S. 98W, Destin, ☎ 904/267–8211) tops the list with 63 holes. The **Indian Bayou Golf & Country Club** (✉ Airport Rd. off U.S. 98, Destin, ☎ 904/837–6192) offers a 27-hole course. The **Santa Rosa Golf & Beach Club** (✉ Rte. 30A, Santa Rosa Beach, ☎ 904/267–2229) has 18 holes.

#### TENNIS
**Sandestin Beach Resort** (✉ 9300 U.S. 98W, ☎ 904/267–7110), one of the nation's five-star tennis resorts, has 14 courts with grass, hard, and Rubico surfaces. The **Destin Racquet & Fitness Center** (✉ 995 Airport Rd., ☎ 904/837–7300) has six Rubico courts.

#### WATER SPORTS
**Big Kahuna's Lost Paradise** (✉ U.S. 98, ☎ 904/837–4061) is a water park with miniature golf and an amphitheater. You can rent powerboats for fishing, skiing, and snorkeling at **Baytowne Marina at Sandestin** (9300 U.S. 98W, ☎ 904/267–7777).

### Shopping
The **Market at Sandestin** (✉ 9375 U.S. 98W, Destin) has 28 upscale shops that peddle such goods as gourmet chocolates and designer clothes in an elegant minimall with boardwalks. **Silver Sands Factory Stores** (✉ 5021 U.S. 98E, Destin) has more than 106 shops featuring top-name merchandise that ranges from gifts to kids' clothes to menswear.

## Valparaiso and Niceville

**❺**   On the northern side of Choctawhatchee Bay, are the twin cities of **Valparaiso and Niceville,** granted their charters in 1921 and 1938, respectively. Niceville evolved from a tiny fishing hamlet called Boggy, whose sandy-bottom bays were rich in mullet. Valparaiso was founded by an entrepreneurial Chicagoan named John B. Perrine, who envisioned it as an ideal city by the sea, or "vale of paradise." Together, the cities have maintained a serene existence, more or less untouched by the tourist trade farther south. Although their character hasn't changed since the 1993 opening of the Mid-Bay Bridge, the link to the beaches of south Walton County has enhanced their viability as a vacation destination.

## Sights to See

**Fred Gannon Rocky Bayou State Recreation Area.** East of Niceville, off Route 20 on Rocky Bayou, are 50 excellent picnic areas, nature trails, boat ramps, and uncrowded campsites with electrical and water hookups in this recreation area. It's quiet and secluded, yet easy to find, and a great venue for serious bikers. ⊠ *Rte. 20,* ☎ *904/833–9144.* ⚏ *$2 per vehicle for day use; campsites $8.56, $10.70 with electricity.* ☉ *Daily 8–sunset.*

**Heritage Museum.** You can take a long step back in time among 8,000-year-old stone tools and early 20th-century iron pots and kettles. A rarity on display here is a steam-powered, belt-driven cotton gin. The museum also maintains a reference library of genealogical and historical research materials and official Civil War records. ⊠ *115 Westview Ave.,* ☎ *904/678–2615.* ⚏ *Free.* ☉ *Tues.–Sat. 11–4.*

## Dining and Lodging

$ ✕ **Nicometo's.** Wedged between a jeweler's and a sporting-goods store, this shopping plaza restaurant dishes up steamed shrimp that makes even the most jaded of diners sit up and take notice. Fried shrimp and chargrilled grouper also go over big with the regulars, but the only concession to red-meat eaters is a New York strip. The decor in the dimly lit dining room is plain and simple—fishing trophies and advertising memorabilia. If you want a jazzier setting, pick a table in the sports bar, where you can throw darts or watch TV. ⊠ *1027 John Sims Pkwy., Niceville,* ☎ *904/678–5072. MC, V.*

$$–$$$ 🏨 **Bluewater Bay Resort.** This upscale resort is carved out of 1,800
★ acres of pines and oaks on the shores of Choctawhatchee Bay. It's still woodsy around the edges, but showcase homes are surrounded by tenderly manicured gardens. Rentals run the gamut from motel rooms to villas (some with fireplaces and fully equipped kitchens) and patio homes. Checkout information in the rental units is translated into German for the benefit of international visitors, who flock to this golf course–rich region. ⊠ *1950 Bluewater Blvd., Niceville 32578,* ☎ *904/897–3613 or 800/874–2128,* 𝖥𝖠𝖷 *904/897–2424. 106 units. Restaurant, lounge, 3 pools, 36 holes of golf, 19 tennis courts, beach, boating, playground. AE, D, DC, MC, V.*

## Outdoor Activities and Sports

### FISHING

Licenses and tackle are available at **Outdoor Sports** (⊠ 1025 Palm Plaza, Niceville, ☎ 904/678–4804).

### GOLF

**Bluewater Bay Resort** (⊠ 6 miles east of Niceville on Rte. 20E, ☎ 904/897–3241), offers 36 holes of championship golf on courses designed by Jerry Pate and Tom Fazio.

### TENNIS

There are 19 courts (12 lighted) featuring two different playing surfaces at **Bluewater Bay Resort's tennis center** (⊠ Rte. 20E, Niceville, ☎ 904/897–3679).

# THE GULF COAST

From Choctawhatchee Bay southeast to Apalachicola Bay, there is an enormous variety of towns strung along the shoreline on U.S. 98. Seaside, a town less than 20 years old, is an interesting experiment; residents hope that a strong sense of community will be inspired by old-fashioned architecture and civic planning. Farther south on U.S. 98 is Panama City Beach, its "Miracle Strip" crammed with classic boardwalk entertainment and junk food. An alternative to neon-lit tourist havens is the quiet, blue-collar town of Apalachicola, Florida's main oyster fishery, where many oystermen still fish by hand, using long-handled tongs to bring in their catch.

## Sights to See

**6 Apalachicola.** About 34 miles east of Port St. Joe is Apalachicola, the state's most important oyster fishery. Drive by the Raney House, circa 1850, and Trinity Episcopal Church, built from prefabricated parts in 1838. Stop in at the **John Gorrie State Museum,** honoring the physician credited with inventing ice-making and air-conditioning. Exhibits of Apalachicola history are displayed here as well. ⊠ *Ave. C and 6th St.,* ☎ *904/653–9347.* ▣ *$1.* ☉ *Thurs.–Mon. 9–5.*

★ **7 Eden State Gardens.** Scarlett O'Hara might be at home here on the lawn of an antebellum mansion set amid an arcade of moss-draped live oaks. Furnishings in the spacious rooms date from as far back as the 17th century. The surrounding gardens are beautiful year-round, but they're nothing short of spectacular in mid-March, when the azaleas and dogwoods are in full bloom. ⊠ *Rte. 395, Point Washington,* ☎ *904/231–4214.* ▣ *Gardens free, mansion tour $1.50.* ☉ *Daily 8–sunset, mansion tours Thurs.–Mon. hourly 9–4.*

**☾ Gulf World.** (⊠ 15412 Front Beach Rd., Panama City Beach, ☎ 904/234–5271) Performers include a bottle-nosed dolphin, porpoises, seals, otters, and sea lions.

**☾ Miracle Strip Amusement Park.** (⊠ 12000 Front Beach Rd., Panama City Beach, ☎ 904/234–5810) This park has dozens of rides, from the traditional Ferris wheel to a roller coaster with a 65-foot drop.

**8 Panama City Beach.** In spite of the shoulder-to-shoulder condominiums, motels, and amusement parks that make it seem like one big carnival ground, Panama City Beach has a natural beauty that excuses its overcommercialization. The incredible white sands, navigable waterways, and plentiful marine life that attracted Spanish conquistadors are a lure for today's family-vacation industry.

**9 Port St. Joe.** Florida's first constitution was drafted here in 1838. Most of the old town, including the original hall, is gone—wiped out by hurricanes—but the exhibits in the **Constitution Convention State Museum** recall the event. There are also provisions for camping and picnicking in a small park surrounding the museum. ⊠ *200 Island Memorial Way,* ☎ *904/229–8029.* ▣ *$1.* ☉ *Thurs.–Mon. 9–noon and 1–5.*

**10 St. George Island State Park** can be reached by a causeway from Eastpoint, east of Apalachicola. You can drive toward the sea along the narrow spit of land, with its dunes, sea oats, and abundant birdlife. The dunes seems to be constantly moving; pine trees have been almost buried here by windblown sand. ☎ *904/927–2111.* ▣ *$3.25 per vehicle with up to 8 people.* ☉ *Daily 8–sunset.*

★ ⑪ **Seaside.** Unlike most developments, whose architecture is contemporary, the Seaside community is all Victorian-style fretwork, white picket fences, front-porch rockers, and captain's walks, and when you visit you can't help but feel as though you have been magic-carpeted to Cape May or Cape Cod. Seaside is the brainchild of Robert Davis, who dictated certain architectural elements that he felt would promote a neighborly, old-fashioned life-style. All houses are on small lots, so none is more than ¼ mile from the center of town, and it's easy to get about on foot. Building didn't start until 1981, so there isn't enough moss in the brick sidewalks to give that "historic district" look, but this architectural-social experiment is a visual stunner nonetheless.

🕃 **Shipwreck Island** (✉ 12000 Front Beach Rd., Panama City Beach, ☎ 904/234–0368) features 6 acres of water rides, ranging from speedy slides and tubes to the Lazy River.

## Beaches

★ **Grayton Beach State Recreation Area** (✉ 357 Main Park Rd., Seaside, ☎ 904/231–4210, 💲 $3.25, ⊘ 8 AM–sunset) is, without a doubt, one of the most scenic spots along the Gulf Coast, with blue-green waters, white-sand beaches, salt marshes, and swimming, snorkeling, and campground facilities. At the **Panama City Beaches** (☎ 800/722–3224), public beaches along the Miracle Strip combine with the plethora of video-game arcades, miniature golf courses, sidewalk cafés, souvenir shops, and shopping centers to lure people of all ages.

🕃 At the eastern tip of Panama City Beach is the **St. Andrews State Recreation Area** (✉ 4607 State Park Ln., ☎ 904/233–5140, 💲 $3.25), which includes 1,260 acres of beaches, pinewoods, and marshes. There are complete camping facilities here, as well as ample opportunities to swim, pier fish, or hike the dunes along clearly marked nature trails. You can board a ferry to **Shell Island**—a barrier island in the Gulf of Mexico that offers some of the best shelling north of Sanibel Island. An artificial reef creates a calm, shallow play area that is perfect for young children. You can reach **St. George Island State Park** (☞ Sights to See, *above*) by a causeway that spans the Apalachicola River; the park has excellent bird-watching and a boardwalk trail through the dunes. ☎ 904/927–2111. 💲 $3.25 per vehicle with up to 8 people. ⊘ Daily 8–sunset.

## Dining and Lodging

$–$$ ✕ **Boar's Head.** An exterior that looks like an oversize thatch-roof cottage sets the mood for dining in this ersatz-rustic restaurant and tavern. Prime rib has been the number-one people-pleaser since the house opened in 1978, but broiled shrimp with crabmeat stuffing, and blackened seafood, are popular, too. ✉ *17290 Front Beach Rd., Panama City Beach,* ☎ *904/234–6628. AE, D, DC, MC, V. No lunch.*

$–$$ ✕ **Capt. Anderson's.** Come early to watch the boats unload the catch of the day, and be among the first to line up to eat in this noted restaurant. The atmosphere is nautical, with tables made of hatch covers. The Greek specialties aren't limited to feta cheese and shriveled olives; charcoal-broiled fish and steaks have a prominent place on the menu, too. ✉ *5551 N. Lagoon Dr., Panama City Beach,* ☎ *904/234–2225. AE, D, DC, MC, V. Closed Nov.–Jan.; Sun. May–Sept. No lunch.*

$ ★ ✕ **Bud & Alley's.** This roadside restaurant grows its own herbs—rosemary, thyme, basil, fennel, and mint. The inside room is down-to-earth, with its hardwood floors, ceiling fans, and 6-foot windows looking out onto the garden. There is also a screened-in porch with a view of the Gulf. The Gorgonzola salad with sweet peppers is a delightful introduction to one of the entrées, such as the seared duck breast with caramelized garlic, wild mushrooms, and cabernet sauce. ✉ *Rte. 30A, Seaside,* ☎ *904/231–5900. MC, V. Closed Tues. Sept.–May.*

$    ✕ **Montego Bay.** Line up with vacationers and natives for a table at any one of the five restaurants in this local chain. Service is swift and the food is good. Some dishes, such as red beans and rice or oysters on the half shell, are no surprise. Others, such as shrimp rolled in coconut and served with a honey mustard and orange marmalade sauce, are real treats. ✉ *4920 Thomas Dr., Panama City Beach,* ☎ *904/234–8686;* ✉ *9949 Thomas Dr., Panama City Beach* ☎ *904/235–3585;* ✉ *The Shoppes at Edgewater, Panama City Beach,* ☎ *904/233–6033;* ✉ *1931 N. Cove Blvd., Panama City,* ☎ *904/872–0098. AE, D, MC, V.*

$$$–$$$$    🏨 **Seaside.** One- to six-bedroom porticoed faux Victorian cottages are
★    furnished right down to the vacuum cleaners, and decor reflects the owners' personalities. Gulf breezes blowing off the water will remind you of the unspoiled, sugar-white beaches just a short stroll away in this idyllic community. Josephine's Inn also offers charming accommodations, with four-poster beds, fireplaces, and claw-foot tubs; the daily brunch is delicious. ✉ *Rte. 30A, 32459,* ☎ *904/231–2992, 800/865–8895, or 800/848–1840,* ⊞ *904/231–4196. 40 units. 2 pools, 6 tennis courts, badminton, croquet, boating, bicycles. AE, MC, V.*

$$–$$$$    🏨 **Edgewater Beach Resort.** Luxurious one-, two-, and three-bedroom
★    units in beachside towers and golf-course villas are elegantly furnished with wicker and rattan. The resort centerpiece is a Polynesian-style lagoon pool with waterfalls, reflecting ponds, footbridges, and more than 20,000 species of tropical plants. ✉ *11212 U.S. 98A, Panama City Beach, 32407,* ☎ *904/235–4044 or 800/874–8686,* ⊞ *904/233–7529. 520 units. Restaurant, lounge, golf, 12 tennis courts, shuffleboard, game room. AE, D, DC, MC, V.*

$$–$$$$    🏨 **Marriott's Bay Point Resort.** Sheer elegance is the hallmark of this
★    pink stucco property on the shores of Grand Lagoon. Wing chairs, camelback sofas, and Oriental-patterned carpets in the common areas recall an English manor house, as do the Queen Anne guest room furnishings. Gulf view or golf view—take your pick. Kitchen-equipped villas are a mere tee-shot away from the hotel. ✉ *4200 Marriott Dr., Panama City Beach, 32408,* ☎ *904/234–3307 or 800/874–7105,* ⊞ *904/233–1308. 355 rooms and suites. 5 restaurants, lounges, indoor pool, 5 outdoor pools, hot tub, 2 golf courses, 12 lighted tennis courts, boating, fishing. AE, D, DC, MC, V.*

$–$$$    🏨 **Boardwalk Beach Resort.** This mile of beachfront has been staked out by a group of four family-oriented hotels: Howard Johnson, Comfort Inn, Gulfwalk, and Beachwalk inns. All share the long beach, and group parties are given regularly by all four hotels. Each has its own separate pool. ✉ *9450 S. Thomas Dr., Panama City Beach, 32408,* ☎ *904/234–3484 or 800/874–6613,* ⊞ *904/233–4369. 627 units. Lounge, 4 pools. AE, D, DC, MC, V.*

# Nightlife and the Arts

## The Arts
Broadway touring shows, top-name entertainers, and concert artists are booked into the **Marina Civic Center** (✉ 8 Harrison Ave., Panama City, ☎ 904/769–1217).

### Nightlife

**Pineapple Willy's** (✉ 9900 S. Thomas Dr., Panama City Beach, ☎ 904/235–0928) alternately features big-band and rock music and caters to the post-college crowd.

## Outdoor Activities and Sports

### Golf

The **Hombre Golf Club** (✉ 120 Coyote Pass, Panama City Beach, ☎ 904/234–3673) has an 18-hole course. **Marriott's Bay Point Resort** (✉ 4200 Marriott Dr., Panama City Beach, ☎ 904/234–3307) is also open to the public and has 18 holes. **Point Resort** (✉ 100 Delwood Beach Rd., Panama City Beach, ☎ 904/235–6909) has 36 holes. **St. Joseph's Bay Country Club** (✉ 650 Country Club Rd., Port St. Joe, ☎ 904/227–1751) offers an 18-hole course.

### Racing

There's pari-mutuel betting year-round and live greyhound racing five nights and two afternoons a week at the **Ebro Greyhound Park.** Simulcasts of Thoroughbred racing from the Miami area are also shown throughout the year. Schedules change periodically, so call for details. ✉ *Rte. 20 at Rte. 79, Ebro,* ☎ *904/535–4048; outside FL, 800/345–4810.* ☞ *$1, clubhouse $2.*

### Tennis

The tennis center at **Marriott's Bay Point Resort** (✉ 100 Delwood Beach Rd., Panama City Beach, ☎ 904/235–6910) has 12 Har-Tru tennis courts.

## Shopping

Stores in the **Manufacturer's Outlet Center** (✉ 105 W. 23rd St., Panama City) offer well-known brands of clothing and accessories at a substantial discount. The **Panama City Mall** (✉ U.S. 231 and Rte. 77, Panama City) has a mix of more than 100 franchise shops and national chain stores.

# LOWER ALABAMA

Near Florida's border with Alabama, in "Lower Alabama," as the locals have labeled it, are several towns worth visiting. Small and unassuming, they often have surprising cultural attributes, such as the voluminous collections at the Robert L. F. Sikes Public Library in Crestview and the Walton-DeFuniak Public Library in DeFuniak Springs. The area also has its share of geologic oddities, such as the plunging pit of the Falling Waters Sink.

## Sights to See

**⑫ Crestview.** At 235 feet above sea level (quite high by Florida standards), this town was dubbed by surveyors of the Louisville & Nashville Railroad Company, which completed a line through northwest Florida in 1882. There's been a settlement of sorts here since the days of the conquistadors, when it was a crossroads on the Old Spanish Trail. Crestview is the sort of small town where the mayor rides shotgun with the police patrol on a Saturday night and folks enjoy the simpler pleasures, such as roller skating and playing softball. The **Robert L. F. Sikes Public Library** and its research center, housed in an imposing Greek revival building, contain more than 44,000 volumes as well as the private papers of its eponym, a former U.S. congressman.

**⑬  DeFuniak Springs.** This small town was the site of the Knox Hill Academy, founded in 1848 and for more than half a century the only institution of higher learning in northwest Florida. In 1885, it was chosen as the location for the New York Chautauqua educational society's winter assembly. The Chautauqua programs were discontinued in 1922, but DeFuniak Springs attempts to revive them, in spirit at least, by sponsoring a countywide Chautauqua Festival in April.

---

NEED A
BREAK?

**Chautauqua Winery** (⊠ I–10 and U.S. 331, DeFuniak Springs, ☎ 904/892–5887) opened in 1989, but already its award-winning wines have earned raves from oenophiles nationwide. You can take a free tour of the winery to see how ancient art blends with modern technology; then retreat to the tasting room.

---

**⑭  Falling Waters State Recreation Area.** This is the site of one of Florida's most recognized geological features—the Falling Waters Sink. The 100-foot-deep cylindrical pit provides the background for a waterfall, and there's an observation deck for viewing this natural phenomenon. ⊠ *Rte. 77A, Chipley,* ☎ *904/638–6130.* ⚏ *$3.25 per vehicle with up to 8 people.* ☉ *Daily 8–sunset.*

**⑮  Florida Caverns State Park.** Take a ranger-led spelunking tour to see an array of stalagmites, stalagmites, and "waterfalls" of solid rock at this expansive park. There are also hiking trails, campsites, and areas for swimming and canoeing on the Chipola River. ⊠ *Rte. 167, Marianna,* ☎ *904/482–9598.* ⚏ *Park $3.25 per vehicle with up to 8 people, caverns $4.* ☉ *Daily 8–sunset, cavern tours daily 9–4.*

**Walton-DeFuniak Public Library.** By all accounts this tiny facility, measuring 16 feet by 24 feet, is Florida's oldest library continuously operating in its original building. Opened in 1887, added to and expanded over the years, it now contains nearly 30,000 volumes, including some rare books, many older than the structure itself. The collection has grown to include antique musical instruments and an impressive display of European armor. ⊠ *3 Circle Dr., DeFuniak Springs,* ☎ *904/892–3624.* ☉ *Mon. 9–7; Tues., Wed., and Fri. 9–6; Sat. 9–3.*

## Dining and Lodging

$   ✕ **McLain's Family Restaurant.** Assorted Wal-Mart art on the walls, piped-in country-and-western music, and a fireplace with a raised hearth give this mom-and-pop establishment a folksy feel that carries right over to the menu. The owners offer an all-you-can-eat buffet three times a day, always with a poached or broiled entrée. All steaks are hand-cut. On weekends, a seafood buffet draws customers from as far away as Alabama. ⊠ *2680 S. Hwy. 85, Crestview,* ☎ *904/682–5286. AE, D, MC, V.*

$   ▥ **Crestview Holiday Inn.** This simple sandstone-and-stucco motel has a typical Florida decor: shell-shape ceramic lamps, seashell-print bedspreads, and oceanic art on the walls. It's a bit south of downtown Crestview and is the "in" place for local wedding receptions. ⊠ *Rte. 85 and I–10, Box 1358, Crestview, 32536,* ☎ *904/682–6111,* FAX *904/689–1189. 120 rooms. Restaurant, lounge, pool. AE, D, DC, MC, V.*

# THE TALLAHASSEE AREA

I–10 rolls east over the timid beginnings of the Appalachian foothills and through thick pines into the state capital, Tallahassee, with its

canopies of ancient oaks and spring bowers of azaleas. Home to Florida
State University, the city has more than a touch of the Old South. South
of Tallahassee is a chain of nature reserves and historic sites, including the expansive Apalachicola National Forest.

# Tallahassee

**⑯** Florida's capital, **Tallahassee,** maintains a tranquil atmosphere quite
different from the sun-and-surf hedonism of the major coastal towns.
Vestiges of the city's colorful past are found throughout; for example,
in the Capitol Complex the turn-of-the-century Old Capitol building
is strikingly paired with the New Capitol skyscraper. Tallahassee's
tree-lined streets are particularly memorable—among the best canopied
roads are St. Augustine, Miccosukee, Meridian, Old Bainbridge, and
Centerville, all dotted with country stores and antebellum plantation
houses. If you visit between March and April, you'll find the flowers
in bloom and the Springtime Tallahassee festival in full swing.

## Sights to See

★ **Capitol Complex.** This downtown area is compact enough for walking, though it's also served by a free, continuous shuttle trolley. To pick
up information about the Tallahassee area, stop at the Visitors Information Center (open weekdays 8–5), on the plaza level of the **New
Capitol,** a modern skyscraper that looms up 22 stories directly behind
the low-rise Old Capitol. On a clear day, you can catch a panoramic
view of Tallahassee and its surrounding countryside from the top floor.
⊠ *Duvall St.,* ☎ *904/488–6167.* ☎ *Free.* ☉ *Hourly tours daily 9–3.*

The centerpiece of the Capitol complex is the **Old Capitol,** a pre–Civil
War structure that has been added to, and subtracted from, several times
over the years. A recent renovation has restored its jaunty red-and-white
striped awnings and combination gas-electric lights to make it look much
as it did in 1902. ⊠ *Monroe St. at Apalachee Pkwy.,* ☎ *904/487–1902.*
☎ *Free.* ☉ *Self-guided or guided tours weekdays 9–4:30, Sat. 10–4:30,
Sun. noon–4:30.*

**Downtown Tallahassee Historic Trail.** A route originally mapped and
documented by an eager Eagle Scout as part of a merit-badge project,
this trail has since become a Tallahassee sightseeing staple; allow at
least four hours for the 8-mile stretch. The starting point is the Old
Capitol, where you can pick up maps and descriptive brochures. You'll
walk through the **Park Avenue and Calhoun Street historic districts,**
which will take you back to Territorial days and the era of post-war
Reconstruction. The trail is dotted with landmark churches and ceme-
teries along with outstanding examples of Greek Revival, Italianate,
and prairie-style architecture. Some houses are open to the public, including the **Brokaw-McDougall House,** which is a superb example of
the Greek Revival and Italianate architectural styles, and the **Megin-
nis-Monroe House,** which served as a field hospital during the Civil
War and is now an art gallery.

**Lake Jackson Mounds State Archaeological Site.** Here are waters to make
bass fishermen weep. For sightseers, Indian mounds and the ruins of
an early 19th-century plantation built by Colonel Robert Butler, ad-
jutant to General Andrew Jackson during the siege of New Orleans,
are found along the shores of the lake. ⊠ *Indian Mound Rd.,* ☎
*904/562–0042.* ☎ *Free.* ☉ *Daily 8–sunset.*

**Maclay State Gardens.** In spring the grounds are afire with azaleas,
dogwood, and other showy or rare plants. Allow at least half a day
for wandering the paths past the reflecting pool, into the tiny walled
garden, and around the lakes and woodlands. The Maclay residence,

furnished as it was in the 1920s, the picnic grounds, and swimming and boating facilities are open to the public. ⊠ *3540 Thomasville Rd.,* ☎ *904/487–4556.* ⊡ *$3.25 per vehicle with up to 8 people.* ☉ *Daily 8–sunset.*

**Museum of Florida History.** Here the long, intriguing story of the state's past—from mastodons to space shuttles—is told in lucid and entertaining ways. ⊠ *500 S. Bronough St.,* ☎ *904/488–1484.* ⊡ *Free.* ☉ *Weekdays 9–4:30, Sat. 10–4:30, Sun. noon–4:30.*

**San Luis Archaeological and Historic Site.** This museum focuses on the archaeology of 17th-century Spanish mission and Apalachee Indian town sites. In its heyday, in 1675, the Apalachee village here had a population of at least 1,400. Threatened by Creek Indians and British forces in 1704, the locals burned the village and fled. ⊠ *2020 W. Mission Rd.,* ☎ *904/487–3711.* ⊡ *Free.* ☉ *Weekdays 9–4:30, Sat. 10–4:30, Sun. noon–4:30; 1-hr guided tours weekdays noon, Sat. 11 and 3, and Sun. 2.*

**Tallahassee Museum of History and Natural Science.** The eclectic collection features old cars and carriages, a red caboose, nature trails, a snake exhibit, and a restored plantation house. ⊠ *3945 Museum Dr., Tallahassee,* ☎ *904/576–1636.* ⊡ *$5.* ☉ *Mon.–Sat. 9–5, Sun. 12:30–5.*

**Union Bank Building.** Built in 1833, this is Florida's oldest bank building. Since it closed in 1843, it has played many roles, from ballet school to bakery. It has been restored to what is thought to be its original appearance. ⊠ *Monroe St. at Apalachee Pkwy.,* ☎ *904/487–3803.* ⊡ *Free.* ☉ *Tues.–Fri. 10–1, weekends by appointment.*

## Dining and Lodging

**$$** ✕ **Andrew's 2nd Act.** Part of a smart complex in the heart of the po-
★ litical district, this is classic cuisine: elegant and understated. If you like pub hopping, there's Andrew's Upstairs, and the Adams Street Cafe (also by Andrew) is next door. For dinner, the veal Oscar is flawless. ⊠ *228 S. Adams St.,* ☎ *904/222–2759. AE, DC, MC, V.*

**$** ✕ **Anthony's.** Often confused with Andrew's, this is the locals' choice for uncompromising Italian classics. Try one of the Italian-style grouper or salmon dishes. ⊠ *1950 Thomasville Rd.,* ☎ *904/224–1447. AE, MC, V.*

**$** ✕ **Barnacle Bill's.** The seafood selection is whale-size, and it's steamed
★ to succulent perfection before your eyes, with fresh vegetables on the side. This popular hangout is famous for pasta dishes and home-smoked fish, too. Children eat for free on Sunday. ⊠ *1830 N. Monroe St.,* ☎ *904/385–8734. AE, MC, V.*

**$$$** 🏨 **Governors Inn.** Only a block from the Capitol, this plushly restored
★ historic warehouse is abuzz during the week with politicians, press, and lobbyists. It's a perfect location for business travelers, and on weekends, for tourists who want to visit downtown sites. Rooms are a rich blend of mahogany, brass, and classic prints. The VIP treatment includes airport pickup, breakfast, cocktails, robes, shoe shine, and a daily paper. ⊠ *209 S. Adams St., 32301,* ☎ *904/681–6855; in FL, 800/342–7717;* 𝐅𝐀𝐗 *904/222–3105. 40 units. Free valet parking. AE, D, DC, MC, V.*

**$$** 🏨 **Holiday Inn Capitol Plaza.** Bustling and upscale, the hotel hosts heavy hitters from the worlds of politics and media who can walk from here to the Capitol. ⊠ *101 S. Adams St., 32301,* ☎ *904/224–5000 or 800/465–4329,* 𝐅𝐀𝐗 *904/224–5000. 244 rooms. Restaurant, bar, lounge, pool. AE, D, DC, MC, V.*

**$$** ☒ **Shoney's Inn.** The quiet courtyard with its own pool and the darkly welcoming cantina (where a complimentary Continental breakfast is served) convey the look of old Spain. Rooms are furnished in heavy Mediterranean style. ☒ *2801 N. Monroe St., 32303,* ☎ *904/386–8286 or 800/222–2222,* FAX *904/422–1074. 113 rooms. Pool. AE, D, DC, MC, V.*

## Nightlife and the Arts

THE ARTS

Florida State University annually hosts 350 concerts and recitals given by its **School of Music** (☎ 904/644–4774) as well as performances of the **Tallahassee Symphony Orchestra** (☎ 904/224–0461) from October through April. The **Tallahassee Little Theatre** (☒ 1861 Thomasville Rd., ☎ 904/224–8474) has a five-production season that runs from September through May.

NIGHTLIFE

Monday through Saturday nights stop by **Andrew's Upstairs** (☒ 228 S. Adams St., ☎ 904/222–3446) to hear contemporary jazz. Top-name entertainment is booked into the **Tallahassee-Leon County Civic Center** (☒ 505 W. Pensacola St., Tallahassee, ☎ 904/487–1691).

## Outdoor Activities and Sports

GOLF

**Killearn Country Club & Inn** (☒ 100 Tyron Circle, ☎ 904/893–2144) has 27 holes.

# South of Tallahassee

South of the capital and east of the Ochlockanee River are several fascinating natural and historical sites. At Wakulla Springs State Park, for instance, an underground river flows into a pool so clear that you can see the bottom, more than 100 feet below. In winter the St. Marks Wildlife Refuge is home to thousands of migratory birds, and if you visit the Natural Bridge State Historic Site in March you can watch a re-creation of the Civil War battle that kept Tallahassee from falling to the Union army.

## Sights to See

**Apalachicola National Forest.** Spreading west of Tallahassee and north of Apalachicola is the Apalachicola National Forest, where you can camp, hike, picnic, fish, or swim. U.S. 319 skirts the forest's eastern border. ☎ *904/643–2282.*

**⑰** **Natural Bridge Battlefield State Historic Site.** In 1865 Confederate soldiers stood firm against a Yankee advance on St. Marks. The Rebs held, saving Tallahassee—the only southern capital east of the Mississippi that never fell to the Union. About 10 miles southeast of the capital and 6 miles east of Woodville off Route 363, the site marks the victory and is a good place for a hike and a picnic. ☒ *Natural Bridge Rd., Woodville,* ☎ *904/922–6007.* 🎟 *Free.* ☉ *Daily 8–sunset.*

**⑱** **St. Marks Wildlife Refuge and Lighthouse.** The once-powerful Fort San Marcos de Apalache was built here in 1639, and stones salvaged from the fort were used in the lighthouse, which is still in operation. The visitor center has information on more than 75 miles of marked trails. ☒ *1255 Lighthouse Rd, St. Marks* ☎ *904/925–6121.* 🎟 *$4 per car.* ☉ *Refuge daily sunrise–sunset; visitor center weekdays 8–4:15, weekends 10–5.*

★ **⑲** **Wakulla Springs State Park,** about 15 miles south of Tallahassee on Route 61, has one of the deepest springs in the world. The wilderness remains relatively untouched, retaining the wild and exotic look it had in the 1930s, when Tarzan movies were made here. Take a glass-bottom boat deep into the lush, jungle-lined waterways to catch glimpses of alligators, snakes, nesting limpkin, and other waterfowl. ⊠ *1 Springs Dr., Wakulla Springs,* ☎ *904/922–3632.* ⌴ *$3.25 per car, boat tour $4.50.* ◷ *Daily 8–sunset, 4 boat tours daily 9:15–4:30.*

NEED A BREAK? The **Wakulla Springs Lodge and Conference Center** (1 Spring Dr., ☎ 904/224–5950), located on the grounds of the Wakulla Springs State Park, serves three meals a day in a sunny, spartan room that seems little changed from the 1930s. Schedule lunch here to sample the famous bean soup, home-baked muffins, and a slab of pie.

### Dining

**$** ✕ **Nicholson's Farmhouse.** The name says a lot about this friendly, informal country place with an outside kitchen and grill. Hand-cut steaks and chops are specialties of the house. ⊠ *From U.S. 27 follow Rte. 12 toward Quincy and look for signs,* ☎ *904/539–5931. AE, D, MC, V. BYOB. Closed Sun. and Mon.*

### The Arts

The **Monticello Opera House** (⊠ U.S. 90E, Monticello, ☎ 904/997–4242) presents operas in the restored gaslight-era playhouse, near Tallahassee.

# THE PANHANDLE A TO Z

## Arriving and Departing

### By Bus

The principal common carrier throughout the region is **Greyhound Lines** (☎ 800/231–2222), with stations in Crestview (☎ 904/682–6922), DeFuniak Springs (☎ 904/892–5566), Fort Walton Beach (☎ 904/243–1940), Panama City (☎ 904/785–7861), Pensacola (☎ 904/476–4800), and Tallahassee (☎ 904/222–4240).

### By Car

The main east–west arteries across the top of the state are I–10 and U.S. 90. Pensacola is about an hour's drive east from Mobile. Tallahassee is 3½ hours west of Jacksonville.

### By Plane

A new, state-of-the-art terminal opened in 1991 at the **Pensacola Regional Airport,** which is served by **American Eagle** (☎ 800/433–7300), **ASA–The Delta Connection** and **Comair** (☎ 800/221–1212), **Continental** (☎ 800/525–0280), **Delta** (☎ 800/221–1212), **Northwest Airlink** (☎ 800/225–2525), and **USAir** and **USAir Express** (☎ 800/428–4322). A trip from the airport via **Yellow Cab** (☎ 904/433–1143) costs about $9 to downtown and $17 to Pensacola Beach.

**Fort Walton Beach/Eglin AFB Airport/Okaloosa County Air Terminal** is served by ASA–The Delta Connection, **Northwest** (☎ 800/225–2525), and USAir Express. A ride from the Fort Walton Beach airport via **Checker Cab** (☎ 904/244–4491) costs $10 to Fort Walton Beach, Niceville, or Valparaiso and $18 to Destin. **A-1 Taxi** (☎ 904/678–2424) charges $12 to Fort Walton Beach and $20 to Destin.

**Panama City–Bay County Airport** is served by ASA–The Delta Connection, Northwest Airlink, and USAir Express. **Yellow Cab** (☎ 904/763–4691) charges about $15–$27 to the beach area, depending on where your hotel is. **DeLuxe Coach Limo Service** (☎ 904/763–

0211) provides van service to downtown Panama City for $6.50 and to Panama City Beach for $11.50–$14.25.

**Tallahassee Regional Airport** is served by **Air South** (☎ 800/247–7688), American Eagle, ASA–The Delta Connection, **Continental Express** (☎ 800/525–0280), Delta, and USAir. **Yellow Cab** (☎ 904/222–3070) travels to downtown for $10–$13. Some Tallahassee hotels provide free shuttle service.

### By Train
**Amtrak** (☎ 800/872–7245) has a Los Angeles-to-Panhandle route; its stops include Pensacola, Crestview, and Chipley.

## Getting Around

### By Boat
The Emerald Coast is accessible to yacht captains and sailors from the Intracoastal Waterway, which turns inland at Apalachicola and runs through the bays around Panama City to Choctawhatchee Bay and into Santa Rosa Sound.

### By Car
It takes about four hours to cross this region from Pensacola to Tallahassee. Driving east–west along I–10 tends to be monotonous, but U.S. 90 piques your interest by routing you along the main streets of several county-seat towns.

U.S. 98 snakes eastward along the coast, splitting into 98 and 98A at Inlet Beach before rejoining at Panama City and continuing down to Port St. Joe and Apalachicola. The view of the Gulf from U.S. 98 can leave you oohing and ahhing if the sun's out to distract you. If not, the fast-food restaurants, sleazy bars, and tacky souvenir stores are a little too noticeable.

Route 399 between Pensacola Beach and Navarre Beach takes you down Santa Rosa Island, a spit of duneland that juts out into the turquoise and jade waters of the Gulf of Mexico. It's a scenic drive if the day is clear; otherwise, it's a study in gray.

Major north–south highways that weave through the Panhandle are (from east to west) U.S. 231, U.S. 331, Route 85, and U.S. 29. From U.S. 331, which runs over a causeway at the east end of Choctawhatchee Bay between Route 20 and U.S. 98, the panorama of barge traffic and cabin cruisers on the twinkling waters of the Intracoastal Waterway will get your attention.

## Contacts and Resources

### Emergencies
Dial **911** for police or ambulance.

HOSPITALS

The following hospitals have 24-hour emergency rooms: **Fort Walton Beach Medical Center** (✉ 1000 Mar-Walt Dr., Fort Walton Beach, ☎ 904/862–1111), **HCA Gulf Coast Hospital** (✉ 449 W. 23rd St., Panama City, ☎ 904/769–8341), **HCA West Florida Regional Medical Center** (✉ 8383 N. Davis Hwy., Pensacola, ☎ 904/494–4000), and **Tallahassee Regional Medical Center** (✉ Magnolia Dr. and Miccosukee Rd., Tallahassee, ☎ 904/681–1155).

### Visitor Information
**Apalachicola Bay Chamber of Commerce** (✉ 84 Market St., Apalachicola 32320, ☎ 904/653–9419) is open weekdays 9:30–4, Saturday 10–3. **Crestview Area Chamber of Commerce** (✉ 502 S. Main St., Crestview

32536, ☎ 904/682–3212) is open weekdays 8–5. **Destin Chamber of Commerce** (✉ 1021 U.S. 98E, Destin 32541, ☎ 904/837–6241 or 904/837–0087) is open weekdays 9–5. **Emerald Coast Convention & Visitors Bureau** (✉ 1540 U.S. 98E, Fort Walton Beach 32548, ☎ 904/651–7131 or 800/322–3319) is open daily 8–5. **Niceville/Valparaiso/Bay Area Chamber of Commerce** (✉ 170 John Sims Pkwy., Valparaiso 32580, ☎ 904/678–2323) is open weekdays 9–4:30. **Panama City Beach Convention & Visitor Bureau** (✉ 12015 W. Front Beach Rd., Panama City Beach 32407, ☎ 904/233–6503 or 800/722–3224) is open daily 8–5. **Pensacola Visitor Information Center** (✉ 1401 E. Gregory St., Pensacola 32501, ☎ 904/434–1234 or 800/874–1234) is open daily 8–5. **Tallahassee Area Convention and Visitors Bureau** (✉ 200 W. College Ave., Tallahassee 32302, ☎ 904/413–9200 or 800/628–2866) is open weekdays 8–5. **Walton County Chamber of Commerce** (✉ 95 W. Circle Dr., DeFuniak Springs 32433, ☎ 904/892–3191) is open weekdays 8–5. **The Information Center** on U.S. 331 at U.S. 98 (☎ 904/267–3511) is open daily 8:30–4:30.

# 12 Northeast Florida

The northeast corner of the state is an area of remarkable diversity. Only a short drive separates the 400-year-old town of St. Augustine from the spring-break and auto-racing mecca of Daytona Beach. The stretch in between is dotted with slender barrier islands—some relatively pristine, all with fabulous beaches. Inland is the university town of Gainesville, the horse country around Ocala, and the backwoods scrub made famous by Marjorie Kinnan Rawlings in her book The Yearling.

Updated by
Pamela
Acheson

 ▮ N NORTHEASTERN FLORIDA you'll find some of the oldest settlements in the state—indeed in all of the United
States—though this region didn't get much attention
until the Union Army came through during the Civil War. The soldiers'
rapturous accounts of the mild climate, pristine beaches, and lush vegetation captured the imagination of folks up North. First came the spec-
ulators and the curiosity seekers. Then the advent of the railroads brought
more permanent settlers and the first wave of winter vacationers. Finally, the automobile transported the full rush of snowbirds, seasonal
residents escaping from harsh Northern winters. They still come, to
sop up the sun on the Atlantic beaches stretching all along the coast;
to tee up in this year-round golfer's paradise; to bass fish and bird-watch
in the forests and parks; and to party in the dance clubs and barrooms
of Daytona (which has the dubious honor of replacing Fort Lauderdale
as the destination of choice for collegiate spring breaks).

This region of Florida is an area of remarkable diversity. Towering, tor-
tured live oaks, plantations, and antebellum-style architecture recol-
lect the Old South. The mossy marshes of Silver Springs and the St.
Johns River look as untouched and junglelike today as they did generations ago. Horse farms around Ocala resemble Kentucky's bluegrass
country or the hunt clubs of Virginia. St. Augustine is a showcase of
early U.S. history, and Jacksonville is a young but sophisticated metropolis. Yet these are all but light diversions from northeastern Florida's
primary draw—absolutely sensational beaches. From the Georgia border straight down through Cocoa Beach, long and slender barrier islands hug the coast. Along the entire eastern side of each of these islands
runs a broad band of spectacular sand. Except in the most populated
areas, development has been modest, and the beaches are lined with
funky, appealing little towns.

## Pleasures and Pastimes

### Beaches
Beaches in northeastern Florida are luxuriously long. Some are hard-
packed white sand, while others have sand with a fine, sugary texture.
The surf is normally gentle, and many areas are safe for swimming.
Bear in mind that the very fragile dunes, held in place by the sea
grasses, are responsible for protecting the shore from the sea. A single
afternoon of careless roughhousing can destroy a dune forever.

The area's most densely developed beaches, with rows of high-rise condominiums and hotels, are in Daytona and Cocoa Beach. Elsewhere,
coastal towns are still mostly small and laid-back, and beaches are
crowded only on summer weekends.

### Canoeing
There are plenty of opportunities to canoe in this part of Florida, including sparkling clear spring "runs" that may be mere tunnels through
tangled jungle growth. The Ocala National Forest and the inland waterway along the Canaveral National Seashore are two of the best canoeing spots.

### Dining
Between the Atlantic Ocean, the Intracoastal Waterway, and the numerous lakes and rivers of this region, seafood is prominently featured
on local menus. In coastal towns, the catches often come straight from
the restaurant's own fleet. Shrimp, oysters, snapper, and grouper are
especially popular.

## Diving

Northeast Florida also offers not only ocean diving but a wide range of cave diving and snorkeling over "boils"—naturally bubbling water that sometimes occurs when an underground spring comes to the surface.

## Fishing

From cane-pole fishing in a roadside canal or off a pier to deep-sea fishing from a luxury charter boat, options abound. There's no charge (or a nominal one) to fish from many causeways, beaches, and piers. Deep-sea fishing charters are available up and down the coast.

## Golf

Although many courses are along the coast, you are never far from the fairways.

## Horseback Riding

Ocala's bluegrass country can be explored on trail rides offered by several outfits. Amelia Island is famous for horseback riding on the beach.

## Lodging

Accommodations range from splashy beachfront resorts and glitzy condominiums to cozy inns and bed-and-breakfasts nestled in historic districts. In general, the closer you are to the center of activity in the coastal resorts, the more you'll pay. You'll save a few dollars if you stay across from the beach rather than on it, and you'll save even more if you select a place that's a bit removed from the action.

## Shopping

Souvenirs unique to northeast Florida include gems and minerals from Deland, beach- and surf-theme merchandise along the coast, and auto-racing items from Daytona Beach. Virtually every beachside town has several appealing one-of-a-kind stores in addition to shops selling T-shirts, bathing suits, and resort wear. From October to August, local grapefruit and oranges are available for shipping.

## Skydiving

Deland is the skydiving capital of the world and the site of high-flying competitions. It is also the home of tandem jumping, which allows novices to swoop down on their maiden voyage in one day. You are attached—literally—at the hip to an experienced instructor-diver.

## Spectator Sports

Daytona Beach is the site of year-round auto and motorcycle racing, including the Daytona 500 in February and the Pepsi 500 in July. There is dog racing in Jacksonville and Daytona. A jai alai fronton can be found in Ocala. The NFL now has a team in Jacksonville, the Jacksonville Jaguars. Golf fans enjoy the Tournament Players Championship held in Sawgrass. Tennis lovers head to Amelia Island for the Women's Tennis Association Championships in April and the Men's All-American Tennis Championship in September.

## Tennis

Virtually every town has at least one public tennis court, and many hotels and motels have courts. Some of the larger resorts have numerous courts and multileveled programs to match.

## Water Sports

Pontoon boats, houseboats, and bass boats can be rented for use on the St. Johns River. Boogie boards, surfboards, and sailboards are available along the beaches.

# Exploring Northeast Florida

This region's tourist territory lies along the Atlantic coast, both on the mainland and on the barrier islands that lie just offshore and where the best beaches are. Besides beaches, each of these spots has something special for visitors. Remote Amelia Island has a 50-block historic district, sophisticated shops and restaurants, and a wide range of accommodations from bed-and-breakfasts to the elegant Ritz-Carlton Amelia Island. Jacksonville is one of the oldest cities in Florida—and the only real high-rise city in northeast Florida—and the downtown riverside area has a number of excellent museums. St. Augustine is the historic capital of this part of Florida; you could easily spend a week and not quite see all the sights. New Smyrna Beach is a sleepy town known for its 7-mile-long, white-sand beach, its national seashore, and its art center. Cocoa Beach's main claim to fame is the Kennedy Space Center and Spaceport USA.

Inland are charming small towns and the sprawling Ocala National Forest. Deland, which is on the eastern side of the forest, is the skydiving capital of the world. Ocala, at the forests' western edge, has become a center for Thoroughbred breeding and training. Gainesville is home to the University of Florida, and visitors are mostly Gator football fans and parents with kids enrolled at the university, so styles and prices of accommodations are geared primarily to budget-minded travelers rather than luxury-seeking vacationers.

## Great Itineraries

Northeast Florida is too large an area to cover, even in 10 days, unless you want to get a brief overview of the region and are willing to spend most of the time in your car. The following suggestions assume you are based somewhere along the coast.

*Numbers in the text below correspond to numbers in the margin and on the maps.*

### IF YOU HAVE 2 OR 3 DAYS

If you're staying in ⊞ **Jacksonville** ①, visit Amelia Island's Fort Clinch State Park to see one of America's best-preserved brick forts and stop by the Jacksonville Art Museum. Take I–95 south to **St. Augustine** ⑤ and see the restored **Spanish Quarter Museum** ⑰ before continuing down the coast to Canaveral National Seashore, accessible either from ⊞ **New Smyrna Beach** ㉑ or ⊞ **Cocoa Beach** ㉒. If the recent movie *Apollo 13* captured your attention, don't miss Spaceport USA at the Kennedy Space Center.

### IF YOU HAVE 4 OR 5 DAYS

From ⊞ **Jacksonville** ①, visit the Amelia Island Historic District as well as Fort Clinch State Park; in town, see both the Jacksonville Art Museum and the Museum of Science and Industry. Going south on I–95, stop in ⊞ **St. Augustine** ⑤, where you can follow the Old City Walking Tour suggested by the Visitor's Center and stroll through the restored **Spanish Quarter Museum** ⑰. Consider driving along the slightly longer but more scenic coastal route A1A to ⊞ **Daytona Beach** ⑲, where you can visit the Museum of Arts and Sciences and the famous beaches. If you're staying in ⊞ **New Smyrna Beach** ㉑ or ⊞ **Cocoa Beach** ㉒ you can reach the Cape Canaveral National Seashore and Spaceport USA at the Kennedy Space Center.

### IF YOU HAVE 10 DAYS

When staying in ⊞ **Jacksonville** ①, make sure to visit Kingsley Plantation, Florida's oldest remaining plantation, besides the attractions in town. On **Amelia Island** ④, spend extra time hiking or picnicking in Fort Clinch State Park before heading to ⊞ **St. Augustine** ⑤, where you can be more leisurely in your exploration of the extensive historic district. Also spend time at the **Lightner Museum** ⑫, housed in one of Henry Flagler's fancy hotels. From ⊠ **Daytona Beach** ⑲, ⊠ **New Smyrna Beach** ㉑, or ⊞ **Cocoa Beach** ㉒ you can cover Daytona's Museum of Arts and Sciences then drive along the shoreline; also see the Canaveral National Seashore and Spaceport USA at the Kennedy Space Center. From any of these bases you can head inland for a day in the Ocala National Forest, a beautiful wilderness area.

## When to Tour Northeast Florida

Northeast Florida can get a bit chilly in December and January and tends to fill up this time of year with Canadians escaping much colder temperatures. Auto-racing enthusiasts should be sure to visit Daytona in February, the height of the racing season. The ocean warms up by March, and college kids on spring break pack the beaches—but this is also the best month to see the azalea gardens in full bloom. Midsummer is breezy and not as hot as in a northern city, as long as you stick to the beaches; inland, the heat and humidity can be stifling.

# JACKSONVILLE AND AMELIA ISLAND

Jacksonville is a city with high-rise buildings and an active downtown area plus a good measure of restaurants and museums. The St. John's River winds through the city, giving it lots of shoreline and pretty vistas across the wide waterway. About 45 minutes north of Jacksonville is Amelia Island; the beautiful historic district in its old seaport town, Fernandina Beach, is one of the best in the country. The east side of the island is one long beautiful beach.

## Jacksonville

*Numbers in the margin correspond to points of interest on the Northeast Florida map.*

**❶** The St. John's River runs through the middle of **Jacksonville** and many bridges cross the water, connecting the two areas of downtown. Two waterfront complexes with shops, restaurants, parks, and museums face each other across the river, and fine-art lovers have their pick of collections, including an impressive hoard of early 18th-century Meissen porcelain.

### Sights to See

**Alexander Brest Museum.** Fine collections of Boehm, Royal Copenhagen, Bing, and Grondahl porcelains can be found here on the campus of Jacksonville University. Also on display are Steuben glass, cloisonné, pre-Columbian artifacts, and an extensive collection of ivories. The home of composer Frederick Delius is also on the campus and is open for tours, upon request. ⊠ *2800 University Blvd. N,* ☎ *904/744–3950, ext. 3371.* ⌑ *Free.* ☽ *Weekdays 9–4:30, Sat. noon–5. Closed school holidays.*

**Cummer Gallery of Art.** Getting a look at the world-famous Wark Collection of early 18th-century Meissen porcelain is just one reason not to miss this stop. Set amid leafy formal gardens, this former baron's estate home now includes 12 permanent collection galleries that display over 2,000 items that cover over 4,000 years of changing styles. There is also an interactive teaching gallery for children and adults. ⊠ *829 Riverside Ave.,* ☎ *904/356–6857.* ⌑ *$3. Free Tues. 4:30–9:30.* ☽ *Tues. 10–9:30, Wed.–Fri. 10–4, Sat. noon–5, Sun. 2–5.*

# Northeast Florida

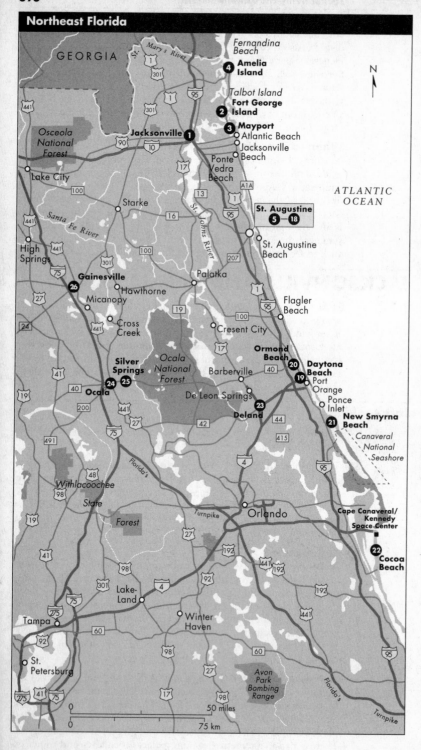

GEORGIA

*Mary's River*

*St.*

*Fernandina Beach*

① 11
301

**4** **Amelia Island**

*Talbot Island*

95

**2** **Fort George Island**

301

**3** **Mayport**

1

**Jacksonville** **1**
Atlantic Beach
Jacksonville Beach

90

10

17

Ponte Vedra Beach

*Osceola National Forest*

Lake City

441

A1A

*ATLANTIC OCEAN*

100

Starke

16

*St. Johns River*

**St. Augustine**
**5** — **18**

95

13

*Santa Fe River*

207

St. Augustine Beach

High Springs

441

75

301

100

Palatka

1

**Gainesville** **26**

Hawthorne

Micanopy

19

Cresent City

95

Flagler Beach

100

24

441

27

Cross Creek

**Silver Springs** **25**

**24** **Ocala**

40

200

441

75

27

*Ocala National Forest*

Barberville

De Leon Springs

**Deland** **23**

42

40

**Ormond Beach** **20**
**Daytona Beach** **19**
Port Orange
Ponce Inlet

44

**New Smyrna Beach** **21**

415

*Canaveral National Seashore*

4

41

491

48

98

19

*Withlacoochee State*

*Florida's*

*Forest*

*Turnpike*

27

**Orlando**

95

*Cape Canaveral/ Kennedy Space Center*

193

**22** **Cocoa Beach**

301

75

98

**Lake-Land**

4

441 192

192

Tampa

92

60

*Winter Haven*

441

192

275

St. Petersburg

60

60

95

275
41
75

17

98

*Avon Park Bombing Range*

*Florida's*

*Turnpike*

0          50 miles
0          75 km

N

**Jacksonville Art Museum.** The collection here includes contemporary and classic art—especially noteworthy are the Koger collection of Oriental porcelains, works by Pablo Picasso, and the rare pre-Columbian artifacts. Special exhibits, film and lecture series, and workshops make this destination worthy of repeat visits. ⊠ *4160 Boulevard Center Dr.,* ☎ *904/398–8336.* ⊑ *Free.* ☉ *Tues., Wed., Fri. 10–4, Thurs. 10–10, weekends 1–5.*

☺ **Jacksonville Zoo.** This sprawling 7-acre veldt is best known for its white rhinos and an outstanding collection of rare waterfowl. You can see 10 species of African birds and animals. ⊠ *Hecksher Dr. E, off I–95,* ☎ *904/757–4462.* ⊑ *$4.* ☉ *Daily 9–5.*

☺ **Museum of Science and History.** Permanent exhibits range from those on pre-Columbian history and the ecology and history of the St. Johns River to the Maple Leaf Civil War Collection and the hands-on Kidspace section. There are also excellent special exhibits, and a popular 3-D laser show in the Alexander Brest Planetarium. Physical science shows are held weekends in the science theater. ⊠ *1025 Museum Circle,* ☎ *904/396–7062.* ⊑ *$5.* ☉ *Weekdays 10–5, Sat. 10–6, Sun. 1–6.*

## Dining and Lodging

**$$$** ✕ **24 Miramar.** This stylish restaurant, with its long, narrow room minimally decorated in black and white, is hidden in a small shopping center on the south side of the river. The superb cuisine captures the essence of California, Asian, Latin, and Italian cooking, and it's difficult to choose among the inventive nightly specials. Try the ravioli appetizer, the delicate angel hair with tomatoes and goat cheese, or the filet mignon. A 16% service charge is automatically added to your bill. ⊠ *Miramar Shopping Center, 4446 Hendricks Ave.,* ☎ *904/448–2424. AE, MC, V. No lunch.*

**$$$** ✕ **Wine Cellar.** Thought by many to be the finest restaurant in Jack-
★ sonville, this elegant, candlelit spot specializes in classic Continental fare. Enjoy the rack of lamb (the house favorite), or choose grilled salmon with dill mustard sauce, veal chop with morel sauce, or chicken topped with crabmeat, asparagus, and béarnaise sauce. Desserts include a bittersweet-chocolate mousse cake and a traditional cheesecake. ⊠ *314 Prudential Dr.,* ☎ *904/398–8989. Jacket required. AE, MC, V.*

**$$** ✕ **River City Brewing Company.** This popular brew pub overlooks the river on the city's south bank. Take one of the daily brewery tours; then sample the day's brew. Sandwiches and salads are featured at lunch, while dinner brings shrimp, fresh fish, grilled steaks, and pasta dishes. There's live jazz for Sunday brunch. ⊠ *835 Museum Circle Dr., Southbank Riverwalk,* ☎ *904/398–2299. AE, MC, V.*

**$** ✕ **Crawdaddy's.** Take it Cajun or cool. This riverfront fish shack, just off I–10 at I–95, is the place for seafood, jambalaya, and country chicken. Lunch is a sumptuous buffet, and there's a very popular Sunday brunch. Dig into the house specialty, catfish—all you can eat—then dance to a fe-do-do beat. ⊠ *1643 Prudential Dr.,* ☎ *904/396–3546. AE, D, DC, MC, V.*

**$$$** ▥ **Jacksonville Omni Hotel.** This 16-story ultramodern facility is the
★ fanciest establishment downtown. The splashy, marble-floored lobby leads to the reception area, an upscale bar and lounge, and a restaurant with cozy banquettes and tables that look up to a soaring atrium. Sunday brunch is popular here. Extra-spacious rooms, many with spectacular river views, are stylishly decorated and include minibars. ⊠ *245 Water St., 32202,* ☎ *904/355–6664,* ℻ *904/354–2970. 354 rooms. Restaurant, lounge, no-smoking rooms, pool, exercise room. AE, D, DC, MC, V.*

$$-$$$ 🏨 **Radisson Riverwalk Hotel.** This bustling five-story hotel, connected to the Riverwalk complex, has modern rooms with either a king-size or two double beds. It's the most conveniently located hotel in the city (and the only riverfront hotel) and is within walking distance of four restaurants, a museum, and water taxis to Jacksonville Landing. Units overlooking the St. Johns River command the highest prices. ⊠ *1515 Prudential Dr., 32207,* ☎ *904/396–5100,* ℻ *904/396–7154. 304 rooms, 19 suites. Restaurant, lounge, no-smoking rooms, pool, 2 tennis courts. AE, DC, MC, V.*

$$ 🏨 **Comfort Suites Hotel.** Located in Baymeadows and central to some currently "in" restaurants, nightclubs, and shops, this all-suites hotel is an unbeatable value. The units, decorated in breezy, radiant Florida hues, include refrigerators, and sleep sofas. Microwaves and VCRs come with master suites. Rates include daily Continental breakfast and cocktail hour on weekdays. ⊠ *8333 Ellis Trail, 32256,* ☎ *904/739–1155,* ℻ *904/731–0752. 128 suites. Pool, spa, laundry. AE, DC, MC, V.*

$$ 🏨 **House on Cherry St.** This early 20th-century treasure is furnished with pewter, Oriental rugs, coverlets, and other remnants of a rich past. Carol Anderson welcomes her guests to her riverside home with wine and hors d'oeuvres and serves a full breakfast every morning. Walk to the parks and gardens of the chic Avondale district. ⊠ *1844 Cherry St., 32205,* ☎ *904/384–1999. 4 rooms. Bicycles. MC, V.*

## Nightlife and the Arts

### THE ARTS

Broadway touring shows, top-name entertainers, and other major events are booked at the **Florida Theater Performing Arts Center** (⊠ 128 E. Forsyth St., Jacksonville, ☎ 904/355–5661). The **Jacksonville Civic Auditorium** (⊠ 300 W. Water St., Jacksonville, ☎ 904/630–0701) also draws various popular entertainment; check local publications for performance schedules. The **Alhambra Dinner Theater** (⊠ 12000 Beach Blvd., Jacksonville, ☎ 904/641–1212) has professional theater with complete menus that change with each play. The **Jacksonville Symphony Orchestra** (☎ 904/354–5479) presents a variety of concerts around town.

### NIGHTLIFE

**Cafe on the Square** (⊠ 1974 San Marco Blvd., ☎ 904/399–4422) has live local blues, jazz, and rock bands Tuesday through Saturday. At **Club 5** (⊠ 1028 Park Ave., ☎ 904/356–5555), there's alternative high-energy techno and disco dance music nightly. **River City Brewing Company** (⊠ 835 Museum Circle Dr., Southbank Riverwalk, ☎ 904/398–2299) has live local jazz or blues bands on Friday and Saturday nights as well as Sunday brunch.

## Outdoor Activities and Sports

### DOG RACING

Greyhounds race year-round in the Jacksonville area, with seasons split among three tracks; in town, the **Jacksonville Kennel Club** (⊠ 1440 N. McDuff Ave., ☎ 904/646–0001) has dog racing from May to September.

### FOOTBALL

The blockbuster event in northeast Florida is Jacksonville's **Gator Bowl** (☎ 904/396–1800) on New Year's Day. The **Jacksonville Jaguars** (☎ 904/633–6000), an NFL franchise, plays scheduled games all season long.

## Shopping

For a huge group of specialty shops and a number of restaurants, roam around the downtown **Jacksonville Landing** (⊠ 2 Independent

Dr. at Main Street Bridge), on the north side of the river. **Riverdale/Avondale Shopping Center** (⊠ 12 Riverside Ave.), in the heart of historic Avondale, has two blocks chock-full of art galleries, restaurants, and boutiques. Stop at the **San Marco Shopping Center** (⊠ 25 San Marco Blvd.), and wander through interesting stores and restaurants in 1920s Mediterranean revival–style buildings.

# Beyond Jacksonville

Jacksonville's main beaches are east of the city and run along the barrier island that includes the popular, laid-back town of Jacksonville Beach. North of Jacksonville Beach are several more barrier islands, including **Fort George Island,** where you'll find Florida's oldest plantation.

## Sights to See

**Fort Caroline National Memorial.** Spread over 130 acres along the St. Johns River is the Fort Caroline National Memorial. The original fort was built in the 1560s by French Huguenots, who were later slaughtered by the Spanish in the first major clash between European powers for control of what would become the United States. An oak-wooded pathway leads to a replica of the original fort—a great, sunny place to picnic (bring your own food and drink), stretch your legs, and explore a small museum. The park is about 13 miles away from downtown Jacksonville. ⊠ *12713 Fort Caroline Rd., Jacksonville,* ☎ *904/641–7155.* ▨ *Free.* ☉ *Museum daily 9–5; closed Dec. 25.*

★ **Kingsley Plantation.** Located on Fort George Island and reachable by ferry or bridge, this site was built by an eccentric slave trader. The Kingsley plantation dates to 1792 and is the oldest remaining plantation in the state. Slave quarters, as well as the modest Kingsley home, are open to the public. ⊠ *Fort George Island,* ☎ *904/251–3537.* ▨ *Free.* ☉ *Daily 9–5; guided tours Thurs.–Mon. 9:30, 11, 1:30, and 3.*

❸ **Mayport and the Mayport Ferry.** Dating back more than 300 years, Mayport is one of the oldest fishing communities in the United States. Today it's home to a number of excellent seafood restaurants and a large commercial shrimp-boat fleet and is the Navy's fourth-largest home port. You can take a fun ferry ride between Fort George Island and Mayport and bring your car along (it's an auto ferry). ⊠ *Mayport Ferry,* ☎ *904/270–2520.* ▨ *$2.50 per car, pedestrians 50¢.* ☉ *Daily 6:20 AM–10 PM every ½ hour.*

## Beaches

**Atlantic Beach** is a favored surfing area. Around the popular Sea Turtle Inn, you'll find catamaran rentals and instruction. Five areas have lifeguards on duty in the summer 10–6.

**Jacksonville Beach** is the liveliest of the long line of Jacksonville beaches. Young people flock to the beach, where there are all sorts of games to play, beach concessions, rental shops, and a fishing pier.

**Kathryn Abbey Hanna Park,** near Mayport, is the Jacksonville area's showplace park. It offers beaches, showers, and snack bars that operate April–Labor Day.

**Neptune Beach,** adjoining Jacksonville Beach to the north, is more residential and offers easy access to quieter beaches. Surfers consider it one of the area's two best surfing sites, the other being Atlantic Beach.

**Talbot Island State Parks.** You'll find 17 miles of gorgeous beaches, sand dunes, and golden marshes that hum with birds and bugs here. Come to picnic, fish, swim, snorkel, or camp. ⊠ *Talbot Island* ☎ *904/251–2320.* ▨ *$3.25 per vehicle with up to 8 people.* ☉ *Daily 8–sunset.*

## Dining and Lodging

$–$$    ✕ **Ragtime.** A New Orleans theme threads through everything from the
★       Sunday jazz brunch to the beignets. It's loud, crowded, and alive with
        a sophisticated young bunch. If you aren't into Creole and Cajun clas-
        sics, have a simple po'boy sandwich or fish sizzled on the grill. ⊠ *207
        Atlantic Blvd., Atlantic Beach,* ☎ *904/241–7877. AE, DC, MC, V.*

$       ✕ **Homestead.** A down-home place with several dining rooms, a huge
        fireplace, and country cooking, this restaurant specializes in skillet-fried
        chicken, which comes with rice and gravy. Chicken and dumplings, deep-
        fried chicken gizzards, buttermilk biscuits, and strawberry shortcake
        also draw in the locals. ⊠ *1712 Beach Blvd., Jacksonville Beach,* ☎
        *904/249–5240. AE, D, MC, V. No lunch.*

$$      🏨 **Comfort Inn Oceanfront.** Every room in this hotel has a view of the
        Atlantic and a private balcony. Four waterfalls cascade into a giant free-
        form heated pool and there is a rock grotto and spa. ⊠ *1515 N. 1st
        St., Jacksonville Beach, 32250,* ☎ *904/241–2311 or 800/654–8776,*
        FAX *904/249–3830. 178 rooms. Deli, lounge, pool, airport shuttle.
        AE, D, DC, MC, V.*

## Nightlife

**Ragtime Taproom Brewery** (⊠ 207 Atlantic Blvd., Atlantic Beach, ☎
904/241–7877) resonates with live local jazz and blues bands Thurs-
day through Sunday.

## Outdoor Activities and Sports

### DOG RACING

**Orange Park Kennel Club** (½ mi south of I–295 on U.S. 17, ☎ 904/646–
0001) has dog racing from November to April. Dogs also race at the
**St. Johns Greyhound Park** (7 mi south of I–95 on U.S. 1, ☎ 904/646–
0001) from March to April.

### FISHING

One popular spot is **Jacksonville Beach Fishing Pier,** which extends 1,200
feet into the Atlantic; the cost to fish is $3, and just to watch 50¢.

### GOLF

**Ponte Vedra Inn & Club** (⊠ 200 Ponte Vedra Blvd., Ponte Vedra Beach
32082, ☎ 904/285–1111 or 800/234–7842) offers 36 holes of golf.
**Ravines Golf & Country Club** (⊠ 2932 Ravines Rd., 32068, ☎ 904/282–
7888) has 18 holes. The **Tournament Players Club** (at Sawgrass (⊠ 110
TPC Blvd., Ponte Vedra Beach 32082, ☎ 904/273–3235 or 800/457–
4653) has 18 holes and hosts the Tournament Players Championship
in March. Ponte Vedra is also the home of the PGA Tour.

### TENNIS

The **Marriott at Sawgrass** (☎ 904/285–7777) offers 19 courts. The
**Ponte Vedra Inn & Club** (☎ 904/285–3856) has 15 Har-Tru courts.

# Amelia Island

❹   Although **Amelia Island** is a bit out of the way, it is worth the trip. The
    town of Fernandina Beach, on the northern end of the island, has 450
    ornate Victorian structures that were built prior to 1927. More than
    50 blocks of these homes and buildings are listed on the National Reg-
    ister of Historic Places. There are also 13 miles of beaches with enor-
    mous sand dunes along the eastern side of the island, and a Civil War
    fort in Fort Clinch State Park.

## Sights to See

★   **Amelia Island Historic District.** Stroll through 50 blocks of historically
    registered homes, including some of the nation's finest examples of Queen

Anne, Victorian, and Italianate mansions, dating back to the haven's glory days in the mid-19th century. Pick up a map for a self-guided walking or driving tour at the **Chamber of Commerce** in the old railroad depot, which was once a stopping point on the first cross-state railroad. ⊠ *Chamber of Commerce, 102 Centre St.,* ☎ *904/261–3248.* ⏱ *Weekdays 9–5.*

**Amelia Island Lighthouse.** You'll probably recognize this frequently photographed landmark—photos of it have appeared in many travel articles and calendars. Built in 1839, this lighthouse is the oldest structure on the island. It is still in operation and is visible 19 miles out to sea. The inside, however, is not open to the public. ⊠ *1 Lighthouse La.,* ☎ *904/261–7378.*

★ **Fort Clinch State Park.** You'll find one of the country's best-preserved and most complete brick forts at Fort Clinch State Park. Fort Clinch was built to discourage further British intrusion after the War of 1812 and was occupied in 1863 by the Confederacy; a year later it was retaken by the North. During the Spanish-American War, it was reactivated for a brief time but for the most part was not used. Today the 1,086-acre park offers camping, nature trails, carriage rides, swimming, surf fishing, picnicking, and living-history reenactments showing life in the garrison at the time of the Civil War. ⊠ *N. 14th St.* ☎ *904/277–7274.* 🎫 *$3.25 per vehicle with up to 8 people.* ⏱ *Daily 8–sunset.*

**St. Peter's Episcopal Church.** was founded in 1859, and is a Gothic Revival structure with Tiffany glass–style memorials and an original, turn-of-the-century L.C. Harrison organ with magnificent hand-painted pipes. It once served as a school. ⊠ *801 Atlantic Ave.,* ☎ *904/261–4293.*

## Beaches

Amelia Island's **eastern shore** is one giant 13-mile stretch of white-sand beach edged with dunes, some 40 feet high. It's one of the few beaches where you are allowed to go horseback riding.

**Fort Clinch State Park** (☞ *above*) on Amelia Island's northern tip, includes a municipal beach and pier; you pay a state-park entrance fee to reach them. Broad and lovely, the beach has parking right on it, bathhouses, picnic areas, and all the facilities of the park itself, including the fort.

## Dining and Lodging

$$–$$$ ✕ **Beech Street Grill.** The hardwood floors, high ceilings, wainscoting, and marble fireplaces in this lovingly restored 1889 sea captain's house create a pleasant environment for a meal, but don't be surprised if small children are running around. You can eat upstairs or in one of the two downstairs dining rooms. An extensive menu includes such house favorites as braised rack of lamb with fresh mint salsa, roasted duck with raspberry sauce, and Cajun shrimp served with andouille sausage over linguine. A blackboard lists four or five fresh fish specials nightly—perhaps a baked grouper with pistachio crust. The outstanding wine list comprises more than 400 labels, including some coveted Californias. ⊠ *801 Beech St.,* ☎ *904/277–3662. AE, MC, V. No lunch.*

$–$$ ✕ **O'Kane's Irish Pub.** Stop here for authentic Irish fare: shepherd's
★ pie, steak and Guinness pie, or fish-and-chips. Also on the menu are sandwiches, ribs, and pasta and an amazing soup that's served in a bowl of sourdough bread—you eat the whole thing! This is one of the few bars in the United States that still prepares Irish coffee the way they do in Ireland—with very cold, barely whipped heavy cream floated on top. ⊠ *318 Centre St.,* ☎ *904/261–1000. AE, MC, V.*

$$$$ ✕▣ **Amelia Island Plantation.** The grounds of the resort, one of the first to be "environmentally sensitive," encompass ancient live-oak forests, marshes, and lagoons and some of the highest dunes in the state. Some homes are occupied year-round, and a warm sense of community prevails. Accommodations range from home and condo rentals to rooms in a full-service hotel; honeymoon villas have private indoor pools. Though the resort is best known for its golf and tennis programs, hiking and biking trails thread through the 1,300 acres. Restaurants range from casual to elegant. ⊠ *3000 First Coast Hwy., 32034,* ☎ *904/261–6161 or 800/874–6878,* ℻ *904/277–5159. 1,100 units. 6 restaurants, 1 18-hole and 3 9-hole golf courses, 25 tennis courts, health club, racquetball, water sports, fishing, bicycles, pro shops, children's programs. D, MC, V.*

$$$$ ✕▣ **Ritz-Carlton Amelia Island.** Considered by many to be the finest
★ resort in Florida, this hotel woos guests with its stylish elegance, superb comfort, and excellent service, plus one of the prettiest and most pristine beaches on Florida's east coast. All units in the eight-story building have balconies and ocean views. Suites and rooms are very spacious and predictably luxurious, with wall-to-wall carpeting, comfortable chairs, and king-size or two double beds. All have a separate dressing and closet area plus oversize marble baths. Public areas are exquisitely maintained, grounds are beautifully manicured, and fine cuisine can be had at a choice of restaurants, including the award-winning Grill, a quietly elegant dining room that is truly outstanding. Chef Matthew Medure has created an unusual menu, and thanks to his talent, it works. Dine on grilled bison tenderloin with stewed Vidalia onions in tuna sauce or salmon escallop with angel-hair pasta in tomato-basil oil. The daring can choose the Adventurous Guest menu, a multicourse meal created on the spot by the chef. (The restaurant is open for dinner only; reservations are essential, and a jacket is required.) ⊠ *Amelia Island Pkwy., 32034,* ☎ *904/277–1100. 449 rooms. 3 restaurants, 3 bars, indoor and outdoor pools, 18-hole golf course, 9 tennis courts, fitness center, beach, bicycles. AE, D, DC, MC, V.*

$$ ▣ **1735 House.** Flower-filled window boxes grace this charming New England-style inn. Ocean-view suites are furnished with wicker furniture, 19th-century sea chests, and captain's bunks. There is also a romantic two-bedroom suite in a replica of a lighthouse. ⊠ *584 S. Fletcher Ave., 32034,* ☎ *904/261–5878. 5 suites. Beach. AE, MC, V.*

## Outdoor Activities and Sports

### GOLF

**Amelia Island Plantation** (⊠ 3000 First Coast Hwy., Amelia Island 32034, ☎ 904/261–6161 or 800/874–6878) has 45 holes. **Ritz-Carlton Amelia Island** (⊠ 4750 Amelia Island Pkwy., Amelia Island 32034, ☎ 904/277–1100) has 18 holes.

### TENNIS

The **Ritz-Carlton Amelia Island** (☎ 904/277–1100) has nine Har-Tru tennis courts. **Amelia Island Plantation** (☎ 904/277–5145 or 800/486–8366) has 25 tennis courts and is the site of the nationally televised, top-rated Women's Tennis Association Championships in April and the Men's All-American Tennis Championship in September.

## Shopping

Within the Amelia Island Historic District are numerous shops, art galleries, and boutiques. Many are clustered along cobblestoned Centre Street, including the **Island Artisans** (⊠ 308 Centre St, ☎ 904/277–9664), which sells handcrafted gifts, jewelry, and custom-designed ceramics.

# ST. AUGUSTINE AREA

St. Augustine is the oldest city in the United States, and you could probably spend a month simply visiting all the historic buildings and attractions in the area. The city is on the mainland and the beaches are on the barrier island to the east, reachable by a causeway. West of St. Augustine are the Ravine State Gardens, an unusual (for Florida) group of steep gorges.

## St. Augustine

**⑤ St. Augustine** was founded in 1565, and the city is a showcase for more than 60 historic sites and attractions, plus 144 blocks of historic houses listed on the National Register of Historic Homes. Several times a year St. Augustine holds reenactments commemorating historic events, such as the Grand Christmas Illumination in December, which marks the British occupation of the town.

### Sights to See

*Numbers in the margin correspond to points of interest on the St. Augustine map.*

**⑥ Basilica Cathedral of St. Augustine.** The cathedral is home of the oldest written parish records in the country, dating back to 1594. Following a fire in 1887, extensive changes were made to the current structure, which dates from 1797. It was restored in the mid-1960s. ⊠ *40 Cathedral Pl.,* ☎ *904/824–2806.* ▨ *Donations welcome.* ☉ *Weekdays 5:30–5, weekends 5:30–7.*

**⑦ Castillo de San Marcos National Monument.** This massive structure looks every century of its 300 years. Park rangers provide an introductory narration, after which you're on your own. This is a wonderful fort to explore, complete with a moat, turrets, and 16-foot-thick walls. The fort was constructed of coquina, a soft limestone made of broken shells and coral. Built by the Spanish to protect St. Augustine from British raids (English pirates were handy with a torch), the fort was used as a prison during the Revolutionary and Civil wars. Garrison rooms depict the life of the era, and special cannon-firing demonstrations are held on summer weekends. Children under 17 must be accompanied by an adult. ⊠ *1 Castillo Dr.,* ☎ *904/829–6506.* ▨ *$2.* ☉ *Daily 8:45–4:45.*

**⑧ City Gate.** A relic from the days when the Castillo's moat ran westward to the river and the Cubo Defense Line (defensive wall) protected the settlement against approaches from the north, the City Gate is now the entrance to the city's popular restored area. ⊠ *St. George St.*

**⑨ Flagler College.** Originally one of two posh hotels Henry Flagler built in 1888, this building is a riveting structure replete with towers, turrets, and arcades decorated by Louis Comfort Tiffany. Now a small liberal arts college, the building is not open for tours, but you can look at the front courtyard. ⊠ *78 King St.,* ☎ *904/829–6481.*

**⑩ Flagler Memorial Presbyterian Church.** For a look at a splendid Venetian Renaissance structure, head to Flagler Memorial Presbyterian Church, which Henry Flagler built in 1889. The dome towers more than 100 feet high, and it is topped by a 20-foot Greek cross. ⊠ *Valencia and Sevilla Sts.* ☉ *Weekdays 8:30–4:30.*

**⑪ Fountain of Youth Archeological Park.** The legendary spring that flowed through folklore as the Fountain of Youth can be found here at a tribute to explorer Ponce de León. In the complex there is a springhouse,

Basilica Cathedral of
St. Augustine, **6**

Castillo de San Marcos
National Monument, **7**

City Gate, **8**

Flagler College, **9**

Flagler Memorial
Presbyterian
Church, **10**

Fountain of Youth
Archaeological
Park, **11**

Lightner Museum, **12**

Mission of Nombre de
Dios, **13**

Oldest House, **14**

Oldest Store
Museum, **15**

Oldest Wooden
Schoolhouse, **16**

Spanish Quarter
Museum, **17**

Ximenez-Fatio
House, **18**

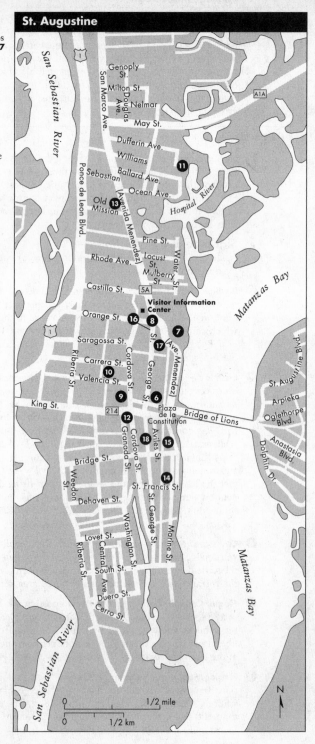

St. Augustine

an explorer's globe, a planetarium, and a Native American village. ⊠ *155 Magnolia Ave.,* ☏ *904/829–3168.* ⌨ *$4.50.* ◷ *Daily 9–5.*

★ ⑫ **Lightner Museum.** In his quest to turn Florida into an American Riviera, Henry Flagler built two fancy hotels in 1888—the Ponce de Léon, which became Flagler College (☞ *above,*) and the Alcazar, which now houses the Lightner Museum. The building showcases three floors of furnishings, costumes, and Victorian Art glass plus a collection of ornate antique music boxes (demonstrations daily at 11 and 2). The Lightner Antiques Mall perches on three levels of what was the hotel's grandiose indoor pool. ⊠ *75 King St.,* ☏ *904/824–2874.* ⌨ *$4.* ◷ *Museum daily 9–5, mall Tues.–Sun. 10–4.*

⑬ **Mission of Nombre de Dios.** The site commemorates where America's first Christian mass was celebrated. A 208-foot stainless-steel cross marks the spot where the mission's first cross was planted. ⊠ *San Marco Ave. and Old Mission Rd.,* ☏ *904/824–2809.* ⌨ *Donation requested.* ◷ *Daily 9–6.*

⑭ **Oldest House.** There has been a structure on this site since the early 1600s. Much of the city's history is reflected here through the building's changes and additions, from the coquina blocks used instead of wood soon after the town was burned in 1702 to the house's enlargement during the British occupation. ⊠ *14 St. Francis St.,* ☏ *904/824–2872.* ⌨ *$5.* ◷ *Daily 9–5.*

⑮ **Oldest Store Museum.** There are high-button shoes, lace-up corsets, patent drugs, and confectionery specialties at this re-creation of a turn-of-the-century general store. ⊠ *4 Artillery La.,* ☏ *904/829–9729.* ⌨ *$4.* ◷ *Mon.–Sat. 9–5, Sun. 10–5.*

⑯ **Oldest Wooden Schoolhouse.** Automated mannequins of a teacher and students relate the school's history. This tiny 18th-century building is built of cypress and cedar and thought to be one of the nation's oldest schoolhouses. Because it was the closest structure to the city gate, it served as a guardhouse and sentry shelter during the Seminole Wars. ⊠ *14 St. George St.* ☏ *904/824–0192.* ⌨ *$2.* ◷ *Daily 9–5.*

**Plaza de la Constitution.** The central area of the original settlement of St. Augustine was laid out in 1598 by decree of King Philip II. Little has changed since in the Plaza de la Constitution. At its center there is a monument to the Spanish constitution of 1812; at the east end is a public market dating from early American days. Just beyond is a statue of Juan Ponce de León, who "discovered" Florida in 1513. ⊠ *George St. and Cathedral Pl.*

⑰ **Spanish Quarter Museum.** You can wander through the narrow streets at your own pace in this state-operated, living-history village with eight sites. Along your way you may see a blacksmith building his shop (a historic reconstruction), and artisans busy at candle dipping, spinning, weaving, and cabinetmaking. They are all making reproductions that will be used within the restored area. ⊠ *Triay House, 29 St. George St.,* ☏ *904/825–6830.* ⌨ *$5.* ◷ *Daily 9–5.*

**Visitor Information Center.** To catch an entertaining film about the founding of St. Augustine, stop by and see *Dream of an Empire.* There are showings every hour from 9 until 4. ⊠ *10 Castillo Dr.,* ☏ *904/824–1000.* ⌨ *$3.* ◷ *Daily 9–5.*

⑱ **Ximenez-Fatio House.** Originally built as a merchant's house and store in 1797, it became a boardinghouse for tourists in the 1800s and is now restored to its condition at the time when it operated as an inn.

✉ *20 Aviles St.,* ☎ *904/829–3575.* ⬚ *Free.* ⊙ *Mon. and Thurs.–Sat. 11–4, Sun. 1–4.*

## Dining and Lodging

**$$**   ✕ **La Parisienne.** Tiny and attentive, pleasantly lusty in its approach
**★**   to honest bistro cuisine, this little place is a true find—and weekend brunches are available, too. Save room for the pastries at this excellent, very French restaurant. ✉ *60 Hypolita St.,* ☎ *904/829–0055. Reservations essential. AE, MC, V. Closed Mon.*

**$$**   ✕ **Le Pavilion.** The Swiss chef's Continental approach spills over from France to Germany with a wow of a schnitzel with spätzle. Hearty soups and breads make a budget meal, or you can splurge on the rack of lamb or escargot. ✉ *45 San Marco Ave.,* ☎ *904/824–6202. AE, D, DC, MC, V.*

**$–$$**   ✕ **Columbia.** An heir to the cherished reputation of the original Columbia, founded in Tampa in 1905, this one serves time-honored Cuban and Spanish dishes including arroz con pollo, filet *salteado* (with a spicy sauce), and a fragrant paella. The Fiesta Brunch on Sunday is a bountiful array of everything from cheeses and cold meats to Belgian waffles. ✉ *98 St. George St.,* ☎ *904/824–3341; in FL, 800/227–1905. AE, D, MC, V.*

**$–$$**   ✕ **Raintree.** The oldest home in its part of the city, this building has been lovingly restored and is worth a visit even though the food is generally not outstanding. The buttery breads and pastries are baked on the premises. Try the brandied pepper steak or the Maine lobster special. The Raintree's madrigal and Champagne dinners are especially fun. The wine list is impressive, and there are two dozen beers to choose from. Courtesy pickup is available from any lodging in the city. ✉ *102 San Marco Ave.,* ☎ *904/824–7211. AE, DC, MC, V. No lunch.*

**$–$$**   ✕ **Santa Maria.** This ramshackle landmark, run by the same family since the 1950s, perches over the water beside the colorful city marina. Seafood is the focus, but there are also steaks, chicken, prime rib, and a children's menu. From the open-air porch you can feed the fish. ✉ *135 Avenida Menendez,* ☎ *904/829–6578. AE, DC, MC, V.*

**$$$**   🏨 **Ponce de León Golf and Conference Resort.** The lavish grounds of this resort are a spacious contrast to the narrow streets and crowds in the old city. You can loll in the sun or seek the shade of century-old live oaks, but the location is a bit out of the way if you intend to spend time sightseeing. ✉ *4000 U.S. 1N, 32095,* ☎ *904/824–2821; in FL, 800/228–2821;* ⬚ᴀX *904/824–8254. 200 rooms, 99 condos. Restaurant, lounge, pool, 18-hole championship golf course, 18-hole putting course, tennis, horseshoes, jogging, shuffleboard, volleyball. AE, D, DC, MC, V.*

**$$**   🏨 **Carriage Way Bed and Breakfast.** A grandly restored Victorian man-
**★**   sion, this B&B is within walking distance of the old town. Innkeepers Diane and Bill Johnson see to such welcoming touches as fresh flowers and home-baked breads. A full breakfast is included in the rate. Special-occasion breakfasts, flowers, picnic lunches, romantic dinners, or a simple family supper can be arranged with advance notice. ✉ *70 Cuna St., 32084,* ☎ *904/829–2467. 9 rooms. Bicycles. D, MC, V.*

**$$**   🏨 **Kenwood Inn.** For more than a century this stately Victorian inn
**★**   has been welcoming wayfarers, and the Constant family continues the tradition. Located in the heart of the historic district, the inn is within walking distance of restaurants and sightseeing. A Continental breakfast of home-baked cakes and breads is included. ✉ *38 Marine St., 32084,* ☎ *904/824–2116. 10 rooms, 4 suites Pool. D, MC, V.*

**$-$$** ⬚ **St. Francis Inn.** If only the walls could whisper, this late 18th-century house would tell tales of slave uprisings, buried doubloons, and Confederate spies. The inn, which has been a guest house since 1845, now offers rooms, suites, an apartment, and a cottage. Furnishings are a mix of antiques and just plain old. Rates include Continental breakfast. ⊠ *279 St. George St., 32084,* ☎ *904/824–6068. 16 units. Pool, bicycles. MC, V.*

### Nightlife

**Scarlett O'Hara's** (⊠ 70 Hypolita St., ☎ 904/824–6535) has live blues, jazz, or reggae bands nightly. **Trade Winds** (⊠ 124 Charlotte St., ☎ 904/829–9336) showcases live bands most nights; call for a schedule. Crowds head to **White Lion** (⊠ 20 Cuna St., ☎ 904/829–2388) for a variety of live music on weekends. Call to find out who's playing and the type of music.

### Outdoor Activities and Sports

GOLF

You'll find 90 holes of golf at the **Sheraton Palm Coast** (⊠ 300 Clubhouse Dr., Palm Coast 32137, ☎ 904/445–3000). The **Ponce de Leon Golf and Conference Resort** (⊠ 4000 U.S. 1N, St. Augustine 32095, ☎ 904/824–2821) offers 18 holes of golf.

TENNIS

**Ponce de Leon Golf and Conference Resort** (⊠ 4000 U.S. 1N, St. Augustine 32095, ☎ 904/824–2821) has six tennis courts.

## Beyond St. Augustine

Stretching between St. Augustine and the Ormond/Daytona Beach area are miles of empty beaches. The inland area is mostly undeveloped, but the Ravine State Gardens park is a stunning place to picnic or hike.

### Sights to See

🔆 **Marineland.** One of the first aquarium attractions with shows ever built in the United States, Marineland is still a magic place. Dolphins grin, sea lions bark, and seals slither seductively to everyone's delight. ⊠ *South of St. Augustine on Rte. A1A,* ☎ *904/471–1111; in FL, 800/824–4218.* 🎟 *$14.95.* ☉ *Daily 9–5:30, shows held continuously.*

**Ravine State Gardens.** For a great picnic spot, make your way to one of the state's great azalea gardens, which began during the Depression as a WPA project. The ravines are atypical of flat Florida. They're steep and deep, threaded with brooks and rocky outcroppings, and floored with flatlands that make a perfect spot for an intimate picnic. Although any month is a good time to hike the shaded glens here, the azaleas are in full bloom February and March. The park is inland about 35 miles west of St. Augustine. ⊠ *Off Twig St. from U.S. 17 S, Palatka,* ☎ *904/329–3721.* 🎟 *$3.25 per vehicle with up to 8 people.* ☉ *Daily 8–sunset.*

### Beaches

The young gravitate toward the public beaches at **St. Augustine Beach** and **Vilano Beach,** while families prefer the **Anastasia State Recreation Area.** All three are accessible via Rte. A1A: Vilano Beach is to the north, across North River, and Anastasia State Park and St. Augustine Beach are both on Anastasia Island, across the Bridge of Lions.

### Dining

**$** ✕ **Zaharias.** This restaurant is a short drive from downtown St. Augustine, across the Bridge of Lions. The room is big, busy, and buzzing with an air of open hospitality. Serve yourself from an enormous buffet instead of, or in addition to, ordering from the menu. Greek and Italian specialties include homemade pizza, a big gyro dinner served with a side order of spaghetti, and shish kebabs, steaks, seafood, and sandwiches. ✉ *3945 Rte. A1A S,* ☎ *904/471–4799. AE, MC, V.*

### Outdoor Activities and Sports

FISHING

Charter the *Sea Love II* (☎ 904/824–3328) or sign up to join a half- or full-day fishing trip.

WATER SPORTS

Surfboards and sailboards can be rented at the **Surf Station** (✉ 1002 Anastasia Blvd., ☎ 904/471–9463).

# DAYTONA BEACH

*Numbers in the margin correspond to points of interest on the Northeast Florida map.*

🕧 **Daytona Beach,** best known for the Daytona 500, has been the center of automobile racing since cars were first raced along the beach here in 1902. February is the biggest month for race enthusiasts, and there are weekly events at the International Speedway. The beach is lined with inexpensive motels and restaurants and is a notoriously popular spring-break destination for college students. The newly restored downtown along Beach Street has been "street-scaped," and neat brick walkways now lead to shops and restaurants.

## Sights to See

**Daytona Beach.** Daytona is one of the few places in the United States where you are allowed to drive on the beach. To get your car on the beach, look for signs indicating beach access via beach ramps. During spring break, race weeks, and summer holidays, expect heavy traffic along this strip of garishly painted beach motels and tacky souvenir shops. Sand traps are not limited to the golf course, though—cars can get stuck. ✉ *Daytona Beach off Rte. A1A.*

**Daytona USA.** Racing enthusiasts will rush to Daytona's new addition, which opened in summer 1996. The interactive motor-sports attraction lets visitors participate in a pit stop on a NASCAR Winston Cup stock car, design their own race car, and talk to their favorite competitors through video. There's also an exhibit of the history of auto racing. ✉ *1801 International Speedway Dr.,* ☎ *904/254–2700.* 🎟 *Unavailable at press time.* ☉ *Daily 9–9.*

**Halifax Historical Society Museum.** Memorabilia from the early days of beach automobile racing are on display along with historic photographs, Native American artifacts, a postcard exhibit, and a video that details the history of the city. There's a shop for gifts and antiques. ✉ *252 S. Beach St.,* ☎ *904/255–6976.* 🎟 *$2, free Sat.* ☉ *Tues.–Sat. 10–4.*

**Museum of Arts and Sciences.** With the addition of the new Humanities Wing, the Museum of Arts and Sciences is now one of the five largest museums in Florida. The new section includes displays of Chinese art and glass, silver, gold, and porcelain examples of decorative arts. The museum also has a large collection of pre-Castro Cuban art and an eye-popping complete skeleton of a giant sloth that is 13 feet long and

130,000 years old. ⊠ *1040 Museum Blvd.,* ☎ *904/255–0285.* ⊡ *$4.* ⊙ *Tues.–Fri. 9–4, weekends noon–5.*

**Ponce de León Lighthouse.** At the southern tip of the barrier island that includes Daytona Beach is sleepy **Ponce Inlet,** where you'll find a small marina, a few bars, and informal restaurants specializing in very fresh fish. Boardwalks traverse delicate dunes and provide easy access to the beach. Marking this prime spot is the bright red, century-old lighthouse, now a historic monument and museum. ⊠ *4931 S. Atlantic Ave.,* ☎ *904/761–1821.* ⊡ *$4.* ⊙ *Daily 10–5.*

**Southeast Museum of Photography.** One of only 12 photography museums in the country, this one contains historical and contemporary exhibits that change throughout the year. ⊠ *1200 W. International Speedway Blvd.,* ☎ *904/254–4475.* ⊡ *Free.* ⊙ *Tues. 10–3 and 5–7, Wed.–Fri. 10–3, Sun. 1–4.*

## Beaches

**Daytona,** which bills itself as the "World's Most Famous Beach," permits you to drive your car right up to your beach site, spread out a blanket, and have all your belongings at hand; this is especially convenient for beachgoers who are elderly or have disabilities. However, heavy traffic during summer and holidays makes it dangerous for children, and families should be extra careful. The speed limit is 10 mph.

## Dining and Lodging

$$$ ✕ **Gene's Steak House.** This family-operated restaurant, located west of town in the middle of nowhere, has long upheld its reputation as *the* place for steaks. The wine list is one of the state's most comprehensive, and there are seafood specialties, but it's basically a meat-and-potatoes paradise for beef-eaters. ⊠ *4½ mi west of I–95/I–4 interchange on U.S. 92,* ☎ *904/255–2059. AE, DC, MC, V. Closed Mon.*

$$ ✕ **Anna's Trattoria.** White table linens and flowers set the scene for
★ delightful Italian fare. Choose from two pages of delicious pasta items: spaghetti with Italian sausage and onions, angel hair with fresh chopped tomatos and garlic, and spinach ravioli stuffed with spinach. There are also many veal and chicken dishes. ⊠ *304 Seabreeze Blvd.,* ☎ *904/239–9624. AE, MC, V. Closed Mon.*

$$ ✕ **Cafe Frappe.** This cozy second-floor restaurant across from a park cooks up such unusual appetizers as a papaya and brie quesadilla. Entrées include beef tenderloin sautéed with herbs and peppers, shrimp in an Asiago-Romano cream sauce, and fresh salmon. ⊠ *174 N. Beach St.,* ☎ *904/254–7999. AE, DC, MC, V. No dinner Sun. and Mon., no lunch weekends.*

$ ✕ **Aunt Catfish's on the River.** This popular place on the southwest bank of the Intracoastal Waterway (off U.S. 1, just before you cross the Port Orange Causeway), just south of Daytona, is crowded day and night. Locals and visitors flock here for the great salad bar, the hot cinnamon rolls and hush puppies that come with any entrée, the Southern-style chicken, and the freshly cooked seafood—fried shrimp, fried catfish, and crab cakes are specialties. ⊠ *4009 Halifax Dr., Port Orange,* ☎ *904/767–4768. AE, MC, V.*

$$$$ ✕▥ **Adam's Mark Resort.** Daytona's most luxurious high-rise hotel,
★ which changed ownership but not much else in 1995 (it was a Marriott), is set right on the beach, near the convention center and the band shell. Every room has a great ocean view and is comfortably furnished in pleasing pastels and blond oak. Guests can lounge around the pool on the spacious deck or head to the beach. There is an elegant restau-

rant, a poolside bar, and numerous other amenities. ✉ *100 N. Atlantic Ave., 32118*, ☎ *904/254–8200 or 800/872–9269*, FAX *904/253–0275. 402 rooms. 3 restaurants, bar, pool, wading pool, beauty salon, health club, beach, playground. AE, DC, MC, V.*

$$$   🏨 **Daytona Beach Hilton.** Most rooms in this beachside high rise have balconies; some have a kitchenette, patio, or terrace. Convenient touches include a hair dryer, lighted makeup mirror, and a bar with refrigerator. ✉ *2637 S. Atlantic Ave., 32118*, ☎ *904/767–7350 or 800/525–7350*, FAX *904/760–3651. 214 rooms. 3 restaurants, lounge, pool, wading pool, hot tub, sauna, exercise room, game room, playground, laundry. AE, D, DC, MC, V.*

$$$   🏨 **Live Oak Inn.** This lovely B&B is in a restored home that is listed in the National Register of Historic Places. Each room is different, but all are beautifully furnished with antiques. Some have long, enclosed porches and look out over the marina or onto gardens. Downstairs is a fine restaurant and a small lounge and reception area. ✉ *488 S. Beach St., 32114* ☎ *904/252–4667. 13 rooms. Restaurant, lounge, whirlpools. AE, MC, V.*

$$–$$$   🏨 **Captain's Quarters Inn.** It may look like just another mid-rise hotel, but the antique desk, Victorian love seat, and tropical greenery in the lobby will change your mind. At this beachfront, all-suite inn, fresh-baked goodies and coffee are served in the Galley, which overlooks the ocean and resembles a family kitchen with a few extra tables and chairs. Each guest suite features rich oak furnishings, a complete kitchen, and private balcony. Penthouse suites have fireplaces. ✉ *3711 S. Atlantic Ave., Daytona Beach Shores, 32127*, ☎ *904/767–3119*, FAX *904/760–7712. 25 suites. Pool. AE, D, MC, V.*

$$   🏨 **Perry's Ocean-Edge.** Long regarded as a family resort, Perry's is famous for its free homemade doughnuts and coffee—a breakfast ritual served in the lush solarium. Three-quarters of the rooms are efficiencies, and most have great ocean views. Choose from several pools (including an indoor one), a wide beach, and a putting green. ✉ *2209 S. Atlantic Ave., 32118*, ☎ *904/255–0581 or 800/447–0002; in FL, 800/342–0102*; FAX *904/258–7315. 204 rooms. Café, indoor pool, 2 outdoor pools, putting green, beach, game room. AE, D, DC, MC, V.*

## Nightlife and the Arts

### The Arts

Broadway touring shows, symphony orchestras and ballet companies from around the world, and popular entertainers appear at the **Ocean Center** (✉ 101 N. Atlantic Ave., ☎ 904/254–4545; in FL, 800/858–6444). **Peabody Auditorium** (✉ 600 Auditorium Blvd., ☎ 904/255–1314) is used for many concerts and programs throughout the year. **Seaside Music Theater** (✉ Box 2835, ☎ 904/252–3394) presents professional musicals in two venues, Jan.–Mar. and June–Aug.

### Nightlife

**Razzles** (✉ 640 N. Grandview St., ☎ 904/257–6236) is the hottest spot in Daytona. DJs spin high-energy dance music from early evening until the early morning hours. Crowds flock to **Billy Bob's** (✉ 2801 S. Ridgewood Ave., ☎ 904/756–0048) to dance to live country music; the band plays nightly. Popular **Wave's Action Bar** (✉ 100 N. Atlantic Ave., ☎ 904/254–8212) is a combination sports bar and DJ disco. And those ready to twist should head to the **Memory Lane Rock and Roll Cafe** (✉ 2424 N. Atlantic Ave., ☎ 904–673–5389), where DJs spin music from the '50s and '60s.

# Outdoor Activities and Sports

### Auto Racing

The massive **Daytona International Speedway** on U.S. 92 (Daytona Beach's major east–west artery) is home to year-round auto and motorcycle racing, including the annual Daytona 500 in February and Pepsi 400 in July. Twenty-minute narrated tours of the historic track are offered daily 9–5 except on race days. For racing schedules, call 904/254–2700.

### Dog Racing

You can bet on the dogs every night but Sunday year-round at the **Daytona Beach Kennel Club** (⊠ U.S. 92, near International Speedway, ☎ 904/252–6484).

### Fishing

Contact **Critter Fleet Marina** (⊠ 4950 S. Peninsula Dr., ☎ 904/767–7676) for full- or half-day deep-sea party trips.

### Golf

**Indigo Lakes Golf Club** (⊠ 312 Indigo Dr., 32114, ☎ 904/254–3607) offers 18 holes of golf. **Spruce Creek Golf & Country Club** (⊠ 1900 Country Club Dr., 32023, ☎ 904/756–6114) has an 18-hole course and a practice range.

### Water Sports

In Daytona Beach you can rent sailboards, surfboards, or boogie boards at the **Salty Dog** (⊠ 700 Broadway, ☎ 904/258–0457). For Jet Ski rentals, try **J&J** (⊠ 841 Ballough Rd., ☎ 904/255–1917).

# Shopping

The **Volusia Mall** (⊠ 1700 W. International Speedway Blvd., ☎ 904/253–6783) has four major anchor stores, including Burdines and Sears, plus many specialty shops. Daytona's **Flea Market** (⊠ I-4 at U.S. 92) is one of the South's largest.

# Side Trips

**②⓪** **Ormond Beach** got its reputation as the birthplace of speed because early car enthusiasts such as Alexander Winton, R.E. Olds, and Barney Oldfield raced their autos on the sands here. Ormond Beach borders the north side of Daytona Beach on both the mainland and the barrier island—nowadays you can't tell you've crossed from one to the other unless you notice the sign.

**The Casements.** The restored winter retreat of John D. Rockefeller now serves as a cultural center and museum. Take a tour through the period Rockefeller Room, which displays some of the family's memorabilia. The estate and its formal gardens host an annual lineup of special events and exhibits; there is also a permanent exhibit of Hungarian clothes, musical instruments, and other utilitarian objects. ⊠ 25 Riverside Dr., ☎ 904/676–3216. ⊡ Donation welcome. ☉ Mon.–Thurs. 9–9, Fri. 9–5, Sat. 9–noon.

**Ormond Memorial Art Museum and Gardens.** Take a walk through lush tropical gardens, past fish ponds and fountains. Inside the museum are historical displays and exhibits by Florida artists. ⊠ 78 E. Granada Blvd., ☎ 904/676–3347. ⊡ Free. ☉ Tues.–Fri. 11–4, weekends noon–4.

**Tomoka State Park.** A scenic park that is a perfect location for fishing, camping, hiking, and boating. It is the site of a Timucuan Indian settlement discovered in 1605 by Spanish explorer Alvaro Mexia. Wooded campsites, bicycle and walking paths, and guided canoe tours on the Tomoka and Halifax rivers are the main attractions. ⊠ *2099 N. Beach St.,* ☎ *904/676–4050.* ⊠ *Year-round $3.25 per car; June–Dec. $8 per day for nonelectric campsite; Jan.–May, $16 per day for nonelectric campsite; additional $2 for electric campsite.* ☉ *Daily 8–sunset.*

**Flagler Beach** is a vast, windswept swath of sand with easy access, about 25 miles north of Ormond Beach.

# NEW SMYRNA BEACH

㉑   **New Smyrna Beach** is a small town with a 7-mile public beach that abuts the Canaveral National Seashore. There are two restored main streets—Canal Street on the mainland and Flagler Avenue, which is beachside and in the process of being restored.

## Sights to See

**Atlantic Center for the Arts.** Gallery exhibits at the Atlantic Center for the Arts change every two months, featuring the works of internationally known artists, and including sculpture, mixed media, video, drawings, prints, and paintings. Intensive, three-week workshops are periodically run by visual, literary, and performing master artists such as Edward Albee, James Dickey, and Beverly Pepper. ⊠ *1414 Art Center Ave.,* ☎ *904/427–6975.* ⊠ *Free.* ☉ *Weekdays 9–5, Sun. 2–5.*

★ **Canaveral National Seashore.** Miles of grassy, windswept dunes, and a virtually empty beach await you at this remarkable 57,000-acre park with 24 miles of undeveloped coastline. But be warned: The dunes are endangered and it's against the law to walk on or play in the dunes or pick the sea grass. Stop at any of the six parking areas and follow the wooden walkways to the beach. Ranger-led weekly programs range from canoe trips to sea turtle talks. Call for a schedule. ⊠ *South end of Rte. A1A,* ☎ *904/428–3384.* ⊠ *Free.* ☉ *Daily, sunrise–sunset.*

**Smyrna Dunes Park.** Here, at the northern tip of a barrier island, 1½ miles of boardwalks crisscross sand dunes and delicate dune vegetation as they lead to beaches and a fishing jetty. Botanical signs identify the flora, and there are picnic tables and an information center. ⊠ *N. Peninsula Ave.* ⊠ *Free.* ☉ *Daily 7–sunset.*

## Beaches

**New Smyrna Beach** has 7 miles of hard-packed white sand and a dune-lined shore, behind which sit beach houses, small motels, and an occasional high rise. (Except at the extreme northern tip, none are higher than seven stories.) Cars are allowed on the beach from sunrise to sunset; the speed limit is 10 mph.

## Dining and Lodging

**$$–$$$** ✕ **Riverview Charlie's Seafood Grill.** A brick walkway winds through tropical foliage to this popular spot, which is jumping day and night. Two cozy dining rooms look out over the Intracoastal Waterway. You can also dine in the high-ceilinged bar, where there is entertainment nightly, or eat outside on the spacious waterfront deck. Fresh fish, including local grouper, are the specialties here, and sandwiches and salads are available for lunch inside and anytime day or night on the deck. ⊠ *101 Flagler Ave.,* ☎ *904/428–1865. AE, MC, V.*

**$$–$$$**   ✗ **Skyline.** Watch private airplanes land and take off at the New Smyrna Beach airport as you dine on secretly seasoned Tony Barbera steaks, veal, shrimp, chicken, and fish. Prices are high for the area, but the fresh fish is usually excellent. ⊠ *2004 N. Dixie Fwy.,* ☎ *904/428–5325. AE, MC, V. No lunch.*

**$**   ✗ **Norwood's Seafood Restaurant.** Crowds head to this casual New Smyrna Beach landmark, which has been open almost 50 years. Fresh local fish and shrimp are the specialties here, but you can also order steak, blackened chicken breast, or pasta. The mashed potatoes and onion rings (both homemade) are outstanding. Prices are incredibly low, and the extensive wine list is extraordinary. ⊠ *400 E. 2nd Ave.,* ☎ *904/428–4621. AE, MC, V.*

**$**   ✗ **Sam's Italian Seafood.** New Smyrna's best-kept secret is this hide-
★ away on U.S. 1, which Sam opened in 1982. He's the chef (his wife, Celeste, is the manager), and he serves some of the best food in New Smyrna Beach. The pasta dishes are superb, particularly the eggplant rollatini. You can count on absolutely fresh seafood here and house specialties include flounder primavera and seafood crepes. The menu is extensive, there are nightly specials, and there is a small but good wine list (beer and wine only). Four small dining rooms and some private rooms with just two tables insure a quiet evening. ⊠ *2392 N. Dixie Fwy.,* ☎ *904/427–1462. AE, MC, V.*

**$**   ✗ **Teddy's.** You wouldn't expect to find a New York-style Greek coffee shop in a small Florida town, but here's a great one. The menu runs the gamut from homemade soups to sandwiches, hamburgers, fresh salads, and steaks plus gyros, Greek salads, and an absolutely superb spinach pie. Early risers flock here for French toast, blueberry pancakes, and western omelets. ⊠ *812 3rd Ave.,* ☎ *904/428–0443. No credit cards. No dinner mid-Apr.–mid-Dec.*

**$**   ✗ **Tony and Joe's.** This longtime favorite opens right onto the beach and has a large terrace perfect for people-watching. Head here for their famous "hoagies," long rolls of fresh bread stuffed with slices of steak, cheese, sweet peppers, and onions and heated until the cheese is perfectly melted. ⊠ *309 Buenos Aires,* ☎ *904/427–6850. No credit cards.*

**$$–$$$**   🖼 **Holiday Inn Hotel Suites.** Families tend to like these comfortable suites, which sleep four, six, or eight people. Bedrooms are raised and set behind the living room, which opens out to a balcony and a spectacular view of the ocean. The furnishings are contemporary, and each unit has a full kitchen. ⊠ *1401 S. Atlantic Ave., 32169,* ☎ *904/426–0020. 102 suites. Restaurant, bar, pool. AE, MC, V.*

**$$–$$$**   🖼 **International Properties.** There are lots of condos and houses available for rent that are on either the ocean or the Intracoastal Waterway. Units, which all have full kitchens, can be rented from three days to a week, a month, or a season. ⊠ *4166 S. Atlantic Ave.,* ☎ *904/424–9173 or 800/227–5581,* 𝖥𝖠𝖷 *904/427–0470. 220 units, most with pools.*

**$$–$$$**   🖼 **Riverview Hotel.** A landmark since 1886, this former bridge tender's home is set back from the Intracoastal Waterway at the edge of the North Causeway, which to this day has an operating drawbridge. Rooms open out to plant-filled verandas and balconies, and views look either through trees to the Intracoastal or onto the private courtyard and pretty pool. Each room is furnished differently with charming antique touches, such as an old washbasin, a quilt, or a rocking chair. A complimentary Continental breakfast is served in your room, and the inn is near many interesting shops. ⊠ *103 Flagler Ave., 32169,* ☎

*904/428–5858 or 800/945–7416,* FAX *904/423–8927. 18 rooms. Restaurant, pool, bicycles. AE, D, DC, MC, V.*

## Shopping

**Flagler Avenue** (North Causeway) is the major entranceway to the beach, and art galleries, gift shops, and surf shops line the street. A few blocks away is the Third Avenue Shopping Center, where there are a number of specialty stores, including the popular **Snow Goose Gift Shop** (⊠ 721 3rd Ave., ☎ 904/423–3100) where you'll need to check out the ceiling as well as the floor to catch everything on display.

# COCOA BEACH

㉒   **Cocoa Beach** is the easiest beach to reach from Orlando and is a popular spot year-round with folks who live in central Florida. Motels and inexpensive restaurants line the beach, and Kennedy Space Center is just 10 minutes away.

## Sights to See

☾   **Brevard Museum of History and Natural Science.** Don't overlook the hands-on discovery rooms and the Taylor Collection of Victorian memorabilia at this museum. Its nature center has 22 acres of trails encompassing three distinct ecosystems—sand pine hills, lakelands, and marshlands. ⊠ *2201 Michigan Ave.,* ☎ *407/632–1830.* ☞ *$4.* ☉ *Tues.–Sat. 10–4, Sun. 1–4.*

★ ☾   **Spaceport USA.** This is perhaps the best entertainment bargain in Florida. There are two narrated bus tours: One passes by some of NASA's office and assembly buildings, including current launch facilities and the space shuttle launching and landing sites. The other goes to Cape Canaveral Air Force Station, where early launch pads and unmanned rockets that were later adapted for manned use illuminate the history of the early space program. Even more dramatic is the IMAX film *The Dream Is Alive,* shown hourly in the Galaxy Theater. Projected onto a 5½-story screen, this overwhelming 40-minute film, most of which was shot by the astronauts, takes you from astronaut training, through a thundering shuttle launch, and into the cabins where the astronauts live while in space. (A second film, *Destiny in Space,* is also worth watching.) ⊠ *Kennedy Space Center,* ☎ *407/452–2121; outside FL, 800/432–2153.* ☞ *Free, bus tours $7, IMAX film $4.* ☉ *Daily 9–6, last tour 2 hours before dark; Closed Dec. 25 and certain launch dates (call ahead).*

**United States Astronaut Hall of Fame.** Stationed at the entrance to Spaceport USA, this museum focuses not only on the milestones of the space program but on the personal stories of the astronauts. Board a space shuttle replica to view videos of historic moments. ⊠ *Kennedy Space Center,* ☎ *407/269–6100.* ☞ *$6.95.* ☉ *Mid-Aug.–May, daily 9–5; June–mid-Aug., daily 9–7; Closed Dec. 25.*

## Beaches

**Cocoa Beach** (☎ 407/868–3274), on A1A, has showers, playgrounds, changing areas, picnic areas with grills, snack shops, and plenty of well-maintained, inexpensive surfside parking lots. Beach vendors offer a variety of necessities for sunning and swimming.

North of Cocoa, **Playalinda Beach,** part of the **Canaveral National Seashore** (☎ 407/267–1110), is the longest stretch of undeveloped coast on Florida's Atlantic Seaboard. Hundreds of giant sea turtles come ashore here May through August to lay their eggs, and the extreme northern area is favored by nude sun worshipers. There are no lifeguards, but park rangers patrol. Take Exit 80 from I–95, and follow Rte. 406 east across the Indian River, then Rte. 402 east for 12 more miles.

## Dining and Lodging

$$$ ✕ **Mango Tree Restaurant.** Dine in elegance amid orchid gardens, with piano music playing in the background. House favorites include fresh grouper with shrimp and scallops glazed in hollandaise sauce and veal française à la Mango Tree (veal scallopini, very lightly breaded and glazed with a mushroom sauce). ⊠ *118 N. Atlantic Ave., ☎ 407/799–0513. AE, MC, V. Closed Mon. No lunch.*

$$ ✕ **Black Tulip.** Two cozy rooms create an intimate setting for this
★ spot's elegant cuisine. Starters include tortellini bolognese, crab-stuffed mushrooms, and a delicious black bean soup. Choose from such entrées as roast duckling with apples and cashews, steak au poivre, or linguini with chicken in a garlic and white wine sauce. Lunch selections are lighter and include sandwiches and salads. ⊠ *207 Brevard Ave., ☎ 407/631–1133. AE, DC, MC, V.*

$ ✕ **Herbie K's.** This diner is a 1950s rock-and-roll landmark. The juke box plays golden oldies and the servers dress, walk, talk, and even dance in the spirit of the times. You'll see saddle shoes and revisit expressions such as "daddy-o" and "doll-face." Famous for its burgers, Herbie K's also serves homestyle blue plates and old-fashioned ice cream desserts. ⊠ *2080 N. Rte. A1A, ☎ 407/783–6740. AE, D, DC, MC, V.*

$ ✕ **Lone Cabbage Fish Camp.** The natural habitat of wildlife and local characters, this one-of-a-kind spot sits on the St. Johns River nine miles north of Cocoa city limits on Route 520 and four miles west of I–95. The catfish, turtle, country ham, and alligator on the menu make the drive well worthwhile. You can also fish from a dock here, buy bait, or rent a canoe for a trip on the St. Johns, making for a fun family outing. ⊠ *8199 Rte. 520, Cocoa, ☎ 407/632–4199. No credit cards.*

$$$ ▥ **Radisson Resort at the Port.** Tame peacocks roam the grounds at this family-oriented resort. While the property is not on the beach, it does provide complimentary transportation to the nearest beaches as well as to restaurants and shopping. Rooms have a Caribbean motif, with wicker appointments and hand-painted wallpaper. The pool is lavish in the best central Florida fashion, tropically landscaped and complete with 95-foot mountain waterfalls. ⊠ *8701 Astronaut Blvd., Cape Canaveral 32920, ☎ 407/784–0000 or 800/333–3333. 200 rooms. Restaurant, pool, wading pool, 2 tennis courts, fitness center, game room, playground. AE, D, DC, MC, V.*

$$–$$$ ▥ **The Inn at Cocoa Beach.** The finest accommodations in Cocoa Beach
★ can be found in this charming oceanfront inn. Each spacious room is decorated differently but all have some combination of reproduction 18th- and 19th-century armoires, four-poster beds, and comfortably upholstered chairs and sofas. There are several suites, some with whirlpool baths. All units have balconies or patios and views of the ocean. Included in the rate is an evening spread of wine and cheese and a sumptuous Continental breakfast with delicious homemade muffins and breads, served in the sunny breakfast room. ⊠ *4300 Ocean Beach Blvd., 32931, ☎ 407/799–3460; outside FL, 800/343–5307. 50 rooms. Pool, beach. AE, D, DC, MC, V.*

$$ ▥ **Wakulla Motel.** This popular motel is clean and comfortable and just two blocks from the beach. Rooms are bright and decorated in tropical prints. The completely furnished five-room suites, designed to

sleep six, are great for families; they include two bedrooms, living room, dining room, and fully equipped kitchen. ⊠ *3550 N. Atlantic Ave., 32931,* ☎ *407/783–2230. 116 suites. Grills, 2 pools, shuffleboard. AE, D, DC, MC, V.*

## Outdoor Activities and Sports

### Fishing
**Cape Marina** (⊠ 800 Scallop Dr., Port Canaveral, ☎ 407/783–8410) has half- and full-day charter fishing trips.

## Shopping

**Ron Jon Surf Shop** (⊠ 4151 N. Atlantic Ave., ☎ 407/799–8840) is a local attraction in its own right—a castle that's purple, pink, and glittery as an amusement park, plunked right down in the middle of the beach community. This multilevel store is packed with swimwear and surfboards and it's open 24 hours a day. It's worth a stop just to see what all those billboards are about. In downtown Cocoa (on the mainland), cobblestone walkways wind through **Olde Cocoa Village,** a cluster of restored turn-of-the-century buildings now occupied by restaurants and specialty shops purveying pottery, macramé, leather and silvercraft, afghans, fine art, and clothing.

# DELAND AND OCALA

Deland, a quiet university town, is home to Stetson University, which was established in 1886 by Stetson hat magnate John Stetson. Ocala is also a peaceful town and is considered to be the center of Florida's Thoroughbred industry. The rolling hills and sweeping fields of bluegrass found here remind one more of Kentucky than of Florida.

## Around Deland

㉓ Other than the university, there is not much to see in **Deland.** But several inviting state parks are nearby, and it's a great place to go manatee-watching during the winter.

### Sights to See
**Blue Spring State Park.** February is the top month for sighting manatees but they begin to head here in November, as soon as the water gets cold enough (below 68°F). The park, once a river port where paddle wheelers stopped to take on cargoes of oranges, also contains a historic homestead that is open to the public.

You can hike, camp, or picnic here. ⊠ *2100 W. French Ave., Orange City,* ☎ *904/775–3663.* ⊠ *$3.25 per vehicle with up to 8 people.* ☉ *Daily 8–sunset.*

**De Leon Springs State Recreation Area.** Near the end of the last century this place was promoted as a fountain of youth to winter tourists, but visitors are now content to swim, fish, and hike the nature trails. ⊠ *Off U.S. 17, De Leon Springs,* ☎ *904/985–4212.* ⊠ *$3.25 per vehicle with up to 8 people.* ☉ *Daily 8–sunset.*

**Gillespie Museum of Minerals.** One of the largest private collections of gems and minerals in the world can be found in the Gillespie Museum of Minerals, on the Stetson University campus. ⊠ *Michigan and Amelia Aves., Deland,* ☎ *904/822–7330.* ⊠ *Free.* ☉ *Weekdays 9–noon and 1–4.*

## Dining and Lodging

**$$** ✕ **Pondo's.** You lose almost half a century as you step into what was once a romantic hideaway for young pilots who trained in Deland during the war. The owner-chef specializes in whimsical veal dishes, but he also does fish, beef, and chicken. The old-fashioned bar will remind you of television's "Cheers," and a pianist entertains Friday and Saturday nights. ⊠ *1915 Old New York Ave., Deland,* ☎ *904/734–1995. AE, MC, V.*

**$** ✕ **Karlings Inn.** A sort of Bavarian Brigadoon, set beside a forgotten highway near De Leon Springs, this restaurant is decorated like a Black Forest inn. Karl Caeners personally oversees the preparation of the sauerbraten, red cabbage, and succulent roast duckling, as well as charcoal-grilled steaks, seafood, and fresh veal. Ask to see the dessert tray. ⊠ *4640 N. U.S. 17, De Leon Springs,* ☎ *904/985–5535. AE, MC, V. Closed Sun. and Mon. No lunch.*

**$** ✕ **Original Holiday House.** This, the original of what has become a small chain of buffet restaurants, is enormously popular with seniors, families, and especially college students. (It's right across from the Stetson University campus.) Patrons can choose from three categories: salads only, salads and vegetables only, or the full buffet. ⊠ *704 N. Woodland Blvd., Deland,* ☎ *904/734–6319. MC, V.*

**$$** 🏨 **Holiday Inn Deland.** Picture a snazzy, big-city hotel in a little college town, run by friendly, small-town folks with city savvy. An enormous painting by nationally known local artist Fred Messersmith dominates the plush lobby. Rooms are done in subdued colors and styles; prestige Suites have housed the likes of Tom Cruise. Tennis and golf privileges at the Deland Country Club are offered. ⊠ *350 E. International Speedway Blvd. (U.S. 92), Deland, 32724,* ☎ *904/738–5200 or 800/826–3233,* FAX *904/734–7552. 150 rooms. Restaurant, bar, pool, nightclub. AE, D, MC, V.*

**$–$$** 🏨 **The 1888 House.** Spacious rooms, fireplaces, family heirlooms, and whirlpool baths make this a particularly enjoyable retreat. The building is of the distinctive Classic Revival style, with steep roofs and broad porches, excellent for rocking. Restaurants and historic sights are within easy walking distance. ⊠ *124 N. Clara Ave., Deland, 32720,* ☎ *904/822–4647. 6 rooms. Bicycles. AE, MC, V.*

**$** 🏨 **University Inn.** For years this has been the choice of business travelers and visitors to Stetson University. Conveniently located on campus, and across from the popular Holiday House restaurant, this motel has clean, comfortable rooms and offers a Continental breakfast each morning. Some rooms have kitchenettes. ⊠ *644 N. Woodland Blvd., Deland, 32720,* ☎ *904/734–5711 or 800/345–8991,* FAX *904/734–5716. 60 rooms. Pool. AE, D, DC, MC, V.*

## Outdoor Activities and Sports

### DIVING

For information about spring and freshwater diving and scuba instruction, try **Dive Tour Inc.** (⊠ 1403 E. New York Ave., Deland, ☎ 904/736–0571).

### FISHING

One of the most savvy guides to St. Johns River bass fishing is **Bob Stonewater** (Deland, ☎ 904/736–7120). He'll tow his boat to meet clients at the launch best for the day's fishing. Rental boats and motors are available from **Blair's Jungle Den Fish Camp** (⊠ 1820 Jungle Den Rd., Astor, ☎ 904/749–2264). **Hontoon Landing Marina** (⊠ 2317 River Ridge Rd., Deland, ☎ 904/734–2474) rents bass boats and offers fishing guide service.

SKYDIVING

Anybody who wants to jump out of an airplane when it's thousands of feet up in the air can do so with the help of **Skydive Deland** (✉ 1600 Flightline Blvd., Deland, ☎ 904/738–3539), open daily 8–sunset.

WATER SPORTS

Pontoon boats, houseboats, and bass boats for the St. Johns River are available from **Hontoon Landing Marina** (✉ 2317 River Ridge Rd., Deland, ☎ 904/734–2474).

# Around Ocala

㉔   **Ocala** is horse country, and outside of town you'll see dozens of horse farms, with their grassy paddocks and white wooden fences. Kentucky Derby winners have been raised in the region's training centers, and sometimes the farms are open to the public. The Ocala National Forest, east of Ocala, has a trio of beautiful, large recreational areas.

## Sights to See

**Appleton Museum of Art.** This three-building cultural complex is a marble-and-granite tour de force with a serene esplanade and reflecting pool. The collection lives up to its surroundings with more than 6,000 pre-Columbian, Asian, African, and 19th-century objets d'art. ✉ *4222 E. Silver Springs Blvd., Ocala* ☎ *352/236–5050.* ☞ *$3.* ☉ *Tues.–Sat. 10– 4:30, Sun. 1–5.*

★   **Ocala National Forest.** A delightful 366,000-acre wilderness with lakes, springs, rivers, hiking trails, campgrounds, and historic sites offers three major recreational areas. From east to west they are: **Alexander Springs** (✉ off Rte. 40 via Rte. 445 south), featuring a swimming lake and campground; **Salt Springs** (✉ off Rte. 40 via Rte. 19 north), which has a natural saltwater spring where Atlantic blue crabs come to spawn each summer; and **Juniper Springs** (✉ off Rte. 40), with a picturesque stone waterwheel house, campground, natural-spring swimming pool, and hiking and canoe trails. ✉ *Visitor center, 10863 East Hwy. 40, Silver Springs,* ☎ *352/625–7470.* ☞ *Free.*

★ ㉕   **Silver Springs.** The world's largest collection of artesian springs can be found at the western edge of the Ocala National Forest at Silver Springs. The state's first tourist attraction, it was established in 1890 and is listed on the National Register of Historic Landmarks. Today, the park presents wild-animal displays, glass-bottom boat tours in the Silver River, a jungle cruise on the Fort King Waterway, Jungle Safari, an antique and classic car museum, and walks through natural habitats. ✉ *Rte. 40 outside Ocala,* ☎ *352/236–2121.* ☞ *$20.* ☉ *Daily 9–5:30.*

**Silver Spring's Wild Waters.** Come here to cool off in the park's giant wave pool and seven water-flume rides. ✉ *Rte. 40 outside Ocala,* ☎ *352/236–2121.* ☞ *$9.95.* ☉ *Late Mar.–July, daily 10–5; Aug., daily 10–7; Sept., weekends 10–5.*

## Dining and Lodging

$$–$$$   ✗ **Fiddlestix, Edibles, & Libations.** This casual spot is extremely popular with locals and visitors alike. The menu offers everything from hamburgers and overstuffed sandwiches to open-pit-grilled steaks, chops, and chicken. ✉ *1016 S.E. 3rd Ave., Ocala,* ☎ *904/629–8000. AE, MC, V.*

$$–$$$   ✗▦ **Ocala Hilton.** A winding, tree-lined boulevard leads to this nine-story pink tower, nestled in a forested patch of countryside just off I–75 and a bit removed from downtown. The marble-floor lobby, with a piano bar, greets you before you enter your spacious guest room, dec-

orated in deeply colored, contemporary prints. Don't pass up **Arthur's**, the hotel's restaurant—filet mignon with port sauce and chicken breast stuffed with spinach and sun-dried tomatoes are house favorites. ⊠ *3600 S.W. 36th Ave., Ocala, 32674,* ☎ *352/854–1400,* FAX *904/854– 4010. 200 rooms. Restaurant, pub, pool, outdoor hot tub, tennis courts. AE, D, DC, MC, V.*

**$$$** 🏨 **Seven Sisters Inn.** This showplace Queen Anne mansion is now an
★ award-winning B&B. Each room has been glowingly furnished with period antiques and has its own bath; some have a fireplace. A wicker-furnished loft sleeps four. Rates include a gourmet breakfast and afternoon tea. ⊠ *820 S.E. Fort King St., Ocala, 32671,* ☎ *904/867–1170. 8 rooms. AE, MC, V.*

### Outdoor Activities and Sports

CAMPING

The **Ocala National Forest** (☎ 352/625–7470) has comfortable camp-sites throughout the park, with showers, bathrooms, and canoe runs nearby—but no electricity. Prices range from $10 to $12.

CANOEING

Try the 7-mile Juniper Springs run in the **Ocala National Forest** (☎ 352/625–7470).

GOLF

**Golden Ocala Golf Club** (⊠ 7300 U.S. 27 NW, Ocala 34482, ☎ 352/622–0172) has 18 holes.

JAI ALAI

The speediest of sports, jai alai is played year-round at **Ocala Jai Alai** (⊠ Rte. 318, Orange Lake, ☎ 352/591–2345).

# GAINESVILLE

㉖ **Gainesville** is a sprawling town, home to the University of Florida. In the surrounding area are several state parks, interesting gardens and geologic sites, and Micanopy, the state's oldest inland town and the former site of a Timucuan Indian Village.

## Sights to See

**Devil's Millhopper State Geological Site.** About 10,000 years ago an underground cavern collapsed and created a geological treat. Now it is a botanical wonderland of exotic, subtropical ferns and trees that have grown in a 500-foot-wide, 120-foot-deep sinkhole. You pass a dozen small waterfalls as you head down 232 steps to the bottom. ⊠ *4732 Millhopper Rd., off U.S. 441,* ☎ *352/955–2008.* 🎫 *$2 per vehicle, pedestrians $1.* ☉ *Daily 9–sunset.*

🖐 **Fred Bear Museum.** This collection is the work of Fred Bear, an avid bowhunter who bagged an impressive array of big-game trophies. The museum also has archery artifacts dating to the Stone Age and a wealth of natural history exhibits. Kids will enjoy seeing the life-size animals and the ancient spears, shields, and arrowheads. ⊠ *Fred Bear Dr. at Archer Rd.,* ☎ *352/376–2411.* 🎫 *$3.50.* ☉ *Daily 8–6.*

🖐 **Florida Museum of Natural History.** Located on the campus of the University of Florida, this museum has several interesting replicas, including a Maya palace, a typical Timucuan household, and a full-size replica of a Florida cave. There are outstanding collections from throughout Florida's history, so spend at least half a day here. ⊠ *Mu-*

*seum Rd. at Newell Dr.,* ☎ *352/392–1721.* 🎫 *Free.* ⊙ *Tues.–Sat. 10–5, Sun. and holidays 1–5; closed Dec. 25.*

★ **Majorie Kinnan Rawlings State Historic Site.** Rawlings readers will feel the writer's presence permeating this home, where the typewriter rusts on the ramshackle porch, the closet where she hid her booze during Prohibition yawns open, and clippings from her scrapbook reveal her legal battles and marital problems. Bring lunch and picnic in the shade of one of Rawlings's trees. Then visit her grave a few miles away at peaceful Island Grove. ⊠ *Rte. 325,* ☎ *352/466–3672.* 🎫 *Grounds free, tours $2.* ⊙ *Daily 9–5; tours Oct.–July, hourly 10–11 and 1–4; closed Thanksgiving, Dec. 25, and Jan. 1.*

**Micanopy.** About 11 miles north of Gainesville on U.S. 441 is Micanopy, site of both a Native American settlement and a Spanish mission. Although there are few traces of the past here, Micanopy is now a beautiful town, with streets lined with live oaks. It's a special draw for antiquers; the main street has quite a few antiques shops, and in fall roughly 200 antiques dealers descend on the town for the annual Harvest Fall Festival. **Paynes Prairie State Preserve.** A 20,000-acre wildlife preserve with ponds, lakes, trails, and a visitor center with museum, this area is a wintering area for many migratory birds and home to alligators and a wild herd of American bison. There was once a vast lake here, but a century ago it drained so abruptly that thousands of beached fish died in the mud. The remains of a ferry, stranded in the 1880s, can still be seen. Swimming, boating, picnicking, and camping are permitted. ⊠ *Off U.S. 441, 1 mile north of Micanopy,* ☎ *352/466–3397.* 🎫 *$3.25 per vehicle with up to 8 people.* ⊙ *Daily 8–sunset.*

## Dining and Lodging

**$$** ✕ **Sovereign.** Crystal, candlelight, and a jazz pianist set a theme of re-
★ strained elegance in this 1878 carriage house. The veal specialties are notable, particularly the saltimbocca (veal sautéed with spinach and cheese). Duckling and rack of baby lamb are dependable choices as well. ⊠ *12 S.E. 2nd Ave.,* ☎ *352/378–6307. AE, D, DC, MC, V.*

**$** ✕ **Market Street Pub.** This British-style pub brews its own beer as well as serving up homemade sausage, fish-and-chips, salads, and hearty sandwiches. Dine indoors or outdoors in the sidewalk café. ⊠ *120 S.W. 1st Ave.,* ☎ *352/377–2927. AE, MC, V.*

**$$** 🏨 **Residence Inn by Marriott.** Studios and two-bedroom suites with a kitchen and fireplace make a cozy pied-à-terre. Cocktails, Continental breakfast, and a daily paper are part of the hospitality. The central location is convenient for the university or business traveler. ⊠ *4001 S.W. 13th St. (at U.S. 441 and Rte. 331), 32608,* ☎ *352/371–2101 or 800/331–3131,* 🖷 *904/371–2101. 80 suites. Pool, exercise room, laundry. AE, D, DC, MC, V.*

**$** 🏨 **Cabot Lodge.** Included in the room rate is a Continental breakfast and a chummy two-hour cocktail reception. Spacious rooms and a club-like ambience make this a favorite with business and university travelers. ⊠ *3726 S.W. 40th Blvd., 32608,* ☎ *904/375–2400; outside FL, 800/843–8735;* 🖷 *352/335–2321. AE, D, DC, MC, V.*

## Nightlife

**DJ Chaps** (⊠ 108 S. Main St., ☎ 352/377–1619) is Gainesville's only country-western dance club; it's always hopping. Crowds head to the **Hardback Cafe** (⊠ 232 S.E. 1st St., ☎ 352/756–0048) for the newest local bands playing live music.

## Outdoor Activities and Sports

### Auto Racing
Hot-rod auto racing goes on at the Gatornationals, championship competitions of the **National Hot Rod Association** (☎ 818/914–4761), and are held each year in late winter at the **Gainesville Raceway** (⊠ 1121 N. Rte. 225, Gainesville).

### Football
The games of the **University of Florida Gators** (☎ 352/375–4683) in Gainesville are extremely popular, and tickets are very hard to get.

### Horseback Riding
Ocala's bluegrass horse country can be explored during trail rides organized by **Oakview Stable** (⊠ S.W. 27th Ave., behind Paddock Mall, ☎ 352/237–8844).

# NORTHEAST FLORIDA A TO Z

## Arriving and Departing

### By Car
East–west traffic travels the northern part of the state on I–10, a cross-country highway stretching from Los Angeles to Jacksonville. Farther south, I–4 connects Florida's west and east coasts. Signs on I–4 designate it an east–west route, but actually the road rambles northeast from Tampa to Orlando, then heads north–northeast to Daytona. Two interstates head north–south on Florida's peninsula: I–95 on the east coast (from Miami to Houlton, Maine) and I–75 to the west.

### By Plane
The main airport for the region is **Jacksonville International.** It is served by **American** and **American Eagle** (☎ 800/433–7300), **Comair** (☎ 800/354–9822), **Continental** (☎ 800/525–0280), **Delta** (☎ 800/221–1212), **TWA** (☎ 800/221–2000), **United** (☎ 800/241–6522), and **USAir** (☎ 800/428–4322). Vans from the Jacksonville airport to area hotels cost $16 per person. Taxi fare is about $20 to downtown, $40 to the beaches and Amelia Island. Among the limousine services, which must be booked in advance, is **AAA Limousine Service** (☎ 904/751–4800 or 800/780–1705), which charges $25 for one to four people going downtown ($8 for each additional person) and $39 for one to four people going to the Jacksonville beaches or Amelia Island.

**Daytona Beach International Airport** is served by American, Continental, Delta, and USAir. Taxi fare to beach hotels is about $10–$12; cab companies include **Yellow Cab** (☎ 904/252–5536), **Checker Cab** (☎ 904/255–8421), and **AAA Cab** (☎ 904/253–2522). **DOTS Transit Service** (☎ 904/257–5411) has scheduled service connecting the Daytona Beach airport to Orlando International Airport, the Sheraton Palm Coast area, Deland, Deland's Amtrak station, New Smyrna Beach, Sanford, and Deltona; fares are $26 one-way and $46 round-trip between the Daytona and Orlando airports, $20 one-way and $36 round-trip from the Orlando airport to Deland or Deltona.

**Gainesville Regional Airport** is served by **ASA–The Delta Connection** (☎ 800/282–3424), Comair, Delta, and USAir. Taxi fare to the center of Gainesville is about $10; some hotels provide free airport pickup.

Although Orlando is not part of the area, visitors to northeastern Florida often choose to arrive at **Orlando International Airport** because of the huge number of convenient flights. Driving east on the Beeline Expressway brings you to Cocoa Beach in about an hour. You can reach

Daytona, about a two-hour drive, by taking the Beeline Expressway to I–95 and driving north.

### By Train
**Amtrak** (☎ 800/872–7245) schedules stops in Jacksonville, Deland, Waldo (near Gainesville), Ocala, and Palatka. The Auto Train carries cars between Sanford and Lorton, Virginia (just south of Washington D.C.). Schedules vary depending on the season.

## Getting Around

### By Bus
**Greyhound Lines** (☎ 800/231–2222) serves the region, with stations in Jacksonville (☎ 904/356–9976), St. Augustine (☎ 904/829–6401), Gainesville (☎ 352/376–5252), Daytona Beach (☎ 904/255–7076), and Deland (☎ 904/734–2747).

Daytona Beach has an excellent bus network, **Votran** (☎ 904/756–7496), which serves the beach area, airport, shopping malls, and major arteries. Exact fare (75¢) is required.

### By Car
Chief north–south routes are I–95, along the east coast, and I–75, which enters Florida south of Valdosta, Georgia, and joins the Sunshine Parkway toll road at Wildwood.

If you want to drive as close to the Atlantic as possible, and are not in a hurry, stick with A1A. It runs along the barrier islands, changing its name several times along the way. Where there are no bridges between islands, cars must return to the mainland via causeways; some are low, with drawbridges that open for boat traffic on the inland waterway, and there can be unexpected delays. The Buccaneer Trail, which overlaps part of Rte. A1A, goes from St. Augustine north to Mayport (where a ferry is part of the state highway system), through marshlands and beaches, to the 300-year-old seaport town of Fernandina Beach, and then finally into Fort Clinch State Park, with its massive brick fortress.

Route 13 runs from Jacksonville to East Palatka along the east side of the St. Johns River, through tiny hamlets. U.S. 17 travels the west side of the river, passing through Green Cove Springs and Palatka, where Ravine State Gardens's mountains of spring azaleas bloom.

Route 19 runs north–south and Rte. 40 runs east–west through the Ocala National Forest, giving a nonstop view of stately pines and bold wildlife. Short side roads lead to parks, springs, picnic areas, and campgrounds.

### By Water Taxi
Connecting the banks of the St. Johns River, the **Bass Marine Water Taxi** (☎ 904/730–8685) runs from 11 to 10 daily (except during rainy or other bad weather) between several locations, including Riverwalk and Jacksonville Landing. The one-way trip takes about five minutes. Round-trip fare is $3; one-way fare is $1.50.

## Guided Tours

### Orientation Tours
City tours of Jacksonville are offered by **Jacksonville Historical Society Tours** (☎ 904/396–6307) for groups and by arrangement.

## Special-Interest Tours

### BIKE AND CANOE TOURS

**Suwannee Country Tours** (⊠ White Springs, ☎ 352/397–2347), run by the Florida Council of American Youth Hostels, organizes bicycle and canoe trips on some of the state's most unspoiled and unusual roads and waters. Stay overnight in country inns, picnic in ghost towns, eat at country churches, and explore forgotten sites.

### BOAT TOURS

In Jacksonville, **River Entertainment** (☎ 904/396–2333) has dinner and dancing cruises on five different boats; schedules vary with the season. **Riverwalk Cruise Lines** (☎ 904/398–0797) offers sightseeing, lunch, dinner, and party cruises. **LA Cruise** (☎ 800/752–1778) has day and evening cruises from Mayport, with live bands, dancing, and gambling.

In New Smyrna Beach, **Coastal Cruise Lines** (☎ 813/428–0201) runs lunch, dinner, sunset, and special-occasion cruises through wetlands. You can often see herons, manatees, and dolphins.

# Contacts and Resources

## Emergencies

Dial **911** for police or ambulance.

### HOSPITALS

The following hospitals have 24-hour emergency rooms: **Alachua General** (⊠ 801 S.W. 2nd Ave., Gainesville, ☎ 904/372–4321), **Fish Memorial Hospital** (⊠ 401 Palmetto St., New Smyrna Beach, ☎ 904/424–5152), **Halifax Medical Center** (⊠ 303 N. Clyde Morris Blvd., Daytona, ☎ 904/254–4100), **Munroe Regional Medical Center** (⊠ 131 S.W. 15th St., Ocala, ☎ 352/351–7200), and **St. Luke's Hospital** (⊠ 4201 Belfort Rd., Jacksonville, ☎ 904/296–3700).

### LATE-NIGHT PHARMACIES

**Eckerd Drug** (⊠ 4397 Roosevelt Blvd., Jacksonville, ☎ 904/389–0314) and **Walgreen** (⊠ 4150 N. Atlantic Ave., Cocoa, ☎ 407/799–9112; ⊠ 1500 Beville Rd., Daytona, P 904/257–5773) stay open 24 hours.

## Visitor Information

**Amelia Island–Fernandina Beach Chamber of Commerce** (⊠ 102 Centre St., Amelia Island 32034, ☎ 904/261–3248) is open weekdays 9–5. **Cocoa Beach Area Chamber of Commerce** (⊠ 400 Fortenberry Rd., Merritt Island 32952, ☎ 407/459–2200) is open weekdays 8:30–5. **Destination Daytona!** (⊠ 126 E. Orange Ave., Daytona 32120, ☎ 904/255–0415 or 800/854–1234) is open weekdays 9–5. **Gainesville Visitors and Convention Bureau** (⊠ 10 S.W. 2nd Ave., Suite 220, Gainesville 32608, ☎ 352/374–5231) is open weekdays 8:30–5. **Jacksonville and Its Beaches Convention & Visitors Bureau** (⊠ 6 E. Bay St., Suite 200, Jacksonville 32202, ☎ 904/353–9736) is open weekdays 8–5. **Ocala–Marion County Chamber of Commerce** (⊠ 110 E. Silver Springs Blvd., Ocala 32671, ☎ 352/629–8051) is open weekdays 8:30–5. **St. Augustine Visitor Information Center** (⊠ 10 Castillo Dr., St. Augustine 32084, ☎ 904/825–1000) is open daily 8:30–5:30.

# INDEX

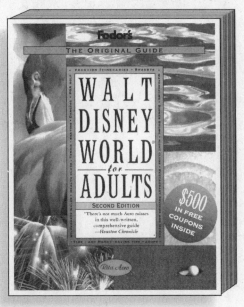

# NOTES

# NOTES

# NOTES

# NOTES

# NOTES

# NOTES

# NOTES

# NOTES

# NOTES

# NOTES

# NOTES

*Escape to ancient cities and*

*journey to* *exotic islands with*

*CNN Travel Guide, a wealth of valuable advice. Host*

*Valerie Voss will take you to*

*all of your favorite destinations,*

*including those off the beaten*

*path. Tune-in to your passport to the world.*

## CNN TRAVEL GUIDE
SATURDAY 12:30 PM ET    SUNDAY 4:30 PM ET

# Fodor's Travel Publications

*Available at bookstores everywhere, or call 1–800–533–6478, 24 hours a day.*

## Gold Guides

### U.S.

Alaska

Arizona

Boston

California

Cape Cod, Martha's Vineyard, Nantucket

The Carolinas & the Georgia Coast

Chicago

Colorado

Florida

Hawai'i

Las Vegas, Reno, Tahoe

Los Angeles

Maine, Vermont, New Hampshire

Maui & Lāna'i

Miami & the Keys

New England

New Orleans

New York City

Pacific North Coast

Philadelphia & the Pennsylvania Dutch Country

The Rockies

San Diego

San Francisco

Santa Fe, Taos, Albuquerque

Seattle & Vancouver

The South

U.S. & British Virgin Islands

USA

Virginia & Maryland

Washington, D.C.

### Foreign

Australia

Austria

The Bahamas

Belize & Guatemala

Bermuda

Canada

Cancún, Cozumel, Yucatán Peninsula

Caribbean

China

Costa Rica

Cuba

The Czech Republic & Slovakia

Eastern & Central Europe

Europe

Florence, Tuscany & Umbria

France

Germany

Great Britain

Greece

Hong Kong

India

Ireland

Israel

Italy

Japan

London

Madrid & Barcelona

Mexico

Montréal & Québec City

Moscow, St. Petersburg, Kiev

The Netherlands, Belgium & Luxembourg

New Zealand

Norway

Nova Scotia, New Brunswick, Prince Edward Island

Paris

Portugal

Provence & the Riviera

Scandinavia

Scotland

Singapore

South Africa

South America

Southeast Asia

Spain

Sweden

Switzerland

Thailand

Tokyo

Toronto

Turkey

Vienna & the Danube

## Fodor's Special-Interest Guides

Caribbean Ports of Call

The Complete Guide to America's National Parks

Family Adventures

Gay Guide to the USA

Halliday's New England Food Explorer

Halliday's New Orleans Food Explorer

Healthy Escapes

Kodak Guide to Shooting Great Travel Pictures

Net Travel

Nights to Imagine

Rock & Roll Traveler USA

Sunday in New York

Sunday in San Francisco

Walt Disney World, Universal Studios and Orlando

Walt Disney World for Adults

Where Should We Take the Kids? California

Where Should We Take the Kids? Northeast

Worldwide Cruises and Ports of Call

## Special Series

### Affordables
Caribbean
Europe
Florida
France
Germany
Great Britain
Italy
London
Paris

### Fodor's Bed & Breakfasts and Country Inns
America
California
The Mid-Atlantic
New England
The Pacific Northwest
The South
The Southwest
The Upper Great Lakes

### The Berkeley Guides
California
Central America
Eastern Europe
Europe
France
Germany & Austria
Great Britain & Ireland
Italy
London
Mexico
New York City
Pacific Northwest & Alaska
Paris
San Francisco

### Compass American Guides
Arizona
Canada
Chicago
Colorado
Hawaii
Idaho
Hollywood
Las Vegas

Maine
Manhattan
Montana
New Mexico
New Orleans
Oregon
San Francisco
Santa Fe
South Carolina
South Dakota
Southwest
Texas
Utah
Virginia
Washington
Wine Country
Wisconsin
Wyoming

### Fodor's Citypacks
Atlanta
Hong Kong
London
New York City
Paris
Rome
San Francisco
Washington, D.C.

### Fodor's Español
California
Caribe Occidental
Caribe Oriental
Gran Bretaña
Londres
Mexico
Nueva York
Paris

### Fodor's Exploring Guides
Australia
Boston & New England
Britain
California
Caribbean
China
Egypt
Florence & Tuscany
Florida

France
Germany
Ireland
Israel
Italy
Japan
London
Mexico
Moscow & St. Petersburg
New York City
Paris
Prague
Provence
Rome
San Francisco
Scotland
Singapore & Malaysia
Spain
Thailand
Turkey
Venice

### Fodor's Flashmaps
Boston
New York
San Francisco
Washington, D.C.

### Fodor's Pocket Guides
Acapulco
Atlanta
Barbados
Jamaica
London
New York City
Paris
Prague
Puerto Rico
Rome
San Francisco
Washington, D.C.

### Mobil Travel Guides
America's Best Hotels & Restaurants
California & the West
Frequent Traveler's Guide to Major Cities
Great Lakes
Mid-Atlantic

Northeast
Northwest & Great Plains
Southeast
Southwest & South Central

### Rivages Guides
Bed and Breakfasts of Character and Charm in France
Hotels and Country Inns of Character and Charm in France
Hotels and Country Inns of Character and Charm in Italy
Hotels and Country Inns of Character and Charm in Paris
Hotels and Country Inns of Character and Charm in Portugal
Hotels and Country Inns of Character and Charm in Spain

### Short Escapes
Britain
France
New England
Near New York City

### Fodor's Sports
Golf Digest's Best Places to Play
Skiing USA
USA Today The Complete Four Sport Stadium Guide

### Fodor's Vacation Planners
Great American Learning Vacations
Great American Sports & Adventure Vacations
Great American Vacations
Great American Vacations for Travelers with Disabilities
National Parks and Seashores of the East
National Parks of the West

# WHEREVER YOU TRAVEL, *H*ELP IS NEVER FAR AWAY.

From planning your trip to providing travel assistance along the way, American Express® Travel Service Offices are always there to help.

---

## *Florida*

American Express Travel Service
32 Miracle Mile
Coral Gables
305/446-3381

American Express Travel Service
330 Biscayne Boulevard
Miami
305/358-7350

American Express Travel Service
3312-14 N.E. 32nd Street
Fort Lauderdale
305/565-9481

American Express Travel Service
2 West Church Street, Suite 1
Orlando
407/843-0004

American Express Travel Service
9908 Baymeadows Road
Jacksonville
904/642-1701

American Express Travel Service
1390 Main Street
Sarasota
941/365-2520

American Express Travel Service
Epcot Center
Walt Disney World Resort
Lake Buena Vista
407/827-7500

American Express Travel Service
One Tampa City Center
Tampa
813/273-9380

**Travel**

http://www.americanexpress.com/travel

**American Express Travel Service Offices are located throughout Florida. For the office nearest you, call 1-800-YES-AMEX.**

# Wet'n Wild®

# $3 OFF

Present this coupon and save $3.00 off the regular all-day adult or child admission price. Coupon good for up to six people. Not to be used in conjunction with any other discounted offer or afternoon pricing.

Expires 12/31/97

# Wet'n Wild®

# $3 OFF

Present this coupon and save $3.00 off the regular all-day adult or child admission price. Coupon good for up to six people. Not to be used in conjunction with any other discounted offer or afternoon pricing.

Expires 12/31/97

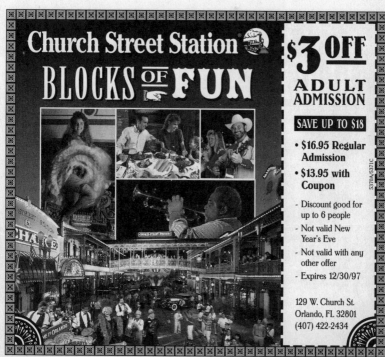

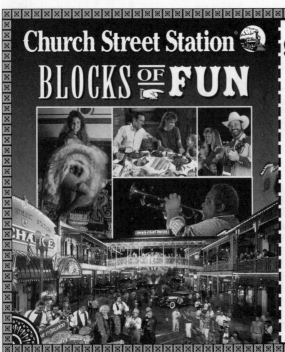

# $3.00 OFF

### All-Day Studio Pass
Regular admission price $38.50 (plus tax)

# RIDE THE MOVIES!

Universal Studios Florida®, the only place on earth where you can Ride The Movies®. Guests can thrill to Back To The Future®...The Ride™, Kongfrontation®, Earthquake®, E.T.®, A Day In The Park With Barney™ and TERMINATOR 2: 3-D BATTLE ACROSS TIME™!

# 20% OFF

### Food and beverages purchased for your party (up to six) at Studio Stars Restaurant or Finnegan's Pub after 4pm.

Present this coupon to your server when ordering. Tax and gratuity not included. This coupon has no cash value and is not valid with any other specials or discounts including happy hour pricing. Valid through 12/31/97.

# $3⁰⁰ OFF

### All-Day Studio Pass

$3.00 discount valid through 12/31/97. Coupon valid for up to 6 people and must be presented at the time of purchase. This offer has no cash value and is not valid with any other special discounts. Subject to change without notice. Parking Fee not included.

6183920001990

# DINE HOLLYWOOD-STYLE

Be a part of the scene at the Studio Stars Restaurant (across from Ghostbusters®) or drop into Finnegan's Pub for Irish spirits, ales and entertainment. Your 20% discount is good for a party of six after 4pm! Remember to present this coupon when ordering.

Cannot be used in conjunction with any other promotion - including happy hour pricing.